Zhang Sheng et al.
The Rape of Nanking

Zhang Sheng et al.
The Rape of Nanking

A Historical Study

With the participation of Guo Zhaozhao,
Jiang Liangqin, Dong Weimin, Wang Weixing,
Yan Haijian and Qu Shengfei

Social Sciences Academic Press (China)

Translated by Evan Villarrubia
B&R Book Program

ISBN 978-3-11-065233-8
e-ISBN [PDF] 978-3-11-065278-9
e-ISBN [EPUB] 978-3-11-065289-5

Library of Congress Control Number: 2021942532

Bibliographic information published by the Deutsche Nationalbibliothek
The Deutsche Nationalbibliothek lists this publication in the Deutsche Nationalbibliografie; detailed bibliographic data are available on the Internet at http://dnb.dnb.de.

© 2022 Walter de Gruyter GmbH, Berlin/Boston
First published as 南京大屠杀史研究 (增订版), Phoenix Publishing & Media Group, Nanking 2015.

Cover illustration: Brandon Chen / iStock / Getty Images Plus
Printing and binding: CPI books GmbH, Leck

www.degruyter.com

Foreword

I was fortunate to be the first to read the soon-to-be published manuscript by Zhang Sheng and his students, and I would like first and foremost to express heartfelt congratulations to them!

The Rape of Nanking[1], which took place during the War of the Japanese Invasion of China, now lies 75 years in the past, and the international trial for this brutal event over 60 years in the past. But to this day, interest in this event seems not to have diminished in the slightest, and discussions about and debates over this event play an important role in shaping Sino-Japanese relations. Therefore, as times change, our vision broadens, and our level of general knowledge improves, our understanding of this event has also continued to deepen. Therein lies the significance of the publication of this work at this time.

Today, 75 years after the event, we are finally able to analyze and study the Rape of Nanking at three levels: as a historical event, as a legal case, and an object in the Chinese people's collective consciousness. These three do not exist in isolation, but rather influence and affect one another.

As a historical event, it comprises all manner of entities, perspectives, standpoints, intentions, and records, their influences upon one another, and their individual persuasiveness or lack thereof. Today, with basically all documents having been studied, we are able to observe a central fact: in December 1937, after Nanjing had been occupied by the Imperial Japanese Army, there took place an act of barbarism unprecedented in modern Chinese history and rare anywhere in the modern history of the entire world. Tens of thousands of Chinese people were slain by Japanese troops under a great variety of pretexts, and the achievements made in Nanjing over a decade-plus of construction were wiped out almost overnight. The effects of the event linger to this day.

At the level of basic facts, we can see Japanese militarism and the bellicosity it incited in the Japanese people in the recent era, changes in Japanese war strategy, the resolve of Matsui Iwane, Prince Asaka Yasuhiko,[2] and others to expand

---

1 This event is known in Chinese as *Nanjing da tusha*, which translates directly to "Great Massacre of Nanjing." As, however, it has been widely known in English for decades as the "Rape of Nanking," this name is retained in this translation for continuity's sake. The spelling "Nanjing" is now preferred for the city in question, and is used in all instances not referring specifically to historical events or institutions known under by the former spelling (translator's note).

2 In China, Japan, and most East Asian countries, the family name precedes the given name. The names of many notorious Japanese figures from this event have been commonly rendered in English by the Western convention of given name + surname; however, in this translation,

the war and punish China; agreements and disagreements among Japanese diplomats and Japanese military officers; different considerations of the Japanese government and the Imperial Japanese Army; "massacre orders" given at all levels; contempt for and vengefulness against China that were pervasive within the Japanese military; and even differing attitudes toward the massacre among officers and soldiers. On the Chinese side, we see the Nationalist government's commitment to fight the Japanese for as long as is necessary, duplicate moves and deployment mistakes; the fierce resistance put up by the Nanjing Defense Garrison and subsequent sudden and total collapse; the decisions by Nanjing residents either to evacuate, or to stay put, and the anticipation among some for what they thought might be the "arrival of a new dynasty"; the comingling of silence and resistance with acceptance of fate and even harming of their compatriots among the Chinese people; massive damages done to the lives and property of city residents as well as their tenacity and resilience; the destruction and reconstruction of communities; the personal integrity of those who vow "not to have lived in vain", and the political equivocation of others; the emergence of traitors to the Chinese race and supporters of the pseudo-regime, and the complex role these individuals played; and so on. As for the Westerners who were in Nanjing, we see their motivations for staying and defending the city, national-interest-driven government responses of Western countries; divergence between popular opinions and official attitudes; how Westerners interacted with the Japanese in terms of processes and policies; operations and functions of the "Safety Zone"; interactions between Westerners and the Chinese residents; the dissemination of information about the Rape of Nanking by Westerners; the impact the presence of Westerners in Nanjing had on the how the Japanese army carried out both the occupation and the colonization of Nanjing, and so on. All these historical facts, now laid bare for all to see, together form a complete picture of Nanjing before, during, and after the war.

The sheer magnitudes of these horrific events defy imagination: the dead bodies of Chinese citizens were piled several feet high on the major thoroughfare of Yijiang Gate; Japanese military trucks drove over the bodies repeatedly, blood squirting from them all over the place. The Sasaki unit alone massacred 15,000 prisoners of war. Another Japanese unit responsible for defending the Taiping Gate area led a massacre of another 1,300 people. The ponds all over Nanjing were full of bodies; Japanese officers and soldiers as well as Chinese residents were forced to drink dirty water that had been colored red. All cash found on

---

all Asian names are rendered the Asian convention of surname + given name, for the sake of unity (translator's note), except for bibliographic references

the bodies of murdered Chinese officers and enlisted men was seized and used as currency in Nanjing; this money was called "stinking bills." Few women of Nanjing escaped violation, regardless of whether they were old ladies in their 70s, girls as young as six or seven, or even female family members of foreign officials or nursing staff in the international Safety Zone. On the single night of December 16, 1937, over 1,000 women were raped near the campus of the University of Nanking. Gang rape was the most common form of sexual violence perpetrated by the Japanese soldiers and most took place in broad daylight or in front of the family members of the victims. Sexual violence was often followed by murders, and sexually-transmitted diseases spread explosively, pregnancies, and unintended births among the victims, as well as post-traumatic stress disorder. Ostentatious advertisements for "comfort women" could be seen all over the city; some women were raped hundreds of times. Rampant organized looting and burning led to massive losses of property in the Nanjing region estimated to be worth USD $100 million, or about one-twentieth of China's gross national product at the time, which was about USD $10 billion. Japanese officers and soldiers profited enormously, with some able to wire as much as 1,000 yen back to Japan every month. Even senior leaders of the puppet Autonomous Committee and the chairman of the Safety Zone Committee were robbed. In order to cover up their own criminal acts, after the looting the Japanese soldiers would incite or otherwise give tacit permission to poor Chinese women and children to steal. Copper, iron, and other metals seized in the Nanjing region were shipped back to Japan as war spoils, along with great quantities of cultural relics and ancient documents and texts. The open and widespread selling of narcotics by the Japanese army led to a spike in drug use in Nanjing, with opium dens sprouting across the city like weeds, all right under the nose of the remaining Westerners, raking in several millions of yuan each month.[3]

The Chinese and Westerners were not the only people who knew about the massacre. Japanese soldiers and officers also wrote of it in detail in their journals and letters, and some even vaunted their "valor" by having photos taken of themselves in front of the severed heads of Chinese people or the still naked bodies of their female Chinese victims. Fully aware of what was going on, high-ranking officials in the Japanese government dispatched geishas and actresses from Japan to Nanjing during the massacre, who would have publicity photos taken of them comforting Chinese children. The Japanese would treat Westerners to del-

---

[3] The currency of nationalist China was widely referred to as "dollars" in foreign texts, but to distinguish it from foreign currencies, in this book the term "yuan" is used in the main text body. When the term "dollars" is used in quotations by Westerners, it usually refers to this same "yuan" (translator's note).

icacies delivered from their homeland, and put out "masterpieces" showing Japanese soldiers carrying elderly Chinese women on their backs, and others carrying water for the locals, all in an apparent attempt to change the international image of the Japanese military as an army of violence and brutality.

Of course, there are also paradoxes in the historical evidence. Japanese soldiers handed out grain outside of the Safety Zone to lure Chinese citizens away from their Western protectors. A number of Japanese soldiers and officers got on well with Westerners, attended religious ceremonies, gifting them with daily necessities, and there were even occasional cases of Chinese civilians being rescued by the Japanese. Some military policemen even received commendation from the Westerners for guarding refugee camps. Military discipline was enforced unevenly among the different units of the Japanese Nanjing Defense Garrison.

The history of the Rape of Nanking is, in itself, a vast and multi-faceted subject. When we examine it as a legal case, we must, amid the numerous and complicated threads of the story, clearly ascertain causal relations, find those who are culpable, and decide how they are to be held to account. At the Nanjing War Crimes Tribunal, which was part of the International Military Tribunal for the Far East and revolved around the trial and sentencing of Hisao Tani, he and the Japanese commanders who led the attack on Nanjing were convicted of carrying out the massacre under international law and the domestic law of China at the time. In the cases of Tanaka Gunkichi, Mukai Toshiaki, and Noda Tsuyoshi, the tribunal found them guilty of the killing of prisoners of war and non-combatants. At the United Nations International Military Tribunal for the Far East (Tokyo), where international law and the rules of procedure ordinarily followed in the United States were applied, the chain of evidence pertinent to and the substance of the Nanking Massacre were established, on the basis of the dereliction of duty by Matsui Iwane, who had failed to take effective action to halt it. The judgments of these two tribunals were accepted by the Japanese government, as was stipulated in the *Treaty of San Francisco*; and they also represent the canonical position on the Rape of Nanking around the world today.

The trial awoke the world's collective memories, and also generated a broad array of social participation. The verdict offered some solace to those in Nanjing who had suffered from the atrocities, and carried out justice. Yet neither of the two trials was without problems and both left behind legacies, albeit to differing degrees. For a variety of reasons, such as political considerations and inadequate supporting materials, the Tokyo trial in particular was unable to produce a comprehensive and thorough account of the historical facts or the war crimes culpabilities. Worse still, evidence presented and arguments marshalled by the defense at the trial would later be co-opted by the Japanese right wing and became the basis for their attempt to overturn the case.

Over the 75 years since the Rape of Nanking, the Chinese people's understanding of the event has continued to change and evolve. In 1945, when Chiang Kai-shek was assessing Japanese war criminals, he "summarily left out" Konoe Fumimaro and 40 others who bore "the political portion of responsibility". He also "summarily exempted" "those who bore military responsibility," including Matsui Iwane. Only those who "had engaged in monumentally heinous deeds," including Doihara Kenji, Itagaki Seishiro, Tojo Hideki, and Tani Hisao would be sent to the dock (Chiang Kai-shek journal entry October 14, 1945). Yet it was this policy of "turning the other cheek," factually baseless and logically incoherent such as it was, that would define the nature of the nationalist government's handling of the Rape of Nanking. This may explain the government's appallingly poor preparations for and shoddy performance at both the Nanjing and the Tokyo trials. After its retreat to Taiwan, and faced with new developments in politics and international relations, the KMT suffered from "selective amnesia", and all but completely forgot these events. On the Chinse mainland, after the eruption of the Korean War, understanding of the role of Westerners, especially the Americans, during the Rape of Nanking, was turned upside down.

For a long time thereafter, the tone of public discourse on the subject was defined by such dubious claims as "the Japanese people were also victims of the war" and "it was only a small handful of Japanese warlords and militarists who instigated the war". Signs that should have set off alarms in a country that had yet to come to terms with its war crimes were dismissed, and soul-searching efforts among progressive forces in Japan were not taken seriously. With the exception of a brief mention in historical accounts of the invasion of China by Japanese imperialism, this episode was all but consigned to oblivion. After 1980, in the wake of the "Japanese textbook controversy," the construction of the "Memorial Hall of the Victims of the Nanjing Massacre by Japanese Invaders" and its exhibitions provided an opportunity to "rediscover" the Rape of Nanking. In the spirit of "remembering and learning from history," uncovering the truth about the past in order to strengthen Sino-Japanese friendship became the fulcrum of research and understanding. The Rape of Nanking quickly became a most prominent factor in Sino-Japanese relations.

Since 1990, thanks to the upsurge of patriotic and nationalist fervor in China, awareness of the Rape of Nanking became practically universal. Constant provocations and irritations by the Japanese right wing, the discovery of great quantities of all kinds of documents, ongoing interviews with victims and eyewitnesses, a growing body of case studies, widespread media coverage, frequent commemorative events, the sounding of sirens around the city honoring the dead all facilitated the dissemination and reconstruction of relevant information, and helped to strengthen the sense of a "community of common destiny" among the Chinese people. At the same time as considerable progress was being made in academic research, understanding of the Rape of Nanking among the Chinese people surged, often in sync with greater political and social trends, and became inextricably entangled with other issues leftover from the war, such as comfort women, germ warfare, chemical warfare, forced labor, and indiscriminate bombing. Under certain circumstances, attitudes toward the Rape of Nanking have become the basis for appraising history and current reality.

In the twenty-first century, the historical study of the Rape of Nanking within Chinese academia has gradually matured into a new and distinct field with its own concepts, scopes, objects of study, document systems, and academic standards. As a new field of academic research, the study of the event's history has gone beyond trying to determine culpability and making general moral judgments about acts of violence. It has also introduced to the Chinese people a range of new issues in relation to this event, including the effects of war on people's humanity, humanitarianism within warfare, the internal complexity of different groups involved in a massacre, the international law of war, comparative analysis of wartime violence, the place of the Rape of Nanking within the broad scheme of the history of humanity as a whole, how the way the Chinese people understand the war not only may affect how people in the invading country understand it but also might propel them toward soul searching regarding their responsibilities both during and after the war, PTSD treatment and rehabilitation, post-war peace reconstruction, and others. This has made fruitful reactions between academic research and public awareness a reality.

I have known Zhang Sheng for a long time, and I have been deeply impressed by his scholarly endeavors in history, especially what he has done to inform his studies with philosophical methodology and analysis. This new work, intended to focus on historical realities, also demonstrates the in-depth reflection he has done over many years on the subject of the Rape of Nanking. I believe that the publication of this book will facilitate further studies and understanding of the event in question among both academics and the public at large. Respect for the dead and the search for truth from facts have been the guiding principles of this book, and are the shared commitments of all historians.

I offer these words to express my feelings upon the imminent publication of this book.

Bu Ping,
Director of the Research Association of the History of the Chinese War of Resistance Against Japan

Beijing, November 2011

Foreword by the First Author

In studying the history of the Rape of Nanking, it is impossible to avoid the following seven issues. These issues are inextricably intertwined with one another at the macro, meso, and micro levels.

In December 1937, during its attack on Nanjing, the Imperial Japanese Army once claimed that it was doing something for which there had been no historical precedence, namely, seizing the capital city of an enemy country in the physical presence of third-party witnesses. This is not exactly true. It was true, of course, that after Nanjing fell, over 20 foreigners from countries that were neutral in the Sino-Japanese conflict remained in the city. However, they were by no means mere observers, but were themselves deeply involved. They organized themselves via the International Committee for the Nanking Safety Zone, the International Red Cross Committee of Nanking, and other organizations, and assumed some management functions of the city government after the nationalist government and special authorities of Nanjing had moved to western China. They interacted with the Japanese military and diplomatic personnel, and the Japan-backed puppet government, and exerted pressure and oversight on the actions of the latter. It is largely owing to their eye-witness account, records, analysis, and dissemination of information regarding the Japanese army's behaviors following the fall of Nanjing that the Rape of Nanking came to be known around world, and became an international event.

Second, before the outbreak of the Sino-Japanese war, both the Kuomintang (KMT) and the Communist Party of China (CPC), the two major political parties in China, had anticipated the war, whose beginning was imminent, to be protracted, and made preparations accordingly. The fall of Nanjing had been expected. But there was a school of thought in the Japanese military, whose proponents included Matsui Iwane, that held that once the nationalist government's capital of Nanjing, seen at the time as a "stronghold of resistance against Japan," was captured, it would be but a short step to vanquishing China's vital force, shattering the country's determination to fight, and effectively bringing China to its knees, and a swift end to the war. This suggests that Nanjing's strategic significance was understood very differently by the Japanese and the Chinese.

Third, there were disagreements among the Japanese after the fall of Nanjing. Some high-ranking officers in the Japanese army who favored a "punitive expedition" against China condoned, turned a blind eye to, or tacitly permitted, the brutality of their troops; the objective existence of a "massacre order" testifies to the intentionality of their criminal acts. But another group, primarily composed of Japanese diplomats, that was more fully cognizant of the international norms governing warfare and the state of the world thought that Japanese brutality would harm the international image of the country and its military. Acting out of what they believed was in Japan's long-term interest, they went so far as to intentionally allow some information about the protestation of some Westerners and their accounts of the violence to reach the outside world, something they thought might put pressure on the Japanese to exercise restraint (in the words of one British diplomat). This schism made it possible for cracks, however small, to open in the city of Nanjing, otherwise sealed off from the world. Of course, this was by no means a clear-cut divide; some members of the Japanese diplomatic corps were as bestial as those in the army, and there were a small number of cases involving Japanese soldiers saving the lives of Chinese people.

Fourth, people in Nanjing before, during, and after the massacre can be roughly divided into three groups: Westerners, Japanese, and helpless Chinese soldiers and civilians. As the Westerners provided humanitarian aid and charitable arrangements, the Chinese naturally gravitated toward and relied on them. The violence of the Japanese army terrified and alienated the Chinese, the same people they needed to put under control in order to establish a colonial order. These conditions gave rise to a two-sided chess game being played by three players. The International Safety Zone was a temporary establishment granted tacit permission by the Japanese army, where strength determined the outcomes: refugees in the Safety Zone gradually dispersed back to their homes under the carrot and stick methods employed by the Japanese army of screenings, "public reassurances," closing of refugee centers, and distribution of grain. Thereafter the International Committee for the Nanking Safety Zone was forced to reorganize as a marginalized humanitarian aid institution under the "new order": the Nanking International Relief Committee.

Fifth, the climax of the Rape of Nanking lasted approximately six weeks, preceded by bombings and siege, and followed by frequent outbursts of violence by the Japanese army. During this entire period, despite the tremendous threats to their survival and the deep trauma they constantly faced, Nanjing's residents nonetheless managed to eke out a living. Under such an extraordinary situation, many residents resorted to extraordinary behaviors and choices. A large number of young women were hastily married. There was migration at an unprecedented scale, with an influx of people from surrounding regions fleeing the war and refugees from places such as Beijing and Shanghai. All these contributed to profound shifts in Nanjing's demographic structure. The departure of governmental bodies, cultural, educational, and research institutions, and factories and mining enterprises led to an intellectual and professional elite hemorrhage. Those who did not leave were those so poor and hapless they had no other choice. Many of those depended on others for the means of basic survival, and lost any meaningful control over their own fate. Following widespread looting by Japanese soldiers, the number of jobs available in Nanjing dwindled, destroying what little economic wherewithal the city's residents had left, plunging the entire region into extreme poverty. To stubbornly survive using all available resources became the overwhelming duty of survivors of the sack; thin congee became the primary food for many people over a long period of time. Some Chinese women and children even turned to theft after Japanese soldiers had plundered provisions from all stores and dwellings.

Sixth, the visible, obvious injuries suffered by victims of the Rape of Nanking were paid great attention even as the event was still unfolding. The accumulation of cases of violence and exposition and propagation of overt injuries being inflicted were focus points in the writings of witnesses. These are actually but the tip of the iceberg as compared to the soft, hidden injuries suffered by survivors of that environment of extreme terror. The truth is that PTSD and other psychological traumas were widespread among survivors of the Rape of Nanking; such afflictions constitute a layer of the event's history that is easily overlooked, despite the fact that their sufferers carried them to the end of their days. The destruction of communities, changes in interpersonal relationships, and overturning of individuals' life histories that accompanied the psychological trauma also often fell and continue to fall outside the field of vision of most people.

Seventh, the verdicts reached by the two post-war tribunals and their conclusions regarding the Rape of Nanking were acknowledged by all governments of the world, including Japan's, in the *Treaty of San Francisco* and other international arrangements; these later constituted the legal bases for discussion of the nature of and responsibility for the event. The verdicts were of enormous significance in determining right and wrong in the event, and constituted the historical starting point for the new life upon which Japan embarked after the war. A thorough study of the two verdicts being made by Chinese academics remains in its initial stages.

I make no claim whatsoever that this book will make accurate responses to the preceding seven issues, but it does reflect our courage in endeavoring to respond, as well as our resolve to continue to strive to endlessly deepen our understanding of those issues.

I am profoundly aware that although we were unintentionally subjected to limitations from outside of academia, we have also been inexorably limited by our educations, our environments, and our levels of understanding. As such, during the long process of deliberating on and writing this book, we paid special attention to listening to voices from Japan, even the sophistical arguments and negations of right-wingers, which we viewed as challenges and encouragements of some significance, which "spurred" us to seek the truth.

The opinions of our friends also pushed us to further reflection. I would like to express gratitude in particular to Mr. Oe Kenzaburo. I once asked him in an informal discussion why these Japanese soldiers, previously good fathers to their children, good husbands to their wives, good sons of their parents, had become monsters who stopped at no evil once they arrived in Nanjing. Mr. Oe lauded the direction of this thinking and then asked a further question: these soldiers who had become murderers, rapists, and looters in Nanjing changed their identities upon returning to Japan, and many again became good fathers to their children, good husbands to their wives, and good sons to their parents; what kind of psychological change belies such a transformation? The mechanisms and processes by which war distorts one's humanity is even now worthy of profound contemplation.

The reflections of our friends illuminated those blind spots that we had long overlooked. Professor Yamada Masayuki (of Osaka Kyoiku University), speaking on the mode of sexual violence perpetrated by Japanese soldiers in Yunnan, noted that atrocities were often committed by Japanese soldiers in groups, demonstrating their clear knowledge that they were engaging in criminal activities in an enemy environment. This was organized tactical behavior, aimed at completely defeating the Chinese psychologically. The occupation of women's bodies indicated their status as conquerors, and Chinese men, unable to save them, were doomed to feel guilt for their impotence the rest of their lives. Professor Yamada believes that military discipline among the Japanese army was by and large rigorous, and so atrocities occurred either under orders from superiors or with their tacit permission. He also believes that General Prince Asaka Yasuhiko, commanding officer of the Shanghai Expeditionary Army, was responsible for atrocities in Nanjing and that Asaka removed the word "miya" [palace] from his official title after the war to cut his ties to the emperor and avoid being found guilty for the emperor's war. In reality, the Japanese government has long taken pains to avoid connecting dirty war crimes with the emperor; this has affected reflection on the war as well as present-day understanding thereof.

Professor Tairako Tomonago (of Hitotsubashi University), Professor Watanabe Norimasa (of Kanto Gakuin University), and Professor Yamashina Saburo (of the Tokyo University of Education) are new friends of mine. They have pointed out that the sense of victimization of the Japanese people has obstructed them from understanding their role as victimizers, and that they should reflect upon their injuries done to the Chinese people and apologize and offer restitution to them. The Japanese government has acknowledged the Rape of Nanking as well as the damage done by their war of invasion to China and the peoples of Asia, but there has also been an unbroken sequence of voices denying these truths; this is not real reflection, and as such it will never be completely forgiven and forgotten by the Chinese people. They have further noted that we must not only study the reasons for and responsibilities underlying Japan's launch of an invasive war, but also investigate the responsibility of the original imperialist nations for the long-term "example" they set in invasion and colonization, and thus make a thorough accounting of the origins and responsibilities for wars that have taken place across the world, to rid humanity of warfare for good. Though we remain far from accomplishing that goal, they tell us we should never lay down the responsibilities of this generation toward that end.

It must be said that our friends' opinions are not always the same as ours. Renowned Rape of Nanking historian Kasahara Tokushi met with Chairman Mao Zedong in his early years, has deeply studied the casualties suffered in Nanjing as a result of the Japanese army's violence, and lays clear blame for the event on the Japanese war. He has, however, consistently referred to this period of history as the "Nanjing Incident" and not the "Rape of Nanking." In our study of the Rape of Nanking, we have no choice but to seek common ground while shelving differences and finding consensus on the basis of sincere academic research.

War means the destruction of or harm to life, especially a war of invasion. Though the war is long past, we must clarify responsibilities in order to truly summarize its lessons. Shortly after the war, the majority of German civilians held that the wartime crimes committed by Germany were matters perpetrated by Hitler and "a handful" of Nazis, and not at all their own fault. With the passage of time and the deepening of their reflections, they have come to realize that every individual as well as the bulk of the German masses all participated to some extent, and as such were at least partly responsible for what happened. In Japan, an overwhelming quantity of evidence indicates the fervor by which the common citizens supported the war on China. The "contest to kill 100 people with a sword" was no isolated incident; thousands upon thousands of Japanese commoners bought sabers at high prices to be delivered to their family members on the front so they too could become "legends of martial valor" on the Chinese battleground. Even the emperor's personal attendant was the recipient of such a sword upon his arrival in China. Every single Japanese citizen bears their own responsibility; we have long overlooked this conclusion reached by many Japanese academics over the years. To push Japanese authorities to "learn from history," our research must be more scientific and more thorough.

As we pass the seventy-fifth anniversary of the Rape of Nanking, we solemnly offer up this book to the dead, to the survivors, and to all those who, like us, look forward to justice and peace.

Zhang Sheng
Nanjing, January 2012

Foreword to the Updated and Revised Edition

On Tomb-Sweeping Day 2012, a press briefing was held at the Memorial Hall of the Victims of the Nanjing Massacre by Japanese Invaders for the publication of the updated and revised edition of *The Rape of Nanking: A Historical Study* (Volumes one and two). It is Tomb-Sweeping Day again today, and the first one since the seventh session of the Standing Committee of the 12th National People's Congress of China declared December 13 of each year "National Memorial Day for Nanjing Massacre Victims."

Solemn ceremonies held on the memorial day have seared the historical event into memory, and this is not just memory of the residents of Nanjing, or the Chinese people, but a collective memory of war and peace belonging to humanity as a whole. There are too many lessons we must learn before all of humanity can unite in a community of shared destiny bound by fraternity and love. The national memorial is a government-organized open-to-the-public ceremony infused with many layers of symbolic significance universally recognized among the Chinese people. The involvement of modern media makes it possible for the peoples of Nanjing, across China, and indeed around the world, to partake in one shared understanding and experience all at the same time.

The national memorial ceremonies are held only on the designated day every year. After several expansions, The Memorial Hall of the Victims of the Nanjing Massacre by Japanese Invaders now provides a public space reserved solely for this purpose. Since the space was finished, it has been able to facilitate personal accounts and expressions. When visitors from around the world enter the space and subjectively experience its concepts, they form an interaction with the words of the space, giving them a panoramic feeling and entry into the experience of the Rape of Nanking.

One could say that the National Memorial Day for the Victims of the Nanjing Massacre and its setting have become a political, social, and emotional force that is impossible to resist; its influence goes without saying.

At the same time, great progress has been made over the past three years in the academic study of the history of the Rape of Nanking. Professor Zhang Xianwen led us in completing *Nanjing da tusha quan shi* [Complete History of the Rape of Nanking]. *Nanjing da tusha yanjiu: lishi yu yanshuo* [Research of the Rape of Nanking: History and Discourse], edited by Professors Zhang Lianhong and Sun Zhaiwei, compiled many new achievements by outstanding researchers. Professor Jiang Liangqin and I have issued a series of dedicated papers on the topic in the periodical *Lishi yanjiu* [Historical Research]. We should note that

Li Yongdong, Li Hongtao, and others are also exploring new routes to deepen study of the Rape of Nanking.

In recent years, the once boisterous Japanese right wing has fallen into a sullen silence, and produced little by way of influential "achievements". Meanwhile, since a consensus has emerged among scholars around the world that the Rape of Nanking was a historical fact, it is no longer as contentious an issue as it had been. In my opinion, however, this is a sign that the history of the Rape of Nanking has become a serious field of study. Now, in this moment of silence on the eve of a breakthrough, the publication of a revised edition of the two-volume *The Rape of Nanking: A Historical Study* is both timely and necessary.

In light of this, I would like to continue forward following the in the academic footsteps of Henri Lefebvre, Pierre Bourdieu, Martin Heidegger, and modern scientists. In my view, the history of the Rape of Nanking is different from other periods in China's history. Its overwhelmingly gargantuan influence on the people of China and its prominent position in the domestic and foreign discourses on modern Chinese history give it a massive "gravitational field," slowing down the time of events within its pull. Time and setting are merged into one within the event, or in other words time has become an organic component of its setting. A view of the history of the Rape of Nanking "cut into slices" and "cut into chunks" using accurate timing standards clearly views the scale and intensity of all aspects of the "gravitational field" as unified, whether viewed in parts or all together.

The existence of history is the foundation of study in the field of history. In the study of history, storytelling at the macro scale and tidying up at the micro level are common occurrences, but both are bounded by specific contexts. In the study of the history of the Rape of Nanking, however, both the macro and micro levels transcend "convention."

At the macro level, it is as though the greatest international event could be made to appear on the screen through a "wormhole" as theorized by modern physics: the judgments and attitudes on conditions in the Far East of U.S. President Roosevelt and his Secretary of State Cordell Hull; competition between the army and navy of Japan as well as the whole nation's "explosion" onto the world scene via the World War; Hitler's cold-blooded, "rational" decision between China and Japan; the supernormal indifference and reverse admonishments of the British Empire toward the violence in Nanjing – calling upon Western missionaries to cease collecting evidence of crimes committed by Japanese soldiers – "that is of no use"; *Pravda*'s reproach of the Japanese army's violence and the rising silhouette of Stalin behind China's War of Resistance; Mussolini's picking sides despite declared neutrality – nobody was truly unaware of the Rape of Nanking during that time of world "policing."

At the micro level, time in historical studies is usually broken down into years, months, and days, but in this event, we have the early morning, the late morning, noon, afternoon, evening, and night, even down to hours and minutes. The result of the minute breakdown has been the "slowing down of time." As John Rabe put it, "The people feel they are afflicted with a major disease, watching the time tick away with a gaze of terror. Time is passing too slowly, as though there were 100 hours in every day and not 24." Minnie Vautrin concluded that "time seemed to have stopped." This "slowing" of time gives us conditions to observe the unlimited number of historical details and open up multiple "windows" through which to observe the event, and engrave the characteristics that the gift of time has allowed us to see deep in our memories.

December 19, 1937 was possibly a "normal" day during the Rape of Nanking. The reason we cite it as an example here is that special reporter Moriyama of the *Tokyo Asahi Shimbun* wrote in a cable from Nanjing that day:

> In the residential district, boys and girls climbed on broken horse carts, singing and dancing... tranquil eulogies issued forth from the church. This is Pastor John Magee leading his now calmed Chinese congregation in the climax of prayers after the smoke of gunpowder had cleared. Today is Sunday... Today in the square within the Japanese embassy compound, Japanese soldiers are issuing refreshments and rice cakes to refugees, as well as cow's milk and cans for the mothers of infants. It is the living image of good will.

The potential truth of "innovative" reports lies in the question of for whom they are intended. The Japanese reporter clearly stated that this was a Sunday, but the only surgeon left in Nanjing at the time – Dr. Wilson of the Gulou [Kulou] Hospital – wrote in his diary: "I guess it's Sunday." He daily performed several operations for victims and was exhausted to the point of delirium. On this morning, he went with other foreigners to lodge protests at the Japanese embassy, where he met with a secretary named Tanaka: "He himself is sympathetic but has no control over the military." On his way home, Wilson discovered Japanese soldiers looting the home of his friend Daniels, whom he drove off. "This afternoon I took out the third eye I have operated on lately and did five other smaller operations." At dinner time, "the Brady's cook and Mr. Chu... had come in to get someone to go over there and interfere with the raping of all their women." He goes on to say that several blocks near "Tai Ping Road" had been set ablaze. He also reports that a Japanese soldier had undressed himself and gotten in bed with nurses of his hospital.

On that same day, a great number of panic-stricken women and girls flooded into the refugee camp in Ginling Women's College. Vautrin's diary records the events down to the hour: "At 8 o'clock a Japanese came in with Mr. Teso from the Embassy. Having been told we had not enough rice for the refugees, I asked him to take me over to headquarters of Safety Zone; this he did, and from there a German car took me over to see Mr. Sone, who has charge of rice distribution. He promised to get us rice by nine o'clock. Later I had to go back with the car to Ninghai Road, the presence of a foreigner is now the only protection for a car. Walking back to college, again and again mothers and fathers and brothers implored me to take their daughters back to Ginling... Later the morning was spent going from one end of the campus to the other trying to get one group of soldiers after another out... in room 538, I found one standing at the door, and one inside already raping a poor girl." That afternoon Vautrin told Japanese officers what had happened. That night, four Japanese "gendarmes" stood guard on the campus. Also that night, she saw the outbreak of at least three major fires in the city.

Time gradually merges with the incident. A picture of the Rape of Nanking clearly emerges with each time sequence, each scene, each perspective, with the chunks of history combining like pieces of a puzzle. The following bit of history drawn from the Safety Zone documents from December 19, 1937 is precise down to the minute:

> 8:30 a.m., Li Wenyuan, driver for American missionary George Fitch, has had his home looted by Japanese soldiers. All eight members of his family were living in the house of a German at number 16 Luojia Road, with a Nazi swastika flag hanging outside. It was looted anyway of seven chests of clothes, two baskets of household implements, six down blankets, three mosquito nets, rice bowls, and 50 yuan in cash, and the household is now reduced to pennilessness.
>
> 3:00 p.m., Japanese soldiers break into the Gulou Hospital. When McCallum and Trimmer ordered them to leave, they opened fire, but thankfully missed.
>
> 3:30 p.m., some drunk Japanese soldiers broke into the residence of Red Swastika Society (note: a private charitable organization in China at the time) chairman Tao Xisan (note: later chairman of the puppet Nanjing Autonomous Committee), located at Number 2 Mogan Road. They broke open his chests. Smythe and Sperling prevented "this likely premeditated looting."
>
> 4:45 p.m., Miner Searle Bates was called to number 16 Cangping Road, where the Japanese had looted and set fire to the building, which was completely destroyed.
>
> 5 p.m., a young man was sent to the Safety Zone headquarters; he had been stabbed in the chest by a Japanese soldier for no reason at all. Fitch and Smythe went to the Japanese embassy to report the violence of the Japanese soldiers and brought the young man to Gulou Hospital.
>
> 6 p.m., six Japanese soldiers climbed into the residence of John Rabe in darkness. When Rabe shined his flashlight on one of them, he pointed his pistol at Rabe, who then ordered

the six to climb back out the way they'd come in. They asked that Rabe let them out by the front door, but "Rabe refused to give them this face."

6 p.m., an employee in the Security Zone came to summon Bates, Fitch, and Smythe to the house at number 19 Hakou Road to drive off four Japanese soldiers presently raping a woman. After they'd been driven off, the woman and her child(ren) were transferred to the main building of University of Nanking.

Incidents at every point in time all encompass a great deal of information and are worthy of detailed dissection and analysis by researchers (who already possess a great deal of "present" knowledge, understanding, and information about the Rape of Nanking and have been molded by such). The "materialization" of time within the Rape of Nanking along with granular and concrete understanding of events therein allow us to feel and experience the Rape of Nanking today several decades hence, just as though we were there; there is still "historical warmth." We can feel the "presence" of the Japanese soldiers at the scenes of each of their crimes, with the "bestial machinery" as described by a German there at the time coming out "in living color." The throngs of Japanese soldiers deliberately committing crimes under orders have been described by Hannah Arendt as "the banality of evil," but in fact their innovative means used in their crimes as well as their breaking through the base lines of humanity were long ago revealed to have been "creative" expressions of far-reaching "evil imagination." The lives of the victimized Chinese were being trampled and stamped out minute by minute, turning time into an "accomplice" of the violence – after 1949, when the Rape of Nanking had long been forgotten, time became another kind of "violence." The neutral Westerners were eyewitnesses to, recorders of, and participators in the "complex of time and events"; today they have come to be guiding emissaries into the events of the Rape of Nanking that stride across history and reality. The history of the Rape of Nanking has its own research concepts and scopes, as well as its own value judgments, and even the routes upon which it relies have their own "norms"; this is precisely the manifestation of its integration with time entities and its reaching of a "higher" plane.

Time has already "begun," and space has already "awoken." Study of the history of the Rape of Nanking within the non-Euclidean space-time complex cannot continue along a "level and smooth track", this means that the demands on us have grown even greater.

The work behind this revision was herculean, with the additions and enrichments of the text going without saying. The redoing of annotations was especially troublesome, adding a great deal of citations of originals in foreign languages to allow those interested in the material to research more on their own. Although I must in advance note that this will sound like a disclaimer, in truth the revised edition still fell far short of encompassing all the new thoughts of the authors, despite the amount of work that went into it. I was also unable to open up the broad world that other researchers might have with their more profound studies and wisdom. So please understand that this is merely one achievement along the road of work in progress, for which I earnestly request comments and critiques.

Zhang Sheng

Tomb-Sweeping Day 2015

Contents

| 1 | The Rape of Nanking in Light of the Japanese Army's Overall Strategic Decisions. Observations Based in Japanese Considerations —— 1 |

2	Changes in the Order of Life for Nanjing Residents Before and After the Massacre —— 15
2.1	The End of the Normal Order of Life and the Dawn of the Order of Life During the Defense —— 16
2.2	Approach, Arrival, and Continuation of the Power Vacuum Period —— 39
2.3	Deadlock and Construction of a "Normalized" Colonial Order in the Transitional Period —— 76
2.4	Transmission of Information Inside and Outside the City —— 90
2.5	Public Security Response —— 103
2.6	Real Estate Issues —— 110
2.7	The Closing and Opening of Commodity Exchange Markets —— 118
2.8	Damages to Water and Electricity Facilities and Their Restoration —— 127
2.9	Transportation Obstructions Inside and Outside the City and Their Clearance —— 134
2.10	Medical Aid —— 140

3	Westerners in Nanjing During the Massacre —— 151
3.1	Westerners in Nanjing before the Fall —— 151
3.2	Westerners and International Rescue Organizations —— 162
3.3	Westerners in the Face of the Rape of Nanking —— 190
3.4	Relations Between Westerners, Japanese, and Chinese —— 237
3.5	Western Diplomats in Nanjing —— 259
3.6	Westerners in the Wake of Massacre —— 270

4	The "German Perspective" on the Rape of Nanking Based in German Diplomatic Documents —— 286
4.1	The Germans behind the "German Perspective" —— 287
4.2	The Core of the "German Perspective": The Truth behind the Rape of Nanking —— 293
4.3	Interaction between the "German Perspective" and British and American Perspectives —— 300
4.4	The "German Perspective" and German Interests —— 307

5 The "American Perspective" on the Rape of Nanking —— 316
- 5.1 The People behind the "American Perspective" and Their Reasons for Staying in Nanjing —— 316
- 5.2 Documents of the American Perspective and Their Dissemination —— 320
- 5.3 The Core of the American Perspective: The Truth of the Rape of Nanking —— 326
- 5.4 The American Perspective and American Interests —— 332

6 The Rape of Nanking in Japanese Historical Sources —— 342
- 6.1 Japanese Military Archives —— 342
- 6.2 Diaries and Correspondence of Japanese Officers and Soldiers —— 365
- 6.3 Memoirs of Former Japanese Soldiers and Military Correspondents —— 380

7 Food Issues During the Rape of Nanking. Focusing on the Safety Zone —— 409
- 7.1 Food Supply Conditions and Food Policies in Nanjing before the Fall —— 409
- 7.2 Food Negotiations between the International Committee and the Japanese —— 420
- 7.3 Food and Living Conditions of Nanjing Residents during the Rape of Nanking —— 441

8 Property Losses of Nanjing Residents during the Rape of Nanking. An Initial Analysis Based on Extant Materials in China —— 455
- 8.1 Surveys and Statistics Made during the War —— 456
- 8.2 Surveys and Statistics from after the War —— 464
- 8.3 Calculating Property Losses of Nanjing Residents during the Rape of Nanking —— 471
- 8.4 Epilogue: Impact of Nanjing Residents' Property Losses —— 481

9 Initial Study of PTSD Among Rape of Nanking Victims —— 486
- 9.1 Introduction of the PTSD Concept —— 486
- 9.2 PTSD Symptoms Among Rape of Nanking Victims —— 489
- 9.3 The Case of Minnie Vautrin —— 495

10 The Nanjing Trials —— 501
- 10.1 Establishment of the Nanjing Military Tribunal —— 501

10.2	Organization and Structure of the Military Tribunal —— 511
10.3	Building Cases for the Rape of Nanking —— 520
10.4	Public Participation in the Trials —— 542
10.5	Reflections on the Post-War Trials of Rape of Nanking Criminals —— 554

11 **The Rape of Nanking Cases in the International Military Tribunal for the Far East Trial Arguments and Their "Legacy". Based in a Study of Cross-examinations —— 559**
11.1	Cross-examination and Calling into Question Witnesses and Sworn Statements of the Prosecution —— 561
11.2	Witnesses and Sworn Affidavits of the Defense, and Cross-examination by the Prosecution —— 570
11.3	Testimony and Cross-Examination of Matsui Iwane —— 583
11.4	The Inheritance of the IMTFE Defense's Legacy by the Japanese Right Wing —— 591

References —— 605

Postscript —— 642

Postscript to the Revised Edition —— 644

1 The Rape of Nanking in Light of the Japanese Army's Overall Strategic Decisions. Observations Based in Japanese Considerations

The great massacre perpetrated by the Japanese army in Nanjing shocked the world. From then until now, there have been relentless attempts to uncover the reasons behind this tragedy. The themes that usually catch the eye are Japanese militarist education, insufficient supply in the Japanese army's rear, as well as the related themes of the policy of local requisitioning, the grievous casualties the army had suffered in the siege of Nanjing and their psychology of retribution, slackening of military discipline, and so on. These studies have doubtlessly added to our understanding of the Rape of Nanking.

However, other works have noted that conditions such as the policy of local requisitioning were part of the overall Japanese invasion of China, but that the massacre of the inhabitants of a captured city such as Nanjing was rare indeed (of course, wherever the tip of the spear of the Japanese army landed, it caused great loss of life and property). Why did the Rape of Nanking occur even as the Japanese army was hoisting the banners of "just war"? To what extent was the Rape of Nanking a random mistake or inevitable within the overall Japanese war of invasion?

Writers have come to feel, through their considerations and studies, that one cannot accurately understand the outbreak of the Rape of Nanking separately from the overall Japanese war plan for the invasion of China. That is because the conflict between Japan and China was the primary conflict in East Asian international relations of the time, and Japan was the primary party of said conflict. If we hold tightly to the Japanese side's thinking and decisions, we can clearly assess the strategic opportunity taken for the Japanese invasion of China.

1.1 Choosing War

The strategic reason Japan chose to launch an all-out war of invasion on China was that China had made breakthrough progress in state organization primarily to resist Japanese power; so if war hadn't been launched immediately, it would not only have been impossible to defeat China, but China may have ultimately reclaimed sovereignty of the Northeast (Manchuria).

The "Marco Polo Bridge Incident" was previously understood as the catalyst for mid to long-range plans for the Japanese following the Eastern Conference, as reflected in the Tanaka Memorial. Shigemitsu Mamoru, Japan's representative at the signing of the unconditional surrender, said: "Later events in East Asia and corresponding actions taken by Japan took place exactly in accordance with the steps outlined in manuals like the Tanaka Memorial, and so it is difficult to clear up foreign suspicions regarding the Tanaka Memorial" (Shigemitsu 1987, 20). The Marco Polo Bridge Incident was certainly one step in Japan's overall invasion of China.

It is, however, undeniable that the there was a degree of "randomness" on the surface of the Marco Polo Bridge Incident. Why did the Japanese launch an all-out invasion of China only six months after the "Xi'an Incident"? Why the Japanese military resolutely push forward its all-out war of invasion while people like Ishiwara Kanji (head of the Japanese Army General Staff Office at the time of the Rape of Nanking), primary planner of the "Mukden Incident," and others opposed war at a time when China's strength was depleted, thereby creating disadvantageous conditions for Japan's preparations for war on the Soviet Union? I will attempt to, on the basis of fragmentary evidence, attempt to assemble a complete picture departing from a few points seldom noticed previously.

Suma Yakichiro served as consul-general of Japan in Nanjing, a position he left on January 18, 1937. On March 15, he gave a speech at the Japan Industrial Association titled "Present and Future of Japan-China Relations." This is an important document worthy of our deep study today because it represents contemporary Japanese judgments of conditions in China at the time, and also demonstrates the logic the Japanese employed in launching their all-out war on China.

In Suma's estimation, the Xi'an Incident demonstrated that China was now unified, and this unity created an unprecedented situation in the history of modern China: "During the First Sino-Japanese War, if you went to Sichuan, Yunnan, or other mountainous provinces, most people did not know their country was currently fighting a war with Japan. Of course, this was also attributable to reasons such as poor transportation links. It was just this China with its complete lack of concern for external affairs that, upon hearing of the Suiyuan Offensive, launched into a nationwide movement of support for the Suiyuan army in all parts of the country, with some places ceasing broadcast of dancing music for three days, and even dance halls in some places sending 20 percent of their revenues in support of the Suiyuan army; you could thus see how zealous they were. What's more, even the inmates of a prison in one place donated funds to the Suiyuan army; this would seem unprecedented anywhere in the world. Where does this zealousness come from? I just spoke of the two levels of Chinese feelings toward Japan – anti-Japan sentiments among the common Chinese people have become very serious, and the Suiyuan Offensive is just the yardstick for measuring that seriousness."

As his listeners were all magnates with their hands on the levers of the Japanese economy, Suma continued in extreme earnestness, concluding that it was Japan's actions that had led to the new conditions in China. "There were two goals, or maybe we should say two situations, that led to this unity. The first was oppression from Japan. Of course, I should rather say that it was just this oppression that gave China an opportunity to move toward unity; I think this is a fact beyond argument. Even though the Chinese are now saying that China's strength is growing with the stabilization of the foundation [of] Chiang Kai-shek's regime that we see today, there are actually two reasons afoot: the first is Japan's invasion, and the second is... It's actually very interesting once you start talking about it. I'll go ahead and say it out loud: it's Yu Youren, director of the Control Yuan." Suma concluded that the reason behind unification was: "This so-called 'unification' could not be brought about on the strength of warlords or the government alone, but was as symbolized by the student movement; it was realized only after the aspiration for unification had deeply penetrated the hearts of the people and become a movement of national unanimity."[4]

According to modern theories on nationalism, external threats and feelings of hatred for an enemy constitute a basic model for the construction of a nation-state (Gellner 2002). Suma provided anecdotal evidence backing this theory: "In 1931, that being six years ago, the nationalist government hired the German Hans von Seeckt. Chiang Kai-shek asked him two questions. The first was how to make China's army strong, and the other was what kind of policy he should adopt toward Japan. To the first question von Seeckt responded: if China wishes to become stronger than Japan, weapons are necessary, airplanes are necessary, but from my experiences in organizing and running the German Defense Force, the most pressing task for China at present is to cultivate among the military a mentality of viewing Japan as the enemy." Here the veracity of Suma's evidence is not important. What is important is that this became the thread that tied his discourse together, i.e. that the unification of China was closely related to Chinese opposition to Japan, or in other words further unification of China necessarily meant intensification of anti-Japan sentiments there, in Suma's estimation.

Suma discussed the example of his meeting with H.H. Kung: "H.H. Kung – the actual director of the Executive Yuan – said that if I wanted to get Japan-China relations on a good track, we couldn't leave the Manchurian issue untreated. I am completely opposed to 'establishing an aside' in the Manchurian issue, he told me. Without a solution to the Manchurian issue, it would be impossible to have a satisfactory dialogue between Japan and China. I took this opportunity

---

4 Further references to this speech will not be cited.

to ask him what kind of a solution he hoped for. He answered that Japanese investments in Manchuria – he is a professional investor himself – seem to be nothing more than investments. If they are indeed simply investments, then we can allow them to stay but we hope that the sovereignty of Manchuria be restored to China. If it is returned to China, then we might take the initiative to either give Manchuria 'dominion' over its own affairs the way Great Britain has done with Ireland or treat it the way Great Britain has treated Canada. China will take the initiative in handling this matter. You can talk until your tongues fall out, but so long as Manchuria is not returned to China, we will have nothing to discuss with you." Suma then commented: "China is already dreaming about Manchuria. We must see this as proof for what I just said, proving that only after internal pacification and unification has China gradually come to notice Japan's soft underbelly, and thus has started feeling us out."

Since Chinese unification necessarily meant antagonism toward Japan, what then did Japan need to do? All those diplomatic documents that mention "peace and guidance" at every turn are full of sparkling rhetoric, but we get a clear picture of the Japanese government's attitude in the recollections of a member of the Japanese Residents in China Association who left Nanjing at the outset of war, Shoji Tokuji:

> I thought of something I said to Colonel Okido shortly before the outbreak of the war: "If the military training of the residents of Nanjing continues another two years, Japan probably won't be a match for them." Colonel Okido replied: "It won't take two years. In another half year we won't be able to take them on." So I don't know if it was fortunate or unfortunate that Japan launched its offensive while it still had a chance at victory. I really think this was the blessing of heaven. I deeply feel that this was the luck of the heavenly kingdom of the rising sun (Japan). At the same time I sincerely prayed that this offensive would be the last in the Japan-China conflict, that this would completely destroy the Chiang regime's resistance against Japan, and that this was a good chance to bring Japan and China back onto the proper course of goodwill for one another.

The idea that Japan should invade before China grew so powerful as to be unconquerable was not shared only among these Japanese residents of China, but was a "public opinion" shared across the Japanese public, and was also clearly the basis of official government policy.

In March 1937, military attaché to the Japanese embassy in China Kita Seiichi, Japanese China Garrison Army Staff Officer Wachi Takaji, and Ohashi Kumao reported to the Japanese Army Staff Headquarters: "The Chiang Kai-shek regime's policy of resisting Japan will, we're afraid, remain in place until Manchuria is restored. It would be an extremely great error to think that concessions in North China will eliminate the policy of resistance against Japan... We cannot assume that ordinary means will reverse the above-mentioned worsening of Japan-China relations." They also tentatively raised the possibility of declaring war on the Soviet Union, noting: "Before launching war on the Soviet Union, we should deal China a blow to damage the foundations of the Chiang regime" (Japanese Ministry of Defense War History Bureau 1987, 293). Thereafter news began to spread in Tokyo that "on the night of the seventh evening of the lunar calendar, something like the Mukden Incident will be reenacted in North China" (Imai Takeo n.d., 16)

On July 6, 1937, after the Japanese had admitted that "there is the possibility for imminent crisis in the conflict between the Japanese and Chinese armies in the vicinity of the Lugou [Marco Polo] Bridge," Japanese Prime Minister Hirota Koki proposed to a meeting of the Cabinet that it would be unlikely that rash wishes for restoration of amity between Japan and China would end in success in the current whirlpool of resistance to Japan and anti-Japan sentiments. Although this gravely dissatisfies Japan, it would nevertheless seem that we have no choice but to resolutely push forward the correct policy: "All cabinet members expressed assent" (Japanese Ministry of Defense War History Bureau 1987, 297). Thus the Marco Polo Bridge Incident became an inevitability amid otherwise ostensible randomness.

1.2 Choosing Nanjing

Japan chose Nanjing as its objective because at the time the Japanese believed it to be the center of Chinese resistance to Japan. Short of capturing Nanjing, the thought went, it would be impossible to punish China for its resistance to Japan and force the country to change policy.

At the outset of the war, Japan's military focus was North China. But then tensions emerged in Shanghai, which Shigemitsu Mamoru analyzes thus: "The sensitivity toward the Japan-China conflict in North China was reflected in Shanghai, where anti-Japan agitations immediately became widespread." He did not mention that Chinese anti-Japan sentiments were the result of Japan's long-term invasion, but rather said that Japan needed to invade because China was resisting Japan; this logic was common across military and political circles in Japan at the time. Shigemitsu, however, was clearly deeply versed in how the Japanese military acted, adding: "The army will create an incident in the North, and the navy will inevitably also provoke some conflicts in Shanghai" (Shigemutsu 1987, 129–130). As a result, the war's focus quickly shifted to the Yangtze River Delta, posing a threat to Nanjing.

When the Battle of Shanghai broke out, however, Nanjing still hadn't been listed as a target for attack. On August 15, 1937, the Japanese Shanghai Expeditionary Army was given orders to "coordinate with the navy, annihilate all enemies in the vicinity of Shanghai, occupy Shanghai and primary battlefronts in the northern region, and protect the subjects of the empire" (Wang and Guoshan 2006, 1). The Japanese Central China Area Army was formed on July 11 of that same year. Chinese forces in Shanghai were near collapsing at that time, but the Central China Area Army was still not commanded to advance to Nanjing: "The Central China Area Army's orders were to coordinate with the navy to break the enemy's willingness to fight and annihilate enemies in the vicinity of Shanghai to find an opportunity to end the war" (Wang and Guoshan 2006, 4). That same day, Japanese military officials designated the combat range of the Central China Area Army as "principally the area to the east of the line running between Suzhou and Jiaxing" (Wang and Guoshan 2006, 6). On November 20, the deputy commanding officer of the General Staff Headquarters telephoned Matsui Iwane to inform him that the army had exceeded its predesignated combat range (Wang and Guoshan 2006, 9). On November 24, the original combat range of the Central China Area Army was abolished (Wang and Guoshan 2006, 10), indicating that high Japanese officials had set their sights on Nanjing. That same day, the Central China Area Army issued these orders: "Coordinate with the China Area Fleet to rapidly seize Nanjing" (Wang and Guoshan 2006, 20).

The Japanese decision to expand the goal from Shanghai to Nanjing was to a great extent related to the personal resolution of Matsui Iwane. In his diary entry from August 16, 1937, he writes: "Our forces should rapidly attack the objective of Nanjing. We must meet up with the Central China Expeditionary Army (about five divisions), and we will inevitably topple the Nanjing government in one blow" (Wang 2005b, 23). Thereafter, he sent an unbroken chain of messages to the Japanese government and highly placed officials in the military, asking for reinforcements. On September 23, Ishiwara Kanji's departure and his replacement by the more radical Shimomura Sadamu must have given hope to Matsui that his wishes were going to be fulfilled. On October 14, seizing the opportunity of a visit to Shanghai by an administrative officer in the navy, he said: "With the tenacious resistance being put up by enemy forces in the Jiangnan region, if we want to finish this war in a month or two, it will be extremely difficult to close that paragraph" (Wang 2005b, 97). He was laying the foundations for subsequent expansion of the war. On October 20, he asked Lieutenant Colonel Suzuki of the General Staff Office, currently in Shanghai, to tell everyone important in the General Staff Office: "Our ultimate military objective is Nanjing" and "the crux of our strategy in the final analysis is to attack Nanjing" (Wang 2005b, 129).

He completely ignored the opinions coming from Japanese commanding authorities at the time. On November 15, Matsui used the opportunity of working under General Staff Office Strategy Department section chief Masaaki Kagesa and Ministry of the Army Military Affairs Bureau director Shibayama Kenshiro to demonstrate to his superior officers the inevitability of an attack on Nanjing, which "they have basically come to understand" (Wang 2005b, 103–104). This gave rise to pressure on all sides. At that time the Central China Area Army had broken out of its established combat range and was already fighting its way toward Nanjing. After the Japanese government and military had finally resolved to attack Nanjing, Matsui writes in his diary: "I elatedly feel that those opinions I did my utmost to stir up are finally having their effect" (Wang 2005b, 140).

Matsui's unwavering opinion that Nanjing must be occupied and that the center of resistance to Japan must be cleared away was broadly shared across all walks of life in Japan at that time:

> When common residents of Nanjing began military training, I thought, that's nothing too special, so I didn't pay much heed. But two or three years later, I noticed that the facial expressions of young adults in Nanjing had become stern, that the light of vitality overflowed from their eyes, and that they stood in powerfully erect posture when working. When I mentioned this observation to Colonel Amamiya, he said: "Everyone who's been through military training is like that; it's nothing special." That's when I realized the true force of education. Thereafter I paid more attention to the results of Chinese military training, and as a result I realized that their military training was quite serious and thorough. I couldn't help but perceive a kind of threat (Shoji 1940).

This is how the Japanese consulate-general in Nanjing reported on conditions in that city following the Marco Polo Bridge Incident: "As the extent of the war grows and expands, the mentality of resistance to Japan in Nanjing has surged to the extreme… radical anti-Japan-ists have begun exerting pressure on our citizens here. Scenic spots in Nanjing's suburbs as well as some mountains in its periphery, previously open to unrestricted sightseeing, have now been forbidden to Japanese, under the pretext that they are restricted military areas. All cinemas in the city are playing anti-Japanese propaganda films, wantonly inciting the feelings of the masses, making the anti-Japan mentality grow stronger on the daily, tension rampant over every quarter of the city" (Japanese Ministry of Foreign Affairs Diplomatic Archives 2001, 205–207).

Staff officer Tanaka Shinichi also describes the significance of occupying Nanjing in his diary: "An attack on Nanjing is necessitated by none other than the disregard for Japan's efforts to put Japan and China back on the road of support and guidance. The ultimate goal behind Commander Matsui's inducing their surrender is also this… We must never relax in punishing the regime that resists

Japan… The world is currently in a period of transformation. If we understand current world conditions, then we must see that China can only successfully organize itself as a nation on a foundation of amity toward Japan…The emergency in China is a tragedy in East Asia, but to put an end to this tragedy, Japan cannot avoid performing a thorough surgery. Seen in this light, the occupation of Nanjing is merely the prelude to the China issue, and a true protracted war begins today" (Japanese Ministry of Defense War History Bureau 2001, 403–404).

How could the personal opinions of Matsui Iwane overpower the existing plans of the Japanese government and military to become facts? This is closely connected with the common practices of the Japanese military at the time. The tradition of *Gekokujō*[5] was still alive in the Japanese military at the time: radical front-line officers and soldiers could exceed limitations set by their government or military superiors and afterward could expect retroactive praise and support, and sometimes even honors and awards. Therefore, "many wanted to be honored for meritorious service in a second Mukden Incident" (Shigemitsu 1987, 112). Matsui had had his eyes on China for a long time, and in 1935 and 1936 had traveled extensively in northern and southern China, reaching this conclusion: "Japan-China relations are worsening in all areas day by day. Recent conditions are as I described before; what pains my heart is that we're nearly in a situation in which we have no choice but to raise an iron hammer to compel Chinese authorities to reflect" (Wang 2005b, 22). Matsui's "pained heart" was given an opportunity to hold power over Japanese civil and military authorities once he'd been appointed commander of the Shanghai Expeditionary Army.

The problem was that China's will to resist couldn't be broken even by the occupation of Nanjing. The truth is that China truly solidified into a unified line of national resistance against Japan only after the occupation of Nanjing; in other words, the Japanese occupation did not break China's will but made it stronger. The question of how to integrate the wishes of the Japanese military to seize Nanjing with practical conditions in China, and to avoid realizing the worst nightmares of the military – becoming bogged down in the mire of a protracted war – drove many in Japan to "reflection." Horiba Kazuo, a firm supporter of Ishiwara Kanji and at one time opposed to expansion of the war into Nanjing, analyzed the situation thus:

> The administration of East Asia must begin from the liberation of China and Japan-China cooperation. China's greatest worry of late has been the Japanese threat and the redding of the Soviet Union. At the same time, Japan should show the way for China, using benevolent

---

[5] Literally "bottom trumps top." In this sense, it means the prerogative of inferior officers to surpass the orders of their superiors (translator's note).

guidance, and help it achieve necessary unification. If we can only eliminate China's feelings of being threatened, then we can alight on the path of Japan-China cooperation... (Horiba 1988, 107).

Here Horiba departed from the unlimited catastrophe the Japanese invasion had instigated in China and indulged in fantastical talk about Japan-China cooperation; as compared with Matsui this was the pot calling the kettle black. Nevertheless, in objective terms "eliminating China's feelings of being threatened" has always been a prerequisite for friendly relations between China and Japan, but the invading Japanese army, unwilling to face squarely the truth that the war had only inflamed patriotism and nationalism among the Chinese people, now made an even more alarming choice.

1.3 Choosing Massacre

Here the primary reason we claim that the Japanese army "chose massacre" is that they established violence as a form of tactical behavior, using terror, barbarity, and extreme measures on the Chinese capital of the time in an attempt to destroy China's willingness and ability to resist, and thereby achieved a war objective.

The United States National Archives possesses the battlefield diary that a Japanese soldier from Yamanashi Prefecture named Hosaka Akira mailed to the Allied Command Military Law Division after the war. In it he claims that on November 29, 1937, somewhere on the outskirts of Changzhou, he killed over 80 civilians with a machine gun "on orders" (Hosaka n.d., n.p.).

This extremely little known diary gives us a hint that the Japanese army's massacre was perpetrated on orders from superiors, and that the massacre had begun well before the army's push to Nanjing. Once there, Imperial Japanese Army 16th Division commander Nakajima Kesago wrote this in his diary entry from December 13, 1937:

> We have basically not carried out a policy of taking prisoners, but have adopted the guiding policy of complete extermination. But since we're dealing with groups numbering in the thousands, the five thousands, and the tens of thousands, not even our arms are sufficient for timely removal... After the fact I learned that Sasaki's troops alone took care of nearly 15,000 people, and a single battalion leader holding Taiping Gate had taken care of 1,300. Another seven or eight thousand had been collectively finished near Xianhe Gate... A large trench was necessary to handle the aforementioned seven or eight thousand, but it was hard to locate one. We've been scheduled to divide them into groups of one or two hundred to carry to appropriate places for disposal (Wang 2005b, 280).

One could say that savagery had become second nature for this division commander who had once issued orders in headquarters that swordsman Takayama test his sword on prisoners (Wang 2005, 278). He chose to directly order his subordinates to instigate a massacre. Matsui Iwane, the highest-ranking commanding officer of the Imperial Japanese Army on hand at the time, chose to adopt an attitude of knowing that atrocities were taking place but doing nothing to stop them, or in other words giving free rein to massacre. The International Military Tribunal for the Far East noted in its judgment that: "He (Matsui) had the power and the duty to control his troops and protect the unfortunate residents of Nanjing. He certainly was aware of what was happening from his own observations and from the reports of his subordinates. He admitted to having heard about illegal behaviors of some extent on the part of his soldiers from military police and consular officials. The court finds that there is sufficient evidence to demonstrate that Matsui Iwane was aware of what was happening. He took no measures whatsoever, no measures that might have put an end to the violence" (Yang 2006, 610–611). As a footnote to the Tokyo tribunal's decision, Matsui's diary entry from December 20, 1937 includes some sensitive information: "For a while there was some looting and raping among a small number of my officers and men; this is always one of those realities that is hard to avoid" (Wang 2005b, 153). The fact that Matsui claimed the perpetrators of the violence to be "my officers and men" and not merely some individual soldiers is, in addition to being particularly frank, worthy of mulling over. The director of the Japanese Foreign Ministry Bureau of East Asian Affairs at the time of the violence, Ishii Itaro, testified that during the Rape of Nanking both he and Foreign Minister Hirota Koki had heard of the violence being perpetrated by the army through many different channels, that Hirota had discussed the matter with War Minister Sugiyama, that Ishii had notified the first chief of the military affairs division of the army, that reports of the violence being perpetrated by the Japanese army in Nanjing never stopped coming, but "Foreign Minister Hirota did not treat with this issue frequently or even many times, only once or twice at most" (Yang 2006, 507–520).

In light of the above, it is clear that the Japanese army from top to bottom adopted an attitude of choosing violence. The question is why did they choose to enact massacre upon Nanjing?

Matsui gives the following two reasons for the Japanese army's violence in Nanjing:

1. Since the army's landing at Shanghai, our officers and men had been constantly engaged in ferocious, difficult combat. This combat caused our men to develop intense feelings of enmity toward our enemy.

2. During an intense and rapid pursuit of the enemy, our army did not receive prompt resupply of food and other necessary materials. (Wang 2005b, 194)

Matsui told part of the truth in this summary, but still it lacks persuasiveness. For example, the intensity of the Battle of Hengyang in 1944 did not pale to that of Nanjing, with the Japanese taking the city only after three months of stiff fighting. Supply was an even bigger problem for the Japanese then; with Chinese and American control of the skies, the Japanese had to drive in supplies only at night, and soldiers were still wearing summer clothes in winter. After the city was occupied, the harm done to Chinese soldiers and civilians was severe, but nothing like the Rape of Nanking happened. So given the lifetime of treacherous efforts Matsui had made to extol Sino-Japanese friendship, which he was still extolling at the time of the Tokyo Trial, the judges concluded that Matsui's writing in his diary that the violence was "hard to avoid" can only be explained as intentionality; he intended for his diary to explain his actions to later generations.

Niu Xianming was a battalion commander in the engineering corps of the KMT's instruction division at the time of the Battle of Nanjing. During the Rape of Nanking, he dressed as a monk and concealed himself in Nanjing's Yongqing Temple and Jiming Temple. He escaped from the city after August. He writes: "Soon I returned to the rear area, where I repeatedly discussed the enemy situation with intelligence comrades. Everybody's conclusion was that the Japanese thought that once they'd taken China's capital, we would certainly come out to discuss peace terms. So they didn't hesitate to engage in collective massacre, in violation of humanitarian and international laws, to weaken our manpower and troop sources" (Niu Xianming 2005, 70). We believe Niu came very close to the truth here. The choice of committing violence in Nanjing was related to Nanjing's special status in the country. The occupation of Nanjing was not merely a military tactical arrangement. Right at the apex of the massacre, the Japanese government installed a puppet regime and attempted to cow the Chinese before their so-called "new order in East Asia." There was certainly political and strategic logic underlying the Rape of Nanking.

So a further question is what were the mechanisms by which the Japanese used the Rape of Nanking to achieve their political and strategic goals?

Professor Yamada Masayuki of Osaka Kyoiku University understands this issue profoundly. In the issue of sexual violence, Yamada explains this as the product of disorder in the ranks, and calls it wrong. He notes that military discipline in the Imperial Japanese Army was severe – no disorder was allowed – and thus all signs indicate that sexual violence during the massacre was conducted under orders, in an attempt to strike at the enemy through sexual violence on their women. He further explains: under threat of force from Japanese soldiers, Chinese men had no choice but to look on as their women were dishonored. This was very depressing and very frustrating. The powerlessness of their men then in turn filled the Chinese women with contempt and regret.

Professor Yamada points to a study he performed in Yunnan, where in one rural village 25 women were subjected to sexual violence by Japanese soldiers. Each woman was gang raped by at least five Japanese soldiers. Yamada infers that the Japanese army viewed the entire environment as hostile, in physiology, safety, and other areas. Such incidents of sexual violence were premeditated acts of organized crime. He continues that there is a contradiction between the privacy of sexual behavior and the openness of collective sexual violence, and that the only explanation is that the acts were carried out on orders from superiors, and that they were executed as part of a combat strategy (Yamada n.d.).

Are there grounds for Yamada's deductions? Let's let the facts speak for themselves.

Truly only an extremely small number of the cases of rape perpetrated by Japanese soldiers during the Rape of Nanking were solo acts. Under the majority of circumstances, these crimes were perpetrated by groups of Japanese soldiers in front of the families of their victims. Chairman of the International Committee for the Nanking Safety Zone John Rabe writes: "Last night up to 1,000 women and girls are said to have been raped, about 100 girls at Ginling Girls College alone. You hear of nothing but rape. If husbands or brothers intervene, they're shot" (Rabe EN, 77). Secretary of the Legation at the German Embassy in Nanjing Georg Rosen writes: "Every night Japanese soldiers break into the refugee camp established in the campus of University of Nanking to either drag women away to rape or to fulfill their evil desires in front of others, including the family members. The cases are innumerable in which accomplices restrain their husbands or fathers, who are forced to witness the ruination of their family's reputation" (Zhang 2005, 327).

Commander of the Nanjing Instruction Corps Impedimentia Battalion Guo Qi, who hid in the Italian consulate in Nanjing, describes in more detail another case, which serves as a typical footnote to Professor Yamada's theory:

> That day a few dozen Jap soldiers came before the door to the foreign-style building next door, wearing black and yellow collar badges, but without serial numbers and without commanding officers. They first drove every man out of the large parlor. Then they assembled all the women past their prime, and right there in the parlor, in front of the children, in broad daylight, as brazenly as possible, they stripped these older women naked and performed their collective farce, three-on-one, five-on-one, over and over without end. How many children witness such terrifying scenes? They were all scared to the point of crying. Outside the parlor, inside the courtyard, the husbands of those women were all completely dejected, bearing red faces and ears. Some cowered on the walls and wailed in lamenta-

tion. Some covered their heads with their hands and stood completely immobile. Once their bestial desires had been satisfied, the Jap soldiers, who still hadn't fastened their pants, walked out onto the road, where they came across another group of Jap soldiers, again numbering in the dozens. This second group burst right back into the house their comrades had just left... (Zhang Lianhong 2005, 167–168).

"Wearing black and yellow collar badges, but without serial numbers and without commanding officers"; this demonstrates that the Japanese soldiers were intentionally concealing their identities. The unbearable nature of the plight of the Chinese men, who were not allowed to leave the scene, demonstrates that the Japanese soldiers accomplished their goal of terrorization. Openly calling their friends to participate demonstrates that the Japanese soldiers knew they would not be punished for raping the women of Nanjing. Matsui admits: "These bad deeds happened in the chaos of battle, and it is thus a fact that we had no power to try those responsible" (Wang 2005b, 194). The major crimes of the Rape of Nanking did not take place "in the chaos of battle," but happened when the Japanese army had complete control of the city, when the Chinese soldiers had already laid down their arms, and when the citizens were completely incapable of resistance. Matsui's explanation actually demonstrates the tacit agreement that existed between Japanese soldiers and officers.

The use of violence as a strategic means was a great "innovation" of the Japanese Imperial Army in its invasion of China. In light of this, there is a clear logical explanation for the Rape of Nanking, and it is thus clear that the event was by no means a random occurrence taking place in the heat of battle. The institution of comfort women that was extended to the entirety of areas under Japanese occupation to keep up troop combat capacity originated from similar strategic considerations.

All the above demonstrate that all links in the strategic decision-making of the Japanese army were connected. Despite some points that consistently defy expectations on the surface, the intrinsic logic to these events was uniform, and the Rape of Nanking was the natural consequence of the evolution of the Japanese military's war strategy. It is only on this basis, in consideration of all reasons near and far, that we can comprehensively understand the occurrence of the Rape of Nanking.

Japanese records, particularly those from commanding officers during the Rape of Nanking, have long given us a series of attention-turning unbroken clues about the fundamental reasons for the occurrence of the Rape of Nanking; these are worthy of our deep contemplation. Take Matsui Iwane and his deputy chief of staff Muto Akira as examples.

On March 8, 1946, Colonel Thomas Morrow questioned Matsui Iwane. Had the Japanese troops that invaded the city from December 13 to 16, 1937 been old or new troops, and were they commanded by highly experienced officers? Matsui answered clearly: "They were well-trained troops commanded by experienced officers... I've never heard of these troops having performed misdeeds anywhere else in China" (Yang 2006, 222–223). During the April 22, 1946 interrogation of Muto Akira, Muto said: "The troops who committed violence in Nanjing and in Manila were recruited in haste and had not undergone regular military education" (Yang 2006, 278). What explains these contradictions? Once you read the rest of the document, you realize that Matsui wanted to prove that the troops under his command were highly disciplined, and that his own requirements were rigorous in the extreme, and as such they could not have possibly committed the massacre. Muto, for his part, wanted to prove that after the dispatching of troops to Siberia in 1915, the Japanese army grew increasingly violent, that there was violence in Nanjing, but that he took great pains to improve the education of the army. The fact that they both underscored different aspects that were nevertheless advantageous to their positions demonstrates that it would be easy for us to lose the forest for the trees by fixating on details such as whether the troops were old or new, or whether they had enough food to eat, as the basis for our discussion of the massacre.[6]

---

[6] The primary contents of this chapter were included in an article published in *Nanjing shida xuebao* 6 (2007). The contents have been revised for inclusion in this book.

2 Changes in the Order of Life for Nanjing Residents Before and After the Massacre

Changes to the order of life for Nanjing residents before and after the Rape of Nanking took place along a clear trajectory. In this book we discuss changes to this order that took place from July 1937 to April 1938 in five distinct phases: "normal order of life," "order of life during the defense," "order of life during the power vacuum," "order of life during the transition," and "'normalized' colonial order of life."

Normal order of life: pre-war Nanjing had developed its own unique character over ten years of construction. As the capital of nationalist China, the city drew in professionals from all walks of life, was endowed with a peaceful, developing, and stable environment, and gave its residents space to pursue life satisfaction and a meaning to their existence. It possessed normal social foundations, which gave the residents of Nanjing a normal order of life.

Order of life during the defense: the Japanese air force began bombing Nanjing on August 15, 1937, gradually grinding commerce in the city down to a halt, greatly damaging infrastructure, driving throngs of residents to evacuate the city, and resulting in the westward evacuation of the government and cultural institutions. The environment of peace, development, and stability gradually disappeared, and the residents of Nanjing entered an order of life of defense against the Japanese attack, which lasted until the fall of the city on December 13, 1937.

Order of life during the power vacuum: after the fall of Nanjing on December 13, 1937, the Japanese Imperial Army entered the city and began the Rape of Nanking, which commanding officers did nothing to stop; during this time survival became the focus of life for Nanjing residents. The Chinese regime had evacuated, but the new regime had yet to be established. Despite the mammoth efforts on the part of the Safety Zone Committee to subdue the Japanese soldiers, that body lacked sufficient legal force, and their 20-plus members were no match for a fully armed criminal army. At this time there was a power vacuum in the city, and its residents entered an order of life under said power vacuum. This situation continued until the end of 1937.

Order of life during the transition: on January 1, 1938, the puppet regime propped up by the Central China Area Army – the Nanjing Autonomous Commit-

Note: Chapter contributed by Guo Zhaozhao.

tee[7] – went into full operation, ending the power vacuum that had existed in control of the city. As the committee became involved in managing the city, the Central China Area Army began actively scouring high and low for Chinese bigwigs to fill out and organize their puppet government for Central China. Several factors prevented the wanton raping, killing, and looting of the Japanese army from coming under control at this time: Tokyo's unclear policies toward Nanjing, the personal plans of high-ranking officers in the Central China Area Army, and insufficient "autonomy" on the part of the autonomous committee to prevent those with real power from becoming criminal entities. Nevertheless, atrocities committed by the Japanese army began to taper off owing to the successful transmission of information in and out of Nanjing, the return of European and North American diplomats, and changing of the army division in charge of defending the city.

"Normalized" colonial order of life: commander of the Central China Expeditionary Army Hata Shunroku established the general line of thought for the Central China puppet government in accordance with the philosophy of "guide actions in accordance with circumstances." Shunroku, in accordance with Tokyo's position, systematically built a "normalized" colonial order of life for the residents of Nanjing. The founding of the reformed puppet government of the Republic of China and the Supervisory Municipal Office of Nanjing were both the results of this work and also the symbols that this work was becoming deeply ingrained.

2.1 The End of the Normal Order of Life and the Dawn of the Order of Life During the Defense

2.1.1 General conditions of the pre-war normal order of life for Nanjing residents

After the founding of the nationalist government in Nanjing in 1927, Nanjing City Hall was established on April 24, later renamed the Nanjing Municipal Government on June 1. Under it were established such bodies as: the Municipal Government Conference Bureau, the Counselor's Office, the Secretariat, the Land Bu-

---

7 The *Nanjing shi zizhi weiyuanhui*, a puppet government established for Nanjing by the invading Japanese army, is known variously in Western sources as the "Autonomous Committee," the "Self-Government Committee," the "Autonomous Government Committee," and other similar names. In this translation unless quoting a primary source, I have preferred the translation "Autonomous Committee" (translator's note).

reau, the Education Bureau, the Social Bureau, the Work Bureau, the Finance Bureau, the Public Security Bureau, the Health Bureau, the Railroad Management Bureau, the Municipal Government Management Office, the Park Management Office, the Municipal Livelihood Office, and so on.

The above municipal government organs assumed relevant functions of city management, and on that foundation the curtain of wide-scale construction of the city was drawn back. After ten years of construction, the city's population had grown rapidly, urban spaces had quickly expanded, infrastructure was continuously improved, and the economy and life grew daily more vigorous. Nanjing was, after all, China's political, military, and cultural center.

2.1.1.1 Population growth and city management

There were somewhat more than 200,000 residents of Nanjing in the first year of the Republic of China (ROC), and up to 360,000 by 1927. In that year population growth accelerated, with the total exceeding one million by 1936. See the following statistics:

Year of the ROC (standard calendar year)	Population
1 (1912)	269,000
2 (1913)	269,000
3 (1914)	377,120
4 (1915)	368,800
5 (1916)	378,200
6 (1917)	377,549
7 (1918)	376,291
8 (1919)	392,100
9 (1920)	392,100
10 (1921)	380,200
11 (1922)	380,900
12 (1923)	401,500
13 (1924)	395,500
14 (1925)	395,900
15 (1926)	395,900
16 (1927)	360,500
17 (1928)	497,526
18 (1929)	540,120
19 (1930)	577,093
20 (1931)	653,948
21 (1932)	659,617
22 (1933)	726,131
23 (1934)	795,955

Continued

Year of the ROC (standard calendar year)	Population
24 (1935)	1,013,320
25 (1936)	1,006,968

Table 1: Population of Nanjing from 1912 to 1936.
Source: Jing Shenghong et al. (2005b, 7–8).

Population in the urban center accounts for the bulk of the above overall population figures. A comparison of birth and death rates in urban and rural regions of Nanjing in June 1937 indicated an urban population of 855,632 and a rural population of 161,182.

Area	Population	Births	Birth rate	Deaths	Death rate
Urban	855,632	1,498	1.75	1,200	1.40
Rural	161,182	281	1.74	146	0.90
Total	1,016,814	1,779	1.75	1,346	1.32

Table 2: Urban and rural populations of Nanjing in May 1937 and comparative birth and death rates.
Source: Jing Shenghong et al. (2005b, 4–5).

In response to rapid growth, in January 1928 the municipal government established the Capital Construction Committee, responsible for establishing the "Capital Construction Plan" and systematically promoting municipal government construction in Nanjing.

The "Plan" subdivided the city as follows: the Central Political Zone to the south of Purple Mountain; the Administrative Zone to the north of Gulou (drum tower) around Fuhougang; the Residential Zone within the old city; the Commercial Zone around the Ming Palace; the Cultural Zone between Gulou and the Wutaishan district; and the Industrial Zone on the northern and southern banks of the Yangtze River. On October 3, 1930, the 96th meeting of the ROC National Congress passed the "Naming Map for Capital Thoroughfares." The following arrangements and naming schemes were adopted under the map:

Axis thoroughfares: including Zhongshan Road, Zhongyang Road, Zhongzheng Road, Zhongnan Road, and Hanzhong Road. Its route was aligned as follows: Zhongshan Road from Zhongshan Gate to the side of Xiaguanjiang. The road was called Zhongshan North Road to the north of Gulou, Zhongshan Road from Gulou to Xinjiekou, and Zhongshan East Road from Xinjiekou to Zhongshanmen. Zhongyang Road began at Gulou and ended in the north at

Zhongyangmen. Zhongzheng Road began at Xinjiekou and ended at Zhubaolang (intersection of Baixia Road and Jianye Road). Zhongnan Road was the southerly section of Zhongzheng Road beginning from Zhubaolang. Hanzhong Road began at Xinjiekou and ended at Hanxi Gate.

Northwestern thoroughfares: named after the 18 provinces of China, with the order of which street took which province's name determined in relation to the area of the province and the amount of taxes it paid to the national treasury matching with the length of roads.

Northeastern thoroughfares: named in accordance with the significance of the name of Wuzhou (five continents) Park, for example Huanhai Road, Guanhai Road, Henghai Road, etc. Thoroughfares in the Central Political Zone in the vicinity of the Ming Palace were given names from the Three Principles of the People, such as Minsheng Road, Minquan Road, Datong Road, Bo'ai Road, etc.

Southern thoroughfares: mostly located in the south of the old city, centered around modern day Zhonghua Road and Hongwu Road. There is a long history in the site of the old city, and so all names of roads there are related to said history (Nanjing Roads Management Office Historical Records Committee 1990, 110–115).

The construction of grassroots political power was also steadily improved in Nanjing. One study concludes: "There were also great changes to political power at the municipal level in Nanjing. When the municipal government had just been established, all areas within the city proper and suburbs as well as of Pukou went under its jurisdiction. The entire prefecture was broken down into three districts, Nanjing City, Jiangning County, and the Sun Yat-sen Mausoleum Park, but corresponding institutions were not established. Thereafter the city was divided into six areas: east, west, south, north, center, and Xiaguan,[8] but still with no district-level government. Beginning in July 1931, local autonomy was promoted in Nanjing, with the establishment of district government organs as an important content of autonomy. Owing to the large quantity of undeveloped land in Nanjing city limits, agricultural development still played an important role in Nanjing's economy. The city was further subdivided into 21 districts to integrate agriculture. District administrative offices were established to handle local autonomy and assist in municipal government work. But district administrative office matters were often the prerogative of a single person, with primitive organization. In 1932 the 21 autonomous districts were redivided into eight autonomous districts,

---

8 The term *Xiaguan* in Chinese means "bottom pass." In Nanjing this was the location of the city's wharf on the Yangtze River, located out of the city proper but of great historical significance in the era of flourishing river commerce. In many foreign texts of the time the name is written "Hsiakwan" (translator's note).

with the same jurisdiction as police bureaus. In 1934, provincial and prefectural boundaries were finalized, with some townships and towns allocated under the administration of Nanjing City, and so the three additional districts of Xiaolingwei, Yanziji, and Shanghxinhe were established; thus there were finally 11 autonomous districts in Nanjing. There was another district: the Sun Yat-sen Memorial District, which had an infinitesimally small population, most of whom were soldiers, managers of the facility (public servants), and a few farmers" (Wang 2001, 60).

There were five organizations under each district administrative office: civil affairs, economy, culture, security, and residency management, each of which facilitated with relevant work from the city government. To increase the transparency of government, the Nationalist Government comprehensively promoted the *Baojia* system at levels below the district administrative office.

When the Nanjing municipal government was established in 1927, it established the Public Security Bureau, entrusted with such matters of public security as maintaining public order, residency management, traffic management, and maintaining social decorum. Beginning in 1928, a series of people advocated for putting the Public Security Bureau under the control of the Ministry of the Interior. On March 2, 1929, the 22nd meeting of the ROC National Congress resolved to change the name of the Nanjing Municipal Public Security Bureau to the Capital Public Security Bureau, and put it under the jurisdiction of the Ministry of the Interior. The congress also resolved that the Capital Police Department was responsible for facilitating the needs of the Capital Special Municipal Government (Wang 2001, 63).

Under the Capital Police Department, there were three sections of general affairs, public security, the inspector's office, and the special affairs group, as well as eight bureaus, nine teams, and two offices. The eight police bureaus had jurisdiction over the eight urban districts of Nanjing, and the nine teams were the police patrol teams over the three districts of Yanziji, Shangxinhe, and the Sun Yat-sen Mausoleum, in addition to the peace keeping squadron, the investigation squadron, the special affairs squadron, the firefighting squadron, and the patrol teams over Bagua Island and Huashenmiao (Wang 2001, 63).

2.1.1.2 Construction of traffic networks and information platforms

Traffic networks in Nanjing could be divided into two constituent parts: long distance and intra-city public transit, and could also be broken into rail transportation, road transportation, boat transportation, and airplane transportation.

Materials indicate that from 1904 to 1911, the completion of the Shanghai-Nanjing Railway and the Tianjin-Pukou Railway gave Nanjing land access to China's two greatest industrial centers of the time: Shanghai and Tianjin (Wang 2001, 13). The Nanjing-Wuhu Railway was constructed between 1934 and 1936. These three land connections provided strong support for transportation in Nanjing. In addition to the railways, there were also highways connecting the capital with the nearby cities of Hangzhou, Wuhu, Shanghai, Yangzhou, Zhenjiang, Chuzhou, and other places, which the Nanjing municipal government continually worked to improve. The shipping industry grew rapidly, with the most influential project thereof being the construction of the Zhongshan Wharf, which was officially opened on March 16, 1936. Boats sailed at fixed times from the wharf to Shanghai, Hankou, Zhenjiang, Yangzhou, Wuhu, and other places. Air transit in Nanjing was ahead of its time, with the construction of the Ming Palace Airport beginning at the end of 1927 and finishing two years later, creating the nation's first civil air route: Nanjing to Shanghai.

The intra-city transportation network was also continuously improved. An intra-city rail line had already been built in the city by the end of the Qing Dynasty, with small trains connecting Xiaguan and Zhongzheng Street (now Tianbaixia Road), with an initial total of six stops in the city: "Jiangkou, Xiaguan, Sanpailou, Wuliang'an (now Gulou), Dushu [Viceroy's Office] (this stop's name was changed nine times in accordance with political changes, but has been known as Changjiang Road station since liberation), and Zhongzheng Street" (Nanjing Local Records Compilation Committee 1990, 17). The Dingjiaqiao station was later added. In 1936, the Nanjing rail network relentlessly continued expanding southward, finally linking with the Nanjing-Wuhu Railway station. In addition to the rail network, there were also passenger horse carts, rickshaws, tricycles, taxis, and other conveyances. The opening of the public bus system in particular brought convenience to the lives of Nanjing residents. On May 5, 1931, the Jiangnan Automobile Company opened with Wu Zhuozhi, who had studied abroad in France on a work-study program, as its manager. The company was first located at Xihua Gate (now next to the Yixian Bridge), and operated long-distances buses between Nanjing and Jurong, Changxing, and Hangzhou. In July 1932 it began operating public buses within Nanjing proper, and developed sight-seeing buses from Xinjiekou to the Sun Yat-sen Mausoleum. On November 10, 1933 the company opened bus line number two within the city. In July 1935 it bought the Xinghua Company and became the only operator of public buses in the city. In October of that year, the Jiangnan Company opened the doors at its new address on Zhongyang Road, and built the first assembly line automobile manufacturing plant in the country. By 1937, it was operating six bus lines in the city, two lines from the mausoleum to the western suburbs, and three long-distance lines. It had expanded its fleet from six to 304 vehicles, of which between 120 and 140 operated every day, with an average of 120,000 person-trips per day. The company boasted 1,600 employees and increased its capital from 100,000 to one million yuan (Nanjing Local Records Compilation Committee 1990, 20).

As Nanjing built its transportation network, it also attached importance to the construction of information transmission platforms. Nanjing originally possessed one wireless radio tower, and in 1928 it built a shortwave radio tower. After years of integration and reorganization, in 1935 the city built the high-power Nanjing Radio Station. At the same time, the Nationalist Government in Nanjing attached great importance to the construction of long-distance telephone systems, installing in the Ministry of Transport and Communications a project office for long-distance calls between nine provinces as well as a dedicated management office for long-distance calls between Shanghai and Nanjing. By the time war broke out, a nationwide long-distance telephone system centered in Nanjing with spokes running to all major cities had been basically completed. The intra-city telephone network was also comprehensively expanded and improved on the foundations of the existing Jinling Telegram Bureau. As for mail, on the eve of the War of Resistance, several dozen post office branches and agencies had been established all over Nanjing, and mail service had been established between Nanjing and all provinces and prefectures of the nation. In addition to radio, telephone, and post, newspapers and magazines were also important channels for the circulation of information both inside Nanjing and with the outside world. After the Nationalist Government had been established in Nanjing, press agencies, newspapers, and magazines sprouted in Nanjing like bamboo shoots after a spring rain, and there was prompt delivery service of Shanghai newspapers and magazines to Nanjing as well.

2.1.1.3 Economic development and public services

Statistics indicate that from 1928 to 1937, "there were a total of 558 factories and mining enterprises in Nanjing, with combined total capital of 30.8736 million yuan, and both the number of such enterprises and their total capital experienced a 10-fold growth from 1927" (Shi 1999, 30). The aforementioned economic development resolved employment problems for some city residents and also changed the city's employment structure, with the service industry, the transportation and shipping industry, and the industrial sector coming to account for a large share of overall employment. There remained, however, many small retailers, as recalled by massacre survivor Mou Xiulan: "My father Mou Shizhen sold cloth, not in a store, but rather he walked through the streets and alleyways of Nanjing hawking cloth that he carried on his body. My entire family relied primarily on my father's income from selling cloth to maintain life; the whole family relied on him. He made just about enough money to cover our needs, and we had nothing to worry about in life" (Zhang and Yuanzhi 2006, 508). Another massacre survivor Xu Qi recollects: "My father did small business. He ran a shop in Changjinglou where he mostly sold handicrafts. All the living expenses of my family came out of the money my father earned in that shop, but no matter how you put it, we had no worries for basic needs; you could say we had peace and contentment in work and life. My mother was a housewife. She took care of chores in the house. Back then women generally didn't have to work outside of the house" (Zhang and Yuanzhi 2006, 522).

There were glaring differences in resident incomes owing to discrepancies in the employment structure. On the whole, in 1930s Nanjing, high level members of the intelligentsia, including government officials, university professors, lawyers, and accountants, all earned high incomes, while the vast majority of residents earned income of less than 20 yuan per month. The lower levels of the income hierarchy were also able to eke out a living owing to low prices.

Over ten years of construction, water and power infrastructure in Nanjing were also greatly developed. Before the construction of a waterworks in Nanjing, city residents had long consumed river and well water. After the ROC established Nanjing as its capital, the municipal government pushed waterworks construction onto the agenda since the river water was polluted and there was insufficient well water. Nanjing mayor Ma Chaojun wrote in a report in February 1937: "Main pipes completed from April 1, year 24 (1935) to the end of December, year 25 (1937), cover the areas of Shanghai Road, Yunnan Road, Yizu School, Guiyuntang, Zhujiang Road, Zhongyang Road, Guangzhou Road, the fourth district of the new residential zone, Chaoku Street and Dashiba Street, the second main pipe entering the city, Jianye Road, Gongyuan Road (between Dazhong Bridge and Fucheng Bridge), Pingshi Road, Caixia Street, Chuanban Alley, Zhongyang Road (from Xuanwumen to Meiling), Zhimaying common residential zone, the AB section of Yuhua Road to Wugui Bridge, Muxu New Village, Hubei Road, Maqun Town to Baishui Bridge, Wawa Bridge, Donghai Road, Yangpi Alley marker 34, Jingwu Road from Wugui Bridge to Dengfushan, and so on, with a total of 44,769 meters of pipe mains laid. Since the water was turned on last year, a total of 138,000 meters of pipe had been laid in the entire city, totaling 130 kilometers" (Jing et al. 2005, 41). Another report reads: "As of the end of March in the year 24 (1936), there were only somewhat more than 1,600 subscribed customers, with total monthly water fee income totaling only a little over 31,000 yuan. As a result of hard work in reorganization and tenacious running of the company, the business is growing more developed daily, with new customers gradually signing on. As of the end of December in year 25 (1937), the number of tap water customers skyrocketed to over 4,000, and monthly income from

Item	Rice	Wheat	Noodles	Soybeans	Maize	Beef	Pork	Fish	Turnips	Cabbage
Unit	Dan[a]	Dan	Dan	Jin	Jin	Jin	Jin	Jin	Jin	Jin
Price	9.63	5.84	0.089	8.83	5.55	0.27	0.34	0.18	0.036	0.29
Item	Bean sprouts	Soybean oil	Sesame oil	Soy sauce	Sorghum liquor	Sugar	Salt	Raw cotton	Coarse cloth	Fine cloth
Unit	Jin	Jin	Jin	Jin	Jin	Jin	Jin	Jin	Chi	Chi
Price	0.036	0.27	0.27	0.08	0.35	0.19	0.12	0.54	–	0.11
Item	Shirt material	Black Jesus	Denim	Towel	Long socks	Thread	Reed	Firewood	Sticks	Coal
Unit	Chi	Chi	Chi	Each	Pair	Roll	Dan	Dan	Dan	Tonne
Price	0.07	0.18	0.18	0.11	0.13	0.007	0.75	0.91	0.70	25.13
Item	Tea, yinchen	Tea, green tips	Cigarettes, good	Cigarettes, poor	Cigarettes	Candles	Kerosene	Soap	Nails	
Unit	Liang	Liang	Liang	Liang	Pack	Bag	Jin	Piece	Jin	
Price	0.05	0.02	0.07	0.02	0.16	0.07	0.19	0.04	0.03	

Table 3: Commodity prices in Nanjing, January–June 1937 (price unit: yuan).
Source: Zhang (2010, 622–623).
[a] Now a *dan* is 50 kg, a *jin* is 0.5 kg, a *liang* is 50 g, and a *chi* is 1/3 of a meter. A footnote in *The Good Man of Nanking* claims a *dan*, written "tan" at the time, was equivalent to 133 pounds (translator's note).

water fees surged to over 63,000 yuan, a miraculous doubling from last year's figure. This year we should find new ways of promotion, to keep the business thriving" (Jing et al. 2005, 39)

Officials in Nanjing attached importance to the construction of electrical infrastructure. Prior to the war, officials improved and completed two routes, the Shangfangmen Power Station six *li* outside of the Zhonghuamen and the Xiaguan Power Station to serve the living and production needs of city residents. The former provided primarily power for streetlights, and the latter was the center of power generation in Nanjing. A 5,000 kilowatt turbine was installed in the Xiaguan Power Station in 1931, to which was added a 10,000 watt generator and a new boiler in 1934, bringing annual power output to 33 million kilowatt-hours. There were 40,000 clients, a ten-fold increase from prior to 1927. In 1937, the Construction Committee merged the Xiaguan Power Station with the Qishu'an Power Station to create the Yangtze Electrical Company, with increased capitalization of 10 million yuan (Wang 2001, 20).

Great progress was also made in Nanjing's medical industry. In April 1927, upon its establishment, the nationalist government took charge of the University of Nanking Hospital, which was renamed Nanjing City Gulou Hospital.[9] In August 1928, the hospital was returned to University of Nanking. The hospital boasted a complete range of facilities, with departments for internal medicine, external medicine, obstetrics, testing, radiology, pharmaceuticals, surgery, and so on; it was capable of providing complete diagnoses and surgical treatments. Central Hospital was established at the same time. It traced its origins to the Central Standard Military Hospital founded in 1929, renamed National Central Hospital the following year. This was the first modern state-founded hospital built by China since the founding of the nation. Former Minister of Health Liu Ruiheng was appointed as the hospital's first director.

In addition to these large hospitals, Nanjing boasted several small charity medical institutions, private hospitals, and teams of private roaming doctors.

2.1.2 From the Marco Polo Bridge Incident to the fall of Shanghai

The nationalist government in Nanjing actively responded to mounting tensions in Sino-Japanese relations. After the January 28 Incident of 1932 in Shanghai, the

---

9 The Chinese term *gulou* means "drum tower." This same hospital is referred to under a number of names in different sources: University Hospital, Drum Tower Hospital, Kulou Hospital, etc. In the text body, I have used Gulou Hospital (translator's note).

nationalist government decided it should build defensive fortifications between Shanghai, China's economic center, and Nanjing, China's political center. The basic conclusion reached at that time was: "The Japanese navy may invade from the Yangtze River or the Bay of Hangzhou. Their air force can raid Nanjing and all other major cities from Shanghai. Their army might land near Shanghai or to the north of the Bay of Hangzhou and split into two columns to attack Nanjing. As such, we ought to divide the region of Nanjing, Shanghai, and Hangzhou into three defensive regions, Nanjing-Shanghai, Shanghai-Hangzhou, and Nanjing itself, with the Nanjing-Shanghai region being the focus" (Huang 1985, 55). Construction of fortifications began in 1934 and was completed in 1936.

The informed decision reached at the time was that the Shanghai-Nanjing route would be the primary route chosen for an attack coordinated between Japan's army and navy, and so it was decided that "the Wu-Fu line (from Suzhou to Fushan) and the Xi-Cheng line (from Wuxi to Jiangyin) would be the primary battlefields of the region, and that rear and forward positions should be established around these areas" (Huang 1985, 56). In order to link the Wu-Fu line and the Xi-Cheng line on the Shanghai-Hangzhou line, it was decided that the "Zha-Jia line (from Zhapu to Suzhou via Jiashan) and the Hai-Jia line (from Haiyan to Wujiang via Jiaxing) would be the primary battlefields, and that a rear position and a forward advancing position should be established around it" (Huang 1985, 56). After deep deliberations about defensive installations in the Nanjing region, the following was decided:

Encircling fortifications and multi-ring defensive fortifications were built outside the city of Nanjing, and alert positions were established in front of the battle positions. It was decided to establish peripheral fortifications along the line running between Wulong Mountain, Qixia Mountain, Qinglong Mountain, Chunhua Town, Niushoushan, and Dashengguan. The wings were established against the natural moat of the Yangtze River to form an arc-shaped defensive perimeter, and the primary defensive direction was established as the southeast. The inner defensive ring was established as Nanjing's city walls, and the outer ring was established on the line between Purple Mountain, Qilinmen, Yuhatai, Xiaguan, and the battery in the fort at Mufushan, forming two defensive circles outside the city to be used in tandem, the inner line for supporting the outer, and the outer for solidifying the inner… In addition, a bridgehead fort was built at Pukou to the north of the river to seal the crossing. The alert position ran across the line from Houtoushan, Dalianshan, Hushu, Molingguan, and Jiangning Town. Despite its relative distance from the outer defensive perimeter, it allowed for ample time to prepare for battle (Huang 1985, 57).

2.1.2.1 Continuation of war and the fall of Shanghai

On August 15, 1937, Matsui Iwane was ordered to take up command of the Shanghai Expeditionary Army. Japanese army headquarters made the following demand: "The commander of the Shanghai Expeditionary Army should coordinate with the navy, annihilate enemies in the vicinity of Shanghai, occupy Shanghai and primary battlefronts in the northern regions, and protect subjects of the empire" (Wang and Guoshan 2006, 1).

Matsui expressed dissatisfaction with these orders, holding that a speedy attack on Nanjing should be the goal. In his diary entry of August 16, he writes: "It seems that Minister of the Army Sugiyama's personal opinions do not differ from those above. But since the opinions of the General Staff Headquarters differ, the Minister of the Army did not express agreement, but rather reminded me that caution and circumspection must surround such words and deeds in places outside of the Ministry of the Army" (Wang 2005b, 24). On August 20 Matsui took charge of the 3rd Division, the 11th Division (minus the Amaya detachment), the independent 7th Machine Gun Battalion, and the 5th Tank Battalion, and brought them out to battle. All these forces identified deeply with Matsui (Wang 2005b, 28).

On August 23 Matsui's forces reached Shanghai, where they were met with heroic resistance from Chinese defenders and suffered great casualties. Matsui used all means available to bring attention to the fighting at Shanghai among high officials in Japan and to be given reinforcements. On September 8, the Japanese army chief of staff cabled Matsui to inform him that four infantry battalions, one artillery battalion, and some other piecemeal battalions of the Taiwan Defense Force under Lieutenant General Shigeto were being dispatched to reinforce the Shanghai Expeditionary Army. Shigeto's forces arrived in Shanghai on September 14. On September 22, the 101st Division arrived. The 9th Division arrived on September 27. Afterward the 5th Wilderness Artillery Battalion of the 13th Division commanded by Lieutenant General Uchiyama landed.

The Japanese army incurred heavy casualties in the battle for Shanghai. Matsui's diary entry for September 28 reads: "Total casualties: 2,286. Total wounded: 6,637. Total sick: 2,825. The great number of casualties is difficult to believe" (Wang 2005b, 79). The Japanese army strengthened its attack on Shanghai, but again the casualties mounted.

	Casualties	Replacements
3rd Division	6,026	Approx. 6,500
11th Division	6,380	5,000
101st Division	2,811	Did not arrive
9th Division	2,894	Did not arrive

Continued

	Casualties	Replacements
13th Division	156	Did not arrive
Shigeto Detachment	998	Did not arrive
Tanigawa Detachment	70	
Total	19,835	11,500

Table 4: Casualty figures for all divisions of the Japanese Army up to October 14, 1937. Source: Wang (2005b, 98).

On October 16, Tokyo informed Matsui it was sending three more divisions to bolster the Shanghai Expeditionary Army. Matsui wrote in his diary that day:

> Today Liutenant Colonel Suzuki of the General Staff Headquarters arrived here. He informed me that the center had created another army (three divisions), and was planning to dispatch this army to join the fighting in Zhejiang in November. This is what I had wanted from the beginning, and was a plan based in our general operational direction, and so I feel extraordinarily happy. This plan shows that the central ministry is slowly changing its mind. I also won't meet the fate of *seppuku* (Wang 2005b, 100–101).

The army he referred to was the 10th under command of Lieutenant General Yanagawa Heisuke. On October 20, 1937, Tokyo issued orders to dispatch the 10th Army: "The 10th Army commander should coordinate with the navy to land on the northern shore of Hangzhou, to enable the commander of the Shanghai Expeditionary Army to successfully complete his mission" (Wang and Guosha 2006, 3). On November 4, the 10th Army arrived in the Bay of Hangzhou and prepared to land.

Matsui assumed complete command of the 10th Army on November 7, per orders from Tokyo, but Tokyo also made a demand of Matsui: "The combat zone of the Central China Area Army is principally the region to the east of the line between Suzhou and Jiaxing" (Wang and Guoshan 2006, 6). By November 9, the Japanese army had encircled Shanghai. That same day, "On November 9, the chairman ordered that our forces divide in two and retreat across the entire line, one part to Hangzhou and the other to Nanjing" (Zongren 1988, 490).

On November 12, Shanghai fell. The Military Affairs Commission of the nationalist government and Chiang Kai-shek both issued "Letters to Compatriots in Shanghai." The commission's letter read: "Beloved Shanghai compatriots, our forces have temporarily retreated back from near Shanghai for strategic reasons. We are doing our utmost to solidify a second battle line, and we will certainly actively press forward in the shortest time possible to reclaim our Songjiang and Shanghai. This was a planned, strategic retreat, and absolutely does not signify defeat in the war. The War of Resistance Against Japan has only truly started at this time, which our compatriots have already come to understand and toward which they can make determined efforts" (Ma Zhendu 2005, 62). Then Nanjing came under attack.

2.1.2.2 Japanese air raids on Nanjing

After the August 13 Incident (the Battle of Shanghai), Japan began evacuating its subjects from Nanjing, a processed completed on August 15. Then Japan began bombing Nanjing. A record from the Japanese consulate in Nanjing reads: "Officer Yasuda and the three remaining police officers escorted the evacuees to the train station at Pukou, and then they returned to the consulate through the dangerous atmosphere by 1:20 pm. It was around this time that the Chinese authorities sounded air raid sirens. About 30 minutes later, seven or eight of our fighters appeared three times in the skies over Nanjing dropping bombs on the Ming Palace Airport and other places" (Zhang 2007, 405). Minnie Vautrin's diary entry of August 15, 1937 reads: "This afternoon two air raids took place in Nanking. They were our first and they were particularly fierce ones."

At this time the residents of Nanjing began the order of life during the defense, in response to the bombing raids, and suffered great casualties. The document "Excerpts Related to Corpse Burying Activities by the Nanjing Branch from the World Red Swastika Society's Questionnaire on Branch Activities in All Localities" reads: "August 15, air raid sirens in Nanjing. Our society's relief team departed upon hearing the sirens. The wounded were brought to hospitals for treatment, total of 373. The dead were encoffined and buried outside the Zhonghua Gate. Among the dead were ten Japanese airmen who had died for their country; these were buried in the potter's field outside the Zhonghua Gate. The following year Japanese Naval Attaché Sugimoto came to our society for discussions. He dispatched his people to the potter's field, where on Sugimoto's instructions, the airmen's bodies were disinterred and cremated. The ashes were returned to their home country. These are the actual accomplishments made by this Swastika Society to save life and rescue the dying in the enactment of humanitarianism" (Sun 2007, 73).

The Chinese Air Force lagged far behind the Japanese in strength. By the end of November, the Japanese Air Force ruled the skies everywhere from Shanghai to Nanjing. Wang Zhuo, then a unit commander under the 5th Battalion of the Chinese Air Force, recalls: "After the August 13 battle had started, the KMT possessed about 250 military airplanes, including some old ones, and most of those were engaged in combat at Shanghai. By November 6, we had in Nanjing only seven airplanes that could still take off, and we had suffered many casualties...

By the end of November, the Air Force General Command and all of our pilots who had survived retreated from Nanjing to Wuhan" (Wang n.d., 360).

The Japanese Air Force's primary bombing targets were military installations, party and government bodies in Nanjing, and important departments. Rear Admiral Mitsunami Teizo testified to the Tokyo tribunal: "On September 20 of that year, we launched an air raid targeting all major government organs in Nanjing, their General Staff Headquarters, and their radio towers" (Sheng and Yang 2007, 123). John Rabe's diary entry of September 22 read: "After the signal (the long signal) came that announced the end of the second air raid, I rode out in my car to inspect the entire city. The Japanese had specifically targeted the central headquarters of the KMT, where the administrative offices and studios of the Central Broadcasting Station were located" (Rabe CN, 10). The Japanese had also bombed Nanjing's public facilities. Acting UK ambassador in Nanking Robert Howe wrote in a September 25 telegram to his Foreign Office: "Nanjing was hit by five consecutive raids today. The Japanese started bombing the city at 9 am and continued until 4 pm. The lighting system and power station have been badly damaged, and cannot function normally. All of Nanjing was enveloped in darkness prior to 9 pm, after which time the authorities restored street lighting by use of a small power plant somewhere in the suburbs. Bombs also fell on the train station located at the Ministry of Railways in Xiaguan and its environs (only about 400 yards from the embassy) and near the civilian airport. I know that the telegram office and waterworks were also hit, because the water supply stopped at the time, although it has now been restored to normal. Other bombs landed between the Central Hospital and the buildings of the Central Health Management Department" (Sheng 2006b, 215).

The Japanese had spies communicating, coordinating, and guiding on the ground during the bombing. Vautrin notes in her diary entry of August 19, 1937:

> Suddenly Chen Mei-yu (1920) came on to the campus all excited and with her hair and clothes covered with dust... Mei-yu thinks there were spies on the campus and that by means of lights they were directing the bombing. An important meeting of the presidents of several government universities was going on in the basement of the library building at the time of the bombing but fortunately no one was hurt.

Robert O. Wilson's letter home of August 22, 1937 reads: "Several citizens have been arrested as traitors. One man, the proprietor of the biggest store near us, who has just put up an additional modern furniture store that looks like 5th Ave. or at least Broadway, was caught giving signals with green and red lanterns on the roof his new store as the bombers came over in our fiercest raid the other night. Another wealthy merchant on Tai Ping Road has also been arrested."

The Japanese air raids on Nanjing were intense and lasted a long time. They were still ongoing up to the eve of the occupation, with the most ferocious bombing happening in September and October. The sustained bombing upset the normal order of life for Nanjing residents.

2.1.2.3 Judgments and responses by Nanjing residents

In response to the bombing, Nanjing officials adopted a series of responses, including the digging of air raid trenches, deployment of anti-aircraft troops, anti-aircraft exercises, restrictions on communications and lights during air raids, and so on. All these activities were a direct message to the people of Nanjing: the war is upon us. Those people in turn made a response to the spreading flames of war.

a. Judgments and responses by officials

Under unified instruction from the nationalist government in Nanjing, family members of officials began being evacuated at the end of July. The July 30 cable from He Yingqin to Liu Guangmi reads: "It was reported at a meeting yesterday (the 29) that residents of all major towns along the river should gradually evacuate. Nanjing's population of over a million is extremely inconvenient in wartime. When it becomes necessary, we can first move the women and children elsewhere, and secret preparations should also be made to remove the families of members of all major government organs, to prevent obstruction of public work and other affairs. As this matter is of the utmost importance, the Military Affairs Commission should hold a secret meeting with all agencies and ministries to discuss and draft an appropriate plan, which should be incrementally enacted once it is revised and approved. I hope this advice will be adopted immediately" (Ma Zhendu 2005, 50). Minnie Vautrin heard the same news, despite being outside the system. She writes in her diary entry of August 2, 1937: "Yesterday it was said that an announcement was made to officials to get their families out of the city. The reason was to lessen the number in Nanking and to free officials of family responsibility – but the result has been to frighten the people terribly. Trains and boats are packed and tickets have been sold for days in advance. Thousands are leaving."

The westward evacuation of the families of public servants was basically completed by the end of October. During this time, the Japanese were also extremely attentive to changes in the order of life for Nanjing residents, dispatching secret agents to obtain intelligence in Nanjing several times during this period. The "Letter from the Japanese Consul-General Okamoto in Shanghai to Foreign

Minister Hirota" of October 27 reads: "The family members of public servants and military personnel in Nanjing have all sought refuge elsewhere, and there has been a precipitous drop in the city's population. A police department survey indicates a current population of somewhat over 530,000, these all being public servants, those with immovable assets, local merchants, and others who need to steadfastly remain in Nanjing to the last. Most people remain tranquil" (Ma Zhendu 2005, 38). The letter goes on: "Small numbers of low-level personnel have been left behind in all government organs. High-level personnel are secretly conducting affairs in other locations. Many public servants have been laid off and many departments have been merged. At present most workers are vigorous young people. With affairs so tense, all volunteer work and conferences have been halted. Public servants are as tense as military personnel, as during the Northern Expedition" (Ma Zhendu 2005, 39).

The fall of Shanghai in early November shocked the nationalist government into accelerating the work of moving the capital. John Rabe, head of the Nanjing office of the Siemens China Company, was in close contact with government officials. He writes in his diary entry of November 15: "I am sure that the government is currently preparing to evacuate Nanjing in the Ministry of Transport and Communications. The halls and offices of the ministry are full of leather suitcases and wooden chests. They're planning to move upstream on the Yangtze River to Changsha. I've been to the Ministry of Railways, where an underling secretly told me that that ministry was going to pack up and move the following day. Why? Because the Japanese have already advanced to near Kunshan, only about 30 miles away from Suzhou. Some even concluded that the Japanese have gotten past Suzhou. But that isn't true. A radio announcer in Shanghai confirmed the news about Kunshan. I paid a visit to German Ambassador Trautmann and his wife for tea. There I spoke with General Spemann, who's come in from Taiyuan. The Kutwo may first deliver the women and some valuable objects to Hankou, and then return to pick up the remaining embassy staff. 'Once the Chinese government leaves, the embassy must also evacuate.' That's what they told me. Otherwise, they'll be in enemy occupied territory" (Rabe CN, 64).

In the face of Japanese pressure, the nationalist government held a highest-level conference of national defense, which formally resolved to move the capital to Chongqing.

b. Judgments and responses of ordinary citizens

Most residents who decided to move west were well-off economically and had few worries left behind them. Many of less solid economic foundations and with more local attachments opted to hide in the countryside. We hear this in the oral account of Rape of Nanking survivor Li Jian: "To avoid the Japanese bombing of Nanjing, on the 11th day of the seventh month of the lunar calendar in 1937, I along with my wife, children, and younger sister took refuge in the country of Hushu Town, Jiangning County. All members of my wife's family also went to the countryside, except an uncle who remained to watch the house" (Zhang and Dai n.d., 75). We hear this in the oral account of another survivor Han Xianglin: "Before the Japanese occupied Nanjing, at the beginning of November, the KMT government decided to move the capital to Wuhan, and high-level officials all began moving westward. In mid-November, some ordinary city residents also sought refuge in the countryside" (Zhang and Dai n.d., 265). When ordinary residents began moving, most left some old family members behind to watch over their property: "Elderly people were often the most reluctant to leave their homes in exposed areas, and they were considered in advance to be safe from wanton attack" (Jiang n.d., 14).

A great number of ordinary residents decided to stay in Nanjing. Tension was unavoidable in the face of Japanese air raids, but they gradually learned to adapt. We read in Rabe's diary entry of October 20, 1937:

> An editor in the (Nanjing edition of the) *Dalubao* [the China Press] says that Nanjing people are used to Japanese air raids. This turn of phrase seems somewhat exaggerated. He goes on to say that air raid sirens have become a daily routine. That, however, certainly is true! When sirens sound the first time, people don't even leave their offices. At most they mechanically organize the things on their desks... Once the danger is past, they calmly return to their work, as if nothing had happened. Of course, sometimes they excitedly discuss the extent of the bombing and what damage it may have caused, but soon afterward they calm down. Everybody's busy doing their work, so they look for some distractions. (Rabe CN, 43)

By the time the fighting in Shanghai was at its direst, common residents of Nanjing began expressing tension and worries. Rabe writes in his diary entry of November 14, 1937: "The Chinese are presently very pessimistic, all of them pacing back and forth with curled lips. This, of course, is understandable. The situation is downright atrocious" (Rabe CN, 63).

c. Judgments and responses of Europeans and Americans

Europeans and Americans fell largely into two categories: the first of diplomatic personnel, and the second of merchants, industrialists, educators, and missionaries. The threat of war affected all of them.

On September 20, 1937, the Japanese government informed the embassies of all nations in Nanjin that the Japanese Air Force would commence wide-scale bombing of Nanjing on September 21, and that all foreign persons of European and North American countries were requested to evacuate the city. This was a predicament diplomatically speaking. The diplomats of the UK, France, and Germany remained resolute, evacuating willing residents to naval vessels on the Yangtze, but themselves remained in Nanjing. On the contrary, the U.S. ambassador took a different tact, himself also taking shelter on a naval vessel. John Rabe writes in his diary entry of September 21, 1937:

> Yesterday news from the Japanese commander in Shanghai came through the German embassy informing us that the bombing of Nanjing would again be intensified starting at midday today (September 21), thus warning all foreigners to leave Nanjing as quickly as possible. The Japanese even asked the embassies of the UK, France, and the U.S., and even those of small countries operating naval vessels on the Xiaguan stretch of the Yangtze River to have their vessels leave their current moorings and move either upstream or downstream of the city, lest they be exposed to damage by bombing; the Japanese expressed they would bear no responsibility whatsoever for any possible damage caused thereby. The British and French said in their replies that they saw no reason to change the current mooring location of their vessels. Conversely, the American ambassador boarded the USS Luzon with all his embassy staff, planning to heed the Japanese recommendation (Rabe CN, 7–8).

The Chinese government and people applauded the former. In a cable to the rest of the world of September 22, acting UK ambassador Howe writes: "The (Chinese) foreign minister expressed deep gratitude today, highly praising our decision to not leave the embassy in Nanjing, because this was an extremely great encouragement to the Chinese people" (Zhang 2006b, 209). The former, however, came under attack. Minnie Vautrin writes in her journal entry of September 20, 1937: "Dr. Wu[10] came in looking disgusted with herself. Said that she had exploded to Mr. Buck[11] and asked him to transfer it to the Embassy telling them what she thinks of their decision to evacuate the Embassy. She feels it is an unfriendly act and doing the very thing that Japan wants foreign powers to do. Buck wrote her a letter later telling her that he transferred her message to Mr. Johnson."

Feeling the pressure from public opinion, Ambassador Johnson quickly returned to the embassy and adopted the same position established by the UK, France, and Germany. In a cable to the outside world of September 22, 1937, acting UK ambassador Howe writes: "The reestablishment of a common position (that the embassies of the various countries should remain in Nanjing) exerted an extremely great influence on the morale of the Chinese government. They expressed high praises for our actions" (Zhang 2006b, 211). In a cable written on

---

[10] President of the Ginling College for Women Dr. Wu Yifang.
[11] Professor in the agriculture department of University of Nanking, former husband of Pearl S. Buck.

September 24 to the UK Foreign Ministry, Howe writes: "If there is a bunker that could be used for defense that would not be exposed to too great a danger, and if meaningful contact can be maintained with the Chinese government, I feel it is extremely important that the embassy remains open as long as possible, out of consideration of national dignity" (Zhang 2006b, 215).

Most non-diplomats who remained had to weigh their lives against their principles. Vautrin writes in her diary entry of August 27, 1937: "9 p.m. A letter by special messenger from the Embassy. They are asking all men and women to evacuate. It was a very clear emphatic statement. All the women at the Embassy are leaving tomorrow. I personally greatly appreciate the attitude of the Embassy." The vast majority of foreign citizens left the city under the direction of their embassies. Those who remained took instructions from their embassies, made emergency contingency plans, and prepared to take refuge on naval vessels on the Yangtze River at any time. Rabe writes in his diary entry of October 9 and 10, 1937: "Dr. Rosen of the embassy has become a permanent resident of the boat; his speech and deportment have left a deep impression on me. He frankly admitted that he was very afraid of the bombing, that he had been taught a lesson. Not everybody is capable of such frankness" (Rabe CN, 27).

The foreigners who decided to remain in Nanjing during the war, such as Minnie Vautrin, Miner Searle Bates, Rabe, Lewis Smythe, George Fitch, and others, did so for many reasons. Rabe writes in his diary entry of September 21, 1937:

> Last night I deeply thought over this situation from all angles. I didn't return here from safe Beidaihe in the North for the thrill of adventure, but first and foremost to protect my property and to represent the interests of Siemens. Of course, the company doesn't expect me to get myself killed for it. I absolutely do not want to rashly risk my life for anything at all. But there's an ethical question here that as an "ethical merchant of Hamburg" I still can't leap over. Our Chinese servants and employees and their families number about 30; they are all looking to the "master." If he stays, then they will loyally hold to their positions until the final moment. If he leaves, not only will the buildings belonging to the firm and of private persons be vacant, but they may be looted down to the last. Leaving aside that last point, I still cannot make any decisions that will betray the confidence that has been placed in me (Rabe CN, 28).

Rabe's words here are heartfelt. Conflicts between personal safety and principles were universal among the foreigners only intensified after the fall of Shanghai, as experienced by John Magee, Ernest Forster, Robert O. Wilson, Eduard Sperling, Christian Kreöger, and others. It was just this group of conflicted idealists who remained in Nanjing to the last, organized the International Safety Zone Committee, and helped the soldiers and civilians of China.

2.1.3 From the attack on Nanjing to the occupation of the fort at Jiangyin

2.1.3.1 Summary of the Japanese advance

On November 12, 1937, Shanghai fell. The Shanghai Expeditionary Army was already planning to attack Nanjing during the Battle of Shanghai. We read the following in the statement of Tada Hayao presented at the Tokyo trials: "The plan to occupy Shanghai was formulated at the time the Shanghai Incident occurred. During the battle of Shanghai we formulated the plan to occupy Nanjing" (Zhang and Yang n.d., 11). On November 20, officials in Tokyo sent a cable to inform Matsui that 10th Army, under his command, had violated its combat orders. Tokyo quickly reversed that decision, however, and on November 24 they rescinded the "Suzhou-Jiaxing halt line," in accordance with the fervent admonitions of Matsui and others, and issued orders to advance on Nanjing. Upon receipt of these orders from Tokyo, Matsui issued the following orders to the Central China Area Army:

> After the Shanghai Expeditionary Army occupies Wuxi, if it possible to blockade the fort at Jiangyin, then attack it. Engage battle in the region of the left bank of the Yangtze River with approximately one division, and then cut off the Tianjin-Pukou railway to the north of Nanjing. Our forces should be concentrated on the line between Danyang and Jurong. First defeat the enemies before you, and then advance to the west of the Mopan mountain range. The 10th Army will proceed to the rear of Nanjing along the line that runs from Guangde to Ningguo to Wuhu with approximately one division. Forces should be concentrated on the line between Yixing and Liyang. First defeat the enemies before you, then proceed to the vicinity of Lishui. Occupy Hangzhou with a portion of soldiers, at your discretion (Wang and Lei n.d., 20).

Tokyo established a headquarters on November 20: "The headquarters is to be composed of staff officers of the commanders-in-chief of the army and navy and all relevant organs; it is to undertake all command matters, participate in setting battle plans, and coordinate between the army and navy" (Wang 2010b, 39). Matsui's diary entry from November 25, 1937, read: "This morning portions of the 9th Division and the 11th Division occupied Wuxi. Troops from the 16th Division followed up by sweeping the city. In so doing we have possessed the rear of the fort at Jiangyin. Now it will be easier to attack Nanjing" (Wang 2005b, 136). A record from the Chinese side reads: "November 26, after our retreat from the Xi-Cheng line, the fort at Jiangyin is isolated" (The Second Historical Archives of China 2005, 455).

On December 1, 1937, Tokyo officially issued "continental order number eight," commanding the Central China Area Army to coordinate an attack on Nanjing with the navy. The next day, Matsui communicated Tokyo's orders to attack Nanjing to his forces. The fort at Jiangyin fell on December 2. The Japanese came to think: "The fall of the fort at Jiangyin has made the Yangtze River blockade, centered on Jiangyin, irrelevant. Our fleet can coordinate with the army to go upstream on the Yangtze and create a major threat in the enemy's rear" (Wang 2010b, 100). At this time officials in Tokyo appointed royal family member General Prince Asaka Yasuhiko commander of the Shanghai Expeditionary Army, to give glory to the royal family.

2.1.3.2 Growing tensions in the defense of Nanjing
With the Japanese attack bearing down on the city, there were differences in opinion within the nationalist government about whether to hold fast in Nanjing. Liu Fei recalls: "After two days, I think it was the 15 and 16 of November, we held the second meeting of high level officials and aides. There were more people attending than at the first meeting. In addition to He Yingqin, Bai Chongxi, Xu Yongchang, and myself, there were also Tang Shengzhi, Gu Zhenglun, and another whose name I can't recall. When we began discussing whether to remain in Nanjing, Tang Shengzhi said we had no choice but to resolutely hold the city. His reasoning was: Nanjing is China's capital, the gaze of the world is fixed here, and it's the site of President Sun's mausoleum. How would we answer the president's soul in heaven if we abandoned Nanjing? So we had to remain even unto our death" (Ma 2005, 348). On November 20, Tang assumed command of the defense forces of Nanjing (orders were not issued until November 24). That same day, the nationalist government announced that it was moving the capital to Chongqing.

On November 25, 1937, Chiang Kai-shek delivered an important speech, after which he organized the defense of Nanjing. Chiang then dispatched a cable: "Respectfully delivered to Commander Tang: the combat order of command for the Capital Defense Garrison has been determined as follows: (1) Commander Tang Shengzhi, (2) Commander Sun Yuanliang of the 72nd Army, (3) Commander Song Xilian of the 78th Army, (4) Gu Zhenglun of the Capital Defense Garrison, (A) the Guangxi Unit, (B) the Military Police Unit, and (5) other special units under unified command" (Ma 2005, 57).

On November 27, Tang Shengzhi delivered a speech titled "We Live or Die with Nanjing," after which he submitted plans for the defense of Nanjing to the highest authorities, determining the following:

> 1. The 88th Division is to center its main force in the vicinity of Yuhuatai and is charged with the defense of the Shuixi Gate and the Zhonghua Gate through the Wuding Gate up to Yuhuatai. 2. The 36th Division is to center its main force in the vicinity of the Longwang Tem-

ple, and is charged with the defense of the Xuanwu Gate, Hongshan, and Mufushan up to the Yijiang Gate, and should coordinate with the Mufushan Fort. 3. The Instructional Unit is to center its main force on Yuxiaoying (to the west of the Central Military Academy), and is charged with the defense of the Guanghua Gate, the Zhongshan Gate, the Taiping Gate, through to Tianbaocheng, is to be commanded by Shao Baichang of the Yituangui Fort, and is also charged with defending the Wulongshan Fort. 4. The Military Police Unit is to center its forces in the vicinity of Qingliangshan, and is charged with the defense of the area from the Dinghuai Gate to the Hanzhong Gate and up to Qingliangshan, and is to dispatch companies at Longtan, Tangshui, and Chunhua to organize scattered soldiers who have been beaten back and await retreat orders. 5. The Police Battalion is charged with the defense of maintaining order within the city and the defense of key transportation points, important warehouses, water towers, the lighting electrical company, and other places. 6. Fort battalions are to staunchly defend the fort areas at Wulongshan and Mufushan and cover the Yangtze River blockade line. 7. The Air Defense Battalion is to establish a 75 mm anti-aircraft gun position near Wutaishan and others at Daxiaochang and Xiaguan, and is primarily charged with defending the city, Daxiaochang, ferries, water towers, and the lighting electrical plant. 8. Transportation, communication, health, supply, and other items will be provided for in other plans (Ma 2005, 33–34).

After plans for the defense of Nanjing had been published, the city was placed under martial law. On November 30 the military attaché to the UK embassy wrote in a cable to the UK Foreign Ministry: "Conditions have dramatically worsened in Nanjing. Of course, everyone is trying to leave the city by any and all means. The following have already vacated the city: ministers of the army and navy, General Chen Cheng, all high officials in the Ministry of Transport and Communications, the mayor, and the 'bankers.' The commander of the Capital Defense Garrison (not Tang Shengzhi) has taken ill, and the police commissioner is dithering. Rumors abound: the police will move out at the first moment in case of need, with the military police behind them, followed finally by combat troops. Unidentified soldiers fill the streets, and the authorities are gradually losing control of the situation" (Zhang 2006b, 220). In a diary entry of December 22, Clarissa Forster writes: "I spent the night in the rr (railroad) station where conditions were pretty bad since more organizations which had been helping have closed up shop and moved away, and those who should be taking responsibility are indifferent. The whole thing is practically on our shoulders now. Some of the British Embassy staff came down to look over the situation. The suffering of the soldiers and the failure of responsible organizations to do their duty by them is hard to see and bear" (Zhang 2005, 95–96).

Even with Chiang Kai-shek still in Nanjing, foreigners in the capital had ominous feelings. Rabe writes in his journal entry of November 28: "Dr. Rosen shared with me the following results of yesterday's conference with the generalissimo: Question: 'Will the defense be limited to areas outside the city or will the battle continue inside the city walls?' Answer: 'We are prepared for both.' Another question: 'Who will be responsible for order if worst comes to worst, that is who will remain behind as the last administrative official in the city and see to it that the power of the police is used to prevent mob violence?' To which the marshal, or maybe General Tang, replied: 'In such a case the Japanese will have to establish order.'" Rabe interpreted that to mean: "In other words: No administrative official will remain here. No one is going to sacrifice himself for the welfare of hundreds of thousands of inhabitants! What a prospect! Good God, if only Hitler would help!" (Rabe EN, 38). Robert Wilson writes in a letter of December 3: "Just as I was leaving the hospital Colonel Huang entered the front door with no less a personage than Madame Chiang and I conducted them up to see the Russians. The Madame is head of the aviation force in addition to her other duties. It was my first glimpse of her and she is certainly all that her sincerest friends claim her to be. It is no wonder that she captivates people. She is a stunning woman with the utmost grace and charm of manner. She said that she and the Generalissimo appreciated what we were doing here, brought some fruit and candy to the invalids, and was whisked away" (Zhang 2006b, 171).

2.2 Approach, Arrival, and Continuation of the Power Vacuum Period

2.2.1 Advance of the Japanese Army and approach of the power vacuum

2.2.1.1 Summary of the Japanese advance

The Japanese army adopted a policy of massive outflanking and massive encirclement in its attack on Nanjing. With the Shanghai Expeditionary Army divided into four routes, the 10th Army divided into three routes, and the Amaya Detachment that crossed the river at Zhenjiang for a massive outflanking and encircling maneuver, the defenses of Nanjing were faced with direct simultaneous attack from eight army routes (Wang 2007a).

Encircling fortifications and multi-ring defensive fortifications were built outside the city of Nanjing, and alert positions were established in front of the battle positions. It was decided to establish peripheral fortifications along the line running between Wulongshan, Qixia Mountain, Qinglong Mountain, Chunhua Town, Niushou Mountain, and Dashengguan. The wings were established against the natural moat of the Yangtze River to form an arc-shaped defensive perimeter, and the primary defensive direction was established as the southeast. The inner defensive ring was established as Nanjing's city walls, and the outer ring was established on the line between Purple Mountain, Qilinmen, Yuhatai,

Xiaguan, and the battery in the fort at Mufushan, forming two defensive circles outside the city to be used in tandem, the inner line for supporting the outer, and the outer for solidifying the inner. In addition, a bridgehead fort was built at Pukou to the north of the river to seal the crossing. The alert position ran across the line from Houtoushan, Dalianshan, Hushu, Molingguan, and Jiangning Town.

The Japanese army advanced rapidly, arriving at Tangshan on December 7. They began to encircle Nanjing from the east and south very quickly. An article in the magazine *Dongfang zazhi* gives us a description:

> The Japanese army divided its vast forces to seize the objectives of Zhenjiang, Jurong, and Lishui, the attacks on which began on the evening of December 3. As these three formed a protective buffer for Nanjing, Chinese military authorities assembled crack troops to hold them, gravely ordering them to defend these places down to the last man, and absolutely not to retreat unless ordered to do so. Intense fighting began in the area of Liyang and Lishui on the morning of December 4, at which time our forces launched a counterattack on Changxing down the highway between Guangde and Si'an, to catch the Japanese by surprise in their rear. Jurong, Lishui, and Zhenjiang all fell in succession on the 4, at which point the Japanese divided their forces into three routes for an attack on Nanjing. The first went around the north of Jurong to the north of Tangshui Town and the rear of Jiuhuashan to attack the Qilin Gate by small back roads. The second proceeded from the Tianwang Temple due south of Jurong to attack Chunhua County to the southeast of our Guanghua Gate along with the Shiwu Road. The third attacked Molingguan from the north of Lishui, to effect a half encirclement of Nanjing. At the same time, the Japanese sent a group to attack Wuhu, to cut off Nanjing's rear. By the 7, Nanjing was in a dire situation, with the sound of artillery clear as bells in all directions. The foreign population of Nanjing all boarded gunboats. The streets of the city were filled with military equipment, and government buildings were all garrisoned with troops, with machine guns in every window. Our forces began systematically destroying arsenals, gasoline stores, airplane hangars, factories, and so on beginning on the 7. After all plans had been carried out, Chairman Chiang (Kai-shek) boarded a plane and left Nanjing. On December 9, Japanese Commander Matsui delivered a letter to General Tang Shengzhi, asking that he hand over the city peacefully, giving him until noon on the 10th to make his reply (Ma 2005, 136–137).

Tang refused to reply, and the Japanese ordered an all-out attack. On the afternoon of December 12, Tang hurriedly ordered a retreat, at which point Nanjing fell into chaos.

2.2.1.2 Final evacuation of the Nanjing government

Chiang Kai-shek left Nanjing on December 7. The head of his bodyguard staff Yu Jiemin recalls:

Chiang Kai-shek boarded the "Mei-ling"[12] and left a little after 5 am, in the interval before enemy planes became active. That day I was on guard at the Ming Palace airport, where under protection of a small squadron of fighters, the "Mei-ling" flew to Lushan, Jiangxi and then to Wuhan via Hengshui, Hunan (Ma 2005, 365).

A slew of high level officials evacuated shortly after Chiang. The diary entry of Jiang Gonggu of December 7 reads: "The sounds of artillery in the region of the capital were clearer today than yesterday. Since after the departure northward of Deputy Chief of Staff Bai tonight left such a large residence with just a few of us to live in it, we couldn't help feelings of loneliness, so we decided to move to the Fuchang Hotel. It was built of a steel frame and concrete, and was unusually solid, which seemed to calm us down psychologically" (Zhang 2005, 55). With the departure of high officials, the meetings of the Committee for the International Safety Zone became much more cold and cheerless. Cheng Ruifang recalls in her diary entry of December 8: "Not a single government official attended the meeting of the International Committee tonight; they had probably all left" (Zhang 2005, 9). That same day, an officer in the U.S. embassy in Nanjing dispatched a cable to his government detailing the departure of the Chinese officials, reading: "I'm sure the mayor has left. He came here a few days ago to tell us that the two officials from the Foreign Ministry who had helped local authorities in talks seem to have disappeared into hiding somewhere today. It's still not easy to pass from the Yijiang Gate to the river shore. But Chinese are still not permitted to enter the city from here. Last night security officials went door to door along the outside of the city walls telling everybody to cross the river to Pukou" (Zhang 2006b, 55).

2.2.1.3 Final evacuation of European and American embassies

Once Chiang had left Nanjing, personnel of European and American embassies also boarded ships to head up the Yangtze River, most Germans on the Kutwo, most Americans on the USS Panay, and most British on the HMS Ladybird. Other foreigners boarded the Whampoa, the Bee, and some other merchant vessels at Xiaguan. These vessels carried not only embassy staff, but also some Chinese refugees on familiar terms with the embassies.

One group of foreigners, however, stalwartly stayed behind, determined to protect immovable property in Nanjing belonging to citizens of all countries as

---

12 Chiang's dedicated airplane, a U.S.-built C47B transport, named after his wife (translator's note).

well as Chinese refugees during the war. Robert Wilson writes in a letter of December 7:

> This afternoon we received the final warning from the Embassy and were told that the U.S.S. Panay was leaving at 9:30 tomorrow with the remaining Americans who were willing to go. From reports during the day we gather that nine are going, mostly Embassy members and newspaper reporters. Thirteen are remaining including our household and the hospital foreign staff. How can we leave the sick patients?... Already hundreds are streaming into the zone and the problems of housing and feeding them are what is occupying the committee's time. The hospital is, of course, an essential cog. The Japanese have now reached a point about 25 miles from the city, a town called Chuyung (Jurong) where earlier there was a large military air base. It was said that gunfire could be heard though I did not hear it myself. It won't be long now, however.
>
> The household now consists of Searle Bates, Lewis Smythe, Plumer Mills, Hubert Sone and myself. Fitch has not moved in. We also have a lad named Steele, reporting for the Chicago Daily News, eating with us. Trim (C. S. Trimmer) is staying in his house. I forgot to mention (James) MacCallum who has moved in with us now that Dick has gone to Kuling. Mac is helping with the business end of the hospital and is a tremendous factor in keeping the wheels going around (Zhang 2006b, 172-173).

2.2.1.4 Comings and goings of common citizens

The rapid evacuation of government officials and foreigners was a major psychological blow to the common citizenry. All remaining families had to begin making their final choices. The flow of humanity was, however, bidirectional: some rushing out of the city, and others flooding in, particularly into the International Safety Zone.

The crush into the Safety Zone came rapidly. Clarissa Forster writes in her diary of December 5: "With the Japanese drawing nearer, so many persons to be responsible for, we thought it best to leave Hsiakwan and bring the Chinese workers in. Yesterday was a busy day with packing and moving. Servants came in the afternoon to get the kitchen ready. We had coolies bring in all the food boxes so we shall have those to live on for a while. We brought in the Victrola and the records. We are bringing in two beds because we shall probably have to take in more people" (Zhang 2005, 96–97). Some farmers from the surrounding region also entered the Safety Zone by climbing over the city walls. A December 8 article in the New York Times by F. Tillman Durdin reads: "This correspondent, motoring to the front, found the entire valley outside Chungshan Gate, southeast of Mausoleum Park, ablaze. The village of Hsiaolingwei, along the main highway bordering the park, was a mass of smoking ruins, and inhabitants who had not evacuated days before were streaming toward Nanking carrying their few miserable belongings and occasionally pausing to take last sorrowing looks at their former homes" (Zhang 2005, 49).

With the great influx of people, the streets of the Safety Zone became crowded. Rabe writes in his diary entry of December 9, 1937: "The streetlights have been turned off, and in the dark you can make out the wounded dragging themselves over the cobblestones. No one helps them; there are no doctors, no nurses, and no medics left. Only Kulou Hospital with its couple of brave American doctors still carries on. The streets of the Safety Zone are flooded with refugees loaded down with bundles. The old Communications Ministry (arsenal) is opened to refugees and in no time fills to the rafters. We cordon off two rooms because our weapons and ammunition are in them. Among the refugees are deserters, who hand over their uniforms and weapons" (Rabe EN, 57). Living space in Nanjing at this time had broken into four distinct levels: city-within-a-city (the refugee camps within the Safety Zone), the inner city (the Safety Zone), the middle city (areas inside the city walls but outside the Safety Zone), and the outer city (outside the city walls).

2.2.1.5 Breaking the perimeter

On the morning of December 12, Tang Shengzhi requested that the Committee for the International Safety Zone display white flags. Smythe writes in a letter to family of December 12: "We were surprised that they had come back at around 11 am, saying that General Tang wanted us to send someone directly to the Japanese to try to reach a three-day truce agreement. So we discussed concrete maters: Sperling would go out waving a white flag saying 'Don't shoot! I have a letter for you!'" (Zhang 2005, 226–227)

At noon on the 12th, Tang signed a retreat order: "1) Enemy conditions are known to you. 2) The Capital Defense Garrison has decided to break through enemy lines tonight and proceed to bordering regions in Zhejiang and Anhui… 6) All units breaking out of the encirclement must avoid highways and must dispatch units to destroy bridges on important highways to prevent their use by the enemy. 7) All officers and shoulders should carry four-day stocks of fried rice and salt. 8) The Capital Defense Garrison headquarters is now being moved to Puzhen" (Ma 2005, 36–37). He issued a follow-up order at 3 pm: "1) All forces under this command are ordered to proceed to regions around Huizhou. 2) All forces under this direct command as well as those of the 36th Division are ordered to cross the river tonight (the 12) and assemble near Wuyi and Huaqiying to await orders. 3) All actions are to be conducted in accordance with regulations" (Ma 2005, 37).

By now the best moment for retreat had already been missed, and Nanjing fell into chaos. George Fitch writes of December 12:

> The general rout must have started early that afternoon. Soldiers streamed through the city from the south, many of them passing through the Zone, but they were well-behaved and orderly. Gen. Tan asked our assistance in arranging a truce with the Japanese and Mr. Sperling agreed to take a flag and message but it was already too late. He [Tan] fled that evening, and as soon as the news got out disorganization became general. There was panic as they made for the gate to Hsiakwan (Xiaguan) and the river. The road for miles was strewn with the equipment they cast away – rifles, ammunition, belts, uniforms, cars, trucks – everything in the way of army impediments.
>
> Trucks and cars jammed, were overturned, caught fire; at the gate more cars jammed and were burned – a terrible holocaust – and the dead lay feet deep. The gate blocked, terror mad soldiers scaled the wall and let themselves down on the other side with ropes, puttees and belts tied together, clothing torn to strips. Many fell and were killed. But that at the river was perhaps the most appalling scene of all. A fleet of junks was there. It was totally inadequate for the horde that was now in a frenzy to cross to the north side. The overcrowded junks capsized, they sank; thousands drowned. Other thousands tried to make rafts of the lumber on the riverside only to suffer the same fate. Other thousands must have succeeded in getting away, but many of these were probably bombed by Japanese planes a day or two later (Zhang 2005, 68).

A small number of soldiers managed to escape. Christian Kröger writes in a private report of January 13: "Fortunately the Japanese attack didn't come as fast as we had imagined. They had planned to arrive in Pukou by the 12. On the evening of the 13, Japanese ships on the Yangtze began to open fire. The sound of their cannons firing and targets exploding was audible until nighttime. It is fortunate that this attack was delayed 24 hours" (Zhang 2005, 318).

2.2.1.6 Foreigners facing reality

There were only a little more than 20 foreigners left in the city at the time of its fall. Fitch writes of December 10:

> We were now a community of 27–18 Americans, 5 Germans, 1 Englishman, 1 Austrian and 2 Russians. Out on the river was the Panay with the two remaining Embassy men, Atcheson and Paxton, and half a dozen others; the Standard Oil and Asiatic Petroleum motor ship with many more, a hulk which had been fitted out as sort of a floating hotel and towed upstream with some 20 foreigners including Dr. Rosen of the German Embassy and some 400 Chinese, and other crafts. How many of them have met their fate we do not know, but it will be a long time before any of them get back. And what a Nanking they will see (Zhang 2005, 67-68).

The foreigners began to worry about conditions in Nanjing. Vautrin writes in her diary entry of December 11: "At Press Conference tonight there were 20 of us – all foreigners. Four press men were present and all the rest were missionaries excepting two Germans and one Russian lad. Searle gave a rather dismal report of breakdown in military authority." What would they do in the face of the advancing Japanese army? The foreigners were becoming very worried indeed. Minnie Vautrin continues in her diary entry of December 12: "Few people will sleep in the city tonight... Just a year ago today General Chang was taken prisoner at Sian." Their only choice was to face reality.

2.2.2 Arrival of the power vacuum period

On December 12, 1937, the Japanese pressed the final stages of their attack on Nanjing. The International Committee, led by Rabe, began to make predictions about conditions in the city, with everyone achieving psychological equilibrium based on "one basic presupposition and two possible directions." The basic supposition was that their fate would be determined by the victorious army. The two possible directions were: Nanjing would fall into total lawlessness, or the Japanese might restore order after a brief period of unrest.

Rabe wrote a great deal that day. His diary entry for December 12 read: "The last thought on my mind before falling asleep was: thank God that the worst is behind us!" (Rabe CN, 133). In a completely different mood, George Fitch wrote: "So ended the happy, peaceful, well ordered, progressive regime which we had been enjoying here in Nanking and on which we had built our hopes for still better days" (Zhang 2005, 69).

Vautrin wrote in her diary entry of December 13:

> The city is strangely silent – after all the bombing and shelling. Three dangers are past – that of looting soldiers, bombing from aeroplanes, and shelling from big guns, but the fourth is still before us – our fate at the hands of a victorious army. People are very anxious tonight and do not know what to expect.

On December 13, Nanjing fell, and the Japanese entered the city. George Fitch wrote: "They were first reported in the Zone at 11:00 that morning, the 13th" (Zhang 2005, 69). Then the power vacuum was fully in place, followed immediately by the rampant killing and looing.

By this time Chinese authorities had already moved westward, and personnel of European and American embassies had boarded ships on the Yangtze. The political order then was completely changed in the city, which now contained a few hundred thousand ordinary Chinese and a little over 20 foreigners. At this point the city consisted of three distinct groups: Japanese soldiers, foreigners of the International Committee and the Red Cross Society of Nanjing, and Chinese civilians and disarmed soldiers. Under these conditions the Japanese had absolute authority and power over life and death. One Japanese soldier wrote to a friend at home: "With the passing of each day, Nanjing is becoming increasingly a Japanese city. I think many interesting things will happen here in the days to come" (Wang 2006a, 378). The presence of the third group, the foreigners, constituted an important and clear buffer between Chinese refugees and Japanese soldiers. Despite their limited powers, they did all they could.

2.2.2.1 Communicating with Japanese commanding officers

The Japanese arrived in the Safety Zone at noon on December 13. Smythe writes in a letter of December 13: "Well on our way home at one we found that the Japanese had reached Kwangchow [Guangzhou] Road. We drove down there and met a small detachment of about six Japanese soldiers, our first – but far from our last!" (Zhang 2005, 229). Vautrin writes that she interacted with her first Japanese soldier at 4:00 that afternoon: "The report came to me that there were Japanese soldiers on the hill west of us. I went up to South Hill Residence to see, and sure enough our West Hill had a number on it. Soon I was called by another servant, who said that one had entered our Poultry Experiment Station and wanted chickens and geese. Immediately I went down and he soon left, after my efforts at sign language telling him the chickens were not for sale."

The foreigners actively confronted Japanese officers. Smythe writes in a letter of December 13: "Back at the office we decided that Rabe and I should immediately find a high-ranking Japanese officer. We found Cola, who speaks Japanese, and together proceeded toward the Japanese to explain three things (to as highly ranked an officer as possible): the Safety Zone, the New Red Cross Committee, and disarmed Chinese soldiers in the Safety Zone" (Zhang 2005, 229).

Near the Nanking Theological Seminary, they found a Japanese soldier on a bicycle who told them they could find an officer on Hanzhong Road near Xinjiekou. Smythe writes in a letter of December 13: "We tried to explain to the officer the Zone and drew it on his map of Nanking, and noted it was not on his map. He said the Hospital would be all right if there was no one in there that shot at the Japanese. About the disarmed soldiers he could not say" (Zhang 2005, 230).

One could say that these three issues constituted the key concerns of the International Committee upon the Japanese entry into the city. But visits with high-level commanders didn't start until the 15th. Rabe writes in his diary entry of that day: "As we were about to say goodbye to the commandant and Mr. Fukuda, General Harata entered and immediately expressed a desire to become acquainted with the Safety Zone, which we show him on a driving tour" (Rabe EN, 71). Rabe then began discussing his top-level plans for the order of life of Nanjing residents with the commander. The Japanese commander responded to the International Committee in summary style:

> 1. Must search the city for Chinese soldiers. 2. Will post guards at entrances to Zone. 3. People should return to their homes as soon as possible; therefore, we must search the Zone. 4. Trust humanitarian attitude of Japanese Army to care for the disarmed Chinese soldiers. 5. Police may patrol within the Zone if they are disarmed excepting for batons. 6. The 10,000 tan22 of rice stored by your committee in the Zone you may use for refugees. But Japanese soldiers need rice, so in the Zone they should be allowed to buy rice. (Answer regarding our stores of rice outside of Zone, not clear.) 7. Telephone, electricity and water must be repaired; so this p.m. will go with Mr. Rabe to inspect and act accordingly. 8. We are anxious to get workers. From tomorrow will begin to clear city. Committee please assist. Will pay. Tomorrow want 100 to 200 workers (Rabe EN, 70–71).

It was crucial to properly handle relations with the Japanese army given the imbalance in power. Rabe writes in his diary entry this day: "People have already become perfectly accustomed to grenades and bombs. Now what we must do is form relations with the occupying army. This wasn't hard for me a European, but to perform this function well as the committee chairman wasn't simple either" (Rabe CN, 144).

2.2.2.2 The Japanese army refutes the Committee's plans

Even as the Committee was working hard to connect with high-level commanders in the Japanese army, violence was already unfolding across the city, and the order to spare no captives was being thoroughly implemented at the division level and below. Commander Yamada Senji of the 103rd Battalion of the 13th Division of the Shanghai Expeditionary Army wrote in his diary entry of December 15: "I dispatched Second Lieutenant Honma to Nanjing to discuss how to dispose of captives and other matters. The orders were to kill all captives" (Wang 2006a, 3). Commander of the 65th Infantry Regiment of the 13th Division Morozumi Gyosaku wrote: "The army issued orders to dispose of all captives!" (Wang 2006a, 16). Second Lieutenant Miyamoto Shogo of the 4th Squadron of the 65th Infantry Regiment wrote in his diary entry of December 17: "This afternoon I participated in the magnificent ceremony for our entry into Nanjing and witnessed this solemn and historically significant scene with my own eyes. When I returned at night, I immediately left to help execute prisoners of war. As they had already killed over 20,000, the soldiers' eyes went red from blood lust, and they unexpectedly attacked friendly forces, killing and injuring several" (Wang 2006a, 32).

Now the power vacuum was complete. Japanese soldiers penetrated into the city claiming to be cleaning up remnant troops, "sweeping" sector by sector. Xu Chuanyin tells us in testimony given to the Tokyo tribunal: "Then the Japanese soldiers began searching door to door, taking food and other times, and also taking among young men and boys of appropriate ages to serve in the army. They tied these up with disarmed soldiers and drove them off to be shot, or else shot them on the spot" (Zhang and Yang n.d., 2). The massacre of young men was also carried out under orders from high-level officials in the Japanese army. Commander of the 6th Infantry Battalion of the 9th Division Akiyama Yoshimichi ordered: "All young men should be arrested and put in jail as remnant troops or plainclothes troops" (Wang and Lei n.d., 111).

The massacre continued into the Safety Zone. Vautrin writes in her diary entry of December 16: "Tonight I asked George Fitch how the day went, and what progress they had made toward restoring peace in the city. His reply was 'It was hell today. The blackest day of my life.' Certainly it was that for me too." News that disarmed Chinese soldiers were being killed in the Safety Zone greatly pained the International Committee. During the great retreat of the night of December 12, many soldiers entered the Safety Zone, where Committee members naively thought that their lives would be spared if they laid down their weapons and surrendered to the Japanese. So they enthusiastically organized mass disarmament of soldiers and engaged in discussions with the Japanese, who ended up betraying their trust. Jiang Gonggu writes in his diary entry of December 28: "Over a thousand of our defenseless brothers were taken by the enemy from the temporary shelter in the Judicial Yuan and were all killed. The foreigners thought this was a failure of the International Relief Committee and heaped blame upon themselves. The American (Charles H.) Riggs even sobbed once over this" (Zhang 2005, 66). Fitch writes in his diary: "Were those four lads from Canton who had trudged all the way up from the south and yesterday had reluctantly given me their arms among them, I wondered; or that all [tall] strapping sergeant from the north whose disillusioned eyes as he made the fatal decision, still haunt me? How foolish I had been to tell them the Japanese would spare their lives. We had confidently expected that they would live up to their promises, at least in some degree, and that order would be established with their arrival. Little did we dream that we should see such brutality and savagery as has probably not been equalled in modern times. For worse days were yet to come" (Zhang 2005, 71–72).

The members of the International Committee were most concerned with three things: the Safety Zone, the disarmed soldiers within the Safety Zone, and the newly established International Red Cross Society. The Japanese completely disregarded their concerns and in so doing directly prolonged the power vacuum period. Committee member Lewis Smythe writes in a letter to "friends in God's Country" of March 8, 1938: "In my studies of Sociology I have heard a lot about the terrors of the 'interregnum.' We passed through the siege of Nanking, the retreat of the Chinese soldiers on the night of December 12th, the period of no authority from the time the Chinese general left Sunday afternoon until the Japanese high command arrived on Wednesday without a single disorder by civilians! The only disorders were by the Japanese soldiers beginning from the night of the 13th. It sounds like a fairy tale and very different from we expected. It may be that the fact that we had the Zone organized, that the heroic Chinese workers kept the light, water, and telephone going until the evening of December 12 which preserved much perfect order in a sea of disorganization. But only a clerk remained of the former City Government and even the head of the police had fled! The burning referred to in news dispatches was outside of the city wall, not inside. In other words, we had here a set-up perfectly arranged for the Japanese to take control of the civilian population peaceably and to have had the essential services going in a day or two. They missed that opportunity by being too blind to see it!" (Zhang 2005, 281–282)

2.2.3 The power vacuum continues – and registration begins

Matsumoto Shigeharu wrote: "The scale of cruel killings by the Japanese soldiers was at its greatest from the 13, after the occupation, until the night of the 17, after the ceremony" (Wang 2010e, 779). The completely unarmed foreigners had no means but to lodge protests in the face of the ongoing atrocities. These protests came in several forms. First, complaints were lodged in the name of the International Committee. Rabe sent protests to members of the Japanese embassy in Nanjing every day for weeks beginning on December 16. On December 19, for example, he reported 70 crimes committed by Japanese soldiers over the course of several days. He reported another 26 crimes on the 20 (serial numbers 71–96). He reported another 26 on December 21 (serial numbers 97–113). Second, the foreigners lodged protests by country. Smythe writes in a letter of December 18: "We drafted a most detailed letter requesting that all possible military means be used to restore order… But conditions grew even worse that day, with Japanese soldiers looting and raping everywhere. Rabe and I decided to act as representatives of the Germans and the Americans to demand action. It was 5:30 pm. We saw only Okazaki in the office, so we spoke with him. Rabe came straight to the point, saying that he was a German Nazi, a recipient of the highest honors of his country, and a representative of German leadership. I stressed that we had only humanitarian interests in protecting the people. Okazaki said that he had already sent Fukuda to talk to the army that afternoon" (Zhang 2005, 236). Smythe clearly recalled all these actions when giving testimony before the Tokyo tribunal: "I was responsible for drafting letters of protest at first, and then Rabe suggested that we take turns signing the letters, since we were citizens of different countries. We sent two letters of protest just about every day during the six weeks following the Japanese occupation of Nanking. One of these was usually delivered in person by myself and Rabe to the Japanese embassy, and the other was delivered by courier" (Yang 195). Third, the foreigners appeared en masse at the Japanese embassy to lodge protests. Vautrin writes in her diary entry of December 21, 1937: "All foreigners in city this afternoon sent in a petition pleading that peace be restored in Nanking – for the sake of the 200,000 Chinese here, as well as for the Japanese army's good. I did not go with the group, having just been there."

The continued protests did yield some results. Counselor to the Japanese embassy in Nanjing at the time Hidaka Shinrokuro testified before the Tokyo tribunal: "Some reports on rumors of evildoing by Japanese soldiers were delivered by foreigners to the consul. However, most of these reports were based on rumor. Since the consul didn't have time to get to the bottom of the matter, he forwarded these reports to the Foreign Ministry in Tokyo and military officials in Nanjing. It seems that the Foreign Ministry in Tokyo then notified the Ministry of the Army of these reports." (IMTFE Exhibit No. 2537). Ishii Itaro, director of the Japanese Foreign Ministry Bureau of East Asian Affairs at the time, said in testimony to the Tokyo tribunal: "Around December 13, our army victoriously entered Nanjing. As a result, acting consul to Nanjing Fukui Kiyoshi returned to his post from Shanghai. The first report he issued from Nanjing to the Foreign Ministry in Tokyo was about the violence of our soldiers there. This caused the prime minister to become alarmed and worried, and he urged me to swiftly take definitive measures to forbid such dishonorable behavior. I replied saying that a copy of the cable had been delivered to the Ministry of the Army, and that I was preparing to admonish military officials into paying attention to such behavior at a joint meeting of the Ministry of the Army, Ministry of the Navy, and Foreign Ministry that was about to take place. This meeting was held soon afterward in my office" (IMTFE Exhibit No. 3287). Ishii goes on: "I was informed that Foreign Minister Hirota had asked Army Minister Sugiyama to swiftly take sharp actions against the incidents of violence in Nanjing."

Japanese authorities expressed extreme displeasure at the "meddling" of foreigners. As depicted in diaries, letters, and reports by high-ranking officers of the Japanese military and Japanese spy departments, the residents of Nanjing were highly dependent on these foreigners. So once the major fighting was over, Japanese authorities began contemplating how to get the Chinese now living clustered around the foreigners to return to their homes. The prelude to this sending home was registration and screening. Rabe writes in his diary entry of December 22, 1937: "Two Japanese from Military Police Headquarters pay me a visit and tell me that the Japanese now want to form their own refugee committee. All refugees will have to be registered" (Rabe EN, 86). The International Committee had no choice but to acquiesce to the demands of the occupying army. Vautrin writes in her diary entry of December 29, 1937: "Registration of the men of this district and many from the city in general continues. Long before nine o'clock a long line extends far beyond the gate. Today they were more severe than yesterday. Then they asked for ex-soldiers to confess, promised them work and pay. Today they examined their hands and selected men whom they suspected. Of course many who were selected had never been soldiers. Countless mothers and wives asked me to intercede in their behalf – their sons were tailors, or bakers, or businessmen. Unfortunately I could do nothing."

The screening left deep impressions on many who were part of the registration. Rape of Nanking survivor Wu Zhisheng's oral account tells us: "On the morning of the 23rd day of the 11th month of the lunar calendar (Kitchen God Festival), Zhikun and I went to buy rice at the Nanjing office of the German Siemens Electric Company (now near Xiaofen Bridge). There were a lot of people buying rice, and it right as it started getting crowded, suddenly three or four Japanese soldiers appeared, grabbing men to check their heads and hands, looking for central soldiers" (Zhang and Dai n.d., 20).

Guo Qi writes in his memoir "Record of Blood and Tears from the Fallen Capital":

> The Imperial Japanese Army's inspection methods were rigorous and thorough, giving every single Chinese person the run down from head to foot, from outside to inside, absolutely not lackadaisically missing any part of the body. There were five gauntlets to pass through. The first was robbery. Any bank notes, pens, watches, copper coins, leather bags, leather belts, or anything of any value whatsoever was first stolen by Japanese soldiers – imperial troops were unwilling to claim prizes from dead bodies in front of watchful eyes. The second was feeling of the head. As most Chinese soldiers shaved their heads during the war, the Japanese would "feel heads" to see how long the hair was. If not long enough, one was led off to be shot. The third was a forehead check. Any men found with marks from a steel helmet on their foreheads were necessarily Chinese soldiers, and were killed on the spot in the same way. The fourth was a waist inspection. Pants were removed to allow for a look. Anyone with the imprint of having worn a belt was determined to be a Chinese soldier, and with a wave of the hand he was taken off to be executed. The fifth was a look at the hands. The Chinese were ordered to hold out their hands for a close look. If any had calluses on their right hand from holding a gun, they were without doubt sol-

diers, and were also executed on the spot without a second thought. If anyone had the incredible luck to make it through these five gauntlets alive, the Japanese immediately dispelled any fantasies that he'd slipped through the devil's hands, because after the aforementioned five inspections, there was an even more terrible juncture to pass: detailed interrogation, on which I will not dwell at great length (Zhang 2005, 185–186).

The Japanese also brought a large number of male refugees to the Ginling Women's College for registration, having female refugees identify and claim their family members. Rape of Nanking survivor Xiong Xiufang recalls thus: "Another time they brought a great many young men from somewhere else. Ms. Hua (Minnie Vautrin) told everyone: 'Go identify your family members so you can rescue your compatriots.' Ms. Hua had a good heart, asking us to go rescue our compatriots. Every one of them who had not been identified was taken by the Japanese to the riverside and mowed down with machine guns" (Zhang and Dai n.d., 503).

2.2.4 Safety Zone operations and the fight for life during the power vacuum

The core of the Committee for the International Safety Zone was comprised of Americans and Germans who had stayed in Nanjing because of personal convictions, but each came from different fields and had distinct personalities.

Prior to evacuating from Nanjing, the Chinese government handed over actual control of the city to the International Committee led by Rabe. In his understanding, his position as chairman came with some drama:

> About two years ago, Dr. Trautmann greeted me at a tea party in Peitaiho with the words: "Ah, here comes the mayor of Nanking!" I was deputy local group leader at the time and somewhat offended by his joke. And now his joke has come true in a way. Of course under normal circumstances a European cannot become mayor of a Chinese city. But since Mayor Ma, with whom we have been working closely recently, left Nanking yesterday and since the committee, with his approval, is forced to deal with all the administrative problems and workings of the municipality inside our Safety Zone, I have in fact become something very like an acting mayor. Enough to give you a fit, Rabe! (Rabe EN, 54).

The International Committee's proposals, plans, and mobilization were all closely related to the war situation. After the fall of Shanghai, the Europeans proposed that an International Safety Zone be established in Nanjing, following the experience of Reverend Jacquinot, who had previously established such a zone in Shanghai, in order to protect refugees during the battle.

Chiang Kai-shek's strategy for the battle for Nanjing was "defense in stages." Rabe's thought of the International Committee's function as "assumption of duties in stages." In his diary entry of December 8, he writes: "As there is no other way out from our current situation, the International Committee had no choice but to assume responsibility for the management of the Safety Zone from Mayor Ma, despite extreme unwillingness to do so. Once the hard times are past, the responsibilities assumed by the committee will end, and the responsibility we've assumed from the city government of Nanjing at their request will be returned to that government" (Rabe CN, 120).

A great quantity of academic materials has accumulated in the study of the Nanking International Safety Zone.[13] We will, on the basis of studies performed before, dynamically demonstrate the efforts and steadfastness of the International Committee during the "power vacuum period" in Nanjing, maintaining focus on the order of life for city residents.

2.2.4.1 Turnover of authority and "legalization" of the International Committee

The Safety Zone was not large in area. It extended to the northern section of Zhongshan Road in the east (from Xinjiekou to the Shanxi Road Plaza), from the Shanxi Road Plaza westward to Xikang Road (the southwestern boundary of the Residential District) in the north, from Xikang Road to Hankou Road (the southwestern boundary of the Residential District) in the west, in a straight line from Shanghai Road to Hankou Road in the southeast, and from the intersection of Hankou Road and Shanghai Road to Xinjiekou in the west. The zone's boundaries were all demarcated by flags with a red cross surrounded by a red circle and three Chinese characters *"nan min qu,"* meaning "refugee zone."

We believe that the legality of the Safety Zone was based in the following five areas: the communal formation of the Committee, its recognition by the Chinese government, forceful support from the members' embassies, its embrace by the masses, and tacit approval from the Japanese.

---

13 Such as: Sun, "Shilun Nanjing da tusha de "anquan qu"" [On the "Safety Zone" in the Rape of Nanking], *Nanjing shehui kexue* 5 (1992); Yang, "Lun Nanjing "anquan qu" gongneng de cuowei ji qi yuanyin" [On dislocations in the functions of the Nanjing "Safety Zone" and reasons], *Kangri zhanzheng yanjiu* 4 (2000); Zhang, "Nanjing da tusha shiqi de rijun dangju yu Nanjing anquan qu" [Japanese authorities and the Nanking Safety Zone during the Rape of Nanking], *Jindai shi yanjiu* 3 (2001); Wang, "Lun Nanjing guoji anquan qu de chengli" [On the founding of the Nanking International Safety Zone], *Minguo dang'an* 4 (2005); Zhang, "Nanjing da tusha shiqi de Nanjing shi zizhi weiyuanhui yu anquan qu guoji weiyuanhui" [The Nanjing Municipal Autonomous Committee and the International Committee for the Nanking Safety Zone during the Rape of Nanking], *Minguo dang'an* 4 (2007); and Pan, "Nanjing anquan qu de zongjiao fuhao fenxi" [Analysis of religious symbolism in the Nanking Safety Zone], *Nanjing shehui kexue* 10 (2008).

a. Communal formation of the team as a prerequisite. Academics widely believe that the formation of the Safety Zone was originally a proposal by a few foreign professors at University of Nanking (Zhang 2002, 85), who later sought Rabe's opinion. Rabe writes in his diary entry of November 22, 1937: "Five p.m. meeting of the International Committee for Establishing a Neutral Zone for Noncombatants in Nanking. They elect me chairman. My protests are to no avail. I give in for the sake of a good cause. I hope I prove worthy of the post, which can very well become important" (Rabe EN, 27). Rabe then writes on December 1: "Dr. Rosen asks the Germans to meet and discuss when people will have to board the Hulk. Herr Kröger, Herr Sperling, young Hirschberg, and Hatz, an Austrian engineer, all want to remain here to help me" (Rabe EN, 46). Not only did the German community support Rabe, but the Americans also expressed unprecedented enthusiasm for him. Vautrin writes in her diary entry of December 7, 1937: "At 10:30 went down to the headquarters of the International Safety Zone Committee to discuss with them the notice concerning articles to be brought in to Safety Zone, etc. Lewis Smythe, Plummer Mills and George Fitch spend all their time on the work in addition to many others. It is fine to see business men – English, German and American – working so closely with missionaries."

b. Recognition by the Chinese government lays the foundation. The Chinese government was extremely supportive of the work of the Safety Zone Committee. Rabe was concerned about the Chinese government's attitude shortly after the committee had been established. He writes in his diary entry of November 25, 1937: "I've just heard on the radio that there are concerns about establishing a neutral zone in Hankou because the Chinese government's opinion had not been solicited" (Rabe CN, 79). The next day Vice Minister Hang Liwu of the Ministry of Education told him not to worry. Rabe writes in his diary entry of November 26: "In answer to my question, Dr. Han(g) Liwu has just told me that we need not worry about the Chinese government's approval for setting up a neutral zone: The generalissimo has personally given his consent" (Rabe EN, 33).

Support from the nationalist government in Nanjing was more than just words; mayor Ma Chaojun actively aided the committee. A report dispatched by a member of the American embassy in Nanjing on December 7 read: "The mayor was still in Nanjing last night. Everyone thinks he's staying behind for the work of the so-called safety zone" (Zhang 2006b, 52). During the tensest period of the defense, the nationalist government, coordinated by Ma, allocated 30,000 sacks of rice and 10,000 sacks of flour to be held in reserve by the Safety Zone Committee. The committee immediately organized transportation for these reserves. Rabe wrote in his diary on December 8: "The food commission must be given a fleet of vehicles to transport the rice and flour stored outside the city into the zone, but this is very difficult under current circumstances (note: the city outskirts are burning). As of last night a total of 12 trucks had transported 6,300 sacks of rice (equivalent to 7,875 dan) of rice into the city" (Rabe CN, 119). They were still moving rice and wheat into the city up to the eve of the Japanese occupation. Rabe's plant manager at Siemens and Rape of Nanking survivor Han Xianglin gives us this oral testimony:

> On December 12 I went to Xiaguan to transport rice, because at the time I was responsible for managing food for the refugees under the International Relief Committee. I and a few others went to Xiaguan from Zhujiang Road. Along the way we saw many scattered soldiers, three to five to a group, walking toward Xiaguan. A city gate to the east of Yijiang Gate had been completely blocked at the time, and one gate to the west had been half opened, just enough for a truck to squeeze through. The surrounding area was full of wire entanglements, sandbags, and other obstacles. On the night of December 12, I brought six or seven porters to Xiaguan to transport rice. All along the way we saw the road full of abandoned bullets, army uniforms, leather cases, suitcases, and other objects, but we saw no other people outside the city. At the time, 80 to 90 percent of the city's residents had fled into the refugee zone (Zhang 2005, 266).

Transporting food was extremely difficult in the wartime environment. The International Committee was unable to transport all the allocated grains into their warehouse, the auditorium at University of Nanking. On January 26, 1938, Rabe summarized the amount of food actually received by the International Committee, as well as the amounts they had been allocated by the Nanjing government.

	Delivery list	Actually received	Confiscated by Japanese	
Rice	20,009 sacks	9,076 sacks	10,933 sacks	96 kg / sack
Flour	10,000 sacks	0 sacks	10,000 sacks	50 lb / sack

Table 5: Amounts of rice and flour allocated by Nanjing City government and amounts actually received by Safety Zone committee.
Source: Rabe CN, 420.

Smythe writes in his letter to "friends in God's Country" of March 8, 1938: "We have been so borne down by the Japanese period of the Safety Zone that we have nearly forgotten the 'Chinese period.' The foresight of the Chinese Mayor of Nanking in giving our Committee over 2,400 tons of rice and 400 tons of flour and $80,000 Chinese currency for our work has been the chief salvation of this population through the winter. Now other funds have been made available in Shanghai" (Zhang 2005, 281).

The International Committee was dissatisfied with the nationalist government for a few reasons. First, despite promises by the commander of the city's defense forces General Tang Shengzhi to demilitarize the zone as quickly as possible, i.e. remove all military installations, he did so too slowly. Second, when it was clear that the city was going to fall, the Safety Zone Committee on two instances requested that the Chinese government hand over the city peacefully, to avoid unnecessary injuries, deaths, and destruction, but they were refused both times.

On December 12, Nanjing came under heavy bombardment from the Japanese army. When the city was about to fall, General Tang approached the Safety Zone Committee and asked them to negotiate an armistice, but the opportunity to do so had clearly already passed. Rabe wrote in his diary that day:

> At 8 a.m. the bombardment resumes. At 11 o'clock Lung and Chow arrive and ask us, on behalf of General Tang, to make a last attempt at establishing a three-day armistice. During these three days the defending forces are to depart, and then the city will be handed over to the Japanese... It's transparently clear that General Tang wanted to conclude an armistice without the generalissimo's consent... And above all, the proposal for an armistice was to be worded so that it would be viewed as having come from the International Committee. In other words: General Tang wanted to hide behind us, because he anticipated and feared severe censure from the generalissimo or the Foreign Ministry in Hankow. He wanted to put all responsibility on the committee, or perhaps its Chairman Rabe, and I didn't like that in the least! (Rabe EN, 63).

c. Strong support from the embassies of the committee members provided a guarantee. A cable dispatched by acting UK Ambassador Howe to the UK Foreign Ministry on November 24 read: "A non-official committee composed of Chinese and foreign members are trying to establish a Safety Zone for refugees in Nanjing, similar to the refugee safety zone established in south Shanghai. The American ambassador and I hope their plan is successful, and that channels for communication with Japanese authorities can also play a role in supporting their actions" (Zhang 2006b, 218).

The German embassy also actively mediated. Rabe wrote on November 22: "The ambassador agrees with the proposal for the establishment of a Safety Zone as drafted by the committee. The proposal will be sent by the American embassy to the American consulate in Shanghai, which will then send it to the Japanese ambassador" (Rabe CN, 73). The Reuters News Agency then revealed this secret. On November 23 Rabe wrote: "Dr. Smythe telephoned to say that the Reuters Agency unintentionally revealed our secret about establishing a Safety Zone when they sent out our cable. We've had someone send a formal apology by cable, to avoid upsetting the Japanese authorities in Shanghai" (Rabe CN, 76).

The German embassy explained that the action had been led by Germans, hoping that the Japanese would understand. Rabe wrote on November 24:

> Dr. Rosen sent the following telegram, via the American Navy, to the German general consulate in Shanghai: "Local international private committee with English, American, Danish, and German members, under chairmanship of German Siemens agent, Herr Rabe, applied to Chinese and Japanese for creation of civilian safety zone should Nanking become directly involved in hostilities. Via general consulate, American ambassador passed the suggestion on to Japanese ambassador in Shanghai and Tokyo. New safety zone to be safe refuge only for noncombatants if needed. Given German chairmanship, I would ask unofficial, but no less warm support of humanitarian proposals. Have only phrase book here. Please pass on to Tokyo and send both your response and answer from Tokyo via American Navy" (Rabe EN, 30–31).

d. Cooperation from the public provided motivation. The Safety Zone was established to protect refugees who hadn't left Nanjing. Wilson Mills wrote in a letter to his wife of March 18, 1938: "Again in September, after the bad raids of that month, I understand the exodus was renewed. But in the last days of November and early December only those remained who could not get away, or who were determined, for one reason or another, so see it through. Then next came the trek into the Zone" (Zhang 2010, 813).

It is noteworthy that the Safety Zone did not receive support from all quarters immediately upon its inception. Rabe wrote in his diary entry of December 4, 1937: "The refugees have slowly begun to move into the Safety Zone. One small newspaper has repeatedly told the Chinese not to move into the "foreigners" refugee zone. These extortionists write that it's the duty of every Chinese to face the dangers that a bombardment of the city may bring with it" (Rabe EN, 49).

In addition, the "Temporary Measures for Sheltering City Residents and Distributing Food" issued earlier by the Safety Zone Committee easily led residents to mistakenly conclude that "one needed an economic foundation in order to enter the Safety Zone." As Rabe wrote in his diary entry of December 4, the Safety Zone Committee did provide a copy of the "Temporary Measures" to the press for publication (Rabe CN, 100–101).

The "Temporary Measures for Sheltering City Residents and Distributing Food" did indeed seem to imply that an economic foundation was necessary for entry into the Safety Zone, and it also declared that the Safety Zone Committee would take actions only when it was necessary. By December 7, the last group of high-level nationalist government officials had left Nanjing, and Rabe issued a news briefing to the press (Rabe CN, 113–114). This press release was markedly different from the previous version issued on the 4th. Although there weren't many changes to the "unspoken words" about needing economic means for survival, it did stress that even the penniless poor could take up residence in the Zone, and that a refugee soup kitchen would provide food.

Refugees soon began converging on the Safety Zone. Rabe wrote in his diary entry of December 7: "Poor people, with a few household goods and bedding, can be seen fleeing into the Zone from all directions. And they are not even the poorest of the poor, they're the vanguard, the people who still have a little money and can pay for shelter with someone they may know inside the boundaries" (Rabe EN, 53).

As the Japanese pressed their final offensive on Nanjing, the Safety Zone began becoming crowded. Fitch wrote in his circular letter of December 24: "On December 10th, the refugees were streaming into the Zone. We had already filled most of the institutional buildings – Ginling, the College and other schools, and now had to requisition the Supreme Court, the Law College, and the Overseas Building, forcing doors where they were locked and appointing our own caretakers" (Zhang 2005, 67).

e. Tacit approval from the Japanese was key. Professor Zhang Lianhong has dedicated an entire paper to this subject (Zhang 2001), clearly noting that the Japanese army did not outright deny the Safety Zone, but nor did they recognize it. The legality of the Zone was greatly discounted as a result, and this exerted a profound influence on the order of life for Nanjing residents during the power vacuum.

2.2.4.2 Work progress without full legality

Rabe and the other foreigners were not punctilious about the insufficient legality of their situation, but rather they actively set about preparing for and running the Safety Zone. Rabe writes in his diary entry of November 30: "They want to establish a neutral zone in Wuhu and have asked for my advice. But we are at a loss to answer them, because nobody among us has ever faced such an arduous task. However, we will complete this task, and must overcome the difficulties no matter what" (Rabe CN, 90).

On that very day, Rabe listed out a series of problems that the Safety Zone Committee needed to urgently resolve (Rabe CN, 91), including funding, police, military installations in the Safety Zone, food, transportation, refugee housing, public facilities, and healthcare. He also listed out the members of the International Committee, in what amounted to an initial deployment of human resources. On December 4 he issued the "Temporary Measures for Sheltering City Residents and Distributing Food," and on the 7th he reissued a revised version to the press, which appeared in a "Letter to the Residents of Nanjing." On December 7 flags began to be raised to demarcate the boundaries of the Safety Zone. Rabe writes in his diary entry of that day: "When we raised the first Committee flags at the entrance to Shanxi Road, we were photographed by Associated Press journalists" (Rabe CN, 112). On that day, Rabe learned that peace proposals made by German Ambassador Trautmann had been rejected, that the highest level government officials had left Nanjing, and that the staffs of various European and North American embassies were boarding ships to leave. He was told by an official from the German embassy named Hürter that the Japanese army had made it to Tangshan, and were about to encircle the city, that the ultimate moment was imminent.

> This afternoon the Safety Zone was demarcated with International Committee flags. What comes next is the moment of difficulty we've long awaited. I first and foremost hope that we will survive hale and healthy. Of course, we're calm and collected, and full of courage! Maybe the situation won't be as horrible as we are imagining. God bless us! God bless us! God bless us! (Rabe CN, 112).

The work of organizing the several dozen refugee shelters within the Safety Zone commenced more or less simultaneously, at the same time that Chiang Kai-shek and embassy personnel were leaving Nanjing. According to one record: "Once news got out that Chairman Chiang had left the capital, the residents of the city flooded into the Safety Zone with their property in an avalanche" (Wang 2010b, 256).

The refugee shelters all had to be expanded to accommodate the swarm of people arriving. Fitch wrote on December 16: "We now had 25 camps, ranging from 200 to 12,000 people in them. In the University buildings alone there were nearly 30,000 and in Ginling College, which was reserved for women and children, the 3,000 was rapidly increased to over 9,000. In the latter place even the space was taken. We had figured to sixteen square feet to a person, but actually they were crowded in much closer than that. For a while no place was safe, we did manage to preserve a fair degree of safety at Ginling. To a lesser degree in the University" (Zhang 2005, 72). Cheng Ruifang wrote in her diary entry of December 22: "There are over 9,000 people living here. You can imagine how crowded it had become. Thankfully it was winter. Had it been spring the stink would've been unbearable" (Zhang 2005, 20).

In this environment of extreme terror, these refugees had no unrealistic expectations. Vautrin wrote in her diary entry of December 15: "[L]ast night was a terrible night in the city and many young women were taken from their homes by the Japanese soldiers. Mr. Sone came over this morning and told us about the condition in the Hsuisimen section, and from that time on we have allowed women and children to come in freely; but always imploring the older women to stay home, if possible, in order to leave a place for younger ones. Many begged for just a place to sit out on the lawn." As for food, those with their own foodstuffs took care of themselves. The extreme poor were fed by the refugee soup kitchens. Vautrin writes: "We are building a mat shed between the two north dormitories and will let men we know sell food there. The rice kitchen outside our front gate is not yet open in spite of all our pressure."

As conditions worsened, the refugee soup kitchens opened despite being ill prepared to do so. The "Nanking International Relief Committee Report" reads: "There are five formal soup kitchens, the second of which having been built by our society, all used to provide food to refugees" (Zhang 2006b, 397). It was extremely difficult to keep the soup kitchens running. Vautrin wrote on December 17: "Went to gate at 7:30 to get message to Mr. Sone who slept down in house with F. Chen. Red Cross kitchen must have coal and rice." That same day, director of the refugee camp in the University of Nanking Middle School Jiang Zhengyun gave Fitch a letter reading: "This morning we received eight sacks of rice from Mr. Sone, but these eight sacks were clearly insufficient considering the great number of people to feed. Please send us eight more. We also lack coal and firewood in addition to rice" (Zhang 2006b, 91–92).

The Japanese army's violence exacerbated their difficulties. Fitch wrote: "The problem of transportation became acute on the 16th, with the Japanese still stealing our trucks and cars. I went over to the American Embassy where the Chinese staff were still standing by and borrowed Mr. Atcheson's car for Mills to deliver coal. For our big concentrations of refugees and our three big rice kitchens had to have fuel as well as rice" (Zhang 2005, 72). Rabe wrote: "The European members of our committee have had no choice but to become truck drivers to deliver food and coal to the refugee camps. Members of the food commission have not dared to venture out of their houses these past two days… Deputy director of the Food Committee (foreigner) Mr. Sone (divinity professor) is protecting the 2,500 Chinese sheltering in the Nanking Theological Seminary, but even he has no choice but to drive a truck to fetch food. Once he's gone, there's nobody left to protect the Chinese" (Rabe CN, 160–161).

Witnesses recorded their efforts for history. Jiang Gonggu wrote in his diary entry of February 15, 1938: "This afternoon Hou Nianyan paid another visit by automobile. At the wheel of the car was the American Riggs, who is a living Buddha who made the greatest efforts to safeguard the refugees. All rice and coal needed by the refugee shelters in the refugee zone had to be transported into the zone from elsewhere. Without Riggs escorting the vehicles, they'd often be confiscated by the enemy, so he was always on the move, day and night, wearing raggedy clothes" (Zhang 2005, 75).

International Committee members other than Hubert Sone and Charles Riggs also actively helped to transport food and fuel. Smythe wrote the following in a December 21 letter to his family: "Riggs has encountered several similar situations. Yesterday after he delivered rice and coal, he felt much better, because by nighttime he could see the results of his efforts. There's really a lot of work involved in providing rice and coal to the refugee camps. No Chinese dares to drive a truck on the roads. On Friday and Saturday Mills also helped transport rice and coal, while Riggs was busy driving off soldiers attempting to commit outrages" (Zhang 2005, 241).

One could say that the initiation of operations in the Safety Zone, particularly the establishment of refugee shelters and the opening of soup kitchens, made a tremendous contribution to enabling refugees to survive the power vacuum period, and also constituted an important support for establishing the prestige of the Safety Zone Committee among the refugees.

As the numbers of refugees grew, there emerged a constant stream of new problems in the management of the refugee camps. Vautrin writes on December 17: "The crowd coming in all day we simply cannot take care of – if we had room we do not have strength enough to manage." Vautrin continues on December 27:

> How Ginling looks as a refugee camp needs greater power of description than I possess. Needless to say it would not receive any blue ribbon for cleanliness. When we had our first 400 refugees we had ideals of cleanliness and tried to have rooms and halls swept very day and paper picked up every day. Not so now. With 10,000 or more here we can do nothing except to persuade people not to use main campus as a toilet. Harriet's ideal of having grass walked on has been realized so fully that there is practically no grass left, and in many places – especially where they serve the rice, there are mud puddles.
>
> The shrubs and trees have been badly used and some of the former have been trampled until they have disappeared. On every sunny day tree and shrub and railing and fence is strewn with diapers and pants of all descriptions and colors. When the foreign men come over they laugh and say they have never seen Ginling look thus.

In the face of these problems, the International Committee conducted a comprehensive study of the life of refugees in their camps at the end of December 1937 and the beginning of January 1938. Rabe wrote on January 3, 1938:

> The reports reviewing our soup kitchens and refugee camps provide an interesting insight into how our committee and its subcommittees have to go about their rather difficult business: Some Chinese are not at all shy about "squeezing." We are in China, and nothing gets done without a "squeeze" (Rabe EN, 111).

Rabe then proceeded to list out the results of the assessments of the over 20 refugee camps, which we have compiled into a table for easier comprehension.

2 Changes in the Order of Life for Nanjing Residents

Serial No.	Shelter	General organizational situation	Special circumstances	Rice distribution problems	Evaluation
1	Army Academy	3,200 ppl. divided in 27 groups, each with a group leader.	Some men serving as coolies for Japanese, sometimes receiving rice from them. There are peddlers and drug users.	Receives 10 sacks of rice daily. About a third of refugees handle their own food. All others are given food. Families cook for themselves. Every adult is given one cup of rice per day, and half a cup for children, all free of charge.	General situation satisfactory. Great efforts required to improve sanitation and change eating habits of refugees to consuming porridge. Two and a half sacks of rice discovered in shelter office.
2	Arsenal Bureau	About 8,000 ppl. and several who spend the night here.	A Chinese police squadron is stationed here. There are delivery rooms for women. There are drug users.	Receives 10 sacks of rice daily. There is a public kitchen which distributes rice porridge twice daily. 3,000 are fed free of charge. About 2,400 handle their own food. About 1,500 pay. Daily revenue 12 yuan. About 600 refugees have money. The income is used to buy daily necessities, and also to buy cigarettes to distribute to Japanese soldiers.	31.5 sacks of rice in rooms (corruption suspected). Sanitation atrocious. Poorly managed by shelter chief. Need oversight for rice sales and income allocation. Reserves brought by refugees from home about to be exhausted.
3	Germany-China Club	444 ppl.	All families cook for themselves.	Two sacks of rice daily. Distribution free of charge. Every person receives one liter of rice per time for two days of use. Same quantities issued for adults and children.	Eating and living conditions decent. Sanitation rules need to be stricter.

2.2 Approach, Arrival, and Continuation of the Power Vacuum Period — 63

Continued

Serial No.	Shelter	General organizational situation	Special circumstances	Rice distribution problems	Evaluation
4	Quaker Missionary House	800 ppl., mostly men.	Some live in straw huts. Japanese soldiers often come to loot and rape.	Two sacks of rice per day. Families cook on their own. Every person is given 7/10 a liter of rice, and sometimes 4/10 a liter, per day. Sometimes a full liter. Rice is distributed free of charge. Same quantities for adults and children.	Need to provide a list of refugees who can handle their own food. Sanitation rules need to be stricter.
5	Hankou Road Primary School	About 1,400 ppl.	Refugees satisfied with leadership.	Two sacks of rice per day. Families cook on their own. Refugees eat cooked rice. Children and adults receive same quantities at distribution time. About 150 people have rice reserves or money to buy rice. This shelter does not have rice for sale.	Rooms extremely crowded, suggest establishing a sanitation team to force refugees to pay attention to cleanliness.
6	Overseas Chinese Club	1,000 refugees and 20 managers.	20 coolies for Japanese army, sometimes earn rice. Leader incompetent, too little education.	All refugees cook indoors. No fixed quantities of rice distribution. Three to five sacks per day. Adults receive one cup of rice and children eight and under receive half a cup per day.	Refugees encouraged to cook outside. Pay attention to sanitation. Hopefully some educated people can assume leadership of this shelter.

Continued

Serial No.	Shelter	General organizational situation	Special circumstances	Rice distribution problems	Evaluation
7	Siemens Overseas Company	602 refugees.	Refugees live in straw huts. Sometimes about 30 people leave to transport coal daily.	Allocated three sacks of rice daily. Adults receive two cups and children one cup daily. Estimated that one sack of rice contains 300 cups. Distributed free of charge. All families cook for themselves.	Space cramped, suggest that some refugees relocate to Judiciary School. Refugees here receive more rice than in other shelters.
8	Zhongshan Road Judiciary School	528 refugees and 9 managers. One man named Wang previously world for envoy to Japan, speaks Japanese.	Under special protection from Japanese army command. 30 coolies for Japanese army. Separate men's and women's toilets. Most rooms contain iron beds.	Allocated three sacks of rice per day. Adults receive one cup and children half a cup per day. Vast majority of rice distributed free of charge. Very few have money to buy rice. People eat only cooked rice. A third of refugees come from outside Nanjing, most of these from Shanghai.	Well led, refugees satisfied. Can consider relocating some refugees from more crowded shelters here.
9	University of Nanking Silkworm Factory	3,304 refugees.	Over 500 sleep in huts. Extremely crowded, sanitary facilities poor, poorly organized.	Allocated four to eight sacks of rice daily. Last two days no rice allocation. One liter of rice per two people every day. Rice is sold. Daily income of about 40 yuan. 120 yuan in till. Friends and family members of shelter chief can obtain rice. Most rice	Many complaints, mostly identical, substantial enough to warrant a thorough investigation of worthiness of shelter chief. Sanitary facilities greatly insufficient.

2.2 Approach, Arrival, and Continuation of the Power Vacuum Period — 65

Continued

Serial No.	Shelter	General organizational situation	Special circumstances	Rice distribution problems	Evaluation
				sold outside of the shelter. Some refugees forced to obtain porridge at University of Nanking.	
10	School of Agriculture	1,658 ppl. There is an ambulance corps and a committee of small group leaders.	Men's and women's toilets separate. There are drug users. 28 people pay two *jiao* per day for food.	Allocated two to three sacks of rice per day. Adults receive one tin of rice per day, children half a tin. People eat rice porridge and cooked rice. There are three layers of control on rice distribution. No rice is given to those who have money, have rice, engage in commerce, or smoke. Families cook on their own.	Very well led. Refugees seem satisfied. Shelter leader very competent, has done very well.
11	Bible Teacher Training School	3,400 ppl.	Often looted by Japanese soldiers, 70% of women raped. Situation improved since military police stationed. Hot water supplied, one copper coin per bucket.	Allocated two to five sacks of rice per day. Most refugees here still able to pay for rice, but money almost exhausted. Shelter income about five yuan per day. Shelter leader often in contact with Mr. Sone.	If conditions don't immediately improve and refugees are unable to return home and take up their occupations, the amount of rice distributed free of charge must be increased. General conditions good, well led.

Continued

Serial No.	Shelter	General organizational situation	Special circumstances	Rice distribution problems	Evaluation
12	Jinling School of Divinity	3,116 ppl.		Allocated two sacks of rice daily. Only old women and widows receive rice free of charge. All other refugees must buy ration cards. About ¾ of refugees are poor. Bills received by Mr. Sone.	
13	Wutaishan Primary School	1,640 ppl.	First shelter to receive refugees, only three hours after Chinese government announcement.	So far this shelter does not receive rice from the International Committee. Refugees receive porridge rations from the Red Swastika Society, but soon may need to rely on International Committee for food provision.	Shelter very well led.
14	University of Nanking Middle School	Run by Jiang Zhengyun, 80 assistants. About 11,000 refugees (was 15,000). 40 small groups.	There is an ambulance corps, a firefighting team, and a clinic run by Chinese doctors and nurses. A consumer union runs a store. Prices unified.	Allocated 12 sacks of rice daily, of which two are sold. Income of about 21 yuan. Money used on necessary shelter expenditures, such as buying rope, brooms, cigarettes for Japanese soldiers, kitchen items, etc. There is a central kitchen, kept very clean and tidy. Coal provided by Mr. Riggs. Running water restored as of January 3.	This is our feeling: the shelter is well organized, and its leadership is methodical. There seem to be tensions between shelter leader Mr. Jiang and school representative Mr. Su.

2.2 Approach, Arrival, and Continuation of the Power Vacuum Period — 67

Continued

Serial No.	Shelter	General organizational situation	Special circumstances	Rice distribution problems	Evaluation
15	Dafangxiang Military Chemical Plant	About 2,800 ppl., all refugee rooms numbered.	Many coolies, under special military protection. Safest place for women to stay. Has committees for hair-cutting, sanitary facilities, commerce, inspection, and price setting.	Allocated six sacks of rice daily, distributed per ration cards. About 100 refugees able to buy rice. We discovered 13 sacks of rice in storage. Distribution takes place in morning. Refugees permitted to leave to fetch water or handle other matters.	The Inspection Committee thinks this shelter is extraordinarily well led. Those in leadership positions are men with education and working experience. Sanitation conditions best of all shelters inspected.
16	Shanxi Road Primary School	About 1,100 ppl.		Allocated three sacks of rice daily. Families cook for themselves. About 100 refugees can buy rice. But no rice sold in shelter. Rice is distributed free of charge to all in shelter. We found 2.5 sacks of rice in storage, allegedly awaiting distribution.	Shelter very dirty. We don't think the shelter chief and his assistants are particularly capable, nor do we think they are interested in their work. Strongly recommend that refugees here eat rice porridge.
17	Gaojia Tavern #55	770 ppl., broken into two placement groups.		Mr. Sone says on average two sacks of rice delivered daily, but shelter chief says he receives only one sack daily, sometimes receiving two sacks every other day. Families cook. About 60 people can buy rice.	Shelter passably well led. Space small and crowded. Sanitation rules should be better enforced. Once difference between Mr. Sone and shelter chief is sorted out regarding daily rice allocation, more rice

Continued

Serial No.	Shelter	General organizational situation	Special circumstances	Rice distribution problems	Evaluation
				Shelter does not sell rice. About 500 people given rice daily free of charge. Adults and children all eat very thin porridge.	should be provided to refugees here.
18	University of Nanking	7,000 ppl., mostly women and children. Men deliver food during the day.	Shelter on difficult times, because Japanese have cut water supply.	Daily allocation of 25–30 sacks of rice and three tons of coal to soup kitchen. Soup kitchen run by Zhou Qingxing, with 50 assistants and 150 workers. Distributes rice porridge twice daily for three coppers per cup, daily income of 50 yuan. Mr. Zhou says only one third of refugees buy porridge. A sample survey indicates that those who do not pay cannot obtain porridge.	Too many assistants and workers. We don't understand why refugees in university library and silkworm factory are forced to buy porridge at Wutaishan. We urgently recommend that the International Committee undertake a detailed inspection of the rice distribution leadership work here.
19	University Library	About 3,000 ppl. in the handicrafts industry, work very hard to make their living.	Refugees live in shacks. Some smoke opium or gamble. Some people very rough and hard to get along with, some of these have taken part in looting.	This shelter does not receive rice from the International Committee. Refugees here were previously fed by the university soup kitchen, but that soup kitchen has denied them food for the past four days.	Dispatch more assistants to the shelter chief and take measures to remove bad elements from shelter. In addition, measures should be taken to provide rice to poor in this shelter.

Continued

Serial No.	Shelter	General organizational situation	Special circumstances	Rice distribution problems	Evaluation
20	Jinling College for Women	5,000–6,000 ppl. (previously 10,000).	Many people still don't dare return home. A detachment of Japanese military police maintain nighttime security.	Allocated 12 sacks of rice daily. Rice is given to over 1,000 relatives to sustain life at the Red Cross of China kitchen across the street from the university gate. 350 people receive free rice from the red ration cards on their clothes. The rest buy cooked rice at a rate of three copper coins per cup. They previously paid in cash, but now they must buy ration cards, the sale of which is undertaken by the university accounting department. Daily income of 80–100 yuan. Most money given to International Committee.	Shelter leader extraordinarily adept.

Continued

Serial No.	Shelter	General organizational situation	Special circumstances	Rice distribution problems	Evaluation
21	Church and Elder Society Missionary School	Shelter chief is a wood merchant from Shanghai. Now 1,000 ppl., previously 2,000. Many people come at night to sleep.	Shelter often looted by Japanese soldiers and women often raped.	About 2/3 of refugees here provide their own food. The rest are completely penniless. Mr. Mills provided three sacks of rice to this shelter on January 5 and is trying to provide the same amount every other day.	

Table 6: Refugee shelter investigation report.
Source: Rabe CN, 270–302.

The results of the Committee's inspections are extremely valuable historical resources, as they expose some management problems for the refugee shelters and express evaluation opinions. In particular they comprehensively expose the basic conditions of life experience of refugees during this time, which are helpful to our all-around understanding of the efforts made by the International Committee to safeguard the lives of refugees in the areas of food and shelter during the power vacuum period.

The International Committee then produced the following "General Recommendations" based on the findings of their survey:

1. We should, along with the staff of the university hospital, take measures to the extent possible to care for the many sick people in the various shelters.

2. The International Committee's ambulance corps should visit each shelter at fixed intervals to oversee strict execution of sanitation rules.

3. All shelters should determine the numbers of women and other people whose husbands or other caretakers have been taken away by the Japanese and not returned, and submit a request to the Japanese authorities that sufficient allocations of money and food be made to support these people.

4. The presence of opium smokers and other rough individuals in all shelters should be given special attention. We should come up with ways and means to remove these bad elements, or provide protection to shelter chiefs to prevent them from coming to harm.

5. In addition, all shelters should determine the number of people whose houses or dwellings have been burned or bombed, and take steps to compensate them.

6. In addition, we must pay attention to the fact that some Chinese are taking women from the shelters and providing them to Japanese soldiers toward unethical ends.

7. We must make a plan to move refugees still living in straw shacks or crowded shelters into better, more spacious shelters.

8. We should convene a meeting of all shelter chiefs as soon as possible.

9. Establish a committee to inspect all shelters.

10. The question of coal provision to the shelters must be considered in a special study.

11. We suggest that morning inspections be made of soup kitchens and rice provisions thereto, to avoid irregularities in rice provision.

12. All shelters selling rice (or porridge or cooked rice), particularly those shelters that require additional expenditures in the course of operations, should have their accounts audited.

13. We should establish behavior standards and post them up in the shelters, and shelter chiefs should be responsible for encouraging refugees to adhere to them.

14. We must establish standardized cards for all shelters to help us keep track of how many refugees pay for food and how many require food assistance free of charge, as well as their names, addresses, etc.

15. We should likewise establish and implement standards and rules for rice distribution.

16. We should commend shelter chiefs and their colleagues for their dedicated contributions to the relief work.

17. The secretary-general of the International Committee should be entrusted with establishing necessary preventative protocols based on the findings of the Inspection Committee (Rabe CN, 302–311).

2.2.5 End of the power vacuum period and initial improvements in public security

2.2.5.1 Japanese considerations and the end of the power vacuum period

The Chinese government refused to surrender, and "some in the Japanese government established the Provisional Government of North China owing to their dissatisfaction with the Chinese government's unclear position following the occupation of Nanjing in December. Wang Kemin was appointed chairman of the government, and so a very influential idea then raised its head: if we prop up the provisional government and later develop it into the central government, Chiang Kai-shek won't be the one we deal with in peace talks" (Imai n.d., 72).

Going along with the policy direction coming out of Tokyo, the Central China Area Army wanted to build a puppet government over Nanjing that would be answerable to itself. Okada Takashi, "commissioned" by Matsui Iwane at this time, gave the following testimony at the Tokyo trials: "I landed at Shanghai at the end of August, at which time this incident was in its initial stage. I immediately sought old friends in the concession to help convey General Matsui's meaning to them. I even had the opportunity to speak with Mr. Tang Shaoyi, an old friend of mine who was a senior Chinese politician at the time. Another person with great understanding of the Japanese situation, Mr. Li Zeyi, also communicated his views to me" (Zhang and Yang n.d., 192). Prior to the encirclement of Nanjing, Matsui again considered the military deployments that would follow the occupation of the city. He wrote in his diary entry of December 2: "The objective established from here forward is: first and foremost expel the nationalist government. If we obtain all of Jiangsu and Zhejiang, then the next step will be to consolidate Anhui, and then establish a regime. If this proves not to work, then we can recreate the nationalist government with important people from among the remnants of KMT officials left around Nanjing, and ultimately establish a nationalist government separate from the one in Hankou. These tasks must be accomplished as we henceforth proceed with the siege and occupation of Nanjing" (Wang 2005b, 143–144).

It was, however, going to be very difficult to establish a puppet regime for Central China. The German ambassador to Japan at the time wrote in a report to the German Foreign Ministry in Berlin: "For the Japanese, it will be much more difficult to organize and administer the provinces they've occupied all together than it would be to occupy new territory, much less to make an enticing display of popular support and good government as well as Sino-Japanese friendship in these regions. That is because, for one, the Japanese lack all basic conditions for autonomously implementing comprehensive management, and for another they must avoid pure occupation of territory or the pursuit of 'territorial goals' to the extent possible. For these reasons the Japanese are anxious to use their traditional methods of using existing management bodies and establish small autonomous units" (Zhang and Yang n.d., 391).

It was under these auspices that, under the "guidance" of the Japanese army, the "Nanjing Autonomous Committee" held a preparatory meeting on December 23. On January 1, 1938, a ceremony was held at the Gulou [Drum Tower] Plaza to celebrate the establishment of the puppet Autonomous Committee, after which said committee began gradually taking over administration of the city.

2.2.5.2 Pressure from Westerners gradually leads to improvements in Nanjing security

After the Japanese had entered the city, officials of the Japanese embassy in Nanjing returned to the city on December 15. Their work was defined as resolving diplomatic conflicts, and in particular to pay attention to the few dozen foreigners in Nanjing and the interests of Western countries. An anonymous letter written on December 15 read: "Today, officials from the Japanese embassy entered Nanjing with the aim of reducing the harm done by Japanese soldiers to the lives and property of foreigners of all nations" (Zhang 2005, 86). Miner Bates wrote in a letter of January 11, 1938 to Mr. Boynton of the National Christian Council in Shanghai: "The Japanese entered the city on December 13. On the 15 their embassy staff announced they were returning to mediate in any damages the Japanese army has inflicted upon foreigners or the property of foreigners. I had talked to Consul Tanaka about this previously" (Zhang 2006b, 98).

At this time a system of forces influencing the order of life for Nanjing residents began to emerge: communication channels were established between the foreigners and the Japanese embassy in Nanjing, and intensive interactions commenced.

Nevertheless, the Japanese diplomatic personnel were in a weak position vis-a-vis the army, unable to stop the violence being perpetrated by their soldiers. For that reason some Japanese diplomats desired that the foreigners would expose conditions in Nanjing to help them pressure the army. A document titled "Summary of Japanese Atrocities Following the Fall of Nanking" transmitted by Bates and later obtained by the nationalist government read: "Only two of the three responsible officers feel deep remorse. The Japanese have asked that we report the truth to help them in negotiating with the Japanese army. This is sufficient to demonstrate that some Japanese civil officials are protecting the army while some are counseling honesty with the army" (Zhang 2006b, 100).

An important objective of the Europeans and Americans was to get personnel from their embassies to return to Nanjing. Fitch wrote of December 20: "Our group here at the house drafted a message to the American Consulate-General in Shanghai asking that diplomatic representatives be sent here immediately as the situation was urgent, then asked the Japanese Embassy to send it via navy radio. Needless to say it was never sent." We see here an instance of feigned compliance by the Japanese embassy (Zhang 2005, 75).

Outside of Nanjing at this time, tensions were mounting between the great powers. On December 24, the Japanese government sent the findings of its investigation into the "Panay" incident, which the U.S. government accepted in principle. The German ambassador to Japan at the time wrote in a report: "The rapid actions taken by the Japanese actions quenched the flames that such a serious incident would ordinarily have given rise to" (Zhang and Yang n.d., 394). The Japanese government adopted a policy of not offending the UK or the U.S. to the extent possible. So the Central China Area Army acceded to the request of American diplomatic staff to return to Nanjing.

Shanghai Expeditionary Army Chief of Staff Iinuma Mamoru wrote in his diary entry of December 29:

> The Area Army chief of staff informed us that we needed to prepare cars, as the staffs of the various embassies are coming to Nanjing on the 29. It was an awkward situation because the Area Army had arranged for these people to come to Nanjing on their own authority. The atmosphere of Shanghai was different from that of Nanjing... Just as I was considering how to receive the staff of the embassies and consulates from the UK, the U.S., Germany, Italy, and other countries, Secretary Fukui (consul to Nanjing) came. According to a Chinese person hired by the American embassy, Japanese soldiers entered the embassy and looted private property belonging to Chinese people on the 23, and looted the residences of staff of the embassy. They used bayonets to force entry and stole calligraphy paintings from the German embassy, and so on and so forth. He returned after depositing a letter written to the consul to the Americans. Some people had committed unspeakable acts. Even if I can't say they were all true, I still need to look into measures for dealing with their fallout" (Wang 2005b, 221).

Shanghai Expeditionary Army Deputy Chief of Staff Uemura Toshimichi, in Nanjing at the time, wrote in his diary entry of December 29: "Last night a report came from the Area Army saying that when the British and German consuls return to Nanjing, we can provide them with cars for their convenience. But today they did not come to Nanjing; they've postponed until tomorrow. Nobody from the Special Service Organ[14] came to coordinate this matter" (Wang 2005b, 251).

Faced with pressure from the returning Western diplomatic personnel, the Shanghai Expeditionary Army stationed in Nanjing began to reorganize military discipline. Uemura wrote in his diary entry of December 30: "(Prince Asaka) assembled the adjutants of all troops stationed in and around Nanjing at 1:30 and demanded that they further rectify discipline and moral standards, particularly in illegal behaviors toward the residences of foreigners. Major General Sasaki (commander of the guard) also raised matters of attention and demands. Staff Officer Nakayama of the Area Army came and delivered a letter to the chief of staff alone expressing regret for the illegal actions that had happened at the foreign residence and for other behaviors in violation of military discipline. He was truly conscience-stricken beyond words. I read the cable sent to the Area Army written jointly by the Minister of the Army and the Chief of the Army General Staff saying that we should pay great attention to trends among all nations as well as nuances therein" (Wang 2005b, 221-222).

In summary, at the end of 1937, the order of life in Nanjing changed slightly for the better. This was felt by most foreigners who remained in Nanjing. Forster wrote in a letter to his wife of December 28: "Things seem to be better in general, as a great many troops seem to have left town, and the people feel freer about walking on streets. They are still scared as stray soldiers are still looting and raping, and men suspected of having been soldiers are still being executed. But it is still much better in many respects than it has been and we are no end thankful. If only more foreigners would come back and help out it would be a great relief to the congested conditions now obtaining. At Ginling College alone there must be over ten thousand women and children" (Zhang 2005, 105–106).

---

14 The *Tokumu Kikan* was an intelligence agency under direct control of the Japanese Imperial General Headquarters charged with espionage, counterespionage, propaganda, and fifth column activities. It has been variously rendered in English as "Special Service Organ," "Special Affairs Department," "Special Services Organization," and so on. In this translation I have preferred the translation Special Service Organ (translator's note).

2.3 Deadlock and Construction of a "Normalized" Colonial Order in the Transitional Period

The Nanjing Autonomous Committee held its founding ceremony on January 1, 1938, at which point the power vacuum period, with no government regime exercising control over the city, ended. A great many documents nevertheless indicate that Nanjing did not immediately enter a "normalized" colonial order once the power vacuum period ended, but rather entered a deadlocked transitional period in which various entities vied with each other for power, and in which public security was sometimes good and sometimes bad. Fitch writes: "It is now the 11th of January, and while conditions are vastly improved there has not been a day that has not had its atrocities, some of them of a most revolting nature" (Zhang 2005, 82).

The transitional period lasted over a month. The wide-scale massacre, raping, and pillaging in Nanjing only began to rapidly come under control with the return of Matsui Iwane to the city in early February. Not long afterward, General Hata Shunroku advanced the establishment of a "normalized" colonial order in Nanjing along the lines of his orders to "establish a new regime in Nanjing in accordance with circumstances." The "Reformed Government of the Republic of China" was founded on March 28, 1938, followed by the founding of the "Supervisory Nanjing City Government Office" in April, both of which provided a clear framework for the "normalized" colonial order of the city.

2.3.1 Background of deadlock during the transition

On January 1, 1938, the Autonomous Committee began operations, but Tokyo's attitude toward China remained unclear at this time. On January 12, 1938, "Hirota Koki asked the German ambassador to transmit a message to the Chinese government that the Empire of Japan would begin to act freely if it had no reply before the 15" (Yu et al. n.d., 95). The nationalist government made no reply. The next day, the Konoe cabinet issued its first declaration on China:

> After capturing Nanjing, the imperial government still gave the Chinese government a final opportunity to reconsider, and we have waited for their response until now. Even so, the nationalist government does not understand the true intentions of the empire, and has rashly launched a war of resistance. Domestically they are unaware of the suffering of their people, and abroad they pay no attention to peace of East Asia as a whole. So henceforth the government of the empire will no longer deal with the nationalist government, but rather hopes that the new ruling regime of China cooperating with the empire can be truly

established and grow, and that normal diplomatic relations can be adjusted with the new regime, and that we can aid in the construction of a new, resurgent China (Imai n.d., 73).

Once they had declared that they would "no longer deal with the nationalist government," Tokyo scrambled to assemble a puppet regime for Central China.

Commander of the Central China Area Army Matsui Iwane did nothing about the war crimes his troops were committing. He was, on the other hand, extremely enthusiastic about establishing a puppet regime for Central China, looking for appropriate candidates while also paying attention to dynamics in Tokyo. Once the declaration that the Japanese government would "no longer deal with the nationalist government" had been made, the Japanese Ministry of the Army, Ministry of the Navy, and Foreign Ministry sat down for consultations and produced a "memorandum" on January 24, the primary content of which was: "In the Central China Area, direction over this part of China must proceed on a foundation of coordination and consultation between the Ministry of the Army, the Ministry of the Navy, and the Foreign Ministry. To this end we resolve that an On-the-Ground Contact Committee be formed of the chiefs of the Special Service Organ of the Army and Navy in Shanghai as well as the consul at Shanghai, and that this committee be charged with necessary planning for on-the-ground conditions and with appointing the people responsible for guidance and their methods" (Yu et al. n.d., 129).

Matsui wanted to establish a puppet regime for Central China that advanced his own plans, so he sent Special Service Organ Chief Harada Kumakichi to Tokyo to make discreet inquiries. Matsui wrote in his diary entry of January 27, 1938:

> Major General Harada has returned. I learned from his report that the government's opinions do not differ from ours in the establishment of governmental and economic strategy. However, the Ministry of the Army has long resolutely supported using the provisional government in Beijing to unify all of China. I am quite alarmed by this. Of course, the Ministry of the Navy and the Foreign Ministry disagree. Army officials seem to have been primarily influenced by the opinions of the North China Area Army. Although the General Staff Headquarters doesn't necessarily support them, such thinking in the army has long obstructed the strategies and combat operations of our Area Army (Wang 2005b, 169).

Clearly, Matsui was very dissatisfied with the Ministry of the Army's support for the North China Area Army's establishment of a "provisional government" to administer the Central China regime. Not long afterward, director of the second (G2) department of the Army General Staff Office in Tokyo Major General Homma Masaharu made inspection visits to Shanghai and Nanjing. Matsui took great pains in receiving Homma, hoping to gain support for his plans.

2.3.2 Deadlock in the transitional period

2.3.2.1 Operations of the Autonomous Committee

The puppet Nanjing Autonomous Committee held its founding ceremony in at the Drum Tower on January 1, 1938. That same day, Japanese consul to Nanjing Fukui Kiyoshi, Nanjing Security Commander Sasaki Toichi, Shanghai Expeditionary Army General Staff Commander Iinuma Mamoru, and Captain Nakahara Saburo of the Imperial Japanese Navy all delivered speeches in an effort to restore order to Nanjing, bring about amity between Japan and China, and create common prosperity for East Asia.

Tao Xisan, who had studied in the Japanese University of Political Science and Law and had chaired the Nanjing branch of the Red Swastika Society, was appointed president of the Nanjing Autonomous Committee. One of the two vice presidents was Sun Shurong, who had served as interpreter for the Japanese embassy in Nanjing, and the other was Cheng Langbo, a Nanjing businessman. Committee members fell largely into two groups. The first was composed of people of different stripes who had lived or studied in Japan and spoke Japanese. The second was composed of the leadership of charity institutions in Nanjing. The committee comprised several sub-offices: the General Affairs Office, the Financial Office, the Relief Office, the Police Office, the Industrial and Commercial Office, and the Transportation Office.

On January 18, 1938, the Autonomous Committee issued the "Autonomous Committee General Regulations and Detailed Work Regulations." Afterward there was a reorganization of internal institutions. The Police Office was broken out into Police Departments, and district administrative offices were established. These offices were primarily responsible for overall affairs, household registration, housing, and relief work, with some overlap with the other offices. A report from the Japanese Pacification Team reads: "Five district administrative offices were established at the end of January, four in the city and one outside the city (Xiaguan). Also in consideration of the requests of the masses for the need to maintain public security, there is great need to add three provisional administrative offices. These were established at the end of March in the three districts of Shangxinhe, Yanziji, and Xiaolingwei Street" (Wang and Lei n.d., 361). On January 21, the Autonomous Committee issued detailed regulations for police work, detailed regulations for administrative offices on January 25, and detailed regulations for the other sub-offices on January 28. At the same time the Autonomous Committee began gradually taking over administration of the city. The committee included many traitors who aided the Japanese army, but also a few upright people who worked to improve refugees' plights.

The goal of the puppet Autonomous Committee was to replace the International Committee for the Nanking Safety Zone. At the time of the preparatory meeting of the Autonomous Committee, the Japanese media announced: "The International Committee will be dissolved at the time of the founding of the Autonomous Committee" (Wang 2010b, 82).

To build up the Autonomous Committee's prestige, the Japanese granted it control of allocations of wartime living materials for Nanjing residents. The day before the Committee's founding celebration, the Japanese put on their best pose: free grain distribution to draw refugees out of the Safety Zone and closer to the Autonomous Committee. Smythe wrote in a letter to his family of December 31: "McCallum got a look at the crowds rushing toward Beimen Bridge carrying rice today, and discovered that the Japanese had opened a rice shop, demanding that the people go fetch their own rice" (Zhang 2005, 258). The Japanese also had the Autonomous Committee open a grain shop outside of the Safety Zone to lure refugees back to their homes. Rabe wrote in his diary entry of January 8, 1938: "Dr. Xu is now an adviser to the Autonomous Committee. He told me that the Japanese were preparing to give 5,000 sacks of rice to that committee, on the condition that it not be distributed in the Safety Zone. They are doing this to impel residents in the Safety Zone to return to their dwellings outside of the Zone" (Rabe CN, 308). In the addendum to his diary entry of January 25, 1938, Rabe attached a memorandum written by Smythe: "At about 6 p.m. yesterday, Mr. Fitch and I went to Shengzhou Road to see the new rice store operated by the Autonomous Committee. We found it with its doors open still doing business. The day before Japanese soldiers tried three times to steal the money inside the store, so the store began operating thus: rice certificates were sold in another place, and that money was delivered to the office, and the goods were delivered in yet another place. This rice store is located on Shuangtang Street, near to the Methodist Society that burned down. Over the past 10 days, the Japanese have given this store 500 sacks of rice. If the weather turns inclement, the Japanese police refuse rice deliveries. The Autonomous Committee wants to open another rice store on or near Baotai Street" (Rabe CN, 417).

The Japanese army made objective efforts to help establish the puppet Autonomous Committee. A situation report made by the Nanjing Pacification Team in March read:

> Relief materials distributed from January 15 to the end of February: 11,200 sacks of rice (2,000 distributed as charity to the poor), 10,000 sacks of flour (2,000 of which distributed as charity to the poor), and 3,670 sacks of salt (300 of which distributed as charity to the poor). In March: 6,000 sacks of relief rice (4,000 of which provided from Wuhu) and 387

vats of soybean oil (from the Pukou warehouse, 200–300 *jin* per vat). (Two) Those in need of relief in Nanjing in January: about 150,000 people; in February: about 75,000 people; in March: about 68,000 people (Wang and Lei n.d., 366).

2.3.2.2 Dissolution of the International Committee

The clustering of Chinese refugees around the foreigners in the Safety Zone was unacceptable to the Central China Area Army. A situation report made by the Nanjing Pacification Team in February read:

> In late November, disregarding clear instructions from our authorities, the International Committee established the Nanjing Safety Zone, gathering all scattered refugees into said zone. After the Imperial Army had entered the city, they continued to offer free medical care, distribute rice, and provide all manner of relief. They also monitored the actions of the Imperial Army in the refugee zone, and actively engaged in malicious dissemination of information to the outside world… If the aforementioned activities of the International Committee continue, clearly they will cause great harm and do no good, and so to put an end to their activities, the Autonomous Committee has sent them a notice, informing them that the Nanjing Autonomous Committee will henceforth assume all the relief activities for refugees in which they have been engaged. Since then we have grasped the opportunity to suppress their disturbances, with the result that the International Committee's activities have basically come to an end (Wang and Lei n.d., 345).

In truth, the Safety Zone Committee engaged in multiple discussions following the beginning of operations of the puppet Nanjing Autonomous Committee. In a letter to his family of January 5, 1938, Smythe wrote:

> Mills had a new idea this afternoon. We've long felt that we're compelled to resolve certain issues through the Autonomous Committee and not directly through the Japanese Embassy. The Japanese urgently want to diminish the stature of the International Committee and turn its authorities over to the Autonomous Committee. So Mills suggested that we work clearly from that basis, handing issues to the Autonomous Committee and greatly encouraging them to raise requests directly with the Japanese. We started with two matters: restoring order to the other parts of the city and get people to return home and stop burning the city. I started drafting a letter on these two points when we returned to the office and asked for opinions from Rabe, Kröger, Mills, and Bates, to make it an even-handed exposition of multiple perspectives. I figured it could be done in stages so as to better restore order before people began returning to questionable areas, and this would also help us observe how things were progressing. This was also an indirect route to get the soldiers out of all parts of the city, but we couldn't accomplish that across the entire city all at once! This was a way of achieving partial success in the Safety Zone, and then spreading outward one step at a time to other parts of the city, possibly beginning from a corner, the southwest corner, where there was the least destruction and where some people still lived (Zhang 2005, 267–268).

There were two primary reasons for these considerations of Smythe: one, the Safety Zone was founded on the principle of "undertaking in stages," and two, the International Committee realized it lacked authority and prestige from its very outset.

On January 6, 1938, the Japanese sent a recommendation to Rabe clearly proposing that the Safety Zone Committee be disbanded. Rabe wrote thus in his diary entry of January 6:

> At 5 o'clock this afternoon, Mr. Fukuda paid me a visit to tell me that by decision of the military authorities our International Committee is to be dissolved and our supplies and moneys are to be taken over by the Autonomous Government Committee. I immediately protest any handing over of our assets and supplies. We have no objection to their taking over our work, but wish to point out that before the city is secure under the rule of law and order, the refugees cannot return to their former homes, which for the most part have been demolished and looted or burned down.

I at once call a meeting of the committee, in which my answer to Mr. Fukuda is discussed and a proposal prepared outlining how we envision the restoration of law and order. I have the feeling that the Autonomous Government hasn't the vaguest idea how to tackle these problems, even though they are being advised by the Japanese. All that interests them are our assets. Their claim is: "You received the money from the Chinese government, and so now it belongs to us!" We are most decidedly of a different opinion and will leave no stone unturned in the defense of our opinion, for which we expect strong support from both the American and German embassies, although as yet we do not know what their viewpoints really are (Rabe EN, 113–114).

In my opinion, the Japanese are asking too high a price of us foreigners (Rabe CN, 297).

> The International Committee, hoping to provide relief to Chinese refugees, formed a cooperative relationship with the "Autonomous Committee" in the food issue through multiple channels, including Xu Chuanyin. The "Nanjing Relief Conditions" report of February 17, 1938 read: "For the past three days our refugee camps have bought rice from the Autonomous Committee store, but since the members of that committee fear opposition from the Japanese, they have asked us to definitely reduce the amount of rice purchased that way. However, the Red Cross Society has bought 1,340 sacks of rice from private reserves inside the city and is currently delivering them to the refugee camps" (Zhang 2010, 510).

At the end of January 1938, the Japanese issued clear orders to the International Committee to disband their refugee shelters by February 4. This created great anxiety among many people and resulted in a false alarm. In a letter to his wife of February 4, 1938, Forster writes: "This was the day by which the people from the refugee centers were to have moved back to the other parts of the city. It was said that force would be used upon those who did not return voluntarily, but I am glad to say that there were no instances of it. We went around to the various centers to observe in case any was used, but everything was quiet" (Zhang 2005, 128). We will go into the reasons the Japanese did not use force shortly.

The foreigners long considered how to reorganize their International Committee per new conditions. Rabe wrote in his diary entry of January 12: "I have come up with a plan for making friends with the Japanese. I shall try to dissolve the Zone Committee and found an International Relief Committee, on which the Japanese will also be represented" (Rabe EN, 124). There was not, however, unanimous support for Rabe's idea on the International Committee. On February 18, 1938, the committee renamed itself the Nanjing International Relief Committee. This day clearly marked a turning point. It was not only the day of the disbandment of the International Committee for the Nanking Safety Zone and the founding of the International Relief Committee but also the day of high-level restructuring of the Central China Area Army and the arrival of General Hata Shunroku to Nanjing. This marked the end of the transitional period in Nanjing, when systematic construction of the "normalized" colonial life order began.

2.3.3 European and American embassy staff strive to break through deadlock of "transitional period"

2.3.3.1 Summary of return to Nanjing by diplomatic personnel

At the end of December 1937, John Moore Allison, an official of the U.S. embassy, was the first to receive permission to return to Nanjing, which he did on December 31. He wrote in a report of that day:

> I reached Nanking at 2:30 this afternoon. The river shore had become the sight of a massacre. Small fires were visible everywhere in the city, accompanied by the sound of gunfire... An English officer told me that no foreigners were allowed to disembark at Nanking. Apparently the Japanese commanding officer has declared that no foreigners are allowed to disembark before January 5. I heard that their justification is that a "sweep" is ongoing, and there is danger (Zhang 2006b, 65).

In a letter to his family of January 5, 1938, Smythe wrote:

> ...three representatives of foreign countries have come and will open a new chapter. Just as Mills said, the Japanese will have no choice but to behave themselves. The expanding foreign community might be most helpful in prompting the return of other missionaries and businessmen. The increase of "neutral observers" will also allow us to not have to be al-

ways submitting letters of protest. I told Mills that we can work with the Autonomous Committee. I am glad that some consuls and foreign representatives had been in Nanjing prior to December 10. They will remember the good order... the city was in at the time. Today they need merely to drive around the city and take a look at superficial conditions to discover how different it is now (Zhang 2005, 265).

Allison finally disembarked on January 6, 1938. Iinuma Mamoru wrote in his diary entry of that day: "Staff Officer Hongo said that the American consul landed before noon and had a favorable impression. Both parties agreed that the military's rule must be abided" (Wang 2005b, 226).

On January 9, diplomats from Germany and the UK also returned to Nanjing. Rosen wrote in a report to the German Foreign Ministry on January 15, 1938: "Before I drove away, Major Hongo bid me farewell in German, and asked why I had returned at the same time as the English. I replied simply: 'why not?' ... He then said: 'I deeply regret that you came with the English.' I did not rebuke him for his impoliteness" (Chen, Zhang, and Dai n.d., 86).

The return of the diplomats increased the numbers of foreigners in the city, and swelled the confidence of the Safety Zone Committee. Rabe wrote in his diary entry of January 11: "All the gentlemen of these three embassies expressed the willingness to assume the daily reporting of crimes by Japanese soldiers, and the submission of these reports to the Japanese embassy or to their own governments. This has greatly reduced the burden on our committee. If these embassies send continuous protests, order may be restored quickly" (Rabe CN, 323).

The Japanese army was dissatisfied with this turn of events. Iinuma Mamoru wrote in his diary entry of January 11: "It is said that as of last night the following foreigners had come to Nanjing: UK, one consul, two military attachés; U.S., one consul, two secretaries; Germany, three secretaries. The English are the most refined, and the Germans are the most abominable. It also seems that they intend to initiate peace talks with Chiang and have budding intentions to feel us out" (Wang 2005b, 228).

2.3.3.2 The Allison Incident

The Americans had high hopes for the return of Allison to the embassy in Nanjing. Smythe wrote in a letter to his family of January 5, 1938:

I spent a considerable time sorting out three copies of each document, one of which was intended for the American representative about to arrive. They were quite surprised that we had raised complaints so directly and so firmly with the Japanese Embassy, but we had felt even more strongly in our hearts than we had written in our letters. All these records are now part of history, but they clearly demonstrate the position adopted by the International Committee during the whole of this event (Zhang 2005, 266).

Allison actively reported on the violence of the Japanese army in Nanjing with the Japanese embassy, the American consulate in Shanghai, the American embassy in Nanjing, and the U.S. Department of State. The Japanese did not approve of Allison's installation of telegram equipment in the U.S. embassy, but Allison disregarded them. Forster writes: "Our Embassy now has a wireless sending set with an operator from the Navy. The J. refused at first, but Allison won out. More power to him! He is awfully nice as being Espy and MacFadyen, the two vice-consuls" (Zhang 2005, 117).

Allison won the respect of the other foreigners in Nanjing. Forster records the role he played:

> Allison and the British and German Consuls are not standing for any nonsense. When their protests, etc. are tabled by the J. Embassy officials, they get into direct communication with Tokyo through Washington, London, and Berlin. This has made the J. awfully mad here, as you may imagine, and they are being told that our gov'ts do not consider a small and unimportant matter to have the property of their nationals looted and people living on those premises for protection carried off by troops whom their officers will not control. One of the J. Consular police is very angry because Allison reported to Washington that he came to the Univ. of Nanking to get women to wash clothing, but when he refused those who offered to go and demanded others who were young and beautiful, he placed his motives under grave suspicion (Zhang 2005, 117).

Allison was struck by Japanese soldiers on January 26, 1938. Forster records the event:

> A girl had been taken by soldiers from one of the Univ. buildings and raped. On her return, the case was reported to the consul and he and Riggs accompanied the girl to the place where she had been taken. It was no less a place than the military police headquarters. Some Military police, Japanese, had accompanied the Consul as they do when he goes out. The girl was asked to enter the building, perhaps to identify her assailants, but Allison and Riggs were not permitted to go along in. They stood about two feet inside the gate. A soldier tried to push them out, and when an officer came along foaming with rage and shouted that they were Americans, a soldier reached over from behind and slapped Allison's face. When one of the Military Police who had accompanied Allison said to the others that he was the American Consul, another soldier grabbed Riggs and shook him by the overcoat collar until he tore it. They waited, however, until the girl was delivered back in their hands (Zhang 2005, 120–121).

The American government immediately lodged a stern protest, to which the Japanese responded swiftly. In a letter to his wife on January 28, 1938, Forster writes:

"According to the radio broadcast at 1 today the J. have issued statements about the slapping of Allison" (Zhang 2005, 122). Iinuma Mamoru wrote in his diary entry of January 29, 1938: "Per an admonishment that came from the home country, the chief of staff has apologized to Allison and two other secretaries of the American embassy to China for the incident in which Japanese soldiers forced their way into the American embassy, or maybe Commander Matsui apologized to the American fleet commander. It was done either in Tokyo or Washington, although I still haven't looked into it, it seems that in any event the chief of staff apologized. A condition was that this would resolve all incidents that have happened to date" (Wang 2005b, 236).

The Allison incident played a role in driving restructuring of the Central China Expeditionary Army's high leadership, and in driving Nanjing out of the transitional period.

2.3.4 Building a "Normalized" Colonial Order

2.3.4.1 Leadership shake-up of Matsui Iwane and other high officers

On February 6, 1938, Matsui Iwane unexpectedly appeared in Nanjing to tighten up military discipline. Iinuma Mamoru writes in his diary entry of February 7, 1938: "At 5:00, Commander Matsui delivered a speech to the members of the Autonomous Committee in the embassy. At 6:30, officers dined together. At the dinner, Commander Matsui made another speech: at this very moment we need 10 soldiers to pacify one Chinese, to make them worship us" (Wang 2005b, 239). Uemura Toshimichi wrote in his diary entry of February 7, 1938: "After it was over, General Matsui talked about his feelings. He admonished the team leader who had come to take part in memorial services and demanded rigorous attention to military discipline. After tonight's dinner with the other officers, he again urged us to be concerned with the Chinese and develop true amity for the Japanese among them. Everybody could be more or less understand the commander's feelings" (Wang 2005b, 268).

There were special reasons for Matsui's performance. At the end of January and the beginning of February, officials in Tokyo began considering a reshuffle of high-level leadership of the Central China Area Army and the Shanghai Expeditionary Army; Matsui felt his time was growing short.

With time growing tighter and Tang Shaoyi unwilling to accept their invitation, the Central China Area Army's Special Affairs Department finally settled on Liang Hongzhi. Special Affairs Department Chief Harada Kumakichi was extremely pleased with the choice of Liang, identifying him as a "politician who's been through the ups and downs in the establishment of regimes and their disestablishment many times" (Yu et al. n.d., 130).

The order to change leadership of the Central China Area Army came soon afterward. Matsui wrote in his diary entry of February 10, 1937:

> Today an envoy came from Tokyo. He brought with him the essential points of the reorganization of the Central China Area Army's command as well as documents related to personnel matters. I learned from these documents that General Hata had been picked as new commander and Major General Kawabe was to be chief of staff. Almost all other personnel selections consisted of capable people within the Area and Expeditionary Armies. In truth, I'm not leaving this post from conceit, as anyone would agree that I haven't been at it very long. This is all the result of the self-importance of figures in the central Ministry of the Army. If I continued in my post under present conditions, I still wouldn't be able to achieve much, so I might as well return home and discuss the nitty gritty details with them there, and come up with new political and military plans for China from the ground up. This is what's most pressing (Wang 2005b, 178).

Matsui was recalled to Japan for the following reasons:

a) Violence in Nanjing. Director of the Japanese Foreign Ministry Bureau of East Asian Affairs Ishii Itaro recalled in his diary entry of January 6, 1938: "A letter came from Shanghai detailing the violent acts of our army in Nanjing. The pillaging and raping described in the letter were atrocious beyond belief. Alas, was this really the Imperial Army? This must have been an expression of how dispirited the people of Japan have become. This was a great social question" (Wang 2005b, 18). The actions of the Japanese army taken under Matsui Iwane egregiously damaged the image of both the army and the nation of Japan as a whole. Rabe confirmed this point in his diary entry of January 7, 1938: "Mr. Fukuda seems to know what's going on now, or at least he's expressed that he understood our thoughts on the matter. As he told me, strict orders have come from Tokyo that order must be unconditionally restored in Nanking" (Rabe CN, 303).

b) Disagreements within the command of the Central China Area Army alarmed Tokyo. There were clear differences in thinking between not only Matsui and Prince Asaka in the Central China Area Army, but also with 10th Army Commander Yanagawa Heisuke. Hata Shunroku wrote in his diary entry of February 8, 1938: "Three Central China Area commanders are running separate schemes and acting willfully toward their own ends. In the beginning Matsui even said we didn't need so many troops, but lately he's said that handling the matters that come after fighting is a more important objective to him than the fighting itself. He also said in the matter of establishing a ruling regime in Central China greater than that in the North, we'd do better with the South supreme and the North following. Commander Yanagawa, for his part, hasn't had a stray thought about politics, and believes that it's enough to leave three divisions in the South and send all the rest of our forces to the North. Commander His Highness thinks we should keep on fighting. It's hard to exert unified control with these three commanders sticking to their own opinions. So now the opinion of the General Staff Office is to set aside the question of military strength for the moment, and that the urgent task is to replace the commanders as quickly as possible" (Wang 2005b, 2).

c) Many incidents involving foreign countries took place during Matsui's tenure. There were frequent incidents involving foreign countries caused by the Japanese army during this time in Nanjing, including the Panay bombing of December 12, the looting of the American embassy, the striking of Americans, the Allison incident, the incident in which Major General Amaya invited foreigners to dinner and then sternly rebuked them, and so on. All these incidents were great embarrassments to Tokyo. Uemura Toshimichi wrote in his diary entry of January 12, 1938: "I was dismayed when I saw the cable from the Chief of the General Staff Office demanding that we increase efforts to maintain military discipline and decorum. The General Staff Office Chief apologized for the offense to the American embassy" (Wang 2005b, 259).

Headquarters in Tokyo dispatched Major General Honma to make observations in Shanghai and Nanjing in late January and early February. Uemura Toshimichi wrote in his diary entry of February 1, 1938: "Major General Honma and his retinue arrived by plane. Major Hongo explained the matters concerning foreigners. Major General Honma said his visit is merely intended to perform liaison work, and is not at all about specifically investigating the matters that have frequently occurred between the army and foreigners in recent days. But it seemed that he intends to perform an on-site investigation of the Panay incident that touched on foreign countries" (Wang 2005b, 266).

As for the recall of Matsui back to Japan, Lewis Smythe, secretary of the International Committee, made a clear analysis. He said: "we raised a storm of protest so strong that finally General Matsui himself came to Nanking to tell his soldiers to behave themselves – but six weeks too late! If he had said that and made it effective on December 17th when he was here before, there would be a different tale to tell" (Zhang 2005, 275).

2.3.4.2 Systematic Establishment of a "Normalized" Colonial Order of Life

Top-level design for the establishment of a "normalized" colonial order of life in Nanjing was undertaken by Hata Shunroku, who was summoned for an audience with the Japanese emperor in Tokyo before leaving for China. Hata records the experience thus:

> His Majesty then asked: "What are your plans?" I answered: "To accomplish the new mission for our army, I will work cautiously and conscientiously, and will in no way act rashly. And I will do my utmost to avoid conflicts with third-party countries. In the end I will accomplish my great mission. In addition, I am preparing a new combat training in accordance with the two guiding principles in accordance with explicit decrees regarding military discipline for our troops." His Majesty nodded his head fervently to express approval upon hearing my response. Then He asked: "How will you treat the Central China Regime?" So I answered: "I will strive to guide affairs in accordance with circumstances." His Majesty then asked: "Do you intend to make that area into a second Manchukuo?" I answered: "I do not have this intention." His Majesty responded in a loud voice: "Very good." (Wang 2005b, 3)

Conditions in Nanjing changed after Hata took up his post. Allison wrote in a report about the American government of February 18:

> The most exciting part of the past few days to report is that conditions have greatly improved in Nanking. Almost all Chinese have left the so-called "Safety Zone" and returned home to their former residences in the city. Although reports continue to come in about disorder and unlawful actions of Japanese soldiers, there has been a reduction in the number of such reports. It is very clear that Japanese authorities are striving to improve living conditions for the residents of Nanking. Limitations on the activities of foreigners are also slowly being alleviated. Doctors of the University of Nanking Hospital who have recently made urgent requests to return have been granted permission to do so (Zhang 2006b, 71).

Hata made great efforts to establish a "normalized" colonial order of life in Nanjing upon taking up his post. The Japanese government issued a detailed program for this process on March 24, with clear explanations on the relationship between the puppet governments of Central and North China. On March 26, 1938, Liang Hongzhi, Wen Zongyao, Chen Qun, Chen Zhuan, Chen Jintao, Ren Yuandao, Wang Zihui and others returned to Nanjing from Shanghai under protection of special agents from the Central China Area Army. On March 28 they celebrated the founding of the Reformed Government of the Republic of China in the Great Hall of the nationalist government.

The puppet Reformed Government consisted of an Executive Yuan, a Legislative Yuan, and a Judicial Yuan. The Executive Yuan consisted of the Foreign Ministry, the Interior Ministry, the Sui-Jing Ministry, the Financial Ministry, the Ministry of Education, the Ministry of Industry, the Ministry of Communication and Transports, the Secretariat, the Department of Civil Service, the Department of Examination, the Department of Statistics, the Department of Ceremonies, the Department of Printing, and the Department of Overseas Chinese. It was further stipulated that: "There shall be a Deliberative Committee in the Executive Yuan with three standing members who will convene meetings of the committee when necessary. The presidents and vice presidents of the Executive, Legislative, and

Judicial Yuan and all presidents of other departments will naturally be members of the committee" (Central Archives et al. 1990, 489).

The operations of the puppet Reformed Government were completely controlled by Japanese military advisers: "Central China Area Army Special Service Organ Chief Major General Harada Kumakichi was the highest ranking adviser; Kanigawa Kozo was the Jing-Sui adviser, and Igarishi Midori was domestic affairs adviser. A team of 27 advisers, including those three, controlled all affairs of the Reformed government" (Zhang n.d., 408). The Japanese army rigorously monitored higher-ups of the puppet government. Per one record: "The Japanese army began controlling and monitoring all areas of work and life starting from when Liang Hongzhi assumed his puppet role. They even sent the beautiful woman Tanaka Sadako to join Liang's entourage, who was there to watch him" (Chen n.d., 85).

By April 1938, the puppet Nanjing Supervisory Municipal Government Office was established, with Ren Yuandao serving as supervisor. "The Municipal Government Office consisted of eight departments and one office: the Secretariat, the Social Department, the Education Department, the Financial Department, the Industry Department, the Work Department, the Health Department, the Advisory Office, and the Police Department, with subordinate district offices, libraries, impressed labor management centers, and so on" (Wang n.d., 10). District offices were established under the Supervisory Municipal Government Office, five urban and three rural per the "Draft Organizational Charter of District Offices of all Districts under the Nanjing Supervisory Municipal Government Office." The monthly funding standards for the district offices were as follows: "1 district manager, 160 yuan; 1 deputy district manager, 100 yuan; 1 interpreter, 60 yuan; 3 group leaders, 150 yuan; 3 level-1 group members, 135 yuan; 3 level-2 group member, 120 yuan; 3 level-three group members, 105 yuan; 10 assistants, 300 yuan, 20 general staff, 240 yuan; 12 custodial workers, 168 yuan; office fees 100 yuan; preparation funds 100 yuan; and constabulary administrative expenses, 400 yuan" (Wang n.d., 76).

With the new puppet regime in place, the "Autonomous Committee" of Nanjing had accomplished its mission and was disbanded at the end of April. Many of its members, however, joined the Nanjing Supervisory Municipal Government Office. Zhan Rongguang became counselor, Sun Shurong secretary-general, Wang Chengdian director of the Social Department, and Wang Chunsheng director of the Police Department.

It was under these circumstances that the Japanese founded the Central China Development Company (CCDC), which was "planned to be centered first in Shanghai, tasked with developing communications, transportation, mining, electric power, aquatic products, and other public enterprises. Its method was to insert Japanese capital and technology into existing Chinese equipment to form and operate joint Sino-Japanese companies" (The Second Historical Archives of China 1997, 1062). One record indicates: "Following the outbreak of hostilities between China and Japan and the successive fall of the various regions of Central China, in order to reconstruct the economy in occupied areas, the Japanese organized and operated Sino-Japanese joint venture companies in all important industries in Central China per the guiding principle of Sino-Japanese cooperation. The first companies thus founded were Central China Mining, Central China Hydroelectric, Shanghai Internal River Transport, Central China Electricity and Telecommunications, and so on. There was a need to create an investment company to execute national policy owing to the needs of controlling and financing the joint companies under this project. Accordingly the plan for the Central China Development Company was announced on March 30 of the 13th year of the reign of Showa (1938)" (The Second Historical Archives of China 1997, 1062).

The CCDC's scope of operations touched on all core areas of economic life. The Japanese established a controlling officer over the company with absolute authority: "When the controlling officer determines it necessary, he may at any time investigate the cash reserves, accounts, materials, documents, or anything else belonging to the company, and may inquire into any business or accounting situation. He may attend shareholders' meetings and other meetings to hear reports and opinions expressed" (The Second Historical Archives of China 1997, 1063).

2.4 Transmission of Information Inside and Outside the City

During the stalemated period of the Battle of Shanghai, Matsui Iwane invited some dozen or so Japanese journalists to a discussion to coordinate propaganda dissemination. "reporters from all the agencies were able to very well understand my meaning. Before the meeting ended, they all expressed they would work hard in their reporting work in response to the tense situation, and would actively cooperate in the work of supporting our army" (Wang 2005b, 92). It was relatively simple to manipulate Japanese journalists, but not so for the European and American journalists. Matsui wrote in his diary entry of October 1, 1937: "Ambassador Kawagoe's envoy brought alcohol to comfort me today... I said that if they wanted to comfort me, they should better control the foreign journalists in Shanghai" (Wang 2005b, 82).

After that, Matsui met several times with foreign journalists. He wrote in his diary entry of October 10: "Today around noon I met with journalists from *The Times* of London (David Fraser) and *The New York Times* (Hallett Edward

Abend), to whom I made a statement declaring my personal position... They seemed to have been basically satisfied with my frankness, judging from the expressions on their faces as they left" (Wang 2005b, 94). On the eve of the Japanese occupation of Shanghai, Matsui met with foreign journalists stationed in Shanghai: "I did my best to not express a tough attitude and informed all present of the guiding principles of our army and my personal intentions. I hoped that the journalists from these countries would be fair and not mislead global public opinion." (Wang 2005b, 126). By the time the Japanese advanced to the Xi-Cheng line (Wuxi to Jiangyin), Matsui again met with the Fraser and Abend to "explain the efforts we had made to protect the interests of the various countries. They were very understanding of my intentions and expressed respect and gratitude for the attitude of fairness for our army had shown them. They also agreed to report the story in all its details to their governments" (Wang 2005b, 141).

The Japanese occupation of Nanjing on December 13, 1937 completely cut off transmission of information between the city and the outside world. The question "what exactly has happened in Nanjing?" became the premise for many actions that followed.

2.4.1 Gradual Obstruction of Information in and out of Nanjing Before the Fall

Mail service. After the bombing of Nanjing began on August 15, mail delivery became sporadic. Vautrin wrote in her diary entry of August 24: "Day after day no mail comes and no newspapers. I received my last North China Daily News on Sunday, Aug. 14th." Employees of the Chinese Post Office still did their utmost to maintain mail service, right up to the end of November. Rabe wrote in his diary entry of November 28, 1937: "At 6 o'clock, a meeting at the British Cultural Association. Postal Commissioner Ritchie informs us that the post office is officially closed. You can still put letters in the mailbox, which will occasionally be emptied. Mr. Ritchie appears a little nervous. His entire vast staff, which has functioned well up till now, is drifting away" (Rabe EN, 38). A report in the Shenbao of December 1 read: "Postal employees are working at this moment amid extreme difficulty. None has left his post despite frequent bombings. Postal authorities in the capital have rented a ship to carry the 350 postal employees and their families there to safety at the last minute" (Ma 2005, 84–85). On December 7, a staff member of the American embassy in Nanjing wrote: "Mail delivery service stopped today, but the post office in Xiaguan is still taking parcels for delivery" (Zhang 2006b, 53). With that, mail service completely shut down in Nanjing.

Telephones. After Japanese bombings, the phone lines of Nanjing were jammed. Vautrin wrote in her diary entry of September 14, 1937: "This evening I tried to get in touch with Eva by long distance. Succeeded by 2:30 this afternoon, so you know how busy the lines are." As city residents began to drift westward, most of them closed their telephone accounts. The manager of military hotlines for the Capital Telephone Authority Wang Zhengyuan recalled: "Beginning in October customers only closed accounts and did not install new telephones. We had lost four-fifths of our users by the end of October... All civilian telephone use was shut down after the middle of November" (Ma 2005, 362–363).

Radio. After August 15, residents of Nanjing went out of their way to hear radio broadcasts with the latest war updates. The Japanese, for their part, did their best to block the transmissions. Wilson wrote: "Dick Brady and I are making it a nightly practice to go over to Mr. Marx' house where we listen to the evening broadcasts from Shanghai, Nanking and Manila. The Japanese run as much interference as they can on the Chinese wave length" (Zhang 2010, 16).

The Japanese bombings caused widespread injury and death among the populace of Nanjing. The nationalist government used their radio stations to report the details of the bombing of Nanjing to the rest of the world, to expose the violence of the Japanese military. The foreigners in Nanjing actively sent out English-language radio broadcasts. Wilson wrote in his diary entry of September 25, 1937: "Mrs. Twinem, who is now doing the English Broadcast for the Central Broadcasting system over the short wave... We helped her word her introduction to tonight's broadcast starting 'Gallons of civilian blood flowed today as Nanking was subjected to three terrific air raids" (Zhang 2010, 37). The Japanese continued seeking opportunities to bomb the radio stations of Nanjing.

In his diary entry of September 26, Rabe wrote:

> Mr. Han (Xianglin) just telephoned to say that the Central Broadcasting Station was severely damaged yesterday, and radio transmission lines in the city have been cut. That is to say that the Japanese achieved their goal: the Central Broadcasting Station in Nanjing has been bombed into muteness (Rabe CN, 15).

Even more distressing to Nanjing residents were the frequent power outages incurred as a result of Japanese bombings of power plants. Among other consequences, this made it impossible to listen to radios, which required electricity. Vautrin wrote on September 30, 1937: "We have not been able to hear the one o'clock broadcast for almost a week – since the bombing of the electric light plant last Saturday." Luckily the power plant was promptly fixed. Rabe was able to hear a radio broadcast from outside the city on December 10, 1937; he wrote: "At noon we heard on the radio that if General Tang does not immediately withdraw his forces, the Japanese will launch a wide-scale attack on Nanjing tomorrow... Japanese radio announces that Nanjing will fall within 24 hours. The Chinese soldiers are already highly demoralized" (Rabe CN, 128).

2.4.2 Non-standard transmission of information after the fall of Nanjing

2.4.2.1 Five war reporters leave the city

There were five European and American war reporters in Nanjing at the time of its fall. They were Paramount Studios cameraman Arthur Menken, C. Yates McDaniel of the Associated Press, Archibald T. Steele of the *Chicago Daily News*, Frank T. Durdin of the *New York Times*, and L.C. Smith of the Reuters News Agency.

On December 14, 1937, Durdin tried to drive to Shanghai, but he was turned back by the Japanese at Jurong. The foreigners remaining in Nanjing paid great attention to the departure of the war reporters, as they were clearly aware that pressuring the Japanese through international public opinion, accomplished through the transmission of information, would help improve conditions in the city. Fitch wrote in his journal of December 14: "Durdin, of the N.J. [New York] Times, started for Shanghai by motor that day, though none of us had much faith he would get through. I hurriedly wrote a letter for him to take, but he was turned back at Kuyung [Jurong]" (Zhang Kaiyuan 2005, 70). Rabe wrote in his diary entry of December 14: "Mr. Durdin of the New York Times plans to drive to Shanghai. This is an idea worthy of commendation. But I don't believe he will make it through. Even so, I gave him a cable to take to Shanghai" (Rabe CN, 140). Wilson wrote in his diary entry of December 15: "When I got home this noon I found that Smith and Steele were leaving for Shanghai on a Japanese destroyer. I had just time to rush upstairs and jam the pages into an envelope which I addressed while they were starting the car" (Zhang 2010, 69). Bates also wrote a record of the Japanese violence upon entering the city, which he entrusted to Steele.

The USS Oahu passed through Nanjing on its way to Shanghai after having dealt with the USS Panay and the HMS Ladybird, so reporters began leaving the city one by one on the 15th to make reports in mainstream international media. The *Chicago Daily News*, for instance, published a special report from Steele: "The Japanese smashed their way into private property of foreigners, including the official residence of American Ambassador Nelson T. Johnson... They've stolen watches and money from nurses in the University Hospital. They've stolen at least two American automobiles and torn up the American flag. They even burst into refugee camps and looted away the last copper coins many poor people had" (Zhang 2005, 93).

Reports from the war reporters called back to the article just published on the 15th in the *New York Times* "Nanking's Silence Terrifies Shanghai": "There has been no news in these last two days since the Japanese army occupied the abandoned Chinese capital. It is difficult to surmise what's become of the fate of the 18 Americans remaining in Nanking. The piecemeal reports we've received through broken telecommunications channels indicate that there have been great casualties among the Chinese Defense Garrison and the civilian population" (Yang and Zhang n.d., 471). The U.S. consulate in Shanghai quickly lodged a protest with the Japanese consulate in Shanghai, requesting that the Japanese transmit letters to the Americans remaining in Nanking.

Letters entrusted to the war reporters by foreigners in Nanjing were circulated among important people. For example, American Consul Gauss in Shanghai dispatched this report to the U.S. Secretary of State on January 5, 1938: "Summary reports obtained on conditions in Nanking following Japanese occupation were sent by cable to the embassy in Hankou at 6 p.m. on December 24. Attached is a record by Searle Bates of the University of Nanking regarding conditions of the Japanese occupation. A copy of this record was given by hand by *Chicago Daily News* reporter Archibald Steele to consulate staff. All information related by Dr. Bates is true. They can be cross-checked with reports from Mr. Steele and other reporters in Nanking at the time of the Japanese Occupation. They are accurate" (Zhang 2006b, 66).

2.4.2.2 Creation of "Nanjing – Shanghai – World" information transmission platforms

After the Japanese bombing of Nanjing, the European and American embassies in the city went into emergency mode, mooring naval and commercial vessels from their countries on the Yangtze River near Nanjing to prepare for an emergency evacuation of their diplomatic staff and all overseas citizens of their countries. The primary foreign naval commercial vessels on the Yangtze near Nanjing at this time were: the USS Oahu, the USS Panay, the HMS Ladybird, the HMS Bee, the SS Kutwo, the SS Whampoa, the SS Meiping, the SS Meihsia, and the SS Meian.

Most foreign vessels congregated between Nanjing and Wuhu for security. What no one expected was the firing upon the Whampoa and the Wantung. On December 12 the UK Yangtze River Command dispatched someone to Wuhu to lodge a complaint with Hashimoto Kingoro. That afternoon, the Japanese bombed vessels on the river once again, this time hitting the HMS Ladybird and the USS Panay, the latter of which ended up sinking. On the 14th, Japanese vessels arrived at the scene of the incident and escorted the Ladybird, the Whampoa, and the Oahu, all of which could still operate, back to Shanghai. Rosen and other German embassy staff, wanting to return to Nanjing, boarded the Cricket, which was not going to Shanghai. On the 18th, Rosen and the others arrived at the harbor of Xiaguan in Nanjing and asked permission to enter the city from Japanese Rear-admiral Kondo, who refused on the grounds that "there are still remnant Chinese forces active in the city." Rosen and the others had no choice but to return to Shanghai. Rosen wrote: "So we, the English, and the others traveling with us decided to join a second escort convoy passing here on the 20. This convoy berthed in Shanghai on the afternoon of the 21 without incident under protection of a Japanese destroyer... I sent a letter to Rabe via the Japanese on the HMS Bee, but I have had no response from him yet" (Zhang 2005, 282).

The letter was delivered by Kondo and an official of the Japanese embassy on December 21 to Rabe, currently in the embassy lodging protests. Rabe wrote a reply to Rosen on the spot, which he entrusted to the official and Kondo:

> I received your letter of December 19 full of concern for us. Thank you very much! I am very happy to report that all 22 foreigners whose names are in the attached list are doing fine. We would be extraordinarily happy if you could celebrate Christmas with us here. By then we may have electric lighting, water, and telephones again. The two German buildings along with my house and that of the ambassador have not been damaged. Dr. Trautmann's car is currently in service of military authorities, as is your car and all other German cars. The gentlemen of the Japanese embassy are all very polite. Mr. Tanaka has enthusiastically agreed to deliver this letter to you (Rabe CN, 194).

Despite its lack of veiled meanings, the Japanese did not deliver this letter.

With no reply from Rabe, Rosen teamed up with the UK and U.S. embassies to pressure the Japanese: "Just like us, the English and Americans have the right to return to Nanjing. We will persist in maintaining this right and oppose all Japanese tricks" (Zhang 2005, 282). Japanese military authorities in Shanghai determined to allow European and American embassy personnel to return to Nanjing shortly.

With permission granted, John Allison of the U.S. embassy was the first to reach Xiaguan on December 31, 1937, but the Japanese refused to let him debark, citing safety concerns. On January 6, 1938, Allison was permitted to enter Nanjing, at which point he delivered a bundle of letters to the Americans in the city. Not long afterward, on January 9, English and German embassy personnel returned to the city. This marked the completion of the "Nanjing – Shanghai – world" information transmission platform, the core of which was composed of embassy officials and Western ships. One person there at the time wrote on January 10, 1938: "Today a friend told me that the ship of some country was going from Nanjing to Shanghai, that we could come up with a way to have it carry our letters to Shanghai, or at least be exempt from 'inspection'" (Zhang 2005, 91).

Rabe writes in his diary entry of January 13: "By way of the English navy I receive a telegram from Siemens Shanghai, dated 10 January, telling me to wind up business here and for Han and me to come to Shanghai as soon as possible. I'll reply tomorrow, saying that at present neither foreigners nor Chinese are allowed to leave the city. Kröger has tried on various occasions to get Japanese permission to travel to Shanghai and has thus far been regularly turned down" (Rabe EN, 128). The Western ships didn't only facilitate telegrams service between Nanjing and the outside world, but also delivered information from Nanjing to Shanghai and other places. Jiang Gonggu wrote in his diary entry of January 13, 1938: "It's said that although the enemy has sealed Nanjing tight to prevent transmission of information to the outside, the International Committee has already written over 500 reports on their beastly violence, which were finally sent out by wireless radio by American naval vessels these past days" (Zhang 2005, 71).

More convenient communication conditions came shortly thereafter. Allison writes in a report to the U.S. government of January 8, 1938:

> Rear Admiral Sheehan installed portable wireless radio equipment in the embassy, so I suggested that he leave a low-grade officer to help run the system. I had, however, predicted that the Japanese military authorities would protest, so I first explained to the Japanese embassy that the wireless radio equipment was entirely to be used in emergency situations. But they responded that this matter must first be looked into by the army. Barring admonitions from other parties, my plan all along has been to first install wireless radio equipment in the embassy (Zhang 2006b, 67–68).

Forster wrote in a letter to his wife of January 24, 1938: "Our Embassy now has a wireless sending set with an operator from the Navy. The Japanese refused at first, but Allison won out. He is awfully nice as being Espy and MacFadyen, the two vice-consuls" (Zhang 2005, 117).

2.4.2.3 Japanese embassy helps deliver letters and packages between Nanjing and Shanghai

During the encirclement of Nanjing, foreigners there attempted to send information out of the city via the Japanese embassy, who subjected their letters to "security inspections." Smythe wrote in a letter of January 5 to his wife:

> All of our letters that pass through the Japanese embassy are "open."… After I returned with a bundle of letters yesterday afternoon, Mills brought a letter of his own. He found out that

Fukuda, Tanaka, and Inami were all busy reading our letters. After they finished reading, they concluded that I needed to be prevented from sending them. Mills suggested that they tear them up, and he brought the pieces back with him. The letters only made one mention of an air raid that wasn't even that severe! This, however, was "military intelligence." In short, now we understand the nature of their screening (Zhang 2005, 264).

It was extremely difficult for the westerners in Nanjing to effectively transmit information out of the city through the screening. For example, upon Rabe's receipt of a letter from Mr. Schaeffer of the German consulate in Shanghai on December 22, 1937, at Fukui's request he wrote a reply, which the Japanese embassy had delivered to the German consulate in Shanghai. Per Rabe's diary entry of December 30, 1937, the letter contained not one word on the violence of the Japanese soldiers, and in fact contained only praise for the Japanese (Rabe CN, 264).

Japanese embassy officials, stuck between their own army and the westerners in an awkward situation, frequently employed words like "sincerely beseech." Rabe wrote in his diary entry of December 29, 1937: "It's been about 40 days since November 19, and I still haven't heard from my wife. Mr. Fukui sincerely beseeched me not to tell people in Shanghai about conditions in Nanjing. That was to say not to include any information that would make the Japanese embassy upset. I agreed. What other choice did I have? If my only option for letter delivery is via the Japanese embassy, then I must obey their commands" (Rabe CN, 245).

It was easier to receive information via that channel. Rabe wrote in his diary entry of December 29: "At 10 a.m. Mr. Fukui and Mr. Takatama paid me a visit to deliver mail from Shanghai. This was quite pleasant. Three letters had been sent by my wife in Shanghai (the last one postmarked December 22). There were also two official documents: one for Kröger from Dr. Bauer of Carlowitz & Co., postmarked December 17. The second was for me from Embassy Attaché Fischer, postmarked December 22" (Rabe CN, 244). There are many similar records of such events.

2.4.2.4 Receipt and transmission of information via radio

Documents demonstrate that the Danish national Sinderberg left his home at Qixia Mountain[15] and moved into the Safety Zone in response to Japanese inspections, bringing with him the first round of radio information the westerners had heard since the city's fall.

---

15 Often referred to by other names from the period, including "Hsi Sha Shan" (translator's note).

At the time, the Jiangnan Concrete Plant at Qixia Mountain was managed by Sinderberg and the German Dr. Karl Günther, who also set up a large refugee shelter. There were a generator and a radio receiver in the plant enabling continuous receipt of radio broadcasts. In a letter to family of December 20, 1937, Smythe wrote: "The young Mr. Sinderberg who oversees the Jiangnan Concrete Plant at Qixia Mountain came to the office today. First he walked 20 miles, and then he boarded a Japanese truck entering the city. Now no foreigners are allowed to enter or reenter the city. There he was hearing news on a Delco radio... We learned some of what had happened outside the city, which restored some vitality and vigor among us!" (Zhang 2005, 238).

Records indicate that electricity was partially restored in Nanjing around New Year, 1938. By then electricity wasn't solely important for lighting. Rabe wrote about news heard on the radio in his diary entry of January 3 (Rabe CN, 267). On January 5 he wrote: "Those with a few hours of access to electricity could listen to intermittent news broadcasts on the radio" (Rabe CN, 295).

Radios allowed only for one-way receipt of information, but even that was exciting. MacCallum of the Gulou Hospital wrote in a letter of January 5, 1938: "Fixed up a radio in the X-Ray room at the hospital with stray equipment picked up here and there and it came in good last night – so communications are again established" (IMTFE Exhibit No. 309). The foreigners then began going to the Gulou Hospital to listen to the radio, after which they edited information for dissemination. Jiang Gonggu recalled: "The New Shenbao established by the enemy was released daily. Of course all of it was counter-propaganda. There was no truth to be found in it. Thankfully we had English-language news reports about the war received on the radio in the Gulou Hospital. The bulletins they compiled there daily were truly detailed and accurate. The bulletins were secretly brought over every day by Xu Xianqing and Qi Gang. We then circulated them among ourselves, vying to be the first one to read them" (Zhang 2005, 74).

2.4.2.5 Fitch's two departures and one return

As already discussed, the departure of the five war reporters set off a round of news dissemination, but their reports were limited to events during the first few days after the fall of the city. Two foreigners departed from Nanjing in mid to late January, first Kröger on January 23 and then Fitch. In February Fitch left again, and Rabe left for the first time.

In late January 1938, the food crisis was growing severe in the Safety Zone as the Japanese had unilaterally denied the legality of the International Committee and brooked no discussions. The committee then added to the agenda the task of sending someone to Shanghai to outmaneuver the Japanese and resolve the crisis. Fitch writes in his diary:

> The question of feeding the refugees is our greatest concern. We'll soon be through our salt reserve. There's a little rice left, but it's almost exhausted. The surroundings for miles around have been reduced to rubble. Nothing is permitted to be brought into the city unless it's for the Japanese. There are starting to be cases of beriberi. We are in urgent need of a great quantity of materials to prevent this disaster. After long talks with the Japanese army, I've finally been granted permission to go to Shanghai aboard the HMS Bee (Zhang 2005, 83).

On January 28 Fitch was granted permission to go to Shanghai for six days. On January 31, Fitch boarded the HMS Bee for Shanghai. He did not recriminate the Japanese in Nanjing publicly. Rabe expresses sympathy: "Fitch arrived in Shanghai yesterday. A radio report has him saying that 'conditions in Nanjing are changing for the better.'... I imagine that Fitch's words are so 'soft' because he wants to be able to return to Nanjing" (Rabe CN, 455).

In private, however, Fitch gave a detailed account of the truth of what had happened in Nanjing to the U.S. Yangtze River Fleet Commander:

> I had my first lunch in Shanghai with Fleet Commander Harry Yanell, later the object of much respect, on his ship. Like others he was eager to hear the most recent news from Nanjing. I had to tell the story over and over, and I met with a few people, but at the same time I bought a shipload of soybeans, rice, flour, and other materials for delivery to Nanjing post haste. Some Americans even asked me to fly to Washington as fast as possible to report on conditions in Nanjing to our government. I already promised Japanese military authorities that I would return no matter what – this was the condition for my permission to leave. Of course, I also wanted to ensure the safe delivery of this food. I promised my friends that no matter what I would immediately negotiate with the Japanese for permission to leave again (Zhang 2005, 83).

On February 12, 1938, Fitch returned to Nanjing on the USS Oahu. Before leaving, Fitch made careful plans for a return to Shanghai, which he did on February 23. He wrote:

> Wilbur gave me a cable in Shanghai (previously arranged): "Return to Shanghai before the 23." I used this cable to obtain permission to leave again. The next morning I boarded a Japanese military train headed to Shanghai at 6:40 a.m. I was huddled with a group of shameless soldiers together. That made me feel tense, because eight rolls of 16 millimeter film negatives recording Japanese violence had been sewn into my camel hair coat. Most had been shot at University of Nanking Hospital. There was no doubt that my bags would be searched in detail upon arrival in Shanghai. What would happen if they found this film? Thankfully they did not find it. I brought them to Kodak to be developed immediately upon my arrival in Shanghai. Most of the film had been shot by John Magee of the

Episcopalian Church, who later became pastor of St. John's Church in Washington. The images were so terrible that nobody could have believed they were real if they hadn't seen the things depicted with their own eyes. Kodak rushed out four developed sets for me. Of course, I was asked to display the films at American community churches and other places" (Zhang 2005, 84).

Before going to the U.S., Fitch had H.J. Timperley write a letter to his good friend, Deputy U.S. Secretary of State Dr. Stanley Hornbeck: "When the suggestion was made to him that he should proceed to the States, George found it difficult to make up his mind, being torn between a desire to go to Washington and tell his story and feeling that perhaps it was not right to desert the little group of foreigners who are still carrying on at Nanking. When he asked me for my opinion I told him that I thought he ought by all means to go to the States and lay the facts of the case before you and, if possible, the Secretary of State" (Zhang 2006b, 184).

As Fitch was leaving Nanjing, Dr. Rosen of the German embassy sent a telegram to the senior commercial officer in the German consulate in Shanghai telling him how to obtain copies of the film brought out by Fitch and how to disseminate them: "Three reports for the Foreign Ministry are attached. Please buy a copy of the film in accordance with the attached letter written by Pastor Magee and deliver it to the Foreign Ministry through a reliable channel" (Zhang and Yang n.d., 411).

The dissemination of this information was bound to create international pressure on Japan in public opinion. Tokyo thus commanded the Imperial Army in Nanjing to restore order to the city.

2.4.3 Gradual Restoration of Information Transmission in and out of Nanjing after the Fall

Restoration of normal platforms for information transmission was both a necessity for preparing Nanjing for the "normalized" colonial order and also an important component of the creation of that order.

2.4.3.1 Mail and telegram service
The Westerners in Nanjing were extremely anxious for restored mail service. Fitch complains at the end of 1937: "the Japanese Embassy tells us that it will still be weeks before the postal services are re-established here" (Zhang 2005, 82). No progress was made, however, on that front until February 1938. Rabe

wrote: "Mr. Ritchie, the postal commissioner, is about to reopen the post office, with the Japanese. Until now he's had no success reopening in any of the destroyed areas" (Rabe EN, 199).

In early March 1938 Ritchie returned to Nanjing for on-site observations to develop plans to restore mail service. Scharffenberg wrote in a report of March 21, 1938: "Postal commissioner Ritchie came to Nanjing in early March this year. He was optimistic. He hopes that five post offices here can be opened by March 25 this year, with one located inside resident zone" (Chen, Zhang, and Dai n.d., 173).

The Japanese accelerated this process in order to establish their "normalized" colonial order. At the same time, they rescinded the rights of the U.S. and UK embassies to send and receive letters on behalf of Chinese people. Vautrin wrote of this on March 5, 1938: "The American and British Embassy has had to withdraw privilege of sending or taking letters from Chinese – which is a pity for to us it means that women stranded here without funds cannot now write for them."

Postal service was quickly restored to the city. Rape of Nanking survivor Song Huifang recalled: "Our family came back with the post office. We hadn't left the city for long. We waited for the situation to calm down in Nanjing to return. By then hadn't they established some sort of puppet government? After we returned, we lived in the same place as before, and my father returned to his work as a postman" (Zhang and Dai n.d., 514).

Postal service was extremely limited at the outset. Bates writes in his "Pseudo-Economic Notes from Nanking" of March 31, 1938: "Post Office reopened on small scale, providing some 700 incomes directly and giving aid or hope to families long separated; service only to Shanghai direct, and no money orders or parcels yet. Part of the employees have the insignia of the Japanese Post Office" (Zhang 2006b, 133).

As for telegrams, the Japanese Consul in Shanghai Hanawa Yoshitaka wrote in a letter to Beiping Attaché Morishima of April 12, 1938: "It's almost been a military branch, as all staff have been taking instructions from the army. But beginning on April 4, per new orders, the bureau must now handle all Japanese, Chinese, and Western language telegram business, private and public, from the general public. 1. Business hours 9 a.m. to 8 p.m. (Japan time). 2. Service categories: Japanese, Chinese, and Western language public and private telegrams. 3. Areas served: Cable sent within or between Shanghai, Qingdao, Hebei Province, Henan Province, and Nanjing. Service for Japanese language telegrams to Japan currently unavailable, but should be available soon" (Jiang et al. n.d., 336). It is thus clear that the telegram service was basically restored by this time.

2.4.3.2 Telephones

Owing to a lack of technicians, progress in this area lagged considerably behind that of the post office. On March 17, 1938, the Nanjing Pacification Team convened a meeting of the Telecommunications Battalion of the Imperial Army stationed in Nanjing, commanders of all divisions, commanders of all army depots, the military police commander, members of the Autonomous Committee, and Japanese residents in the city to give testimony, and also entreated the Chief of the Special Service Organ in Shanghai multiple times to dispatch technicians to Nanjing to resolve the following:

> 1. Owing to the extreme difficulty in the urgent task of restoring telephone service, we are provisionally providing rotary-style telephones to satisfy the most basic public needs in public security and general contacts.
>
> 2. Restoration of the central telephone bureau must be completed in accordance with the Army Special Service Organ's guiding principles, and a suitable company should be appointed to the work of this restoration.
>
> 3. The switchboard should be located within a Special Service Organ office.
>
> 4. The Army Telecommunications Battalion will be responsible for providing labor and supplying outside lines.
>
> 5. Telephones already in possession of the Special Service Organ from China will be used. If not sufficient, Special Service Organ offices will come up with means to supplement.
>
> Locations for installation of telephones as applied for by the public (including the Chinese) will be chosen by the Special Service Organ.
>
> Per the above resolutions, this organ is temporarily allocating rotary-style telephones collected by the Autonomous Committee to management by the Army Telecommunications Battalion. We will also make and turn over a list of places where there is a need to install telephones for private use.
>
> Hereafter the Shanghai Special Service Organ will dispatch three telegram-delivery technicians to Nanjing by the end of the month, so we will discuss the demands for complete restoration of service here with them in detail (Wang and Lei n.d., 373–374).

Telephone service was incrementally restored to Nanjing in April, and then the telephones were handed over to the newly-established Central China Company for management. The Central China Company was established under Japanese guidance, first under the name "Central China Telecommunication Company", and then later renamed "Central China Electric Communication Company" (The Second Historical Archives of China 1997, 1084).

Restored telephone service was mostly used in service of the Japanese army and the puppet government, and did not make a great impact on the lives of ordinary residents of Nanjing. That said, restored telephone service did carry symbolic significance.

2.5 Public Security Response

2.5.1 Public Security Response Before the Fall

The police are the force that maintains public security. During the air raids, the Nanjing Police Department painstakingly maintained social order in the city. On October 17, 1937, Rabe wrote a letter to Hermann of the *Far East Journal*, vividly describing the actions of the Nanjing police force:

> The buses, similarly painted black, are still operating. They are packed full when the central ministries and other departments let off work, because government officials are still working, even on Sundays! There's nothing to criticize in order on the streets. Soldiers, policemen, and civilian patrols are modestly and properly carrying out their duties. Half an hour after two bombs exploded the gravel road along the major thoroughfare of Zhongshan Road, the hole had already been filled in, and the road was walkable again. Traffic was not held up at all while the road was being repaired (Rabe CN, 37–39).

Even Japanese intelligence reports affirm the role played by the Nanjing police force: "As usual, the city is guarded by military police, regular police, and armed security forces. Important areas are extremely well guarded, with an absolute prohibition on entry and exit… During air raids, the alarm is sounded 30 minutes in advance, and the emergency siren is sounded 10 minutes beforehand, at which point pedestrians all take cover underground, vehicles and horses all park in fixed locations, and the streets are completely emptied. The thorough commands of military police and the civil defense corps and the orderly behavior of city residents allow for the air raid sheltering to take place under conditions of extremely good order" (Ma 2005, 38–39).

In late November 1937, the Japanese Air Force attained control of the skies over Nanjing. Rosen wrote in a report to the German Foreign Ministry of December 24, 1937, with the army closing in: "As the Chinese we may have considered here lacked sufficient courage, they have all chosen to flee to Hankou and not remain in the capital. Thereafter the Committee had no choice but to manage the Safety Zone on its own, making Mr. Rabe play the role of actual mayor of Nanjing" (Zhang 2005, 277). He said "during this period, my English and American colleagues and I took a step in Chiang Kai-shek's office to explain to him that establishing an institution for city residents to maintain order by the police would be extremely beneficial to Nanjing if the city became occupied. The only result of this step was that Chiang asked the Police Department Commissioner Wang Gupan, who has been close with us and speaks German very well, to stay behind. This latter refused, and was subsequently relieved of his position" (Zhang 2005, 278).

The police force broke out of the encirclement as a unit after the city fell. As recorded in the report "Actual Conditions of the Nanjing Capital Police during the War of Resistance":

> Armed with only rifles and grenades, after several rounds of hand-to-hand combat, only a few police officers managed to make it to the north shore along with the retreating soldiers by crossing at Jiangxin Island. We counted only a little over 300 in the roll call. Fortunately these 300 were led by Deputy Commissioner Fang Chao and Sixth Police Bureau Chief Ren Jianpeng and retreated with the army on the morning of the 13 northward along the Jin-Pu line (Tianjin to Pukou) and were incorporated into the military ranks along the way. Only a few dozen policemen escaped danger by swimming across the river. Upon arrival in Xuzhou we reordered our strategy and then arrived at Hangao. The Police Department's public security force, which had previously numbered over 1,700, was reduced to a little over 100 after the war. It is still led by Captain Zhao Shirui of the public security force, who made it to Hankou and was ordered to rearrange the force into the Interior Ministry's police unit (Ma 2005, 237).

Another police unit made its way into the Safety Zone. Rabe records discussions of the Safety Zone Committee had with the Japanese regarding this issue: "In addition yesterday we requested that the 450 armed policemen assigned to our Safety Zone by the Chinese government be reorganized into a Japanese-led police force. We also hoped that the 90 armed policemen we had previously mentioned would be included within this force. As for the 45 'volunteer police,' we hoped that they would be returned to our headquarters, or that we would be informed where they had been assigned to work. We had a registry of the names of the 450 armed policemen assigned to our Safety Zone. If needed, we can provide this registry to you" (Rabe CN, 162).

2.5.2 Public Security Response After the Fall

On December 17, 1937, after the ceremony for entry into the city, the Central China Area Army resolved to make the 16th Division, led by Major General Sasaki Toichi, responsible for all security throughout the city. Sasaki's command of the Nanjing Guard began on December 21, 1937 (Wang 2005b, 321) and lasted until January 22, 1938, when the 16th Division left the city and Major General Amaya assumed command of the Nanjing Guard (Wang 2005b, 322).

The primary public security problem of this time was the massacring, pillaging, and burning of the Japanese army itself. On January 10, 1938, Bates wrote a letter which he surreptitiously delivered to friends outside of Nanjing: "Most of the refugees were robbed of their money and at least part of their scanty clothing and bedding and food. That was an utterly heartless performance, resulting in utter despair on every face for the first week or ten days" (Zhang 2005, 17). The violence had not abated at all by the time Amaya took over. Rabe wrote in his diary entry of February 2, 1938: "We have had to register 88 offenses by Japanese soldiers over the last three days. That is even worse than what we experienced in this regard in December. Hidaka, into whose hand I press our report, apologizes for these 'Japanese rascals,' but offers as an excuse that such things occasionally happen when troops are being relieved" (Rabe EN, 170–171). Uemura Toshimichi wrote in a February diary entry: "I saw the military police report. There are still many incidents concerning military discipline, and many matters in violation of regulations as well as unimaginable matters. These were all the result of drunkenness, and I feel extreme remorse" (Wang n.d., 270).

Tokyo did make a statement regarding the violence of Japanese soldiers in Nanjing. On January 8, 1938, Army General Staff Chief Prince Kan'in Kotohito sent a cable to the commander of the Central China Area Army regarding demands for military discipline: "Matters despicable in the view of military discipline have happened sporadically of late, and are increasing in number. Truly I wish not to believe them, so I do remain skeptical. I presume that it's individuals who lose control, and yet an individual can influence the true value of the entire contingent. The error of a contingent can harm the sacred mission of the entire army" (Wang and Lei n.d., 15). Shanghai Expeditionary Army Deputy Chief of Staff Uemura Toshimichi wrote in his diary entry of January 8, 1938: "There have been many actions in violation of military discipline per military police reports. I truly regret the shameless second lieutenants and warrant officers who should be reining their troops in" (Wang 2005b, 257).

After the fall of Nanjing, there were still entities in charge of public security. First and foremost were the army's own military police, whose job was to control their soldiers. Second, despite their lack of direct control over their own army, the Japanese embassy in Nanjing did restrict the unlawful behaviors of their soldiers within a certain extent from concerns over incidents involving foreign countries. Third, the foreigners in Nanjing themselves actively prevented criminal actions by Japanese soldiers and protected the lives and property of Chinese people. Those three entities all took up part of the burden of maintaining public security, but all three had different characteristics.

2.5.2.1 Crime prevention and participation in crimes by military police

The Japanese military police headquarters was located at Xiaofen Bridge in Nanjing, and some military police did prevent fellow soldiers from committing crimes. Vautrin wrote in her diary entry of December 18, 1937: "I went to the [Japanese] Embassy… I reported our difficult experiences and also the Friday night incident and then asked for a letter which I could carry with me in order to drive out the soldiers, and also for some proclamations for the gate. I received both and came home grateful beyond words. Also Mr. Tanaka, a very understanding and distressed person, said he would go and get two gendarmes to keep guard during the night… With Mills and two gendarmes at the gate I went to bed in peace for the first time for days and felt that all would be well." A week later on December 24, Vautrin wrote: "Stray groups of soldiers have almost ceased to come to the campus since we have the guard and patrol at the gate. This lessens the strain for me a great deal." The next day, Christmas Day 1937, Vautrin continued: "The night again was one of peace – with our guard of twenty-five at the gate patrolling both Hankow and Ninghai Roads. For the first time in weeks and weeks I slept soundly through the night."

Bates found some Japanese military police directly engaging in looting and raping. He wrote in a letter of January 10, 1938 to the American embassy:

> Please allow me to report on an incident that touches on American property and one American resident of the city. This incident clearly reflects the lack of discipline on the part of soldiers and the character and behavior of the military police in this area that are hardly satisfying… Two soldiers brought two women they'd found to a house across Tianjin Road from Xiaotaoyuan (the language school, now part of the university's agriculture department)… The descriptions of the two women of the surrounding buildings, gates, and types of architecture indicate that the place they were taken was the military police headquarters… Everyone in the surrounding area, Chinese and foreign alike, expresses dissatisfaction with the military police, finding them excessively cruel and unworthy of trust. Also, all families of Chinese living on Hankou Road have said that the military police come grab women whenever they please (Zhang 2006b, 95–96).

2.5.2.2 Mitigation by Japanese embassy officials and consular police

Consular police returned to Nanjing on December 14, following the army's occupation of December 13. On December 15, Japanese embassy personnel returned. Bates gave testimony to this effect to the International Military Tribunal for the Far East: "Almost daily for the first three weeks I went to the Embassy with a typed report or letter covering the preceding day, and frequently had also a conversation with the officials regarding it. These officials were Mr. T. Fukui, who had the rank of consul, a certain Mr. Tanaka, vice-consul, Mr. Toyoyasu Fukuda. The latter is now secretary to the Premier Yoshida. These men were honestly trying to do what little they could in a very bad situation, but they were terrified by the military and they could do nothing except forward these communications through Shanghai to Tokyo" (Yang 2006, 84). Some officers of the Shanghai Expeditionary Army expressed rage at the actions of the consular officials. Fukuda Tokuyasu testified at the Tokyo War Crimes Trial: "I heard that because of some colonel – Mr. Fukui might know his name – one day he came to the embassy and threatened to burn it down, because the embassy was revealing the unlawful actions of soldiers to Tokyo" (Yang 2006, 293).

Officials of the Japanese embassy could not only intervene with the Shanghai Expeditionary Army, but also had control over the consular police force for management of public security. Vautrin wrote about this many times in her diary, for instance on December 25, 1925: "Tonight we have no guard. One police has been sent to us from the Embassy." She continued on December 26: "Another night of peace. Only one Embassy police at front, but his presence was a help in that it gave a feeling of safety."

All foreigners at the time despised a Japanese consular policeman named Takatama. Magee wrote in a letter to his wife of January 11, 1938: "Workers in the Japanese consulate, other than one scoundrel of a policeman, are all willing to help us. They feel ashamed of what the Japanese army is doing, and are doing their utmost to protect the property of foreigners" (Zhang 2005, 165).

2.5.2.3 Interventions by foreigners

Although the foreigners lacked much of a say in public security management while the city was under Japanese control, they made the greatest efforts to protect the lives of Nanjing residents.

Safety Zone Secretary Smythe wrote in a letter to his family of December 27, 1937:

> On the one hand they say they're restoring order, and on the other they destroy everything and threaten the people. Talking to them is of no use. Rabe spends most of his time at home protecting his property and the 600 refugees there. Kröger is also watching over his property. So are Magee and Forster, protecting the refugees who fill their houses. Minnie Vautrin and Mary Twinem dare not leave the Ginling Women's College. They even need a foreigner on guard at the college all day and all night. It's the same at University of Nanking. Once Bates ever leaves on an errand, he's sought everywhere. So he's busy all day running around chasing off Japanese soldiers. These days the only people with a sense of accomplishment are Riggs and Sone, as they are delivering goods and escorting coolies, and watching carefully over their trucks. The rice and coal they deliver help to fill people's bellies, but it's hard for them to meet the daily needs of everyone. Gradually trucks and cars are disappearing (Zhang 2005, 253).

Security began improving in March, 1938. Smythe summarized the thoughts common to all Westerners in Nanjing at this time in his "Letter to Friends in God's Country" of March 8, 1938:

> There is no danger from the Chinese snipers for us! The only danger we have faced is that from Japanese soldiers. How we all escaped when we were <u>almost</u> "insolently" policing the Japanese Army – they claimed their 17 military police in the city were inadequate (as they were) but 22 foreigners made a good attempt at it – is more than any of us can ever explain. One night when things were at their worst – two days after Matsui's triumphal march through the city – the fellows at our house remarked at supper, "The first fellow that gets killed we are going to carry his body over and put it in the Japanese Embassy." Several piped up, "Well, I am willing to either be so carried or do the carrying!" Each night the doctor acting as "Mama" of the household would look around the eight of us and wonder who would be missing the next night. He said, "We just can't <u>all</u> get through this alive." Well, we did. The worst was a bayonet scratch in the neck that McCallum got the day after the Allison incident (Zhang 2005, 276–277).

2.5.2.4 Sperling led the Safety Zone police.

Rabe appended a letter from Sperling to Rosen in the German embassy in his diary entry of January 22, 1938:

> The undersigned, along with other gentlemen, remained in Nanking at his own peril during this time of war and at the founding of the International Committee was named inspector general for the Nanking Safety Zone. As such and in the course of my tours of inspection, I observed many things with my own eyes, the good as well as the bad, but more of the latter. My field work was not easy, but 650 well-drilled native policemen, plus a well-organized private corps of police stood at my side. We maintained public order, and I must once again state herewith that I have great regard and respect for the Chinese race, who, as I have often witnessed, are willing to bear their pain and sorrow without complaint or murmur (Rabe EN, 150).

Sperling remained on the front lines for the entire duration. Smythe wrote in a letter to family: "Sperling is the chief inspector of headquarters. All day long he's periodically called out. He's been to nearly every house in the area. Now whenever Japanese soldiers see him they run away. These are fully armed soldiers" (Zhang 2005, 241).

Under Sperling's guidance, the Safety Zone police force actively carried out their duties, including organized lining up at soup kitchens, maintaining order in refugee shelters, and assisting in refugee registration. In times of dire need, however, they still had to call on the Westerners for help. Magee wrote in a letter to his wife of January 4, 1938: "While I was walking and talking with Mr. Sone on the street, a policeman ran over and said that someone had been killed... Before I got in the car, another policeman ran over to say that Japanese soldiers had returned. I ran back as fast as I could and saw three Japanese soldiers. When I asked them to leave, they left" (Zhang 2005, 161).

Safety Zone police were subject to threats to their lives, as their legal status wasn't solid. Rabe wrote in his diary entry of December 16, 1937: "Our police are obstructed in the execution of their duties. Yesterday 50 police carrying out judicial duties were arrested. An officer present said they were going to be taken away and shot. Another 45 of our 'volunteer police' were similarly taken away yesterday afternoon" (Rabe CN, 153).

The personnel shake-up in the Central China Area Army of February 1938 was intended to lay the groundwork for putting an end to the interminable city-wide violence. A report on conditions by the Nanjing Pacification Team of February 1938 read: "To help Imperial Army troops in the city quickly restore peace to Nanjing, the Autonomous Committee made plans for the establishment of a police department immediately upon its founding. These police are to uphold the peace under guidance of workers in the Special Service Organ and the military police, and have made some good progress. Peace is still, however, maintained by soldiers and military police; this goes without saying. The work of directly maintaining peace will be transferred from the soldiers to the military police, and then again from the military police to the Autonomous Committee" (Wang and Lei n.d., 343–344).

As a result more refugees returned home and ordinary citizens began emerging onto the streets. A report written by Scharffenberg of the German embassy on conditions in Nanjing of March 4, 1938 read:

> Nanjing Guard Commander Major General Amaya rules with an iron fist: we no longer hear of violent incidents, and order has been greatly restored. All the trees chopped down by Chinese to obstruct tanks have been moved to the sides of roads, and so now all roads around the Sun Yat-sen Mausoleum are once again unobstructed. Half of the refugees in the Safety Zone have now left. Now many people can be seen in the city in the evening. There are only a few rickshaws, however, and no horse carriages, although sometimes there are carts pulled by donkeys. There has been an increase in the number of traffic police. Sometimes we see Japanese patrols passing through the Safety Zone with two Chinese policemen carrying a white flag on which is written "Safety Zone Clean-up." It's clear that violence is not being used. We've often seen children playing games with a few of the Japanese sentries (Chen, Zhang, and Dai n.d., 152–153).

The International Relief Committee recorded cases No. 445 to 459 from February 3 to February 28 and cases No. 460 to 470 from February 27 to March 20, a marked reduction over the number of cases recorded in January. This was a clear reflection of the improvement in public security in Nanjing. The "Summary of Present Conditions" made by the Safety Zone Committee on March 3, 1938 read: "Over the past two weeks order has been greatly restored" (Zhang 2010,

534). By early April, the number of refugees in their shelters quickly fell to 22,000.

There were still instances of atrocities committed by Japanese soldiers, but their days of burning, killing, and looting in the open were now over. The initial results of the systematic establishment of a "normalized" colonial order were making themselves felt.

2.6 Real Estate Issues

2.6.1 War and property destruction

The Japanese bombing of Nanjing resulted in enormous damages to city real estate. The Chinese also caused some damage to properties in the city in preparation for the defense of the city. After the city fell, buildings over an even greater area were burned down by the Japanese.

There are ubiquitous records of damage to property caused by Japanese air raids. One is the August 1947 report of Cheng Zhifang of the Replacement Chongshu Primary School of Nanjing: "Forty-five houses in Nanjing's Daquanfu Alley were destroyed by enemy bombing on September 19, 1937, causing damages of 90,000 yuan" (Xia, Guo, and Jiang n.d., 484).

Much of the damage to real estate during the Battle of Nanjing was the result of Chinese soldiers deliberately setting fires from tactical considerations. As A.T. Steele wrote in a dispatch for the *Chicago Daily News* on December 9: "Last night I went to a village outside the West Gate. The villagers were all gathering there things, preparing to head to the refugee zone. They said that the army had issued an order to burn the village, so they had to leave in the middle of the night. Many people are flooding into the refugee zone like ants moving house" (Zhang 2005, 52).

The Japanese burned residential buildings over a large area upon entering the city. McCallum wrote in his diary entry of December 29, 1937: "Today I tried to estimate the extent of the property damage. About 50% of buildings from the hospital to Zhongshan Road and Baixia Road have been destroyed. About 50% of buildings on Baixia Road are destroyed, and about 60% of buildings from Zhongshan Road to Jiankang Road. A similar percentage of buildings at the southern end of town were burned, as were 20 to 30% of buildings from the Drum Tower southward to the eastern city wall" (IMTFE Exhibit No. 309). There were also records kept among the Japanese soldiery, as evidenced in this record by Akao Junzo: "Notices regarding orders from the army commander to all subordinate troops to maintain 'strict military discipline' were posted by military police in all important areas of the city long ago. Nevertheless, shortly thereafter when the sun came up, we didn't know who did it, but a fire was spreading in all corners of the city. Bright red flames rising like towers burned the skies. The flames consumed buildings and property in the city little by little" (Wang 2010e, 401). Squad Leader Maeda Yoshihiko of the 7th Squadron of the 45th Infantry Company of the 6th Division wrote in his diary entry of December 19: "On the way back when I passed a crossroads on the road south to Qinhuai River, I was surprised to see what looked like black smoke billowing from a three-story Western-style building along the road, and tongues of flame began emitting from downstairs. This morning when I came nowhere was on fire. These fires were all set by the collection team with permission" (Wang 2006a, 500).

Smythe presents a panoramic picture of the destruction of property in Nanjing in his "War Damage in the Nanking Area":

> Outside the wall, 62 per cent of the buildings were burned, even 78 per cent in the case of Tungchimen. Inside the wall, the percentage was 13, ranging from 29 in Men Tung down to 0.6 in the Safety Zone and 3.5 in the sparsely built Cheng Pei (Jiang et al. n.d., 19).

Buildings not burned were subject to looting. Smythe wrote: "Looting grossly affected 73 per cent of the buildings within the wall, but is reported for only 27 percent outside the wall, where so much was burned, reaching 34 percent in Hsiakwan. Inside areas ran as high as 96 per cent for Chen Pei and 85 for Cheng Pei Tung; the only below 65 was the Safety Zone Area, in which the low report of 9 per cent appears for buildings showing damage by looting" (Jiang et al. n.d., 19).

The Japanese also occupied many buildings as barracks. Maeda Yoshihiko wrote in his diary entry of December 15, 1937: "The division commander has occupied roads to the south of the city center. Banks, jewelry shops, hotels, restaurants, and many grand and majestic buildings have been used as quarters for the Telecommunications Battalion, the Wilderness Combat Hospital, the sick horse farm, the weapons battalion, and others. It's as though a sign were erected reading 'this place belongs to the commander,' who despises us dirty soldiers" (Wang 2006a, 495).

2.6.2 Use and management of buildings in the Safety Zone

By comparison, most buildings in the Safety Zone were preserved. During the darkest hour, an enormous amount of refugees squeezed into this zone that occupied only one-eighth the area of the city of Nanjing. Smythe wrote in "War Damage in the Nanking Area":

> Some idea of the crowding, the price willingly paid for partial security, is indicated by the fact that 43 per cent of the population, 14 weeks after the fall of the city, was living in an area which had only 4 per cent of the total number of buildings noted in the Survey, and which comprised roughly one-eighth of the total area within the walls.
>
> The fact that practically no burning occurred within the Zone was a further advantage, and suggests the generally preferential treatment given to the Zone area as compared with the destruction and violence outside, even though the Zone was not officially recognized by the Japanese authorities (Jiang et al. n.d., 8–9).

Only limited housing resources were available for such an enormous quantity of people. So the macro allocations of housing and management of shelters in the Safety Zone were no easy affairs.

Optimized housing resources. When the Safety Zone Committee was founded, it established a housing group to plan housing for refugees. Public properties go without saying; as the Chinese government wholeheartedly supported the work of the Safety Zone Committee, it allowed for use of public buildings at times of need. Before leaving the city, Zhang Qun even handed his villa over to the Committee to be used as they saw fit. Because the foreigners remained in Nanjing, foreign owned properties like University of Nanking and Women's College could be used to shelter refugees. The problem lay with "houses of officials and residences of the intelligentsia and the middle class" in the northwestern part of the Safety Zone. To increase its stock of housing, the Safety Zone Committee deliberated with the city government for the use of this category of new residence and received permission from mayor Ma Chaojun: "At this time the mayor's permission is granted for this Committee along with members of the police to enter unoccupied residences, store all movable assets in one or two rooms, and then allow all other rooms therein to be used by refugees entering the city from elsewhere" (Zhang 2006b, 393). At the same time, refugees were encouraged to move into private houses using personal connections or by talking with people overseeing private residences. One record reads: "How to proceed for housing and shelters in the refugee zone: The resolution of the housing question for refugees shall be carried out per the following principles. First make exhaustive efforts to negotiate with private owners to make all possible preparations therefrom. Leave aside all public buildings and properties in the case an expansion is needed. We fear that when the crisis arrives, all buildings in the Zone will be full to capacity, and the poorest households remaining outside the Zone will still flood in" (Zhang 2006b, 393). Rape of Nanking survivor Ding Rongsheng revealed: "When the Japs came close to Tangshan, my cousin's mother-in-law said that we couldn't live here anymore. So we again fled into the city. Among those fleeing into the city were 12 young women. When we got to the charitable institution at the corner of Hanzhong Road, we saw a one-story house that had just been built. It had seven rooms and nobody living inside, but there was someone managing it. So we rented it and moved in" (Zhang and Dai n.d., 478).

Increasing housing usage efficiency. When the International Committee was founded, it also established a housing management group with Xu Chuanyin as its director: "The Refugee Committee had a great quantity of subordinate housing groups, which divided the refugee zone into eight districts, each with an office area for the management. They also took detailed measurements of usable space, to come up with measures for maximum potential usage" (Zhang 2006b, 393). In addition, several hundred policemen and patrolmen helped out in the management, as recorded: "The work of this Committee at this time truly relies on friendly, effective cooperation with the 400 policemen and patrolmen who did not leave the city. Fewer than six people have been arrested from among the refugees for cause, as the refugees all behave themselves with the utmost decorum" (Zhang 2006b, 393–394). The goals of the strict management were clear: "We've used either rational persuasion or threat of force to squeeze the masses of people into private homes, to ensure that all livable housing is being used properly" (Zhang 2006b, 393).

With the Japanese attack bearing down and refugees streaming into the Safety Zone, the housing group resolved "private houses shall be measured by each floor. Once the maximum capacity of occupants is reached, the larger houses will be opened and filled floor by floor, opening a new floor only when the previous is full, to prevent any refugees from partnering up to occupy an outsized amount of space" (Zhang 2006b, 393).

Dynamic management. Statistics indicate that "the average number of people per refugee shelter was 70,705 in the second half of December; 62,500 in January; 36,800 in February; 26,700 in March; 21,750 in April; and 12,150 in May" (Zhang 2006b, 395).

For the over 20 refugee centers under their purview, the International Committee did their utmost to maintain orderly ways: "For the University of Nanking, Ginling Women's College, and the Nanking Theological Seminary, the housing group asked personnel from all said institutions to open up housing to accommodate refugees, and the housing group appointed managers from among said institutes to help coordinate" (Zhang 2006b, 394).

For houses with nobody watching over them, "those shelters established in private homes will be managed by a manager appointed by the housing group (sometimes by a deputy manager). Many houses will be managed by a single person. There will be differences in conditions and personnel of such shelters"

(Zhang 2006b, 394). For houses with someone watching them, "For other private houses, the housing group, with permission of the person in the house, will be responsible for the house's management, which it will entrust with those people temporarily residing within. Sometimes those people staying within the city walls of Nanjing who are familiar to the members of the housing group will be appointed as managers by the group. In other cases the housing group will seek out suitable people from within the shelters to serve as managers. Exceptional people among the refugees whose talents come to the attention of fellow refugees, and those with certain ambitions, will also be appointed by the housing group as managers. There will be fixed and unfixed attributes to these positions. There will be those who achieve remarkable results, those who are inadequate, and those who attempt treachery; this is unavoidable given the circumstances" (Zhang 2006b, 394).

On the whole, however, the Safety Zone's housing stock was very well managed: "In summary, during the existence of the shelters, they lacked electricity, running water, channels for expelling wastewater, telephones, and policemen of a friendly and adequate nature to be sought in times of need. Most people in the city walls have moved on. Those remaining are the poorest, the handicapped, and the incapable. Under these conditions, collective living has been a grand enterprise. This grand enterprise is often criticized by outsiders, who say "only Chinese can endure this. Only the Chinese can work together with one heart with no major conflicts between them'" (Zhang 2006b, 394).

2.6.3 Damages to foreign-owned property and conflict resolution

The Japanese Air Force's indiscriminate bombing of Nanjing threatened the lives and property of foreigners in the city, and all nations present lodged frequent protests. Acting UK Ambassador Howe wrote in a cable to his Interior Ministry of September 23, 1937:

> Yesterday's air raid indicates that Japan has started acting on its threat of destroying Nanjing. Their military actions to date have mostly been limited to the south of the city, but yesterday the bombs fell mostly in the north of the city, with a large concentration of foreigners and foreign interests, and also the location of the diplomatic quarter. During the first round of fierce bombing, UK citizens and their property came to harm, and employees of an English company died in the bombing (see my cable No. 480). The head of the Japanese Foreign Ministry has promised that they have informed authorities of the army and navy to take precautions to ensure the lives and property of foreigners, but their actions in fact have been alarming (Zhang 2006b, 213).

The European and American embassies began their final evacuations in early December 1937. Prior to leaving, they handed authority over embassy property to their Chinese employees, and they informed the governments of other countries and Japanese diplomatic authorities about this authorization. A report titled "Protecting Americans in Nanjing" to the outside world and the American government from the American embassy in Nanjing on December 9, 1937 made this very clear:

> While personnel of the embassy are gone, management of the U.S. Embassy building, its two auxiliary buildings, and its air raid trench has been entrusted to two Chinese secretaries: T. C. Deng and Wu Yechao. Service personnel of the embassy and their family members and Chinese employees will reside within the embassy with 17 special police we have hired. They have all been given identification papers (Zhang 2006b, 58).

Once the personnel of the British, American, and German embassies had been evacuated to Shanghai, they immediately began simultaneously pressuring the Japanese about damages to their interests. A high-level order was thereafter sent from Japan to Nanjing, upon which the Japanese embassy in Nanjing ordered consular police officer Takatama to investigate instances of harm done to foreign-owned property. Rabe wrote in his diary entry of December 23, 1937: "Yesterday evening Police Chief Takadama paid me a visit and asked for a list of all damage or loss of property suffered by foreigners here" (Rabe EN, 88).

Per Takatama's request, the Westerners performed a survey of damage to their property. Smythe wrote in a letter to his family of December 23, 1937: "This morning Rabe came over to say that the consular police want a list of foreign-owned property that has been looted as of 2 p.m. today. So this became something we urgently attended to. Of course we could only provide a report on general conditions. As to the extent of looting, later a document confirmed by the American embassy declared that it (indirectly) reserved rights. It was said that 38 of 47 German houses were looted, as were 158 of 174 American houses" (Zhang 2005, 245).

When embassy staff began returning, they began intensively interacting with their expatriate populations. Rabe, Bates, Smythe, and other Westerners in Nanjing at the time made concentrated reports of conditions in the city after the evacuation of diplomatic personnel. Smythe wrote in a letter to his family of January 9, 1938: "We hadn't planned to do so much to protect American property, but when people from the Japanese Embassy came, we quickly ascertained that they were interested only in protecting foreign property – unfortunately they had only the smallest amount of interest – but the Chinese had no interest whatsoever in this matter. We used this advantage as much as possible, because we Americans had the majority of refugee camps in our property" (Zhang 2005, 268).

Surveys performed by citizens of the various Western nations exerted enormous pressure on the Japanese. Forster writes in a letter to his wife of January 12, 1938:

> I think the presence of the officials of the American, German, and British Embassies are responsible for the difference. The J. have no face at all over the looting of foreign property (even the Embassy) by their troops, and they cannot put the blame on the shoulders of the Chinese for very often when the foreign officials go around to examine the state of the foreign property they find J. soldiers on the premises in the act of looting. They stole all motor cars they could get, even took out cars that were put in the American Embassy for safekeeping. Now the J. Embassy is trying to collect all they can get back from the military as a face-saving gesture. But I don't think it's setting very well with the foreign officials (Zhang 2005, 112).

The International Committee made concentrated reports of these incidents, not only hoping for reparations from the Japanese, but also that the embassy would report on these matters to the American government, which would, for one, report the violence of Japanese soldiers in Nanjing to the world, and for another, put international pressure on Japan to put an end to the atrocities. They hoped that Tokyo would halt the rampage their soldiers were unleashing on foreign property in Nanjing and provide some protection. This motivation was extremely clear, because the majority of refugees were living in foreign-owned property. Forster writes to his wife in a letter of February 2, 1938:

> This morning there was a meeting of the managers of the refugee centers which I attended. At present there are about 58,000 people being cared for in all these centers by the International Committee. These centers are all located in the Refugee Zone. It is interested [sic] to see how they are distributed. 36,271 or 62% in American property; 601, or 1% in German property; 17,900 or 31% in Chinese government property; 3,139 or 6% in private property, Chinese. The Japanese are insisting that the people must move out of these centers by Feb. 4th or they will be driven out by force. Notices to this effect have been posted in all the centers and some people have begun to move back into the areas designated as safe by the J. authorities. But at the meeting this a.m. practically every camp manager have reported incidents which have caused people to come back into the refugee centers. Women suffered from raping and men from robbery by the soldiers. Ginling college alone has more than forty authenticated cases which have happened since Jan. 28th when the people started moving back. Other centers also had many cases to report. All these will be presented to the J. as an indication that they are not carrying out their promises to protect the people if they go back to their homes (Zhang 2005, 125–126).

2.6.4 Establishment of district administrative offices and return home of refugees (p. 90)

The Japanese army was extremely upset about the concentration of Chinese refugees dwelling in Western-owned property. A report from the Nanjing Pacification Team read: "It was said that there were about 250,000 refugees in the city at the time we entered. They were concentrated in the so-called Refugee Zone established by the International Committee, which was like a city of beggars. Not only did this present a major obstacle to maintenance of public order and the progress of restoration, but living under the administration of the International Committee engendered among the refugees a dysfunctional psychological dependency on the Europeans and the Americans. To counter this, we should establish an autonomous committee as soon as possible and establish norms of self-rule" (Wang and Lei n.d., 343). So the Japanese "guided" the establishment of the Autonomous Committee and its subordinate grassroots organizations and urged refugees to leave the Refugee Zone for their homes. The Nanjing Pacification Team wrote again: "The plan to make refugees return to their original dwelling places was enacted beginning January 10. The city was divided into five districts, not counting the Japanese area in the center of the city. Each district had a manager, and refugees were gradually prompted to return to the various districts. Housing is provided for those with no homes to return to. We predict that basically all refugees will be distributed among the various districts by about the end of January, at which point the Refugee Zone can be formally abolished" (Wang and Lei n.d., 339)..

At this point public security in Nanjing changed for the better. Paul Scharffenberg wrote on February 17, 1938: "When driving through the city center, I noticed some vitality. Of course, most of those I saw were young people. The Autonomous Committee has announced that 100,000 have already returned to the city, that is to say have left the Safety Zone" (Chen, Zhang, and Dai n.d., 143).

To facilitate the construction of a "normalized" colonial order of life, the district administrative offices provided housing per Japanese demands to take in refugees in need of relief, to compel refugees out of the Safety Zone, and to finally end the refugees' reliance on the Europeans and Americans. A February 1938 report of the Nanjing Pacification Team read: "The numbers of people returning to their original dwelling places is gradually growing. The number as of the end of February was: 172,502" (Wang and Lei n.d., 345–346).

By the end of March, even more people had returned home. Smythe's "Notes on the Present Situation" of March 21, 1938 read: "An inspection of the southern part of the city reveals that many streets are now populated which were deserted a month ago. This extends even to the southeastern section of the city" (Zhang 2010, vol. 2, 546).

In summary, the Autonomous Committee and the District Administrative Offices it established used housing placements to serve the Japanese establishment of a "normalized" colonial order of life. Once the vast majority of refugees had left the Safety Zone, the final complete emptying of the few remaining shelters went on the Japanese agenda. Bates wrote in a letter to his wife of April 20, 1938: "Various reports from Self-Gov't people that Japs are after them for dealing with us, and also that we are to cease operations from May 1" (Zhang 2010, vol. 1, 199).

The Japanese gradually built a "normalized" colonial order of life starting from the flood of refugees into the Safety Zone in December 1937 through their piecemeal dispersal ending in spring 1938. Rape of Nanking survivor Ma Changfa recalled: "We later returned to our original residences, but the houses had been destroyed. We built another house. I used my workmanship to make a living from small capital and keep the family alive. Some of the baked cakes and fried dough strips I made were wholesaled, and some I hawked from the door" (Zhang and Dai n.d., 497).

2.7 The Closing and Opening of Commodity Exchange Markets

2.7.1 Gradual shutdown of markets for commodity exchanges in Nanjing before the fall

Feelings of danger gradually mounted among Nanjing residents after air raids began on August 15. These raids also gave rise to sensitivity in markets, and eventually to a hoarding mentality. Vautrin wrote in her diary entry of August 18, 1937: "The day closed without a single air raid – what a welcome relief. This evening Catharine and I went to the street to buy food in case of a siege but we found little. Our regular store was sold out of butter, crackers, and cookies, and milk. As you walk along the streets you can feel that there are many fewer people in Nanking."

This was followed shortly thereafter by a general closing of stores. On August 21 Vautrin wrote of a shopping trip: "Streets are not as crowded as formerly and you can well believe that tens of thousands have moved out. Many shops were closed and locked. I went to two Indian stores to see if I could get material for dresses – but both stores were locked." By late September, there were even fewer stores operating normally. Vautrin wrote on September 21: "This morning

Mr. Francis Chen went to the main business streets of the city to see if he could buy the red, white and blue cloth for the big flag we intend to make – but alas he said that every store was shut up tight and locked."

Prices in Nanjing rose accordingly. Wilson wrote in his diary entry of August 22: "It is very difficult for my cook to find anything to buy on the street and what he does buy he has to pay fancy prices for" (Yale Divinity). The prices of some daily necessities rose even faster. Rabe wrote in his diary entry of November 19, 1937: "The price of a can of kerosene has risen from 4.7 to 7 yuan. A ton of coal now costs 28 yuan, no longer 20. I've been able to store a ton of coal and four cans of kerosene. It seems that I won't be able to get my hands on any more" (Rabe CN, 69).

Even the Japanese noticed Nanjing's rising prices. Japanese Consul Okamoto in Shanghai wrote in a letter to Foreign Minister Hiroda of October 27, 1937: "Most stores in the city are closed. Fewer than one-fourth of businesses around Taiping Road are open. The larger restaurants are all closed. There is a lack of imported goods and sundries, and of cotton cloth, silk goods, and woolen goods. Prices have doubled from prior to the incident. The same for cigarettes. Rice prices run from about 10 yuan per dan (high quality rice) to eight yuan per dan (middle quality rice). It has not become inconvenient to procure other local products. Buses now run only on the Xiaguan and Fuzimiao lines. There is disorder in the coming and going of ships, owing to the movements of refugees" (Ma 2005, 38).

2.7.2 Great loss of commercial vitality after the fall

In a report to the American government of January 8, 1938, Allison wrote: "I inspected the commercial streets in central Nanjing. The signs of wide destruction spread before my eyes. Stores and all buildings looking out on prosperous streets were looted completely empty, and nearly burned out. It seems that the majority of destruction was perpetrated after the Japanese entry into the city" (Zhang 2006b, 69). Fitch wrote in a letter to Peter Shih of February 14, 1938: "You will be greatly distressed to see Nanking as it is today. About 80% of the stores have been burned down and nearly 50% of the houses" (Zhang 2005, 88).

The Westerners performed an on-site inspection of damages to buildings and other property along major commercial streets:

Street	Losses in dollars	Military Operations	Fire	Looting	Unknown
1. Zhonghua Road	12,452,145		77.0	18.5	4.5
2. Zhongzheng Road	11,088,775	1.7	86.6	11.7	
3. Taiping Road	9,327,530		49.7	29.0	21.3
4. Zhongshan Road	5,591,070		39.2	60.8	
5. Jiankang Road	4,306,030		97.8	2.2	
6. Baixia Road	3,819,095	4.2	69.3	26.5	
7. Shengzhou Road	2,129,655		35.4	46.9	17.7
8. Zhuque Road	944,725		16.6	72.3	11.1
Total	49,659,025	0.7	65.2	28.0	6.1

Table 7: Losses by damage and looting of buildings and contents on main business streets, according to cause (shown in percentages).
Source: Jiang Liangqin et al. (n.d., 61).

Scharffenberg writes sadly of the destruction to commercial streets in a report on January 13, 1938: "All has stopped: there are no hotels, cinemas, pharmacies, stores, markets, and so on. It's all gone" (Chen, Zhang, and Dai n.d., 83).

Smythe's "War Damage in the Nanking Area" gives us more details:

> When we compare the groups of the employed, we find that those engaged in trade were two-thirds of the former number, but earnings were only 26 per cent of former earnings; those in agriculture, under one-half, with 27 per cent of former earnings; in domestic and personal service, under one-sixth, with 47 per cent of former income; in manufacturing and mechanical industries, under one-tenth, with 35 per cent of former income; in general labor, under one-eighth, but wages of those employed were 73 per cent of old wages. Public service employment practically disappeared, as did professional service; while clerical occupations literally were not found (Jiang et al. n.d. 16).

2.7.3 Markets near the Safety Zone after the fall

Markets continued to exist in Nanjing following the Japanese occupation, for the key reason that the "marketized" management of the Zone by the International Committee kept them alive. Sun Baoxian recalled in a document of December 14, 1937: "The Committee sold rice for eight yuan per bag. When I heard that, I wasn't afraid anymore, although I'd gone hungry for two days already, because I still had over 70 yuan that I could use. I lived with three soldiers of the 52nd Division on the third floor. I learned from talking to them that they were eating two meals of rice porridge per day, and not getting full on it. Every person received only one big bowl of porridge at every meal. I gave them money to buy rice, and asked them to come up with a way to cook it for everyone to eat.

That kept us going for five or six days" (Zhang 2005, 104). Smythe wrote in a letter to his family of December 31, 1937: "We're not in great need of rice, but private reserves will soon be exhausted, and people urgently need to buy more. So there are very long lines in the mornings and afternoons at the store we set up at No. 5 Ninghai Road. The business there is brisk, as it's the only place where people feel safe. In addition, some of the big refugee camps are selling rice to those who can buy it. We've also delivered some goods in private. The latter has grown rapidly in the past days. This morning we decided: we are charged one yuan per sack (1.25 dan) of rice, which we still sell... at nine yuan per dan. This way the price per dan is still less than 10 yuan. We are charged 0.5 yuan per sack of flour delivered, and we sell it at five yuan. We hope that in this way we can control purchasing to keep people from hoarding food. We allow for purchases of only one dou per person at the store" (Zhang 2005, 256–257).

It must be explained that the International Committee was not trying to earn profits, but was rather trying to optimize allocation efficiency of reserve grains in the Zone by limiting sales, limiting the quantity of sales, and combining methods of free distribution and paid distribution.

By around December 21, self-emerging markets for commodities exchanges began appearing around the periphery of the Safety Zone. Jiang Gonggu recalled in a diary entry of December 21, 1937: "People on the outside say that all stores of valuables in private and public housing have just about been plundered to the last by the enemy and brought back to their country. Distressed compatriots connived to take out all the remaining things of no value and sell them in a scheme to shift the blame off themselves. The military hospital warehouse at Longpanli near the West Gate, for example, has had all its white sheets stolen and sold at one yuan per four of five, and four pillow cases for only a copper. They're all marked with Red Cross insignia, but they're being used as portable bags for selling cigarettes. This was unbearable to me at an unconscious level" (Zhang 2005, 63).

Markets around the Safety Zone grew quickly, from individual transactions and flea markets to entire commercial streets. Vautrin wrote in her journal entry of December 30, 1937: "You should see Shanghai Road! If the area outside the Safety Zone is deserted as 'No Man's Land' certainly the streets inside the Zone look as if a 'Big Market' day is on. There are crowds, and all kinds of business is being done. They say a regular market is starting up on Shanghai Road."

The Westerners were unusually moved by this development. Rabe wrote in his diary entry of January 2, 1938:

> The streets of the Zone are still packed with people: Untold thousands just stand around or barter and trade. The sides of the streets are taken over by peddlers, most of them offering

food, tobacco, and old clothes. Everyone is running around with Japanese armbands or flying Japanese flags (Rabe EN, 108–110).

International Committee members were very understanding. Smythe wrote in a letter to his family:

> The most severe problem at present, and the one we cannot find an effective solution to, is that there is no economic life for community of 200,000… Under these conditions it is difficult to operate such simple institutions as exchange shops and rice shops; these conditions make you respect for well ordered and organized life. The small shops along the streets are doing a decent business, with little risk and very decent income. So they're still operating, and their stocks are full. We've even wondered if they've stolen good from the burned areas outside the Safety Zone, but anything that we can get our hands on now is a treasure. It's as Mills said: "In my view Zhongshan Road is no longer the major thoroughfare. Shanghai Road and Ninghai Road are!" There the people crowd in because order has been restored. Both sides of the streets are lined with peddlers. Hankou Road is a vegetable market, extremely crowded every morning, just like Beimen Bridge before. The rest of the city seems to have been abandoned (Zhang 2005, 257–258).

It was hard to make ethical inquiries into the goods being sold under wartime conditions. Scharffenberg wrote in a report of January 28, 1938: "The Chinese still do not dare to leave the Safety Zone, except during the day. But even then it's only old women and children. Now they happily steal and plunder under the eyes of the Japanese. Our impression is that the Japanese are happy to see this, as it helps remove the blame from themselves. The only things left in the houses are those that the Japanese passed over. The Safety Zone has thus become a bustling 'thieves' market" (Chen, Zhang, and Dai n.d., 102).

By the end of January and the beginning of February, goods from the outside world started becoming available in the Safety Zone. Forster wrote in a letter to his wife of January 30, 1938: "One egg when procurable costs eight cents and meat, varying much in quality, around fifty cents a pound, fish around 70 cents, chickens and ducks around $1.50 depending on the size; besides these things all are scarce. Gradually, however, some of the people outside the city are managing to bring more in, but if they carry in or buy much, it is very apt to be taken by J. soldiers" (Zhang 2005, 124).

Things ordinarily expensive in peacetime became extremely cheap. Rabe wrote in his diary entry of January 24, 1938: "My manservant Chang today bought an electric fan for $1.20 (valued at around $38), which I had no choice but to be happy about. Some Ming vases are selling for only $1 apiece (Rabe CN, 411)… If I felt like it, I could fill the entire house with cheap curios—meaning stolen and then sold for a song on the black market. Only food is expensive these days:

A chicken now costs two dollars, the exact same price as those two Ming vases" (Rabe EN, 153).

2.7.4 The Beginning of Japanese army "commercial controls" on Nanjing

To support operations of the Autonomous Committee, the Japanese army first began handing over confiscated grains and other materials to the Committee to sell or distribute. This was done from political considerations, primarily to boost the legality of the Committee, which did, after all, require funding.

A report by the Nanjing Pacification Team read:

> To scrounge together funds for the Autonomous Committee, all parties are currently doing their utmost to come up with solutions, but owing to a lack of economic resources, and because no fewer than 70,000 out of the population of 380,000 are in need of relief, the task of establishing a treasury as quickly as possible has become extremely difficult. Consequently at the same time that we have imposed controls on grains for refugees, we have made profits from the direct sale of grains the primary income of the Committee. Nevertheless, as enemy-owned resources in the vicinity of Nanjing have been exhausted, we are currently working to bring in materials produced in regions in the rear. Moreover, the Committee has provisionally been empowered to take over and sell any stores of salt in this area, as continued storage would subject it to humidity which might render it unusable. The Committee will establish public salt houses and set up accounts for the sale of salt. In addition, we are beginning to repair the rickshaws dispersed throughout the city. So far seven-hundred and some dozens of rickshaws are operating in the city, and the rickshaw tax has begun to be levied. We have also ordered sanitation teams to collect scrap iron while sweeping the streets. So far they have collected about 600 tons worth (Wang and Lei n.d., 362).

At the same time, the Central China Area Army actively built a Japanese-led central wholesale market. When the market opened for business on February 15, 1938, it dealt primarily in grains and sundries. The organization and primary business activities of the central wholesale market were as follows:

> 1. Joint-stock organization, capitalized with 100,000 yuan (one registered share 10 yuan). 2. Forty percent of profits distributed to shareholders, 10 percent to an accumulation fund, 20 percent to subsidize the Autonomous Committee, 10 percent in special profits to the initiators, 10 percent as a premium to the initiators, and 10 percent to a relief fund for those unemployed as a result of controls. 3. All daily necessities in the city are to be sold at unified administration centers, with all income going to the city commercial lending fund. 4. To prevent unethical merchants from manipulating prices and settle people's livelihoods, we will raise adequate funds to sell all necessities at fair prices. A price-setting committee will be established from wholesale merchants of all commodities and members of the Autonomous Committee's Industrial and Commercial Office to exert unified controls over prices (Wang and Lei n.d., 349–350).

The occupying army also actively supported Japanese-owned commerce and established an "Overseas Japanese Exclusive Zone." Shanghai Expeditionary Army Chief of Staff Iinuma Mamoru wrote in his diary: "The planned region for an exclusive overseas Japanese zone in Nanjing includes over two-thirds the area of Chengbei [the north of the city] and a rather large portion to the south of the foot of Purple Mountain, to be allocated as a residential zone to Japanese (mostly commercial operators) currently taking shelter in Nagasaki and other places. Foreigners and Chinese are to be prohibited from living in the central locations where the zone touches Chinese streets. This plan has been approved by His Highness" (Wang 2005b, 212).

With support from the army, Japanese-owned stores in Nanjing began going into business in droves. A January 1938 report from the Nanjing Pacification Team read:

> More Japanese people are gradually entering Nanjing as progress has been made in the city's resurgence and transportation has been restored. The Japanese quarter is located in a convenient part of the city, occupying 220 *jongbo* [Japanese unit for measuring area]. The quantity of military-operated stores, food stores, clock stores, barber shops, general stores, hotels, and so on has been gradually growing, up to about 60 at present, and some others are currently applying for business licenses. There are about 300 Japanese living here in addition to military personnel and their family members. The army's policy is to provide as much convenience as possible to Japanese merchants coming to Nanjing, so we predict that the Japanese quarter will grow rapidly. But owing to inconvenience in shipping, all stores other than those operated by the military are increasingly feeling the difficulties of bringing goods into the city. Special convenience has been accorded to the Japanese who have evacuated here from Hankou. Most who currently live here are these we have mentioned. Those merchants who came initially found it difficult to obtain a place of their own (Wang and Lei n.d., 340–341).

By April 1938, there was a sizable community of Japanese engaged in various commercial enterprises. Allison of the American embassy wrote in a report of April 15, 1938: "Yesterday a report in the *Nanjing minbao* said that there were a total of 810 Japanese living in Nanjing as of March 31 (420 male and 390 female), per a report from the Japanese Consul. The report went on to say that these Japanese are engaged in 45 different occupations, including powder manufacturing, construction, cinemas, insurance, printing, electronics, camera shops, doctors, shipping, pharmaceuticals, food stores, hotels, restaurants, tea houses, liquor stores, cosmetics, etc." (Zhang 2006b, 72).

With finance inseparable from commerce, the Japanese army began issuing military bank notes upon occupying Nanjing, building up a colonialized finance order. A February 1938 report of the Nanjing Pacification Team read: "Wages of military coolies are all paid in military bank notes, so the army finds it necessary to offer exchanges of these notes. To this end, a first military bank note exchange center, operated directly by the army, was established on January 5 in the Refugee Zone, exchanging a sack of rice against 10 yuan in military currency and a sack of flour against 2.5 yuan in military currency. This center was later closed on January 15 in accordance with the guiding principle of dissolving the Refugee Zone, but others were established in all other districts (excepting Xiaguan)" (Wang and Lei n.d., 349)

To facilitate the issuance of military currency, the Japanese army decreed that only such notes could be used to purchase goods in Japanese stores. Chinese had to exchange these notes in order to buy goods. Cheng Ruifang recalled in her diary: "Japanese soldiers stole Chinese rice and rough flour to sell for money. In order to buy it, people must first buy their military currency, and use these to buy rough flour. They come up with so many schemes! The rough flour they sell is cheap if bought with military currency. The people seek petty advantages and so they crowd in. Sometimes Japanese soldiers strike them, saying they'll only sell to young women. Some people buy in their stores and sell at a high markup elsewhere. These young women put on their makeup to go buy. I don't know how many sold cigarettes. White flour could be bought too. With so many people to feed, what choice did the Chinese have!?" (Zhang 2005, 32).

The Japanese army made some "institutional" arrangements to increase the scope and value of their military currency. A Nanjing Pacification Team report read: "In the beginning not only military-operated stores but also ordinary stores were forbidden to sell goods to Chinese. Only personnel from public enterprises and people employed or impressed into service by the Japanese army were given certificates authorizing them to purchase goods from Japanese-owned stores using military currency" (Wang and Lei n.d., 353). "To satisfy the refugees' needs for daily necessities, 13 Japanese-owned stores in addition to the existing military-operated stores were allowed to sell daily necessities to the Chinese, using military currency, beginning on February 16" (Wang and Lei n.d., 350).. Elsewhere, "Designated stores could exchange the military currency obtained from sails at the army accounting department for Japanese bank notes. In addition to military exchange centers, Chinese can exchange military currency with the Autonomous Committee in times of need. Restrictions can be placed on such exchanges in times of need. The army accounting department, command headquarters, military police, and Special Service Organ will all produce one member to form a price control committee, which will control prices in designated stores. (Note) this document was approved by the army chief of staff and the chief of the army accounting department on February 14" (Wang and Lei n.d., 356).

At the same time they were issuing military currency, the occupying army also allowed for settlements of goods transactions in Japanese yen. Bates wrote in his "Economic Notes from Nanking" of March 31, 1938: "Japanese shops began business only in yen, receiving Chinese money directly or indirectly at a heavy discount. There was some shaking down to a ratio of 11/10 or 10/9, with some inside deals at even exchange. Recently some of the shops have been holding the yen high, and predicting a collapse of the Chinese dollar. Now there is good evidence for a Japanese order to local authorities for fixing a rate of one dollar to seventy yen" (Zhang 2006b, 134).

As they were establishing Japanese stores around the city and creating an economic order, the Japanese army began breaking up markets within the Safety Zone in February 1938. Cheng Ruifang recalled in her diary entry of February 6: "People in shacks on Shanghai Road were informed long ago that their shacks would be destroyed, that they needed to move to areas designated by the Japanese to conduct business. They wanted them to return to the south of the city. The Japanese soldiers were very casual about this. This is the Safety Zone, where there are many foreigners, where they can't act so casually. The shacks were all dismantled by the 8. Those not dismantled by then were forcibly demolished" (Zhang 2005, 40). This dismantling was basically completed by mid-February. The special markets that emerged during this unique period had accomplished their historic mission.

The dismantling of markets in the Safety Zone was closely connected with the dissolving of the International Committee and the return home of refugees, and demonstrated the resolve of the Japanese to end the refugees' mentality of reliance on foreigners.

By March, changes had taken place in the commercial districts of Nanjing. Mills wrote in a letter to his daughter Harriet of March 1938:

> I said above that you would find Mo Tsou Lu today just as it always was. That is not quite true. In one respect it is greatly changed. It is now one of the busiest streets in the city! From having been a rather quiet street, it is now daily lined on both sides of the street with an extensive curb market. Wang-si-fu says you can now buy anything you want in front of our house! There are two explanations of this. First when the people were compelled to the early part of February to move out of the Safety Zone, the shops that had opened in little temporary quarters along Shanghai Road moved, many of them, just south along Mo Tsou Lu. The other explanation is that most of what is now being sold on the streets, aside from occasional food stalls, is salvaged stock from former stores and shops. This is offered in a kind of curb market for whatever it will bring. What seems a busy street is really an evidence of the extent to which the normal life of the city has been upset (Zhang 2010, vol. 2, 811).

It would have been difficult to re-establish the order of economic life in Nanjing relying solely upon Japanese stores. Later the Japanese army began allowing for the resurgence in the private economy of Nanjing. A March report by the Nanjing Pacification Team titled "General Conditions of the Reconstruction of Nanjing" reads:

> Since our entry into Nanjing, the foremost issue we've considered in the city's resurgence has been entry therein by Japanese, with primary efforts made in the supervision and control of Japanese, with no attention paid to resurgence of the economy of Chinese people, the primary entity of which is composed of refugees. As conditions have calmed, we first established a chamber of commerce, and as the city began to open up, all manner of business began to emerge. Consequently this organ began cooperating with the chamber of commerce in late March to provide lateral support. Per a survey conducted by the chamber of commerce, the number of stores that have begun operations is now 747 (Wang and Lei n.d., 368).

In an informal note of March 9, 1938, Rosen writes: "A chamber of commerce was established in Nanjing on the 7 of this month. The chamber's president is the deputy of the Autonomous Committee Cheng Langbo, who was previously manager for Guohua Bank. The two vice presidents are Hu Qifa and Wang Mingwu. At the chamber's founding meeting, the president gave a speech mentioning the four important tasks of the chamber" (Chen, Zhang, and Dai n.d., 163).

In summary, the private economy of Nanjing became freer than it had been over the two previous months. Of course the Japanese guided this process, but it was fundamentally motivated by the survival instincts of the common people.

2.8 Damages to Water and Electricity Facilities and Their Restoration

2.8.1 Increasing difficulty operating water and electric facilities before the fall

One of the first targets of the Japanese bombings in Nanjing was the waterworks. Damages to this facility created great inconvenience in the lives of Nanjing residents. There were, however, many wells in the city, which helped the city through the crisis. Forster wrote in a letter to his wife of December 12, 1937: "The Safety Zone is packed full of people and there is practically no way to control them.—The water supply has ceases so that we are reduced to drawing water from wells and ponds, and the likelihood is that the electricity will also cease to function very soon" (Zhang 2005, 100). Rabe wrote in his diary entry of December 11: "8 a.m. Water and electricity are off" (Rabe CN, 129).

The power plant was also made a primary target for Japanese bombing. Due to timely repairs, however, power was not cut off to the city until its ultimate fall. Sixteenth Division Commander Nakajima Kesago wrote in his diary entry of December 13, 1937: "We found out after the fact that the electric light plant of Nanjing was still operating through the morning of the 13" (Wang Weixing 2005b, 278).

The water and electric facilities of Nanjing were able to hold out for so long for two main reasons.

The first was the highly interconnected electric grid. Vautrin wrote in her diary entry of September 25, 1937: "Evidently the city light plant has been injured. In about half an hour the street lights were turned on, but we were told that the current was from an emergency plant which had previously been erected." The "emergency plant" to which she referred was the electric plant at Shangfangmen. The plant at the Jin-Pu Railway Station could also be connected to the city grid. Rabe wrote in his diary entry of September 26, 1937: "Per this evidence I have just obtained, the power plant at the Jin-Pu Railway Station has been connected to the municipal grid in Nanking" (Rabe CN, 14–15).

The second reason was that the Siemens Company, under Rabe's control, had contracted to service many electrical installations in Nanjing. The company provided not only products, but also a seasoned engineering team stationed in Shanghai to be called upon in emergencies. Rabe wrote in his diary entry of September 28, 1937: "7 a.m., Dr. Probst and installation specialist Riebe have come here from Shanghai. Their job is to inspect the Xiaguan power plant, which has been bombed, and discuss how to restore the plant to service with its management" (Rabe CN, 17–18). Rabe then wrote in his diary entry of October 26, 1937: "Herr Riebe has finished the job at the electricity works. He could have left for Changsha, but a telegram arrived from Shanghai: "Letter to follow – don't rush the work!" In all my twenty-seven years with Siemens, I have yet to receive such a lovely telegram. (Rabe EN, 16). I'd really like to become a turbine installer myself!" (Rabe CN, 49).

2.8.2 Gradual restoration of water and power facilities after the fall

The Japanese army needed electricity after its occupation of Nanjing. On December 15, 1937, the Japanese commander sent a summary response to the International Committee, stressing "telephones, water, and electricity must be restored as soon as possible. We plan to inspect these facilities this afternoon with Mr.

Rabe, and will establish measures after the inspection" (Rabe CN, 143). Rabe wrote in his diary entry of that day: "As we were about to say goodbye to the commandant and Mr. Fukuda, General Harata entered and immediately expressed a desire to become acquainted with the Safety Zone, which we show him on a driving tour. We make an appointment for this afternoon to visit the electricity works in Hsiakwan" (Rabe EN, 71). Earlier on that same day, Rabe wrote: "At 11 o'clock we receive Mr. Fukuda, the attaché of the Japanese embassy, with whom we discuss the details of our agenda. Mr. Fukuda agrees that it is obviously both in our interest and that of the Japanese authorities to have the electricity works, waterworks, and telephone system repaired as quickly as possible. And we, or I, can be of help to him" (Rabe EN, 69).

Precisely because it was in the interests of the Japanese army, restoration of power and water facilities was quickly added to the agenda of the 16th Division in charge of guarding Nanjing. Nakajima Kesago wrote:

> Although there were still electric lights and running water in Nanjing on the morning of the 13, the engineers and staff were all disposed of in the tumult following the army's entry into the city, so there's nobody to turn on the machines. Although the army is considering solutions, so far there's nobody to do the job. Nobody knows when this problem will be solved. So, since I have no faith in our headquarters, I immediately began searching among my soldiers for those who had previously worked as technicians in power plants of waterworks, and I ended up finding 40 or 50. I ordered a technician second lieutenant in the engineering corps to collect together all those soldiers who had worked as technicians and with them inspect the machines and have them running by the 18. The power plant in Xiaguan used American-style machinery, whereas in Japan we use mostly German-style machinery, so the technicians were somewhat unfamiliar with it initially. So I encouraged them to bravely try to get the machinery running. In the end, the little power plant in the south of the city was the first to start generating electricity. Then we eliminated the obstacles in the machinery in the Xiaguan power plant, and the coal burner began operating. The results of these efforts were that the lights came on in all quarters at 7:30 on the evening of Lunar New Year's Eve. The happiness that the arrival of lighting aroused is hard to describe in words; we were overwhelmed with emotion. I then rushed to order the management battalion to bring out an amphora of alcohol for them to celebrate with. The next day the technician second lieutenant came to wish me a happy New Year and express gratitude. Then we've been busy these past few days getting the power lines in order. The area of electricity provision continues to grow. The nights of Nanjing are gradually lighting up. On around January 7, running water began flowing to the first floor. But nobody of the general public has expressed gratitude for the efforts of the division, let alone praise (Wang 2005b, 292).

Water and power were restored in sync with one another. A 1938 report of the Nanjing Pacification Team read:

As water provision was deeply reliant on electricity, the priority was first placed on restoring power, after which the water would naturally come back.

The lack of drinking water in Nanjing became increasingly acute, however, so diesel generators were brought in to facilitate the restoration of running water. On the other hand, efforts to restore electricity were begun at the Xiaguan power plant, but the enormity of the machinery there necessitated auxiliary power to keep fans blowing and water flowing into the plant, as without these there was potential danger in running the boilers. So the Japanese immediately started attempting to get the power plant running at Shangfangmen six *li* outside the Zhonghua Gate. It was at this time that the Japanese discovered that transmission lines outside the city had been seriously damaged, but night-and-day efforts allowed partial provision of electricity and water to the army beginning on January 1 (Wang and Lei n.d., 357).

Related documents indicate that running water was initially restored to the city on January 1, 1938. Smythe wrote in a letter of that date to his wife: "This morning Sperling couldn't find that rice seller, but he told us that running water had been restored to the city. But until they fix the damaged pipes, the pressure is too low, so we still don't have running water here" (Zhang 2005, 261). Rabe wrote in his diary entry of that day: "This morning Han's house had water again. It seems that some of the pipes have been restored to service. Here the water doesn't flow even to the kitchen at a height of two meters. It's said that many pipes were destroyed, and the pressure is too low" (Rabe CN, 258).

The army restored power and water especially quickly from concerns that an epidemic might break out and spread to their troops. Rabe wrote in his diary entry of January 10: "We also wanted to use this opportunity to again discuss a problem we frequently explore in private conversations with the gentlemen of the Japanese Embassy. Ponds polluted by dead bodies have been greatly reduced, or perhaps have completely eliminated, our water sources in the Safety Zone. The danger of a long-term lack of water under these conditions needed to be mentioned, particularly since very few water pipes have been restored within the city" (Rabe CN, 322). This issue was also of great importance to the Japanese, who restored running water to faucets across the city by the end of January. Jiang Gonggu wrote in his diary entry of January 29: "Many service workers... at the waterworks and electric light plant were killed for their country when the enemy troops entered the city. Now the enemy is urgently trying to restore them, but ordinary workers are absolutely unwilling to cooperate with them. They were only willing to begin work once the German Sperling guaranteed their safety; in fact he served as foreman. Now running water has been restored to the entire city. Electricity, however, is only running on one cable; only the enemy and the various foreigners enjoy the right to turn on the lights" (Zhang 2005, 73).

While seeking workers to get the power running again, Rabe and the others learned that over 40 power plant employees had been killed by Japanese soldiers. Smythe wrote in a letter to his wife of December 22, 1937: "Poor Rabe, desperate to get the power plant running again, signaled a willingness to cooperate. But when they went searching for workers today, they found that only 11 remained of the original 54. The Japanese killed the other 43 a few days ago... So cruel and barbarous!" (Zhang 2005, 242–243). Fitch also wrote: "Mr. Wu, engineer in the power plant which is located in Hsiakwan, brought us the amazing news that 43 of the 54 employees who had so heroically kept the plant going to the very last day had finally been obliged to seek refuge in the International Export Company, a British factory on the river front, had been taken out and shot on the grounds that the power plant was a government concern – which it was not" (Zhang 2005, 76).

According to Nakajima Kesago's diary, electricity was gradually restored to Nanjing beginning at 7:30 p.m. on December 31, 1937. Fitch wrote: "We are at last in touch with the outside world through the radio and that is a great blessing; for last Sunday I got our house connected up and we now have electricity. Fortunately too for our stock of candles and kerosene was just giving out" (Zhang 2005, 82).

Uemura Toshimichi wrote in his diary entry of January 3, 1938: "Tonight the electric lights of the restaurant were formally powered up. We've been fated to have no electric lights for four months now, and now we more sincerely feel the advantages of electric lights" (Wang 2005b, 255). Forster wrote in a letter to his wife of that same day: "Today for the first time in many weeks we have electric lights again which means also that we can get radio news. Unfortunately, John's is not functioning..." (Zhang 2005, 109)

Electricity was only provided to certain quarters. The vast majority of refugee shelters still didn't have electricity by the end of January 1938. Rabe wrote in his diary entry of January 26, 1938: "The Japanese brought in three Japanese engineers from Shenyang today. They restored operations of the generators in the central power plant with help from Chinese workers. Now I won't need to go to Xiaguan anymore. The Chinese said that turbine units nos. 2 and 3 were put into operation with boilers from the Parsee Company. Outside of Japanese military organs, very few buildings in the Safety Zone have electricity. To prevent air raids, street lights are also not lit" (Rabe CN, 422).

Once water and power were restored, these facilities came under management of Japanese companies. A February report of the Nanjing Pacification Team read:

To date, the enterprises of water and power provision have been under direct management by the Japanese army. Of course, the army is highly mobile, so these facilities were first managed by the 16th Division, then by the accounting department of the Expeditionary Army, and finally by the accounting department of the 13th Division. Owing to insufficient quantities of technicians and laborers in the beginning, all efforts were initially concentrated on meeting the needs of the army, and power provision only began elsewhere once permission had been granted by all subordinate units. But since water and power are indispensable elements of daily life, and as this has been the best motivation for the work of propaganda and pacification, now water and power are both provided free of charge to a large area. As for the questions of insufficient technicians and laborers, the Army Special Service Organ has issued orders to the Central China Development Company to commission an electrical consortium to dispatch eight electrical workers and to the city of Tokyo to dispatch two waterworks workers to Nanjing, to undertake all specialized work in support of the army. The Central China Development Company must make many preparations to take over management of these two enterprises from the army. The first is the question of staffing. In addition to the aforementioned, it is also planned for nine power plant workers (thermoelectric group) and fifteen power line workers to be brought over from Tokyo. It is planned that the former group will arrive on the 9 of this month, to work on running power lines in and out of the city with electricity workers; the Company plans to increase the number of workers in this area. As for transportation capacity, there are right now two trucks, 12 bicycles, and one car, with plans to add three trucks. As for remunerations, first housing will be provisionally arranged for as previously, and an understanding was reached for food with the 3rd Division, which will assume responsibility for such until transportation and general economic conditions are restored. Wages will provisionally be paid per prior precedents. The Central China Development Company has made its headquarters in the Bank of Jiangsu building on East Zhongshan Road, where it is making various and sundry preparations. Once it takes over operations from the army, it will prepare to move the Xiaguan headquarters into the city and expand the company's area. Through these preparations, the company has internally planned to take over operations from the 3rd Division on March 15 (Wang and Lei n.d., 357–358).

On April 12, 1938, Japanese Consul-General to Nanjing Hanawa Yoshitaka wrote a letter to the Beiping Chief of Staff Morishima: "Now the 3rd Division's management department is in charge of operations. It is now generally forbidden to install electricity anywhere but to primary Japanese facilities, foreign embassies, and primary Chinese organs, owing to the controls placed on lights. Soon management will be transferred to the Central China Development Company, at which point ordinary citizens will be permitted to use it" (Jiang et al. n.d., 334). He continued: "A tributary of the Yangtze River has been designated as the water intake point. Electric power is being used to prevent breakdowns; a diesel engine (500 horsepower) has been prepared. Although there has been no other damage to the water intake point, the iron pipes running through Qingliang Mountain were damaged in the bombing, with serious leakage. Now the 3rd Division is operating these facilities and fixing the pipes, and as with the electric light plant, it will soon turn over these operations to the Central China Development Company, which will provide water for general usage" (Jiang et al. n.d., 334).

The Central China Development Company quickly handed over operations to the Central China Water and Electric Company. One document read: "After the Japanese army had occupied Shanghai, power generation and water provision were both put under the management of the army, owing to military needs, and the army undertook the work of restoring them. The majority of Chinese water and electric facilities were under management of the Central China Development Company after the fourth month of the 27th year. Two-hundred and seventy-five million Japanese yen was on the third of the sixth month to found Japanese companies to initially take over water and power facilities in areas outside of the concessions in Shanghai, and this was gradually extended to cover all occupied areas in Central China" (The Second Historical Archives of China 1997, 1074).

Once the Central China Water and Electric Company took over Nanjing's water and power facilities, it gradually started charging city residents for these services. Per a record from the UK embassy in Nanjing on August 18, 1938: "The Central China Water and Electric Company is a China-Japan joint venture company that provides water and electricity in a belt across Central China. They began charging fees at the end of May. These fees are not collected based on figures from power meters, but rather based on how many light bulbs are used per month. One light bulb costs one yen, and no considerations at all are made to how many lights are used. This standard for fee collection is unfair in most situations, and the amount is alarming. It is also reported that the company will begin charging for water using similar methods. Owing to low water pressure many houses are without water. Water is available generally only to the first story and to buildings... directly connected to water mains. Registration of water users has been begun" (Zhang 2006b, 242–243).

Of course, operations of water and power were comprehensively included within the overall plans for a "normalized" colonial order of life. Water and power provision services were greatly harmed in the transition from one normal to another "normal." Per statistics: "The Nanjing waterworks provided 1,125,500 cubic meters of water per day before the incident, down to 55,000 after" (The Second Historical Archives of China 1997, 1080). And another statistic: "Power output by the Capital Power Plant in Nanjing averaged 30,000 kilowatts per day prior to the incident, and 11,000 afterward" (The Second Historical Archives of China 1997, 1078).

2.9 Transportation Obstructions Inside and Outside the City and Their Clearance

2.9.1 Gradual stoppage of transportation in and out of Nanjing before the fall

Once the bombing started, military, civil, and education officials in Nanjing were ordered to move westward in successive waves. All city residents with means followed.

The Yangtze River is an important transportation waterway to the hinterlands. It quickly became difficult to buy tickets on boats heading upriver. Vautrin wrote in her diary entry of September 13, 1937: "Lung is leaving tomorrow morning for Wuchang. It has been almost impossible to get a boat ticket for him." Boat tickets became even harder to obtain in November. Rabe wrote on November 19: "Mr. Han still can't buy a boat ticket to Hankou. He is still unable to get his family to a safe place. The servants come and go with their eyes wide from terror, because everybody thought I was going to leave on the Kutwo. I have clearly told them that I won't leave Nanjing under any circumstances. Now they've become happy again" (Rabe CN, 69).

The shortage inevitably led to a sharp rise in ticket prices. A manager for the Capital Telephone Authority's "military hotline" Wang Zhengyuan recalls: "Steamship tickets became difficult to buy in Nanjing before the end of November. Once the city authorities announced we were in a state of war, those fleeing the impending disaster swarmed out of the city, and tickets were four to five times their original cost. Tickets resold on the black market could go as high as ten times their original cost" (Ma 2005, 362).

Some people spared no efforts to leave Nanjing aboard foreign ships, and "looking for connections" became imperative under the tense conditions of the time. Rabe wrote on November 6: "My friend Mr. Wang and his wife just paid me a visit. He's an engineer from the Military Communication Academy, and his wife is Austrian. They want to get on the Kutwo. I sent a request to the ambassador, who refused. The wife could board, but the husband, like all Chinese, is not allowed on board. There are only 50 sleeper berths on the Kutwo, but it must be used to accommodate all 112 Germans who might decide to board it" (Rabe CN, 66). Again from Rabe on December 26: "I've heard that a police-like disciplinary inspection team has been formed on the Kutwo, led by Major Brunder. This is very necessary, because it has been discovered that the second-class section reserved for Germans was occupied by Chinese when the Germans boarded. These Chinese were surreptitiously brought on board by the Chinese staff (in the tea-room, of course they charged a great fee for this service)" (Rabe CN, 82).

At the same time, people still continued traveling from Shanghai to Nanjing. Forster wrote in a letter to his wife of November 23, 1937: "Conditions at the railroad station more frightful and disorganized today than ever before. There were 250 wounded at the station when I arrived, and 750 more came before the night was over. Some Boy Scouts were on the job, but, due to rain and cold and lack of transportation, no other volunteer showed up. Most of the men were serious wound cases—John Magee is still trying to get plans for more volunteer help through the Ministry of Health and also more ambulances" (Zhang 2005, 93).

A Japanese document from the time, a letter from Japanese Ambassador Kawagoe in China to Foreign Minister Hirota, tells us about conditions on the Shanghai-Nanjing line prior to the fall:

> 1) All travel between Shanghai and Nanjing completed in automobiles, usually via this route: Shanghai, Qingpu, Kunshan, Suzhou, Wuxi, Yixing, Jurong, Nanjing. The long route that passes through Hangzhou can also be taken. There are many trucks moving in both directions on the highways. Roads have been severely damaged, and there has been no time to repair them (worst damage between Qingpu and Wuxi), making automobile transportation difficult. There are dozens of overturned and destroyed vehicles on the roadsides. Most automobile traffic proceeds at night, with little during the day; military trucks seldom travel this route. The aforementioned condition was articulated by a Chinese of the Military Committee. Most military transportation happens on waterways to avoid bombing by airplane. Only unimportant military materiel is transported by truck. Many refugees are now observed fleeing from Shanghai by the waterway between Beixinjing in Shanghai and Suzhou. No refugees are visible along the highways; only a few dozen refugees were observed in a sleeper car near Yixing... 3) Military police inspections of pedestrians on the route are particularly rigorous. Permission to proceed is not granted unless proper identification is produced. The cars of foreigners are often inspected one by one. Inspections at the Tianwang Temple in Jurong County are the most rigorous, with stops along the way of each individually verified by telephone. I spent about two hours in this place alone... 13) There are many ships headed upriver from Nanjing, as British and Chinese ships are traveling in sync. Airplanes are still flying between Nanjing and Hankou. The daily fast train between Nanjing and Shanghai and the ordinary train between Nanjing and Suzhou are often stopped due to bombing. Although fast trains still run daily between Pukou and Jinan on the Jin-Pu Line, they are never on time due to military transportation and air raids (Ma 2005, 37–39).

The nationalist government implemented unified control over all conveyances to facilitate the war effort. The same letter from Kawagoe to Hirota read: "Since the establishment of the Unified Automobile Headquarters, 200 of the 600 vehicles in the city's fleet have been incorporated. One-hundred and fifty of those were sent to the front, with the remaining 50 being used by the military police headquarters" (Ma 2005, 40). As a result, public transit in Nanjing completely stopped at the end of November, which in turn led to sustained increases in the price of rickshaw trips. Rape of Nanking survivor Pan Kaiming recalls: "With refugees all taking flight, the rickshaw business boomed. Trips from Xinjiekou to Xiaguan could run as high as four jiao" (Zhang and Dai n.d., 232–233). The cost of transporting luggage to Xiaguan was likewise alarming. Eyewitness Lu Yonghuang recalls: "A week before the fall, order in the city started disintegrating. The residents started evacuating on their own, taking refuge everywhere. Luggage was stacked into a mountain at the Nanjing-Wuhu Railway Station and at the steamship dock at Xiaguan. Rickshaw drivers charged extortionate prices of between 10 to 20 yuan. Those leaving the city are on hard times. The military police are still in forceful presence, and I have not heard of any armed robberies" (Zhang 2005, 517).

The closing of city gates was placed on the agenda in preparation for the defense of Nanjing. A report on conditions in the city written by a staffer of the American embassy on December 3, 1937, read: "All city gates have been sealed with earth. Only three remain partially open: Zhongshan Gate, Yijiang Gate, which leads to the shore of the Yangtze River, and the South Gate, which leads toward Wuhu" (Zhang 2006b, 51). Soldiers began sealing the Yijiang Gate on December 9, 1937. The closing of this gate, which led toward Xiaguan, presaged the coming of a tense time. A report by an American embassy staffer read: "Yijiang Gate was being sealed with earth when we passed through it, and wide areas around Xiaguan and near the city walls outside the city have been burned to ashes" (Zhang 2006b, 59).

2.9.2 Slowdown in transportation after the fall, and the restart

2.9.2.1 Gradual shutdown of transportation

After the occupation, the Japanese army completely sealed Nanjing off from the outside world. Transportation out of the city was suspended indefinitely, and the major thoroughfares of the city fell into extreme disorder. Squad Leader Maeda Yoshihiko of the Japanese army wrote: "We've finally entered Nanjing city proper. The asphalt roads are about 20 meters wide. There is row upon row of Western-style stores of two to three stories each on either side of the roads, an extremely magnificent sight. There are air raid trenches and bunkers everywhere along the roads, as well as enemy bodies, weapons, and vehicles (including some new quick-firing guns) yet to be disposed of. Broken power lines droop down in tangles everywhere. There are even some gigantic bomb craters in some places. We're like Arab tramps who've come from a wilderness where civilization has been wiped out into a luxurious metropolis. Motorcycles emitting deafening roars drive past these mountain monsters with unkempt whiskers wearing unspeakably tattered clothes" (Wang 2006a, 495).

In those days when the entire city was subjected to rampant burning, killing, and looting, there were very few movements of people out of Nanjing. There was however, an extremely minuscule quantity of such movements: on the 15 and 16 of December five British and American war reporters left the city on naval vessels. A few days later, the Dane Bernhard Sindberg went to the Safety Zone from Qixia Mountain. Rabe describes this incident in his diary entry of December 20: "Returning to Ninhai Lu, I make the acquaintance of Herr Bernhard Arp Sindberg of the Kiangnan Cement Works in Hsi Sha Shan. Sindberg had wanted to bring several wounded Chinese to Nanking, since he had heard on the radio that Nanking was perfectly calm, with its electricity and waterworks as well as its telephone system fully restored. He was not a little amazed to learn about current conditions. About halfway here he had to send the wounded Chinese back to Hsi Sha Shan, since the Japanese wouldn't let him through. He took it into his head, however, that he had to press on to Nanking no matter what and walked a good part of the way before being picked up by a Japanese truck that brought him safely to the North Gate. Now the question is how to get back home" (Rabe EN, 83).

On January 6, 1938, personnel from the American embassy returned to the city, followed three days later by UK embassy personnel. At this point transportation restrictions in the city were relaxed.

In mid- and late January 1938, transportation conveyances and pedestrians began appearing on the streets of the Safety Zone. Vautrin wrote in her diary entry of January 25, 1938: "Rickshaws? I haven't seen one on the street since December 12, I believe it was." Nevertheless all vehicles passing through city gates were still subject to rigorous inspections. A report by the Nanjing Pacification Team of January 21 read: "Restrictions on transportation in and out of the city were lifted once preparations such as the resolution of the food problem and the city sweep were completed. Now only a certain extent of free travel in and out of the city by families living near the perimeter of the city is permitted, from considerations of relations between family members living inside and outside the city" (Wang and Lei n.d., 339). Again in a report from the Nanjing Pacification Team: "In the matter of refugees entering and leaving the city… free entry and exit was permitted beginning February 25" (Wang and Lei n.d., 346).

At this time a group of survivors who had survived this long sought opportunities to leave the city.

The Shangxinhe route led both to Wuhu and to Wuhan further west, and was connected to the city by the Hanxi Gate. Sun Baoxian recalled: "I decided to flee Nanjing after taking a look at Shuixi Gate. Upon returning, I gathered together some old subordinates and a few colleagues from the Instruction Unit who'd kept in touch with me and deliberated a plan for escape. The result was that six people were willing to fly from Nanjing with me… We decided to depart at 7:30 a.m. on March 2 and split into four groups when going out the Shuixi Gate, two to a group, with a gap of over 200 meters between the groups. After the decision was made, we all returned for things we could carry. I ordered them to prepare to look like poor refugees" (Zhang 2005, 112).

Another disguised group of soldiers left the city by the Yijiang Gate and departed on trains or steamships from Xiaguan. The army doctor Jiang Gonggu and his party fled by this route. Jiang wrote in his diary entry of February 27, 1938: "We awoke around 3 a.m. and prepared our luggage. At 5 a.m. I left in the first group with the section chief and Mr. and Mrs. Huang Ziliang. We departed from the residence on Hankou Road and went down Zhongshan Road out the Yijiang Gate to the train station, whereupon we finally discovered that the original refugee trains would be traveling that day and the following, but the enemy still suspected that many of us officers and enlisted men remained in Nanjing, so they registered everybody going to Shanghai. Once proven not to be a native, these were subject to search" (Zhang Lianhong 2005, 81–82).

Officer Guo Qi of the Instruction Unit also vividly described his trip out of the city via Xiaguan: "At dawn the next day, March 11 of the 27th year of the Republic of China, our group of 11 left out the back door of the Hutchison Whampoa Company's headquarters and quietly boarded the fishing boat we'd hired without a soul noticing. All 11 of us squeezed into the boat's hold, daring to say nothing in a loud voice, and the boat left the dock" (Zhang Lianhong 2005, 265).

Some of the remaining Westerners also left the gates to seek resources in the city's periphery. McCallum wrote in his diary entry of January 15, 1938: "Today I drove the ambulance out, and Grace Bauer drove the other to transport Chinese cabbage. He picked up the cabbage outside of the Tongji Gate and returned safely. We foreigners have no problems getting in and out of the city, which is great" (IMTFE Exhibit No. 309).

2.9.2.2 Initial restoration of transportation, led by the Japanese

The Japanese arranged for all transportation and transit in Nanjing to come under the purview of the Central China Development Company. On March 9, 1938, the Company brought in two buses from Shanghai, which went into operation the following day. A March 1938 report from the Nanjing Pacification Team reads:

After the long wait by everybody, two new buses finally went into operation on March 10. Their routes are as follows: route 1 from the Nanjing Railway Station to the Zhongshan Gate via Xinjiekou, with return service; route 2 also from Nanjing Railway Station to Taiping Street via Xinjiekou, also with return service. Their operating schedules, departures, and arrivals have been coordinated. The first bus runs at 6:40 a.m., and the last at 7 p.m., with approximately one bus per hour. The routes are divided into six fee zones, costing five coins per zone, half price for military personnel. Owing to the great demand for buses from the army depot, they have been granted the special price of six yuan per hour to rent a bus. The operating conditions for the buses are very good, often with full ridership. One bus runs 990 kilometers per day, consuming 94 gallons of gasoline, providing an average daily income of 63 yuan for the Chinese drivers and the female attendants (Chinese) (Wang and Lei n.d., 379).

By November 1938, transit in Nanjing was handed over to the Central China Urban Automobile Company, a subsidiary of the Central China Development Company (The Second Historical Archives of China 1997, 1092).

In addition to buses, the traditional conveyance of rickshaws came into wider use in the city. A January report of the Nanjing Pacification Team read:

The Autonomous Committee, currently in a transitional period, still lacks funding. So from today on, in addition to income from military grain sales and the rickshaw tax about to be levied (about 1,000 in service), preparations are being made for the Autonomous Committee to directly operate fish and vegetable markets, the income from these enterprises going to fund the committee (Wang Weixing and Lei Guoshan n.d., 339).

At this time, the Japanese began planning and operating transportation between Nanjing and external points. A report from Consul-General Hanawa Yoshitaka of April 12, 1938, read: "Steamships, light-oil truck, and trains are used for transportation between Nanjing and Shanghai. One Nissin steamship departs every three to five days. Two trains run daily, and one light-oil truck. There are also trains and steamers between Nanjing and Wuhu, but ordinary merchants and citizens need military permission to board trains and steamers. Ordinary foreigners need to obtain travel permission from the army to board Nissin steamers or Japanese naval vessels to travel to Shanghai or other places" (Jiang Liangqin et al. n.d., 335).

The Japanese army initially handed control of transport out of the city to the Nissin Company, waiting for conditions to ripen before handing it over to the Central China Development Company. One record reads: "In mid-March of the 27th year of the Republic of China, the Japanese established the Zhejiang Steamship Company, with the Nissin Steamship Company as its primary entity, to be sole operator of domestic water transport, forbidding all other ships from domestic waterways, in order to consolidate transportation by water in Central China.

The company was later dissolved, and a more organized controlling company was established. That company's founding was announced on July 28" (The Second Historical Archives of China 1997, 1079).

The railways were initially managed by the army, but the Central China Railways Company was founded the following year. One record reads: "By spring of the 27th year, it was resolved to establish a special Chinese legal person and to organize a company for unified control over transportation by railways and long-distance trucks in Central China. A company was established on April 13 of the 28th year with capital of 50 million yuan with control over about 800 kilometers of track in the Jiangnan region. The military retains management of railways in the Jiangbei region, the operation of which has been entrusted to this company. Military management was abolished in April of the 31st year" (The Second Historical Archives of China 1997, 1098).

Military oversight was particularly stern as transportation in and out of Nanjing was being restored. Consul-General Hanawa wrote in an April 1938 report: "No special limitations on Chinese have been established for intra-city transport, but all carried items are rigorously searched once they pass the city gates to prevent secret exchanges of guns and ammunition between Chinese. When moving between Nanjing and other places, they need special permission from the army. Free transportation within the city is permitted to foreigners, but outside the city they are allowed to freely walk in the walking area (from the Zhongshan Gate to the Sun Yat-sen Mausoleum and the Ming Xiaoling Mausoleum). To go anywhere else they need permission from the army and a military police escort. The primary intra-city conveyance is the rickshaw. Other than these, there are two buses belonging to the Central China Development Company" (Jiang Liangqin et al. n.d., 334–335).

In summary, the restoration of transportation in and out of Nanjing served the construction of Japan's "normalized" colonial order.

2.10 Medical Aid

2.10.1 Medical issues in Nanjing before the fall, and responses

Healthcare facilities were also targets of the Japanese campaign of indiscriminate bombing. Vautrin wrote in her diary entry of September 26, 1937: "5 p.m. Dr. Wilson took Dr. Wu, Grace Bauer, and me over to Central Hospital to see the results of yesterday noon's bombing. Although on the roof there was a large red cross painted in bold colors, yet there were 16 bombs deliberately dropped in that compound which houses the Central Hospital and the Ministry of Health."

The nationalist government in Nanjing announced it was moving the capital on November 20, at which point most medical workers in the city rapidly fled westward with the government. Rabe wrote in his diary entry of November 24:

> ... I could have used these two cars to help injured soldiers. The problem of injured soldiers is growing worse. Dr. J. Henry Liu, director of the Central Hospital, has fled, as have the two managing doctors he left behind. Without the American missionary doctors holding fast, I don't know what would have become of so many injured soldiers (Rabe CN, 78–79).

An even bigger problem was that most of the medical personnel of the University of Nanking Hospital also fled Nanjing on December 1. Wilson tells us in his testimony at the Tokyo trials:

> Our staff feared for their lives and wished to leave, and we attempted to calm their fears by saying that under martial law they would have nothing to fear in Nanking after the city fell. We were unable to convince them, however, and they left to up-river, leaving the hospital with Dr. Trimmer, another American doctor, and myself, five nurses who elected to remain behind, and some of the servant class who elected to stay with us. They left the city about the first of December. All together, about twenty Chinese doctors and forty or fifty nurses and student nurses left (Yang 2006, 43).

During the crisis, the University of Nanking Hospital assisted the Safety Zone Committee's health group to organize operations. When the Safety Zone Committee was being designed, the health group's tasks were handed over to the University of Nanking Hospital. There were two main foreign doctors, Wilson and Trimmer; an administrator, McCallum; and a nursing team led by the 60-plus year old Iva Hynds. A dispatch from F. Tillman Durdin published in *The New York Times* on December 6, 1937, read: "There are only three doctors in the University Hospital, which is the only true hospital in the city other than army emergency medical centers. Dr. Frank Wilson drives the only ambulance into bombed areas to provide treatment to the wounded" (Zhang 2005, 42).

The International Committee together with Chinese military doctors who had remained in Nanjing provided emergency care to wounded Chinese soldiers. Wilson wrote in a letter home on September 27, 1937: "The Central hospital has temporarily abandoned their quarters and are reorganizing as a military hospital in the Orphanage just outside of the city. They are preparing to take care of two thousand wounded from the Shanghai front" (Zhang 2010, 40). By early December, the military doctors remaining in Nanjing were organized under the leadership of the German-speaking Dr. Jin Songpan, who consolidated all wounded soldiers and military hospitals into the Foreign Ministry compound and the Ministry of War compound, which served concurrently as shelters and treatment centers. In September, Jin proactively approached the Safety Zone Committee to discuss emergency management procedures. Rabe wrote in his diary entry of December 10, 1937:

> Dr. King [Jin], who speaks German, offers the committee his help. He has eight military hospitals under his command, all outside our Zone. Only the lightly wounded are housed in these eight field hospitals, and most of them, or so Dr. King says, have wounded themselves in order to get out of danger. Dr. King would like to place those with self-inflicted wounds inside our Zone. That is in fact contrary to our agreement, but I hope the Japanese won't object when they learn about it, and I refer Dr. King to Dr. Trimmer, the chairman of our medical division at Kulou Hospital. According to King, he's still in charge of 80 Chinese doctors, about whom we knew nothing before now; but we would be very happy if they really do exist and were to join us; the more, the merrier. Over 1,000 people have been wounded in the city over the last two days (Rabe EN, 57–58).

The International Committee came up with a middle road: to have the International Red Cross Society take over the hospital in name and establish the Nanjing International Red Cross Hospital, to give the institution an air of legitimacy. This task was spearheaded by John Magee and Ernest Forster, and funded with money that two military officers from the nationalist government had granted to the International Committee. Vautrin wrote in her diary entry of December 13, 1937: "Searle Bates came over about eleven and reported... that $50,000 has been given to the International Red Cross for use for the Military Hospitals. The first one will be established in the Ministry of Foreign Affairs. A committee of seventeen has been organized."

2.10.2 Problems in providing medical care after the fall, and responses

2.10.2.1 New problems emerge in healthcare

Japanese harassment of hospitals. A letter of December 19, 1937, from Dr. Wilson to the Japanese embassy read:

> I respectfully beg to call your attention to an incident occurring last night, December 18, at the University Hospital where we have over one hundred and fifty patients together with nurses, doctors and hospital staff and where in the past we have been privileged to serve various members of staff of the Japanese Embassy with medical care.
>
> Three soldiers entered the hospital compound by the rear door and tramped up and down the hospital corridors. This was at approximately eight P.M. Miss Hynds, a 63-year old American nurse, met them and accompanied them. They took her watch in spite of her protes-

tations that it was her own. They also took several (six) other watches and three fountain pens. Two of them departed and the third disappeared without leaving.

At nine fifteen my attention was called to the fact that a Japanese soldier was in the nurses' dormitory. I went there with a lantern and found one soldier in a room with six nurses. He was partially dressed and I found that he had been in bed with three of the nurses before I arrived. All the nurses in the building were terrified beyond description (Rabe CN, 171).

Per Wilson's later testimony, by the time he arrived on the scene to obstruct the soldier's misdeeds, the soldier pointed a gun at him, but did not fire. Countless similar events unfolded in the days that followed. Even the hospital's administrator McCallum was subject to a violent attack by Japanese soldiers, suffering a bayonet wound to the neck.

Epidemic looms. After the fall of Nanjing, over 200,000 refugees were living in the Safety Zone, with danger of an epidemic outbreak constantly looming, causing great worries among the members of the International Committee. Rabe wrote in his diary entry of January 22, 1938: "There are only two foreign doctors in the city, so there is little hope in case an epidemic breaks out. There have now been two cases of diphtheria, and many people have caught colds in this cold, humid weather. An increase in illness is something we should expect" (Rabe CN, 399).

The Japanese army refused to permit the Westerners in Nanjing to enter the Foreign Ministry and Ministry of War to offer aid to wounded soldiers. The hospital for wounded soldiers was the product of deliberations between military doctor Jin Songpan and the International Committee prior to the fall of Nanjing, operating in the name of the International Red Cross Society. The Japanese attempted to scuttle this arrangement. Nakajima Kesago wrote in his diary:

There was a temporary hospital for the Chinese army inside the compounds of the Central University, the Foreign Ministry, and the Ministry of War. Chinese medical staff have all fled; only a handful of foreigners are straining themselves to care for the wounded soldiers. Not allowed to enter or leave the facilities, the soldiers there were bound to die sooner or later owing to a lack of resources. The reason they'd chosen those buildings to shelter wounded soldiers might be that the foreigners (many of them?) and important officials of the Chinese central government had come to an agreement. So if the Division needs these buildings, it will ask them to vacate. Also, the Japanese army refuses to treat their wounded, as we have enough of our own (Wang 2005b, 279).

As for direct interference by high-ranking officers of the Japanese army, on December 14, 1937, Magee, Forster, Kröger, and the other Westerners were forbidden entry. In January 1938, the Safety Zone Committee was informed of current conditions there, as Rabe wrote in his diary entry of January 25, 1938:

Confidential file on conditions in the Red Cross Hospital in the Foreign Ministry

1. Patients:
There are over 300 patients in the hospital, all of them wounded Chinese soldiers. Fifty to sixty have already recovered but aren't allowed to leave the hospital.

2. Staff:
21 Chinese female nurses
40 Chinese male nurses
70–80 Chinese handymen
About 20 Chinese doctors
2 Japanese doctors
4 Japanese male nurses

3. Food supply
Two meals per day for Chinese workers, served at 10:00 and 16:00, with rice and extremely small portions of cabbage served. Only Dr. Tu eats somewhat better. He has two friends among the Chinese doctors, and sometimes he invites them to eat with him. Patients are also served two meals a day, at the same time, served only three bowls of very thin rice porridge.

4. Treatment of patients

Per the news that has reached me, the doctors punish patients on orders of the Japanese. Some have even been tied up and taken away by the Japanese. There must have been many more patients there than now, but the exact number is now impossible to determine. There were many bodies in the basement when the Red Cross took up management of the hospital, some buried near the pavilion. Also, it has been reported to me that many patients died during this time, and some escaped by jumping over the wall of the Foreign Ministry.

Conditions at the Red Cross Hospital in the Ministry of War
There were about 200 patients at the hospital in the Ministry of War a week ago. Previously three nurses from the hospital in the Foreign Ministry went to this hospital accompanied by Japanese soldiers, the last time being one week ago. It is said that conditions in this hospital are deplorable. The wounded lie directly on the ground, and there is no one to look after them except a lone Chinese doctor. The female nurses come only to help change bandages (Rabe CN, 414).

2.10.2.2 University of Nanking Hospital (Gulou Hospital) working over capacity

The Safety Zone Committee and the Nanjing branch of the International Red Cross Society did their utmost to support the University of Nanking Hospital. Red Cross Nanjing branch Secretary Ernest Forster wrote in a report of January 12, 1938:

> What the people of Nanking can celebrate is that the Kulou Hospital continues to operate in the face of so much adversity. The International Red Cross of Nanking, after completing

temporary services for wounded soldiers, turned its attention to developing medical care for the poor and sick, which it has accomplished very well. The Society's work in the area of medicine requires only cooperation, and not direct participation. The Red Cross Society is providing support for the staff, funding, and supply needs of the Kulou Hospital. The Society is also imploring everywhere it can for aid to the hospital. The agreement between the Society and the Kulou Hospital is that we send the poor sick to them, and sometimes we provide cash payments to the hospital for medical services, or otherwise we pay the bills for patients (Zhang 2006b, 406).

Outside of normal medical responses, the University Hospital used most of its energies on surgical emergencies. Fitch wrote on December 17, 1937: "the hospital is rapidly filling up with the victims of Japanese cruelty and barbarity. Bob Wilson, our only surgeon, has his hands more than full and has to work into the night" (Zhang 2005, 73). Rape of Nanking survivor Sha Guanchao recalled in oral testimony: "The wound was excruciatingly painful after I returned to the Refugee Zone. My wife was alarmed when she saw it. She supported me by the arm and brought me to the Gulou Hospital. The doctors took a look and wanted me to stay in the hospital for treatment. I was there for 11 days, and I recall sleeping in bed no. 267. I was in no way at peace staying in the hospital, because Japanese soldiers frequently came to make inspections. The doctor told me not to say I had been stabbed by a Japanese soldier, but that I'd been injured in the bombing" (Zhang and Dai n.d., 19).

In addition to surgical emergencies, the staff of the University Hospital also had to respond to the aftermath of rapes: unintended pregnancy. Bates wrote in a letter to his wife of February 13, 1938: "Now the long-foreseen problem appears. A woman has brought her daughter to the University today, asking for abortion to relieve the engaged girl from continuing a pregnancy resulting from Japanese rape" (Zhang 2010, 183).

Doctors in the University hospital successively came down with illnesses themselves from too many consecutive days of nonstop labors. Rabe wrote in his diary entry of December 26, 1937: "Liu and his child are sick. I drove them to Dr. Wilson at the Kulou Hospital. Right now he alone is in charge of all the work in the hospital, because Dr. Trimmer is sick" (Rabe CN, 227). Wilson himself succumbed at the end of January, 1938 (Rabe CN, 441–442).

2.10.2.3 Medical aid in other institutions

The Nanjing Red Swastika Society also set up a refugee hospital. Cheng Ruifang wrote in her diary entry of January 21, 1938: "There is a refugee hospital on Huaqiao Road. It doesn't cost much. Fees can be waived if I write a note. I send them over there for treatment" (Zhang 2005, 35). A medical team composed of the military doctors was concealed in the Red Swastika Society's hospital. Eyewitness Zhu Qingchuan wrote:

> Here's what I heard from Deputy Chairman Chen Guanlin... Prior to the 13 of this month, those of my rear medical team with implements and drugs who had not escaped through the Yijiang Gate and were hiding in the Safety Zone came to the Society to ask for shelter. They were willing to provide care to refugees. We have placed them near all major shelters in the Safety Zone in clinics under the name of the Red Swastika Society. For several days since the city fell they have been providing emergency care and delivering babies. I was ordered to pay attention to protecting this corps of military medics. Chen reminded me to be particularly attentive to Director Sun Shurong (Zhang 2005, 475).

As the Red Swastika Society had previously assisted in relief efforts following the Tokyo earthquake, they collected the bodies of Japanese airmen who'd been shot down and buried them. After Nanjing fell, high-ranking officials from the Japanese army paid a special visit to express gratitude. After that, the Society operated with few hitches. One record reads: "Plague broke out in the wake of the turmoil of war. No public or private hospitals or clinics have been restored. There is nowhere for the sick to be treated. This Society specially established two clinics for care in all branches of medicine, internal and external. The society provides both doctors and medicine to provide relief to the poor. Care is daily provided to 200 to 300 people in each clinic, and the total of those treated thus far exceeds 60,000. Over eight months many public and private hospitals have been restored to previous conditions, so the Society's clinics are now coming to an end" (Sun 2007, 75).

Chongshantang, another charitable association in the city, also provided medical care. A document titled "Status of Chongshantang Activities such as Burying Bodies" reads: "Since entry into the Refugee Zone on December 11 of the 26th year, this society has provided rice to refugees. This provision has been sporadic since May. We opened clinics in the Refugee Zone on January 6 of the 27th year to provide treatment to refugees. These are still operating. We began burial work on January 23 and stopped on March 29" (Sun 2007, 145). The Red Cross Society of China also participated in medical relief work. The document "Excerpts from the Red Cross of China Nanjing Branch Summary on Refugee Relief Work" reads: "The area around Xiaguan was the part of Nanjing most devastated by war, so the sick refugees there had nowhere to seek medical treatment. This branch thus established a clinic and pharmacy in Xiaguan. The clinic is divided into two sections, internal and external medicine. The internal medicine clinic is staffed with Traditional Chinese Medicine doctors and provides Chinese medicine. The external medicine clinic is staffed with Western-style doctors and provides Western medicine. Most patients to the internal medicine clinic are suffering from intestinal and stomach ailments, and ninety percent of patients to the external medicine clinic suffer from skin disorders. Both of these conditions arise because of the poor environment for the refugees, who are incapable of providing proper sanitation. Considering the extreme lack of drugs in Nanjing following the incident, once epidemics start breaking out in summer, we'll have doctors but no medicine, and this is a singular cause of worry" (Sun 2007, 177).

2.10.2.4 Sanitation and epidemic prevention work

Infant care. Vautrin wrote in her diary entry of December 27, 1937: "To date we have had fourteen births and four deaths. Mrs. Tsen [Cheng Ruifang] is the only nurse we have and she is terribly overworked." Conditions in other places were even worse, as Rabe wrote on December 30: "Over the last two nights, here in the straw huts, in the muck and mud of my refugee camp, the so-called Siemens Camp, two children were born, a boy and girl... No doctor, no midwife, no nurse to help. There aren't even any bandages or diapers. A few wretched dirty rags were all that the parents had for their newborn infants" (Rabe EN, 106).

In January 1938, the International Committee was finally able to communicate regularly with charitable organizations in Shanghai once communications had been restored. They had a shipment of milk powder delivered in haste on European and American naval vessels. Cheng Ruifang wrote: "Now a great quantity of cod liver oil has been delivered from Shanghai for refugee children to eat. There is also milk powder for infants. Distribution of these began today, with many already having signed up. Every day from 1 p.m. to 3 p.m. they are checked to see if they regularly consume milk powder or cod liver oil. I must prepare the milk powder for them to eat. Many children have been born here with no milk to eat. If the adults have nothing to eat, then where is the milk to come to feed the children? I weigh them once a week to see how much they've grown. I've found three intellectuals among the refugees who help me deliver milk powder and mix milk powder, because it needs to be brought to six buildings" (Zhang 2005, 38–39).

Once communication had been restored, the Westerners actively sought doctors and drugs from outside the city. Smythe wrote in a letter to his family of January 9, 1938: "In the cable to Secretary Feng we also requested two foreign doctors and two foreign nurses. We want to do more medical work and build mobile medical stations in the refugee camps" (Zhang 2005, 272). The International Committee also actively requested medical support from Shanghai. In a letter to Director Boynton of the National Christian Council in Shanghai, Rabe wrote: "Please send 1,000 pounds of cod liver oil (in big packages) and 200 pounds of surgical gauze on the English cannon boat on the 23 (Sunday) to the University Hospital. Please ensure that the 20,000 orders of diphtheria medication ordered from the international dispensary on January 10 are also delivered no matter what" (Rabe CN, 392).

The Japanese army imposed strict restrictions on entry and exit in and out of the city by foreigners at this time, but it was impossible for them to simply ignore the sustained entreaties by the foreigners, so they proposed allowing for Japanese doctors to help in medical aid, to brush aside their concerns (Rabe CN, 393).

Full-out efforts against contagious diseases. The first case of diphtheria was discovered in the Safety Zone in January 1938. Cheng Ruifang writes in her diary entry of January 10, 1938:

> A child came down with diphtheria. The hospital won't take the child, so I had no choice but to move him to the laundry room behind no. 500… The child with diphtheria symptoms died, as did his little sister. Now a total of 15 children have died, as have four adults, two old people, and two middle-aged people (Zhang 2005, 31).

By the middle of February, other contagious diseases appeared in the Safety Zone in the wake of the diphtheria outbreak. After repeated entreaties from the foreigners in Nanjing, Dr. Brady came to Nanjing on February 21, 1938, to inoculate refugees with cowpox. Vautrin wrote on February 25, 1938:

> Vaccination began at 2 with babies and lasted until 5:20. Vaccinated a total of 1,117. Dr. Brady came with three helpers. Place – between the two South dormitories out in the sunshine.

No major outbreak of contagious disease occurred in the Safety Zone, owing to the great care taken in this regard. A later report by the Nanking International Relief Committee read: "Despite the ordinary high death rate among the refugees (particularly among children), no serious disease has broken into an epidemic. Truly there are many suffering from beriberi, measles, and scarlet fever, but these caused few deaths considering conditions at the time. In the vaccination campaign among the shelters in spring 1938, 16,265 people were inoculated with cowpox, and over 12,000 received intravenous vaccinations against typhoid and cholera, including patients in the Gulou Hospital and in the clinics supported by the Red Cross" (Zhang 2006b, 406–407).

Active treatment of beriberi. The first case of beriberi was discovered in early February 1938. Smythe wrote in a cable to Fitch, in Shanghai at the time: "We've discovered many cases of beriberi. Please send 10 gallons of vitamin B water as soon as possible (we stress that it be vitamin B!), as well as 60 milliliters of diphtheria antitoxin – please place priority on getting these two to the Ministry of

Health. The doctors recommend using soybeans as a preventative food. Please send 100 sacks of broadbeans on the Oahu. If there's not enough, please send as much as possible" (Rabe CN, 489). Fitch, per the cable's request, bought broadbeans in Shanghai. He then returned to Nanjing on February 12 and waited for the foodstuffs and drugs to arrive.

The shipment and distribution of these 100 tons of broadbeans was also subject to interference from the Japanese army. First the army claimed it was unaware of any cases of beriberi in Nanjing (Rabe CN, 541). Second, the Japanese demanded that the broadbeans be given to the Autonomous Committee for distribution. The Safety Zone Committee communicated with the Autonomous Committee quietly via mediation from the U.S. embassy, with this result: "Mr. Allison from the American embassy arrives with news that the 'green bean problem' has now been settled. The beans can be imported and distributed both inside and outside the Zone" (Rabe EN, 198). The bean problem was not ultimately resolved until the end of February.

2.10.2.5 Japanese participation in medical care and the building of a "normalized" colonial order

After the Japanese had occupied the city, Dr. Hirai, then chief of the Japanese Army Medical Staff, began talking with the Shanghai Expeditionary Army about providing medical care to refugees. He was met with a stern refusal. Iinuma Mamoru wrote in his diary entry of December 21, 1937:

> The medical staff chief came here and said that a great quantity of healthcare materials had been collected in Nanjing. He also recommended that our army provided care to locals, to prevent an epidemic from breaking out in our ranks. This care is not at all intended for propaganda or pacification aims. It's as though everything were turned upside down. So he was asked to use... remaining forces to accomplish this task (Wang 2005b, 212).

Clearly, the Japanese army hadn't thought too much about the establishment of a "normalized" colonial order at this time.

The Japanese began participating in the provision of medical care to Nanjing residents in late January and early February 1938. A March report from the Nanjing Pacification Team reads:

> First district administrative office: since January two Chinese doctors, two Chinese nurses, and two Chinese pharmacists had been dispatched, a total of six, to provide medical care. A Japanese doctor was added to the first district administrative office after March for support (still unpaid). Offices of the first district administrative office will be moved into the former military police headquarters in early April. Now the first district administrative office will be opened on Nanjing Public Hospital (originally the Public Hospital). This is currently

being planned. Funding support for this project may come from the Foreign Ministry's Cultural Service, which has already undertaken this matter. The second, third, and fourth district's administrative offices also established Japanese army clinics in early March and are providing medical care free of charge. In another matter, as drugs and other materials here are insufficient in quantity, we are using enemy products. Considering that this is a city of 380,000 inhabitants, there are many problems requiring study (Wang and Lei n.d., 366).

3 Westerners in Nanjing During the Massacre

3.1 Westerners in Nanjing before the Fall

3.1.1 Evacuation of Westerners before the fall

Western countries began evacuating their citizens from Nanjing after the Japanese air raids commenced, with women and children being the first moved further inland in China. American women and children began evacuating Nanjing on the evening of August 16, 1937, as Vautrin wrote that day: "They are being sent up river to Kuling or Hankow." A New York Times article of August 28 repored that as of August 27: "Most American women and children have been sent to safer places further up the Yangtze River. Some others will leave before the weekend, reducing the ranks of American expatriates here to 34 men and 19 women, including the staff of the embassy" (Yang and Zhang n.d., 324). That same day the German embassy once again implored all German citizens who were not staying for professional or other emergency reasons to leave Nanjing (Rabe CN, 6).

The sustained Japanese bombing of Nanjing endangered the lives and property of Westerners in the city and resulted in protests from all major Western nations (Zhang Sheng 2006b, 2). In complete disregard of these protests, on September 19 the commander of the Japanese 3rd Fleet issued a warning to the diplomatic organs of third-party countries that even larger air raids were going to be launched on Nanjing, with a request that all overseas citizens and diplomatic personnel remaining in Nanjing be evacuated, to "end the present hostilities as quickly as possible" (Jing 2005b, 159).

In response to the Japanese actions to "frighten the diplomatic personnel of all countries into evacuating the capital at Nanjing," China's representative to the League of Nations Wellington Koo (Gu Weijun) "sent a diplomatic note on this issue to the League of Nations Secretary-General" (Koo n.d., 492). On September 28, the League of Nations unanimously passed a resolution censuring Japan: "In response to such military actions that make the whole world feel terror and indignation, we declare there is no space for explanation, and hereby sternly rebuke the aforementioned behavior" (Zhang 2006b, 7).

Nevertheless, "Washington wanted to stay out of the matter by all means" (Tuchman n.d., vol. 1, 248). On September 22, "Nanjing was subject to over 20 raids by light and heavy bombers between 10:50 and 13:45. Many bombs landed near stations on the way as well as all over the city." At this time much of the

---

Note: Chapter contributed by Dong Weimin.

staff of the U.S. embassy took refuge aboard the USS Luzon and USS Guam, returning to the embassy only after the bombing had ended in the afternoon (Zhang 2006b, 4).

This action by the American embassy imposed a dilemma on the other embassies in the city. The French foreign minister soon expressed that the "immediate action by the American embassy to evacuate Nanjing... baffled him." In the end most officers of other diplomatic organs in Nanjing "stayed in place and did not move." This unilateral action by the U.S. also aroused "indignation from the government in Nanjing" (Koo n.d., 494). American public opinion even held that the action might "arouse hostility toward Americans in Nanjing. The U.S. Department of State "paid great attention" to the matter (Zhang 2005, 11).

Conditions continued to worsen thereafter. On November 16 a meeting of highest-ranking defense officials in the nationalist government resolved to move the capital to Chongqing, with the Executive Yuan, the Legislative Yuan, the Judicial Yuan, the Control Yuan, and the Examination Yuan in its train. The Ministry of Foreign Affairs and the Ministry of Finance moved to Wuhan.

On November 16, 1937, the German embassy's Expatriate Rescue Group issued "Notice No. 1" to its citizens in China, giving detailed explanations of plans that had been made to evacuate them, with each family allowed to bring one servant along (Zhu 2007, 147–148). Rabe received the notice that night, and thought he might bring his assistant Han Xianglin on the boat as his servant (Rabe CN, 66).

"...the American embassy... like all other embassies, has ordered its citizens to leave Nanking" (Rabe EN, 32). Officers of the American embassy felt that if conditions in Nanjing grew to the point of "excessive chaos and danger," it might "imperil the safety of foreigners," and so "all Americans have been sent onto American gunboats." They were not, however, forced to leave Nanjing, as Minnie Vautrin wrote on November 19, 1937.

On the evening of November 22, 1937, the Kutwo left for Hankou, with the staff of the German embassy leaving Nanjing on board (Rabe CN, 76). Most of the staff of the embassy headed to the new location of the Chinese government's Ministry of Foreign Affairs, Hankou. A small group of only three diplomats remained in the "emptied-out embassy." France, Italy, and other nations evacuated all their overseas citizens from the city (Rabe CN, 72–73).

On November 28, the Americans remaining in Nanjing were called to the American embassy for a meeting. The "expatriate evacuation expert" Paxton said "that as many as possible should leave at once, and those who cannot leave immediately should be prepared to go out when and if Embassy leaves for the U.S.S. Panay." Paxton even considered the city gates: "If city gates are closed two places were designated as points for going down over city wall by ropes" (Yang and Zhang n.d., 373). Vautrin wrote on November 28 that she and Searle Bates "feel that our responsibilities make it necessary to stay through. Our explanations were accepted and respected."

On December 1, Tokyo issued orders to establish the "Central China Area Army," and subsequently ordered this army to work with the navy in an attack on Nanjing (Wang and Lei n.d., 7–8). On this day the American embassy called its expatriates to another meeting, where they were divided into three groups, as Vautrin wrote on December 1: "those who can and should get away today on a commercial boat; those who must stay on for the time being and will get out the last minute on the U.S.S. Panay – going down over city wall by a rope if necessary; and those who expect to stay through." The German embassy also called its expatriates to an assembly that day, "to discuss when people will have to board the Hulk" (Rabe CN, 94).

On December 3, the American embassy sent out its final warning asking that Americans leave Nanjing. The embassy gave them the following three choices, "(1) flee on your own; (2) flee on board the USS Panay; (3) stay in the city", and asked that they sign statements declaring their decision (Zhu n.d., 96); "Though there's a war proceeding before their eyes, some Americans are planning to stay in Nanjing to the very end." This was "extremely difficult for the embassy staff remaining in the city" (Zhang 2005, 33).

On December 8, Japanese forces began pressing upon Nanjing. Japanese Consul-General Okamoto wrote a letter to the Norwegian Consul-General Jahr, leader of the consular corps, requesting that he transmit a message to other consuls that the Japanese request foreign citizens to leave Nanjing (Ma 2005, 116). The small group remaining in the American embassy, prior to boarding the USS Panay, sent out a notice titled "Read – to Americans in Nanking" to all Americans still in the city, establishing Bates as their contact (Zhang 2006, 53–54).

Scharffenberg wrote that on December 11, "officers of the British and American embassies decided to leave Nanjing en masse. Dr. Rosen, Scharffenberg, and Hürter then also boarded a storehouse boat of the Taigu Company berthed upriver from Nanjing" (Chen, Zhang, and Dai n.d., 62). The Yijiang Gate, which led from the city toward the wharf at Xiaguan, had been closed, and all transportation in and out of the city was basically halted. The evacuation of Westerners thus came to an end. Two days later, the Japanese occupied Nanjing.

3.1.2 Structure of Westerners in Nanjing and their motivations

3.1.2.1 Origins and organization of Westerners in Nanjing

Rabe was in Nanjing before, during, and after the Japanese occupation. During this time, he undertook the organization of Westerners in Nanjing, serving as chairman of the International Committee for the Nanking Safety Zone until he finally left the city on February 23, 1938 (Rabe CN, 583). Among his remaining papers are some lists of the Westerners who stayed in Nanjing during this time. One of them was the "List of International Committee for the Safety Zone":

Name	Nationality	Address
John Rabe, Chairman	German	Siemens China Co.
Lewis S. C. Smythe, Secretary	American	University of Nanking
P. H. Munro-Faure	British	Asiatic Petroleum Co.
Rev. John Magee	American	American Church Mission
P. R. Shields	British	International Export Co.
J. M. Hansen	Danish	Texaco
G. Schultze-Pantin	German	Shingming Trading Co.
Iver Mackay	British	Butterfield & Swire
J. V. Pickering	American	Standard Oil Co.
Eduard Sperling	German	Shanghai Insurance
Dr. M. S. Bates	American	University of Nanking
Rev. W. P. Mills	American	Presbyterian Mission
J. Lean	British	Asiatic Petroleum Co.
Dr. C. S. Trimmer	American	University of Nanking
Charles Riggs	American	University of Nanking

Table 8: Members of the International Committee for the Nanking Safety Zone (November 29, 1937). Source: Rabe EN, 44.

Rabe goes on to note: "The gentlemen whose names are in italics left Nanking before the siege" (Rabe EN, 44). Rabe added Kröger and Fitch to his list after the fact, noting that they remained in Nanjing and participated in the work of the International Committee the entire time (Rabe CN, 92).

Second, Rabe included a letter from the International Red Cross Society Nanjing Branch to the Japanese embassy in his diary entry of December 15, 1937, in which he included a list of the members of the Nanjing branch of the International Red Cross Society:

No.	Name	Position
1	Rev. John C. Magee	Chairman
2	Mr. Li Chuin-nan	Vice-Chairman (Chinese Red Cross Society of Nanking

3.1 Westerners in Nanjing before the Fall — 155

Continued

No.	Name	Position
3	Mr. W. Lowe	Vice-Chairman
4	Rev. Ernest H. Forster	Secretary
5	Mr. Christian Kroeger	Treasurer
6	Mr.s Paul de Witt Twinem	
7	Miss Minnie Vautrin	
8	Dr. Robert O. Wilson	
9	Mr. P. H. Munro-Faure	
10	Dr. C. S. Trimmer	
11	Rev. James McCallum	
12	Dr. M. S. Bates	
13	Mr. John H. D. Rabe	
14	Dr. Lewis H. D. Smythe	
15	Rev. W. P. Mills	
16	Mr. Cola Podshivoloff	
17	Pastor Shen Yu-shu	

Table 9: List of International Red Cross Committee.
Source: Rabe CN, 145.

Numbers 2, 3, and 17 of the above list were Chinese. Number 6, Mary Twinem, was originally American. Although she was white, she became a Chinese citizen after marrying a Chinese man. Consequently, she is not included as a foreigner in statistics compiled by the American embassy, the Japanese embassy, or even among the Westerners themselves (Kasahara n.d., 170, footnote). Vautrin wrote on October 17, 1937: "Mary Twinem is here and doing a fine piece of work helping wherever she is needed – but she no longer counts as a foreigner." Number 9, P. H. Munro-Faure, left Nanjing before the fall (Rabe CN, 92).

On December 21, 1937, the Westerners in Nanjing delivered to the Japanese embassy a letter of protest signed by all 22 foreigners in the city. Here are their names:

Name	Nationality	Address
1. Mr. John H. D. Rabe	German	Siemens Co.
2. Mr. Eduard Sperling	German	Shanghai Insurance
3. Mr. Christian Kröger	German	Carlowitz Co.
4. Mr. R. Hempel	German	North Hotel
5. Mr. A. Zautig	German	Kiesseling and Bader
6. Mr. R. R. Hatz	Austrian	Mechanic for Safety Zone
7. Mr. Cola Podshivoloff	White Russian	Sandgren's Electrical Shop
8. Mr. A. Zial	White Russian	Mechanic for Safety Zone

Continued

Name	Nationality	Address
9. Dr. C. S. Trimmer	American	University Hospital
10. Dr. R. O. Wilson	American	University Hospital
11. Rev. James McCallum	American	University Hospital
12. Miss Grace Bauer	American	University Hospital
13. Miss Iva Hynds	American	University Hospital
14. Dr. M. S. Bates	American	University of Nanking
15. Mr. Charles H. Riggs	American	University of Nanking
16. Dr. Lewis S. C. Smythe	American	University of Nanking
17. Miss Minnie Vautrin	American	Ginling College
18. Rev. W. P. Mills	American	Northern Presbyterian Mission
19. Rev. Hubert L. Sone	American	Nanking Theological Seminary
20. Mr. George Fitch	American	Y.M.C.A.
21. Rev. John Magee	American	American Church Mission
22. Rev. E. H. Forster	American	American Church Mission

Table 10: Westerners in Nanjing (December 21, 1937).

Note: two members of this list are noted as "White Russian," which at the time denoted any Russians who had fled from the Soviet regime following the October Revolution. The Soviet Union did not acknowledge them as citizens, making them men without a country. Source: Rabe CN: 195.

There were also Westerners living in the suburbs of the city, including the German Karl Günther and the Dane Bernhard Sindberg.[16] They were hired to guard the Jiangnan Concrete Plant near Qixia Mountain shortly before the Japanese arrived, to prevent the Japanese from occupying it. They were in contact with the Westerners inside the city (Zhang 2005, 172–175).

There were also a handful of Western war reporters covering the Sino-Japanese conflict who were in the city at the time it fell. Four were American: Frank Tillman Durdin, C. Yates McDaniel, Arthur Menken, and A. T. Steele (Zhang 2006b, 57–58). There was also a British reporter from Reuters: Leslie C. Smith. Vautrin wrote in her diary entry of December 15, 1937: "Our four reporters went

---

16 There is a theory that Günther and Sindberg hired three "white Russians" as part of their team at the Jiangnan Concrete Plant (see Chen Kejian 2005, Jiangnan shuinichang nanmin ying [Refugee camp in Jiangnan Concrete Plant]. In *Shiji* 4; and Zhang Shuoren (2005), Kangzhan shiqi de Jiangnan shuini gongsi [The Jiangnan Concrete Company during the War of Resistance], Nanjing Normal University Institute of Social Development masters dissertation, accessed from the Chinese renowned masters dissertations database). As far as we can tell, however, this theory remains unsubstantiated, so we have not included mention of these three "white Russians" in our book.

to Shanghai today on a Japanese destroyer." Actually only McDaniel left on a Japanese Destroyer, the Tsuga, and that was on December 16 (Zhang 2005, 117). The other three American reporters and the British reporter left Nanjing on the USS Oahu on the 15th. The above 29 Westerners were present in Nanjing and its environs during the massacre.

On the eve of the Japanese occupation, all diplomats remaining in Nanjing evacuated to naval and merchant vessels on the Yangtze near the city to avoid the danger of combat. After the Japanese occupation, British, American, and German diplomats requested permission to return: "The three officials from the American embassy, Mr. Allison, Mr. Espey, and Mr. McFadyen, arrived here today aboard the USS Oahu from Shanghai by way of Wuhu. They were already outside Nanking once before on 31 December, but were not allowed to land and so went on to Wuhu" (Rabe EN, 113). By this time the Japanese had occupied the city for over three weeks.

On January 8, 1938, Fukui of the Japanese embassy gave Rabe some News: "Dr. Rosen, Hürter, and Scharffenberg will be arriving tomorrow with two gentlemen from the British embassy" (Rabe EN, 115). On January 9, the aforementioned German diplomats arrived in Nanjing aboard the HMS Cricket with three British diplomats, not the "two gentlemen" mentioned by Fukui. Rabe mentioned them in his diary entry of that day: "Consul Prideaux-Brune, Colonel Lovat-Fraser, and Mr. Walser, an air-force attaché, who, however, was not permitted to land, since the Japanese alleged that they had not been informed of his arrival" (Rabe EN, 118).

On January 29, 1938, British Consul Prideaux-Brune left Nanjing for Shanghai on the HMS Cricket, on board which Fitch carried some of Rabe's diary entries out of the city (Rabe CN, 436). In a letter to his wife Dora, Rabe wrote that Prideaux-Brune introduced his successors Mr. Jeffery and Mr. Williams to Rabe before he left the city. This letter was attached to his diary entry of January 27, 1938, but the letter itself was dated January 28 (Rabe CN, 430). This is the earliest mention of these two British diplomats' presence in Nanjing.

After the city's fall, the earliest mention of non-diplomatic Westerners arriving in the city comes from Rabe's diary entry of January 26, 1938: "Today a young American arrived by car, accompanied by a Japanese guard. He wants to sell some large timber holdings of an Anglo-American lumber company to the Japanese" (Rabe EN, 156). This young American's name was Bishoprick, and the company he represented, the China Export and Import Lumber Co., was "a British company that represented many American interests" (Zhu Chengshan n.d., 84). Rabe writes in his diary of Bishoprick's journey: "This man, who is attached to the British embassy, reports that on his trip from Shanghai they encountered a total of perhaps 60 people in the first 50 miles, and that Nanking is the only city with any number of inhabitants worth mentioning. All the other cities between here and Shanghai are as good as dead" (Rabe EN, 156). He planned to leave the city for Shanghai by car on February 4, but since it was a "wet and cold snowy day," he had to postpone his trip. He still hadn't left by February 12 (Zhang 2005, 127–128).

Based on the above, we can conclude that a total of 41 Westerners were in Nanjing, having been there the entire time or recently arrived, between December 13, 1937 and the beginning of February 1938.

Nationality	American	German	British	White Russian	Danish	Austrian
Number	22	9	6	2	1	1

Table 11: Nationalities of foreigners in Nanjing.

In February 1938, only a handful of Westerners returned to the city, including Dutch and French diplomats, the American missionary Father Kearney (Vautrin, Feb. 8 and 11, 1938), and Dr. Brady. On March 4, 1938, Scharffenberg of the German embassy criticized the harsh controls imposed by Japanese officials on foreigners' entry and exit of Nanjing: "The Japanese here impose strict controls on entry and exit of Nanjing. That is to say that they strictly control entry and exit of Nanjing by foreigners." He went on to say that the Westerners were "stuck here, like rats hiding in a hole, and the Japanese are the cat" (Chen, Zhang, and Dai n.d., 154).

On April 25, 1938, Cabot Coville, military attaché to the U.S. embassy in Japan, paid a visit to Nanjing, where Allison of the Nanjing embassy told him: "There have been a total of 34 Americans in Nanjing since December 12, including myself. There have been a total of 50 Westerners in Nanjing since December 12, including officers on American and British gunboats" (Zhu n.d., 83).

3.1.2.2 Motivations of Westerners for staying in Nanjing

Karl Günther was born in Tangshan, China, in 1903. His father, Hans Günther, had been a German geological engineer employed by the Chee Hsin Cement Company's Tangshan Cement Works. As the Japanese closed in on the Jiangnan Cement Plant, the Chee Hsin Company, an investor in the Jiangnan Plant negotiated with the German equipment supplier Siemssen & Co. to have them dispatch their employee Günther as the managerial agent. The Chee Hsin Company also arranged with the Danish F.L. Smidth Company, the Jiangnan Cement Plant's foremost creditor, to send someone to guard the plant. They sent Bernhard Sindberg.

Prior to mid-November 1937, Sindberg had been the assistant to renowned British journalist Pembroke Stephens, who was killed in a bomb blast that also injured Sindberg (Chen, Zhang, and Dai n.d., 333). It was at this time that F.L. Smidth found him. Sindberg wrote in a letter of December 1937: "I just got a new job. A Danish concrete plant built in Nanjing by F.L Smidth is right in the combat zone. I've been assigned to head there to raise the Danish flag and represent the company" (Chen, Zhang, and Dai n.d., 337).

On November 27, 1937, Karl Günther left Tangshan accompanied by a Chinese engineer. They first arrived in Shanghai, where they joined up with Sindberg. They then left Shanghai together, taking the long way around the combat zone in a northern loop, passing from Tongzhou to Yangzhou to Zhenjiang and finally to the Jiangnan Cement Plant at Xixia Mountain (Chen, Zhang, and Dai n.d., 270–271). The German embassy gave Günther a document demonstrating that he was to defend the Jiangnan Cement Plant: "Our citizen Günther has been ordered to proceed to the Jiangnan Cement Plant near Nanjing to guard the plant and defend the interests of the German company Siemssen & Co. We hereby declare that he is the bearer of this certificate" (Chen, Zhang, and Dai n.d., 267). Sindberg wrote an indemnity on his potential death before leaving: "I hereby declare myself willing to proceed to the Jiangnan Cement Plant at Qixia Mountain near Nanjing, where I will remain during wartime. I bear responsibility for the risks myself. If I am injured, maimed, or killed, I will not seek any claims against F.L. Smidth or any other party (except for reasonable medical fees)" (Dai n.d., 34).

Unlike these two, the Westerners remaining in the city received repeated notifications and warnings from their embassies. What's more, their colleagues, friends, and family members who had been living and working with them in Nanjing had all left the city in the name of safety; these Westerners stayed because they chose to do so. Rabe's mentality was typical.

Rabe was born in Hamburg in 1882. He began work in China in 1909. During the First World War, after China declared war on Germany, he became an overseas citizen of a hostile country in China. He wasn't imprisoned, but was subject to tight surveillance. When Germany lost the war, Rabe lost most of the assets he had accumulated over more than 10 years, and his entire family was repatriated to Germany. He later came back, and in 1931 began working for Siemens again, first in Beiping and then in the Nanjing offices of the company.

In his diary entry of September 21, Rabe wrote that he spent the entire previous night "thinking deeply about all aspects" of conditions in Nanjing. Rabe wrote frankly: "It wasn't because I love adventure that I returned here from the safety of Peitaiho, but primarily to protect my property and to represent Siemens's interests. Of course the company can't—nor does it—expect me to get myself killed here on its behalf" (Rabe EN, 5).

Rabe continued: "Our Chinese servants and employees, about 30 people in all including immediate families, have eyes only for their 'master.' If I stay, they will loyally remain at their posts to the end." Rabe knew this from his prior experience with wars in the north: "If I run, then the company and my own house will not just be left deserted, but they will probably be plundered as well." He then cited the most important reason: "Apart from that, and as unpleasant as that would be, I cannot bring myself for now to betray the trust these people have put in me. And it is touching to see how they believe in me, even the most useless people whom I would gladly have sent packing during peacetime" (Rabe EN, 5).

In mid-November, when Rabe had some luggage placed upon the Kutwo, his servants thought this meant he was going to leave Nanjing: "The servants walk about with large, terrified eyes, because they think I'll be leaving on the Kutwo as well. They'll be happy again once I explain straight out that I am definitely staying on in Nanking, come what may" (Rabe EN, 25). "The heroic spirit is contagious," Rabe wrote (Rabe CN, 8). He was not the only one affected by that heroism: "Herr Kröger, Herr Sperling, young Hirschberg, and Hatz, an Austrian engineer, all want to remain here to help me" (Rabe EN, 46).

On November 19, the news that Rabe had decided to stay in Nanjing got out, at which point the American missionaries planning to establish the Safety Committee asked him to join them. On November 23, the German Wolf Schenke, passing through Nanjing, paid Rabe a visit. He found that Rabe "still kept his old good humor," although added "but it seemed to me to be more of a gallows humor now." Schenke then wrote: "Rabe had not remained in Nanking for business reasons, but in order to erect a zone of refuge for the 200,000 noncombatants of Nanking, similar to that created by Pater Jacquinot in Shanghai." Schenke expressed skepticism about the plan to Rabe, who responded: "Well, after working here for 30 years and spending most of your life here, it's worth taking the risk" (Rabe EN, 30–31).

Among the Westerners who decided to remain, Americans comprised the majority. Prior to this time they had not been on close terms with Rabe or the other Germans. Rabe met Smythe for the first time only on November 19, 1937, after having been invited to Smythe's home for dinner (Rabe CN, 69). In fact, Rabe still did not know who Minnie Vautrin was as of December 26 (Rabe CN, 231). Paxton of the American embassy had read Japanese warnings to Vautrin and the other Americans, encouraging them to "leave for a few days," as Vautrin wrote in her diary on September 20. A few hours later on the same day she wrote a letter to Paxton saying: "we were staying on with our co-workers – that it was in such a time as this that we felt we could be of greatest help... We made it clear that we were staying at our own risk and that we did not in any way – no matter what might happen – want either our Government or the College to feel responsible for us." Vautrin detailed that on September 18 Smythe wrote "a long article for the World Call in which he condemns missionaries going out at the command of the Embassy or Statement [sic.] Department." He went so far as to use the word "running" to censure missionaries leaving the city. On the 20th she detailed that Smythe, still "not recovered from an illness," "is spending untold energy in organizing an ambulance corp for the Drum Tower Hospital." Wilson wrote in a letter of August 24th that he also thought of American doctors as examples for their Chinese colleagues, holding that if the Americans left, then the Chinese would too, and the hospital would have no choice but to close (Yale Divinity n.d.). Bates kept in close contact with the American embassy, because he was "not intending foolish risks," adding "there is so much of big importance to be done, and so few to do it" (Zhang 2010, vol. 1, 153). At the request of University of Nanking president Chen Yuguang, Bates became chairman of the University Emergency Committee, entrusted to protect university property along with Smythe, Riggs, and others.

Of course, the missionaries were also concerned about the Christian missions to which they had devoted themselves. Vautrin stressed on September 18: "Our greatest investments are in friendly relationships and in cooperation with the members of a young church – to leave at the time when we are most needed seems to me to be missing one of the greatest opportunities for service which comes to us." Forster was of a similar opinion: "Successfully implementing the neutral zone plan is the only thing we can do for our workers and congregations." With the "front pressing closer to the city every day and conditions growing worse," "this is the best opportunity to apply Christianity to practice in a concrete way" (Zhang 2005, 96–97).

The other missionaries had also lived in China for many years, some even having worked in regions swamped with warlord fighting and banditry. They had clear ideas of what could happen to them in this war, and signed their names on an American embassy notice confirming their willingness to accept the consequences of remaining in Nanjing. In signing, they were prepared to face "'any foreseeable tragedy' that might result from staying in Nanjing" (Zhu n.d., 250).

The words most mentioned in the documents left behind are "service" and "duty"; they were willing to do their utmost to save the lives of Chinese refugees: "They did not mention any heroic mettle that compelled them to stay. They stayed out of duty alone, to protect their churches' property, to give confidence to their Chinese colleagues, and to assist with the Safety Zone then being planned. This was a matter of hundreds of thousands of Chinese live" (Zhang 2005, 33).

During the Rape of Nanking, the efforts of the Westerners in the city helped save the lives of hundreds of thousands of Chinese refugees. Rabe's experiences during this time "made him become much more than an unremarkable Hamburg businessman, and wrote an indelible page in modern Chinese history" (Rabe CN, introduction 2). Can the same not be said about the other Westerners? The German Günther and the Dane Sindberg ran a shelter for over 10,000 refugees in the concrete factory they were guarding. Their actions were noble, although they did not come to Nanjing in the first place "from motivations of earthshaking nobility" (Dai n.d., 8). An analysis of the practical motivations that led the Westerners to stay in Nanjing does not negate their accomplishments. It is only by looking at the "uncommon" nature of these "common" people that we can understand why these Westerners – missionaries and Nazis alike – came to have such love for the Chinese people; this is the only way to see the glimmers of humanity through complex and often paradoxical historical phenomena.

3.2 Westerners and International Rescue Organizations

3.2.1 The International Committee for the Nanking Safety Zone

3.2.1.1 Organization of the International Committee for the Nanking Safety Zone

As early as August 12, 1937, some Western preachers and members of their congregations "got together to discuss how Christians in the city should face the national crisis." They established the "Women's and Children's Relief Committee," which on September 26 was expanded into the "Nanking Christian War Relief Committee" (NCWRC) with 12 executive committee members appointed on October 3: "University of Nanking President Dr. Chen Yuguang serving as chairman, and Nanking Theological Seminary President Handel Lee and Ginling Women's College President Dr. Wu Yifang (one of the very few renowned female educators in China at the time) serving as vice chairpersons." Also on the committee were Han Lih-wu [Hang Liwu], Mills, Smythe, Vautrin, and others. The committee's job was: "(1) Relief work and work related to the Nanjing University Hospital, which was tasked with saving the lives of common citizens injured in air raids, and providing relief to refugees from the fighting in Shanghai who arrived by Xiaguan. (2) Public communication work, raising funds for relief expenses, and informing Chinese friends abroad of matters in the city" (Zhu n.d., 137–138).

As fighting spread, on November 7 Vautrin wrote that the NCWRC formed a "new section, called Reception for Wounded Soldiers at Hsia Kwan," with "Pastor Chu" of the Y.M. church at Xiaguan and John Magee leading its work. Later, Minister Ernest Forster of the American Episcopal Mission returned from Yangzhou to Nanjing, where he became involved with this work (Zhang 2005, 92).[17]

By mid-November, 1937, faced with extremely severe conditions, all departments of the nationalist government in Nanjing were making preparations for evacuation. How to help refugees in the city through "the most difficult time" became the question for Vautrin and other missionaries in the city. Not long before, the Shanghai Safety Zone had been successfully established by Father Robert Jacquinot de Besange. The 59 year-old Jacquinot was a Catholic priest from France, a professor in Aurora University, director of the China International Famine Relief Commission, member of the International Relief Foundation Committee, and director of the Shanghai International Relief Committee's Relief Group, as well as Refugee Committee Chairman of the Shanghai International Committee of the Red Cross; he devoted his life to charitable and relief work in China. During the "January 28 Incident" of fighting in Shanghai between the Japanese and Chinese in 1932, Jacquinot risked his life running into combat zones rescuing wounded soldiers and refugees, and had his right arm amputated after having it injured in an explosion in Zhabei.

After the outbreak of the Battle of Shanghai in 1937, Jacquinot and others pushed for the establishment of a safety zone for refugees in the south of the city. He first worked for informal approval from charitable organizations in the city as well as the British, French, American, and other consulates, after which he contacted Chinese and Japanese authorities. He received formal approval from both sides on November 5. Flags began to be erected to demarcate the now official Safety Zone on November 8, a task which was completed on November 9. Several hundreds of thousands of Chinese refugees were sheltered in the Zone during the fighting.

The Shanghai Safety Zone was a great inspiration for the community in Nanjing concerned with refugees' lives. Mills wrote in a letter to his wife: "With regard to the Safety Zone, we got our inspiration of course from the success of Father Jacquinot's zone in Shanghai. I have called it his zone, just because his name was so prominently associated with it" (Zhu n.d., 175). Miner Bates testified at the International Military Tribunal for the Far East about the founding of the International Committee: "Following the exemplar of the inter-

---

[17] Mrs. Forster returned with her husband to Nanjing, but she later evacuated to Hankou and then Hong Kong "to allow the men to work more freely."

national committee organized by Father Jacquinot a French priest in Shanghai, which was of considerable help to a large body of Chinese civilians there, we attempted in Nanking to do something similar in our very different condition" (Yang 2000).

Per the recollections of Han Lih-wu, it was he who first suggested establishing a safety zone: "I assembled about ten or twenty foreigners, and I said we should establish a refugee zone. They all agreed. They thought of this as a humanitarian action which they should approve" (Han Lih-wu n.d., n.p.). Han made his suggestion around November 16, 1937. On November 17, Vautrin, completely unaware of Han's suggestion, wrote a letter to a Mr. Peck in the American embassy containing a very similar proposal. Peck replied: "The Embassy would be very welcoming of such a center if it were founded, and would notify Japanese military authorities about it" (Wang 2005a, n.p.). Around 5 p.m. that day, the Americans Mills, Bates, and Smythe paid a visit to Peck's home regarding the founding of a safety zone. Peck spoke of his concerns about the plan from his perspective as a member of the staff of the American embassy: "If it came to be known that the founding of a non-combatant zone was thought up by Americans (and this may come to pass), the result would be that if either country broke the agreement, then the person who came up with this plan would without a doubt be hated by everyone. So he suggested that the people proposing and implementing this plan should adopt a faultless method to avoid coming under censure for the plan's failure, and that Chinese military authorities should themselves attempt to participate in the plan." Peck further noted that the American embassy would have to have assurance of Chinese official approval of the plan before notifying Japanese authorities of the safety zone.

Mills and the others agreed with Peck's advice. Mills further suggested: if the ambassador was planning to meet with Dr. Sun Ke and others that evening, "it would be a good idea for him to try to feel out this issue." Before leaving, Mills and the others said that some of them would return the following day to continue discussing the safety zone plan (Zhang 2006b, 84–85). It is thus clear that "the founding of the Safety Zone wasn't the idea of one person, but rather an idea at which both Chinese and foreigners arrived by coincidence." In any event, Han Lih-wu was one of the first people involved in the plan (Wang 2005a).

On November 19, Rabe wrote: "An International Committee has been formed, made up primarily of American doctors from Kulou Hospital and professors from Nanking University, all missionaries. They want to try to create a refugee camp, or better, a neutral zone inside or outside the city, where noncombatants can take refuge in case the city comes under fire. Since word has got around that I intend to stay on, I was approached about whether I would like to join the committee. I agreed and at dinner this evening at Professor Smythe's home, I made the acquaintance of a good number of the American members" (Rabe EN, 25).

On November 21, a report on preparations being made for the Nanjing Refugee Zone signed by Han Lih-wu, Mills, Bates, and Smythe was presented to the Nanjing municipal government. (Huang Huiying: 157). The next day, before the German ambassador left the city, Rabe introduced Committee Secretary Smythe to him, and asked for his approval for the Safety Zone plan. The American and British embassies had already assented by that time. At this time "there were no more French or Italians in the city, so there were no representatives of those two countries on the committee." Bates later testified to the International Military Tribunal for the Far East: "The committee was organized at first with a Danish chairman, with German, British, and American members" (Yang 2000, 124). Rabe was chosen as the committee's chairman at a meeting that night. The committee drafted a cable of recommendations for the Safety Zone, signed by 15 members, which it then dispatched to the American consulate in Shanghai, which then forwarded the cable to the Japanese embassy: "The committee decides that the text of the telegram should not be published before the Japanese ambassador in Shanghai has received it" (Rabe EN, 28).

On November 26, Han Lih-wu told Rabe that the "generalissimo has expressed assent." (Rabe CN: 82). That same day, another report, this time signed by more than 10 members of the International Committee, was submitted to the Nanjing municipal government, raising some key issues in the founding of the Safety Zone: "The extent of the Safety Zone is planned to be: the eastern border running from Xinjiekou to the Shanxi Road Plaza along Zhongshan North Road; the northern border running from the Shanxi Road Plaza to Xikang Road; the Western border running from Xikang Road southward along Shanghai Road to the intersection with Hankou Road; and the southern border running from Hankou Road to Xinjiekou" (Huang n.d., 174).

Chinese authorities granted approval to the report, formally acknowledging the Safety Zone's founding, giving corresponding authorities to the International Committee within the Safety Zone, and offering support in personnel, funding, and materials (Huang n.d., 175–176). Rabe wrote on November 29: "At 6 o'clock the regular meeting at the British Cultural Club. The mayor formally announces the formation of the International Committee" (Rabe EN, 40). At this time the International Committee was composed of 15 German, American, British, and Danish nationals. On December 1, the German embassy turned over to the Committee the house at Number 5, Ninghai Road, formerly the home of Minister "Chang Chun" [Zhang Qun], who had put the house at the embassy's disposal. The next day, the International Committee established the house as its headquarters (Rabe CN, 93).[18]

The great support from Chinese authorities was a boost in morale, but the International Committee felt "it was very difficult to resolve to continue the work of founding a safety zone" as they had not "received a reply from Japanese authorities" (Rabe CN, 95). On December 2, Father Jacquinot sent a cable from Shanghai reading: "Japanese authorities have duly noted request for safety zone but veto it" (Rabe EN, 46). On December 5, the American consulate in Shanghai forwarded the Japanese embassy's formal reply:

> 4. Although the Japanese government acknowledges the noble motivations of the leadership responsible for this recommendation, under such circumstances, the Japanese government cannot take responsibility for ensuring that the described zone will not be subject to attacks or bombing.
>
> 5. You may construe the following conditions as an expression of our attitude: the Japanese army does not intend to launch attacks on locations not used by the Chinese military or in areas where Chinese troops and military installations have not been deployed (Rabe CN, 104).

The International Committee took the Japanese response as "tacit assent" for their plan. The Japanese "intentionally used some unclear wording, but it was enough for us to believe that the plan's implementation had been permitted" (Zhang 2005, 96).

In addition to external factors, the International Committee had some internal organizational issues to sort out. Of the 15 who comprised the committee at its outset, only eight remained after the city fell. Per one record, before the fall of the city, "the one Danish member and three of the British members were taken away by their companies or governments" (Yang and Zhang n.d., 624). On April 25, 1938, American Foreign Service Officer Cabot Coville met with the British businessman Shields, previously a member of the International Committee, aboard the HMS Scarab. Shields told Coville: "The Nanking Safety Zone is a mistake" (Zhu n.d., 88). His criticism of the Safety Zone was, in a way, an affirmation of the great efforts made by the International Committee in the face of enormous difficulties and the achievements they made anyway.

---

18 This being the private residence of Chinese Foreign Minister Zhang Qun (written Chang Chun at the time), which Zhang gave to the German embassy to use, and which in turn the German embassy turned over to the International Committee.

3.2.1.2 Preparations and initial operations of the Safety Zone before and after the city's fall

At the beginning of preparations for the Safety Zone, the Committee's members assumed that it would be a safe zone sheltered from fire from both sides for Chinese citizens during the fighting for the city, and that it would serve during the "power vacuum" as authority over the city transitioned between regimes. It was assumed that after the fighting ended, the winning side would be responsible for managing the city, and the Safety Zone's mission would be over.

The first task to which the International Committee set itself was to solicit support from the embassies of all the members. The day Rabe was elected chairman, German Ambassador Trautmann was preparing to leave Nanjing by boat. Prior to leaving, Rabe managed to introduce Committee Secretary Smythe to Trautmann: "The German ambassador, to whom I introduce Dr. Smythe shortly before he leaves to board his ship, gives his consent to the text of a telegram to be sent to the Japanese ambassador by way of the American consulate general in Shanghai, which has a wireless" Before that, the Committee had already gotten "the permission of the English and American ambassadors" (Rabe EN, 27–28).

As stated above, Chinese authorities also supported the Safety Zone's establishment. Upon receiving a formal reply from the Japanese, the International Committee sent a cable back to the Japanese authorities on December 6, expressing their attitude regarding continuing the work of establishing the Safety Zone: "1. The International Committee has received the reply of the Japanese authorities, and has already recorded its contents. Chinese authorities are currently reducing the number of military installations within the Zone and also evacuating military personnel from it. The Committee has begun to demarcate the Zone with flags. The pattern of the flags is a white background with a red cross inside a red circle (the red circle symbolizes the Safety Zone). Large banners with the same insignia are also being hung vertically on corners and on the roofs of buildings inside the Zone. 2. Owing to the difficulties presented by the gradual retreat of the remaining Chinese military personnel within the Safety Zone and the flooding into the Safety Zone of tens of thousands of refugees and other ordinary citizens, the Safety Zone Committee hopes that the Japanese will not bomb the Zone during the preparation period or after its establishment, or launch any form of attack on the Zone. The International Committee will do its utmost to complete the work that has been entrusted to it. 3. The International Committee has learned of a promise made by Japanese authorities in paragraph 5 of their response; for this we express gratitude. The Japanese promise is as follows: the Japanese army does not intend to launch attacks on locations not used by the Chinese military or in areas where Chinese troops and military installations have not been deployed. 4. The International Committee hereby informs Japanese authorities that 15 to 20 foreigners are voluntarily assuming management of the Safety Zone. The continued presence of these foreigners in the city demonstrates that the assurances made by both Chinese and Japanese authorities regarding the Safety Zone are honest and believable, and that the Committee will resolutely bear responsibility for fully implementing all stipulations regarding the Safety Zone" (Rabe CN, 109–110). No reply came from the Japanese this time. The International Committee took this silence as tacit approval of the contents of their cable.[19]

On December 3, the Safety Zone Committee submitted a request to Chinese military authorities to vacate their personnel from the Safety Zone. General Tang Shengzhi, commander of the Nanjing Defense Garrison, had previously "promised us that all military personnel and installations would be kept out of the refugee zone," but "we now learn that three new trenches and/or foundations for antiaircraft batteries are being dug in the Zone. I inform General Tang's emissaries that I will resign my office and disband the International Committee if work is not stopped at once. Written promises to respect my wishes are provided, but I am informed that carrying them out may take some time" (Rabe EN, 48–49). That day Tang wrote to Rabe promising to remove all military personnel and installations from the zone (Rabe CN, 106).

On December 4, the Safety Zone Committee learned that "Soldiers continue to build new trenches and install military telephones inside the Safety Zone" (Rabe EN, 49). On December 5, Rabe, Bates and Sperling paid a visit to General Tang, "in order to get his consent to have all military personnel and establishments removed from the Zone at once. Imagine our amazement when General Tang tells us that this is quite impossible, that at best it will be another two weeks before the military can vacate the Zone. A nasty blow" (Rabe EN, 50). On December 6, Rabe wrote another letter to Tang. After "expressing sincere gratitude for your approval of the Committee's work and support for assistance of the refugees and ordinary citizens of Nanjing," Rabe listed out the "detailed assurances" Tang had "made for matters concerning the Safety Zone": 1. no new military installations, trenches, or other bunkers would be established in the Safety Zone, nor will any artillery be left in the Zone; 2. once the Safety Zone was clearly demarcated, orders would be issued prohibiting all military personnel from entering the Safety Zone; and 3. all military personnel belonging

---

19 By this time the International Committee had already established communications channels with Japanese authorities via Western consulates in Shanghai as facilitated through Father Jacquinot. This cable was most likely received by Japanese authorities, yet they did not respond.

to command centers or other departments would be gradually withdrawn from the Safety Zone. Rabe reminded Tang that "the fate of many Chinese people depends on the Safety Zone" (Rabe CN, 110–111). On December 8, Bates reported the presence of Chinese soldiers in the Safety Zone to Rabe (Rabe CN, 118). An agreement was finally reached on December 10 with Chinese military authorities regarding the southwestern boundary of the Safety Zone near Wutaishan. That afternoon Vautrin wrote that she "went to our west boundary to help put up Safety Zone flags. The hope is that all military will be out by tomorrow and that telegrams to that effect can be sent to both parties."

On the day of the Japanese occupation, December 13, Rabe wrote: "Returning to headquarters, I find a great throng at the entrance. Unable to escape by way of the Yangtze, a large number of Chinese soldiers have found their way here while we were gone. They all let us disarm them and then vanish into the Zone. Sperling stands at the main entrance with an earnest, stern look on his face and his Mauser pistol—without any bullets in it, by the way—in his hand and sees to it that the weapons are counted and placed in neat piles, since we plan to hand them over to the Japanese later on" (Rabe EN, 67).

The Committee negotiated while also proceeding with all areas of work with great intensity. On December 1, the International Committee held a meeting in Pingcang Alley, where Rabe revealed: "We assign various tasks and put together a list of the people involved." Mayor Ma Chaojun attended the meeting at the head of a throng of assistants, and promised to deliver to the Committee "30,000 sacks of rice and 10,000 sacks of flour" (Rabe EN, 44). The Committee established the Safety Zone Management Commission to handle the various issues related to operating the zone. The International Committee was composed of several sub-committees, with over 20 members, Chinese and foreign, in charge of concrete tasks. By December 4, Rabe wrote: "The refugees have slowly begun to move into the Safety Zone" (Rabe EN, 49).

On December 7, the Committee published the Safety Zone's rules at its daily press meeting at 6 p.m. The Committee also issued its "Letter to the People of Nanjing" to inform the press of the reasons for the founding of the Safety Zone as well as relevant details thereof:

Letter to the People of Nanjing

Not long ago, during the Battle of Shanghai, the International Committee there made recommendations to both Chinese and Japanese authorities that a Safety Zone be established in the south of the city. This was approved by both sides. Chinese authorities promised that Chinese military personnel would not enter the appointed area. Since there were no troops stationed there, the Japanese agreed not to attack it. This agreement was respected by both parties. Despite terror and destruction taking place in other parts of the city, this Safety Zone was spared, along with the lives of tens of thousands of people.

Now the International Committee of Nanking has made a similar recommendation, the Safety Zone here being contained within the following boundaries: "The eastern boundary running along Zhongshan Road from Xinjiekou to the Shanxi Road Plaza; the northern boundary running from the Shanxi Road Plaza along Xikang Road (the southwest corner of the new residential zone); the western boundary from Xikang Road southward to the corner with Hankou Road (the southwest corner of the new residential zone); and the southern border from the intersection of Hankou Road and Shanghai Road to the original starting point of Xinjiekou." This zone's boundaries have been demarcated with flags. There are red crosses inside of red circles on these flags, as well as the three characters "*nan min qu*" [Refugee Zone].[20]

...

International Committee for the Nanking Safety Zone

December 8, 26th year of the ROC (Rabe CN, 114 – 116)

On December 9, Japanese "front-line troops have already occupied areas near Purple Mountain and Yuhuatai, and are drawing gradually closer to the city" (Wang 2005b, 147). Tension in the city drove remaining residents to flee in droves to the security of the Safety Zone: "The streets of the Safety Zone are flooded with refugees loaded down with bundles" (Rabe EN, 57). The International Committee then issued "Safety Measures for the Safety Zone":

1. Nowhere is absolutely safe in wartime (even in the international concessions of Shanghai, more than 1,000 people died from stray bullets, anti-aircraft fire, artillery shrapnel, bombing by the Japanese, and accidental bombing by Chinese fighters).

2. We must remember that the Japanese have never promised not to attack or bomb our Safety Zone.

3. The Japanese have promised only to not intentionally attack the Safety Zone given that there are no Chinese soldiers or military installations there.

4. So we urgently call on residents to hide in dugouts or basements during air raids (tile-roofed houses can also prevent harm from anti-aircraft shrapnel).

5. If the city comes under artillery attack or bombing, everybody who can should hide in dugouts or basements.

6. Even if only the sounds of rifles or machine guns are audible in the city, you should still hide in air raid dugouts or basements, or seek protection behind enclosing walls. While shooting is active, people inside brick houses should not remain near windows.

---

20 In Chinese the Safety Zone was often referred to as the *nanmin qu* or "Refugee Zone," but always as the "Safety Zone" in English.

7. If a person is on the street when an air raid, artillery shelling, or machine gun fire commences, and that person cannot quickly reach a safe place, that person should seek shelter in a ditch or behind a wall if possible.

8. If fighting breaks out in the city or in nearby areas, pedestrians should not walk in groups, but should separate to the extent possible.

9. Treatment can be sought for the wounded at the Gulou Hospital. For ambulances, call 31624.

10. Please call the following numbers in case of a fire:

Dafangxiang fire station: 31058

Gulou fire station: 31093

International Committee for the Nanking Safety Zone (Rabe CN, 122–123)

Under such chaotic conditions, the Committee was unable to complete all planned preparations for the Safety Zone, despite doing their utmost.

On December 13, the Japanese army entered Nanjing through the Guanghua Gate and other places. As they entered, actual control of the city changed hands, and the International Committee was faced with a new situation. In the "Important Notice to Refugees in Shelters" issued that day, the Committee asked refugees to protect themselves and not resist any Japanese soldiers entering the Safety Zone: "1. We urgently call on everyone to not linger on streets to the extent possible. 2. In the most dangerous times, we suggest that you hide in buildings or in places where you can't be seen. 3. We must note that the Refugee Zone was established for refugees. We note with regrets that the Refugee Zone is not authorized to provide protection to Chinese soldiers. 4. If the Japanese come to inspect or tour the Refugee Zone, you must let them through. Do not put up any resistance to them" (Rabe CN, 136).

"Thank God the worst is past!" (Rabe CN, 133). That was Rabe's feeling the night before the city fell. Almost all the foreigners in Nanjing at the time felt the same way; some were even grateful for the shortness of the fighting (Zhang 2006a).

On December 13, Rabe and the others risked their lives by leaving the Safety Zone and heading in the direction of the Japanese attack to make contact, but the officers they encountered were all of low rank. On December 14, the International Committee drafted a letter to the Japanese commander. Rabe and the others took a translator along and "met with six Japanese officers," who told them to "contact Army General Tani Hisao, who will arrive tomorrow or the day after" (Rabe CN, 137–138).

On the afternoon of the 14th, some members of the Japanese diplomatic corps returned to Nanjing close on the heels of the invading army (Zhang 2007, 407).

On the 15th, Fukuda, attaché to the Japanese embassy, paid a visit to Rabe to "discuss the details of our agenda. Mr. Fukuda agrees that it is obviously both in our interest and that of the Japanese authorities to have the electricity works, waterworks, and telephone system repaired as quickly as possible." Rabe agreed to offer help to Fukuda in these matters (Rabe EN, 69).

Fukuda's visit demonstrates that the Japanese recognized the difference of the Safety Zone from the rest of the city, and to a certain extent acknowledged the status of the International Committee. The next day, Japanese Consul-General Okazaki paid a visit to Rabe asking him to note that though the Japanese had not acknowledged the International Committee, "it is being treated as though it has been acknowledged" (Rabe CN, 151). On the morning of the 16th, the Japanese embassy's translator Kikuchi wrote a letter to Rabe informing him that the Japanese were going to search the Safety Zone for Chinese soldiers (Rabe CN, 145–146). This move demonstrated that the Japanese de facto acknowledged that the International Committee was in charge of the Safety Zone, and as such needed to communicate with the Committee officially. This allowed the Committee to serve as a buffer to refugees in the Safety Zone, to a certain extent.

The organization of the International Committee for the Nanking Safety Zone was based on that of Jacquinot's organization in Shanghai, with some changes based on actual conditions in Nanjing at the time. On December 3, the International Committee passed a resolution on the areas of responsibility of members of the Safety Zone Management committee:

Organization of Safety Zone Administration

I. Officers:

1. Chairman of International Committee: John H. D. Rabe.
2. Secretary of International Committee: Lewis S. C. Smythe.
3. Director: George Fitch.
4. 2nd Director: Dr. Han Liwu.
5. Treasurer: Christian Kröger.
6. Chief of Chinese Secretariat: Dean Tang.

II. Commissions:

1. Inspector General: Eduard Sperling.
2. Food Commission: Han Hsiang-Lin, Chairman.
    Hubert L. Sone, Associate.
3. Housing Commission: Wang-Ting, Chairman.
    Charles Riggs, Associate. Charles Gee.
4. Sanitation commission: Shen Yü-shu, Chairman.
    Dr. C. S. Trimmer, Associate.
5. Transport Control: E. L. Hirschberg, Chairman.
    R. R. Hatz, Associate (Rabe EN, 253)

Many Chinese participated in the various committees actually controlling the Safety Zone; these worked under the guidance of the Westerners. Statistical reports demonstrate that over 1,500 Chinese people directly participated in settlement and relief work in the Safety Zone (Zhang 2006b, 391).

The day after occupying the city, the Japanese army began to search the Safety Zone. On December 13, 16th Division Commander Nakajima Kesago wrote: "We have found almost no enemy soldiers in the city. There is only a refugee camp in the region of the 9th Division, where most are women, children, and old people." He inferred that "It's not difficult to imagine that there are certainly many defeated soldiers now in plainclothes there" (Wang 2005b, 279). The 9th Division occupied the part of the city containing the Safety Zone, and discovered that the streets surrounding the Safety Zone were "covered with Chinese military uniforms," as recorded in the diary of Mizutani So (Wang 2006a, 378). From 6 to 8 p.m. on the 13th, wrote Ike Mataichi, 9th Division troops "proceeded to the international refugee zone to sweep for remnant enemy forces" (Wang 2006a, 133).

Not only was it impossible to prevent the Japanese army from sweeping the Safety Zone and carrying off Chinese men suspected of being "remnant enemy forces," but it was also difficult to effectively stop roaming Japanese soldiers from raping Chinese women.

The International Committee did possess the municipal government's management functions within the Safety Zone, but it had not been sufficiently prepared. Rabe wrote: "Dr. Smythe announces that the police, who are now nominally under our control, have arrested a 'one-item thief' and want to know what to do with him. The incident provokes general amusement, since until now we hadn't even thought about our having to take the place of the courts. We sentence the thief to death, then pardon him and reduce his sentence to 24 hours in jail, and then for lack of a jail, simply let him go" (Rabe EN, 61). Later certain "bad elements" were discovered in the various refugee shelters, smoking opium, gambling, stirring up trouble, and generally harming the general order; all that could be done was to "toss them out" (Rabe CN, 302). Fortunately, this problem was not acute while the Safety Zone existed, and "no more than six of the refugees were arrested for cause" (Zhang 2006b, 393–394).

On the whole, the "safety functions established" under the Safety Zone plan "did not play the role they should have played; housing and relief functions became elevated to the highest position" (Yang 2000, 137).

3.2.2 Nanjing branch of the International Committee of the Red Cross and other organizations

Other Westerners were involved in relief organizations outside of the International Committee for the Nanking Safety Zone at the same time. These organizations were coordinated in their relief work, but each had its own focus, and they all played an important role during the Rape of Nanking.

3.2.2.1 Nanjing branch of the International Committee of the Red Cross

In the last few days leading up to the Japanese occupation, John Magee and others were planning the establishment of a Red Cross organization in Nanjing, hoping to, as quoted in the *New York Times*, "do our utmost in the final minutes to protect the several thousand wounded Chinese soldiers in the military hospitals of Nanjing" (Yang and Zhang n.d., 425). On December 5, the small group organized by Magee sent a cable to the Red Cross leadership in Hankou, "requesting details on how to organize such a branch." Magee planned to "build a localized Red Cross body" and "send a request by telegram to Japanese military authorities that they acknowledge the organization in 12 military hospitals in Nanjing." Magee was attempting to place the hospitals treating wounded soldiers under the auspices of Western-led charitable groups. His plan was approved by the director of the Chinese Ministry of War's Department of Medicine, but no response was received from the Japanese (Yang and Zhang n.d., 425).

The tempestuous Rabe criticized Magee for his circumspection: "What a shame! In his shoes I wouldn't boggle. If you can do some good, why hesitate? Consent is sure to arrive in due course" (Rabe EN, 58).

A Chinese military envoy approached the International Committee on December 12, asking "if we could accept wounded soldiers." Smythe and the rest "discussed the matter and immediately decided to found a branch of the International Red Cross" (Zhang 2005, 226). Finally, on the morning of December 13, after the Japanese had begun entering the city but before they had reached the Safety Zone, a branch was founded. Rabe wrote: "Upon arrival at committee headquarters, it takes us ten minutes to found a branch of the International Red Cross, whose board of directors I join. Our good John Magee, who has been mulling over the same idea for weeks now, is chairman" (Rabe EN, 65). Ernest Forster, an Episcopalian minister like Magee, served as secretary, and 17 others served as committee members, including Rabe, Bates, and Vautrin (Zhang 2005, 147–148).[21]

As only a small number of Westerners inhabited the city at the time of its fall, there was a great overlap of membership of the International Committee for the Safety Zone and the Red Cross committee, with most Westerners playing important roles on both. We can also ascertain from Secretary Forster's letters that the Red Cross Committee even shared an address with the International Committee, at Number 5 Ninghai Road (Rabe CN, 144).

On December 15, Forster wrote a letter to the Japanese embassy: "There are presently many wounded soldiers and civilians. To respond to the difficulties this situation has presented, we have established a Nanjing branch of the International Red Cross. We have taken the necessary steps to ensure that our branch will be acknowledged by the International Red Cross Society in Shanghai and the Chinese Red Cross." In the letter Forster also asks that the Japanese embassy help the Nanjing Red Cross branch "receive approval from Japanese military authorities in Nanjing, to help us carry out our humanitarian work" (Rabe CN, 144).

Most of the funding for the Nanjing Red Cross branch came from Chinese sources. As the city was falling, a Chinese military officer donated 23,000 yuan to Magee, who used these funds specifically to care for wounded soldiers (Rabe CN, 123), although it was difficult to access these funds for a long time as the Japanese sealed off the city (Rabe CN, 536). The branch also received considerable amounts of help from charitable organizations in Shanghai once it was able to contact the outside world (Rabe CN, 508).

On the afternoon of December 12, Magee "went to the Ministry of Foreign Affairs where I found many wounded soldiers but no medical officers or nurses." Magee scrambled to make arrangements, and "by evening" of the 13th, "the hospital for wounded soldiers began to take on some semblance of order as the hundred or so dressers had begun to get to work" (Zhang 2005, 148).

Once in the city, Japanese soldiers commenced a city-wide search for Chinese men suspected of being soldiers. Ike Mataichi wrote that they discovered "many wounded soldiers in the Red Cross Hospital (Ministry of Foreign Affairs)" (Wang 2006a, 133). Magee was obstructed from entering the hospital for wounded soldiers in the former Ministry of Foreign affairs on December 14. A month after the city fell, the Japanese still didn't let Magee inspect the hospital for wounded soldiers. Consequently, Magee wrote a letter of protest to the Japanese

---

[21] This list taken from the list of members of the International Red Cross Society Nanjing Branch. Please note that Munroe-Faure was on the list but "boarded an English naval vessel at the last minute having been ordered to leave the city."

embassy on January 15, 1938 (Rabe CN, 344). Actual conditions inside the hospital at this time were deplorable. On the pretext of going out to do some shopping, a female nurse from the wounded soldiers hospital in the Ministry of Foreign Affairs made her way to the Red Cross Committee, where she made a report: "The daily ration, she says, is just three little bowls of rice broth. The patient was beaten, and when he asked, once the beating was over, if they had beaten him because he was hungry, the Japanese took him out into the courtyard and bayoneted him. The nurses watched this execution from the windows" (Rabe EN, 142). Conditions in the Red Cross hospital in the Ministry of War building were even worse: "There were still about 200 patients in the Ministry of War hospital a week ago. Previously, three female nurses from the Ministry of Foreign proceeded to the hospital once daily escorted by Japanese soldiers. The last time that happened was one week ago. Conditions there are deplorable. The wounded lie directly on the ground. Nobody is there to care for them except one Chinese doctor. The nurses come only to help change bandages" (Rabe CN, 414–415).

From the perspective of the Japanese soldiers, the fates of those wounded Chinese soldiers were sealed the moment the city fell. Japanese soldier Hayashi Masaaki recorded their attitudes toward wounded Chinese soldiers: "Our troops entered Chinese government buildings before the first month of the lunar year. There were over 200 wounded Chinese soldiers in there, regaining their strength day by day. What should be done about these guys? If they recover, they'll obviously want to return to their units. What should our friendly forces do about them? It's against international precedent to kill wounded soldiers. If they recover, though, then we can walk them to the shore of the Yangtze, point our guns at them, and send them off into their long sleep. If they don't recover, then they'll die all on their own. These miserable Chinese wounded soldiers are truly pitiable… There are also a few thousand wounded Chinese soldiers in the Red Cross hospital. Many of them are faking wounds. Now they've all fallen into our hands" (Wang 2005b, 631).

Magee and Forster sent wounded refugees with no money to pay for treatment to the Gulou Hospital, where they were treated free of charge; the Red Cross then paid the hospital. The accounting records of the hospital demonstrate that more than 5,000 people were treated in third-class hospital wards free of charge every month during this time, all paid for by Magee's Red Cross (Rabe CN, 558). Jiang Gonggu writes that with help from that hospital, Magee founded an emergency hospital behind the Gulou Hospital, "as a place for treatment and shelter for wounded civilians and soldiers" (Zhang 2005, 70). Many Chinese military doctors, who had previously worked in the hospital for wounded soldiers, now served here (Zhang 2005, 155).

Once Sindberg made contact with the Westerners inside the city, Magee ventured out to inspect the Jiangnan Concrete Plant, where he helped establish a basic hospital (Dai Yuanzhi n.d., 143).

3.2.2.2 Gulou [Drum Tower] Hospital

The Gulou Hospital was founded by the Canadian missionary Dr. William Edward Macklin with assistance from the U.S.-based Church of Christ, under the name Nanjing Christian Hospital. In 1914, it was merged with the University of Nanking, and was renamed the University of Nanking Gulou Hospital. The Western community referred to it as the University Hospital of Nanking. As of 1936, there were 22 doctors and 88 nurses employed in the hospital (University of Nanking Bulletin n.d.).

The Central Hospital of Nanjing was severely damaged during Japanese bombing raids in October 1937, at which time that hospital's director Liu Ruiheng [Hengry Liu] asked for assistance from the Gulou Hospital (Zhang Sheng 2010, vol. 1, 121).

Prior to the city's fall, the majority of the hospital's staff was evacuated, but a few Americans remained behind. Forster wrote: "The Nanking University Hospital is carrying on valiantly with a small staff of two foreign doctors, one Chinese doctor, and two foreign and several Chinese nurses. They are about worn to a frazzle through pressure of work and lack of personnel, since the Chinese superintendent and about 49 other doctors and nurses connected with the hospital deserted and went to Hankow for safety" (Zhang 2005, 132).

The night before the city fell, the hospital recruited some new nurses and workers. Vautrin wrote on November 26, 1937 that she even recommended some: "All the nurses from University Hospital have evacuated leaving 200 patients for others to take care of. McCallum has become business manager and is taking on people. I have recommended one nurse, two amahs and one errand boy to him today."

The Gulou Hospital was located on the edge of the Safety Zone. Magee wrote that upon discovering Chinese soldiers building military installations in the streets near the hospital, Dr. Wilson and others entered negotiations with Chinese military officials, asking that they not allow fighting to break out near the edges of the Safety Zone. Hospital staff also moved the drugs stored in its street-facing pharmacy, to avoid danger (Zhang 2005, 147). In the end, there was no fighting in the vicinity of the hospital, but occupying Japanese soldiers still managed to cause unexpected catastrophes in the hospital.

We get a glimpse of conditions in the hospital from a letter of protest Wilson wrote to the Japanese embassy: "Three soldiers entered the hospital compound by the rear door and tramped up and down the hospital corridors. This was at approximately eight P.M. Miss Hynds, a 63-year old American nurse, met them and accompanied them. They took her watch in spite of her protestations that it was her own. They also took several (six) other watches and three fountain pens. Two of them then departed and the third disappeared without leaving... At nine fifteen my attention was called to the fact that a Japanese soldier was in the nurses' dormitory. I went there with a lantern and found one soldier in a room with six nurses. He was partially dressed and I found that he had been in bed with three of the nurses before I arrived" (Rabe CN, 171).

Wilson's protest achieved no results whatsoever. As was the case for other places in the Safety Zone, the Gulou Hospital was long the target of constant harassment by Japanese soldiers. Only the appearance of a Westerner was sufficient to drive them off. Wilson, McCallum, and others were subject to threats of violence from Japanese soldiers when trying to drive them away. McCallum was even shot at (though not hit), and had his neck wounded by a bayonet.

Atrocities committed by Japanese soldiers also led to increases in the numbers of wounded refugees, as demonstrated by hospital records. One case attended to by Dr. Wilson involved a 13-year old girl: "When the Japanese came to the city on the 13th she and her father and mother were standing at the entrance to their dugout watching them approach. A soldier stepped up, bayonetted the father, shot the mother, and slashed open the elbow of the little girl, giving her a compound fracture. She has no relatives and was not brought to the hospital for a week. She is already wondering what to do when she has to leave. Both the father and mother were killed" (Zhang 2005, 339–340). Wilson went on to say that on December 15, 30 people entered the hospital but nobody checked out (Zhang 2005, 334), and "About ten of the hundred and fifty cases are medical and obstetrical and the rest are surgical" (Zhang 2005, 335). McCallum wrote that of patients brought to the hospital after the city's fall, "nearly all came in with bayonet or bullet wounds" (Zhang 2005, 207). "We have every bed filled," wrote Wilson of his hospital during the height of the uncontrolled rampage (Zhang 2005, 340).

Most Nanjing residents with economic means fled the city before the fall. After the fall, the hospital, already in dire straits, fell into financial crisis. Most remaining residents were from the poorest strata, unable to pay for their treatment. McCallum wrote that "the most severely wounded" were sent to the hospital during the period of Japanese violence, and the hospital had no choice but to take them (Zhang 2005, 205).

John Magee's Red Cross did its utmost to help the wounded, and in so doing cooperated with the Gulou Hospital. Nevertheless, the hospital's financial reports demonstrated that: "The actual amount that the hospital receives from the relief fund for patients treated free of charge is about 80 cents per patient per day." The hospital's "budgets for the last two months were replenished or balanced by the local Red Cross branch." The Red Cross "gave us 5,000 yuan in January," but the hospital's "actual expenses were around 6,00" (Rabe CN, 558).

Even patients discharged from the hospital required an escort from a Westerner. McCallum wrote: "Everyone who leaves the hospital must be accompanied by a foreigner. I am the official bodyguard for even the police. We are so crowded that we are glad to get some out. So many have no place to go to and no money and no clothing that it is quite a problem. We cannot heal them and then kick them out to die of neglect or starvation, or to be killed or reinjured" (Zhang 2005, 207).

Once Western diplomats returned to Nanjing, the Gulou Hospital was able to contact the outside world and ask for help. Hospital materials were replenished to a certain extent by deliveries from American and British gunboats (Rabe CN, 548). What the hospital needed more than materials, however, was staff, especially Western doctors. Dr. Trimmer wrote in a cable: "Now mare than ever we need to increase our staff... Now we have only 14 qualified Chinese female nurses, one American nurse, three Chinese doctors with little schooling, and two American doctors. The hospital is now able to maintain only extremely limited clinical services owing to personnel shortages. The 60,000 people in our 25 refugee shelters have no clinical treatment services (repeat: none whatsoever)" (Rabe CN, 415–416).

3.2.2.3 The Jiangnan Concrete Plant Refugee Shelter

On December 28, 1937, Christian Kröger slipped past Japanese sentries and risked his life on a journey to inspect conditions outside the city walls. He wrote: "The Japanese troops, however, were not to be outdone, and continued to set fire to things on a grand scale, indiscriminately shooting farmers, women, and children out in the fields, all under the motto: 'Find the evil Chinese soldiers!' In the fields and beside the highway lay a lot of dead water buffalo, horses, and mules, already badly eaten by dogs, crows, and magpies. By day the farmers flee to the mountains with their few possessions, and only the old women and men remain behind. Even their lives are in danger: For an hour's drive I did not see a single live human being, not even in the larger villages. Everything has been burned down or is dead or flees the moment a car comes into view. At Thousand Buddha Mountain a large refugee camp had formed with over 10,000 people, all farmers from the vicinity. The Japanese soldiery doesn't let that stop them, either. Even here they randomly select young boys to be shot, rape the girls, and drunken Japanese soldiers make a sport of using bayonets to skewer or slash whomever they take a dislike to, especially where there is no medical help to be had. Temple images are stolen or destroyed, and even monks are in no way safe from such mistreatment. Confronted by two Europeans—a German, Dr. Günther, and a Dane—the terror has more or less come to halt outside the cement works. There, too, about 4,000 refugees have settled, bringing what they could carry" (Rabe EN, 144–145).

In truth, Sindberg and Günther hoisted German and Danish flags over the plant with the help of remaining employees on December 5, 1937. To avoid Japanese bombing, they painted an enormous Danish flag, 1,300 square meters per Sindberg's telling, inside the plant for pilots to identify from the sky (Chen, Zhang, and Dai n.d., 365). As word got out that the plant was being protected by foreigners, residents from the area as well as refugees flooded in from the outside started to seek shelter there. Magee wrote in a report on his trip to the plant that the shelter there was established at the periphery of the plant and divided into a northern and southern section. Refugees built their own straw huts along the plant's enclosing wall. There were about "25 managers" of the shelter, who managed the refugees under coordination by Sindberg and Günther (Zhang 2005, 173).

After Chinese forces withdrew from Qixia Mountain around December 9, the area fell under Japanese control. Günther and the others organized a plant security team, with sentries and patrols. The order given was that once a sentry sighted Japanese soldiers, he was to run to Günther and Sindberg on the second floor of the plant's club, at which point they would go talk with the Japanese soldiers. The two Western representatives of the plant "courteously received and socialized with" Japanese officers, leading to monthly expenses of "three to four hundred yuan" (Dai n.d., 80).

The Jiangnan Concrete Plant had a diesel generator, and so a radio receiver could be used. Misguided by propaganda being sent out over the radio, Sindberg mistakenly thought that order had been restored in Nanjing. On December 20, 1937, he and some others attempted to bring some wounded to the city for treatment. They encountered Japanese sentries, who would not let them proceed, so Sindberg sent the wounded back to the plant with the others in his party, and then proceeded toward the city alone. After walking a long distance, Sindberg boarded a Japanese truck, which finally bore him to the Safety Zone, where he met with Rabe and his crew. Sindberg later borrowed the car of Rabe's assistant Han Xianglin, which he drove back to the concrete plant (Rabe CN, 188).[22] After

---

22 Sindberg wrote a receipt for the borrowed car to Rabe in Rabe's name, but per Rabe's diary

this, Sindberg became the bridge connecting the Jiangnan Concrete Plant outside the city with the International Committee inside the city.

An article in a Danish newspaper of the time tells us that Sindberg made many trips into and out of the city, carrying with him reports of Japanese violence taking place in the vicinity of Qixia Mountain and petitions from locals; he even successfully brought monks from the Qixia Temple into and out of the city (Chen, Zhang, and Dai n.d., 340). On December 23, Sindberg entered the city with two petitions to Japanese authorities from the refugees of Qixia Mountain, signed by 17,000 refugees, asking that the authorities stop the harassment of their soldiers. That day Rabe sent a letter to Tanaka in the Japanese embassy with the petitions attached (Rabe CN, 217–218).

On February 3, 1938, Sindberg brought another letter from the abbot of the Qixia Temple, titled "To All Concerned Persons in the Name of Humanity," signed by "20 renowned local people." This letter listed out daily violent acts by Japanese soldiers and described conditions in the area of Qixia Mountain: "Eighty percent of the refugees here have lost everything. Their houses have been destroyed, their livestock slaughtered, their valuables looted to the last. Many women have also lost husbands, and children have lost fathers. Most young men have been killed by Japanese soldiers. Others are wounded and sick, laying up here without medicine. Nobody dares go out for fear of being killed, and we have only very small remaining food stores. Our farmers lack both water buffalo and seed rice. How will they plant their paddies this spring???" The refugees implored anyone who could help them in the most pitiful manner: "We beg you, no matter who you are, please just help us prevent this inhuman violence from happening again" (Rabe CN, 469–471). Sindberg also compiled cases of Japanese violence he had personally witnessed and submitted them to the International Committee (Zhang 1995, 84–89).

Upon learning of food shortages among the Westerners in the city, Sindberg brought some food into the city on all of his trips, including eggs, vegetables, and fowl. With Sindberg's donated foodstuffs, the Americans living at Number 3 Pingcang alley were able to celebrate with "Xmas dinner" (Rabe CN: 225). After posting someone to guard the refugees at his house, Rabe managed to "spend a quarter of an hour or so together with my American companions in adversity" (Rabe EN, 95).

It was through this channel that the International Committee became aware of rural conditions in the Qixia Mountain area, and began to provide assistance

---

we know that the car belonged to Han Xianglin. It is possible that Han lent it to Sindberg in Rabe's name.

to refugees there. On February 16, 1938, Sindberg and Magee made an on-site inspection of the refugee center in the Jiangnan Cement Plant. It had been more than two months since this area fell to the Japanese. On the way, Magee photographed the corpses scattered everywhere and widespread destruction between Nanjing and its eastern suburbs, as well as those wounded by Japanese violence and sent to the refugee hospital in the cement plant for treatment. Magee wrote a report about his trip, which he submitted to the International Committee (Zhang 2005, 172–175).

The efforts of Günther and Sindberg were without a doubt an enormous help to the refugees sheltering in the Jiangnan Cement Plant. They were applauded by both the refugees in the plant and the International Committee. Günther was even awarded the second-degree Red Cross medal by the German government (Dai n.d., 217).

3.2.3 Nanking International Relief Committee

Upon occupying the city, the Japanese tacitly acknowledge the Safety Zone's existence, but "soon the Japanese army came to believe that the Safety Zone's existence was obstructing their establishment of a 'new order' in Nanjing. Then Japanese authorities began "adopting various means to put pressure" on the Safety Zone, "until it was finally replaced by the 'Autonomous Government'" (Zhang Lianhong 2001, n.p.). Under pressure from the Japanese, the International Committee for the Nanking Safety Zone reorganized as the Nanking International Relief Committee, which continued to work to provide relief to refugees in the city.

3.2.3.1 Founding of the International Relief Committee

On December 16, the Japanese Consul-General paid a visit to Rabe to tell him that the Japanese government was going to treat the International Committee as though its status had been de facto acknowledged. On the 17^t, Rabe wrote a letter to Fukui of the Japanese embassy saying: "We hereby reiterate that we do not intend to continue fulfilling the half-administrative functions we have been fulfilling on behalf of the municipal government of Nanjing. We hope that you will assume these functions as soon as possible, to allow us to continue our work as a purely relief-oriented organization" (Rabe CN, 154). Rabe also wrote: "Mayor Ma of the Nanjing city government gave us nearly all administrative functions over the city during the special time, including management of police affairs, public organs, fire stations, rights to manage and allocate housing, food distribution, city sanitation, and so on… Of course, the plenary rights granted to us do not exceed the boundaries of the Safety Zone, and even in the Safety Zone we do not possess sovereign rights" (Rabe CN, 151–152).

The Japanese also perceived the presence of the Safety Zone and its administrative organizations within the city. As the International Committee was still of some use, it was most advantageous for the Japanese to adopt an attitude of cooperation (Rabe CN, 158). It is within such reality that Japanese authorities and the International Committee gave consent to the bottom line of mutual tolerance.

After the puppet autonomous regime had been founded, discussions were held within the International Committee, which decided that "we should find a way to continue the existence of the Committee." The standards for judging suggestions for cooperation were "whatever best serves the (International) Committee's goals or is most advantageous to the (International) Committee's goals" (Rabe CN, 269).

On January 6, 1938, a member of the Japanese embassy visited Rabe "to tell me that by decision of the military authorities our International Committee is to be dissolved and our supplies and moneys are to be taken over by the Autonomous Government Committee." "We have no objection to their taking over our work," wrote Rabe, but "I immediately protest any handing over of our assets and supplies" (Rabe EN, 114).

The Japanese did not disband the International Committee by force, but they did exert pressure and throw up obstacles wherever possible. On January 9, 1938, Wang Chengdian of the Autonomous Committee told Rabe that the Japanese no longer permitted the International Committee to sell rice to refugees (Rabe CN, 317). On the 10th, Major Ishida of the Japanese materials provision office refused to continue fulfilling the agreement already made and stopped rice sales to the International Committee (Rabe CN, 319). On the 13th, the Autonomous Committee took over the Safety Zone police force, which the municipal government had entrusted to the International Committee prior to evacuating. That afternoon, on the pretext of seeking a bag of stolen clothes, a large group of armed military police surrounded the International Committee's headquarters and climbed the walls to search the premises (Rabe CN, 325). The seasoned and pragmatic Rabe recognized that he must make changes to end ongoing tensions with the Japanese. "To get on good terms with the Japanese," Rabe came up with the idea of the Committee resolving to disband itself, "and founding an International Relief Committee," on which the Japanese were also to be represented (Rabe CN, 326). Other members of the Committee did not agree with Rabe's plan, being concerned that a new committee might "not be paid the least attention" by the general public (Rabe CN, 327).

In January 1938, the 10th Battalion of the Japanese 11th Division was ordered to defend Nanjing. Battalion Commander Amaya Naojiro took over command of the Nanjing Defense Garrison. To give the outside world the impression that order and prosperity had been restored to the city, upon taking charge he ordered: "All refugees must return to their original dwellings by February 4 (seven days from the order's issuance). If they do not return, the Safety Zone and refugee shelters will be disbanded by force, and lingering refugees will be driven from refugee camps by Japanese soldiers" (Zhang 2006b, 353). After receiving intense protests from the International Committee, and with the return of Western diplomats to their embassies in Nanjing, the Japanese ultimately decided to drop the use of force. Rosen of the German embassy met with Hidaka Shinrokuro of the Japanese embassy to discuss Hidaka's idea that the Japanese army disband the Safety Zone by force. Hidaka later told Rabe that the dissolution of the Safety Zone had been postponed, but he "asks that we not tell the Chinese that the Japanese will not employ force to disband the Zone, in order not to bog down the process even further" (Rabe EN, 171).

On February 18, 1938, the International Committee held a meeting in its headquarters at Number 5, Ninghai Road, with councilors Rabe, Bates, Mills, Trimmer, Magee, Sperling, Smythe, and others in attendance. At the meeting it was resolved: "The 'International Committee for the Nanking Safety Zone' will henceforth continue work under the name 'Nanking International Relief Committee.' This new name better conforms to the nature of its present work. Committee Secretary Dr. Smythe has been charged with informing all embassies and relevant relief organizations in Shanghai of the name change." To allow for someone to take charge of the committee in case of Rabe's absence, the Committee resolved, at Rabe's suggestion: "Pastor Mills has been selected vice chairman. Thus once Mr. Rabe departs, there is no need to elect a new chairman" (Rabe CN, 565). The election of Mills ensured a smooth transition of control after Rabe's departure.

On February 16, Committee Secretary-General George Fitch notified the Autonomous Committee in writing: "All administrative functions formerly entrusted to the International Committee by the government terminate upon the founding of the Autonomous Committee, and will be handed over all now completed duties to your organization. From now on, our committee is a purely private relief organization. Per our considerations, the Safety Zone no longer needs to exist." The Autonomous Committee then designated the area containing the Safety Zone as District Four, and appointed a district manager over it (Rabe CN, 552).

3.2.3.2 The International Relief Committee's Survey

Economic conditions in Nanjing were severely set back by the war. The long period of violence by the Japanese army, which Japanese officials were unable to rein in, nearly completely destroyed the city's economic foundations. In February 1938, the International Committee discovered that: "There are no indications of any rapid economic recovery. There is little present hope for economic access to Nanking, and there is no local production going on. It is difficult even to start spring farming on truck gardens inside or outside the city walls. Furthermore, much property – buildings, productive equipment and supplies – has been destroyed. Finally, there is a very small amount of paid labor in the community employed by the Japanese Army or by any others. All of these facts forbid any considerable economic revival in the next few months" (Miner Searle Bates Papers 1938, n.p.).

To become clear on actual circumstances in post-combat Nanjing and allow the relief work to proceed in a targeted manner, the Relief Committee conducted two surveys, which were the specialties of Professors Smythe and Bates of the University of Nanking, into wartime economic loses in Nanjing and agricultural conditions in the counties adjacent to Nanjing. In March 1938, under Smythe's guidance, the International Relief Committee sent 13 surveyors into households in the city and in the five adjacent counties to conduct a detailed survey that lasted several weeks. The survey had two objectives: to determine the extent of damage to economic life and to illuminate conditions of the people several months after the fighting. The report was finished in July 1938 and published under the name "War Damage in the Nanking Area," by Dr. Lewis S.C. Smythe (Zhang 2006b, 392).

Smythe had long experience in conducting sociological surveys. He had previously participated in "the Economic Survey made on behalf of the National Flood Relief Commission by the Department of Agricultural Economics of the College of Agriculture and Forestry of the University of Nanking, under Professor J. Lossing Buck," as well as "the Survey of the Rural Areas Affected by the Shanghai Hostilities (1932)" (Jiang Liangqin et al. n.d., 2–3). Some members of the Relief Committee had also participated in these surveys. Bates participated in writing the report and analyzing survey results (Jiang Liangqin et al. n.d., 7). The surveys' results are startling at first glance, as demonstrated by the following two tables detailing urban and rural losses.

Item	Average per family	Total	Cause				
			Military operations	Fire	Military robbery	Other robbery	Unknown
Buildings (owned)	271.56	12,855,600	496,800	12,291,200	78,600	17,700	1,300

Continued

Item	Average per family	Total	Cause				
			Military operations	Fire	Military robbery	Other robbery	Unknown
Movable property							
1. Machinery, tools	16.00	759,200	—	424,000	269,200	29,000	37,000
2. Shop equipment	65.01	3,084,600	—	1,833,500	1,025,000	150,000	76,100
3. Materials for manufacture	19.55	927,500	—	163,300	710,200	37,000	17,000
4. Stock for Sale	186.71	8,859,300	6,000	2,607,700	4,178,000	1,911,400	156,200
5. Rickshaws	3.60	171,000	11,500	65,500	79,200	—	14,800
Total movables for economic uses	290.87	13,801,600	17,500	5,094,000	6,261,600	2,127,400	301,100
6. Household furniture utensils	110.37	5,237,200	63,000	1,886,800	1,619,800	796,800	870,800
7. Clothing, bedding	115.43	5,477,200	24,200	1,196,300	3,155,800	782,900	318,000
8. Family food and supplies	7.93	376,400	3,500	50,300	290,300	15,200	17,100
9. Bicycles	2.59	122,800	12,500	6,000	102,300	—	2,000
10. Cash, jewelry	9.53	452,000	—	16,500	427,800	2,500	5,200
11. Other	29.83	1,415,300	57,100	149,000	1,167,300	26,000	15,900
Total movables for domestic uses	275.68	13,080,000	160,300	3,304,900	6,763,300	1,623,400	1,229,000
Total all movable property	566.55	26,882,500	177,800	8,398,900	13,024,900	3,750,800	1,530,100
Grand total	838.11	39,768,100	674,600	20,690,100	13,103,500	3,768,500	1,531,400
Percentage		100.0	1.7	52.0	33.0	9.5	3.8

Table 12: Losses of buildings and movable property for families remaining in Nanking, by cause. Source: Lewis S.C. Smythe, "War Damage in the Nanking Area," in Jiang Liangqin et al. (n.d., 55).

Items	Average amount lost per family	Unit value (yuan)	Value of average loss per family (yuan)	Total losses of all farm families	Total value of losses for all farm families (yuan)
1. Buildings	1.656	77.90	129.00	308,100	23,999,500
2. Labor animals	(head)		35.84	(head)	6,668,100
Water buffaloes	0.313	70.00	21.91	58,200	4,076,500
Oxen	0.317	55.00	7.55	25,500	1,404,600
Donkeys	0.213	30.00	6.38	39,600	1,187,000
3. Farm implements	(pieces)		28.17	(pieces)	5,241,100
Plows	0.509	6.50	3.31	94,700	615,300
Harrows	0.449	5.50	2.47	83,700	460,000
Pumps	0.618	33.00	20.41	115,100	3,798,100
Hoes	1.976	1.00	1.98	367,700	367,700
4. Stored cereals	(shih tan)		22.44	(shih tan)	4,175,900
Wheat	1.002	5.00	5.01	186,400	931,800
Barley	0.451	3.00	1.35	84,000	252,000
Rice	2.507	3.00	7.52	466,400	1,399,100
Corn	0.234	2.75	0.64	43,500	119,700
Soybeans	1.563	4.30	6.72	290,800	1,250,300
Other	0.300	4.00	1.20	55,700	223,000
5. Winter crops	(shih tan)		4.11	(shih tan)	765,200
Wheat	0.616	5.00	3.08	114,600	572,900
Barley	0.212	3.00	0.63	39,500	118,300
Rapeseed	0.019	4.50	0.08	3,500	15,700
Broad beans	0.042	4.00	0.17	7,700	31,000
Field Peas	0.035	4.20	0.15	6,500	27,300
Total			219.56		40,849,800

Table 13: Losses of farm families with detail of items.
Source: Lewis S.C. Smythe, "War Damage in the Nanking Area," in Jiang Liangqin et al. (n.d., 64).

Bates, who helped write the survey report's conclusions, wrote: "I have learned of a great number of facts that make me tremble, demonstrating the depth of the needless suffering of the ordinary people" (Zhang Kaiyuan n.d., 48).

3.2.3.3 The Committee's relief work

In the Nanking International Relief Committee's reports through April 30, 1939, relief work was "naturally divided into two periods," the first period running from December 1937 to the end of May 1938. This period ends when it does because refugee shelters were disbanded then. The Committee's headquarters also moved from Number 5 Ninghai Road to a building of the University of Nanking at Number 4 Tianjin Road (Zhang Sheng 2006b, 390). Although the Safety Zone ceased to exist when the International Committee was reorganized, the Relief Committee maintained close contacts with shelters in the Zone.[23]

Food relief. The Relief Committee continued providing food assistance to refugee shelters. Reports from the Committee give us the following figures:

> In March, the average occupancy of all 22 refugee shelters combined was 26,700. Of those, 17,300 were fed by daily rice provisions of 59 sacks, for a total of 1,821 on the month.
>
> In April, the number of shelters was reduced to 16, with an average occupancy of 21,750, of whom 11,300 were provided with daily allotments of 31 sacks of rice and 12 sacks of wheat per day by the Committee. This Committee provided 5.5 sacks of rice to the Red Swastika Society's soup kitchen. Public relief and special donations totaled about 18 sacks of rice per day. A total of 930 sacks of rice and 1,059 sacks of wheat were allocated to a total of 16,000 people seeking food.
>
> In May, there were seven shelters housing about 12,150 people, of whom 7,250 relied on cereal allocations from this Committee. Every day we provide 4 sacks of rice and 10.5 sacks of wheat. We also make daily allocations of 4 sacks of wheat to the Red Swastika Society to be used for public relief and other special donations, accounting for about 18 sacks per day. Their monthly total of rice is 474 sacks and 969 sacks of wheat, going to feed 11,650 people (Zhang Sheng 2006b, 398).

There were nutritional deficiencies among the refugees, who for long periods were able to obtain only enough food to survive. The Relief Committee also obtained broad beans and other foodstuffs from charitable groups in Shanghai for distribution to refugees: "This Committee has taken great pains to obtain 87 tons of broad beans from Shanghai after weeks of discussions. This is to be divided into 1,077 sacks, each weighing 161.55 pounds, to facilitate distribution to all refugees. Per our calculations, 17,500 of refugees in shelters in the two months of March and April were of the poorest class; each person may obtain an average allocation of 2.25 pounds." Besides, though "adding large amounts of coarse grain to their cereals," the problem of a single diet for refugees over a long period of time was mitigated, this after months of eating the same thing every day (Zhang 2006b, 399).

---

[23] Refugee shelters within the Safety Zone were not disbanded immediately upon the termination of the Zone, but rather they came under management of the Autonomous Committee, as the new government authority in the city. Nevertheless, these refugee shelters continued to rely heavily upon support from the International Relief Committee.

By March 1938, the reorganized sub-committees under the Relief Committee had already established "main offices and four sub-bureaus" and were working "full steam ahead."

Cash relief. A report of the reorganized committee read: "By the end of March, there were 12,145 households. Cash distributed totaled 42,725 yuan, an average of 3.52 yuan per household. About one-seventh of Nanjing households received relief funds from us."

Work for relief. "For example, we helped the Red Swastika Society hire 200 laborers to bury bodies and coffins. We helped the second district of the Autonomous Committee to hire 100 laborers to clean streets, and 100 to 200 farmers for the University of Nanking to plant the fields outside the Taiping Gate. We hired workers to clean the Safety Zone."

3.2.3.4 Mail service for refugees

As the ordinary postal service had yet to be restored, it was hard for refugees in the city to write to their friends and relatives elsewhere to send help. The Relief Committee wrote letters on behalf of refugees seeking aid for them: "For example, the husband of one woman in our Shuangtang shelter named Mrs. Luo Nanping worked in the Customs Bureau in Yichang. She was later brought by Bates to the University Hospital to give birth. After the Shuangtang shelter was closed, we brought her to the relief center in the University of Nanking."

The Relief Committee reached out to the Customs Bureau in Shanghai, which was able to put them in touch with Mr. Luo Nanping.

Bates, who participated in all the work of the two committees, summarizes thus: all the work done by the International Committee for the Nanking Safety Zone and later by the International Relief Committee "has been a romance of struggle to rescue refugees, worthy of giving one's life and blood, going to hell, or crying. This story of cooperation between a German Nazi, English businessmen, and us American missionaries transcends our nationalities. Some of our numbers are also Muslims, Buddhists, and Catholics. Several Chinese workers have shown excellence in heeding the call of these urgent times. These are the real accomplishments we've made faced with weapons, faced with unending orders to 'disband' and under conditions of distrust in cooperation between the Chinese and us" (Zhang 2005, 49).

3.3 Westerners in the Face of the Rape of Nanking

The reason the Westerners who remained in Nanjing after its fall in 1937 are remembered today is that their decision to stay placed them in the middle of a cyclone of barbaric violence unequaled in modern history: "As far as the International Committee for the Nanjing Refugee Zone was concerned, 'fighting with the Japanese army' only truly began once the attack on Nanjing had ended and the Central China Area Army had occupied the city" (Kasahara n.d., 122).

3.3.1 Recording and stopping Japanese atrocities

3.3.1.1 Negotiating with the Japanese to stop the massacre

A report issued by the International Committee on the eve of the Japanese occupation clearly called on refugees to allow Japanese soldiers to enter the Zone unobstructed, with no resistance (Rabe CN, 136). The Westerners discovered a large amount of Chinese soldiers seeking shelter in the Safety Zone prior to the Japanese occupation. The Committee stipulated that they must lay down their arms to be admitted to the Zone and concentrated them within a few public buildings in the Safety Zone (Rabe CN, 138).

On December 13, Smythe and Rabe "found Cola, who speaks Japanese, to go explain three things to the Japanese (trying especially to communicate with high-ranking military officers): the Safety Zone, the newly established Red Cross Society, and the disarmed Chinese soldiers in the Safety Zone" (Zhang 2005, 229). They assumed that these disarmed soldiers would be treated as prisoners of war at the very least. On December 13 when leaving the Safety Zone on his way to talk with the Japanese, Rabe came across some Chinese soldiers on the street. He encouraged them to throw down their weapons. Rabe thought that he had been "able to save three detachments of about 600 Chinese soldiers by disarming them" (Rabe EN, 66). "And we still had the hope that these fully disarmed troops would face nothing worse than being treated by the Japanese as prisoners of war" (Rabe EN, 67).

Nevertheless, when Japanese soldiers began searching the Safety Zone, the Westerners witnessed both disarmed soldiers and young men suspected of being such tied up and carried away by the Japanese to be shot en masse without even the pretense of a trial. Rabe wrote on December 13: "Of the perhaps one thousand disarmed soldiers that we had quartered at the Ministry of Justice, between 400 and 500 were driven from it with their hands tied. We assume they were shot since we later heard several salvos of machine-gun fire" (Rabe EN,

68). Fortunate survivors of these Japanese massacres who were able to return to the Safety Zone confirmed what had happened.

One Western reporter made this observation in the *New York Times:* "Tens of thousands of prisoners have been massacred by the Japanese. Most Chinese soldiers in the Safety Zone have been massacred en masse. The Japanese have carried out detailed searches of buildings throughout the city, looking for people with rucksack imprints on their shoulders or other signs that they may have been soldiers. All these people are put together and executed" (Zhang 2005, 114). These conditions put the Westerners on high alert. Fitch wrote about his feelings at the time: "Our own hearts were lead. Were those four lads from Canton who had trudged all the way up from the south and yesterday had reluctantly given up their arms among them, I wondered; or that all [tall] strapping sergeant from the north whose disillusioned eyes as he made the fatal decision, still haunt me? How foolish I had been to tell them the Japanese would spare their lives. We had confidently expected that they would live up to their promises, at least in some degree, and that order would be established with their arrival. Little did we dream that we should see such brutality and savagery as has probably not been equaled in modern times" (Zhang 2005, 72).

In the face of the organized massacre perpetrated by the Japanese army, the Westerners' first instinct was to attempt to intervene. On December 15, Rabe stood guarantee for some disarmed Chinese soldiers "as a German citizen." He said that these soldiers "would fight no longer and should be freed." They were, nevertheless, tied up and taken away by the Japanese. Rabe, Smith, and Mills tried again to save them, but it ended up being a "waste of words." Rabe and Smythe even went to make an entreaty at the Japanese embassy, but to no avail (Rabe CN, 143).

That day, the International Committee sent a letter to the Japanese embassy, actively taking the blame for not being able to separate Chinese soldiers from civilians: "That night, owing to the disorder and chaos, as well as the fact that the soldiers had already cast aside their uniforms, the Committee was unable to separate disarmed Chinese soldiers from civilians." The letter continues: "The Committee further hopes that the Japanese Army will in accordance with the recognized laws of war regarding prisoners and for reasons of humanity exercise mercy toward these former soldiers" (Rabe EN, 70). Rabe went so far as to suggest that Chinese prisoners of war be put to work as laborers, so long as the Japanese spared their lives (Rabe CN, 141–142).

On December 16, Japanese soldiers took a large group of disarmed Chinese soldiers away from the Ministry of Justice, as well as a group of Safety Zone police. McCallum and Riggs witnessed what came next. Riggs tried to stop the Japanese soldiers from taking off Safety Zone police, but was "threatened with a saber" by a Japanese officer three times, and then beaten (Rabe CN, 164). This incident was recorded in a memorandum to the Japanese embassy under the name "Ministry of Justice Incident."

Smythe wrote: "We exhorted the Japanese to not shoot disarmed soldiers. The question of disarmed soldiers has been one of the most serious we faced in the first three days. This question was immediately answered, however, as the Japanese simply shot everybody. At the very least the unending string of incidents that followed has made us believe this. In the end they drove out all the Chinese soldiers and shot them" (Zhang 2005, 230).

The comprehensive sweep of the city by Japanese soldiers following the city's occupation was sped up to allow for the victory celebration, but the searches did not stop with the City Entry Ceremony held on the 17th. On December 21, the Japanese 16th Division took up defense of the city. On December 22, the Japanese army issued a notice calling for all refugees to be registered: "On December 24, this commanding officer will issue population reassurance passports to all refugees and civilians. The only goal of this action is to ensure peace and contentment of the people. All people must report to places where the Japanese army is issuing these documents and receive one of the aforementioned passports. It is not permitted to have someone else pick up a document on your behalf; the document's bearer must report in person. The elderly, weak, and infirm should have family members accompany them to report. This is mandatory. Anyone later found without a passport will not be permitted to reside in the city of Nanjing. This is very important" (Zhang 2006b, 309). The so-called "refugee registration" was nothing more than an extended search of the city. During the registration, all "suspicious" refugees were arrested, and most of these were then killed en masse. McCallum wrote: "Several men were forcibly carried away from Ginling, Magee's place, and other places, accused of being soldiers. The men had friends among the group who could identify them as civilians, but because they had calluses on their hands, they were branded without further investigation as soldiers in spite of the protests voiced. Many rickshaw and San-pan men as well as other laborers have been shot simply because they have the marks of honest toil upon their hands" (Zhang 2005, 206).

Records left behind by the Westerners demonstrate the rare instances in which they were able to obstruct the Japanese in their organized searches and killings. They were more likely to succeed at obstruction in cases of willful killings by disorganized bands of soldiers. Vautrin wrote on December 16 that she twice saved workers in the Ginling Women's College by telling Japanese soldiers, "No soldier. Coolie." The result was that "they were released from the fate of being shot or stabbed."

One rescue attempt by Magee was less successful. On December 19, the two younger brothers of his driver were carried off by Japanese soldiers, and the driver's wife asked Magee to intervene. Magee wrote that he went off with her to search, and "she ended up seeing her two young men." Magee then talked with the Japanese officer in charge, to whom he said "two civilians, not soldiers." Magee said the officer then "looked at me with a look of extreme repugnance, and said something to me in a most loathful manner, which I guessed meant 'get out.'" Magee then said to the woman: "there's no hope." So they went home (Zhang 2005, 150).

3.3.1.2 Recording and stopping sexual violence

Shortly after the Japanese entry into the city, the Westerners discovered that "the most horrible thing now is the raping of women which has been going on in the most shameless way that I have ever known. The streets are full of men searching for women" (Zhang 2005, 151).

There were a great quantity of rapes perpetrated by the Japanese over a long period of time. Rabe had this to say about the Safety Zone: "Last night up to 1,000 women and girls are said to have been raped, about 100 girls at Ginling Girls College alone. You hear of nothing but rape" (Rabe EN, 77). Wide-scale raping began immediately upon the Japanese entry into the city. The Japanese academic Kasahara Tokushi places the approximate end of the period of raping as the founding of the "Reformed Government of the Republic of China" on March 28, 1938, at which point public security conditions calmed. Academician Sun Zhaiwei agrees, holding that atrocities by the Japanese army, including rape, "extended into March 1938" (Sun Zhaiwei 2005, 97).

When it came to rape, Jiang Gonggu writes that the Japanese soldiers "didn't care about age. So long as it was a woman, any woman they stumbled upon, whether an old lady of 70 or 80 or a young girl of eight or nine, none escaped" (Zhang 2005, 62). Of course nighttime saw the most cases, but a great many rapes happened in broad daylight. Cheng Ruifang wrote about the refugee shelter in Ginling Women's College, harboring up to 10,000 women at the time: "During the day today two soldiers came to (building) number 500. One stood at the door, and the other went in and shoed off the people inside, leaving only a girl, whom he raped" (Zhang 2005, 18). Minnie Vautrin writes that she drove off Japanese soldiers in the middle of a rape on December 19. Li Xiuying, six months pregnant and sheltering in the American school at Wutaishan, says she was stabbed 19 times while fending off Japanese soldiers trying to rape her (Zhang 2005, 72). On the afternoon of December 20, Japanese officers forced their way into the shelter at the Hankou Road Primary School, drove workers out of the office, and there raped two women, according to the report "Cases of atrocities committed by Japanese soldiers in the Safety Zone" (Zhang 2006b, 302).

Japanese soldiers perpetrated most rapes in groups, and were extremely vicious in doing so. Smythe wrote that "groups of three to seven scattered soldiers" marauded along the streets, entering refugee shelters at will. When Westerners found them, they would claim they were "looking for Chinese soldiers!" (Zhang 2005, 279). During these "so-called searches, the only real objective was to see if there were any women present to be hauled off and raped at night" (Rabe CN, 168). On December 17, Rabe received this letter: "There are about 540 refugees crowded in Nos. 83 and 85 on Canton Road. Since Dec. 13th, up to the 17th those houses have been searched and robbed many many times a day by Japanese soldiers in groups of three to five. Today the soldiers are looting the places mentioned above continually and all the jewelries, money, watches, clothes of any sort are taken away. At present women of younger ages are forced to go with the soldiers every night who send motor trucks to take them and release them the next morning. More than 30 women and girls have been raped" (Rabe EN, 81). Even Western diplomats witnessed the corpses of Chinese rape and murder victims. One officer of the German embassy in a conversation with Magee "described seeing a woman with a golf club inserted in her. He called this 'Japanese technology'" (Zhang 2005, 167).

The verdict of the International Military Tribunal for the Far East summarizes the typical case of Japanese violence in Nanjing: "There were many cases of rape. Death was a very common punishment for anyone who resisted, either the victim trying to protect herself or her family members. Many young girls and elderly women were raped throughout the city. There were also instances of perversion and sadism along with rape. Many women were killed after being raped, and then had their bodies violated. In the first month after occupation, there were nearly 20,000 cases of rape in the city of Nanjing" (Yang 2006, 607).

Westerners witnessing the brutalities being done to Chinese women did their utmost to protect them. In the words of Magee: "The other foreigners and I are busy about all kinds of things, but in most cases we're busy protecting women from being dishonored by Japanese soldiers" (Zhang 2005, 153). The Westerners themselves admitted that despite their best efforts, many innocent Chinese women were subject to the awful fate of rape every single day. In her "Review of the first month (December 13 – January 13)," Vautrin wrote: "Women in those days faced a terrible dilemma – meaning that even if they were spared rape by Japanese soldiers, their husbands and suns would face the risk of being taken away or killed. Even during this dangerous period, we did our best to encourage older women to stay home with their husbands and sons. This exposed them to the danger of rape, but it allowed for the younger women to seek protection with us. These horrible, bestial rapes continue. Even in the Safety Zone they're unavoidable" (Zhang 2005, 318).

All relevant records indicate that the mere appearance of a Westerner was most often enough to drive off a Japanese soldier attempting to rape a Chinese woman. Under most conditions, however, these soldiers were not brought to their officers for punishment, because to do so would have exposed the Westerners themselves and the Chinese around them to additional risks. Vautrin wrote on February 18, 1938 of her attitude when she saved one woman from being raped: "My first impulse was to snatch his dagger – which I had a good opportunity to do, and call on the group of servants which had congregated by that time, to help me catch him, but I decided that was not the part of wisdom so did nothing worse than to make him climb over the fence."

3.3.1.3 Records of other forms of violence

Japanese soldiers in Nanjing engaged in many criminal actions other than massacre and rape, including looting, arson, enslavement, beatings, etc.

With tacit permission granted in orders and from commanding officers, the looting of all kinds of goods from the city became a means for the invading Japanese army to replenish its stores. The day the Japanese entered Nanjing, Rabe and others witnessed Japanese soldiers smashing into stores and looting the food and other goods stored within. Magee wrote that the Westerners observed Japanese soldiers driving lines of cars down the streets and looting whatever they could get their hands on, all under direction of their officers (Zhang 2005, 238).

Even many homes of Westerners were often subjected to looting; the Chinese living inside them dared not object. Wilson wrote: "The looting continues. They carried off the Daniels' rugs today, one of them requiring four men to take. The poor people who stay in the house can of course do nothing about it and can only tell about it later. J. Lossing Buck has no idea how extremely lucky he is to date. His house, by virtue of the fact that there are eight Americans in it, has so far been spared the ravages of looters. Thompson's house next door has also been left untouched. The remaining houses are mere shells" (Zhang 2005, 341).

The International Committee lists out cases of looting by Japanese soldiers in one of its first reports on Japanese criminal activities in Nanjing:

2. A carriage loaded with rice was taken on December 15th at 4:00 p.m. near the gate of Ginling College by Japanese soldiers.

3. Several residents in our second sub-division were driven from their homes on the night of December 14th and robbed of everything. The chief of the sub-division was himself robbed twice by Japanese soldiers (Rabe EN, 253).

6. On December 14, 30 Japanese soldiers clearly without an officer in charge searched the University Hospital and female nurses' bedchambers. Hospital staff were subject to organized theft. Items stolen include: six fountain pens, 180 yuan in cash, four watches, two rolls of hospital bandages, two flashlights, two pairs of gloves, and one sweater.

7. Yesterday, December 15, reports from everywhere, shelters, public places, and even university buildings, inform us that Japanese soldiers have been breaking in everywhere and robbing Chinese refugees multiple times.

8. On December 15, the door of the American embassy was forced, and the embassy was looted, with several small objects now missing.

9. On December 15, Japanese soldiers climbed the wall behind the Ginling Women's College, broke a window, and made their way into the department of medicine. Nothing was stolen, as all movable objects stored in the department had been moved on December 13.

11. Our rice shop on Ninghai Road was subjected to inspection by Japanese soldiers in the afternoon of December 15. They bought three sacks of rice (3.75 dan) but paid only five yuan. The current price for rice is nine yuan per dan. So the Japanese army now owes the International Committee 28.75 yuan.

13. On December 14, Japanese soldiers broke into the residence of American missionary Miss Grace Bauer, stealing a pair of leather gloves, drinking all the milk left on her table, and emptying her sugar jars with their hands.

14. On December 15, Japanese soldiers broke into the garage of American doctor R.F. Brady (at Number 1 Shuanglong Lane), breaking a pane of glass on a Ford automobile. They later returned with a mechanic and attempted to start the car (Rabe CN, 148–149).

The report highlighted 15 instances of criminal activity by Japanese soldiers, of which nine were looting. The Westerners' concern for looting is clear. In each instance the details are clearly recorded, including time, place, and objects stolen.

Looting went hand in hand with massacre and other forms of violence, causing tension among the Westerners. Wilson wrote about his experience: "This noon I came as near to being shot as I ever hope to be. On my way home the police in front of the girls' dormitory at the University told me that a Japanese soldier was inside and begged me to see to it. As that is getting to be an old story now I barged in and ordered him out in no uncertain terms. He was having them pump up one of their own bicycles for him to ride but I put a stop to that and kept urging him out. He also wanted to take a rickshaw and bicycle pump along and I roughly objected to that but that is where I overplayed my hand as he had brought the rickshaw along himself with the poor coolie in tow. We were now no longer friends and he proceeded to calmly load his rifle and play around with it a little. The Chinese then told me that he had brought the rickshaw and pump so I told him to take them and get along which he did. He then went outside and as I passed loaded several more cartridges in his rifle. I fully expected to be shot in the back as I went beyond him towards our house. He must have lost his nerve" (Zhang 2005, 341).

Diplomats returning to the city also witnessed looting by Japanese soldiers. Scharffenberg wrote on January 28, 1938: "The Japanese are excellent at looting. One example is when they tried to move a grand piano from a bank into a stable. First they pushed the piano down the stairs, snapping all the cords. It's still in the bank like that now. Mr. Aman's office is in that bank. The Japanese broke a hole in the concrete wall above the safe and looted the office to the last" (Chen, Zhang, and Dai n.d., 102).

To deflect blame away from themselves, the Japanese tried to create the impression that Chinese people had been responsible for the looting. Scharffenberg wrote again on January 28: "The Chinese still do not dare to leave the Safety Zone, except during the day. But even then it's only old women and children. Now they happily steal and plunder under the eyes of the Japanese. Our impression is that the Japanese are happy to see this, as it helps remove blame from themselves. The only things left in the houses are those that the Japanese passed over. The Safety Zone has thus become a bustling 'thieves' market'" (Chen, Zhang, and Dai n.d., 102).

Arson went along with the looting. In the short span of time between the city's fall and December 20, 1937, the Westerners witnessed several cases of arson:

> Japanese soldiers set fire to the house at Number 16, Pingcang Alley. Sperling and the Safety Zone fire battalion rushed to the scene but were unable to put out the fire, as our pumps and all other firefighting equipment had been stolen by Japanese soldiers a few days ago. That same day, a house at the corner of Zhongshan Road and Baotai Road burned to cinders. More fires were detected that night in the direction of Guofu Road.

> Between 5 and 6 p.m. on December 20, Mr. Fitch and Dr. Smythe found an entire street full of Japanese military trucks and vehicles along Taiping Road southward to Baixia Road. The Japanese were unloading them. Beginning at the small river on the south side of Zhujiang Road all the way to Baixia Road, they encountered small detachments of 15 to 20 Japanese soldiers. Some of them seemed to be observing the houses burning on either side of the road under the eyes of detachment ringleaders. Others were moving merchandise out of stores. Fitch and Smythe saw some soldiers setting fire to the shops for fun. They kept going along Zhonghua Road, where they saw similar conditions. A large fire was already engulfing the northern half of the YMCA building. The fire had, beyond any doubt, been

set from within the building, because the outside of the building was not on fire. Japanese sentries paid no heed whatsoever to these two gentlemen.

Around 9 p.m. on December 20, Kröger and Hatz were driving down Zhongzheng Road toward Baixia Road, planning to turn east onto Zhonghua Road, but Japanese sentries stopped them and prevented them from driving south. The YMCA building had by this time long been burned to ashes. They took an inventory when driving north along Taiping Road. There were 10 fires actively burning on either side of the street, not counting houses already completely burned out. When they reached the corner of Zhongshan Road and Zhujiang Road, they saw a large fire on the north side of Zhujiang Road. At this point a Japanese patrol stopped them and prevented them from driving eastward. Japanese soldiers are everywhere on the streets, in great numbers, but they clearly do not plan to put out the fires. On the contrary, many of them are busy moving away merchandise (Rabe CN, 202).

The Westerners were powerless to stop the arson. The fire trucks and other firefighting equipment given to the International Committee by the former municipal government had mostly been stolen by Japanese soldiers, leaving them with no means to stop the conflagrations, as documented in cases of criminal acts reported by the International Committee (Zhang Sheng 2006b, 311).

3.3.2 Saving Chinese civilians

3.3.2.1 Organization and management of refugee shelters

Per the earliest conceptions, the Safety Zone's primary function was to provide combat-free shelter to refugees in wartime, to allow refugees to survive the chaos during the transition of power. The majority of buildings in the Safety Zone were the private property of Chinese citizens, and not subject to direct management by the International Committee. The International Committee thought most refugees with some economic means or with personal connections should be able to live with friends or family in the Safety Zone or at least rent a house there. Only a very small minority of refugees without economic means and unable to make a living would need to rely on the International Committee for housing and food, the thinking went.

In organization, the majority of refugee shelters under the purview of the International Committee arose organically, and were approved by the Committee only after the fact. The managers of all refugee shelters were monitored by the International Committee, which provided both guidance and material supplies to them. The following is a list of refugee shelters given by the International Committee to Japanese authorities.

Number	Building name	Number of refugees	Designation
1	Former Ministry of Communication	10,000+	Families
2	Wutaishan Primary School	1,640	Families
3	Hankou Road Primary School	1,000	Families
4	Army Academy	3,500	Families
5	Xiaotaoyuan Nanjing School of Languages	200	Families
6	Military Chemical Store (behind Overseas Chinese Hotel)	4,000	Men
7	University of Nanking Middle School	6,000–8,000	Families
8	Bible Teacher Training School	3,000	Families
9	Overseas Chinese Hotel	2,500	Families
10	Nanking Theological Seminary	2,500	Families
11	Ministry of Justice	Vacant[24]	
12	Supreme Court	Vacant	
13	University of Nanking Silk Factory	4,000	Families
14	University of Nanking Library	2,500	Families
15	German Club	500	Families
16	Ginling Women's College	4,000	Women, children
17	Law School	500	Families
18	Agriculture Department	1,500	Families
19	Shanxi Road Primary School	1,000	Families
20	Unviersity of Nanking dormitories	1,000	Women, children
Total:		49,340–51,340	

Table 14: List of refugee shelters in Safety Zone (December 17, 1937).
Source: Zhang Sheng (2006b, 287).

Per a report by the subsequent Nanking International Relief Committee, the Committee established a total of 25 "permanent" shelters, all within the Safety Zone. In addition, within the Safety Zone there were also "organizations independently formed by a group of refugees that subsequently asked for coordination and oversight by the International Committee, a few hundred in the Quaker Society and a few hundred in Huiqingli." There were also autonomously organized groups outside the Safety Zone that also asked for help from the Committee, such as the Shuangtang shelter (Zhang 2006b, 395). Chinese people were in charge of the vast majority of these shelters. From December 31, 1937 to January 5, 1938, the International Committee conducted a survey into the majority of shel-

---

[24] The Ministry of Justice and Supreme Court were left vacant as a result of aforementioned Japanese searches, ending in the taking off of most young men in those buildings, with the result that remaining refugees there did not dare linger (Zhang 2006b, 287).

ters under their purview. The survey's results demonstrate their internal organization.

The above table demonstrates that all shelters were led by directors, that these directors had to answer to the International Committee and subject themselves to inspection, and that assistance came from the Committee in the form of material provisions – rice, coal, medicine, medical supplies, etc. – and in technology. The primary matters for which these directors were responsible were food distribution, housing allocations, internal security and management, sanitation and cleaning, and so on. In small shelters, directors with a handful of assistants directly watched over all these matters. In larger shelters, committees were formed under the leadership of the director to handle these affairs. Some shelters even established committees to "receive" harassing Japanese soldiers, giving them cigarettes, tea, and other services, to prevent them from harming refugees or looting the shelters.

It is also clear that levels of competence varied among shelter directors. Some directors were suspected by the International Committee of incompetence or immorality. The inspection team asked that unqualified directors be replaced. The team also created a list of suggestions for shelter improvements:

General Recommendations

1. Measures should be taken along with University Hospital personnel to the extent possible to provide care for the many sick people in the various shelters.
2. The International Committee's ambulance corps should visit all shelters at fixed intervals to strictly enforce sanitation rules.
3. All shelters should make a count of women and other people whose husbands or caretakers have been taken away but not returned by the Japanese. An appeal should then be made to Japanese authorities to provide money or food needed to care for these people.
4. Special attention should be paid to opium smokers and ruffians in shelters. We should find means and methods to remove these bad elements, or provide necessary protection to directors to prevent them from coming to harm.
5. Also, shelters should make a count of people whose houses or residences have been destroyed by fire or bombing, and take steps to compensate them.
6. We should also pay attention to the fact that some Chinese are taking women from shelters to provide them to Japanese soldiers for immoral purposes.
7. We must create a plan to move refugees living in straw huts or overcrowded shelters into more spacious shelters.
8. Convene a meeting of all shelter directors as soon as possible.
9. Appoint a standing committee to inspect all shelters.

3.3 Westerners in the Face of the Rape of Nanking — 201

No.	Shelter name	No. of refugees	Internal organization	Surveyor's assessment of shelter management
1	Army Academy	About 3,200 ppl.	Director: Mr. Zhao Yongkui. Refugees divided into 27 groups, each with a group leader. Director of public affairs: Mr. Zhou. Secretary: Mr. Yi. Human affairs secretary: Mr. Pu. Social Affairs Department: Mr. Xie. General Affairs Department: Mr. Ma.	General conditions satisfying. Shelter director has made efforts to maintain order. Sanitary facilities require great improvement.
2	Armaments Department	About 8,000 ppl., as well as many who come just to spend the night.	Director: Mr. Lu Chengmei, with about 40 assistants.	Organization and leadership need improvement. The director seems honest and competent and is working hard to complete his duties, but he has yet to firmly control his subordinates.
3	Germany-China Club	444 ppl.	Director: Zhao Tangrong.	Refugees well treated, both with food and housing..
4	Quaker Missionary Society	About 800 ppl., mostly men, more women than children.	Director: Mr. Zhang Gongsheng.	Not much organized work visible, but refugees seem satisfied.
5	Hankou Road Primary School	About 1,400 ppl. (was 1,500).	Director: Mr. Zheng Dacheng.	Refugees seem satisfied with leadership.
6	Overseas Chinese Club	1,100 ppl.	Director: Mr. Mao Qingliang, with 19 assistants.	Leader seems incompetent, low level of education.
7	Siemens China Company	602 ppl.	Director: Mr. Han Xianglin (works at International Committee headquarters during the day).	
8	Zhongshan Road School of Justice	528 ppl.	Director: Mr. Tong Xiechen, with 8 assistants.	Well led and organized.

Continued

No.	Shelter name	No. of refugees	Internal organization	Surveyor's assessment of shelter management
9	University of Nanking silk factory	3,304 ppl.	Stand-in Director: Mr. Jin Zheqiao (former director arrested by Japanese on suspicion of being a Chinese soldier)	Seems lacking in appropriate organization.
10	School of Agriculture	1,658 ppl.	Director: Mr. Shen Jiayu, with 20 assistants. There are group leaders who must report on their work to the director. The director and group leaders are in charge of looking into all disputes. Shelter has a rescue team and a group leader committee.	Well led. Refugees seem satisfied. Leader very competent, has made many achievements.
11	Bible Teachers Training School	3,400 ppl.	Director: Missionary preacher Guo Junde, with assistants. Shelter possesses various committees, for management, inspection, guard work, sanitary facilities, and also for providing food and drink to Japanese soldiers who attempt to break in.	General conditions very good, very well led.
12	Nanking Theological Seminary	3,116 ppl.	Director: Mr. Tao Zhongliang, with 20 assistants.	
13	Wutaishan Primary School	1,640 ppl.	Director: Mr. Zhang Yili, with assistants.	Shelter is well led.
14	University of Nanking Middle School	11,000 ppl. (was 15,000).	Director: Mr. Jiang Zhengyun, with about 80 assistants. Refugees divided into 40 groups. There is an emergency rescue	Shelter is well organized, leadership is methodical.

3.3 Westerners in the Face of the Rape of Nanking

Continued

No.	Shelter name	No. of refugees	Internal organization	Surveyor's assessment of shelter management
			team, an inspection team, and a firefighting team.	
15	Dafangxiang Military Chemical Plant	About 2,800 ppl.	Director: Mr. Wang Chengzhai and Mr. Sun Pingliang, with some assistants. All refugee rooms have serial numbers, making them easy to find. The shelter has various committees, including for management, sanitary facilities, commerce, inspection, price setting, and so on. The work of these committees seems satisfactory.	The inspection committee finds this shelter excellently led. The gentlemen in charge are educated and have work experience. The shelter is well organized, and workers are exceptional.
16	Shanxi Road Primary School	About 1,100 ppl.	Director: Mr. Wang Youcheng, with assistants.	We don't find the director and his assistants very competent, or that they are interested in their work.
17	Gaojia Tavern #55	770 ppl., divided into two groups.	Director: Mr. Ling Enzhong, with a few assistants.	Led acceptably well.
18	University of Nanking	7,000 ppl., most of whom are women and children. Men come during the day to bring food to family members.	Director: Mr. Qi Zhaochang, with assistants.	Compared to number of hired laborers at Ginling Women's College, there are too many assistants and hired workers distributing rice here. We urgently recommended that a further detailed inspection be made of leadership in this shelter by the International Committee.
19	University Library	About 3,000 ppl.	Director: Mr. Liang Kaichun, with some assistants.	Send more assistants to director and find a way to eliminate bad elements.

Continued

No.	Shelter name	No. of refugees	Internal organization	Surveyor's assessment of shelter management
20	Ginling Women's College	5,000–6,000 ppl. (was 10,000). Mostly women and children, with an extremely small number of elderly men.	Director: Miss Minnie Vautrin, with assistants.	Leadership excellent.
21	Presbyterian Church and Missionary School	1,000 ppl. at present, was 2,000. Many people come only at night to sleep.	Director: Mr. Chen Luomen.	Director is a wood merchant from Shanghai who was on business in Nanjing but unable to return home. He has proven to be a competent shelter director.

Table 15: Internal organization of refugee shelters.
Source: Rabe CN, 284–293, 299–301.

10. A special study must be made in the question of coal provision to all shelters.
11. We suggest morning inspections of soup kitchens and rice provisions thereto, to prevent abnormalities in rice allocations.
12. All shelters selling rice (or porridge and cooked rice), especially those incurring additional expenses in their operations, should have their accounts audited.
13. We should write behavioral rules and post them in all shelters, and make shelter directors responsible for encouraging refugees to obey these rules.
14. We must make standard cards for all shelters to facilitate their quick grasp of numbers of refugees paying for food and those receiving food for free, including names, addresses, and so on.
15. We should also create standards and rules for rice allocations.
16. We should commend all directors and their colleagues who have happily contributed to relief work.
17. We should have the International Committee's secretary-general establish necessary preventive measures per the findings of the inspection committee's survey (Rabe CN: 308–309).

After the comprehensive survey had been conducted, the International Committee convened a meeting of all shelter directors on January 11, 1938, attended by more than 20 of them. At the meeting, they discussed "follow-up work, improvements to sanitary facilities, the takeover by the Autonomous Committee, and many other problems" (Rabe CN, 323).

By February 1, 1938, the International Committee had compiled further statistics gleaned from the meeting of shelter directors, as Forster writes in a letter to his wife: "At present there are about 58,000 people being cared for in these centers by the International Committee. These centers are all located in the Refugee Zone. It is interested [sic.] to see how they are distributed. 36,271 or 62% in American property; 601, or 1% in German property; 17,900 or 31% in Chinese government property; 3,139 or 6% in private property, Chinese" (Zhang 2005, 125).

In addition to large shelters, there were also many private dwellings in the Safety Zone used for housing refugees. The Safety Zone Housing Management Committee even divided the Zone into districts with managers responsible for houses in their district. A report of the International Relief Committee reads: "A large housing group has been established by the Refugee Zone Committee;

this has divided the Refugee Zone into four districts,[25] each district with an office and detailed measurements of usable locations to maximize utilization. We need to encourage with good words or pressure with authority those people crowded in private houses to allow for appropriate usage of all inhabitable houses" (Zhang 2006b, 393).

3.3.2.2 "Safety" mechanisms in the Safety Zone

The International Safety Zone never received formal approval from the Japanese, a fact that cast an enormous shadow over the Zone. During the zone's planning phase, the Chinese government offered complete guarantees for the Zone. When the Chinese defenders retreated, those soldiers who could not join the retreat dispersed into the Safety Zone. These soldiers never engaged in fighting or creation of disturbances within the Zone, and never harmed anyone therein, but in any event they provided the Japanese with a pretext for violating the Safety Zone. During their searches, the Japanese intentionally greatly exaggerated the threat posed by these soldiers and even arrested young men who had never before held a weapon. Even more egregiously, the Japanese killed soldiers and innocent refugees alike without trial. This was something the International Committee had not expected.

In addition, Japanese soldiers roamed the Safety Zone in groups of three to five inflicting all manner of atrocities, creating additional calamities for the people in the Safety Zone. The Safety Zone's police force was far from sufficient to do anything; many police themselves were targets of Japanese violence. In the face of these circumstances, both the Chinese and the Westerners in the Safety Zone learned that the only way that had any chance of stopping atrocities was for a Westerner to appear. So a fragile safety mechanism was built around the core of Westerners.

The German Eduard Sperling was the Safety Zone's inspector-general, in charge of the Safety Zone's police force. Only an appearance by Sperling was enough to "intimidate" Japanese soldiers in the commission of violence. As such, Sperling made frequent patrols of the entire Safety Zone, often responding to Chinese appeals to chase off Japanese soldiers in the middle of violent acts. Vautrin was also constantly called on to chase off Japanese soldiers in Ginling Women's College. Rabe set a sentry in his house that was serving as a shelter.

---

25 Before Rabe left Nanjing, a meeting was held among the directors of all refugee shelters, where it was resolved that they would attempt to prevent Rabe from leaving. The letter they wrote to him was signed by 25 shelter directors from nine districts of the Safety Zone (Rabe CN, 572).

Every night he slept in his clothes, because he was frequently awoken by the sentry's whistle whenever Japanese soldiers climbed the walls into his courtyard. Rabe appeared as quickly as possible every time to send them away.

There were also internal political issues to resolve in the Safety Zone in addition to harassment by Japanese soldiers. At its peak, the tiny area of less than four square kilometers contained between 200,000 to 300,000 refugees. To maintain order, the shelters established a volunteer police force with arm band insignia to bolster the official police force. The International Committee, however, lacked courts and jails. The only option the Committee had for dealing with law breakers was to kick them out of Safety Zone shelters.

Since the supply of running water and electricity was cut off during the battle for the city, the shelters all established sanitation groups responsible for arranging sanitary drinking water and the disposal of human waste.

There was no way to guarantee absolute security in the Safety Zone, but security there was much better than elsewhere in the city.

3.3.2.3 Food provision

The Committee had considered that there might be difficulties if food provision into Nanjing were cut off because of the fighting. The Committee listed the quantity, storage, and distribution of food in the Safety Zone as one of the important issues to resolve while planning for the Safety Zone. Of the five sub-committees established on December 3, 1937, two were involved in this issue: the food commission, of course, and also the transport commission, responsible for bringing food and fuel into the Safety Zone (Rabe CN, 102–103).

The International Committee was deeply concerned with the food issue; in fact, this issue was baked into the cake of the Committee's founding. In testimony given to the International Military Tribunal for the Far East, Bates spoke of the International Committee's thinking on this subject: "The committee expected that its chief duties would be to provide housing and if necessary some food during a period of a few days or possibly of a few weeks when the city was under siege and when Chinese civilian authority might have disappeared but Japanese military authority would not yet have been established" (Yang 2006, 75). The Committee had anticipated a "power vacuum" of only about one week. The Committee issued a notice prior to the city's fall, asking that: "All people moving in now should bring with them at least enough food for a week" (Rabe EN, 253).

Chinese authorities were indeed highly supportive of the Safety Zone plan, and provided great quantities of funds and materials to the International Committee. The Chinese military had also provided, as the Committee writes in a letter to Fukuda on December 16, "three trucks to use for hauling rice for feeding civilians" (Zhang 2006b, 276). By December 8, the International Committee told the press its food sub-committee had "collected a total of 6,300 sacks of rice (equivalent to 7,875 dan) on 12 trucks."

Nanjing was already feeling pressure from the Japanese attack by the time this transport began. In his diary entry of December 9, 1937, Rabe described how a truck and people were hit by artillery fire: "We are still busy transporting rice from outside the city. Unfortunately one of our trucks was damaged in the process. One of our transport coolies lost an eye and was taken to the hospital" (Rabe EN, 55). [26] Rabe wrote of another incident: "The crew of another truck arrives back sobbing and weeping. They were at the South Gate, which is being shelled. The guards there didn't want to let the truck out, but were finally talked into it. When the truck returned, of the entire guard unit—about 40 men—not one was still alive" (Rabe EN, 55–56).

The Nanking International Relief Committee wrote in a 1939 report: "The municipal government allocated to this committee 20,000 sacks of rice, 10,000 sacks of flour, and 80,000 yuan in cash. Owing to difficulties in transportation, only 9,067 sacks of rice were able to be brought into the city before the siege. The only flour we could get into the city was the 1,000 sacks donated by the Datong flour factory; none of the municipal government's flour was received. The municipal government donated 350 sacks of salt."[27] The Japanese occupied the city before all grain reserves could be moved in.

High-ranking officers of the Japanese army did not effectively enforce military discipline, and the city fell into chaos as violence erupted in all quarters. Looting became "a routine military operation" under guidance of officers (Rabe CN, 236). Japanese soldiers often stole cars. To deliver food to refugees in urgent need thereof, Smythe wrote that the Westerners had no choice but to "deliver rice to

---

26 Fitch writes about a similar incident: "one [driver] lost an eye with a splinter of shrapnel." The two men might have been writing about the same incident (Zhang 2005, 67).

27 Records differ in the quantities of rice allocated by the Nanjing municipal government to the International Committee. Rabe writes in his diary of "30,000 sacks of rice". Other records commonly quoted claim "30,000 *dan*" or "20,000 sacks." Rabe writes in a letter of January 26, 1938, to the American, British, and German consulates, that a detailed inventory had been taken of the sources and quantities of grain reserves for the Safety Zone: "On December 2 we received a waybill for 15,000 sacks of rice, and another on December 5 for 5,009 sacks. We actually transported only 8,476 sacks into the Zone. That in addition to the 600 sacks intended for distribution to refugees at Xiaguan comes to a total received by us of 9,076 sacks, equivalent to 11,345 *dan*." These figures gel well with other records. Our estimate based on all records is that the municipal government allocated somewhat more than 20,000 sacks of rice, or a little more than 25,000 *dan*. See "Report of the Nanking International Relief Committee" (Zhang 2006b, 391) and Rabe CN, 420.

refugee shelters in private cars, to ensure that they wouldn't go hungry for two days or longer" (Zhang 2005, 277). International Committee members Zial and Riggs were both either detained or beaten by Japanese soldiers for protecting food and cars.

On December 21, the entire foreign community of Nanjing submitted a letter of protest to the Japanese embassy, claiming: "The present situation is automatically and rapidly leading to a serious famine" (Rabe CN, 191). Rabe and others met with Mastui Iwane that day in the Japanese embassy, but Rabe found the Japanese unwilling to even discuss the food issue: "The Japanese themselves are short on rations and are not interested in whether or not we can make do with our supplies" (Rabe EN, 85).

Most refugees carried rice and bedding with them into the Safety Zone, where they set up their own stoves, and each family cooked its own rice, or many families took turns cooking rice, as attested by Ma Liangyou (Zhang and Dai n.d., 508). With the Japanese making replenishment of rice stores difficult, most refugees had no choice but to reduce their daily food consumption, most often limiting themselves to two meals daily, mostly consisting of thin porridge. Once their rice stores had been exhausted, some people took their lives into their own hands to leave the Safety Zone and fetch more from home. The German diplomat Scharffenberg recorded how one 14 year old girl was "shot in the head and died" when leaving the Safety Zone to fetch some vegetables (Chen, Zhang, and Dai n.d., 102). Scharffenberg wrote on January 13 that the Japanese were also plundering and setting fires left and right. Those food stores not stolen by soldiers were in many cases burnt to ashes: "All streets outside of the Safety Zone are completely abandoned. Amid the ruins one sees only desolation" (Chen, Zhang, and Dai n.d., 83).

The refugees had no means to cope with the food crisis other than seeking assistance from refugee shelters and soup kitchens. Soup kitchens in the Safety Zone were mostly established by the Red Swastika Society, the Red Cross Society, and the International Committee. The Red Swastika Society, Smythe wrote in a letter home, had set aside some rice prior to the city's fall, and had even obtained 3,000 sacks of rice from Japanese monks to use in their soup kitchens (Zhang 2005, 257).[28] Afterward, however, the Society mostly relied on the International Committee for food.

---

[28] Red Swastika Society Director Tao Xisan had studied abroad in Japan and later served as chairman of the Autonomous Committee, maintaining close links with the Japanese throughout the occupation.

All shelters made their own rules about food distribution per the economic conditions of refugees. Refugees with economic means were asked to pay for rice, or to buy porridge from soup kitchens. Refugees with no economic means whatsoever were separated out by their shelters and given free food: "Red insignia were stitched onto the clothes of people truly too poor to afford food; these were fed first." On December 22 Vautrin wrote that she "prepared tickets for those who do not get rice each day – it always runs out before we get around – so that they will come first on the next serving." The International Committee paid particular attention to food distribution situations in refugee shelters in its surveys. Those conditions have been described above.

A 1939 report of the Nanking International Relief Committee recalls food relief conditions in the city after its fall:

> From December 17 to 31, the Safety Zone Committee daily provided 84.5 sacks of rice to its 25 shelters, in addition to 28.5 sacks to soup kitchens, three sacks to police and sanitation workers, and 20 sacks in special donations (including to the Red Swastika Society). There were five formal soup kitchens, two of which founded by this committee, located in refugee shelters; two others were set up by the Red Swastika Society, these feeding mostly refugees in shelters; the last was set up by the Red Cross Society, all of its food going to refugees in shelters. The average occupancy in all refugee shelters at this time was 70,750, of which 25,150 ate in their shelters, and 8,200 ate in nearby soup kitchens. Eight thousand people received special donations. So about 38,350 people were fed by this committee. Some of these were able to supplement their diets with their own vegetables, oils, or peanuts. Meat is rare in shelters, and there is a very small quantity of green vegetables and beans served in shelters; these are extremely expensive. The total quantity of rice distributed is 2,035 sacks.
>
> Grain distributions for the second half of December and every month after it are made based on every day in the period. The number of people actually receiving rice and other grains is greater than in our statistics, but some people received rice and grains on fewer days than were recorded. We estimate that one sack of rice, cooked into thick porridge, can feed 300 people per day; our standard is 250 people fed per sack of rice per day. There are many cases of people receiving relatively little rice; these might eat only once daily in soup kitchens, and the rice they receive is less than the predetermined amount. The rice stored by this committee is all of middle to low quality, and each sack weighs on average 212.25 pounds, or about 77.5 kilograms, equaling about 1.25 *shi dan*.
>
> The average occupancy of refugee shelters in January was 62,500, of which 22,250 ate in their shelters, which received 79 sacks of rice daily from this committee, distributed across 25 shelters. Another 4.5 sacks went daily to feed the police, sanitation workers, and other workers, including some working in shelters. Yet another 4.5 sacks went to the Red Cross Society and other groups with special connections. So a total of 27,125 people rely on free food provisions from this committee to stay alive. During this month, the soup kitchens run by the Red Swastika Society had no further need for large rice provisions from this committee. Those run by the Red Cross Society were integrated into shelters. This month this committee distributed a total of 2,721 sacks of rice.

There was a dramatic reduction in refugee shelter occupancy in February, down to an average of about 36,800, most of these belonging to the poorest classes, and many of whom had no more private food reserves whatsoever. 20,800 people ate in shelters, to which this committee provided 69 sacks of rice daily. This month this committee's workers were paid in cash, but all other special donations were stopped. Total of 1,935 sacks (Zhang 2006b, 397–398).

The Autonomous Committee was founded on December 23, 1937, and held its founding ceremony on New Year's Day, 1938. Smythe wrote about the fallout in multiple letters. "The Japanese urgently want to weaken the International Committee and hand its functions to the Autonomous Committee" (Zhang 2005, 267). To this end, the Japanese attempted to "close by force" the International Committee's rice shops and distribute a small quantity of free rice outside the Safety Zone "to bribe the people into returning to their damaged homes" (Zhang 2005, 270). The Japanese distribution of rice was merely a symbolic gesture aimed at "pacification," because during the three months following the Japanese occupation, "rice sold wasn't sufficient for even two weeks of consumption." The rice requisitioned by the Japanese army in Nanjing, however, "could feed the city for three months!" (Zhang 2005, 277).

Although the Westerners did not hold the Autonomous Committee in high esteem, Bates felt that "rice is the most urgent task," and Smythe felt that "we have no choice but to rely on these people to bring rice in." Under these conditions, the foreign community "all agreed to work with it as much as possible" (Zhang 2005, 266). Smythe wrote that the same was true for the coal desperately needed by the soup kitchens. The Japanese did not agree to hand coal over to the Westerners, so the International Committee "let people from the Autonomous Committee handle its transport"; the International committee supplied trucks and gasoline to assist the process. Riggs of the Transport Commission "only dispatched trucks," to make the contributions of Westerners less conspicuous (Zhang 2005, 266).

Wilson made this critique of the role Safety Zone refugee shelters played in food relief: "The populace is crowding into the refugee camps even from the private residences within the Zone as the degree of safety is slightly greater even though there is no guarantee anywhere. If it were not for the way the International Committee had gathered rice beforehand and done what they could to protect the population there would be a first class famine and the slaughter would have been considerably less than it has" (Zhang n.d., 339).

3.3.2.4 Births and babies in refugee shelters

Even as the Japanese were snuffing out untold numbers of lives in Nanjing, some new lives were just beginning in the direst of times. Even amid all their other troubles, the refugee shelters, occupied mostly by women, had to attend to the issues of delivering babies and providing care for infants. The shelter in the University of Nanking conducted a detailed survey into the women who had given birth there, and also provided assistance to the new mothers.

In her diary entry of December 27, 1937, Vautrin wrote of the Ginling Women's College refugee shelter: "To date we have had fourteen births and four deaths. Mrs. Tsen [Cheng Ruifang] is the only nurse we have and she is terribly over worked." With the help of the International Committee, the shelter there was able to provide milk powder and fish liver oil, along with other supplements, to the new mothers and newborns, as well as a decent living environment.

3.3.2.5 Soothing wartime trauma

The long period of ruthless violence by Japanese soldiers inflicted a nameless terror on the refugees, a great number of whom saw family members, friends, and neighbors killed, or themselves barely escaped the clutches of death. All these experiences inflicted enormous psychological trauma on them. Magee wrote about a Chinese preacher who felt no way out, and, despite the exhortations of Forster and others, killed himself (Zhang 2005, 161). The German diplomat Scharffenberg wrote on February 3, 1938 about Chinese women he witnessed who had lost their minds after seeing their sons killed, and spent the entire day in hysterical states (Chen, Zhang, and Dai n.d.,121).

During the reign of terror, the Westerners already started thinking about how to mitigate and soothe the psychological trauma inflicted on Chinese refugees, how to give them the hope to live on. Magee, who had previously lived outside the city walls at Xiaguan, brought his congregation with him to live inside the Safety Zone prior to the city's fall. Even at the height of the troubles, he never stopped preaching or giving services, in an attempt to help his flock make it through the darkest hour with the power of religion.

Religion was also used on the University of Nanking campus to solace refugees. Forster wrote about one religious activity he attended on the campus: "This was a real gospel meeting, not a bible reading class, although it was based in Matthew 29 because most people in attendance weren't Christian. A professor from the University of Nanking (a Christian from Xiaguan) told me that he estimated the audience at 400, the largest congregation they've had so far. The meeting was held in the large lecture hall of the college of science. It was truly packed to capacity, but everybody listened attentively" (Zhang 2005, 118).

Name (Most names given as father – mother surnames)	Former address	Current Address	Date of birth	Sex	Miscarriage	Current age of child	Remedy for insufficient milk	Mother's milk quantity	Date of death
Gao – Song	No. 250 Houzaimen	U. of N. Dormitory C	10, 10th month of lunar calendar	Boy		3 months	Rice powder	Insufficient	
Chen – Ying	No. 141 Shuiximen	Dormitory C	21, 9th month of lunar calendar	Girl		3+ months	Porridge	Insufficient	
Fan – Li	No. 384 Zhujiang Road	Dormitory C	9, 11th month of lunar calendar	Boy		2 months	Porridge	Insufficient	
Wang – Zhou	No. 25 Tongjimen	Dormitory B	23, 9th month of lunar calendar	Boy		3+ months	Porridge	Insufficient	
Xia – Yang	Waguang Temple	Dormitory B	2, 10th month of lunar calendar	Boy		3+ months	Porridge	Insufficient	
Chen – Yao	No. 84 Pingshi Street	Dormitory B	27, 9th month of lunar calendar	Girl		3+ months	Porridge	Insufficient	
Liu – Zhang	Banbianying	West Building	7, 10th month of lunar calendar	Boy		3 months	Porridge	Insufficient	
Li – Ma	No. 29 Zhangjiafu	Dormitory C	21, 12th month of lunar calendar	Girl		3 weeks	Porridge	Insufficient	

Continued

Name (Most names given as father – mother surnames)	Former address	Current Address	Date of birth	Sex	Miscarriage	Current age of child	Remedy for insufficient milk	Mother's milk quantity	Date of death
Chen – Yang	No. 20 Zhongshanmen	Dormitory C	24, 2nd month of lunar calendar	Girl		3 weeks	Porridge	Insufficient	
Zhang – Xu	No. 22 Zhongshanmen	West Building	11, 12th month of lunar calendar	Girl		1 month	Porridge	Insufficient	
Tong – Ding	Huapailou	East Building	9, 11th month of lunar calendar	Boy		2+ months	Milk cake		
Wang – Tao	Tongzuofang	East Building	6, 1st month of lunar calendar	Girl		1 week	Milk	Insufficient	
Feng – Jin	No. 4 Xijiaxiang	Same as above	11, 1th month of lunar calendar	Girl		2 months	Milk	Insufficient	
Zhang – Wang	No. 3 Zhubaolang	Same as above	26, 10th month of lunar calendar	Boy		2+ months	Milk	Extremely insufficient	
Guo – Guo	No. 8 Shangxinhe	Same as above	12, 10th month of lunar calendar	Boy		3 months	Milk porridge	Insufficient	
Wang – Wang	No. 29 Maxiang	Same as above	9, 10th month of lunar calendar	Girl		2+ months	Milk sufficient	Excess	

3.3 Westerners in the Face of the Rape of Nanking — 215

Continued

Name (Most names given as father – mother surnames)	Former address	Current Address	Date of birth	Sex	Miscarriage	Current age of child	Remedy for insufficient milk	Mother's milk quantity	Date of death
Liu – Sun	No. 11 Nanputing	Same as above	9, 10th month of lunar calendar	Girl		3 months	Milk	Extremely insufficient	
Zhu – Kong	No. 14 Tangfangiang	Same as above	25, 11th month of lunar calendar	Boy		1+ month	Milk	Close to sufficient	
Wang – Jiang	No. 30 Xiaoshiqiao	Same as above	20, 7th month of lunar calendar	Girl		Half week	Porridge		Mother deceased
Cai – Xu	No. 12 Taipingxiang	Dormitory I	7, 12th month of lunar calendar	Boy		1+ month	Porridge	None	
Shen – Hong	No. 53 Changshu Dongmen	Dormitory I	7, 12th month of lunar calendar	Boy		1+ month	Milk porridge	Insufficient	
Ma – Mo	No. 94 Pingshi Street	Same as above	14, 12th month of lunar calendar	Girl		1 month	Milk	Sufficient	
Tian – Xu	No. 17 Shuangtang	Dormitory H	11, 11th month of lunar calendar	Girl	Baby died	2 months	Milk		23, 11th month of lunar calendar
Guo – Li	No. 82 Gang Street	Dormitory I	3, 1st month of lunar calendar	Boy	Baby lived	9 days	Milk	None	

Continued

Name (Most names given as father – mother surnames)	Former address	Current Address	Date of birth	Sex	Miscarriage	Current age of child	Remedy for insufficient milk	Mother's milk quantity	Date of death
Nie – Li	No. 225 Zhima Village	Dormitory G	5, 11th month of lunar calendar	Boy	Baby lived	2+ months	Porridge	None	
Wu – Chen	No. 125 Shiba Street	Dormitory G	25, 12th month of lunar calendar	Girl	Baby died	1 month			28, 12th month of lunar calendar
Zheng – Lin	No. 96 Mianhualou	Dormitory G	5, 1st month of lunar calendar	Girl	Baby lived	7 days	Milk	Sufficient	
Diao – Zhang	Wuding Bridge	Gym	25, 12th month of lunar calendar	Boy	Baby lived	Half month	Milk	Sufficient	
Wang Yong	No. 25 Donghanmen	East Building	6, 11th month of lunar calendar	Boy		2 months	Milk	Sufficient	
Zhang Yongfu	No. 12 Shiba Street	U. of N. Library	7, 2nd month of lunar calendar	Girl		4 days	Suckle	Sufficient	
Yang Ruiwu	Sandao Gaojing	Same as above	5, 11th month of lunar calendar	Girl		2+ months	Porridge	Insufficient	
Tao Jizhong	Fuminfang	Same as above	5, 11th month of lunar calendar	Boy		2+ months	Porridge	Insufficient	

Continued

Name (Most names given as father – mother surnames)	Former address	Current Address	Date of birth	Sex	Miscarriage	Current age of child	Remedy for insufficient milk	Mother's milk quantity	Date of death
Xu Shuyi	No. 111 Taiping Road	Same as above	3, 12th month of lunar calendar	Girl		1+ month	Porridge	Insufficient	
Mo Peijie	Daxinggong	Same as above	28, 12th month of lunar calendar	Boy		1+ month	Porridge	Insufficient	
Liu Enfu	No. 27 Guanghuamen	Same as above	21, 11th month of lunar calendar	Girl		1+ month	Porridge	Insufficient	
Luo Sijin	No. 4 Wutaishan	Same as above	12, 11th month of lunar calendar	Girl		2 months	Porridge	Insufficient	
Ma Qianren	Fengfuxiang	Same as above	15, 11th month of lunar calendar	Boy		2+ months	Porridge	Insufficient	
Xie Daolong	Baoshan County North Gate	Same as above	5, 1st month of lunar calendar	Girl		1 week	Porridge	Insufficient	
Wu Jingqi	No. 36 Guanghuamen	Same as above	20, 11th month of lunar calendar	Boy		1+ month	Porridge	Insufficient	
Cui Youcai	No. 216 Pingshi Street	Same as above	22, 12th month of lunar calendar	Girl		3 weeks	Porridge	Insufficient	

Continued

Name (Most names given as father – mother surnames)	Former address	Current Address	Date of birth	Sex	Miscarriage	Current age of child	Remedy for insufficient milk	Mother's milk quantity	Date of death
Dong Guoxing	No. 80 Wuxueyuan	Same as above	19, 12th month of lunar calendar	Girl		3 weeks	Porridge	Insufficient	
Tao Yuming		Same as above	11, 11th month of lunar calendar	Girl		2 months	Porridge	Insufficient	
Pan Bingyuan	No. 62 Caixia Street	Same as above	24, 11th month of lunar calendar	Boy		1+ month	Porridge	Insufficient	
Tang Mingyu	Same as above	Same as above	Same as above	Boy		1+ month	Porridge	Insufficient	

Table 16: University of Nanking refugee birth survey (February 11, 1938).
Source: Chen, Zhang, and Dai (n.d., 440–443).

Vautrin also found that when things were at their worst, some people who had never believed in religion even started attending their services for spiritual solace. She wrote on January 2 that not long after the Japanese occupation of the city, she and others began holding religious activities in the Ginling Women's College shelter: "Religion has become a vital sustaining force in many lives."

Also in her diary entry of January 2, 1938, Vautrin wrote about the religious services held that day: "Mr. Li and I went over to Drum Tower to Church. They had a very, very fine service – the speaker, who used to be in our Sunday School work at South Gate, then left distinctly religious work for a business career, largely selfish, shared by his sermon that he had learned a deep spiritual lesson through his suffering. There must have been eighty at the service. Religion has become a vital sustaining force in many lives. James McCallum said they had a fine service last Sunday also. The church was decorated in red, and really looked festive. This afternoon at 4:30 the English service was revived – after four or five Sundays of omission. I went to the service this morning and Mary this afternoon. We do not both like to leave the campus at the same time – in fact one of us is always here with the Japanese police letter to drive off stray soldiers. We have had three services on the campus today. Our 7:30 prayer service this morning, a 2 o'clock service this afternoon for women, and a 7:30 service this evening for campus servants. We have enough helpers on the campus so we can take turns – Miss Wang took morning meeting, Miss Lo afternoon, and Ms. Chen the evening."

Forster writes that he and Magee were "invited to a New Years' Supper along with all the refugees from #25 and #17 who get their food from our common kitchen (there are a good many who cook their own.) The food was placed in circles on the floor of #25 and we sat around on kneeling cushions to eat it. In order to save rice and money, the people have been taking only two meals a day and they are chiefly vegetarian with thick rice congee. The managing committee asked for permission to serve dry cooked rice and an extra bowl of food. John readily agreed. In addition I contributed $5 as from you and me and John contributed $5 as from himself and Faith, so they were all able to have two extra dishes of meat. It was a grand party, about fifty people and everybody ate to his heart's content for once" (Zhang 2005, 123–124).

Rabe also discovered that the refugees housed on his property lived in fear all day. To mitigate their feelings of desperation and inspire confidence in the future, Rabe distributed red envelopes of money on Christmas, New Year, and Chinese New Year and also increased food provisions, to drum up good feelings among his refugees (Rabe CN, 443).

3.3.2.6 Arrangements for new lives for refugees

While the Rape of Nanking was still unfolding, the International Committee began thinking about how the refugees would pick up the pieces of their lives after the catastrophe had passed. The Japanese occupation and subsequent outbursts of violence deprived many refugees in the Safety Zone of family members, as well as physical materials upon which their lives depended. Once out of the camps, these people would have to face the pressure of making a living with no resources whatsoever. Vautrin wrote on January 13: "With 70,000 soldiers living off the land for a little time there are few or no chickens, pigs, or cows left. Donkeys are being killed for meat, and horses also."

Vocational training classes were held in the shelters in the University of Nanking and the Ginling Women's College. The Westerners hoped that refugees could use skills acquired in the classes to make a living. Bates and others taught literacy and vocational courses in the University of Nanking for refugees. Bates wrote in a circular of November 29, 1938 that the university "is trying hard to open primary schools of some size in different places, vocational classes for young farmers, remedial verbal and mathematics classes for children who dropped out in middle school, and some illiteracy elimination work as well" (Zhang 2005, 48).

(Morning)			
8:00—9:00	Men's physical training	Every day	Maximum students (under normal conditions): 10
9:00—10:00	Advanced Japanese	Every day	20
10:00—11:00	Advanced English	6 days	10
	Basic English	6 days	40
	Basic Japanese	6 days	20
	Sunday Service	Sundays	150
11:00—12:00	Women's physical training	Every day	10
(Afternoon)			
1:00—2:00	Advanced Chinese	Every day	60
	Basic Chinese	Every day	60
2:00—3:00	Advanced Chinese	Every day	60
	Basic Chinese	Every day	60

Continued

(Afternoon)			
3:00—4:00	Women's hygiene	5 days	20
	Bible class	2 days	120
4:00—5:00	Hymn singing class	3 days	60
	Basic science	3 days	20
7:00—9:00	Bible study	Every day	60

Table 17: Refugee classes in primary University of Nanking buildings.
Source: Zhang (2010, vol. 1, 482).

Bates wrote in the same circular of November 29 that the most important work of providing new lives for refugees was done by the reorganized sub-committees of the International Relief Committee, through "cash relief, refugee camp management, public relief projects, clothing, health and sanitation, and small loans for trade and production" (Zhang 2005, 48). The Reorganized Committee established a main office as well as district offices in the south city district, the city center district, the north city district, and the Shuangtang district. These offices were charged with conducting detailed surveys of households in their districts. On February 3, 1938, the offices of the reorganized Committee conducted surveys of over 17,000 households.

Number of households surveyed	March 1–10	March 11–20	March 21–31	March	February	February and March combined
Main office	2,432	1,825	1,822	6,079	3,198	9,277
City center	1,348	750	796	2,894	558	3,452
South city	417	655	789	1,861	—	1,861
North city	38	540	793	1,371	—	1,371
Shuangtang	—	416	909	1,325	—	1,325
Totals	4,235	4,186	5,109	13,530	3,756	17,286

Table 18: Statistics compiled from household surveys conducted by all offices of reorganized committee (February and March 1938).
Source: "Comparative statistical report of reorganized commissions of the Nanking International Relief Committee" (Zhu n.d., 157).

On the basis of these detailed surveys, the reorganized committee was able to provide assistance to refugee households in many areas, including bringing the sick to hospitals for treatment, distributing cash, and supplying all other kinds of relief materials.

	March 1–10	March 11–20	March 21–31	March	February	February and March combined
Sets of bedding distributed	107	81	464	652	16	668
Free food tickets distributed	200	293	451	944	247	1,191
Towels distributed	12	16	11	39	12	51
Cloth jackets distributed	10	158	382	550	8	558
Broad beans distributed (dou)	—	103.7	284.5	388.2	—	388.2
Milk powder distributed (pounds)	—	27	40.5	67.5	—	67.5
Fish liver oil distributed (ounces)	—	311	810	1,121	—	1,121
Coffins distributed	1	—	—	1	—	—
Job placements	26	366	838	1,230	—	1,230

Table 19: Statistics of materials distribution and job placement by the reorganized committee (February and March 1938).
Source: "Comparative statistical report of reorganized commissions of the Nanking International Relief Committee" (Zhu n.d., 159).

Number of households assisted	
Main office	7,259
South city district office	1,930
City center office	1,174
North city office	762
Shuangtang office	1,020
Total	12,145
Cash distributed to refugees	
Main office	27,201.00
South city district office	7,080.00
City center office	3,263.00
North city office	2,709.00
Shuangtang office	3,472.00

Continued	
Cash distributed to refugees	
Total	42,725.00

Table 20: Cash relief distributed by reorganized committee (February 7 to March 31, 1938). Original note: 3.52 yuan per household on average. Source: "Comparative statistical report of reorganized commissions of the Nanking International Relief Committee" (Zhu n.d., 160).

In addition, the reorganized committee also provided assistance to refugee households through public works relief. Statistics demonstrate that from March 8 to 31, 1938, the reorganized committee paid a total of 490.20 yuan in wages to 1,237 laborers hired directly by the Committee, as reported in the "Report of the Nanking International Relief Committee on daily replacement of charity with labor" (Zhu n.d., 160–162).

3.3.2.7 Case study: the Siemens China refugee center

During the Rape of Nanking, Rabe led comprehensive efforts to save the lives of Chinese refugees, and also meticulously ran a refugee shelter in his own home. As a result of Rabe's efforts, nobody died from Japanese violence inside this shelter, nor was any woman sheltered there dishonored. His house was an "island of safety" in a tumultuous sea of violence by Japanese soldiers.

Prior to the city's fall, the numbers of Chinese seeking shelter from air raids in Rabe's dugout grew steadily. Rabe even affixed a large poster written in German, Chinese, and English to the doorway of his dugout:

> A Bulletin for My Guests and Members of My Household: Anyone using my bomb shelter must obey the rule giving the safest seats, meaning those in the middle of the dugout, to women and children— whoever they may be. Men are to make do with other seats or stand. Anyone disobeying this instruction may not use the dugout in the future (Rabe EN, 14).

Chaos ruled the streets at the time of Nanjing's fall, so Rabe shut his gates. Some people, however, climbed the walls into his compound. Women and children fervently knocked at his gates, begging to be admitted. "I can't listen to their wailing any longer, so I open both gates and let everyone in who wants in. Since there's no more room in the dugouts, I allocate people to various sheds and to corners of the house. Most have brought their bedding and lie down in the open" (Rabe EN, 64).

An enormous German flag was spread out across Rabe's courtyard, originally as a signal to Japanese bombers not to target this place: "A few very clever sorts spread their beds out under the large German flag we had stretched out in case of air raids. This location is considered especially 'bombproof'!" Rabe himself could no longer access his air raid shelter. Wearing his steel helmet, "I run through the garden like a watchdog, moving from group to group, scolding here and calming there. And in the end they all obey my every word" Later that night Rabe wrote: "Every joint in my body hurts. I've not been out of these clothes for 48 hours. My guests are settling in for the night as well. Around 30 people are asleep in my office, three in the coal bin, eight women and children in the servant's lavatory, and the rest, over a hundred people, are in the dugouts or out in the open, in the garden, on the cobblestones, everywhere!" (Rabe EN, 64–65).

As refugees thronged to the Safety Zone, Rabe's house came to be considered the safest place in the city; an unbroken chain of refugees sought shelter there. Every time his gates were opened to let a car in or out, women and children would rush in and begin to kowtow. On December 24, the Japanese demanded that Chinese refugees in the Safety Zone be registered, and began issuing "good citizen certificates." Prior to this point, Rabe had thought there were 350 to 400 people in his courtyard. However, his assistant Han Xianglin made an accurate count: "There are a total of 602 people living in the office and courtyard (302 male and 300 female, with 126 under the age of 10, and one 2-month-old infant). These figures do not include the 14 company employees, domestic workers, and their family members, who bring the total up to 650."[29] Rabe's courtyard was about 500 square meters in area; one can imagine the degree of crowding. After its inspections of refugee shelters, the International Committee suggested moving a portion of these refugees into a less crowded shelter, but nobody was willing to leave.

Germany was Japan's ally at the time, so Rabe flew a German flag from his roof and posted notices on his gate from the German and Japanese embassies, but this did not prevent harassment by Japanese soldiers. During those days and nights of terror, the "women and children" in Rabe's courtyard "silently huddled together, staring at one another with their panicked eyes. Half of them were doing this for warmth, and half to boost courage. Everyone's hope was that this 'foreign devil' could drive away the real devils!" (Rabe CN, 151)

---

29 For the complete list see Appendix One of Chen, Zhang, and Dai, eds., *Deguo shilingguan wenshu*.

One night when Rabe was returning home at 6 p.m., some Japanese soldiers were climbing the walls into his compound: "One of them had already removed his uniform and opened his belt, and was attempting to rape a girl refugee." Rabe ordered him to climb out the way he had come in. On December 23, when Rabe was working at International Committee headquarters at Number 5 Ninghai Road, a servant ran in to inform Rabe that a Japanese soldier had broken in and was rummaging around Rabe's personal office, trying to open the safe. By the time he and Kröger got to the office, "The intruder had just absconded. He'd been unable to open the safe by himself" (Rabe EN, 88–89). As they were sitting down to eat, three more Japanese soldiers climbed in; Rabe made them go back out the way they'd come in. Kröger volunteered to house-sit for Rabe that afternoon. Right as Rabe was leaving, another six Japanese soldiers came over the wall (Rabe CN, 216).

These intruders were pursuing two goals: loot and rape. One intruder Rabe chased off threatened him with a weapon. One Japanese soldier pointed his bayonet at Rabe. Another pointed his pistol at him. Every time similar events occurred, Rabe sternly rebuked the soldiers and pointed at the swastika insignia on his sleeve. Once Rabe protested at the Japanese embassy about the illegal entry into his house of Japanese soldiers. The chief of the embassy police replied with a "shrug, and the problem has been dealt with as far as he is concerned" (Rabe EN, 89).

Once when Rabe was not at home, a Japanese soldier broke in and began chasing after women. It just so happened that a Japanese translator from the Japanese embassy was in the house at the time. The translator blocked the soldier and made him leave, ending the matter. Another time, a Japanese soldier attempting to rape a woman was caught in the act by Rabe and a Japanese army officer. The officer slapped the soldier twice, and then let him go. It was very dangerous for refugees to leave Rabe's house at this time. On December 31, two men sheltering in Rabe's house left and were kidnapped by Japanese soldiers and forced to carry booty for them. When Rabe returned home that noon, the wife of one of the men kneeled before Rabe imploring him to bring them home, lest they be killed. Rabe took this woman, dressed in rags, out in his car to find the men. After talking with 20 fully armed Japanese soldiers, he finally got the men released from the clutches of the most unwilling Japanese soldiers. Once home, Rabe scolded the two men in front of the rest of the refugees, exhorting the crowd to not frivolously leave the compound (Rabe CN, 255).

In addition to providing security, Rabe also provided means of subsistence for these refugees. At one point he brought 60 straw mattresses to his compound for the refugees. It was right in the middle of winter, so the refugees used these mattresses along with broken doors and other materials in the courtyard to build shacks to keep out the cold and snow (Rabe CN, 157).

The International Committee, led by Rabe, provided food to the refugees in his courtyard. The Committee provided a daily allotment of three sacks of rice, with about 300 cups of rice per sack, to this shelter. Adults received two cups per day, and children one cup. This rice was distributed free of charge. The day-to-day management of this shelter was handled by Rabe's assistant at Siemens Han Xianglin, who also served as director of the Safety Zone Food Commission. Refugees in this shelter were better fed than those elsewhere, so much so that the International Committee's surveyor wrote of it: "There is obviously much more rice distributed in this shelter than in the others" (Rabe CN, 309).

A blizzard struck Nanjing in late January 1938. "You really don't have to be softhearted to feel pity for these poor people here." Rabe's courtyard became one big mud puddle: "Little channels have been dug around the tents and straw huts to let some of the snow water run off." Of most concern to Rabe were the fires: "More than once I've just closed my eyes when I've spotted open fires under those low straw roofs. In the driving wind and snow, fires are impossible outside. So if people are to have any warmth at all, we simply have to run the risk" (Rabe EN, 142).

To improve living conditions for refugees, Rabe had a few thousand "stolen" bricks brought from a half-built house in his neighborhood so the refugees could build narrow paths between their shacks to avoid walking in the mud. Rabe even had a brick wall built around the outhouse to make the camp a little more "elegant."

On December 27, Rabe found time to play Santa Claus and gave out 20 cents each to all the children refugees in his house (126 in total), only adding to the crowding and chaos there: "They almost tore me to pieces, and when I saw that fathers holding babies were in danger of being crushed, I had to give up trying to distribute the money. Only about 80 or 90 children received their gift." Rabe said he'd seek out the remaining children "as opportunity arises" (Rabe EN, 99).

January 30, 1938 was New Year's Eve in the Chinese lunar calendar. After two days of blizzard, the snow began to melt, and Rabe's courtyard turned into a swamp. Rabe and Han raised 100 yuan in cash and distributed one yuan to each of the poorest refugees, "which made them all very very happy." The International Committee also agreed to grant a special subsidy of five yuan to this relatively small shelter to buy spices for a New Year's dinner. What's more, "everyone is to receive (on the sly) one teacup of rice in addition to their daily very scant ration of two cups." These very small contributions made them "extremely grateful" (Rabe EN, 164).

December 25, 1938 was Christmas. Rabe was also extremely grateful on this day: "I've just received a Christmas present better than any I could have wished. I have been given 600 human lives" (Rabe EN, 97). When the Japanese "refugee registration commission" came to Rabe's house, all the men were called out one by one and registered according to a strict procedure, with women and children standing on the left and men on the right. Rabe offered cigars and Siemens notebooks to the officials in charge, and the process went smoothly, with nobody hauled off. Refugee registration in this area had been completed by the afternoon of December 26. Even the 20 people who had sneaked into the compound were given "good citizen certificates" (Rabe CN, 226–227). Rabe's refugees had been spared a looting. The Japanese "cleared out" 20,000 people from other areas of the Safety Zone, some of whom were put to work, and the rest of whom were killed.

In late January 1938, newly appointed commander of the Nanjing Defense Garrison Amaya Naojiro ordered that all residents of the Safety Zone return to their homes by February 4. On February 3, the day before the deadline, the Zone's shelters were full of depressed and sobbing refugees. Seventy girls and women in Rabe's courtyard got on both knees and kowtowed over and over, wailing, imploring Rabe: "You are our father and our mother. You have protected us till now, don't stop half way! If we are going to be violated and have to die, then we want to die here!" Rabe permitted them to stay. Only a few older people left (Rabe EN, 171).

The selfless help given by the Westerners in the face of disaster earned them the respect of the common Chinese. Rabe was no longer seen as an abominable "foreign devil," and the Chinese in his house revered him "like a god" (Rabe CN, 156). On New Year's Day 1938, Rabe wrote: "When I return home in my car, I am received with a royal salute." The refugees in his courtyard formed into two lines outside his house and set off fireworks they'd gotten from the Japanese to celebrate the founding of the Autonomous Committee, in homage to Rabe: "Then all my six hundred parishioners surround me and give me a New Year's greeting written in red ink on white wrapping paper, which reads 'We sincerely wish you a happy new year! Make a fortune as money keep pouring in!'... They all bow three times and are very happy when I bow my head in gratitude and fold up the greeting and put it in my pocket" (Rabe EN, 108).

3.3.3 Records and Expositions of the Massacre

3.3.3.1 Documents of the Nanking Safety Zone

In 1939, Professor Shuhsi Hsu [Xu Shuxi] of Yenching University compiled some of the documents that had "fortunately survived" of the International Committee into a book titled *Documents of the Nanking Safety Zone*, later published in Shanghai. In the book's foreword, Xu explains that some of the book's contents had been published in *Riben zhanzheng xingwei* [Japan's War Actions], edited by Xu, and in the appendix of Harold Timperley's *What War Means: The Japanese Terror in China*, but "since these were important sources of materials for historiography and international legal research, as well as important evidence of the noble actions of a few righteous men and women, it was clearly a moral act to independently publish as many of these documents as possible as a dedicated collection" (Zhang 2006b, 269).

The book contains 69 documents from the Safety Zone, spanning a period from the day after the Japanese occupation, that being December 14, 1937, through to the collection's last letter, written on February 19, 1938, informing embassies that the International Committee for the Nanking Safety Zone was being reorganized as the Nanking International Relief Committee.

Shortly after the Japanese occupation of the city, Rabe felt that "the previous period during which we experienced vicious bombing raids and a sustained attack now seems like nothing at all compared to the horrible times we're in now" (Rabe CN, 146). His only solace was the thought that military discipline would be restored once high-ranking officers of the Japanese army arrived. On December 16, however, the International Committee wrote a letter to Fukuda, attaché to the Japanese embassy, describing general conditions in the Safety Zone (Rabe CN, 146). The letter pointed out: "We refrained from protesting yesterday because we thought when the High Commander arrived order in the city would be restored, but last night was even worse than the night before, so we decided these matters should be called to the attention of the Imperial Japanese Army, which we are sure does not approve of such actions by its soldiers" (Rabe EN, 74). Attached to the letter was a report titled "Violence by Japanese Soldiers in the Nanking Safety Zone," which listed out 15 "well documented" cases of Japanese violence reported by the International Committee (Rabe CN, 147–149).

From that point onward, writing letters of protest detailing instances of violence by Japanese soldiers became a daily activity for the Committee. Smythe, the Committee's secretary, wrote in a letter to his family: "The crimes happen so fast I can hardly keep up, so I've started to use shorthand. If I wait for someone else to record them, it'll be too late, because the embassy asks us to report only conditions from the present day. So now I'm using shorthand all the time" (Zhang 2005, 240).

Smythe continued: "Since the 14 I've had to have Bates compile details at the university nearly every day for a letter of protest and records of crimes committed by Japanese soldiers, with an attached letter of censure. In addition, Minnie Vautrin lodges protests at the embassy every day. We've gone two or three times. It should be enough, but we've not seen any great use to it" (Zhang 2005, 243). Rabe wrote in his diary entry of December 18: "At 8 o'clock Herr Hatz shows up in a truck with a Japanese police commissioner and a whole battery of gendarmes, who are supposed to guard Ginling College tonight" (Rabe EN, 80). Nevertheless, not only were these "gendarmes" unable to stop crimes from happening, but some of them even participated. Vautrin wrote in her diary entry of December 21: "After breakfast we collected facts about the harm done by our guard of 25 last night (two women raped)."

The Japanese right-wing fanatic Matsumura Toshio titled one section of his book "Radical Changes in the International Committee's Documents," censuring the Committee for suddenly "gradually increasing the quantity of reports of violence by Japanese soldiers" on the 16th despite no such reports on the 14th and 15th (Matsumura, 43). The truth is that these reports on crimes by Japanese soldiers were made at the request of Japanese diplomats. In testimony given before the Nanjing War Crimes Tribunal, Smythe said of the protests submitted to the Japanese: "We only started the reports after the Japanese had asked us for proof" (Hu 2006, 368).

The International Committee then began submitting letters of protest to the Japanese embassy at fixed intervals, attaching numbered reports of crimes committed by Japanese soldiers in the Safety Zone. Originally all the letters were drafted in the name of Committee Secretary Smythe, but later Rabe had the idea of "taking turns signing the letters," since they came from different countries (Yang 2006, 195). It was thus that Smythe and the others "sent out two letters of protest nearly every day during the first six weeks after the Japanese occupation." Usually one of the letters was "delivered in person to the Japanese embassy" by either Rabe or Smythe, the other being delivered by the International Committee's courier (Yang 2006, 195).

Smythe explained the situation: "Before drafting letters of protest and delivering them to the Japanese embassy, I did my utmost to verify the accuracy of the cases reported. Even if I had to determine where the representative of the International Committee who reported the case was, I did my best to interview them. All the cases we reported to the Japanese embassy were those I found to be accurate and reliable" (Yang 2006, 195).

Rabe wrote in his diary entry of December 15: "What we need to do now is get on good terms with the occupying army. This should not be difficult for a European, but it's no easy task to perform well as committee chairman" (Rabe CN, 144). It is precisely for these reasons that when reading reports of Japanese crimes submitted by the International Committee, we should note that other than the so-called "Ministry of Justice incident" (Zhang 2006b, 286), when 50 Safety Zone policemen were taken away by Japanese soldiers, very few of the Committee's records touch on organized searches or massacres by the Japanese army.

It is precisely because these reports were submitted to Japanese authorities that there are so many differences between the International Committee's official records and the private records made by Westerners. There are many records of Japanese massacres of Chinese "remnant troops" or young men suspected of being soldiers in internal Safety Zone dossiers and the private diaries and letters of Westerners in the city at the time; none of these made it into the official reports.

In early January 1938, when American, British, German, and other diplomats began returning to the city, the International Committee began sending copies of reports of atrocities committed by Japanese soldiers to these embassies. In these letters, the International Committee made highly explicit critiques of the kind not used in reports delivered to the Japanese embassy. For example, in a letter to Allison of the American embassy on January 10, 1938, Smythe expressed his view on cases reported thus far: "Incident #185 clearly demonstrates the inhumanity of Japanese soldiers executing civilians, but more importantly also touches on the threat to our lives and health and those of residents here, because the entire Zone is full of bodies, particularly the ponds... Incident #187 demonstrates that there are some of vile character among the Japanese military police, whom the Chinese and we are supposed to trust" (Zhang 2006b, 324).

The Japanese warned not only civilian foreigners but also diplomats about reporting on Japanese violence. Rabe wrote: "The Japanese have asked him [Rosen of the German embassy], just as they have asked me, to be somewhat cautious in his reports" (Rabe EN, 119).

The International Committee was not the only body issuing reports to the Japanese. Bates, chairman of the University of Nanking Emergency Committee, also submitted reports to the Japanese embassy on all manner of crimes committed by Japanese soldiers on the university campus. Taking Rabe's advice, Bates "submitted an independently written report to the Japanese embassy nearly every day detailing crimes committed by Japanese soldiers in the largest refugee shelter in the Safety Zone, the one inside the university. The crimes included: 1,720 illegal entries by Japanese soldiers into the campus, forcing 647 people away to serve as laborers, dishonoring 290 women, and more than 60 cases of murder" (Hora 1987, 92).

Another portion of the "Documents from the Safety Zone," other than letters of protest, is composed of back-and-forth letters between the Committee and the Japanese embassy about providing relief to refugees. Especially in its attempts to contact the outside world for food relief, the Committee communicated multiple times with the Japanese embassy.

Some of the reports in the collection were never submitted to the Japanese, including the "Memorandum on Refugee Registration in the University of Nanking (December 26, 1937)." This document called Japanese rule directly into question and directly censured Japanese authorities for organized massacre.

3.3.3.2 Foreigners' dissemination of the truth about the massacre

A common goal emerged among the foreign community in Nanjing: to record violence by Japanese soldiers in Nanjing and spread the word, to use international public opinion to pressure Japanese authorities into reining in their troops.

A few American and British reporters were in the city when it fell. They witnessed the violence perpetrated by Japanese soldiers during the first few days of the occupation. They were then "politely escorted" out of the city by Japanese troops on December 15 and 16, after which point nobody but Japanese were permitted in or out of Nanjing. All means of communication with the outside world – telephones, telegrams, and the post – were all cut off. Even people with radios had no way to use them, as electricity had not been restored. The Chinese and foreigners in Nanjing at the time were completely cut off from the rest of the world.

The Westerners remaining in Nanjing started reporting on instances of violence by Japanese soldiers to Japanese authorities three days after the occupation. Bates wrote in a circular of April 12, 1938: "We feel that there is a certain moral necessity to make known the terrible facts in a constructive way. Only ourselves or people working with us can do that. Others are gaining access to the materials more and more freely by indirect means and are bringing them out in semi-commercial form" (Zhang 2005, 35). Magee's thinking was that despite the difficulty of publicizing Japanese atrocities to the world, "we should record them so that these undying truths will become part of the world's legacy" (Zhang 2005, 163).

Officials of the Japanese embassy returned to Nanjing on December 14 and even helped the Westerners get word of their safety to family members, but clearly they weren't going to allow letters or telegrams that touched in the very least on violence perpetrated by Japanese forces. Some Japanese merchants and military officers occasionally helped carry letters from Westerners out of the city, but Vautrin, who had a letter carried for her to Shanghai by a Japanese colonel, wrote on January 6: "It was a most difficult letter to write." The Japanese embassy clearly called upon Westerners to say "nothing bad about the emperor." The foreigners were extremely conscious of the enormous risk they would run by exposing Japanese violence while living in Nanjing under Japanese military occupation.

In early January 1938, with the return of Western diplomats to the city came channels of information dissemination for exposing the Rape of Nanking outside the control of Japanese authorities. American and British gunboats ran between Shanghai and Nanjing, bringing letters into and out of the city. The radio transmitters on these boats provided a means for Westerners in Nanjing to contact the outside world. They wrote an enormous amount of letters to family members, friends, companies, and religious organizations outside the city; in these they provided detailed accounts of atrocities committed by Japanese soldiers during this period.

More reports came from Westerners leaving Nanjing. McCallum wrote in a letter to his wife: "They would like to have had us all out of Nanking but now that we have stayed so long and know so much, we are not allowed to leave – we are virtually prisoners" (Zhang 2005, 211). The Japanese did not start permitting foreigners to leave until after the end of January 1938; most who left at this time went to Shanghai. Upon arriving there, they began giving reports to religious organizations and delivering public lectures to get the word out about Japanese atrocities in Nanjing. They had their own concerns in so doing, because other Westerners remained in Nanjing. Forster again wrote in a letter to his wife: "Please be circumspect about retailing news about conditions here, since the J. are anxious to keep as much under cover as possible" (Zhang 2005, 107).

There were practical difficulties for the Westerners in Nanjing to get word of Japanese atrocities out of the city: only detailed accounts given by eyewitnesses could lend credibility to the news. But to do so they would have to attach their names to the reports, or otherwise interlace their reports with clues as to their identities, which would reveal the sources of information to Japanese authorities, which might expose them to harm in Nanjing.

Harold Timperley's *What War Means: The Japanese Terror in China* was the first book published in English detailing the Rape of Nanking. He drew his contents mostly from the records of Bates and other Americans in Nanjing at the time. After receiving Timperley's plan, Bates, still in Nanjing, wrote on March 21, 1938, that "Mills, Smythe, and I, who have taken the responsibility, decided to approve going ahead" even though they "understood you would be gathering facts from these sources [their letters] but not that they would constitute so much of the book per se" (Zhang 2010, vol. 1, 257). Bates, facing a dilemma between protecting people and getting the truth out, made a great deal of suggestions to Timperley:

> 6. We enclose our only copy of Sindberg's notes from Tsehsiashan [Qixia Mountain]. His name must not be disclosed, as the company is very cautious...
>
> 10. We have eliminated the names of Chinese who reported cases, as protection against retaliation.
>
> 11. Some people think that as a matter of principle and of expediency, no Japanese should be mentioned unfavorably by name. My correspondence hits Takatama hard, chief of the Consular Police attached to the Embassy, and a dangerous man. I have no urging for or against, but raise the question whether his name should be eliminated.
>
> 12. There is little use to pretend to try to cover George and me. Any of the Japanese in or near the Embassy here, some in Shanghai, some in Tokyo, could identify either of us on first reading of those main chapters...
>
> 18. List of western nationals in Nanking. This might help to keep things clear for careful readers and those with personal or institutional connections in Nanking (some thousands over the course of years). Also, it avoids confusion from the notes on persons which often include absentees – e.g. Fenn's house, and so on (Zhang 2010, vol. 1, 258–260).

Fitch made a trip to Shanghai to seek aid for Nanjing from charitable organizations there. He hid negatives of photographs taken by Magee of Japanese atrocities in a special compartment in his coat, but he was extremely cautious in public statements made in Shanghai, as he wished to return to Nanjing (Rabe CN, 455). The next time he left Nanjing, it was on a trip to the U.S., where he displayed Magee's documentary and gave public speeches on Japanese atrocities. When news of his actions reached Nanjing, members of the Japanese embassy expressed outrage, claiming that Fitch had "tricked" them and "went to the U.S. only to encourage that country to take an aggressive stance toward Japan."

There were other political factors limiting the extent to which Westerners in Nanjing could expose what they had seen. Rabe wrote and organized his diary on events in Nanjing meticulously, but he had this to say on the title page: "I wrote and compiled this diary not for the public, but for my wife and family. If one day it is suitable to publish it, the assent of the German government must first be obtained, but today it goes without saying that it is absolutely not possible" (Rabe CN, foreword). The case was the same for the diary of another German, Christian Kröger. It was only after Kröger died at the age of 90 that his son Peter found his diary entitled "Days of Fate in Nanking" in his father's desk drawer; he later gave the diary to Iris Chang. A line at the end of Kröger's diary explains why he kept the diary a secret for so long: its contents "are contrary to the perspectives of the present regime of Hitler. So I must be extremely cautious about this report" (Chang n.d., 256–257).

When Nanjing fell, there were five British and American reporters in the city who sent out reports on atrocities being perpetrated by the Japanese army. After this first burst, however, Western reporters were denied permission to return to Nanjing for a long time afterward.

Western diplomats returning to the city learned of Japanese atrocities through their own observations and the reports of their compatriots. They also started disseminating news of the Rape of Nanking to government bodies in their home countries, but they were all filed as intelligence reports and not widely disseminated, and thus had no impact on public opinion. Only the "Allison incident," the "piano through a wall incident," and other incidents affecting the safety and property of Westerners went wide in the West to form diplomatic pressure on Japan.

The truth was hidden, and lies traveled in its place. In April 1938, Magee, on a trip to Shanghai, wrote a letter to a Reverend McKim in New York, in which he revealed that he had lived through Japanese atrocities committed in Nanjing: "It has been brought to my attention that you have been writing letters to the *Times* saying that the stories of Japanese atrocities in Nanking were false. Perhaps by this time you will have learned that they were only too true" (Zhang Kaiyuan 2005, 175 and 177).

Nevertheless, it was precisely because Westerners in Nanjing like Magee revealed the truth of the Rape of Nanking that in February 1938 Matsui and several other high-ranking officers of the Central China Area Army were recalled to Japan. The document "Battle records of the 23rd Urban Infantry Company" reveals: "At the time, it was forbidden to report on this matter in Japan, but censures coming in from around the world put the army central command in an extremely awkward predicament; they even admonished Commander Matsui" (Wang 2010a, vol. 2, 557). The verdict from the Tokyo War Crimes Tribunal details more: "Reports of atrocities by the Japanese army were disseminated everywhere. Minami Jiro, then governor-general of Korea, acknowledged having read such reports in newspapers. Once this news casting Japan in a bad light came out, the Japanese government recalled Matsui and about 80 of his subordinate officers to Japan under global pressure in public opinion, but no punishment measures were taken on any of them" (Yang 2006, 609).

3.3.3.3 Case study: the making and dissemination of Magee's films

Member of the International Committee and chairman of the Nanjing branch of the International Red Cross Society Reverend John Magee risked his life to document the atrocities around him using the 16 mm home movie camera he previously used to spread the Gospels.

At the time the Japanese army strictly controlled all actions of foreigners in the city; without a doubt, they would not have granted permission to Magee to record their atrocities on his camera. In the introduction to his film, Magee wrote in the introduction to his documentary: "I had to act cautiously and circumspectly, and absolutely not let any Japanese see when I was filming. I could not directly film executions or any scenes of the great amount of corpses piled up in the city" (Zhang 2005, 179).

Xia Shuqin and her younger sister were in the Safety Zone taking reports from refugees at the time. Her family's sad story caught Magee's attention. He and Red Swastika Society Deputy Director Xu Chuanyin paid a visit to their home at Number 5 Mendong New Road (Number 5 Zhonghua Gate Inner New Road) to record the calamity that had taken place there on film. Xu gave the following testimony at the Tokyo War Crimes Tribunal: "The young girl was raped on the table; and while I was there the blood spilled on the table not all dry yet. And we also see the corpses because they were took away, not far away, only a few yards from that house, all the corpses there. Of those corpses Mr. Magee and I took pictures of them because they were naked and shows the crimes there" (Yang 2006, 59).

Filming conditions were deplorable. George Fitch's granddaughter recalled Fitch having told her how Magee had filmed through a window a scene of civilians and women on their knees begging not to be taken away by Japanese soldiers. Magee himself recalled in the introduction to his film: "I would have shot more scenes if I'd had more film and more time" (Zhang 2005, 178–179).

The Japanese army imposed strict restrictions on the movements of foreigners in the city to keep the truth of the Rape of Nanking from getting out. After several attempts, YMCA Director George Fitch was finally granted permission to travel to Shanghai aboard a train. He carried a portion of Magee's films in a compartment stitched into his camel-hair greatcoat, which the Japanese did not detect. Timperley, also in Shanghai at the time and a journalist for the *Manchester Guardian*, helped edit the films, which both men broke into sections given English titles.

The Kodak Company in Shanghai made four copies of the documentary. One was given to the English missionary Muriel Lester of the Fellowship of Reconciliation. Another was given to Dr. Rosen of the German embassy. Another was carried by Fitch to the U.S., and the last made its way finally to the American Congress, and is now stored in the U.S. National Archives.

The copy given to Lester was brought to Japan and exhibited there, but it was quickly banned. In the 1990s the Japanese broadcaster NHK found seven people who had watched the film. The whereabouts of the copy given to Rosen are unknown. In the "Rosen files," there are descriptions of atrocities witnessed by Rosen personally. In his report to the German Foreign Office of February 10, 1938, Rosen wrote a passage describing Magee's documentary as "the most persuasive proof of atrocities committed by the Japanese" (Chen, Zhang, and Dai n.d., 130). He attached the English titles of the film's shots and asked that it be shown to Hitler:

> During the Japanese reign of terror in Nanjing – which lasted a very long time – Reverend John Magee of the American Episcopal Church – who has lived here for a quarter century already – shot this film, which is the most persuasive proof of atrocities committed by the Japanese.
>
> Mr. Magee – I request that special attention be paid to keeping his name top secret – has been doing his utmost to care for Chinese refugees in the house of a German consultant. He pays more attention to German affairs than most of his colleagues, because his now deceased sister was married to an Austrian foreign service officer. He refuses to allow his films to be used for commercial purposes. He paid to have the Kodak Company in Shanghai copy the film, and he has provided one copy to the embassy. These facts demonstrate his selfless and noble character. The film will be sent to the Foreign Ministry through reliable channels.
>
> This film presents events over the entire span of time, with descriptions given of each section and English translations attached. The descriptions, like the film itself, are a soul-stirring documentation of this time (Chen, Zhang, and Dai n.d., 130).

Both Fitch and Magee screened the film upon returning to the U.S. Nearly 100 stills from the film were developed into standalone photographs, and 10 of those were published in the May 1938 edition of *Life* magazine in the U.S.

For various reasons, Magee's documentary was forgotten after the war. The discovery of Rosen's report in 1990 reminded the world of the film's existence. In the late 1990s, the New York Foundation for Reparations from Japan published an announcement in the *New York Times* that it was compiling historical materials on the Rape of Nanking. George Fitch's daughter Edith saw the ad and contacted the Foundation, ultimately telling them about her father's experiences during the Rape of Nanking. The United States Memorial Union for Massacre of Nanjing Victims later obtained George Fitch's diary from Edith, titled *My Eighty Years in China*, detailing how he secretly brought Magee's film to Shanghai and had four copies made. Fitch's granddaughter Tanya Quentin donated copies of the film to both the Memorial Union and China's Second Historical Archives.

In August 1991, Magee's son David Magee found both a copy of the film and the 16 mm camera among his father's belongings. On October 2, 2002, David

Magee donated the camera to the Memorial Hall of the Victims in Nanjing Massacre by Japanese Invaders.

3.4 Relations Between Westerners, Japanese, and Chinese

After its fall, Nanjing was essentially cut off from the outside world. In this sealed environment, a delicate, nuanced struggle emerged between the Westerners, the Japanese, and the Chinese over Japanese atrocities and provision of relief to refugees. Despite their weak position, the Westerners used their special status in the city to provide assistance to Chinese refugees, in an even weaker position than themselves.

3.4.1 Westerners and Japanese authorities

3.4.1.1 Westerners and Japanese military personnel

After the fall of Nanjing, the Japanese army established its rule at the tip of bayonets.

On December 18, after attending the city entry ceremony, high commander of the Central China Area Army Matsui Iwane convened a meeting of high-ranking officers. Iinuma Mamoru wrote how Matsui stressed his conviction in handling international issues: "The means by which we should make the Chinese reflect is to make them realize: the Japanese are not at all afraid of foreigners, but we cannot make foreign countries unhappy with us in the area of emotions when it is of no benefit to us. We must be harmonious and cordial in dealings with Chinese. With the UK, the U.S., and other countries, we must be reasonable and firm." In his speech, Matsui also claimed that he was "intimately aware that the British and American governments realized the extent of Japanese power in the Far East, and so a guiding policy of cooperation with Japan should be adopted. They have not, however, adopted policies that transmit this idea to their peoples, most particularly the British government." Matsui demanded that his subordinate officers be "calm and unhurried, and adopt the bearing of a great power" (Wang 2005b, 209).

Shanghai Expeditionary Army Deputy Chief of Staff Uemura Toshimichi summarized Matsui's orders this way: "Our attitude toward the UK, the U.S., and other countries must be firm but proper. Toward China we must be warm, to get them to renounce dependence on the UK and the U.S." (Wang 2005b, 246). The order to be "warm" to the Chinese was mere lip service. On December 16 Uemura wrote "I have heard of a few instances of poor military discipline by troops in the city" (Wang 2005b, 244). The Japanese military was much better at being "firm" with British, Americans, and other foreigners.

Before the Japanese occupation, the International Committee had presented its plans for the Safety Zone to Japanese authorities and received "tacit" acknowledgment from them. In orders to the Central China Area Army titled "Issues of Note in the Siege and Occupation of Nanjing," the commander wrote: "As indicated in the overall plan, it is absolutely forbidden to approach areas of foreign interest, particularly diplomatic bodies.[30] In particular it is forbidden to enter the neutral zone proposed by foreign diplomats and refused by our army except when absolutely necessary. Sentries should be set at necessary locations" (Wang and Lei n.d., 27). The extent to which the orders to not approach "areas of foreign interest" and not to enter the Safety Zone were respected is up for debate,[31] but these orders demonstrate beyond any doubt that Japanese military authorities were aware of the Safety Zone's existence.

The fates of both the foreigners and Chinese residents of Nanjing were in the hands of the victors. The International Committee began actively communicating with Japanese authorities immediately following the occupation out of hope to restore order as quickly as possible. In the Committee's first letter to the Japanese on December 14, they actively proposed cooperation: "We should restore water, electricity, and telephone service as quickly as possible." The letter also discloses to the Japanese that some Chinese soldiers had entered the Safety Zone (Rabe CN, 137). The Westerners quickly realized, however, that the Japanese army was extremely unwilling to play host to "neutral observers" during their occupation of Nanjing.

On December 15, Rabe and some others met with officers of the Japanese Army Special Service Organ in their headquarters at Xinjiekou. This was the first formal meeting between members of the International Committee and representatives of the Imperial Japanese Army. The army granted the meeting in response to two letters written by the Committee. In its form, the meeting was entirely dedicated to allowing the officer from the Special Service Organ to give statements in response to the questions raised in the Committee's letters. According to the "Notes on meeting with authority from the Japanese Special Service Organ" within the "Safety Zone Documents" collection, there were no "questions

---

30 Original translator's note: here by "diplomatic bodies" Matsui is referring to the small number of non-official foreigners in Nanjing at the time. See the December 8, 1993 revised edition of Nanjing War History Compilation Committee, *Nanjing zhan shi ziliao ji (yi)* [Compilation of materials on the history of the war in Nanjing (one)] (Tokyo: Kaikosha, 1993).
31 Current research demonstrates that there was a "massacre order" issued to the Japanese army in Nanjing. Please see related works by Cheng Zhaoqi.

asked or discussions" (Zhang 2006b, 274). The nature of the meeting demonstrates that Japanese military authorities acknowledged the International Committee as an entity to be dealt with, qualified to ask questions of the Japanese. They did not, however, acknowledge the Committee's formal status, nor its right to negotiate with the army.

The Japanese officer's statements indicate that the Japanese were aware of the existence of the Safety Zone and were not planning to disband it immediately. They even promised to "station guards at the entrances to the Zone." The Japanese acknowledged the limited governmental authorities entrusted to the International Committee and expressed willingness to cooperate with the Committee in some areas.

The International Committee raised the question of disarmed Chinese soldiers in the Safety Zone in their letter of December 14. A letter written to Fukuda on the 15th was devoted entirely to explaining this situation (Zhang 2006b, 273). The Japanese did not criticize the foreigners for accepting Chinese soldiers into the Safety Zone, but rather blithely expressed that "the Imperial Japanese Army will treat them with a humanitarian attitude." The Committee raised the question of housing arrangements for refugees in the Safety Zone in their letter of the 14th, to which the Japanese did not respond, only mentioning that "refugees should return to their original residences as soon as possible," as noted in the Committee's letter to the Japanese embassy of December 17 (Zhang 2006b, 279).

In her diary entry of December 15, Vautrin wrote: "Mr. Rabe and Lewis [Smythe] are in touch with the commander, who has arrived and who is not too bad. They think they may get conditions improved by tomorrow." After witnessing wholesale executions of disarmed Chinese soldiers and other atrocities committed by Japanese soldiers, the Westerners' attitudes toward the Japanese changed. Vautrin wrote the following day: "From a military point of view, the taking of Nanking may be considered a victory for the Japanese army but judging it from the moral law it is a defeat and a national disgrace – which will hinder cooperation and friendship with China for years to come, and forever lose her the respect of those living in Nanking today."

In addition to slaughtering Chinese people, Japanese soldiers also insulted and beat up Westerners attempting to protect the interests of refugees. Smythe wrote in a letter to his family that American instructor at the University of Nanking Charles Riggs was "struck twice" by a Japanese officer at noon on December 16 and "came back in tears" (Zhang 2005, 234). On December 17, Vautrin wrote that she was slapped in the face for not opening the door quickly enough to a group of Japanese soldiers looking for Chinese soldiers.

Nevertheless, with the Japanese in actual control of the city, the Westerners had no choice but to hold back the enmity they felt for the Japanese in order to protect Chinese refugees. Rabe realized quickly that "we must now get on good terms with the occupying Japanese army" (Rabe CN, 144). In his letter to Fukuda on December 14, Rabe actively sought to cooperate with the army to restore water and electricity as quickly as possible. On the 15th Rabe still believed he could have "engineers and workers restore operations of the plants" (Rabe CN, 141). By the 16th, however, Rabe felt: "I am willing to help, but given the incredible behavior of the Japanese soldiery, prospects are slim that I could drum up the 40 to 45 workers needed." Rabe continued: "And given the circumstances, neither would I like to risk having the Japanese authorities call one of our German engineers back from Shanghai" (Rabe EN, 75). But on the 17th, having been urged to do so by the Japanese, Rabe sent a telegram through the Japanese authorities to the Siemens Company headquarters in Shanghai: "Japanese authorities would like German engineer to come to Nanking to restart the local power plant" (Rabe EN, 79).

The primary feeling of Westerners in Nanjing toward the Japanese was one of being compelled, to differing degrees, to cooperate. Bates succinctly summarized relations between the foreigners and Japanese military authorities in a letter to his wife of February 2: "Naturally we don't take this lying down, yet we cannot directly oppose their police order from military authorities" (Zhang 2005, 28).

3.4.1.2 Westerners and Japanese diplomats

The primary function of the Japanese government's diplomatic organs in Nanjing was to communicate with the Chinese government. Once the Chinese government had evacuated, however, Japanese diplomats centered their work on the 20-plus Westerners in the city, as well as the foreign legations that gradually returned.

At 11 a.m. on December 15, the Japanese embassy's military attaché Fukuda paid a visit to the International Committee, "with whom we discuss the details of our agenda" (Rabe EN, 69). At a meeting on December 16, Japanese Consul-General Okazaki told Rabe: "The International Committee has no basis for existence from a legal point of view." He also bid the Committee to note that although the Japanese had not agreed to acknowledge the Committee, the Committee would be treated as though it had been acknowledged (Rabe CN, 151).

At the request of the Japanese embassy, the International Committee began compiling records of crimes committed by Japanese soldiers in the Safety Zone and submitting them to the embassy, ultimately to no real effect. Smythe wrote in a letter to family that the Westerners themselves realized that their written and oral protests to the embassy "were of no great use." What's more, "people from the embassy say they can't raise any more protests with their military department." (Zhang 2005, 243). No member of the embassy staff ever denied the atrocities reported to them by the Westerners. On the contrary, they constantly promised to communicate the reports to army officials in order to improve conditions. Magee wrote in a letter to his wife that when new Japanese troops were rotated into the city, embassy officials told the Westerners that the new batch "had a somewhat better reputation" (Zhang 2005, 156).

When Rabe wrote about the attitude of one member of the Japanese embassy: "Hidaka, into whose hand I press our report, apologizes for these 'Japanese rascals,' but offers as an excuse that such things occasionally happen when troops are being relieved. The old bad troops were ostensibly sent off on 28 January and behaved badly yet again before being sent off. I've heard this particular excuse before, but we believe we have proof that the rapes, etc. that have been reported were committed by the new troops" (Rabe EN, 170–171). Smythe wrote that he felt similarly about Japanese embassy officials: "The staff of the Japanese embassy seem to want to make our plight more bearable, but it seems they can't get past their own compatriots (military personnel)" (Rabe CN, 241).

The psychology of the Japanese army reveals itself in the orders given by the Special Service Organ to the Autonomous Committee, as recorded by Rosen in notes of February 1, 1938: "Nanjing is a city that the Japanese army has occupied in war. You must understand that under these circumstances, any unexpected event should be considered normal" (Chen, Zhang, and Dai n.d., 118).

Other documents indicate that Japanese diplomats in the city were somewhat empathetic with the Westerners, especially in their feelings about Japanese military actions. Forster wrote in a letter to his wife: "The Japanese Embassy people have been decent, but have lost face over their inability to accomplish anything with the military" (Zhang 2005, 102). Scharffenberg had this praise for Fukuda: "He is the friendliest of the Japanese officers." Magee wrote in a letter to his wife: "The Japanese consular staff, with the exception of one contemptible scoundrel of a policeman, have all been willing to help us. They feel ashamed of the actions of their army and are doing what they can to protect foreign property" (Zhang 2005, 165).

Of course, the Westerners understood the position the Japanese diplomats were in. Rabe wrote: "The Japanese embassy's attitude indicates that some of them have long felt ashamed of the actions of their military. They'll do anything they can to attempt to cover these actions; one of their means is to prohibit movement in and out of the city" (Rabe CN, 419). Fukuda told the Westerners he could carry letters for them to Shanghai, but Smythe wrote in a letter to his family that the Westerners knew that "letters are subject to his surveillance!" Knowing this, Smythe sent out a scantily worded telegram: "Merry Christmas, we are all doing well, hope you are too" (Zhang 2005, 245). According to Smythe, it was hard for American missionaries to draft telegrams they knew would be read by Japanese embassy officials (Zhang 2005, 241). Fukui of the Japanese embassy had this warning for Rabe: "If you report bad things, you will annoy the Japanese military and will not be allowed to return to Nanking!" (Rabe EN, 186).

Sperling wrote in a report: "On 17 December, Herr Hürter's automobile was stolen. By chance Herr Hatz and I happened to be nearby, along with an official of the Japanese consulate, so that we were able to halt the thief at the next street corner, and with great difficulty and long speeches to regain possession of the vehicle. —During this incident I noticed how little power Japanese civil servants have. With many bows and scrapes, the consular official bade his farewell to these military brigands" (Rabe EN, 151).

The truth is that not even Japanese language decrees issued by the Japanese embassy were respected by Japanese soldiers: "From December 17 to 20, 1937, Tanaka of the Japanese Embassy drove to all foreign residences and had people post notices on them written in Japanese that were intended to protect them (I later found that many of these vile notices had been torn down and thrown to the ground). Nevertheless, Japanese soldiers continued to break in and loot these houses to the last" (Rabe CN, 397).

To "show respect" for the International Committee, the Japanese embassy held an informal dinner on January 15. Rabe wrote: "Dinner at the Japanese embassy went off without incident. We were 13 people in all. Besides the officials of the Japanese embassy, nine representatives from our committee showed up: Miss Vautrin, Miss Bauer, Dr. Bates, Mills, Smythe, Dr. Trimmer, Kröger, and I. And after we had sat down to eat, John Magee appeared as well, who always tends to bring up the rear, but is otherwise a fine fellow" (Rabe EN, 132).

At the dinner Rabe gave a carefully written speech, intended not to offend his hosts. He then wrote these thoughts about the speech in his diary: "I don't know what the Americans thought of my speech. I am aware that I spoke a little against my own conscience, but I thought it useful for our cause and followed the Jesuit principle: "The ends justify the means." There is no denying that it was the officials of the Japanese embassy who helped us to some extent— were the only ones who could help us by passing on our reports to the Japanese military and interceding for us a bit. That they did not have the success we wished surely lies in the fact that diplomats in Japan must defer to the military, who have the first and last word in the Japanese government. The embassy personnel, Fukui, Tanaka, and Fukuda, could therefore rightly be praised a little if one was to praise at all, which after our bitter experiences was indeed hard enough to do" (Rabe EN, 133–134).

Rosen wrote in a report of February 16 to the German consulate in Bombay: "Mr. Fukui formerly worked in the Foreign Ministry's Treaty Department, the embassy to the U.S. in Washington, and the embassy to Canada in Ottawa. It is clearly because of his absolute submission to the military (like then Ambassador Kawagoe Shigeru) that he was chosen for this post. Like the rest of his ilk, his primary duty was to organize feasts and celebratory activities. They tried to hoodwink foreign legations into ignoring conditions here, to hide the truth" (Chen, Zhang, and Dai n.d., 141–142).

The Westerners did not harbor innate biases against the Japanese, but rather began to oppose them after having witnessed their crimes. That is why the Westerners were capable of noticing the scant good deeds done by the Japanese. Magee wrote in a letter to his wife: "I don't wish to blacken everything, because to be fair, some Japanese have done some good deeds. For example, yesterday I saw a woman who had been injured in many places by machine gun fire during an air raid before the Japanese occupation. She had lost an eye. She had several children. To be able to save most of them, she had no choice but to abandon a three month old child outside the city. The Japanese saw this and gave her some help. Our florist was taken by the Japanese to work for a few days, but they paid him 50 cents per day and gave him food" (Zhang 2005, 165).

3.4.2 The Westerners and the Chinese Public

3.4.2.1 Refugees flock to the Westerners

Even though Nanjing was the capital of Republican China, statistics from 1936 reveal an illiteracy rate of 53.36% among city residents, these being the city's poor (Zhang 2002, 86). They had no means to flee, and so could only wait for the unexpected results of war to come crashing down on them. Survivor Lin Changsheng recalled: "At that time there were very few people who read newspapers, much less listened to radio broadcasts. We got to have some impression of current events from gossip on the streets, but we paid no attention to matters that didn't concern us; these went in the one ear and out the other... Mr. Xu was concerned that the bread and cake had been ruined, but he told us not to fear, saying: 'The Japs have fought for many years in the three provinces of the Northeast, and then they fought in Shanghai, but they still haven't won. Shanghai is 600 to 700 *li* away from Nanjing. There won't be any impact on Nanjing.' We, who had never been through war before, could not then feel any threat that the war might pose to us. We weren't nervous in the least. We continued our daily work in a most orderly fashion in the bakery" (Zhang 2005, 545). For the poorest classes, "their only choice once war came was to remain in Nanjing" (Zhang 2002, 86). The vast majority of residents with any status at all fled from the city, to such an extent that it was difficult for the Japanese to scrape together enough "prestigious" people in the city to organize a "dignified" Autonomous Committee.[32]

A report in the Japanese newspaper *Asahi Shimbun* of December 21, 1937, read: "It seems clear that there are no intellectuals left. It's hard to find any among the refugees who can write, despite the city's being the capital of a literary country. Only one in a hundred is literate" (Zhang 2005, 241).

Prior to the war, the Westerners and common Chinese saw little of each other despite living in the same city, as they ran in different circles. Outside of a very few Chinese people who provided services to the Westerners, the vast majority never came into contact with them, let alone had the opportunity to communicate with them. For the lowest class of citizens with poor literacy rates, street gossip provided the majority of what they knew about Westerners. Once tragedy had descended upon the city, however, the only choice for most refugees was to throw themselves at the mercy of the foreigners.

The government's departure in mid-November 1937 left the public terrified and gave rise to a tremendous rumor mill. Helpless citizens sought shelter anywhere they could find it. Vautrin wrote on November 28, 1937 that many Chinese people living in the vicinity of Ginling Women's College attended religious services there just to find out if they would be allowed to shelter there when the hammer fell.

The Safety Zone became the primary destination for Chinese refugees. Also on November 28, Vautrin wrote: "Again and again I met groups of women and children in search of the 'Safety Zone.' They had heard of it in a vague way and wanted to make sure of its location."

Refugees began flooding into the Zone on December 7, before the Zone had even become official. "As a result of a rumor that houses near the gates inside the walls are to be burned down as well, panic has broken out among the poor living near the South Gate. Hundreds of families are streaming into our Zone, but now that it's dark they cannot find any shelter" (Rabe EN, 53–54). Vautrin wrote on December 7: "Thousands of people from South Gate crowded into the zone…"

---

[32] There were nine members of the "Nanjing Autonomus Committee." Tao Xisan was chairman, and Sun Shurong and Cheng Langbo were vice chairmen. Zhao Weishu, Zhao Gongjin, Ma Xihou, Huang Yuexuan, Hu Qifa, and Wang Chunsheng were ordinary members (Sun 1997, 464). None of them were "prestigious," and in particular none had served as high officials in the previous government. The members of this committee were particularly lackluster compared to similar bodies established by the Japanese in other occupied Chinese cities. Even Matsui Iwane was dissatisfied with the members of the Autonomous Committee.

On December 8, the International Committee issued its "Letter to Residents of Nanjing," beginning the formal acceptance of refugees into the Zone. Rabe writes: "Thousands of refugees are fleeing into our so-called Safety Zone from all directions; the streets are thronged with more people than in peacetime... As it grows dark some families, unable to find shelter anywhere, stretch out to sleep in nooks and alcoves of buildings, or simply on the street, despite the cold" (Rabe EN, 54). On December 10 Rabe wrote: "The streets of the Zone are packed with refugees. Many of them are still camping in the streets because they couldn't find any suitable shelter" (Rabe EN, 58).

For several weeks after the Japanese occupation, the trend in refugee movement was that people outside the Safety Zone clustered into the Zone, and people already within the Zone flocked to refugee shelters, particularly those under direct Western management.

As Japanese atrocities mounted, the Chinese refugees saw the Westerners as their last line of defense. More than 20 refugees in the Safety Zone wrote the following letter to Rabe:

> We (those concerned for our sons, husbands, and others) had nowhere to turn, did not know to whom to address our cries for help, but we knew that you have a good heart and compassion, so we again implore you to help us finds methods and means to return our young people to us, to restore breadwinners to their families, to save our lives. Please tell us: what can you do for us? Are those young people still alive? Where are they right now? (Alive or dead?) Can they still return to us? When can they come back? Please hold nothing back from us. Please give us all the details. We have faith in your good heart and compassion, and for this we will be grateful to you the rest of our lives (Rabe CN, 555–556).

3.4.2.2 Case study: Rabe and his neighbor the cobbler

Rabe refers many times in his diary to "my neighbor the cobbler," paying special attention to how the cobbler's attitude toward Rabe changed after the city fell. Rabe had not been enamored of the cobbler, who overcharged him for shoes, "because he always included the reduction to servants in his fee." Rabe "closed one eye" to this but never forgot. In his diary entry of September 22, Rabe wrote of his impressions of the cobbler, who had come to hide in his air raid shelter. On September 22 there were "about 28 Chinese squatting" in Rabe's air raid shelter, of whom he knew less than half. Rabe wrote: "My air raid dugout is not that much better than any other, but it was built for a German, so it must be especially strong" (Rabe CN, 10).

On November 22, water got into Rabe's air raid shelter: "My neighbor the cobbler can go to hell! Whenever the *jing bao* sounds, he comes running with his wife and children, grandfather and grandmother, and God knows how many other relatives, but now that there's three feet of water to be bailed in the dugout he's nowhere to be seen." Later Rabe realized he was wrong about the cobbler: "As for the cobbler, all is forgotten and forgiven. He, his wife, his three children, and a half dozen of his relatives have been busy bailing away" (Rabe EN, 27).

The cobbler tried to win Rabe's trust with his proactivity, and in the process earn himself a security guarantee. By November 19 it was clear to the Westerners that all the rich had fled, and everyone else of even meager means was also trying to get out: Vautrin wrote on November 19: "The trek continues but now it is mostly rickshaws filled with baggage, the past few days it has been cars and busses." On November 20, "At 6 p.m. an extra edition of a Chinese newspaper announces that the Chinese government has been moved to Chungking. Nanking Broadcasting confirms the news" (Rabe EN, 26). We have no means of knowing why the cobbler decided to stay in Nanjing, but we can be sure that he asked himself what he would do for himself and his family when the Japanese came. His German neighbor became the only person upon whom he could rely.

A few days later Rabe's relationship with the cobbler had completely changed: "My neighbor, the cobbler, that miserable cobbler, has now become my friend. We are bosom buddies. He and his family have been bailing water from the dugout all day, and on the side he has made me a lovely pair of brown boots for ten dollars. I volunteered an additional dollar to further cement our friendship" (Rabe EN, 32). The same happened between Rabe and his servants. There was also fighting in the north where they came from, so they too had no choice but to rely on Rabe's support. They were frightened when they thought Rabe would leave the city with the other Germans: "The servants walk about with large, terrified eyes, because they think I'll be leaving on the Kutwo as well. They'll be happy again once I explain straight out that I am definitely staying on in Nanking, come what may" (Rabe EN, 25).

After the city fell, the cobbler and his family sheltered in Rabe's courtyard. Rabe wrote about him again on December 23: "My neighbor, the cobbler, has resoled my old boots for Christmas; he also made a leather case for my field glasses. I gave him 10 dollars, but he just pressed the money back into my hand, not saying a word." A servant explained why: "Chang says that the man could not possibly take money from me; he is far too much in my debt as it is, the poor fellow!" (Rabe EN, 89).

3.4.2.3 The role played by Westerners and gratitude of Chinese refugees

Minnie Vautrin witnessed the flight from Nanjing of its residents from the richest down to those of even very meager means. Ignoring multiple warnings from the

American embassy, she decided to stay. In truth, she had had a close call during fighting for Nanjing in 1927. This time she felt her life might be endangered again because she was American. She had even made plans to leave in the case that her status as an American endangered the Chinese people around her. Nevertheless, she ultimately stayed behind to offer her assistance to the poorest Chinese women and girls.

Bates had been in the same predicament as Vautrin in 1927, but he too was undaunted and was one of the earliest participants in the planning of the Safety Zone.

Upon observing great numbers of wounded Chinese soldiers transported to Xiaguan with nobody to care for them, Magee organized his church's forces to provide treatment. A fellow Episcopalian priest, Forster, sent his wife and children to the interior and himself rushed to Nanjing from Yangzhou to help Magee.

They had been concerned that the city would descend into chaos in the interim between the Chinese government's evacuation and the Japanese occupation, and that there would be looting perpetrated by routed Chinese soldiers and by civilians. So once the Japanese entered the city, the Westerners were sure that the worst was behind them. Nevertheless, atrocities by Japanese soldiers only became worse day by day, even as high-ranking officials entered the city, and even after the official ceremony for entering the city had been held. Cheng Ruifang, dormitory warden for Ginling Women's College who was in intimate contact with the foreign community this entire time, wrote: "The International Committee lost face this time. In the beginning they were afraid of looting by our soldiers. They thought that the Japanese army was good. They always talked that way at meetings. Now they have found they were wrong, that not even the Safety Zone is acknowledged. Now that they know how ferocious the Japanese army is, they too are afraid" (Zhang 2005, 13).

Rabe wrote on December 23: "My refugees stand tightly pressed together in the rain and mutely watch the lovely horrible inferno. If these flames were to reach our house, these poor people would have no idea where to go. I am their last hope" (Rabe EN, 89). That was the tenth day of the Japanese occupation. "These are times of endless terror," Rabe concluded (Rabe CN, 216). Vautrin wrote on November 23: "Fear is permeating down to even the poor – and there is little wonder when so many of the better classes have fled from the city. The servants are afraid that when the Japanese come they will be made to serve as soldiers, or be beheaded. Rumors are wild" McCallum wrote in a letter to his family: "We could write up hundreds of cases [of crime] a day; people are hysterical; they get down on their knees and 'Kotow' any time we foreigners appear; they beg for aid" (Zhang 2005, 203–204). Many of the other Westerners made similar observations.

The Westerners also came to see themselves as "saviors" in the eyes of the Chinese refugees. Magee wrote in a letter to his wife: "We need more foreigners, because there aren't enough of us to protect the Chinese." When the "worst division" of the Japanese army was about to be rotated out of the city, Magee wrote: "I feel great sorrow for the people of the place that this division is going, because they won't have foreigners to protect them" (Zhang 2005, 158–159).

Vautrin recorded an event in her diary entry of March 30, 1938: "One funny incident happened on the way back which is really too good to keep. A little boy called out 'Foreign devil' when he saw me riding along on my bicycle, but another little boy, not far away, vehemently corrected him, saying 'Why that is Hwa Siao-dzie!' [Miss Vautrin]."

At the time of Vautrin's entry, the Japanese had already been in the city for more than three months. Vautrin keenly noted on March 30, 1938: "Really the deference showed to some of us from the mere fact that we remained in the city is almost too much." The war had changed people's perspectives, and also gave the Chinese public a chance to come to know the foreigners who had remained in the city on intimate terms. Owing to their extremely low literacy rates, the refugees left behind very few records, despite their great numbers. We have to rely primarily upon the records of others, particularly those written by the Westerners themselves, to understand the Chinese public's attitude toward them.

Vautrin also recorded how she was treated by an elderly Chinese couple in her diary entry of the same day, March 30:

> Soon after we had turned into Scissor's Lane, we were met by the old Mr. Hu, with his wife, who refugeed at Ginling for about 20 days. He insisted that we must go to his home for a cup of tea. We promised to go if they would not go to the bother of serving anything else, but he won. Before we left he and his good wife had served peanuts, watermelon seeds, and very nicely cooked lotus root in sugar. His little row of three rooms had not been burned, although the main house of which they had been a part was entirely burned. As he took us into one of the rooms that had barely escaped burning – the paper on the ceiling was scorched – he said he had escaped because his idol, the Goddess of Mercy, had protected him. Surely the old couple had been fortunate, for not one of his sons, or grandsons or great-grandsons – he has three of the latter – had been touched. The old people do not live with the sons because the latter eat too much meat. He and his good wife are devout vegetarians. They told us of one family – a gardener's – who lived not far from them, who had lost 16 out of 18 members of the family. Also several other tales too inhuman to repeat here. It is little wonder that they feel the invaders are beasts.

The couple, having survived disaster, treated Vautrin to "peanuts, watermelon seeds, and very nicely cooked lotus root in sugar" despite a promise to not serve anything but tea. When recounting the story of the gardener who had lost 16 family members, Mr. Hu must have felt immense gratitude for the 20 days under Vautrin's protection during the hardest time.

Prior to leaving Nanjing, Rabe accepted Vautrin's invitation to Ginling Women's College for a farewell party. Rabe wrote about what happened when he was preparing to leave: "The refugees at the university—there are still 3,000 women and girls there—besieged the door and demanded that I promise not to leave them in the lurch, that is, not to leave Nanking. They all went down on their knees, weeping and wailing and literally hanging on to my coattails when I tried to depart. I had to leave my car behind, and once I had fought my way to the gate, which was instantly closed behind me, had to return home on foot. This all sounds very exaggerated and lugubrious. But anyone who has witnessed the misery here understands what the protection we've been able to give these poor people really means. It was all so obvious, none of it has anything to do with heroics." (Rabe EN, 199–200).

3.4.2.4 The complex feelings of the Westerners toward Chinese refugees

Rabe and the others were able to experience the deep gratitude their actions had won from Chinese refugees. Rabe wrote wistfully about his preparations to leave the city: "Contrary to expectation, I've managed to come up with some crates. There's a carpenter among my lao bai xings [common people], that is, among the refugees in my garden, and through his connections I've been able to round up 20 crates, and not just crates, but straw as well. For the grand sum of two dollars and by pouring rain, several of the refugees carried three cartloads of straw from well beyond the Han Hsi Men city gate, and the carpenter is helping me pack free of charge. You see: The friendship of these poor people is worth something after all, sometimes, as in this case, worth a great deal, for wood has all but vanished from the marketplace" (Rabe EN, 194).

The Westerners saw clearly the adversity facing the Chinese refugees. The prosecutor for the International Military Tribunal for the Far East wrote that the "submissive attitude of the Chinese populace was extremely tragic and pitiable" (Yang Xiaming 2006: 396). The Westerners who chose to stay in Nanjing made the same observation. Forster wrote about one case in a letter to his wife: "Another instance in the same neighborhood was that of a man who had been carried off to Wuhu by the soldiers. He succeeded in making his way back to find his home gone and his womenfolk in hiding. Tired and hungry he had just prepared a bowl of cabbage when a Japanese soldier came along, demanding money and women. When the man could produce neither, the soldier urinated into the bowl of cabbage and went off" (Zhang 2005, 117).

Rabe wrote of a similar case: "There is one case that we don't record: A Chinese worker, who has worked all day for the Japanese, is paid in rice instead of money. He sits down in exhaustion with his family at the table, on which his wife has just placed a bowl of watery rice soup: the humble meal for a family of six. A Japanese soldier passing by plays a little joke and urinates in the half-full rice bowl and laughs as he goes on his merry way." Rabe then commented: "The incident made me think of the poem 'Lewwer duad üs Slaav'[33]; but one simply can't expect a poor Chinese worker to behave like a free Frisian. The Chinese are far too downtrodden, and they patiently submitted to their fate long ago. It is, as I said, an incident that is given the scantest notice. If every case of rape were revenged with murder, a good portion of the occupying troops would have been wiped out by now" (Rabe EN, 154).

3.4.3 Case studies in three-way relations

During the Rape of Nanking, there were the Japanese establishing their reign at the tips of bayonets, Chinese people being ruled under the bayonet, and also Westerners, observers very much involved. The struggles over food and "comfort stations" that ensued demonstrate the nuanced relationship between the three parties.

3.4.3.1 The food problem
The Japanese reign of terror caused a food crisis in the city. On the one hand, combat forced some residents to abandon their regular lives, including decreases in food production. On the other, the war put an end to interregional food trading; the obstruction in food circulation caused tension in food provision in Nanjing. The great quantity of refugees forced into the Safety Zone by the violent rule of the Japanese army exacerbated the famine.

The Japanese army's so called "storming of Nanjing" put their troops in a constant forced march to strike at retreating Chinese forces. To provide for their front line troops, the Japanese army primarily had to "live off the land." Sone Kazuo, a member of that advancing Japanese army, wrote:

> Five or six days after leaving Shanghai, the combat troops attacking Nanjing began growing far from our depots. The only supply possible was of ammunition, indispensable to the at-

---

[33] "Better dead than a slave." From footnotes to Rabe EN, 243 (translator's note).

tack; it was impossible to get food to soldiers on the front lines. No matter how valiant a soldier may be, once he's hungry it becomes very difficult to continue acting.

There were only two possible outcomes if this condition continued: to temporarily halt the attack and allow supplies to catch up from the rear, or continue fighting until we've all starved to death. The IJA battle commanders with their spirit of never giving ground did not allow their combat troops to rest, but rather issued orders to "requisition food where you are and keep yourselves alive." The requisitioning order seems to make sense at first blush, but actually there's no difference between it and plundering food from locals. We had lived off the land before, but before receiving these orders, we all felt it was reproachable behavior. Our feelings of guilt evaporated once the order came down, and the soldiers became bandits thieving and plundering cereals and fowl to fill their bellies wherever they arrived (Sone n.d., 983).

By December 7, the Japanese forces had already arrived outside Nanjing, where Nakano Masao wrote that they were "entirely relying on requisitioning for food" (Ono n.d., 84). Endo Takaaki wrote that once Japanese forces were inside the city, "it was difficult to maintain relying solely on requisitioning, so headquarters asked us to appropriately deal with prisoners" (Ono n.d., 161). Food shortages became an excuse for the massacre of Chinese prisoners of war. Second Lieutenant Miyamoto Shogo wrote on December 15: "Now we can hardly supply our soldiers with food. Clearly it's not easy to find food for prisoners." So the next day his unit brought "about 3,000" prisoners to the shore of the Yangtze, where they were shot (Ono n.d., 99–100).

The Japanese army rapidly cleared out all stores and grain warehouses in Nanjing, and, as Fitch wrote in his diary, "locked up all coal and rice supply" (Zhang 2005, 75). On December 13, Rabe saw "with his own eyes": "The Japanese march through the city in groups of ten to twenty soldiers and loot the shops... Some Japanese soldiers dragged their booty away in crates, others requisitioned rickshaws to transport their stolen goods to safety" (Rabe EN, 67). Looting even became a "routine military operation" under supervision of officers (Rabe CN, 236). Smythe wrote in a letter to his family that the lone rice shop in the Safety Zone, run by the International Committee, was also subjected to harassment by Japanese soldiers. Japanese soldiers hauled off "entire sacks of rice" as well as workers (Zhang 2005, 233). Vautrin wrote on December 28, 1937 that Japanese soldiers even frequently stole food from the refugee camp in Ginling Women's College. Survivor Wu Biyi revealed that even household grain stores were looted (Zhang and Dai n.d., vol. 1, 35–36).

Japanese soldiers also frequently stole cars upon entering the city. Fitch wrote: "The problem of transportation became acute on the 16th, with the Japanese stealing our trucks and cars" (Zhang 2005, 72). Not only was it impossible to transport grain into the Safety Zone, but it was difficult to distribute grain already stored there to the various refugee shelters. Smythe wrote in a letter to family: "No Chinese dares to drive a truck on the streets... It's been like a war to prevent Japanese soldiers from stealing coolies and trucks" (Zhang 2005, 241). To get grains to hungry refugees, claimed Smythe in a letter to friends, the Westerners had no choice but to "deliver rice to camps in private cars, to keep them from going hungry for two days or more" (Zhang 2005, 277).

The serious food shortage was caused by the successful invasion of the Japanese army. On December 20, Matsui Iwane received a report on food in Nanjing. He wrote in his diary: "It is said that when it evacuated, the government of Jiangsu Province entrusted 100,000 silver dollars and all current grain reserves in Nanjing to an employee of the Siemens Company, but I'm not sure if that's true or not. However, there are over 10,000 dan of grain currently stored in Nanjing. There is also some hidden grain. I've come to understand that there will be no food shortages among the population in the short term" (Wang 2005b, 152). The Siemens employee Matsui refers to is probably Rabe. Matsui's understanding about the more than 10,000 *dan* of grain in the city was not far off from reality. His conclusion about "no food shortages among the population in the short term," however, could not have been more wrong.

Most refugees brought some food into the Safety Zone with them. Some people, upon exhausting their personal reserves, were forced to leave the Safety Zone to bring rice from home, risking their lives in the process. The case of refugee Sha Guanchao was typical: he and six neighbors returned home together to find grains. On the way they came across a group of Japanese soldiers, who bayoneted them all. Sha's six neighbors all died immediately, but Sha survived despite taking several bayonet wounds. Because he "was a rickshaw driver and could run fast and knew the big streets and back alleys alike," he was able to make his escape, although he took a bullet in his arm while getting away. Upon returning to the Safety Zone, his family members brought him to the Gulou hospital, where he was treated for several days (Zhang and Dai n.d., 18–19).

Rabe and the others entered negotiations with the Japanese to retrieve the grain gifted to the International Committee by the city government which the Japanese army had seized. The following is a list of correspondence between the International Committee (and its successor the International Relief Committee) and the Japanese regarding the food issue.

Serial No.	Date	Sent to	Signed by
Z1	12.14	Japanese commander	John H.D. Rabe
		This letter was meant to establish a connection with Japanese authorities but also contained a request to transport uninsured rice.	
Z6	12.15	Memorandum on meeting with chairman of special services department	Smythe
		During this meeting, the chairman of the Special Services Department responded to the letter of the 14 and the request for rice: We are permitted to use insured rice and assured that uninsured rice will be inspected.	
Z21	12.27	Japanese embassy	John H.D. Rabe
		A letter to Mr. Fukui asking for permission for us to ensure safety of rice and flour held by military.	
Z40	1.19	Messrs. Allison, Prideaux-Brune, John H.D. Rabe, and Rosen	
		A letter about discussing the rice and flour issues as well as giving support for propaganda.	
Z44	1.27	Japanese embassy	John H.D. Rabe
		A letter about discussing the rice and flour issues and asking the embassy to put pressure on the army about this issue.	
Z54	2.6	Mr. Allison	John H.D. Rabe
		A request that the Nanjing Autonomous Committee provide rice and flour.	
Z61	3.2	Colonel Hirota	W.P. Mills
		Attempting to reestablish consultations.	
Z66	3.18	Mr. Hanawa Yoshitaka	Lewis S.C. Smythe
		Another outline of consultations, including attachments z1, 6, 44, 54, and 61.	
Z67	3.18	Mr. Hanawa Yoshitaka	W.P. Mills
		A letter briefly summarizing Z66 and "Memorandum on Rice and Flour" by Hubert Sone, who became the International Committee's food commissioner on December 13. A list of the locations of rice and flour which Chinese authorities requested we guarantee. W.P. Mills	
Z69	4.13	Mr. Hanawa Yoshitaka	W.P. Mills
		A request to farmers in the Nanjing region to exchange seed rice in exchange for 10,000 sacks of flour, requesting that the rice be delivered between May and August to support relief work.	

Table 21: Letters between the International Committee (Relief Committee) and Japanese regarding food.
Source: Zhang (2010, 565–566).

When diplomatic personnel from the U.S., Germany, and other countries began returning to Nanjing in January 1938, the Westerners in the city gained channels to communicate with the outside world. The International Committee immediately used these channels to contact charitable groups in Shanghai and elsewhere to ask for resupply of food, drugs, and other goods. Smythe wrote in a letter to his family that he asked in a cable to the Red Cross Society in Shanghai to have "broad beans, peanuts or oil, and vegetables or substitutes delivered from Shanghai" (Zhang 2005, 271). On January 15, Rabe wrote that he had received word from Shanghai: "Six hundred tons of food already loaded on ships ready to be delivered" (Rabe CN, 341). The Japanese army, however, refused to allow the ship to unload at Nanjing. The International Committee also contacted the Commercial Reserve Bank of Shanghai to purchase "3,000 sacks of rice and 9,000 sacks of wheat (these grains are stored at Xiaguan, Sanchahe, and outside of the Hanxi Gate)"[34] (Rabe CN, 335–336). The Japanese embassy later confirmed that those grains had been confiscated by the army.

To prevent the spread of beriberi, on February 6 Smythe sent a telegram to George Fitch in Shanghai asking him to buy broad beans. He arranged for the purchase and shipment of 100 tons of broad beans, which the Japanese initially refused to allow into Nanjing; they later granted permission to bring them to Nanjing so long as they were not distributed within the Safety Zone. After negotiations, the Japanese army proposed "having the beans distributed by the Autonomous Committee," with "no additional restrictions" on distribution in the Safety Zone or elsewhere (Rabe CN, 553). The International Committee was forced to consent.

After the food crisis had passed, the Japanese began to use food as bait to entice Chinese refugees to submit to their rule; this led to deaths from hunger and hunger-caused disease following on the heels of direct massacre. The infant mortality rate in the shelter at Ginling Women's College, for example, was very high. Cheng Ruifang wrote that even some adults there "went to sleep at night and died, with no disease. They were fine the night before, but their bodies were weak and they'd been subjected to too much fear, and there wasn't good food this month. Their energy couldn't keep up, and they died" (Zhang Lianhong 2005, 31). The food crisis was one consequence of Japanese atrocities, as well as a component thereof.

The Westerners adopted an attitude of cooperation with the Japanese when it came to food. They did not even demand credit for their work, giving away the rights to distribute the food they had transported into the city, so long as they could provide substantive assistance to refugees. At a speech given in New York on June 25, 1941, in answer to the question of whether their relief work helped the Japanese establish their puppet regime, Bates answered: "The Japanese profited very little from this work, and the benefit to the ethics and characters

---

[34] Grains stored by said bank in warehouses at Xiaguan and other surrounding areas of Nanjing.

of the Chinese greatly surpassed anything we did for the Japanese" (Zhang 2005, 61).

Uemura Toshimichi wrote that Matsui ordered his high-ranking officers to be "firm" with "the UK, the U.S., and other countries," but "cordial" toward China (Wang 2005b, 246). In reality, the Japanese were butchers, and Chinese refugees their meat. Even the "puppet" Autonomous Committee was viewed by the Japanese as a slave organization with no status whatsoever: "Even the wives of members of the Autonomous Committee have been targeted for rape by Japanese soldiers just like those of ordinary citizens" (Rabe CN, 486).

3.4.3.2 Establishment of "comfort stations"
Upon their entry into the city, rapes of Chinese women occurred in great numbers, even as the Japanese were busy massacring civilians, setting fires, and looting. Magee wrote in a letter to his wife: "the most horrible thing now is the raping of women which has been going on in the most shameless way that I have ever known. The streets are full of men searching for women" (Zhang 2005, 151). Day and night, Japanese soldiers cruelly subjected Chinese women, from little girls all the way up to old women, to rape. They often killed their victims after the deed to destroy the evidence, and often the killing was perpetrated in the most inhumane way. "Resistance means the bayonet," writes Fitch, whenever a Japanese soldier fixed his gaze on a Chinese girl or woman (Zhang 2005, 73). "If husbands or brothers intervene, they're shot" (Rabe EN, 77). The scale and cruelty of Japanese atrocities that continued for a long time were utterly shocking to the Western observers.

High-ranking Japanese officers were aware of the atrocities being perpetrated against Chinese women. In addition to the nearly daily reports on atrocities being delivered by the International Committee to Japanese authorities, Japanese military police also began receiving similar reports very early. Matsui Iwane wrote in his diary that he was aware that "looting and raping have emerged among a small number of people," but he concluded this was "difficult to avoid" (Wang 2005b, 153). Aware of the mounting atrocities committed by their troops, high-ranking officers did not consider the problem from the perspective of reducing the number of atrocities, but rather attempted to establish military "comfort stations" to contain the "calamitously unchecked sexual desire" of their soldiers within "orderly bounds."

On December 4, 1937, before the Japanese army arrived in Nanjing, chief of the first office of the Shanghai Expeditionary Army's general staff Nishihara Issaku wrote that he heard: "The impedimenta battalion of the 11th Division carried off 12 and 13 year old girls by force, and dishonored them as the army advanced."

A military policeman wrote in a report that "there are many cases of similar events" and "I feel there is a need to establish comfort stations" (Wang 2005b, 108). A comfort station was established by military police in Huzhou in December 1937 under command of a colonel. Tenth Division Staff Officer Yamazaki Masao wrote in his diary entry of December 18: "In the beginning there were only four" comfort women, "and now there are seven... There were no notices posted, nor any signs posted at the entrance... The service was poor, and there were many problems. Complaints were heard everywhere." Nevertheless the enterprise prospered: "I don't know where the soldiers heard, but they're coming in droves, and the scene is boisterous" (Wang 2006a, 466).

Shanghai Expeditionary Army Deputy Chief of Staff Uemura Toshimichi wrote that he realized that "bad behavior among the troops is daily increasing." On December 28, 1937, he had the second office of the general staff headquarters "convene officers from all units to give reports on this matter." It was resolved that "stern preventative measures" would be implemented beginning at 10 a.m. on the 30th. That same day, Uemura deliberated the "Plan on Establishing Comfort Stations in Nanjing" submitted by the second office (Wang 2005b, 251).

Ogawa Sekijiro, chief of the 10th Division Legal Affairs Department, knew about all manner of atrocities committed by Japanese soldiers in great detail owing to the nature of his job. There are many cases of rape and rape followed by murder recorded in his diary. When a colonel asked him about "many cases of rape not being followed up," he reported an unexpected perspective:

> I responded that maybe this is the case, but I have to consider war conditions, the psychology of the accused at the time, the moral conceptions Chinese women have in this matter, the relative number of cases not reported or reported haphazardly of rape (a great number in fact) to date, and so on. Furthermore, theoretically speaking, under conditions of the time, according to Article 178 of the Criminal Code, rape is submission without capacity to resist, but we can't conclude that this is the case in all such situations. In some cases the person very readily submitted to the demands of the actor. If we judge from this article, it would be rash to immediately conclude that all cases of illicit sexual relations are rape. We should first make a deep study of conditions at the time and then decide how to proceed. For these reasons, I was unable to immediately respond to the colonel's demand (Wang 2006a, 420).

Ogawa was of the opinion that "we can prevent increases in rape cases if we establish comfort facilities" (Wang 2006a, 420). On December 21, Ogawa became aware of the "comfort station" experience in Huzhou: "It was mentioned at this provisional combat meeting that when the comfort station for soldiers was first opened in Huzhou, it was extremely busy. There were a dozen or so Chinese women there, but their numbers continuously increased. The business there was excellent, with soldiers forming long lines to get in" (Wang 2006a, 417).

Once the Japanese had passed their resolution, they found women through the Chinese collaborators [*Han Jian*] serving them. The highest concentration of female refugees in Nanjing at the time was in the shelter at Ginling Women's College, which was property of an American church and under management by Minnie Vautrin. Members of the puppet government proceeded there to select women with help from the Japanese. So Chinese, Japanese, and Western people were all involved in the establishment of "comfort stations" in Nanjing.

On December 24, 1937, Vautrin was summoned to her office, where a Japanese officer was waiting for her. The officer told Vautrin the purpose of his visit through a Chinese language interpreter from the Japanese embassy: to choose 100 prostitutes from among the 10,000 female refugees in the college. They told her that if a military brothel could be established, Japanese soldiers would no longer harass decent Chinese women. They also promised to only take away willing volunteers, and that no decent women would be forced off. Vautrin agreed to allow them pick from among the female refugees at a meeting in the college assembly hall. The officer remained in Vautrin's office as the assembly was arranged. Ultimately 21 women volunteered to join the comfort station after hearing the pitch made by the Chinese people under Japanese supervision.

From a moral perspective, the Westerners all fervently opposed the establishment of "comfort stations," the American missionaries most of all. Their attitudes changed slightly, however, after witnessing unchecked atrocities perpetrated by Japanese soldiers. They faced a dilemma between their Christian doctrine and their consciences, on whether to sacrifice a few women, who were already prostitutes, to preserve the honor of a great many decent Chinese women. Rabe wrote that Vautrin "is not going to hand over even one of them willingly. She would rather die on the spot; but then something unexpected happens. A respectable member of the Red Swastika Society, someone whom we all know, but would never have suspected had any knowledge of the underworld, calls out a few friendly words into the hall—and lo and behold! A considerable number of young refugee girls step forward. Evidently former prostitutes, who are not at all sad to find work in a new bordello" (Rabe EN, 99). Smythe wrote in a letter to his family: "Bates had hinted that this might happen, but Riggs was extremely alarmed when it happened" (Zhang 2005, 248).

Records left behind by Chinese survivors mention their powerlessness under the Japanese rule. Cheng Ruifang wrote: "Today some chief of staff brought a few Chinese here to find prostitutes. If these prostitutes were turning their trade outside, the soldiers wouldn't come to the shelter so often. Their words are reasonable, to the end of preventing decent women from coming to harm. There are many prostitutes here, so they were permitted to have a look. Some Chinese people here know prostitutes. Some Japanese prostitutes have come in the last two days. Under these conditions they can do whatever they want. If the people are humiliated, the government is to blame. It's all so tragic" (Zhang 2005, 22).

The German diplomat Rosen gave a strong nod to the Autonomous Committee's establishment of "comfort stations" in a report to the German Foreign Office written on January 20, 1938:

> The first thing Jimmy did was to open a brothel. He sought necessary personnel from among the women who formerly worked at the entertainment facility near the Confucius Temple, and provided furniture free of charge from among his personal stock. As Japanese women came later, now he is charging. No matter how you slice it, Jimmy did a good thing for their people, because previously many upright women were previously subject to rape and dishonor at the hands of the devils, and now with the opening of a proper brothel, the sexual needs of the Japanese army thugs have been brought into bounds that won't cause more harm (Chen, Zhang, and Dai n.d., 335).

The Japanese viewed the founding of "comfort stations" as a means for eliminating the rape problem. Most Westerners found the stations to be the lesser of two evils. Planned by the Japanese, run by Chinese puppets, and tacitly approved by the Westerners, "comfort stations" came into existence in Japanese-occupied Nanjing.

Such tensions between ethics and pragmatism run through the entire time period of the Rape of Nanking. The Westerners could not ignore the miserable plight of Chinese refugees caught between the reality of Japanese control of every aspect of life and their own struggle for survival, but nor could they openly resist Japanese authority. Rabe wrote of the concert the Japanese embassy invited him to attend: "It was a tall order to expect men who have been walking in the morning among Chinese murdered by Japanese soldiers to sit that same afternoon among those soldiers and enjoy a concert, but anything is possible in this dishonest world" (Rabe EN, 185). The foreigners also knew, however, that in order to do good for Chinese refugees, it was necessary "to get along peaceably with the Japanese here somehow" (Rabe EN, 134). This fact forced them into frequent awkward compromises. To reduce the degree of harm done to refugees, the Westerners had to stoop to "currying favor" with Japanese soldiers. Forster wrote in a letter to his wife that he "finds that the occasional cigarette offered to Japanese soldiers is extremely helpful" (Zhang 2005, 121).

3.5 Western Diplomats in Nanjing

3.5.1 Western diplomats return to Nanjing

In mid-November 1937, the nationalist government decided to move its capital and continue fighting, at which point foreign embassies moved along with it. The embassies of the UK, the U.S., Germany, and other countries with concentrated interests in Nanjing all left behind small groups of embassy personnel to watch over said interests. The British and Americans anchored gunboats on the river off Xiaguan to serve as temporary offices for their embassies and shelters for their expatriates. Germany, without a military presence in China, rented British commercial vessels to transport its expatriates.

On December 11, Nanjing was in imminent danger. Prior to the closing of the Yijiang Gate, which leads toward Xiaguan, the small diplomatic teams of the various embassies all retreated aboard ships anchored on the river at Xiaguan to stay safe. Their plan was to return to the city immediately after the fighting stopped. On December 12 many British and American gunboats and commercial vessels came under attack by the Japanese air force. The USS Panay was sunk, causing the deaths of many American servicemen and civilians. British, American, German, and other diplomats were also put in danger during the Japanese attack. Once out of danger, they remained on these vessels moored close to Nanjing, some even docking at the Xiaguan wharf, but Scharffenberg wrote that none was given permission from the Japanese to disembark (Chen, Zhang, and Dai n.d., 64). Magee wrote in a letter to his wife that the Japanese claimed that "no invading army would allow for the presence of neutral observers" (Zhang 2005, 163).

The USS Panay incident created tensions in Japan-U.S. relations. Utsonomiya Naokata wrote that it was considered possible at the time that its repercussions could be as serious as those of the sinking of the USS Maine (Wang 2006b, 11). Although the Japanese claimed that the bombing had been "entirely not the result of intentional actions," they said government did apologize and offer reparations very quickly. According to an "Oral memorandum given by Japanese Foreign Minister to American ambassador," the Japanese government also promised that "strict orders" had been issued by the army, air force, and Foreign Ministry, and that there would be "no more incidents of unreasonable interference in or harm to the rights and property of the U.S. or any other third party country" (Zhang 2006b, 39). One measure adopted to alleviate tension in relations with the U.S. was to have the Central China Area Army grant earliest permission to American diplomats to return to Nanjing.

On December 28, American diplomats arrived at Xiaguan aboard an American naval vessel with a telegram from the Central China Area Army granting them permission to enter Nanjing. Iinuma Mamoru wrote that the Shanghai Expeditionary Army, occupying Nanjing at the time, felt that "the atmosphere in Nanjing is different from that in Shanghai" and complained that "the Area Army's arranging for these people to return to Nanjing on their own initiative has created great awkwardness for us." Shanghai Expeditionary Army commander Prince Asaka Yasuhiko issued orders to "not let them return very soon." So the Japanese soldiers at Xiaguan refused to allow the American diplomats to disembark on the pretext that their telegram's "date has passed, and thus invalid" (Wang 2005b, 220).

The Japanese army could not, however, keep out Western diplomats indefinitely, especially under mounting diplomatic pressure. Inuma wrote that the Japanese Minister of the Army and Chief of the Army General staff sent a joint telegram exhorting their forces in central China to pay attention to trends among all nations and to maintain good relations with the great powers (Wang 2005b, 222). The Japanese army in Nanjing had no choice but to study the question of "how to handle" Western diplomats.

Inuma reveals that on January 6, 1938, Secretary Allison of the U.S. embassy disembarked at Xiaguan with two other embassy officials, Espy and MacFadyen. On January 9, Secretary Rosen of the German embassy, along with two other German embassy officials Scharffenberg and Hürter, as well as Consul Prideaux-Brune, Colonel Lovat-Fraser, and air-force attaché Mr. Walser of the British mission, arrived in Nanjing aboard the HMS Cricket (Wang 2005b, 227–228).

3.5.2 Western diplomats and Japanese authorities

The Japanese had no choice but to ultimately bend to diplomatic pressure and allow the diplomats to return to Nanjing. Their return to the city had a marked effect on conditions there.

3.5.2.1 Friendly overtures and trickery by the Japanese

Prior to the return of Western diplomats to Nanjing, Matsui Iwane wrote that while in Shanghai he noticed: "There have been more incidents of soldiers looting cars and other goods from foreign embassies in Nanjing. I am quite enraged by the stupid and crude actions of these soldiers. The prestige of the Imperial Army will be destroyed by such incidents. This is extremely regrettable." Matsui immediately dispatched Staff Officer Nakayama Hayato to Nanjing "to take urgent measures to deal with the aftermath" (Wang 2005b, 156). Iinuma Mamoru wrote that the Japanese army began setting guards at the various embassies and convened "all aides-de-camp of all units in and near Nanjing" to a meeting to restore military discipline, and in particular stamp out "illegal actions toward foreign embassies" (Wang 2005b, 221).

Rosen wrote in a report to the German Foreign Office of January 15, 1938, that to destroy the evidence of their atrocities, the Japanese army began "urgent clean-up work...The bodies of innocent civilians, women, and children and the twig-thin corpses littering the streets were all cleaned up" (Chen, Zhang, and Dai n.d., 326).

As they were busy covering up their atrocities, the Japanese army also did its utmost to get on good terms with the personnel of foreign embassies. Forster wrote in his diary that on the one hand they strove to restore all vehicles stolen from embassies by Japanese soldiers "to assume a face-saving posture" (Zhang 2005, 112). On the other hand, the "Japanese embassy will allow new automobiles to be brought from Japan for the gentlemen at our embassy, and presumably at other embassies as well, to replace the cars that were stolen" (Rabe EN, 117). The Japanese embassy also provided great conveniences to the staff of Western embassies, including "beef, eggs, apples, oranges, and canned fruit," as noted by Scharffenberg on January 20 (Chen, Zhang, and Dai n.d., 123). Japanese diplomats also frequently invited their Western counterparts to dinners.

In a report of February 10, Scharffenberg recounts the scene of one dinner thrown by the Japanese embassy: there were abundant plates of food and "geishas just for pouring alcohol," as well as singing, dancing, and drinking: "All the Japanese got drunk." The dinner, which had started at 6:00 p.m., ended "with farewells in an atmosphere of extreme cordiality" at 11:30 p.m. At a concert arranged by the Japanese, an "orchestra brought in from Tokyo made a grand impression." The orchestra's conductor had studied music in Paris, and "had a high degree of professionalism." During intermission, the geishas "poured tea and handed out cigarettes," and "a great number of print and film reporters vied with one another to take photos and film," in an attempt to show the rest of the world "an image of closeness and peace between the Japanese and foreigners in Nanjing" (Chen, Zhang, and Dai n.d., 135).

As the Japanese tried to get on friendly terms with the Westerners, they did not forget to enforce strict controls in the name of safety. "You must submit to the army's[35] rule" was a precondition for the army's allowance of diplomatic person-

---

35 Here "army" refers to the Shanghai Expeditionary Army.

nel to disembark at Nanjing, wrote Iinuma Mamoru (Wang 2005b, 226). The Japanese army not only restricted the scope of activities in which the diplomats could engage, but also assigned them obligatory military police escorts that followed them whenever they went out. Once British diplomats were late to a dinner thrown by the Japanese embassy because the guard in front of the UK embassy had received orders that "nobody may leave the embassy without a military police escort." As the military police had already been relieved of duty for the day, the two British diplomats had "no choice but to spend half an hour convincing the guard" before he finally consented to let them go to the Japanese embassy, as recounted by Scharffenberg in his report of February 10 (Chen, Zhang, and Dai n.d., 406–407). Uemura Toshimichi praised "easygoing" British diplomats in his diary: "They can accept demands from the Area Army; we get along just fine" (Wang 2005b, 258).

Iinuma Mamoru wrote that when Rosen disembarked, he expressed dissatisfaction at the use of the "unfriendly and impolite term 'submit'" used by the Japanese to demarcate his relations with their authority; Rosen was found to be "most deplorable" by Japanese military authorities (Wang 2005b, 227). Rosen wrote in his report of January 15 that when he paid a visit to the Sun Yat-sen Mausoleum "on his own initiative" without permission, he was stopped and rebuked by Japanese officials. Fukuda of the Japanese embassy went so far as to "take out a pen and paper and write an apology letter on the spot," which he demanded that Rosen sign (Chen, Zhang, and Dai n.d., 87). To frighten Rosen and the other Westerners "running around wantonly," the Japanese embassy issued a notice to them: "There are still some Chinese soldiers in plainclothes in Nanjing. Japanese troops have received orders allowing them to shoot anyone suspicious. So we are dispatching guards to protect the safety of all diplomatic personnel" (Rabe CN, 431). Even the Chinese saw the underlying intentions of this move. Cheng Ruifang wrote: "There are many places the foreigners are not allowed to go; that is because there are many corpses they're afraid to let them see" (Zhang 2005, 29).

The Japanese army even changed up its methods in an attempt to pin its crimes on Chinese people. The majority of the houses of foreign diplomats and foreigners in general in Nanjing were looted following the fall of the city. Forster wrote in his diary that the Japanese tried to blame this on Chinese people, but in many cases the Westerners had "seen Japanese in the act of looting" (Zhang 2005, 112). Rosen wrote in a report to the German embassy in Hankou of February 28, 1938 that he inspected several German houses that had been looted and confirmed that "those soldiers who stole cars were part of the Sasaki detachment, and those who stole bicycles belonged to the Katagiri detachment" (Zhang 2005, 418). He also wrote in a report to the German Foreign Office of February 14 that at the behest of their French colleagues, he and Scharffenberg inspected the French embassy, where they found that the embassy had been cleaned out by Japanese soldiers, but the doormen asked Rosen in a terror-stricken manner not to say so, "because the Japanese threatened to beat them to death, demanding that they claim Chinese people had done the looting" (Chen, Zhang, and Dai n.d., 138). Cheng Ruifang wrote that she observed that the Japanese "ordered Chinese to go loot, and once they had done so bayoneted them to death. Then they called foreigners to see that it was Chinese that had done the looting rather than themselves. Under this ruse they both killed more Chinese and had something to show to the foreigners" (Zhang 2005, 32).

3.5.2.2 Atrocities witnessed by Western diplomats

The Westerners in Nanjing thought that the return of their diplomats would mean an improvement in conditions. Cheng Ruifang wrote that even the Chinese thought that with the "return of people from various nations to the shore" the Japanese would "have to attend to their face in a few matters, and would have to appear somewhat better" (Zhang 2005, 31). Smythe wrote in a letter to his family that he felt that the diplomats' "presence will be a deterrence to the Japanese army and will be clearly effective" (Zhang 2005, 268). Fitch wrote that he thought that the return of Western diplomats would mean "a little more assurance that conditions will still further improve" (Zhang 2005, 82). Forster wrote in his diary on January 10: "Officials of the British and German embassies have returned too, which ought to make things better" (Zhang 2005, 112).

Japanese atrocities continued at full steam even as the army attempted to display a sterling image. Rabe invited the German diplomats to dinner the night of their return, writing in his diary that during the dinner "A fire has broken out behind the Shanghai Commercial Savings Bank. It seems that the return of embassy personnel will not at all deter Japanese soldiers from officially mandated arson" (Rabe CN, 318). Magee wrote in a letter to his wife that a British diplomat found the body of a Chinese woman into whom a golf club had been inserted (Zhang 2005, 167). Rosen wrote in a report to the German Foreign Office of February 10 that he witnessed the massacre of four civilians by Japanese soldiers: "One old man carrying two chairs was shot by a Japanese soldier who did not even flinch. His younger sister had gone into hiding when the Japanese arrived. She called two acquaintances, who made a litter from a door, two bamboo poles, and some thick rope, and prepared to carry the injured old man away. The Japanese, upon sighting them, shot all four to death: the injured old man, his younger sister, and the two people carrying the litter" (Zhang 2005, 375–376).

In fact, some Western diplomats had witnessed scenes of massacre on the shore of the Yangtze prior to disembarking. Rosen wrote in a report to the German Foreign Office from Shanghai of December 23 that on December 21, 1937, as the HMS Bee passed Xiaguan, he "saw serious damage" and "many piled bodies" wearing civilian clothes (Zhang 2005, 282). On the afternoon of December 31, as the American naval vessel he was aboard passed Nanjing, he noticed that "the shore has become the scene of a massacre. I could also see that there are small fires all over the city, and I could hear gunshots" (Zhang 2006b, 65). In addition to recording atrocities they themselves witnessed, these diplomats also widely collected statements on Japanese atrocities and recorded them into their diplomatic reports.

Magee wrote in a letter to his wife of the Japanese army's attitude toward crimes committed by its soldiers: "The greatest crime would be to have their acts discovered and reported in foreign newspapers" (Zhang 2005, 171). As the Western diplomats returned to Nanjing, British and American naval vessels began docking at Xiaguan, providing channels for communication not under Japanese control. The Japanese army was extremely unwilling to allow news about criminal actions to be disseminated via these naval vessels' shipboard radios. Forster wrote in his diary: "Our Embassy now has a wireless sending set with an operator from the Navy. The J. refused at first, but Allison won out" (Zhang 2005, 117).

The Japanese repeatedly exhorted Western diplomats not to disseminate news of Japanese atrocities. Rosen was warned by the Japanese to "be somewhat cautious in his reports" (Rabe CN, 320) and not to speak ill of the Japanese army. Rabe was sure that the Japanese were attempting to cover up their atrocities: "They try to cover things up wherever it's even vaguely feasible. And the ban on anyone entering or leaving is one of their ways of keeping the world ignorant of Nanking's present state. Even though that can last only for a short time, because ever since the Germans, Americans, and British restaffed their embassies here, hundreds of letters have been sent to Shanghai describing local conditions in precise detail, not to mention all the embassies' telegraphed reports" (Rabe EN, 157).

The greatest headache for the Japanese came from the Western diplomats, official representatives of their countries, who held a trump card against the Japanese of reporting their actions to the world. Forster wrote in his diary of the Western diplomats: "When their protests, etc. are tabled by the Japanese Embassy officials, they get into direct communication with Tokyo through Washington, London, and Berlin. This has made the Japanese awfully mad here" (Zhang Kaiyuan 2005, 117).

When head of the Japanese consular police Takadama sought "washerwomen" in the shelter at Ginling Women's College his motives were questioned when he insisted that they be young and beautiful. This incident came to the attention of Allison in the American embassy, who reported it to Washington. This infuriated Takadama, who insisted that "his reputation be restored... Dr. Smythe, who took down the minutes of the entire discussion, promises him that the various embassies will be notified. That, of course, really rubs Takadama the wrong way, and he departs in great disgruntlement, after first expressly asking that the embassies not be bothered" (Rabe EN, 154).

3.5.2.3 The Allison incident

On January 18, 1938, the UK Foreign Ministry received the following report from China: "The American embassy sent a diplomatic note to the Japanese government on January 17, strongly protesting the looting of American property, the tearing down of notices, and the tearing down of American flags in the midst of military operations in Nanjing, Hankou, and other places. The American government finds these actions to be in contradiction to the assurances made by Japan in the wake of the sinking of the USS Panay, and that the Japanese government is not taking enough measures to protect American rights. They are demanding that the Japanese government stress orders already given to effectively prevent the re-occurrence of atrocities" (Zhang and Chen n.d., 542).

The UK Foreign Ministry came to this conclusion about the American embassy's protest in that report: the Americans "have certainly received an assurance that the Japanese government has again sent out relevant orders. But it remains a question whether atrocities will now stop, because the Japanese army is now out of control. It's a good thing that they are coming to recognize this fact from one hard lesson after another. They're going through the same course as we did, and I fear they will come to the same conclusion: oral arguments have no force against the Japanese army" (Zhang and Chen n.d., 543).

Still, in the same report on damages to American property, British diplomats made fun of American colleagues who are "keeping cool and avoiding radical actions that may inflame popular sentiments" in an attempt to come to a "friendly resolution" in the current stage of issues with Japan. The British experience had caused them to "abandon all hope long ago... The American Department of State may ultimately realize that the actions of low-level Japanese army officers have not in the slightest violated the Empire's policies (eliminating Western influence in China), but are, to the contrary, a forceful embodiment of those policies" (Zhang and Chen n.d., 544).

On January 26, as Allison was on his way to the University of Nanking to investigate cases of Japanese soldiers raping Chinese women, he was abused by a Japanese officer and slapped by a soldier. UK Consul Prideaux-Brune made a record of this incident:

> The Allison Incident
>
> On January 25, two Japanese soldiers abducted a Chinese woman from the workshop of the agriculture department of the University of Nanking. The workshop is American property, a fact highlighted in a notice posted there by the Japanese embassy. The two Japanese soldiers tore down this notice upon entering the premises.
>
> Japanese soldiers have been systematically looting American property, with incidents occurring nearly every day. Allison's protests to the Japanese embassy bore no fruit. Fukui accused him of placing too much credence in gossip and reports made by Chinese. So Allison decided to investigate this matter himself. He had spoken previously with the Japanese embassy about his investigation into this matter.
>
> On the afternoon of January 26, Japanese consular police chief Taketomi and two Japanese military policemen paid a visit to the workshop's American manager Charles Riggs. It seems that it was arranged for the investigation to happen somewhat later on that same day. Nevertheless, they all went to see Allison at the American embassy. Together they proceeded to the workshop from which the Chinese woman had been abducted. The Japanese soldiers had taken her to a nearby building and later released her back to the workshop.
>
> Allison, Riggs, and the Japanese came to the workshop. The Japanese wanted the abducted woman to take them to the building where she had been held. They were all taken to the place. The building was not American property, but was probably owned by a third party. The building had already been occupied by the military, but this was not possible to determine immediately from its exterior.
>
> After the Chinese woman had entered, Allison and Riggs followed. They had taken a step or two inside the door when a guard suddenly appeared. Allison was slapped, and Riggs had his collar torn off. An officer stepped forward and loudly scolded the Americans. The Japanese military police in their train attempted to intervene, but they too ended up in a screaming match with the military personnel. The moment they mentioned that the two foreigners were Americans, all soldiers present immediately became infuriated.
>
> This matter was reported to the Japanese embassy. The following afternoon, Major Hongo and the Army Staff Headquarters Communications Officer paid a visit to Allison in the American embassy to apologize on behalf of the commanding officer of the offending soldiers and assure him that the same would never occur again. At the same time, it appears that Japan disseminated a distorted version of the event over the radio, using provocative language (Zhang and Chen n.d., 540–541).

The matter was also reported by telegram to Washington, whereupon the American government immediately lodged a protest with Tokyo. The "Allison incident," in which an American diplomat was struck by Japanese soldiers, was widely reported in American and British media, but Forster wrote in a letter to his wife: "Allison does not know yet whether to report the incident as he is afraid it may have serious results, as far as the relations between the two countries are concerned" (Zhang 2005, 120). Uemura Toshimichi, a high-ranking Japanese officer, however, found Allison to "exhibit symptoms of neurosis, lodging groundless complaints of bad conduct to the consulate" (Wang 2005b, 263). Uemura wrote that nevertheless, the matter "involved the higher-ups," and so all that was possible was to dispatch people to apologize to Allison and send up the offending officer for a court martial in Tokyo (Wang 2005b, 264).

3.5.3 Western diplomats and expatriates

Prior to the return of Western diplomats to Nanjing, the foreigners in the city had been living under the Japanese army's reign of terror in complete isolation from the rest of the world. They had to both keep their refugees alive and run left and right driving off Japanese soldiers in the commission of atrocities, spreading their energy thin. Rabe wrote: "What we need is people (Europeans) to come here to help us, but the Japanese won't permit anyone to come to Nanjing." (Rabe CN, 241). Vaturin expressed a similar sentiment in her diary entry of December 29: "To date we are still cut off from the outside world and no foreigner from outside has been able to get in." The news of the imminent return of Western diplomats was a great encouragement to Chinese and foreigner alike in the city. On January 5, 1938, Cheng Ruifang wrote that she expected that "it will be good if the American consul truly returns to Nanjing" (Zhang 2005, 29). When Rabe heard from the Japanese embassy that Rosen and the rest of the German diplomats were returning, he called it "a very welcome bit of news" (Rabe EN, 111).

The Westerners could barely contain their jubilation when their diplomats returned to Nanjing. Vautrin wrote on January 6 that the day they arrived, she "was able to collect ten [eggs] ... and was glad to present them as a gift." Rabe was overjoyed, writing in his diary on the day of the return of the American diplomats: "HURRAH! The three officials from the American embassy... arrived here today" (Rabe EN, 113). Rabe continued about of the return of the German diplomats: "Kröger, Hatz, and I went to the German embassy at 2 o'clock this afternoon and at about 3 the three German officials arrived, accompanied by Mr. Tanaka and Mr. Fukuda of the Japanese embassy, and we welcomed them with a bottle of champagne that Kröger had 'commandeered' somewhere." That night Rabe invited Rosen to dine in his house (Rabe EN, 113).

Smythe wrote in a letter to his family that he felt himself "relieved of a burden" when the American diplomats returned. Once the British and German diplomats returned, he "felt as though a relief force had arrived – as though relief had come to people in a siege" (Zhang 2005, 268).

Japanese soldiers broke into refugee shelters to perpetrate all manner of crimes every day after the occupation. The Japanese did not, however, pay heed to protests lodged by Westerners in residence in the city. Cheng Ruifang estimated that not only would their protests be of no avail, but on the contrary they would cause the Japanese to bear grudges. She writes "Now the consuls have returned. There are some matters that when reported by them carry more force" (Zhang 2005, 30).

On January 10, 1938, Rabe and Mills paid a visit to the American embassy, where Allison promised to help the International Committee in the work of filing protests. On the 11th, Rabe visited the British embassy, where Rosen and Allison were waiting. Consuls from all three nations expressed willingness to take daily reports from the Committee on crimes committed by Japanese soldiers, and also promised to forward these reports to the Japanese embassy or to their own governments (Rabe CN, 323).

On that day, the 11th, Japanese military police surrounded the International Committee's headquarters at Number 5 Ninghai Road and conducted a thorough search. The next day Rabe paid visits to the three embassies to discuss the previous day's event. With Rabe's report in hand, Rosen wrote a letter to acting Consul-General Fukui of the Japanese embassy demanding that "no more such unlawful entries into German properties occur." If the Japanese army thought "such a search was imperative, and had sufficient reason to demonstrate the necessity of such an action," Rosen indicated that he would "be very happy to accompany any such search group, or send along a member of the embassy or another German representing me." Rosen ended on a veiled threat: "I hope we can handle matters like this on the ground here, and that there is no need for me to report on them to my own government" (Chen, Zhang, and Dai n.d., 92). On January 27, McCallum was attacked by two Japanese soldiers in the Gulou Hospital and "wounded in the neck" by bayonet. Rabe wrote that "the American and Japanese governments will be informed at once by telegram" (Rabe EN, 159). Under relentless diplomatic pressure, Tokyo had no choice but to dispatch Major Hongo of the General Staff Headquarters to Nanjing to resolve disputes with the three foreign legations.

The Japanese controlled contacts between Nanjing and the outside world before the return of the diplomats. When Westerners occasionally were able to get letters out via Japanese officials, these letters were subject to screening. On December 19, 1937, Rabe, aboard a ship docked at Xiaguan but not allowed to disembark, sent a letter to Rabe via the Japanese inquiring about conditions in the city. In his reply, Rabe noted that lighting, water, and telephone service had been cut off in the city, and that only "two German properties have not been damaged, that of the ambassador and my own. Mr. Trautmann's car is currently serving the Japanese army, as are your car and other German cars" (Rabe CN, 194). The Japanese were highly displeased with Rabe's words and "refused to send out this telegram." Smythe wrote in a letter to his family that the Japanese refused to send out his telegram even after six revisions, and he found "conditions growing tenser every day," whereas the Japanese said "conditions are growing better day by day" (Zhang 2005, 240). The Japanese embassy once asked that Rabe "not report any events that would make the Japanese embassy unhappy." Rabe had no choice but to consent, because "the only way to send out the letters was through the Japanese embassy" (Rabe CN, 245).

The return of the diplomats gave the Westerners in Nanjing channels for transmitting information. Cheng Ruifang wrote: "Now every letter we receive is like a treasure, as we haven't received letters for a long time. These letters are delivered on American naval vessels. Now it's much more convenient" (Zhang 2005, 31).

Every move by foreign embassies to help the International Committee in its quest to preserve refugee lives was met with fervent disapproval by the Japanese. During a dinner thrown by the Nanjing Defense Garrison, its commander Major General Amaya openly warned foreign diplomats: "Please don't interfere in my dealings with the Chinese!" (Rabe EN, 189). Rabe later "expressed deepest gratitude for help" given by the foreign diplomats to the International Committee (Rabe CN, 570).

In summary, the activities of Western diplomats during the Rape of Nanking played a real role in helping Chinese refugees and curtailing Japanese atrocities. Their reports not only influenced their governments' understanding of the Japanese government and military and provided reference materials for the drafting of their government's Japan policies, but also ensured that a great quantity of records of Japanese atrocities were stored in Western diplomatic archives. Many of their reports and letters were used as evidence by prosecutors in the International Military Tribunal for the Far East (see "Prosecutors' evidence related to the Japanese army's Rape of Nanking" in Yang Xiaming 2006).

Despite their alarm at Japanese atrocities and empathy for the plight of Chinese refugees, the foreign diplomats generally based their conclusions in national interests and relations with Japan. Allison suggests in a report of April 15 to the American government that Americans should strive to win the markets of Nanjing: "If no effective plan is conceived, and if American and other foreign enterprises have to wait until they're allowed to return to Nanjing, the vast majority of their previous market share will certainly have been usurped by Japanese" (Zhang 2006b, 72).

Some individual diplomats were not enthusiastic about their expatriates' relief activities. Scharffenberg wrote in a report of February 10: "The accomplishments of Mr. Rabe, chairman of the International Committee, are outstanding, but in my opinion he trusts the Americans too much and has become their pawn, serving American interests and American proselytizing ministers" (Chen, Zhang, and Dai n.d., 134). Scharffenberg recorded a great number of Japanese atrocities, but also wrote in a report of February 10 that "the bloody incidents of looting and murder by the Japanese... have no connection whatsoever with our Germany" (Zhang 2005, 407). In a report of February 1, he wrote that he also felt that the Allison incident had been "of his own creation" (Zhang 2005, 362). In the report he also frequently criticized his colleague Rosen, who could "not keep anything hidden in his heart," and frequently incited incidents with Japanese authorities (Zhang 2005, 363).

3.6 Westerners in the Wake of Massacre

During the Rape of Nanking, the heroic efforts of the handful of Westerners in the city provided inestimable service to the throngs of Chinese refugees. They were an inextinguishable light shining in the long darkness of the massacre, giving hope to desperate Chinese people and leaving a lasting impression of friendship and peace on the Chinese people and the world at large.

3.6.1 Westerners in war crimes tribunals

3.6.1.1 The Tokyo Trials

After the end of the Second World War, the Allies conducted international war crimes tribunals to punish the war criminals who had instigated the war. General Matsui Iwane, previously commander of the Central China Area Army, was executed by the International Military Tribunal for the Far East. Many Westerners who had been in Nanjing testified for the prosecution in his trial.

Dr. Wilson, Dr. Bates, Reverend Magee, and others testified for the prosecution during the Tokyo trials. Smythe, Fitch, McCallum, and others provided statements to be read in court. Other records created by Westerners were also used as evidence in the trials: "Documents of the Nanking Safety Zone," diplomatic correspondence from the American embassy, Rabe's correspondence, letters written by German Ambassador Trautmann to the German Foreign Ministry, and so on.

3.6 Westerners in the Wake of Massacre — 271

The statements of these foreigners played a key role in the verdicts reached in trials regarding the Rape of Nanking. It is clear from the verdicts that the tribunal trusted their statements to a great degree.

Summary of prosecutor's evidence: overall conditions at the time of the fall of Nanjing	All resistance by Chinese forces in the city came to a full stop when Nanjing fell on December 13, 1937.
Westerners providing evidence	Wilson, Bates, Magee, etc.
Relevant contents from verdict statement	When the Japanese army entered the city on the morning of December 13, 1937, all resistance had come to an end.
Summary of prosecutor's evidence: 1. Murder and massacre	(2) Testimony of Dr. Robert Wilson: After Nanjing fell, the University Hospital, which had contained 50 patients, became full of patients of all ages in only a few days. The stories they told made him believe more firmly that these people had been sacrificed in Japanese atrocities. He mentioned one 40-year old Chinese woman, who had had a chunk of her neck cut off by a Japanese soldier. He also mentioned an eight-year old boy whose stomach had been pierced by a bayonet. He mentioned one man whose head and neck had been badly burned, who prior to dying said that he had been the only survivor of a large group of people who had been tied together, had gasoline poured over them, and burned alive. He also mentioned an old man injured by a Japanese soldier's bayonet and was left on the scene to die. A seven-year old girl's elbow had been cut open by a Japanese soldier, prior to which the same soldier had killed her father and mother before her eyes. He recognized Captain Liang (Tingfang) and Wu Changde as having received treatment from him. Their wounds had been inflicted by Japanese, and both gave testimony in the same case. (4) During one of their frequent searches of the Safety Zone, Japanese soldiers once carried off 1,500 refugees despite the protests of International Committee Chairman Rabe. These were broken into groups of 10 to 15, had their hands tied together, and in the words of Mr. Fitch and Dr. Hsu, these civilians were all shot to death by machine guns. Their bodies were all piled into a small pond. (5) In his testimony, University of Nanking Vice President and member of the International Committee for the Nanking Safety Zone M.S. Bates said he witnessed a great number of shootings of individual civilians with no warnings or clear reasons cited prior to the shootings. Bates said in testimony: "The total spread of this killing was so

extensive that no one can give a complete picture of it." In his own "sure knowledge," 12,000 civilians, men, women, and children, were killed within the city walls: "There were many others killed within the city outside our knowledge whose numbers we have no way of checking, and also there were large numbers killed immediately outside the city, of civilians. This is quite apart from the killing of tens of thousands of men who were Chinese soldiers or had been Chinese soldiers." The International Committee arranged for the burial of 30,000 Chinese soldiers, who had, after surrendering, been killed by machine gun fire on the shore of the Yangtze. It was impossible to estimate the number of bodies thrown into the river or disposed of through other means. Over the course of three weeks, the Safety Zone was searched every day. Anyone with calloused hands or with hat marks on their foreheads were accused of being former Chinese soldiers and dragged off by Japanese troops to be killed. The vast majority of those killed were common carriers or laborers.

(6) Bates continues: "In some cases a peculiar form of treachery was practiced to persuade men to admit that they had been soldiers... Japanese officers urged Chinese men to come forward, saying, 'If you have previously been a Chinese soldier, or if you have ever worked as a carrier or laborer in the Chinese Army, that will all now be forgotten and forgiven if you will join this labor corps.' In that way, in one afternoon, two hundred men were secured from the premises of the University of Nanking and were promptly marched away and executed that evening along with other bodies of men secured from other parts of the safety zone."

(7) John G. Magee, resident in Nanjing from 1912 to 1940, testified that the massacre of civilians began as soon as the Japanese took the city, and grew steadily more intense, until "there was organized killing of great bodies of men. Soon there were bodies of men lying everywhere, and I passed columns of men being taken out to be killed. These people were being killed by rifle fire and machine gun principally. Also, we knew of groups of several hundred being bayoneted to death."

Magee goes on to discuss the evening of December 14: "I passed two long columns of Chinese all tied up with their hands in front of them, four by four. I should say that, the very least, there were a thousand men in those two columns, or there may have been closer to two thousand." All were killed. On December 16 a group of 1,000 refugees, including 14 from a Christian congregation and the 15-year old boy of a Chinese pastor, were taken to the shore of the Yantze and "mowed down with cross-fire machine guns from either end."
(8) Magee along with another American and two Russians witnessed

another killing: "A Chinese was walking along the street before this house in a long silk gown; two Japanese soldiers called to him, and he was so frightened; he was trying to get away. He hastened his pace, was trying to get around a corner in a bamboo fence, hoping there was an opening, but there was no opening. The soldiers walked in front of him and couldn't have stood more than five yards in front of him, and both of them shot him in the face – killed him. They were both laughing and talking as though nothing had happened; never stopped smoking their cigarettes or talking – they killed him with no more feeling than one taking a shot at a wild duck, and then walked on."

(9) Magee testified that he saw piles of dead Chinese at the wharf, hundreds of bodies to the pile, many of them charred, indicating that they had been burned after having been shot. Some streets were impassible due to the large numbers of corpses. He also took photos of Chinese women kneeling before Japanese soldiers begging them to spare their men, who were in a line being driven off by Japanese soldiers. When he attempted to ask a Japanese soldier to release two of their number, his driver and his driver's brother, he was rudely scolded by an officer.

(10) George A. Fitch was born in China. He served as secretary of the Young Men's Christian Association (YMCA) International Committee in China for about 36 years. In his statement, Fitch recounted a few passages from his diary. "On December 15, I saw approximately 1300 men, all in civilian clothes, just taken from one of our camps near our headquarters, lined up and roped together in groups of about 100 by soldiers with fixed bayonets. In spite of my protests to the commanding officer, they were marched off to be shot."

"On December 22, 1937, I saw about fifty corpses in some ponds a quarter of a mile east of my office. All were dressed in civilian clothes, most of them with hands bound behind their backs, and one with the top half of his head completely cut off. Subsequently I saw hundreds of bodies of Chinese, mostly men but a few women, in a similar condition, in ponds, on the streets, and in houses."

(11) James McCallum was an American missionary in Nanjing. In his diary he recorded many instances of killings of civilians by Japanese soldiers after their entry into the city: "It is absolutely unbelievable, but thousands have been butchered in cold blood – how many it is hard to guess, some believe it would approach the 10,000 mark."

The next day he recounts how people were taken away from the Safety Zone, called Chinese soldiers by the Japanese. He writes: "The men had friends among the group who could identify them as civilians, but because they had calluses on their hands they were branded without further investigation as soldiers in spite of the protests voiced. Many rickshaw and sampan men, as well as other laborers have been shot simply because they have the marks of honest toil upon their hands."

(27) On January 25, 1938, the American embassy published an official report from a deputy consul in Nanjing recounting crimes committed in Nanjing between December 10, 1937, to January 24, 1938. The report claimed that over 20,000 were killed by Japanese soldiers within the first few days after the city's fall, all because they were suspected to have been soldiers. The report goes on: "It seems that no measures whatsoever are taken to distinguish former soldiers from whose who have never served in the armed forces. If one is suspected of being a soldier, he is doomed to death." The report later reads: "In addition to small detachments of Japanese massacring soldiers, there are also groups of two to three Japanese soldiers marauding the streets at all hours. It is precisely the burning, killing, and looting of these soldiers that are creating the great terror in the city. We still do not know if these soldiers were authorized to burn, kill, and loot at will or if the Japanese army has completely lost control. Japanese soldiers still swarm on the streets of Nanjing committing crimes too numerous to record. Per reports given by numerous foreigners, Japanese soldiers have, like barbarians, ravaged this city in the most brazen manner. Untold numbers of men, women, and children have been killed around the city."

Westerners providing evidence	Wilson, Fitch, Rabe, Bates, Magee, Allison, and others.
Related contents from verdict statement	Per one eyewitness, Japanese soldiers were completely unrestrained and profaned the city like a nomadic tribe. Per the eyewitness, the city was like prey fallen into the hands of the predators, the Japanese soldiers, and not like a city occupied after organized fighting. The victorious Japanese troops then committed untold numbers of atrocities on their prey. Japanese soldiers roamed the city individually or in groups of three to five, committing murder, rape, looting, and arson, with no discipline to speak of. Many soldiers were extremely drunk. As the soldiers idled around the city, they indiscriminately killed Chinese men, women, and children, without having been provoked and for no clear reason, filling the city's streets and alleys with corpses. In the account of another eyewitness, Chinese were hunted like rabbits. Anyone who ran was shot. During the first two or three days of the Japanese occupation, 12,000 non-combatants – men, women, and children – were indiscriminately slaughtered.

3.6 Westerners in the Wake of Massacre — 275

Summary of prosecutor's evidence: 3. Rape

(1) From December 13, 1937, to February 6, 1938, women in Nanjing aged nine to 77 were subjected to cruel rape and gang rape. In a report delivered to the German Foreign Ministry, International Committee for the Nanking Safety Zone Chairman John Rabe writes that more than 20,000 women were raped by Japanese soldiers during the first month after the fall of Nanjing. Thousands of women were killed while being ravaged by Japanese soldiers, and many more were killed afterward. Japanese soldiers inserted sticks, alcohol bottles, and other foreign objects into the vaginas of their victims after savaging them, and then left their corpses out in the open. Such infuriating crimes never ceased. If a victim's family members, or even children, tried to intervene in these shameless crimes, they were doomed, either beaten or shot to death on the spot.

(2) For the first four to five weeks following the fall of Nanjing, Japanese soldiers attempted to burst into Ginling Women's College every day. The college was inside of the announced Safety Zone and sheltered over 10,000 women and children. More than 40,000 refugees sheltered on the campus of the University of Nanking, also declared within the Safety Zone. Despite the valiant efforts of Vautrin, Mrs. Twinem, Mrs. Cheng, and International Committee workers and other foreign residents, Japanese soldiers continued to openly rape girls and women on the university grounds. Some soldiers even selected pretty girls to be taken to officers' dwellings to be raped. After the fall of Nanjing, the unchecked Japanese army committed crimes for a sustained period of over six weeks.

(3) Speaking to sexual crimes committed by Japanese soldiers, Bates gave the following testimony: "That was one of the roughest and saddest parts of the whole picture. Again, in the homes of my three nearest neighbors, women were raped, including wives of University teachers. On five different occasions, which I can detail for you if desired, I, myself, came upon soldiers in the act of rape and pulled them away from the women. The safety zone case reports, to which we have previously referred, and my own records of what occurred among the thirty thousand refugees on the various grounds and in the building of the University of Nanking, hold a total of many hundreds of cases of rape about which exact details were furnished to the Japanese authorities at the time. One month after the occupation, Mr. Raabe [sic.], the Chairman of the International Committee, reported to the German authorities that he and his colleagues believed that not less than twenty thousand cases of rape had occurred. A little earlier I estimated, very much more cautiously and on the basis of the safety zone reports alone, some eight thousand cases. Every day and every night there were large numbers of different gangs of soldiers, usually fifteen or twenty in a group, who went about through

the city, chiefly in the safety zone because that's where almost all the people were, and went into the houses seeking women. In two cases, which I remember all too clearly because I nearly lost my life in each of them, officers participated in this seizing and raping of women on the University property. The raping was frequent daytime [sic.] as well as night and occurred along the roadside in many cases. On the grounds of the Nanking Theological Seminary, under the eyes of one of my own friends, a Chinese woman was raped in rapid succession by seventeen Japanese soldiers. I do not care to repeat the occasional cases of sadistic and abnormal behavior in connection with the raping, but I do want to mention that on the grounds of the University alone a little girl of nine and a grandmother of seventy-six were raped."

(4) Wilson testified that he had driven off Japanese soldiers committing rape and taken in a girl who had caught syphilis after being raped by a Japanese soldier.

(6) In his testimony Magee affirmed the magnitude of the rapes and cited a few cases of his own. One case involved a 10-year old girl raped on December 20 and a 15-year old raped six times on February 1. There was a 40-year old widow raped eight times, and a 37-year old widow raped twice on her way to the University of Nanking. In another case, an old woman of 80 years was shot in the head simply for saying "I am too old." Once when a Japanese officer came across a soldier raping a woman, the only punishment given was a slap on the face. When Magee told a Japanese sentry that a rape had just occurred, the sentry "only laughed."

(12) The American missionary McCallum writes in his diary: "Rape! Rape! Rape! – We estimate at least 1000 cases a night, and many by day. In case of resistance or anything that seems like disapproval there is a bayonet stab or a bullet. We could write up hundreds of cases a day. People are hysterical; they get down on their knees and 'Kowtow' anytime we foreigners appear. They beg for aid... Women are being carried off every morning, afternoon, and evening. The whole Japanese army seems to be free to go and come anywhere it pleases, and to do what it pleases." He continues on January 3, 1938: "each day has a long list of bad reports. A man was killed near the relief headquarters yesterday afternoon. In the afternoon a Japanese soldier attempted to rape a woman; her husband interfered and helped her resist; but in the afternoon the soldier returned to shoot the husband. This morning came another woman in a sad plight and with a horrible story. She was one of five women whom the Japanese soldiers had taken to one of their medical units – to wash their clothes by day, to be raped by night. Two of them were forced to

satisfy from 15 to 20 men, and the prettiest one as many as 40 each night. This one who came to us had been called off by three of the soldiers into an isolated place, where they attempted to cut off her head. The muscles of the neck had been cut but they failed to sever the spinal cord. She feigned death but dragged herself to the hospital." He continues on January 8: "Some [Japanese] newspaper men came to the entrance of a concentration camp and distributed cakes and apples, and handed out a few coins to the refugees, and moving pictures were taken of this kind act. At the same time a bunch of soldiers climbed over the back wall of the compound and raped a dozen or so of the women. There were no pictures taken out back."

(13) On December 25, 1938, after the American vice consul returned to Nanjing, he wrote an official report to the American embassy summarizing events that had occurred in the city following its fall: "It is reported that Japanese soldiers find and rape women wherever women can be found. Attached to this report are some reference materials on these matters. In the initial period following the Japanese occupation, it is estimated by the foreigners here that 1,000 such cases occurred every night. One American calculates that there are 30 cases of rape per night in American property alone."

Westerners providing evidence	Rabe, Vautrin, Bates, Wilson, Magee, McCallum, and others.
Relevant contents from verdict statement	There were many cases of rape. Death was a common outcome both for rape victims and their family members who attempted to protect them. Even young girls and old women were not spared. There were many cases of perversion and sadism accompanying rape. Many women were killed after being raped, and their bodies were further disgraced. In the first month of occupation, there were nearly 20,000 cases of rape in the city of Nanjing.
Summary of prosecutor's evidence: 4. Looting, robbing, and wanton destruction of property	(2) Prior to the occupation, only a small number of buildings in the city had been damaged. Nanjing was reduced to a rubble pit during the first five to six weeks of occupation, with Japanese soldiers wantonly destroying residences, shops, churches, schools, and public buildings. See Bates' testimony: "Practically every building in the city was entered many, many times by these roving gangs of soldiers throughout the first six or seven weeks of the occupation. In some cases the looting was well organized and systematic, using fleets of army trucks under the direction of officers. The vaults in the banks, including the personal safe deposit boxes of German officials and residents, were cut open with acetylene torches… With the exception of one of two minor fires, apparently started by drunken soldiers, there was no burning until the Japanese troops had been in the city five or six days. Beginning, I believe, on the 19th or 20th of

December, burning was carried on regularly for six weeks. In some cases the burning followed the looting of a line of stores, but in most instances we could not see any reason or pattern in it. At no time was there a general conflagration, but the definite firing of certain groups of buildings each day. Sometimes gasoline was used, but more commonly chemical strips, of which I secured samples." When questioned whether the buildings of the Russian embassy were burned by Japanese soldiers, Bates responds: "Yes, they were burned at the beginning of 1938. Also, just to illustrate the range of the burning, the Y.M.C.A. building, two important church buildings, the two chief German properties with the Swastika flying upon them, were among those burned."

From Magee's testimony: "The Japanese soldiers took from the people anything that struck their fancy: wristwatches, fountain pens, money, clothing, food. I took to the hospital in those first few days of occupation a half-witted woman of forty-one who was stabbed in the neck because she grabbed at some bedding that a Japanese soldier was taking away from her... The burning continued day by day in different parts of the city. One of our own Episcopal church missions was partly burned, and later on they finished the job on January 26. The Christian Disciples Mission was burned – one of their school buildings was burned, the YMCA, the Russian Embassy, and a great many homes of the people outside of our Safety Zone. Every once in a while these soldiers would leave behind little black sticks of some substance which may have been termite [sic.]. It was highly inflammable, and it was no doubt what they were using to set fire to the buildings."

Fitch writes in his diary entry of December 20: "Vandalism and violence continue absolutely unchecked. Whole sections of the city are being systematically burned. At 5 PM Smythe and I went for a drive. All Taiping Road, the most important shopping street in the city, was in flames. We drove through showers of sparks and over burning embers. Further south we could see the soldiers inside the shops setting fire to them and still further they were loading the loot into army trucks. Next to the YMCA – and it was in flames – evidently fired only an hour or so ago... That night I counted fourteen fires from my window, some of them covering considerable areas."

McCallum writes in his diary entry of December 29, 1937: "Every foreign house is a sight to behold, untouched until the Japanese army arrived, nothing untouched since. Every lock has been broken, every trunk ransacked. Their search for money and valuables has led them to the flues and inside pianos... Nanjing presents a dismal appearance. At the time the Japanese Army entered the city little harm had been done to buildings. Since then the stores have been stripped of their wares and most of them burned. Taiping, Chung Hua, and practically every other main business road in the city is a maze of ruins."

General von Falkenhausen submitted one German eyewitness report to the German Foreign Ministry in a top secret report, describing the conduct of the Japanese in Nanjing from December 8, 1937 to January 13, 1938: "They stole everything they could from the refugees – food, wool blankets, clothes, watches, in a word anything worth stealing. One Japanese soldier brought four coolies to load the booty of his looting; this was a very common sight. This organized looting persisted for 14 days, and even now, personal safety is not assured." The report goes on to discuss how most places in the city had not been destroyed prior to the occupation, but only in the aftermath of the occupation: "Under the Japanese army's rule, Nanjing's complexion changed greatly. Not a day went by without arson. Now it is the turn of Taiping Road, Zhongshan East Road, Guofu Road, and Zhujiang Road. All of the south of the city and the Confucius Temple have been completely burned. If I had to put it in a percentage, I'd say that 30 to 40% of Nanjing has been burned."

(4) The official report submitted to the American Department of State reads: "[The Japanese army] took no steps to put out the fires."

Westerners providing evidence	Bates, Magee, McCallum, Kröger, Allison, etc.
Relevant contents from verdict statement	Japanese soldiers plundered whatever they wanted at will. Everywhere soldiers stopped civilians not wearing military uniforms for searches. If nothing of value was found, they were shot on the spot. Many residences and stores were illegally entered and then looted. The spoils were then hauled off in trucks. After looting stores and warehouses, Japanese soldiers often set them afire. Taiping Road, the busiest commercial street in Nanjing, as well as a large swath of commercial district in its environs, were burned to cinders. Soldiers burned private homes for no reason. A few days afterward, arson seems to have assumed a fixed pattern and lasted for six weeks. About one-third of the city was burned in this way.
Summary of prosecutor's evidence: 6. The reign of terror persisted for more than six weeks	(1) Dr. Wilson describes conditions of several civilians brought to his hospital for treatment after being wounded by Japanese soldiers and then states: "Cases like this continued to come in for a matter of some six or seven weeks following the fall of the city on December 13, 1937."

(2) When asked about the duration of sustained atrocities, Bates responds: "The terror was intense for two and one-half to three weeks. It was serious to a total of six to seven weeks."

(3) When asked how long had been the duration of the cruel treatment of Chinese civilians by Japanese soldiers he had described, Magee answers: "After about six weeks it began to taper off although many things happened – individual things happened after that."

Westerners providing evidence	Wilson, Bates, Magee, etc.
Relevant contents from verdict statement	As stated in testimony by Bates, the most intense terror lasted for two to three weeks after the Japanese occupation, but remained serious for six to seven weeks.
Summary of prosecutor's evidence: 8. Reports from the International Committee for the Nanking Safety Zone	(1) The International Committee for the Nanking Safety Zone was composed of German, British, American, and Danish citizens who remained in Nanjing before and after its fall. From December 14, 1937, to February 10, 1938, the German Mr. John Rabe was chairman of the International Committee, and Dr. Lewis S.C. Smythe served as its secretary. The names and nationalities were recorded on pages 4508 and 4509 of the trial transcripts. The objective of the committee was to provide a small zone free of fighting where refugees could avoid the threat of warfare.

(2) The International Committee delivered reports by individuals to Japanese diplomatic organs in Nanjing every day. The Committee delivered written reports to Japanese consuls and representatives of Japanese diplomatic organs in Nanjing every day, recounting in detail atrocities committed by Japanese soldiers in the Safety Zone. These reports contained 425 numbered cases spanning December 16, 1937 to February 2, 1938 (some reports contained 30 different cases of rape or other incidents). Smythe writes in his statement: "We filed nearly two protests every day for the first six weeks of the Japanese occupation. Usually one of these was taken to the Japanese Embassy by Mr. Rabe and myself in person; the other was sent by a messenger... In the almost daily conferences that Mr. Rabe and I had with the Japanese Embassy, they at no time denied the accuracy of these reports. They continually promised that they would do something about it. But it was February, 1938, before any effective action was taken to correct the situation."

In his testimony, Dr. Bates tells us:
Almost daily for the first three weeks I went to the Embassy with a typed report or letter covering the preceding day, and frequently had

also a conversation with the officials regarding it. The officials were Mr. T. Fukui, who had the rank of consul, a certain Mr. Tanaka, vice-consul, Mr. Yoyoyasu Fukuda. The latter is now secretary to the Premier Yoshida. These men were honestly trying to do what little they could in a very bad situation, but they themselves were terrified by the military and could do nothing except forward these communications through Shanghai to Tokyo.

In the letter of December 16th I complained of many cases of abduction of women from the University's properties and of the rape of thirty women in one University building the previous night.

In the letter of December 17th, besides detailing the specific cases by rote, the reign of terror and brutality continues in plain view of your buildings and among your neighbors.

In the letter of December 18th I reported that on the previous night rape had occurred in six different buildings of the University of Nanking. For three days and three nights many of the thousands of women on our property had not been able to sleep and, in the hysterical fear that was developing, violent incidents might occur. I reported the saying common among the Chinese that where the Japanese Army is, no house or person is safe.
In a letter of December 21st, I complained that many hundreds of refugees had been taken away for forced labor.

On Christmas Day I reported that in one building of the University about ten cases per day of rape and abduction were continually occurring.

On the 27th of December, after a long list of individual cases, I wrote: "Shameful disorder continues and we see no serious efforts to stop it. The soldiers every day injure hundreds of persons most seriously. Does not the Japanese Army care for its reputation?"

(3) Bates goes on to testify that the situation began to improve markedly only after February 5 or 6, 1938. He claims to know that the reports he submitted to the Japanese embassy in Nanjing were passed along to the Japanese Foreign Ministry in Tokyo. He says: "I have seen telegrams sent by Mr. Grew, the Ambassador in Tokyo, to the American Embassy in Nanking, which referred to these reports [those written by Bates] in great detail and referred to conversations in which they had been discussed between Mr. Grew and officials of the Gaimusho [Japanese Foreign Ministry], including Mr. Hirota" (Hirota was a defendant in the tribunal).

(4) On December 16, International Committee Secretary Smythe wrote a letter to Mr. Fukuda of the Japanese embassy listing out in detail instances of disorder by Japanese soldiers in the Safety Zone: "yesterday the continued disorders committed by Japanese soldiers in the Safety Zone increased the state of panic among the refugees."

(5) International Committee Chairman Rabe wrote a letter to the Japanese embassy on December 18 describing in detail atrocities committed by Japanese troops in the Safety Zone, beginning the letter as follows: "We are very sorry to trouble you again but the sufferings and needs of the 200,000 civilians for whom we are trying to care make it urgent that we try to secure action from your military authorities to stop the present disorder amongst Japanese soldiers wandering through the Safety Zone."

(6) A letter by the Committee Secretary to the Japanese Embassy of December 19 lists out even more disturbances caused by Japanese soldiers in the Safety Zone: "I am also very regretful to have to report that the situation today is as bad as ever."

(7) On December 20, Chairman Rabe begins a letter to the Japanese embassy thus: "Herewith is the sad continuation of the story of disorders by Japanese soldiers in Nanking, cases Nos. 71 to 96. You will note that of these 26 cases reported to us since yesterday, that 14 of them occurred yesterday afternoon, night and today. Consequently there does not seem to be much improvement in the situation."

(8) A letter of December 21 from Secretary Smythe to the Japanese embassy lists out the cases of the previous afternoon: "We must remember that the husbands of some of the women who have been daily raped in our Safety Zone are ministers, are workers at the YMCA, are lecturers in the university, are people who lead dignified lives…"

(9) A letter of December 21 submitted by the entire foreign community of 22 people to the Japanese embassy pleads that in the name of humanity and for the sake of the more than 200,000 civilians in Nanjing, that a stop be immediately put to the arson and other outrageous actions committed by Japanese soldiers in the city, and that their actions to date had already caused great hardships.

(10) A letter from the Committee of February 2, 1938, lists 77 individual cases of rape, four cases of murder, and 13 cases of looting, all of which having occurred in the last week of January 1938.

(11) In his testimony, Magee mentions several cases of outrages committed by Japanese soldiers to the Japanese embassy in addition

	to the Committee's reports. He says: "On December 21, Vice Consul Tanaka told me that the rather deplorable division in Nanjing was about to be replaced by a better division. He thought that everything could be resolved after December 24, but the situation did not clearly change for the better after December 24."
Westerners providing evidence	Bates, Smythe, Magee, Rabe, etc.
Relevant contents from verdict statement	International Committee for the Nanking Safety Zone Secretary Lewis Smythe submitted two letters of protest daily for the first six weeks.
Summary of prosecutor's evidence: 9. Foreign Ministry in Tokyo aware of conditions in Nanjing	The Japanese took no effective actions to improve conditions in Nanjing for over six weeks, even after reports of atrocities committed by Japanese soldiers were reported to Japanese diplomatic organs and army leadership. These atrocities were permitted to continue in full knowledge of Japanese military and civilian authorities, proving correct the secret report Ambassador Trautmann submitted to the German Foreign Ministry in Berlin on December 16, 1938. That report included the records of events in Nanjing as observed by a German eyewitness: (1) the defeat of Nanjing defense forces; (2) there was a lack of discipline among Japanese troops. Atrocities and criminal acts were not limited to a few individuals, but were perpetrated by the entire army, all Japanese present: "This is how the Japanese wage war on China without declaring war."
Westerners providing evidence	Kröger et al.
Relevant contents from verdict statement	The German representative informed his government that "atrocities and criminal acts are not limited to individuals, but it's the whole army, that is the Japanese." Later in the report the Japanese are referred to as "bestial machinery."

Table 22: Comparison of degree of trust expressed in Westerners' testimony in verdict statements from prosecutors' summaries.
Source: "Prosecutor's Summary of Evidence" (Yang Xiaming 2006, 390–408) and "Verdict (Related to Rape of Nanking)" (Yang Xiaming 2006, 606–610).

We can see from the above table of evidence that the Westerners had a grasp on the macro situation taking place in all of Nanjing as well as on the granular detail of individual cases.

3.6.1.2 The Nanjing Trials

In February 1947, Smythe and Bates, recently returned from the Tokyo trials, took the witness stand again in another war crimes tribunal, giving testimony on Japanese atrocities committed during the Rape of Nanking. Smythe "submitted three books on the events of the Rape of Nanking to the court: *Documents of the Nanking Safety Zone*, *Records of Japanese Atrocities* [also known as *Japanese Atrocities Witnessed by Foreigners*], and *War Damage in the Nanking Area*" (Hu 2006, 367). The evidence they provided played a great role in the Rape of Nanking cases of the Nanjing War Crimes Tribunal (see relevant sections of this book for more details).

3.6.2 Historical legacy of the Westerners in Nanjing

The contributions of Westerners were widely applauded by Chinese refugees. Many received commendations from the Chinese government or their own governments. At the same time, they bore a heavy burden from having lived through the Japanese atrocities, and they too were victims. Many were unable to escape the pall cast over their lives by the Rape of Nanking after conditions had calmed, and even after they themselves had left Nanjing.

Vautrin wrote on December 18, 1937 that a Chinese chauffeur working for the American embassy told her: "The only thing that had saved the Chinese people from utter destruction was the fact that there were a handful of foreigners in Nanking." Nevertheless, Vautrin's mental state deteriorated after the Rape of Nanking, to the point that she could no longer continue her work in China. She attempted suicide aboard the ship that took her back to the U.S., but was discovered in time. She never recovered. In 1941, Vautrin, who had provided assistance and solace to so many Chinese women, left this world by ending her own life.

Dr. Robert Wilson, whose tireless work had saved so many lives, also experienced psychological and physical after-effects. He finally stopped working only in June 1938, when he took a furlough to Shanghai. By 1940, "sickness and mental breakdown" forced Wilson to abandon his work in China and return to the U.S: "He never returned to China again, and never fully recovered from a state of tension" (Chang n.d., 247).

John Magee's son David Magee believed that "the psychological pressure of dealing with the Japanese during the Rape of Nanking caused his father to die young." George Fitch's daughter also believed that her father's experiences from that time caused "frequent amnesia" (Chang n.d., 247).

John Rabe brought his records of Japanese atrocities committed in Nanjing back to Germany, where he gave public lectures on Japanese atrocities and submitted evidence thereof to the German government. The result was his arrest by the Gestapo. Rabe ended up losing his job under the Nazi regime, allied to Japan, and he fell on dire straits. It is possible that the aid given to Rabe by the victorious government in Nanjing gave him some small solace.[36]

When, in the 1990s, the Japanese right wing politician Ishihara Shintaro gave a speech denying the Rape of Nanking, the journalist Tillman Durdin, still alive and well in the U.S., "took direct action. He temporarily suspended his retired life in San Diego and convened a press conference to refute Ishihara's speech." John Magee was already dead by then, but his son attended and "was interviewed by the media, participated in a conference about the Rape of Nanking, and read his father's correspondence at the conference, and even displayed the camera his father used to record Japanese atrocities" (Chang n.d., 264).

The foreigners who have already passed away will continue to make contributions in maintaining the historical record through the documents they left behind. John Rabe's diary has been published in Germany, China, Japan, and the U.S., and the original is now in a Chinese collection.

In October 2009, during a conference jointly undertaken by China Radio International, the Chinese People's Association for Friendship with Foreign Countries, and the State Administration of Foreign Experts Affairs of China, and hosted by an international website, John Rabe received the second most votes, coming behind only the Canadian doctor Norman Bethune, in a public vote for the international friend who has made the most contributions to China, is most beloved by the Chinese, and has the most destiny with China in the past 100 years.

The heroic acts of foreigners during the Rape of Nanking were a ray of light in the darkness. This light illuminates not only the past, but also the way into the future for lovers of peace.[37]

---

[36] In early 1948, the Nanjing City Council passed a resolution to found a committee to raise money to send relief to Rabe. The committee ended up raising $2,000 USD, which it sent to Rabe. Shen Yi, mayor of Nanjing at the time, bought four big bags of food and sent them to Rabe, to "express the gratitude of the people of Nanjing for his righteous acts." The city government continued to send Rabe a bag of food once per month from June 1948 until April 1949, when the nationalist government evacuated Nanjing. On January 5, 1950, Rabe died of a stroke in Germany (see Huang n.d., 324–335).

[37] Dong Weimin earned his doctorate in history from Nanjing University in June 2011 with a dissertation of the same name as this chapter. It was heavily revised before being used in this book.

4 The "German Perspective" on the Rape of Nanking Based in German Diplomatic Documents

Germany was a friend to both China and Japan when war broke out between them, but they differed in degrees of importance to Hitler. On the one hand, Japan and Germany were allies under the Anti-Comintern Pact, and both shared common global interests. On the other hand, the nationalist government of China was cooperating closely with Germany politically, economically, and militarily. At the time, German military advisors continued to help Chiang Kai-shek organize his resistance to Japan, and arms sales from Germany to China were brisk. The best option for the Germans would have been to remain neutral in the conflict between China and Japan, had it been possible. German Ambassador Trautmann in China and German Ambassador von Dirksen in Japan actively mediated between China and Japan at this time, precisely from such considerations. This illogical but pragmatic stance gave Germans a unique perspective on the Sino-Japanese conflict, one that is of great value to us today.

As the Japanese army pressed in on the Chinese capital at Nanjing in November 1937, the German legation to China left behind a small crew headed by Political Secretary Georg Rosen. There were also a handful of German merchants who decided to stay against orders from their government and participate in the work of the International Committee. They, along with the missionaries, merchants, journalists, and Westerners of other stripes who stayed behind, became third-party eyewitnesses to the Rape of Nanking and collaborators in international relief efforts. A few other Germans also became aware of Japanese atrocities committed in Nanjing, to differing extents, either through work contacts or personal friendships with Germans in Nanjing or through other channels, and these too had their perspective on matters.

The "German perspective" discussed in this chapter consists of the observations, records, and analyses of the Rape of Nanking made by Germans at the time, primarily foreign service personnel; these are highly distinct documents relating the history of the Rape of Nanking. In this chapter we attempt to expose the historical significance of these documents through analysis thereof and of related issues, relying primarily on German diplomatic records.

4.1 The Germans behind the "German Perspective"

Oskar Trautmann, German ambassador to China, was transferred from Nanjing to Hankou on November 11. Beginning on October 22, he was busy playing mediator between China and Japan. He grew severely angry with Japan during the course of his mediations, writing the following telegram to the German Foreign Ministry on January 11, 1938:

> Japan has again submitted revised peace conditions, which we have delivered to China. This is a "shameless trap," and in truth Japan is playing with us, and has caused us to completely lose face before the Chinese government (Liu n.d., 50).

Trautmann had already arrived in Hankou before the fall of Nanjing. The Japanese indiscriminate bombing of Nanjing had been an alarming portent of things to come. Thankfully Japan was allied with Germany, and the word "Deutsch" carried a degree of deterrence with Japanese soldiers (Rabe CN, 157–158). So Trautmann did not need to be overly concerned for his expatriates remaining in the city. As for the Rape of Nanking, Trautmann had the option of pulling rank on Rosen and the rest to force them to cooperate with the Japanese, as instructions from Hitler had indicated, but he consistently forwarded reports on events in Nanjing written by Rosen, Scharffenberg, and the rest to the Foreign Ministry in Berlin, adding his own summaries and conclusions ill-disposed toward Japan. Of course, as an ambassador, he focused on analyzing the far-reaching consequences on international relations in the Far East of the Sino-Japanese conflict and German responses.

Georg Rosen, political secretary in the German embassy to China, fled aboard a British naval vessel on the Yangtze River on the eve of the Japanese occupation of Nanjing. He made a trip to Shanghai under escort from a Japanese gunboat and returned to Nanjing on January 9, 1938. On September 11, 1945, he wrote a letter to the Chinese ambassador to the United States:

> The intent of this letter is to alert the Chinese government of the large quantity of materials on the Japanese invasion of China discovered in the German embassy and consulate to China. ...
>
> There are many reports written by me in Nanjing between November 1937 and June 1938, from when I was temporarily assigned to run the German embassy until my recall and firing (in June 1938). I spent many weeks of that period aboard a British ship on the Yangtze. During my brief stay in the consulate at Shanghai, I dictated reports on these events (the sinking of the USS Panay). I also made several reports through my friend in Nanjing John Magee, who is now in Washington, D.C. (Central Archives et al. 1995, 133).

Aboard the British ship, Rosen, Scharffenberg, and Hürter witnessed the consequences of the indiscriminate attack by the Japanese army. Rosen's anger with the Japanese immediately elevated to a level he could not contain. His insistence on making observations all over Nanjing at scenes of massacres also put the Japanese on their guard against him. Japanese Consul-General Fukuda Tokuyasu once told Scharffenberg in a vexed mood, as he writes in a letter to Lautenschlager of February 1, 1938: "I already know that the Americans and English view Japan with hostility, but why would Germans be that way too?" (Zhang 2005, 361). German diplomatic records clearly demonstrate that Japanese diplomatic and military personnel arranged multiple luxurious banquets, including gorgeous geishas to pour alcohol, in an attempt to win Rosen's good will and cooperation. Rosen, however, refused to relent, up to the day of his recall and firing. As the saying goes, like attracts like, and of everyone in Nanjing at the time, Rosen got along best with Third Secretary Allison of the American embassy, at the center of the great diplomatic scandal after he had been struck by a Japanese soldier.

Paul Scharffenberg, office administrator of the German embassy to China in Nanjing, later regretted taking refuge on the British naval vessel with Rosen, writing in the same letter to Lautenschlager that this action "nearly caused irredeemable consequences" (Zhang Sheng 2005, 361). After returning to Nanjing, he became completely disgusted with Japanese attempts to cover up atrocities through "publicity tricks." On February 8, 1938, the Japanese consulate arranged another entertainment for foreign diplomats in Nanjing: "There was a pause after four acts. During the intermission the corridor was filled with food, cakes, desserts, pastries, fruits, and more meandering across a long table like food reserved for the Russian czar. The food was all laid out in orderly fashion. Then the geishas came with tea. The alluring posture they assumed when lighting cigarettes aroused particular attention from the many photographers, who captured images of the scene to show in films or newspapers to the rest of the world, unaware of conditions here, how well the Japanese and foreigners get along." Scharffenberg added a criticism: "This is entirely the back side of a medal. Their disguise was laid bare!" (German Foreign Ministry Archives: 2718/2081/38). His disgust for the Japanese originated in the brutality of their soldiers. In a report to Trautmann he wrote: "From one single pond near Dr. Schröder's house, for example, they fished out over 120 bodies, their hands tied behind them with wire. Herr Rabe was there and saw it all. I myself have frequently seen Japanese soldiers fetch water in their cooking pots from these pools. Bon appétit!" (Rabe EN, 190).

John H.D. Rabe, manager of Siemens China Company and chairman of the International Committee for the Nanking Safety Zone, was in the city through the entire ordeal. As he had served in this important post, an Allied tribunal declared Rabe to be "denazified" after the end of the war (Rabe CN, 599). In 1908 Rabe first arrived in China, where he lived for 30 years, excluding a period during the First World War. Rabe had great empathy for the plight of the Chinese people. When he was recalled by Siemens in March 1938, he had saved the lives of tens of thousands of Chinese people from the maw of the Japanese war machine. Rabe writes in the diary entry "returning home after 30 years" that after he had submitted a report on Japanese atrocities to Hitler, the Gestapo forced his silence (Rabe CN, 588), which goes to demonstrate the shocking nature of Rabe's perspective on events.

Eduard Sperling, employee of the German-owned Shanghai Insurance Company and inspector-general of the International Safety Zone, also remained in Nanjing for the duration. On December 12, 1937, he volunteered to mediate a ceasefire between Japan and China to allow Chinese forces to retreat and the Japanese to enter the city peacefully (German Foreign Ministry Archives: 2722/1011/38). On January 10, 1938, when Jiang Gonggu of the Nationalist Army's wilderness combat rescue team approached Sperling, Sperling held out a map of China to him, saying sternly: "The enemy has occupied only a few percent of the area of your country. Your only way out is to resist, or else you'll be slaves!" (Zhang 2005, 84). His frank response demonstrates his sympathy for the Chinese cause as well as a certain German calmness and solemnity.

Christian Kröger, engineer for the German-owned Carlowitz and Co. and member of the International Committee, was also in Nanjing for the duration. His first contact with the Japanese army came late at night on December 12, 1937, where a Japanese officer displayed an "extremely friendly" demeanor after a short inspection of the hospital for wounded soldiers in the former Foreign Ministry building, giving Kröger the impression that the Japanese army was highly disciplined: "Unfortunately this impression was very quickly overturned." By the 14th, Kröger wrote in a private report to the German Foreign Office of January 13, 1938 that "conditions have dramatically worsened," and that the atrocities committed by Japanese soldiers reminded him of the seventeenth century's "Thirty Years War."

Karl Günther was a German residing in Tangshan, China. Before the fall of Nanjing, the Tianjin board of directors of the nearly completed Jiangnan Concrete Plant hired him to pretend to be a representative of the German company Siemssen and Co. and to proceed to Nanjing to prevent occupation of the plant by the Japanese army using his status as citizen of a non-belligerent country. The board simultaneously asked that the Danish company F.L. Smidth send a representative; they ended up sending Bernhard Sindberg. Upon arrival, Günther and Sindberg erected German and Danish flags at the plant, established a refugee camp, and offered protection to more than 10,000 Chinese people. Günther repeatedly risked his life traveling between the plant and the city of Nanjing to take letters on Japanese atrocities from his camp and the population of the outskirts of the city to the Westerners inside, to help Magee film his documentary, and to bring food to the nutritionally-deprived foreigners in the city. In recent years it has been discovered that Günther also kept a large amount of documents, pictures, and materials on the Rape of Nanking.[38]

Martin Fischer, German consul-general in Shanghai, was in Shanghai during the Rape of Nanking. Despite his impoliteness toward Matsui Iwane in Shanghai, Fischer did not share the intense anger about Japanese atrocities of Rosen and the others. He wrote to Rosen in a letter of January 21, 1938: "You cannot overlook the fact that the city is militarily occupied. Everyone knows that military officials will not permit any discussion of matters they find essential to their cause." Clearly he had no idea the massacres, rapes, looting, and arson witnessed by Rosen and the rest were not "essential to their cause," and so he asked Rosen to "maintain friendly moderation for the moment" with the Japanese (German Foreign Ministry Archives n.d.).

Dr. Heinz Lautenschlager, legation councilor to the German embassy in China, was in Hankou during the Rape of Nanking. A good friend of Scharffenberg, Lautenschlager heard a great deal of complaints about Rosen and Rabe from him before Scharffenberg realized the true nature of the Japanese. For example, Scharffenberg wrote in a letter to Lautenschlager of February 1, 1938: "A few days ago Rosen and Rabe again left the embassy in Rabe's car without a military police escort. Major Hongo gave Rabe a stern warning, which he wanted passed along to Rosen, to not go out again without a military police escort. Hürter, myself, and the other Germans all deal politely with the military police in front of the embassy, but Rosen doesn't even look either of them in the eye. It's as though he's pointed the spear of his anger at the entire Japanese army... When discussing this issue, he angrily said in front of Rabe and myself: 'Just like Fischer's attitude toward Matsui in Shanghai, I don't plan to sit at the same table with these murderers'" (Zhang 2005, 361–362). In truth, Rabe thought it was wrong of Rosen to refuse a Japanese escort, finding that Rosen's attitude toward cooperation with the Japanese made him "unpopular" and negatively affected Rabe's negotiations with them (Rabe CN, 431 and 442–443). Lautenschlager and Rabe, however, seem to have had a good relationship; Rabe once served as Nazi local party group leader in his place (Rabe CN, 596).

---

38 Günther's achievements provided by Mr. Dai Yuanzhi of the *Zhongguo qinnian bao* and the Jiangsu Journalists' Station.

Willey Noeble was a military attaché to the German embassy in Japan, where he was during the Rape of Nanking. His insights into the events in Nanjing and their consequences were penetrating. He wrote in a report to the German Foreign Office of March 3, 1938: "No matter what, foreign governments and international opinion now hold that the impossible has come true. Japan's General Army Staff Headquarters has lost due to a conflict in opinion with groups led by extreme nationalist civilian officials... It seems that the peremptory, high-handed actions of General Matsui have not only caused conflicts with the great powers in Shanghai, but have also caused conflicts with the Japanese government in Tokyo. In the end he will become the victim of his own sacrifice. This action may have been intended to pacify the UK, which is growing increasingly displeased with Matsui's rule. Nevertheless, the recall of Matsui does not necessarily imply that a scapegoat has been found for the Rape of Nanking" (Zhang 2005, 427 and 429).

German Ambassador Herbert von Dirksen in Japan, retired Lieutenant Colonel Brinkmann, North Hotel manager Hempel, State Secretary Ernst von Weizsacker of the German Foreign Office, Military Attaché Bidder of the German embassy to China, and German citizen Hans Stoltenberg-Lerche were also components of the German perspective on the Rape of Nanking.

The rigorousness of the German perspective is the foundation of its value. Japanese academic Yokoyama Hiroaki says of Rabe's diary that its "influence over the direction of discourse on the Rape of Nanking is absolute," that it is "a super first class resource," and as such, the German perspective is one of the greatest sources of discomfort for Japanese right wing deniers, who have consistently come up empty-handed in repeated attempts to knock down Rabe's writings (Cheng 2002a, 125–168). The characteristics of the German perspective's rigorousness also give us a chance to note that the Japanese cover-up of the truth about the Rape of Nanking began while it was still ongoing. On March 10, 1938, Nazi Party member Hans Stoltenberg-Lerche wrote a letter to German Vice Consul Kempe in Guangdong (also a Nazi Party member), in which he mocked the article "The Front Line Air Battle in China" by Japanese Air Force Captain T.H. carried in the German newspaper Deutsche Post as "quite a special piece of propaganda." Stoltenberg-Lerche went on to note that the Captain "writes this about Guangdong in the article: They opened fire from tennis courts in European residences. That is to say that he was fired upon from there (!), while American gunboats targeted nothing but the sky with their cannons. In another article of a few days ago, this author claimed – and to a certain extent this was an apology for the sinking of the Panay – that it is impossible to clearly identify national flags from an airplane (as we all know, these flags are wide enough to block out the sun). Yet he sighted the long thin barrel of an artillery piece!?! Then he heard the siren that usually goes off 15 minutes before airplanes appear and 'grazed roofs flying over.' We eyewitnesses on the ground here have to strain our eyes to identify those tiny black specks in the sky. All this forces us to question the truth of this article." It is quite a pity that the German media actually published such an article (German Foreign Ministry Archives: 240/948/38). Stoltenberg-Lerche cited another case with German foreign service officer Altenburg, also in Guangdong, about an article written by the same Japanese air force captain: Nanjing "residents are all fleeing to Pukou on the other side of the Yangtze River, with tens of thousands making the crossing daily. The bridge is now unusable." Altenburg then pointed out the far-sight of the Japanese fabrication of news about the bridge over the Yangtze River at Nanjing to the German Foreign Office: "If the political direction of German newspapers is guided by grand political considerations, we must express empathy and understanding for Japanese actions in China, and the Germans here have no choice but to keep silent on the matter. But what the people here will never understand is that these repeated pure lies and stupid fabrications should not be seen by the German public" (German Foreign Ministry Archives: 240/948/38). Trautmann later told the German Foreign Office that he had already reminded them many times that such brazen lies and fabricated reports should not appear in German media (German Foreign Ministry Archives: 2722/2452/38).

We should pay particular attention to the fact that though these Germans saw maintaining German interests as their duty, they also felt great sympathy for the Chinese who had fallen on calamity. There were, however, differences even within the German community; highly educated people like Rabe cracked jokes about "uncouth" men like Sperling in the historical record. The greatest contradiction, we must note, was between Rosen and Scharffenberg, who frankly said that he did not feel happy working under Rosen. Scharffenberg thought Rosen's attitude of non-cooperation with the Japanese was unwise. At the outset, he thought that there were polite gentlemen among the Japanese with whom he dealt, and that Allison's incident was to a large degree caused by his own actions. He wrote in his letter to Lautenschlager of February 1 that he thought that Rosen "might be hit twice or three times in the face" if the Japanese army were not so muddled. He wrote: "Ever since I returned here (Nanjing), conditions have grown worse daily owing to his great hostility toward the Japanese" (Zhang 2005, 360 and 362). Rosen repeatedly mentioned atrocities committed by Japanese soldiers in front of Japanese foreign service officers, actions Scharffenberg found "outmoded." He also felt that the British and Americans played a special role in Rosen's anger: "Not only have the British and American colleagues who discuss these matters with him not stopped Rosen from acting rashly, but have rather poured oil on the fire" (Zhang 2005, 362). Scharffenberg also thought that

"Rosen's offensive attitude is of no use to the work of the International Safety Zone Committee." He thought that Rabe felt the same as himself, and he hinted that "the Japanese will find out sooner or later" that Rosen was accepting invitations to dine with English and American diplomats while refusing theirs (Zhang 2005, 364–365). Scharffenberg was clearly of the opinion that a display of goodwill would meet a similar response from the Japanese, but he soon realized the cruel nature of the Japanese army, and many important reports on Japanese atrocities were recorded under his pen. The changes in Scharffenberg's attitude are worthy of epistemological study.

Communication and information dissemination within the German perspective came, on the one hand, from diplomatic telegrams and ordinary letters, i.e. those passing between Germans in Nanjing and those on the outside, in places like Hankou, Shanghai, Tokyo, and Berlin, and extending even as far as Guangzhou, London, New York, Los Angeles, Chicago, and other places. Nanjing was the center of crucial information collection, Hankou the policy center, and Shanghai the primary place from which information flowed to the outside world. The other source was face to face communication, limited to residents of Nanjing. It is now clear from the materials that their mutual supplementation and provision of proof has helped fill out the historical record on the Rape of Nanking.

4.2 The Core of the "German Perspective": The Truth behind the Rape of Nanking

As Germans in Nanjing witnessed the Rape of Nanking, the Nazi persecution of Jews in Europe had already begun. Some of these observers were Nazis, including Rabe and Sperling, who said they had no idea that the Nazis were committing atrocities in Europe. Nearly without exception, they criticized Japanese atrocities as "medieval barbarism." Presently available records also demonstrate that the Germans were among the first in the world to refer to the incident as "the Nanjing Massacre" (*Nankinger Massacre* in German) (German Foreign Ministry Archives: 2722/4279/37).

So far as we know, Rabe took the most detailed notes on the Rape of Nanking of all the Germans. His diary serves as a daily chronicle of the event; we can find records of nearly all kinds of Japanese crimes committed in Nanjing in its pages. As chairman of the International Committee, he had to attend to keeping alive hundreds of thousands of refugees, and so he had to cooperate with the Japanese at some level, sometimes only at surface level. Rabe felt disgusted with the Japanese after witnessing their atrocities and reading reports of many more, but at the same time, he favored removing from the Committee's official reports particularly nauseating sections. For example, in one report Sperling wrote: "A naked Japanese soldier lay atop a young pretty girl"; Rabe felt that this needed to be deleted (Rabe CN, 478). So one gets a feeling of superhuman "tranquility" reading his reports of Japanese atrocities – there are very few adjectives in his diary.

On December 13, 1937, Rabe and the others had 1,000 disarmed soldiers enter the building of the Ministry of Justice, from which the Japanese forced away 400 to 500 to be shot. Rabe wrote: "These events have left us frozen with horror" (Rabe EN, 68). This initial shock was quickly replaced by a sustained nightmare. The body of a Chinese soldier tied to a bamboo bed and killed by Japanese soldiers was left unburied outside of Rabe's house, serving as a menacing notice from the Japanese army to Rabe for six weeks: The events of December 13 were but the beginning. And truly enough, on December 17 Rabe wrote that 1,000 women had been raped the previous night inside the Safety Zone (Rabe CN, 156). Rabe wrote on December 22: "While cleaning up the Zone, we find many bodies in the ponds, civilians who have been shot (30 in just one pond), most of them with their hands bound, some with stones tied to their necks... I promised the Japanese to help them look for employees of the electricity works and told them to look, among other places, in Hsiakwan, where 54 electricity plant workers were housed. We now learn that about three or four days ago, 43 of them were tied up and led down to the riverbank and machine-gunned, ostensibly because they were the employees of an enterprise managed by the Chinese government" (Rabe EN, 86–87). As he was unaware of the circumstances of the massacre from Xiaguan to Yanziji, Rabe sincerely wrote on January 3 about 60,000 Chinese soldiers imprisoned or killed, and mentions concern that 2,000 disarmed Chinese soldiers and thousands of civilians had been killed, but he prayed "I hope it's no more" (Rabe CN, 269). He later wrote about a woman whose entire family, even her children, had been shot by the Japanese: "With what little she had left, she bought a coffin so she could at least bury her father. Hearing news of this, Japanese soldiers ripped the lid from the coffin and dumped the body onto the street. Chinese don't need to be buried, was their explanation" (Rabe EN, 115). On January 25 he writes about a Chinese man who had labored all day for the Japanese before returning exhausted to his home, where his wife had prepared a few bowls of congee for all six members of the family; A Japanese soldier came in, urinated in the bowl, and left glibly (Rabe CN, 417). On February 7 Rabe wrote: "This morning... Mr. Sone and I visited a somewhat out-of-the-way field in the vicinity of Sikiang Road, where the bodies of 124 Chinese have been fished out of two ponds, all of them shot, about half of them civilians. The victims had all had their hands tied, were then mowed down by machine guns, doused with gasoline, and set on fire. But when the burning took too long, the half-burned bodies were simply tossed into the ponds" (Rabe EN, 181).

Rabe calmly wrote: "People might think that the Japanese army is composed of released prisoners, as normal people could not do such things!" (Rabe CN, 395). He also felt pained by the resigned submission of the Chinese, but even this he recorded calmly: "If every case of rape were revenged with murder, a good portion of the occupying troops would have been wiped out by now" (Rabe EN, 154). Ultimately Rabe succumbed to deep fatigue after the unending cycle of calamity, and hoped to escape Nanjing, where the tragedy made one lose faith in humanity. On the eve of his return to Germany, 3,000 women from the University of Nanking refugee shelter encircled Rabe's car. He quietly got out of the car and left the Safety Zone, of which he had been chairman, on foot. Of course, when he left Nanjing aboard the HMS Bee, he took with him a disguised former Chinese air force pilot posing as his domestic servant (Rabe CN, 571).

Rosen accepted an invitation to board an English steamer on the Yangtze near Nanjing prior to the Japanese occupation, allowing him to avoid Japanese atrocities in the city for a while. The Japanese army, however, gave him a most particular reminder of their actions: "In the morning (of December 12), Japanese infantry killed several innocent civilians on tugboats and pontoon boats per their custom on land and on sailboats." Later when the request of Rosen and the ship's British captain to return to Nanjing was denied, he wrote: "The real reason was that Japan does not want us to see the deplorable scene of rape, burning, killing, and looting that the completely unbridled Japanese army has unleashed on the civilians of Nanjing." On December 21, passing by Xiaguan on a British naval vessel bound for Shanghai, Rosen saw "several piles of bodies in addition to severe destruction – the bodies were all wearing civilian clothes" (German Foreign Ministry Archives: 2722/8432/37).

On January 9, 1938, work began again in the German embassy in Nanjing. In his first formal report to the German Foreign Office, Rosen wrote that when foreign diplomats mentioned returning, the Japanese army immediately set to disposing of bodies. The scale of the massacre, unprecedented in modern history, was simply too great, so the Japanese army was unable to completely destroy the evidence of their crimes. Rosen wrote: "This arson, organized by the Japanese military, is still going on to this day—a good month after the Japanese occupied the city—as is the abduction and rape of women and girls. In this respect, the Japanese army has erected a monument to its own shameful conduct." Rosen was most upset by the plight of women in the city: "At the American Mission Hospital women are constantly being admitted, the most recent case occurring only yesterday, who have suffered grave bodily harm from rape committed by packs of men, with the subsequent infliction of bayonet and other wounds. One woman had her throat slit half-open, a wound so severe that Dr. Wilson himself is amazed that she is still alive. A pregnant woman was bayoneted in the belly, killing the unborn child. Many abused girls still in their childhood have likewise been admitted to the hospital, one of whom was violated 20 times in succession. On 12 January, my English colleague, Consul Prideaux-Brune, the English military attaché Lovat-Fraser, and the English air-force attaché Commander Walser visited the house of Mr. Parsons of the British-American Tobacco Company and discovered there the body of a Chinese woman into whose vagina an entire golf club had been forced. There are documented cases in which accomplices have forced the husbands and fathers of victims to witness the violation of their domestic honor" (Rabe EN, 120–121).

The Japanese were clearly sure that the Chinese would sue for peace as soon as their capital had been occupied, and so they told some "secrets" to the Westerners in Nanjing without reserves. Unfortunately for them, Rosen came to learn of these "secrets," which he included in a report to the German Foreign Office. From December 18 to 20, 1937, Rosen was aboard the HMS Bee: "While we were aboard the British gunboat Bee, anchored outside Nanking from 18 to 20 December, the Japanese rear-admiral Kondo declared to Holt, the British admiral, that on a large island downstream from Nanking there were still 30,000 Chinese soldiers who would have to be removed. This removal or 'mopping up,' as it was called in Japanese communiqués, consists of murdering what are now defenseless enemies and is contrary to fundamental principles of humane warfare. Besides mass executions by machine gun fire, other more individual methods of killing were employed as well, such as pouring gasoline over a victim and setting him afire" (Rabe EN, 145). In truth, the stretch of shore along the Yangtze from Xiaguan to Yanziji was one of the primary sites of Japanese execution of unarmed Kuomintang forces; this is one reason that it is so difficult to accurately count the number of killed. In his records of the massacre on Bagua Island, Rosen helps make up for our shortcoming with abundant details.

It must be pointed out that Rosen was as rigorous as Rabe in recording the events of the Rape of Nanking. While John Magee was making his famed documentary, Rosen was on the ground making observations: "I too have been to the site, where I saw four victims of this week's heroics by the Japanese army. One old man carrying two chairs was shot by a Japanese soldier who did not even flinch. His younger sister had gone into hiding when the Japanese arrived. She called two acquaintances, who made a litter from a door, two bamboo poles, and some thick rope, and prepared to carry the injured old man away. The Japanese, upon sighting them, shot all four to death: the injured old man, his younger sister, and the two people carrying the litter" (Central Archives et al. 1995, 155).

Scharffenberg's style was different from Rosen's, but he did no less than Rosen to reveal Japanese atrocities. As the atrocities mounted, Scharffenberg finally realized that he was like a "political prisoner" of the Japanese, or in other words the Japanese were a cat and he was the mouse hiding in his hole (German Foreign Ministry Archives: 2718/2608/38 scene to a great deal of evidence of the massacre, and this clearly did not adhere to the Japanese army's demand that foreigners be presented a good image. So the work of cleaning up bodies was accelerated there. In a March 4 report to Trautmann, Scharffenberg wrote: "The work of removing bodies from the city is picking up pace. The Red Swastika Society has been permitted to bury 30,000 bodies in Xiaguan, and is accomplishing 600 burials per day. The bodies are wrapped in straw mats with only their two legs uncovered. They are then covered in lime and transported off in trucks to be buried in mass graves, where more lime is added. It is said that about 10,000 have thus far been buried" (German Foreign Ministry Archives: 2718/2608/38).

Kröger had his car stolen by Japanese troops, his servant forced to open his door at bayonet-point, and had a great deal of his property stolen, but to him the worst of all were the three bodies left at his doorstep for several weeks. On December 28, 1937, Kröger had already begun observing Japanese atrocities at Qixia Mountain during the peak of the massacre. There he discovered that the Japanese army had "indiscriminately shot down all farmers in their fields, men, women, and children, on the pretext that they were 'eliminating Chinese communist soldiers.'" He goes on to admit, however, that he "lacked the courage to be heroic."

He witnessed looting, killing, and raping perpetrated by Japanese soldiers, as he documented in his private report to the German Foreign Office of January 13, 1938:

> When both combat troops and soldiers who were famished and undernourished from the fierce attack were let into the city, they unleashed a cruel attack on destitute residents and innocent civilians that nobody could have predicted. They stole rice from refugees. Actually they stole anything they could, blankets, suits, watches, gongs, and so on. Anything they though valuable was stolen. If the people being robbed hesitated for even a moment, they were immediately stabbed to death by bayonet. Many fell victim to such barbarous behavior.
>
> Their victims already numbering in the thousands, these ruthless soldiers began breaking into scattered houses in the Safety Zone, with the goal of stealing what previous soldiers had left behind. There are hardly any houses in the city that have not been subjected to break-in and coarse searches and looting.

> There has been no difference with their searches of refugee shelters, which have been repeated wantonly multiple times. The result has been that with no military tribunals and without a single shot fired by city residents, five to six thousand have been shot to death. To dispense with the bother of burying bodies, the majority of shootings have taken place on the river bank. These numbers are conservative estimates.
>
> Another disturbing matter has been the mistreatment and rape of thousands of women and girls. Truly, such violent behavior can happen among any army. Especially in the Far East. What has been absurd is the mistreatment of young girls and boys, some having their hands and feet cut off for no reason at all. All of this has been done by the forces of Imperial Japan guided by their ideal of *bushido* and their ancient warrior spirit (Zhang 2005, 319–321).

One often hears from the mouths of right wing Japanese deniers that the fires that reduced most of Nanjing to ruins were set by Chinese soldiers. In truth, the Ministry of Communications and a few other buildings in the city as well as some residences outside the city were indeed burned by Kuomintang forces under their "scorched earth" strategy. On the whole, however, Kröger's description of what he witnessed in late January 1938 paints a clear picture of what happened:

> The Japanese have been systematically burning this city beginning on December 20. To date they have successfully burned a third, especially the main commercial district in the south of the city, including all sops, houses, and residential areas near our territory. The burning has abated somewhat, meaning that they're burning only individual buildings they had previously failed to notice or had passed over. What's more, all buildings are looted to the last by organized teams with plans before they are set alight (German Foreign Ministry Archives: 2722/1508/38).

Sperling was a veteran of the First World War. During the Siege of Tsingtao (Qingdao), he was captured and spent four years as a prisoner in Japan. Jiang Gonggu wrote that he was known to his colleagues on the Relief Committee as the "committee's fortress" as he spent all day every day chasing after Japanese soldiers and succoring Chinese refugees (Zhang 2005, 85). As head of the Safety Zone's force of about 650 Chinese police, Sperling demonstrated "respect and admiration for these Chinese, as I often observe their spirit of bearing humiliation without complaint." As his work was limited to the Safety Zone, Sperling estimated the number of civilians murdered by Japanese soldiers at between 5,000 to 6,000.

Many of the 200,000 refugees forced from their homes were women with infants, shivering in their mothers' embraces as they suckled. Many of them arrived at the Safety Zone with nothing more than their lives:

> On New Year's Day, several Japanese soldiers were making themselves especially comfortable. The mother of a pretty young girl called upon me and pleaded on her knees amid tears that I help her. I drove with her to a house in the vicinity of Hankow Road. Upon entering the house, I saw the following: A Japanese soldier lay fully unclothed atop a pretty young girl who was weeping terribly. I yelled at the fellow in dreadful tones and in every conceivable language, wishing him "Happy New Year," and in no time he hastened on his way, trousers in hand (Rabe EN, 151–152).

Despite such constant hardships, Sperling was one of the few foreigners who kept his head held high for the duration. He said proudly: "I was summoned many more than 80 times by Chinese civilians to drive off Japanese soldiers who had broken into Safety Zone residences to brutally rape women and girls. There was no difficulty at all in driving any of them off" (German Foreign Ministry Archives: 2718/1789/38).

The Japanese soldiers did not, however, halt the course of their atrocities because of Sperling's hard work. Unimaginable atrocities were still being committed in March 1938, despite Sperling's best efforts to protect the Chinese under his purview. Sperling wrote in a letter to Rosen of March 22, 1938 stored in the German Foreign Ministry Archives: "In the building of the German-owned Schmidt Company live company representative Mr. Xiao, a company employee, and their wives. Japanese soldiers broke in there nearly every day, looting and destroying German property, and raping their wives in the most savage of fashions. The wife of Mr. Liu screamed for help through sobs, because they just couldn't take it any longer. They kneeled before me begging that I rid them of these bestial devils. – I took these two households into our house."

Most reports by Germans were passed on to the Foreign Office by Trautmann with his signature. In addition to passing on the terrifying reports he was receiving to German officials and others in the outside world, Trautmann also added his own analysis, concluding that the Rape of Nanking was the natural product of the national character of Japan, a profound insight. He wrote in a report of January 23 to the German Foreign Office:

> The most heartrending has been the Japanese army's actions in Nanjing. Here the excitement of battle is long past, and now Chinese soldiers are led off in groups like rabbits and shot down in cold blood.
>
> Once angered, Japanese soldiers are capable of far greater cruelty than those of other countries. I am reminded of an incident that occurred when I was an adviser in the Tokyo embassy. It happened not long after the great Kanto earthquake of 1923. In order to kill the family members of a socialist leader, a Japanese military policeman gave some sweets to their young children, and as the children were delighting in the sweets they had received,

he hung the adults with rope right behind them.[39] Such Asiatic barbarism has been fully laid bare before the people of China. In Nanjing many civilians have been shot to death, and many houses have been looted, including those owned by Europeans, and Chinese women have been raped. According to the American ambassador, 13 women have been forcibly abducted from the homes of American missionaries alone, and the looting of European residences continues to this day (Zhang 2005, 344).

In the same report Trautmann also noticed the effects of the massacre on the Chinese people: "The war has certain moral advantages for China. China has awoken. The Japanese army has caused hitherto undiscovered patriotism long buried in the hearts of the Chinese people to sprout. All attempts by the Japanese to establish an independent government produce only an image that they can persist only at the tip of Japanese bayonets... The future of China will demonstrate whether China can find the last forces toward national resurgence from this 'baptism by fire'" (Zhang 2005, 344). This observation was born out by an American observer, who wrote the following in an article for Ken magazine: "The defiance in the faces of these Chinese, even as they were led away on that last death march, is the greatest proof I could offer that China is at last a nation as we 'patriotic' westerners understand the word." (Ken n.d., 12–15).

The massacre's role in shaping the new national identity of China has long been overlooked. Trautmann's observation was prescient indeed.

4.3 Interaction between the "German Perspective" and British and American Perspectives

Reports on the Rape of Nanking by Britishers and Americans are an important reason that the event became known to the world.[40] There was close interaction between the "German perspective" and these Britishers and Americans.

---

39 Per materials provided by the Japanese Nanjing Incident Research Association, the Japanese government proclaimed martial law after the Great Kanto Earthquake of September 1923. Captain Amakasu Masahiko of the military police brought the anarchists Sakae Osui and Noe Ito, along with Sakae's six-year-old nephew Munekazu Tachibana, to his headquarters and killed them. Amakasu spent three years in prison, and after his release during a general amnesty was later appointed to the Concordia Association of Manchukuo and served as the head of the Manchukuo Film Association.

40 We should note that the American public had ample opportunity to learn the details of the Rape of Nanking at the time as a result of efforts by some reporters and missionaries and information disseminated by the nationalist government, with major media outlets like the *New York Times*, the *Chicago Daily News*, the *Washington Post*, the *Los Angeles Times*, *Reader's Digest*, and others carrying multiple articles about the event, but the American public paid limited attention

Four of these Britishers and Americans played a little known but very important role in the event: *New York Times* reporter Tillman Durdin, *Chicago Daily News* and *New York Herald Tribune* reporter Archibald T. Steele, Reuters News Agency reporter Leslie Smith, and Paramount Studios cameraman Arthur Menken. All four were present in Nanjing when the Japanese army entered the city on December 12, 1937, and most reports in the international media about the Rape of Nanking appearing shortly after the event were penned by them. As the Germans involved in the event were either busy working in the Safety Zone or aboard British gunboats on the Yangtze at the time, they had limited contacts, and so interviews of these five reporters became an important source of the German perspective.

For example, Steele reported on early war crimes committed by the Japanese army in Nanjing in successive *Chicago Daily News* articles appearing on February 3 and 4, 1938. There was, of course, a time lag in the publication of these articles, owing to concerns that their publication would be harmful to the position of Westerners remaining in the city, and because of Japanese news censorship in Shanghai. The primary contents of these articles, however, appeared under the title "Nankinger Massacre" in a report of December 30, 1937, by Dr. Bidder of the German embassy's Beiping bureau to the German embassy. The articles published in the newspaper had been redacted, with scenes of Japanese atrocities described in limited detail, and abnormal behaviors of Chinese people during their calamity hardly mentionable in the same breath. Bidder of the German embassy's Beiping bureau wrote in a report to the embassy in Hankou of December 30, 1937:

> As Japanese searches intensified, some soldiers experienced mental disorders resulting from prolonged terror. I once saw a soldier steal a bicycle with brute animal force and then atop the bicycle charge into a detachment of Japanese soldiers a few hundred yards

---

to Japanese atrocities taking place in the remote Far East. A report of May 1939 issued by the Kuomintang's Central Propaganda Ministry's New York office reads: "In the beginning American films from the Far East including the Japanese bombing of the Panay, Japanese strafing of the English embassy, intense fighting around the edges of foreign concessions, and others were once widely heralded, but now times have changed, and such materials are no longer of news value. Even the bombing of American property overseas warrants only the tiniest mention in newspapers." The report goes on: "Films about Japanese atrocities in Nanjing are being played everywhere, earning great revenues. But because of the terrible nature of the films, many cinemas are unwilling to screen them. These films, with eloquent explanations from Dr. Hua De'er, incite great sympathy among the masses. Too bad there are so few like Dr. Hua." See "Niuyue banshichu di 184 hao baogao (5 yue 30 ri)" [New York Office Report No. 184 (May 30)], China Second Historical Archives Kuomintang Central Propaganda Ministry Archives, archive number 718 (4), document number 4723.

away. After pedestrians on the street had told him this was dangerous, he suddenly turned around and charged in the opposite direction. He then suddenly leapt off the bicycle and ran into a civilian. I finally saw him stripping off his uniform and attempting to steal the civilian's clothes. Some soldiers ride horses aimlessly around the city streets firing their guns wildly into the air. One of the few remaining foreigners in the city, a burly German, decided to teach him a lesson, so he pulled the man down from his horse, took away his pistol, and punched him in the face. He took the blow without making a sound (German Foreign Ministry Archives: 2722/4279/37).

Losers of the First World War, Germans were acutely aware that they were not entirely on the same side as the British and Americans. But as the sources abundantly demonstrate, Germans took the words of British and Americans, fellow Westerners, more seriously than those of Asians. In truth, Chinese newspapers in Hankou like the *Dagongbao* and *Xinhua ribao* gave detailed reports of the Rape of Nanking, but Trautmann, located in Hankou at the time, wrote in a report to the German Foreign Office on January 6, 1938, that a speech by Reuters reporter Leslie Smith demonstrated: "It seems that reports on the actions of the Japanese army making a stir locally are not exaggerated." Trautmann then goes on to report Smith's account:

> On the morning of December 14, the Japanese army had still not assumed a hostile attitude toward ordinary Chinese citizens. But by noon that day, there were small detachments of Japanese soldiers six to 10 strong everywhere in the city. They tore off their unit insignia and began looting every house they came upon. Chinese soldiers had stolen only food, but the Japanese soldiers stole everything. Their plundering of the city was organized and thorough.
>
> Before I left Nanjing on December 15, from what I and other Europeans witnessed, all Chinese houses without exception and most European-owned houses were looted clean by Japanese soldiers.
>
> I ran into Herr Rabe outside the firm of Kiessling & Bader. He and the owner were currently throwing out several looting Japanese soldiers who had torn down the German flag.
>
> Great numbers of Chinese young women and girls have been abducted from their homes. It is impossible to know what has become of them, as they have not been seen again.
>
> On December 15, the Japanese granted foreign correspondents permission to board a Japanese gunboat leaving Nanking for Shanghai. It was later decided that British gunboats could take the same route. When the wait for departure lasted longer than expected, we used the time to undertake a short investigative walk. We saw how the Japanese had tied up some thousand Chinese out in an open field, and watched as small groups of them were led away to be shot. They were forced to kneel and were then shot in the back of the head. We had observed some 100 such executions, when the Japanese officer in charge noticed us and ordered to leave at once. Previously we had seen about 100 instances of such executions. I don't know how the rest of the Chinese are (German Foreign Ministry Archives: 2722/1105/38).

The above became the basis for the early descriptions of the Rape of Nanking among nearly all Germans outside the city at the time.

In addition to the reporters, British and American officers of the Safety Zone also provided a great deal of information to the Germans. Most importantly, they provided records of Japanese atrocities to Rabe nearly every day. Taking December 30, 1937 as a random example, on that day Rabe recorded ten typical cases of Japanese atrocities, numbered 155 to 164, the cases being reported by Wilson, Bates, Mills, Riggs, and Smythe, all Americans. Taking February 1, 1938 as another example, on that day 10 cases were also reported, numbered 210 to 219, these from Sone, Wilson, Bates, Smythe, Mills, McCallum, Magee, and Rabe himself; all American except Rabe. Magee's secret documentary of the Rape of Nanking was known to Germans in and out of Nanjing, and copies were given to some Germans.

Miner Searle Bates was a professor in the history department of the University of Nanking. With his sensibilities as a historian, he knew that the Rape of Nanking must be recorded for posterity. So he disseminated information on happenings in the city to the outside world through as many channels as possible. Trautmann and Bidder received his initial report shortly after the city's fall: "At Nanking the Japanese army has lost much of its reputation, and has thrown away a remarkable opportunity to gain the respect of the Chinese inhabitants and of foreign opinion... in two days the whole outlook has been ruined by frequent murder, wholesale and semi-regular looting, and uncontrolled disturbance of private homes including offences against the security of women... Squads of men picked out by Japanese troops as former Chinese soldiers have been tied together and shot. These soldiers had discarded their arms, and in some cases their military clothing. Thus far we have found no trace of prisoners in Japanese hands other than such squads actually or apparently on the way to execution, safe for men picked up anywhere to serve as temporary carriers of loot and equipment... Thousands upon thousands of private houses all through the city, occupied and unoccupied, large and small, Chinese and foreign, have been impartially plundered. Peculiarly disgraceful cases of robbery by soldiers include the following: scores of refugees in camps and shelters had money and valuables removed from their slight possessions during mass searches" (German Foreign Ministry Archives: 2722/4379/37). Bates thereafter sent out an unbroken series of secret reports on new happenings, which circulated among all Westerners in the city, including the Germans. In his last report to the Foreign Office before leaving Nanjing of March 24, 1938, Rosen wrote about Japanese "ronin" selling opium obtained from Japanese military secret service departments; he had gotten this information from Bates (German Foreign Ministry Archives: 2718/2404/38). Bates proudly describes himself in a letter to Timperley of March 3, 1938:

"I am the hardest working correspondent for the University of Nanking" (Zhang 1999, 36).

The interactions ran both ways. Observations and records from Germans also constitute an important source for the British and American perspectives of the Rape of Nanking. The International Committee provided special reports to press correspondents for a long time after the Japanese occupation of the city. Much of the information collected by Rabe and the others was sent out by telegram aboard the HMS Bee, possibly allowing the British to have most up to date information on the Rape of Nanking in real time (of course the British embassy was extremely concerned about this for fear of infuriating Japan). Recently discovered documents about the Rape of Nanking in British and American archives are worded very similarly to Rabe's diary; this is not coincidence.

The Germans were happy to feed ammunition to the British and American public opinion machines to put pressure on Japan. When Kröger was permitted to travel from Nanjing to Shanghai at the end of January 1938, the Japanese granting permission clearly had no idea how much he wanted to tell his story. In Shanghai he wrote many reports on Japanese atrocities, but he also thought that his efforts were far from sufficient when compared to Japanese propaganda. He suggested to Rabe: "We should make a big stir in public opinion through newspapers, with headlines like 'Japanese Army Starving Population of Nanjing.' For American sentiments, propaganda like that is extremely effective... If possible, we should write a news report every day and ensure that new information is reported in every issue, or else we'll never keep up with those uncouth fellows working in the Japanese army!" He mailed to Rabe a copy of *North China Daily News* reporting on Japanese atrocities, and expressed regret that he had nothing to say about the "Allison incident" (Rabe CN, 499–500).

There are many instances of interaction between the "German perspective" and the British and American perspectives. For example, the similarities between the following two passages are striking.

First, a report by Rosen of March 4, 1938:

> The Japanese have brought along pretty full-color picture posters featuring an affable Japanese carrying a box of rice with a Chinese child on his shoulders and the child's poor, sincere peasant parents gazing with gratitude and happiness upon this kind-hearted uncle. The pity of it is that this color picture poster has nothing to do with reality, and should be thought of only as an advertisement to boost the tourism business! (German Foreign Ministry Archives: 2722/1896/38).

Second, a June 2, 1938 article in *Ken* magazine:

Japanese bombers dropped handbills onto the city. "Your friends in the Imperial Japanese Army will provide food and clothing to all decent Chinese people who return to their homes," said the handbills. "Japan hopes to become the friendly neighbor of all Chinese not devilishly deceived by Chiang Kai-shek's forces." On the handbill was a full color picture of a handsome Japanese soldier holding a Chinese child in his arms like Jesus, with a Chinese mother kneeling at his feet in gratitude for a sack of rice he has given them (Ken 1938, n.p.).

Documents from the Nanking Safety Zone contains many important records by British and American sources on the Rape of Nanking. The book *What War Means: The Japanese Terror in China* by *Manchester Guardian* reporter Harold Timperley made the Rape of Nanking known to the world. In fact, this book caused extreme anger and alarm toward Japan among the British and American publics, who began to express great sympathy for the plight of the embattled Chinese people. The publication of this book would have been impossible without the efforts of Bates and the others. Nevertheless, reports by Germans like Rabe, Sperling, Kröger, and Hempel were also important components of the Safety Zone documents, and Rabe's organizational skill was the linchpin to the Safety Zone's operations.

The close interaction between the "German perspective" with Britishers and Americans goes to demonstrate the tight cooperative relationship of Germans with the British and Americans in Nanjing. However, just as the German perspective was rooted in German national interests, the interests of the British and Americans involved were also clear. For example, an article in the *Chicago Daily News* of December 10, 1937, on the Safety Zone provides food for thought:

> ...the International Committee, composed of 13 Americans and four Germans, manages this newly formed territory occupying two square miles of the capital.
>
> The committee, composed mostly of missionaries and doctors, has made incomparable humanitarian achievements in the short span of a week. Their achievements may end up saving tens of thousands of innocents. International YMCA Committee Secretary George Fitch, of Wooster, Ohio, is in charge of the committee's administration, and Lewis Smythe of Chicago, a professor at the University of Nanking, is the committee's secretary.

The article goes out of its way to mention that the committee is "composed mostly of missionaries and doctors," excluding the Germans, neither missionaries nor doctors, and mentions the Committee's chairman Rabe not once.

The "USS Panay incident," in which Japanese bombers sank the American naval vessel Panay on the Yangtze river near the capital, happened during the Rape of Nanking. As a result of the incident, the U.S. became aware of the sharp contradictions and differences of opinion between the Japanese army and navy. They came to realize that it was Colonel Hashimoto Kingoro of the army who ordered the Japanese navy's fighters to bomb the Panay (Nanjing Incident Investigation and Research Association n.d., 80–85). Although the Japanese navy openly blamed Hashimoto for the event to the Americans, in the end the navy took full responsibility for various reasons, and made Rear Admiral Mitsunami Teizo, commander of the Second Combined Air Group, the scapegoat for the incident, and placed him on reserve duty (Nanjing Incident Investigation and Research Association n.d., 51–52 and 80–85; Powell n.d., 305–319). The U.S.'s quick forgiveness of Japan and new awareness of disagreements between branches of the Japanese military are not reflected in German diplomatic records, demonstrating that there was a limit to the friendship between the U.S. and Germany. Truly, the U.S. displayed unprecedented forgiveness for the sinking of the Panay, even though it was proven to be intentional.[41] A response from American Ambassador to Japan Joseph Grew to Japanese Foreign Minister Hirota Koki does not mention the fact that Japan had not punished the incident's instigator (note: this had been an American demand), but demonstrated a quick willingness to move on: "The American government is satisfied with the quick acceptance of responsibility, the apology, and the pledge for compensation made by your government in its official document of December 14" (Nanjing Incident Investigation and Research Association n.d., 75–76). Thus we cannot eliminate suspicion of "instigation" looking back on Scharffenberg's criticism of Rosen's "pour oil on the fire" in his dissatisfaction with the Japanese in matters related to the British and Americans. On April 25, 1938, Cabot Coville, military attaché to the American embassy to Japan in Tokyo, paid a visit to Nanjing to make observations. Coville asked Rosen if "German foreign relations with Japan were obstructing the protection of German interests here," to which Rosen answered: "Under Chinese rule, the treatment of foreigners wasn't great, but at least we could do much more of what we wanted to do. But if we're talking about the strict rules of the Japanese army, they're intolerable." Coville said of Rosen: "At first glance it's clear that he hates the Japanese" (Nanjing Incident Investigation and Research Association n.d., 110–121). The shrewdness of his questions and the hatred written on Rosen's face provide a contrast worthy of our reflection in the study of the Rape of Nanking.

So we should consider the special complex factors behind the interactions of Germans with British and Americans during the Rape of Nanking. These factors are hidden within the overarching theme of "Westerners in Nanjing during the

---

[41] The U.S. launched the Spanish-American war due to the sinking of one of its ships, and joined World War One because of the sinking of the Lusitania.

massacre": Germany lost its extraterritorial privileges in China to Japan because of its defeat in the First World War, but it was allied to the present occupier Japan, meaning that the Japanese army was somewhat more concerned with Germans. This is an important reason that Rabe was elected to chair the International Committee. The Americans and British still had extraterritorial rights in China under their treaty systems, and furthermore the nationalist government at the time repeatedly reminded the UK and the U.S. that the Japanese invasion not only endangered the integrity of China's territorial sovereignty, but also the interests of those two countries in China, in an attempt to draw them into the war. The UK and the U.S. had a relatively lenient attitude toward Japan in their Far East policies, and they encouraged China and Japan to resolve differences through talks.[42] The Japanese army, however, was highly opposed to any British or American intervention in Nanjing; the bombing of American ships, the Allison incident, and the striking of the American Charles Riggs by a Japanese soldier in the Safety Zone are all pieces of this overarching background.

German Foreign Minister von Ribbentrop calculated that the British were ready to improve relations with Italy and Japan and were willing to pay a price; this calculation was set against the German global strategy of preventing the UK from allying with France and becoming involved in the Franco-German conflict. So Germany established an anti-UK alliance and strengthened relations with Italy and Japan (Wang n.d., 160). Furthermore, although there were no direct hostilities between Germany and the U.S. at the time, the U.S. had already identified Japan as a threat to American interests in the Far East. The cooperation, interaction, and friendship through common adversity of Westerners in Nanjing during the massacre naturally faded with time as a result of these factors.

4.4 The "German Perspective" and German Interests

It is undeniable that the Germans recorded Japanese atrocities with the rigor of historians and strove to save the lives of tens of thousands of Chinese soldiers and civilians because of their great humanitarian spirit. This humanitarianism was shared by all Europeans and Americans in Nanjing at the time, regardless

---

[42] Chiang Kai-shek sent a letter to Roosevelt saying: "We are fighting for the freedom of the nation of China and against the common threat to humanity as a whole." Roosevelt responded: "Your reconciliation will become the foundations on which friendly relations and long-lasting peace rest" (Nanjing Incident Investigation and Research Association n.d., 213–214 and 216–217).

of country, creed, or political orientation. They came to a strong consensus and acted together when times were worst to save the lives of Chinese people. This is the part of the great historical calamity of the Rape of Nanking that lets us feel the bright light and warmth of humanity.

Of course, we likewise should not deny that German national interests were the most important factor behind the German perspective throughout the entire Rape of Nanking. Their focus remained on concrete interests, from strategic relations between Germany and Japan, between Germany and China, and the entire system of international relations in the Far East, all the way down to the properties of individual Germans located in Nanjing. Rosen explains this frankly in a report to the Foreign Office of January 15, 1938: "For me German national interests have always been the highest priority" (Central Archives et al. 1995, 149). Truly, even Rabe put German national interests first when he was forbidden by the Gestapo to publish his diary, writing: "Should its publication, which for obvious reasons has at present been prohibited, ever seem appropriate, that should be done only by permission of the German government" (Rabe EN, introduction). He even pledged to Hitler: "I have no intention to sing a tune contrary to that of German policies and German authority" (Rabe CN, 558, footnote). When the upright Kröger discovered that China was still buying goods from Germany, he said: "This is a matter of the greatest importance to us" (Rabe CN, 501).

The Germans' strong concern for their national interests means that we must pay special attention to the fact that as the German embassy was demanding protection from the Japanese for German interests in Nanjing, it wrote a letter to the Chinese Foreign Ministry on January 5, long after the fall of Nanjing, making this demand: "The German embassy will be unceasingly grateful to the Chinese Foreign Ministry if it can ask Chinese controlling departments, particularly air force command departments, to ensure that Germany's imperial subjects and German property not come under attack from air raids" (German Foreign Ministry Archives: 2722/1057/38). This "neutrality" based in German national interests allows us to observe the impact of the Rape of Nanking on the international community from a different perspective, and also enables us to view the complex inner psychological world of Germans in Nanjing, as well as their compassion and willingness to save Chinese lives.

Trautmann personally strongly empathized with the fierce Chinese resistance. In a summary of international relations in the Far East before and after the Rape of Nanking, Trautmann wrote in a report to the Foreign Office of January 23, 1938: "Right as China was making enormous changes in all areas to transform from a medieval country into a modern one, it was taken by surprise in this war." He seemed about as cold as Sperling for the next line: "The truth of General von Seeckt's line that 'weak countries threaten peace' has been proven here." In Trautmann's view: "Japan is trying to accomplish what it could not in the (First) World War, to submit China entirely to its control and eliminate the influence of the white man from China." He saw some conflicts of interest with Germany's strategic interests: "That will mean the end of Germany's enormous commercial activities here, and will cause Germany to lose its investments in China." As for exchangeables between Germany and Japan, "we can place 'hope' in future political possibilities" (Zhang Sheng 2005: 347–348).

Trautmann's hopes for political possibilities of the future not only frequently opened up holes in his compassion for China, but also makes his somewhat early emphasis on the Anti-Comintern Pact seem hypocritical. Trautmann wrote in a report of November 5, 1937, that in a meeting with him on November 4, Chiang Kai-shek and H.H. Kung told him that the result of a defeat of the nationalist government by sustained Japanese attack would be a red regime in China. He thought that such an outcome would be an extreme misfortune for China (Chen Renxia n.d., 214). Trautmann wrote in a report of November 9 that in a meeting with H.H. Kung on November 8, he said he hoped China would reduce its demands in the German-led mediation with Japan, because a sustained war would expose China to a communist threat (Chen Renxia n.d., 216).

Rosen, on the other hand, did not at all cover up his friendliness for the Chinese of Nanjing and enmity toward the Japanese. The primary reason he hated the Japanese was the utter lack of humanity displayed by the Japanese army, completely at odds with his own conscience. He also thought that Japan's intentions and acts to date were at odds with Germany's political goal of preventing the development of communism, and that Germans should be soberly aware of this contradiction. He expressed hope that "the British spirit of jovial friendship and willingness to help others on the Yangtze will in the near future manifest itself in a format of global significance to Germany" (German Foreign Ministry Archives: 2722/8432/37). During the secret talks taking place between the UK and Germany, clearly this global strategic view among the Germans of Nanjing was somewhat naive.

It seems that there was a consensus within the German perspective that Japan was not a valuable strategic partner in the fight against communism. In a letter to Count Strachwitz of March 18, 1938, retired Lieutenant Colonel Brinkmann attached the personal experiences of "a German" in Nanjing. From the document's contents and most particularly its recounting of conditions at the refugee camp at Qixia Mountain, it is extremely likely that this is the first time Kröger's efforts in Shanghai bore fruit. The document's conclusions are clear: "This bestial machine's (note: the Japanese army) pose as the vanguard in the fight against communism now seems like a joke. It loudly proclaims to the rest of the world that their doing such and such is in order to liberate and reform China, but the truth is that life under their iron heel will only cause true communism to flourish and bring all the bad elements to the surface" (German Foreign Ministry Archives, no. N/A). The disgust felt by Germans as well as their analysis of the Japanese false pretext of combating communism go to demonstrate their values.

The Germans felt that stressing their role as military advisers and an emphasis on their "foresight" could augment Germany's prestige, and this was also an important method by which they demonstrated German interests in China. They tended to think that Chiang Kai-shek's ignoring the advice of his German military advisers had imperiled great numbers of Chinese forces, who were sacrificed to Japanese massacres. Rosen stressed this point in a report to the Foreign Office of December 14, 1937: "General von Falkenhausen encouraged Chiang Kai-shek weeks ago to abandon the defense of Nanjing situated where it is in a bend of the Yangtze. After evacuating from Shanghai, Chinese military leaders have displayed no military competence whatsoever in open regions, or even made any real efforts to hold the forts between Shanghai and Nanjing. They have rather preferred to put on a show of resistance in mostly very poorly fortified areas, unnecessarily sacrificing their troops and civilians – the poorest of the poor" (German Foreign Ministry Archives: 2722/8432/37). In Trautmann's report of January 23, he wrote that it was a lack of national strength that had made China succumb to the fierce attack of Japan, "a power armed with all manner of modern weaponry." Nevertheless he also saw a "miracle" in the Chinese defense, and he cites a phase from Madame Chiang Kai-shek to explain the reason for the miracle: "It is wonderful that the German military advisers grasped methods for very patiently treating with the Chinese" (Zhang 2005, 348).

The German flag and Nazi flag were symbols of German interests and occupy an important place in German records of the Rape of Nanking. Likewise images of Hindenburg and Hitler, as well as written protection certificates in the German embassy, were also seen as symbols of Germany's national prestige, respected by both China and Japan.

In truth, the Germans did not find Chinese military forces any more trustworthy in terms of morality or discipline before the Rape of Nanking. Kröger, in charge of this work, observed the actions of Chinese soldiers on the afternoon of December 13 and that of Japanese soldiers many times afterward. He wrote in a letter to the German embassy at Nanjing of January 11, 1938 that he came to the conclusion that suspicions that scattered Chinese soldiers had damaged German property were unfounded, but that Japanese soldiers had looted houses flying the German flag under the eyes of their officers. This, he writes, was behavior worthy of censure and contrasted sharply with the temporary breakdown of discipline of panicked, retreating Chinese soldiers (German Foreign Ministry Archives, No. N/A). As reports like this mounted on his desk, Trautmann asked the German Foreign Office for instructions in cable number 25 to the Foreign Office of January 15 (German Foreign Ministry Archives). The reply he received from State Secretary Ernst von Weizsäcker in cable number 30 of January 22 was extremely clear: "Please submit a protest to the Japanese government regarding all proven cases of disrespect by Japanese troops to German houses flying the German flag and all damages to German property caused thereby, and ask for full compensation" (German Foreign Ministry Archives). Despite multiple consultations between German and Japanese officials, Trautmann reports that Kröger was ultimately able to report the truth: "Although the German flag is more respected than the American flag, it has not prevented severe looting of German properties" (German Foreign Ministry Archives: 2722/1508/38).

Clearly, bringing the grave yet hypothetical issue of German national honor into the question of protection of tangible German assets in Nanjing may have been based in strategic interests common to both sides, but it was not practical in Nanjing at that time if the goal was to seek an overall resolution to the problem. The Japanese thought of collateral damages to civilians and third parties as common occurrences in war. Rosen wrote in a report of February 7 that a member of the Japanese embassy even bluntly told Rabe: "Germans did the same in Belgium!" (German Foreign Ministry Archives: 2722/1096/38). The overbearing and sophistical nature of the Japanese army was the practical working environment in which the Germans had to work. The maintenance of tangible interests, particularly the protection of German properties in Nanjing, became one of the major daily tasks of Germans in Nanjing. Given the conditions in which tens of thousands of Chinese people had their lives constantly at risk, these concerns come off as discordant.

As early as November 18, 1937, the German embassy to China asked its consulate-general in Shanghai to find a detailed map of Nanjing for the Japanese embassy to give to the Japanese army, to ensure the protection of German assets there. On December 7, all German-owned properties in the city were clearly visible on the map (German Foreign Ministry Archives: PO: 4, L, 8).

Not even such meticulous planning could ensure that German assets in Nanjing could come through the war unscathed. Even the North Hotel managed by Mr. Hempel fell prey to vicious luck. Kröger wrote in his letter of January 11 to the embassy in Nanjing that when he inspected the hotel on December 21, 1938 with Takadama of the Japanese embassy, he found its rear building in a blaze of fire (German Foreign Ministry Archives). In truth, nearly all German-owned properties in Nanjing were illegally entered and looted, making Rosen, as overseer of German interests in Nanjing, extremely irritable and sensitive, which was precisely the cause of Scharffenberg's displeasure with him.

One typical case was on January 17, 1938, when Rosen wrote a strongly worded letter of protest to Japanese Consul-General Fukui, noting two matters. The first was two illegal entries by Japanese soldiers into Scharffenberg's house and demand that the Chinese living there hand over his radio on January 16, even though the house had long before been looted in the most savage of ways. The second was the entry of Japanese soldiers into Rabe's office at Number 5 Ninghai Road and mistreatment of Chinese there on the 11th. These were egregious offenses in the eyes of people coming from an era of peace, but in the heyday of Japanese crimes in Nanjing, these were "light" offenses indeed. Rosen sternly warned Fukui that if the matter were not resolved immediately, it would be reported to the German government (German Foreign Ministry Archives: 5719/1004/38).

Rosen's attitude toward these matters was clear: Japan must compensate "all losses caused after the end of combat actions" perpetrated by the Japanese army. The intent of this statement was to separate out loses that "may have" been caused by retreating Chinese forces. He writes:

> Many Germans, including apartment owner Mrs. Rode, hotel owner Hempel, and the baker Scheel of the Kiessling and Bader bakery lost their livelihoods due to serious looting (Mrs. Rode) or having their property burned (Hempel and Scheel), and require full compensation for their property losses. They will clearly use the term "consolation money" to make their requests easier on the ears. I will also persist in receiving full compensation for other smaller losses. Thankfully our most precious German assets were transferred to the rented English steamer Kutwo, another expense attributable to the Japanese government. The imperial government has to pay $700 US dollars per day for this vessel in addition to fuel costs for many months. This has been an exorbitant price to pay for the safety of some chattels of our citizens. So for all remaining German property that has been burned or looted maliciously, the empire has cause to demand full compensation, and not some small charity.

Trautmann was also clearly a defender of German interests, but he was more concerned about higher, more comprehensive interests. While Rosen was raging, Trautmann ordered the German consulate general in Shanghai to talk with Japanese officials there, who replied that "Rosen is wasting his time resisting local regulations." Trautmann then asked Fischer to ask Rosen to keep calm, sent him some food as solace, and "ask the Japanese to pay him some special care" (German Foreign Ministry Archives, cables 35 and 36 of January 20, 1938).

Rosen's calm or lack thereof was not based in Japan's reaction to his demand. The truth is that Japan's attitude toward compensation of German property losses was very clear after Rosen was removed from his post in Nanjing, as indicated in this report of the German consulate-general at Shanghai of July 2, 1938:

> It remains unclear whether German losses in Nanjing were caused by Japanese or by Chinese. Even if the damages are proven to have been caused by Japanese people, the Japanese government is not liable, because the actions of Japanese soldiers were out of self defense in response to provocations by China. As for British, American, and other countries' losses, some special regulations should be made as those done for German requests for compensations; it is not possible to do so at this time (German Foreign Ministry Archives: 5720/4637/38).

One could say that the German government did not do its utmost to preserve German interests. If, however, we examine relations between China, Germany, and Japan at the macro level from the second half of 1937 through Chinese New Year of 1938, we see that the German government's concern for the property of its individual citizens was utterly flaccid, in some cases even comical, as the Nazi government advanced its plans toward world war. In brief, "German interests" as understood by Germans on the ground in China were different from those valued by Hitler and von Ribbentrop.

Although there was a great quantity of trade between Germany and China at the time, the Nazi government did not place economics at the forefront of its considerations of relations with China and Japan. It was clear that: "People did not believe – primarily in economics – that 'in opposing China we can gain from Japan what is lost in China.' 'China is clearly much more important than Japan for German exports.'" Hitler "maintained a perspective of cooperation with Japan in principle." With the Sino-Soviet Non-Aggression Pact in place as well as increased cooperation between Chinese nationalists and communists, the red threat constantly brought up by the Japanese seemed to have been "proven." At the same time, Japan continually protested against German fence-riding. By October 1937, "After repeated Japanese threats to withdraw from the Anti-Comintern Pact and the failure of secret talks between Germany and the UK, Hitler weighed the pros and cons and decided to improve relations with Japan and strengthen the alliance." That month, Germany announced a stop to all new loans to China (Wang 1995, 210–211).

Germany's gradual favoring of Japan over China seems to be related to Hitler's strong personal enmity toward communism. He said the following to the German assembly in a speech acknowledging the Japanese puppet state of Manchukuo: "I do not believe that China is strong enough spiritually or materially to resist any Bolshevik attacks on its own" (Kirby n.d., 281). Hitler had previously said that a Chinese victory in the war against Japan would be a victory for Bolshevism in the Far East, "a victory of benefit to nobody except the international Jew" (Kirby n.d., 293). H.H. Kung had, however, offered a defense against this position in a letter to Hitler of 1937, explaining that China was a totalitarian state under Confucian rule that would absolutely never become a communist country.

Kung argued that it was Japan, with its weak parliamentary rule and enormous industrial proletariat, that was likely to become a paradise for the communist party (Kirby n.d., 285). Hitler did not, however, refuse to engage with communist countries at all. His signing of the Treaty of Non-Aggression between Germany and the Union of Soviet Socialist Republics caused the cabinet of Japanese Prime Minister Hiranuma Kiichiro to resign (Shigemitsu n.d., 180). That is to say that opposition to communism was the pretext Hitler used to abandon China, but what really motivated the decision was probably a comparison of the strength of China and Japan and the alignment of German and Japanese global strategic interests. This determined Germany's basic policy toward China, and so Hitler applied a different kind of logic when addressing how the Rape of Nanking had "tarnished" the alliance's image. Rosen, virulently anti-Japanese, wanted Hitler to watch Magee's film, because, as he wrote in a report to the Foreign Office of February 10, it was "the most shocking documentary of its age" (German Foreign Ministry Archives: 2722/1113/38). Nevertheless, Rosen wrote in his letter to the Chinese embassy to the United States of September 1945 that "the Nazi government forced me to leave my diplomatic post and to leave China" (Central Archives et al. 1995, 133). Rabe thought that with the prestige he had earned, he merited a personal visit with Hitler, but what he really got was a search, arrest, and interrogation by the Gestapo (Rabe CN, 587–588).

On February 4, 1938, Hitler approved the firing of German Defense Minister von Blomberg and Foreign Minister von Neurath, both pro-China. Another pro-China German, Economic Minister Hjalmar Schacht, had resigned in September 1937. On February 21, 1938, newly appointed Foreign Minister von Ribbentrop issued instructions to German diplomats in China: the German acknowledgment of the Japanese puppet state of Manchukuo "is merely the result of pragmatic German policy, and is unrelated to Germany's attitude to the conflict in East Asia" (Chen Renxia n.d., 275). Once Rabe, Rosen, Trautmann, and the other Germans had returned, the Rape of Nanking was locked away in German files and forgotten.

In summary, the "German perspective" on the Rape of Nanking is significant for five reasons. First, the records they left behind as impartial third party observers demonstrates the ineradicable truth of the history of the Rape of Nanking. Second, among the Germans at Nanjing were merchants, First World War veterans, and even Nazis, but they all stood up in the face of great danger when the Chinese people needed them most and saved hundreds of thousands of lives; for this they are commendable as great humanitarians. This then goes to demonstrate the complexity of historical personages: any simplified linear version of events that takes a part of the story as a whole will run into awkward predicaments when faced with the entire truth. Third, the Germans of this story described the Japanese as "Asiatic" and "medieval," which in their context meant "backward." The Germans, for their part, demonstrated "industrial" and "modernized" brutality in the assembly line style operations of their concentration camps and massacre of Jews. In truth both kinds of brutality are forms of extreme contempt and abuse of the dignity of life. Fourth, national interests have ever been important bases for the actions of historical figures, but national interests can never possibly all be interpreted identically. There are logical explanations for both the overlaps and the divergences in conceptions of national interests between the Germans, the British, and the Americans in this story. There were even differences between individual Germans in the story regarding which interests to maintain and how to maintain them, demonstrating the unlimited abundance of the giant system of history. Fifth, the Rape of Nanking incited a patriotic fervor among the Chinese people to resist Japan to the last man, playing the same role as the overall war on uniting the country and people of China. On April 24, 1938, Rosen told Cabot Coville: "Japan's brutal actions have solidified the Chinese people's will to resist, and so it must destroy itself. Japan will lose. The Chinese, fighting on their own territory, will never surrender to these barbaric invaders. Guerrilla squadrons are vying with the 'big gorilla,'' and so the 'big gorilla' must suffer defeat. All the forces and appeals for so-called culture and civilization are behind China." Bates and Smythe had expressed a similar sentiment to Coville on April 22: "Sustained pressure from unpredictable attacks by Chinese forces and the Chinese spirit of revenge will ultimately force the Japanese army to retreat... As for the legends about the orderly and disciplined nature of the Japanese army and the selflessness of Japanese military authorities, these have been completely destroyed by the penetration deep into the hearts of the Chinese people of the Japanese army's barbarism and criminal acts. So there is no meaning whatsoever for the Chinese people to any rule by Japan over them. The Chinese people may have already realized this, and their sorrows will continue to drive them to keep up the attack, until the Japanese army is finally driven out" (Nanjing Incident Investigation and Research Association n.d., 110–121).

The German perspective on this issue reminds us that perhaps we can observe the historical status of the Rape of Nanking from a different perspective, even as we focus our research on Japanese atrocities. The event turned out to be one of the dear prices China paid in the course of its transformation into a modern country.[43]

---

[43] This chapter was first published in *Nanjing daxue xuebao* 1 (2007) under the title "Qin Hua Rijun Nanjing da tusha de 'Deguo shijiao' – yi Deguo waijiao dang'an wei zhongxin" [The "German Perspective" on the Japanese army's Rape of Nanking – Centered in German Diplomatic Documents]. It has been revised for inclusion in this book.

5 The "American Perspective" on the Rape of Nanking

In this book the "American perspective" refers to the reports, observations, records, analyses, and policy directives made by Americans living in Nanjing and others concerned with the incident before, during, and after the Rape of Nanking.

These Americans left behind a great quantity of documents; in fact American documents constitute the most abundant portion of third-party records on the Rape of Nanking. Not only did these play an important role in both the Tokyo and Nanjing trials after the war, but they are now the keystone of historical research on the topic in refuting absurd denials of the event. In this chapter, we will analyze the extent to which the American perspective was disseminated, its contents and values, and also expose the national interests underlying the American perspective, all of which are of great academic value.

This chapter is built on a foundation of existing research.[44] We humbly request that readers point out to us any inaccuracies or places requiring improvement.

5.1 The People behind the "American Perspective" and Their Reasons for Staying in Nanjing

Three classes of people comprise the American perspective. The first were reporters: C. Yates McDaniel, reporter for the Associated Press; Archibald Trojan Steele, reporter for the *Chicago Daily News*; Frank Tillman Durdin, reporter for *The New York Times*; and Arthur Menken, cameraman for Paramount Pictures. All four were present for the fall of Nanjing. McDaniel left Nanjing for Shanghai on a Jap-

---

44 For the academic history of the Rape of Nanking, see C. X. George Wei, "Politicization and De-politicization of History: The Evolution of International Studies of the Nanjing Massacre", *The Chinese Historical Review* 15 (2008). See also Wei, "Lishi yu lishi xuejia: haiwai Nanjing da tusha yanjiu de zhengyi zongshu" [History and historians: summary of disputes in overseas study of the Rape of Nanking], *Lishi yanjiu* 5 (2009).

Existing research has given us considerable leeway in writing this chapter in the areas of degree of substantiation of documents, the composition of the American perspective, the integrity of the American perspective, the propagation of the American perspective at the international level, American national interests belying the American perspective, internal disagreements and limitations within the American perspective, and other areas.

https://doi.org/10.1515/9783110652789-008

anese naval vessel on December 16. The other three left one day before for Shanghai aboard the USS Oahu along with Reuters reporter L.C. Smith. In addition, Hallett Edward Abend, *The New York Times* reporter in Shanghai, and John B. Powell of the *China Weekly Review* paid close attention to events in Nanjing, despite not being there.

The second class of Americans was comprised of government officials, including Third Secretary John Moore Allison, Vice-Consul James Espy, and embassy staffer A. A. McFadyen. All three men returned to Nanjing on January 6, 1938. In addition the U.S. ambassador to China Nelson T. Johnson, U.S. ambassador to Japan Joseph C. Grew, and U.S. consul-general in Shanghai C.E. Gauss all paid great events in Nanjing at the time, despite not being physically present. U.S. Secretary of State Cordell Hull and President Franklin Roosevelt expressed principles and positions on the Rape of Nanking as American policymakers. In addition, other officials such as military attaché to the U.S. embassy to Japan Cabot Coville and U.S. Asiatic Fleet Commander Admiral Harry E. Yarnell were extremely concerned with events in Nanjing.

The third class was comprised of American members of the International Committee for the Nanking Safety Zone (founded November 29, 1937 and reorganized into the Nanking International Relief Committee in February 1938) and the International Red Cross Committee of Nanking (founded December 13, 1937); Americans working for the University of Nanking, the university's Kulou Hospital, and the Ginling Women's College, including Charles H. Riggs, Miner Searle Bates, Lewis S.C. Smythe, C.S. Trimmer, Robert O. Wilson, Grace Bauer, Iva Hynds, James H. McCallum, Minnie Vautrin, and others. Most of these were of religious backgrounds, and many were sent by American church missions to China. There were also full-time missionaries, priests, and preachers, including Ernest H. Forster, Hubert L. Sone, John G. Magee, W. Plummer Mills, George A. Fitch, and others. J.V. Pickering of the Standard-Vacuum Oil Co. was also in Nanjing before and after the massacre, but he left few historical records behind.[45] Albert N. Steward, professor of botany in the University of Nanking, came to Nanjing after the peak of the massacre, and also left behind some records. The members of the above three classes were the primary writers of American records on the Rape of Nanking.

---

45 Per the Safety Zone Documents, there were seven Americans on the International Committee for the Nanking Safety Zone: Smythe, Magee, Pickering, Bates, Mills, Trimmer, and Riggs. There were nine on the International Red Cross Committee of Nanking: Magee, W. Lowe, Forster, Wilson, Trimmer, McCallum, Bates, Smythe, and Mills; Mary Twinem, born in the U.S., was also on the committee, but by now she was a naturalized Chinese citizen (see Zhang 2006b, 271–271).

The following were the four primary motivations for Americans to either remain in Nanjing during the incident or come to Nanjing shortly after:

1. Professionalism. A.T. Steele was the resident reporter in Nanjing for the *Chicago Daily News*. As the capital was coming under encirclement, he left Jinan and headed southward via Xuzhou, against the flow of outpouring residents, arriving in Nanjing on December 2. Steele knew before his sojourn that Nanjing was "doomed" (Zhang 2005, 31–32), but this did not prevent him from venturing into the midst of danger. Other reporters showed equal levels of professionalism, such as Menken and Durdin, who remained on Zhongshan East Road to witness the resistance and ultimate sacrifice of many Chinese defenders (Zhang 2005, 104).

2. Protection of church property and dissemination of the Christian creed. Most Americans who stayed in Nanjing were fervently religious. In a letter to his wife of December 5, 1937, not long before the city fell, Forster wrote: "All we can do is to pray and bear a Christian witness of fidelity to our charge. We are helpless but God isn't" (Yale Divinity n.d.). Vautrin wrote on December 12 that that morning, in the final moments before the city's fall, her Church Emergency Committee even gave a service. Even at the peak of the atrocities, the missionaries inspected church property "every day or every other day," wrote McCallum in a series of letters to his wife from December 29 to January 15 (Zhang 2005, 204). In their reckoning: "The needs and opportunities for Christian services in Nanking are great" (Bates and Mills n.d., n.p.).

3. Protection of American national interests on orders from the U.S. government. When American diplomats returned to Nanjing, they immediately investigated damages done to American interests. Forster wrote in a letter to his wife of January 24 that the American embassy, despite interference from the Japanese, "has a wireless sending set with an operator from the Navy" (Yale Divinity n.d., n.p.). Not long afterward, Allison and Charles Riggs were struck and abused by Japanese soldiers when investigating the abduction of a girl from the University of Nanking. Nevertheless, the actions of diplomats on behalf of the American government did exert pressure on the Japanese. Cabot Coville writes that when he arrived in Nanjing in April 1938, Allison had been compensated USD $6,000 in addition to 10,000 yuan local money as a result of the incident (Zhang 2006b, 80).

4. Providing relief to Nanjing residents and general humanitarianism. Vautrin wrote in her diary entry of November 19 that when the embassy ordered American expatriates to vacate the city, she responded: "I felt that I could not leave my group at Ginling and in neighborhood; that they were depending on me." Bates wrote in a circular to friends of November 29 that he was "fighting for people's lives," "defending truth and humanitarianism," and acting as "an

impulse and shock to the spirit" amid extreme danger (Zhang 2005, 51). On December 3, 1937, the American embassy sent out its last warning to expatriates to vacate the city, but Forster and Magee both chose to stay. Forster's wife Clarissa wrote of this decision in a letter to his wife of that day: "To remain in the city. John and I have decided on the latter, since we feel it will require the cooperation of as many foreigners as possible to insure the success of the neutral zone plan which is the only way left now to provide for our workers and Christians. Also, we have been using our decision to stay to encourage nurses and dressers to be faithful to their duty" (Yale Divinity n.d., n.p.). After the peak of the massacre had passed, Smythe reflected in a letter to his friends of March 8, 1938: "Do I hate the Japanese? No… if I am ever given the opportunity of doing the same as we have done her for 250,000 Chinese men, women, and children, I would do the same right over again" (Zhang 2005, 281–282 and 285).

The majority of Americans who stayed in Nanjing during the event shared woe and weal with city residents. They did so not for any expected fame or fortune. Most had been educated in renowned institutions and were keen observers of international conditions and China's situation therein. They understood the nuances of the very complex situation around them and were capable of taking appropriate measures, and in so doing were able to take effective measures to check the Japanese in Nanjing. They effectively used the platforms and mechanisms they had established in advance to make enormous achievements in relief and humanitarianism, much greater than what they had originally thought themselves capable of.[46] They demonstrated both the power of knowledge and the height to which their subjective initiative could bring them even during the bloodiest of wars.

We should point out that some motivations overlapped. For example, missionaries not only actively protected church property, but also tended to other American-owned property. Most importantly, they were the primary force of international relief efforts in Nanjing, effectively reducing the extent of violence the Japanese army could inflict on the Chinese.

---

[46] The American church folk cited an appraisal of them in a *Boston Globe* article of the time: "When the Japanese entered Nanjing, a group of foreigners, mostly Americans, organized the Safety Zone Committee, in the hopes of creating a safe spot for non-combatants to escape the ravages of war. The committee was composed of university staff and churchmen, professors and preachers. This is an extremely rational composition. It was precisely these cultured, elegant people who stood up when civilization itself was imperiled" (see John W. Wood n.d.).

5.2 Documents of the American Perspective and Their Dissemination

The documents left behind by the above-mentioned Americans and which comprise the American perspective can be divided into the following six categories:

1. Documents of the Nanking Safety Zone. The Americans in non-governmental positions in Nanjing created a great quantity of records in the course of reporting and stopping Japanese atrocities and in providing relief to Chinese civilians. These along with testimonials by Chinese eyewitnesses were compiled into a collection titled "Documents of the Nanking Safety Zone" by Professor Xu Shuxi[47] of Yenching University, who translated them into Chinese and published them in 1939. The collection consists of 69 documents, including correspondence between the International Committee and the embassies of Japan, the UK, the U.S., Germany, and also the puppet Nanjing Autonomous Committee. There are also notes on conditions in refugee shelters under management of the International Committee as well as 444 documented cases of atrocities perpetrated by Japanese soldiers in and near the Safety Zone between December 15, 1937, and February 7, 1938.

We should note that the International Committee felt compelled to cooperate with the Japanese – granted, to the lowest extent possible – in their efforts to provide relief to refugees, owing to their complete powerlessness to halt organized searches and mass killings by the Japanese army. There are, consequently, few records of mass killings in the Safety Zone Documents, which focus rather on rape, looting, arson, and problems of concern to refugees such as food, fuel, and medicine. This is, in fact, one characteristic of the American perspective (see "Nanking Safety Zone Documents" in Zhang 2006b, 269–388).

2. Yale University Divinity School Library Special Collections. Dr. Bates of the University of Nanking studied at Oxford University and later at Harvard University, and in 1920 was dispatched to China by the United Christian Missionary Society. He later received his doctorate in Chinese history from Yale University. Bates was twice commended for his services to the residents of Nanjing during the Rape of Nanking by the nationalist government (Yale Divinity n.d.). He wrote in a circular letter to friends of April 12, 1938: "We feel that there is a certain moral necessity to make known the terrible facts in a constructive way." He went on to say that all people in the world "have a right to know this significant chapter in the experience of our times" (Zhang 2005, 35). Bates's documents occupy a special place within the American perspective. We subsequently refer to

---

[47] Known at the time as Hsu Shuhsi (translator's note).

all of his documents and many others now stored in the Yale University Divinity School Library as the "Yale documents." Diaries and correspondence of American missionaries in Nanjing during the event comprise an important component of the Yale documents, which were first translated and published in China by Mr. Zhang Kaiyuan.

The primary components of the Yale documents are the many letters written by Bates to media outlets in China and abroad, the Nanking Safety Zone Documents, John Rabe's diary, and Minnie Vautrin's diary. They also include photos taken by Ernest Forster and others, documents from the United Board for Christian Higher Education in Asia, reports to American diplomats in Nanjing, documents based in missionary reports from the Foreign Christian Mission Society, and telegrams between Americans and other Westerners and the Japanese. Bates had performed a great quantity of analyses of trends in Sino-Japanese relations before the war, and during the war he secretly investigated the organized, systematic sales of narcotics by the Japanese army in occupied Nanjing. He also studied the monopoly Japan exerted on Nanjing's economy, the responses of Chinese to Japanese occupiers, resident life in Nanjing after the fall, the activities of the International Relief Committee, and more. The Yale documents, then, are a crystallization of the collective memories of Americans in Nanjing during the event, particularly of Bates.

3. American diplomatic documents. Before the fall of Nanjing, American foreign service members in the city submitted a great quantity of documents to Ambassador Johnson, some of these describing the founding of the International Committee for the Nanking Safety Zone (FRUS Volume III, 768–769; 781–782). Upon their return to the city, they wrote a great many eyewitness testimonials and analysis reports. Many Westerners also sent copies of their correspondence with Japanese authorities to the American embassy, some of which the embassy passed on to the U.S. Department of State. Many were distributed within the American government with the signature of President Roosevelt or Secretary of State Hull, and became the basis of the American government's dealings with Japan during this time. After the war, some of these documents were even submitted to the International Military Tribunal for the Far East.

4. Reports in the U.S. periodicals *Chicago Daily News*, *The New York Times*, *Readers Digest*, *Washington Post*, and *Life*, most of which were written by American journalists. Some other American reporters wrote articles based on accounts of Americans who had been in Nanjing.

5. The testimony and statements of Bates and others given to the International Military Tribunal for the Far East. In May 1946, Bates, Wilson, and Magee all appeared in Tokyo at the trials to give testimony and be cross-examined, providing detailed accounts of the Rape of Nanking and refuting Japanese defendants'

intentional distortions and attacks. Wilson, Smythe, Fitch, and McCallum all also provided sworn affidavits to be read into the tribunal record (see Yang 2006; Zhang and Yang n.d.).

Manchester Guardian reporter Harold John Timperley's book *What War Means: the Japanese Terror in China*, published in 1938 in New York and London, made a big splash internationally. Bates did a great deal of on the ground leg work for this book's writing, promising to provide to the author Smythe correspondence, reports from Qixia Mountain, Vautrin's diary, unpublished draft articles by Forster and Wilson, and correspondence of Fitch and Bates himself (Yale Divinity, *Bates to Timperley*, March 14, 1938). Bates even gave Timperley 18 concrete recommendations for improvements to the manuscript (Yale Divinity, *Bates to Timperley*, March 21, 1938). Magee filmed a documentary in Nanjing, which Fitch secretly took out of the city and had developed in Shanghai, and which was later shown in China and the U.S., with a copy even making its way to Germany. In spring 1938, Smythe led his students in performing a field survey of Nanjing and its environs, which resulted in the pamphlet *War Damage in the Nanking Area, December 1937 to March 1938*. Bates wrote in the preface that "we venture merely to point out that losses to life and property from actual warfare are shown by these surveys to be one or two percent of the total," as the survey was conducted under the eyes of the puppet Autonomous Committee (Jiang Liangqin et al. n.d., 2). It is, nevertheless, a valuable source of information. In addition, John Powell's memoir, Fitch's diary, and Cabot Coville's report on observations made in Nanjing are also organic components of the American perspective.

The scope of activities of American private citizens in Nanjing is the spatial foundation for the American perspective. Theoretically speaking, they were a neutral third party, but their activities were subject to severe restrictions by the Japanese army, and sometimes even threats to their lives. On December 16, 1937, Japanese soldiers searched refugee camps for Chinese soldiers. Housing commission Deputy Chairman Charles Riggs treated with the soldiers time and again to convince them not to carry of innocent civilians, but he was met with three threats of being bayoneted from a Japanese officer and a beating (Rabe CN, 164). McCallum actually suffered a bayonet wound to the neck from a Japanese soldier. As Bates reported in a circular to friends of January 10, 1938, other Westerners in Nanjing at the time had similar experiences. The private American citizens in Nanjing at the time were brave, but they did not actively seek death, so they limited their activities mostly to the confines of the Safety Zone, which occupied only one-eighth of the area of the city. Only under special circumstances, such as when exhorted by Chinese people seeking aid, did they venture out.

Owing to Japanese fears that a bad image of their army be spread abroad, they were not easily permitted to leave the city (Zhang 2005, 19–20).

The diplomats had a somewhat larger scope for their activities, but even they had to follow Japanese "rules," accept "escorts" wherever they went, and saw only areas that had long before been "cleaned." Political Secretary Rosen of the German embassy wrote in a report to the German Foreign Office of January 15, 1938: "The news given to me by Germans and Americans tells me that frantic clean-up work commenced as soon as foreign delegations announced their intention to return to Nanjing. The bodies of innocent civilians, women, and children, bones scattered across the roads, and emaciated corpses have all been cleaned, and a semblance of cleanliness restored" (Zhang 2005, 326).

The stretch of Zhongshan Road (now Zhongshan North Road) from the Drum Tower in the city's center running to the Xiaguan Railway Station and wharf was Nanjing's primary thoroughfare in and out of the city, the road that Americans had to take on their exits and entries. This street was the northwestern perimeter of the Safety Zone, but it allowed for movement beyond the zone's bounds. The sojourn of John Magee to the refugee camp in the Jiangnan Concrete Plant held down by the German Günther and the Dane Sindberg is one important exception in the scope of observations of the American perspective.

As discussed above, there were objective limits to the physical area covered by the American perspective. There are few mentions in American records of happenings in riverside locations like Caoxiexia, Mufushan, Yanziji, Shangxinhe, Sanchahe, and so on, where the massacre was particularly concentrated. Mostly their writings about happenings in those places were limited to hearsay.[48] That is to say that even though the Americans in the city were important eyewitnesses, they cannot testify to the full extent of the massacre. This is another important characteristic of the American perspective.

The extent of the dissemination of the American perspective, however, was enormous. First was the area under control of the KMT. The author of this chapter found a letter written by Bates in The Second Historical Archives of China. In it Bates wrote: "Marauding soldiers attack residents, plunder goods, and dishonor women, some suffering this fate ten times in a day, others six times in a night; truly these cases are beyond numbering... Many in the city have been driven by hunger and cold to extreme conditions. As their food and valuables have all been stolen by soldiers, and their clothing and bedding looted to the last, they are un-

---

[48] For example, Minnie Vautrin writes in her diary on February 16, 1938, that when a Mr. Yan called on her, he told her that "he had heard" that 10,000 were killed at Sanchahe, 20,000 to 30,000 at Yanziji, and another 10,000 at Xiaguan. As she did not go investigate the claims herself, her record remains hearsay.

able to withstand the harsh winter, and most are sick beyond treating. How will the Japanese authorities deal with this problem?" (The Second Historical Archives of China, no. 718(5)/15). Media outlets in nationalist-controlled China, such as the *Ta Kung Pao*, quoted *New York Times* Shanghai reporter Hallett Abend's article: "Some Japanese forces in China have lost all discipline, surpassing even the bandits of yore in China in every way" (*Dagongbao* December 25, 1937). Once Timperley's book was published, the nationalist government immediately had it translated into Chinese and printed. The International Propaganda Office gave 20 copies to Chiang Kai-shek as well as copies to all major governmental organs and important officials, to a furious reaction. With ferocious demand for the book all over the country, the International Propaganda Office sent this letter to the Cultural Services Office on August 20, 1938: "Your office has given us 17,000 copies of *What War Means: the Japanese Terror in China*, but we have very few copies left after having disseminated previous printings to all offices in the government. Copies have still yet to be sent into combat zone number 482 or to guerrilla forces and peace-keeping forces. We hereby request that you print another 30,000 or so copies for us to continue undertaking their dissemination. Given the aforesaid, we trust you will undertake this, as the printing capacity in Wuhan is limited. Thus before the end of this month print at least 5,000 copies and send them to us, and come up with a plan for printing and shipping out the full 30,000 as quickly as possible, to keep up with demand" (The Second Historical Archives of China, no. 718(4)/4711).

The second area of dissemination was the Communist Party of China (CPC) base of resistance against Japan. In 1939, the Yan'an Current Events Research Association compiled and printed the book *Riben diguozhuyi zai Zhongguo lunxian qu* [Japanese imperialism in fallen zones of China]. The first article of the third chapter of the third volume relates to Japanese atrocities in Nanjing based on letters of protest submitted by the International Committee to Japanese authorities, and in particular the infringement of American rights by the Japanese. Mao Zedong wrote the book's preface, titled "Yanjiu lunxian qu" [Studying the fallen zones] and wrote the book's abbreviated name of *Riben zai lunxian qu* [Japan in the fallen zones] (Yan'an Current Events Research Association).

The third area was Europe. The UK learned a great deal of information about the Rape of Nanking from the American perspective. One British diplomat makes this critique of Timperley's book: "More exposition won't yield any results. In particular as we have come to understand, this is even more the case as conditions have changed a great deal recently" (Zhang 2006b, 229–230). In May 1938, when Pedlar of the UK Treasury sent a letter from Reverend Sargent to Howe in the British Foreign Office, he attached George Fitch's diary entry of Christmas Day, 1937. In his reply, Howe wrote: "We have already received nearly identical reports from other sources" (Zhang 2006b, 238–240). As for the Germans, the reports of Bates and Steele were copied and attached to reports sent from the German embassy's bureau in Beiping to the embassy in Hankou (Zhang 2005, 288–295).[49] Magee's film and his written introduction thereto were included within Rabe's dictionary and Rosen's reports. Rosen even specifically requested that Hitler view the film, as it was "the most shocking documentary of its age" (German Foreign Ministry Archives: 2722/1113/38). The Soviets also quoted articles from American media. A report in Pravda reads: "Durdin, a reporter for the New York Times, has reported on Japanese atrocities committed in Nanjing. Durdin writes that the Japanese army undertook wide-scale looting, raping of women, and killing of civilians for the first two days after their occupation of Nanjing, as well as the gunning down of Chinese prisoners of war. Nanjing has become a city of terror, its streets littered with corpses" (Zhang and Yang n.d., 241).

The fourth place was the U.S., which was, naturally, the primary area of dissemination of the American perspective. The Rape of Nanking was revealed in all its facets in American mainstream media, in diplomatic reports, in reports of the Foreign Christian Missionary Society, and in private correspondence, as detailed above. When Timperley's *What War Means: the Japanese Terror in China* was published in London and New York, 300,000 copies were distributed (The Second Historical Archives of China, no. 718(4)/4711). Earl H. Leaf, British subject and overseas employee of the KMT's International Propaganda Office, contacted a Ms. Brady of the Harmon Foundation to have Magee's film screened (Wen n.d.).

George Fitch's speech tour in the U.S. is a very good example of dissemination of the American perspective. On January 24, 1938, Fitch left Nanjing for Shanghai. At the end of February, he accepted the invitation of Guangdong provincial government Chairman Wu Tiecheng to give a speech about Nanjing's events in Guangzhou; "there were no empty seats in the house." He arrived in California in early March, where he gave three speeches. "I showed the film during one speech, and it got the crowd into a great uproar." He was interviewed by the Los Angeles Times. In April Fitch arrived in Washington, where he met with Deputy Secretary of State Stanley Hornbeck and Chinese Ambassador Wang Zhengting and others. He showed Magee's film to the U.S. House Committee on Foreign Affairs, the Office of War Information, and the press in general. One Japanese present threatened Fitch: "He attached a document on me to a report to the Foreign Ministry in Tokyo." Many American commentators highly

---

[49] This report, titled "Report to German embassy to China (Hankou)" from the German embassy's Beiping bureau makes the first use of the term "Nankinger Massacre."

praised Fitch's reports. Fitch also gave speeches in New York and Chicago (Zhang 2006b, 185–188).

5.3 The Core of the American Perspective: The Truth of the Rape of Nanking

The Americans in Nanjing initially suspected that occupation by the Japanese would restore order. Vautrin wrote on December 1, 1937: "It does seem as if the end of all things is near at hand." The ensuing massacre, however, instead showed them, in George Fitch's words, "hell on earth" (Zhang 2006b, 246).[50]

First, the American perspective recorded the massacres perpetrated by the Japanese army.

When Steele left Nanjing, he estimated that between 5,000 and 20,000 soldiers had been massacred (Zhang 2006b, 96, 92). Durdin wrote in an article titled "Japanese Atrocities Marked Fall of Nanking After Chinese Command Fled" printed on January 9, 1938, in the *New York Times:* "The last thing I saw was a group of Chinese who had been executed before a city wall near the river's shore, about 300 in total. A pile nearly knee-high of corpses was already there... When departing from Xiaguan, this reporter had no choice but to drive his car through a pile of corpses five feet high. This is also how Japanese trucks and artillery pieces passed" (Yang and Zhang n.d., 516–517). Durdin affirmed the report of Steele, who wrote: "there was no hope left for the now disarmed Chinese soldiers preparing to surrender. They were searched and executed methodically... It is extremely possible that 20,000 Chinese soldiers have been thus executed" (Zhang 2005, 96, 92).

In a letter of January 9, Dr. Wilson recorded the testimony of a 17-year-old boy from January 3, 1938: on December 14, 1937, about 10,000 Chinese boys and men from 15 to 30 years old were taken to the river levee near the ferry wharf and killed, with only three surviving. About 6,000 of these had been soldiers, and the other 4,000 were civilians (Yale Divinity n.d.).

We feel particular admiration for the sense of "responsibility" borne by Americans in Nanjing, and their good intentions; these elevate the credibility of the American responsibility. Mills wrote in a letter to his wife of February 9, 1938: "we did think that the Japanese would treat unarmed men properly, and so when the men came to us, we told them that we thought that if they gave

---

50 See also Hubert Sone's "Letter to Dr. Price" (Zhang 2005, 354).

up their arms and entered one or another of the refugee camps they would be safe... They too were doubtless among the many killed" (Yale Divinity n.d., n.p.).

American government officials also received information on the Rape of Nanking. On January 21, 1938, Ambassador Johnson passed on to the embassy a secret intelligence report from the British: "the Japanese Embassy officials who reached Nanking shortly after the entry of the Japanese troops were horrified when they saw the orgy of drunkenness murder rape and robbery which was going on openly in and around the refugee zone. Failing to make any impression on the military commander, whose attitude of callous indifference makes it probable that the army was deliberately turned loose on the city as a punitive measure, and despairing of getting cables through to Tokyo owing to army control, Embassy officials had even suggested to the missionaries that the latter should try and get publicity for the facts in Japan so that the Japanese government would be forced by public opinion to curb the army" (IMTFE no. 328). Third Secretary Allison of the American embassy writes in a detailed report to the American government of February 2: "All ex-Chinese soldiers and persons suspected to have been such were systematically shot. Although no accurate records are obtainable, it is estimated that well over twenty thousand persons were executed in this manner" (IMTFE no. 328).

The death toll continued to mount. In March 1938, an American periodical in Wuhan wrote: "To date, the Japanese army has killed at least 80,000 Chinese in Nanjing" (Zhang Sheng 2005, 184). Vautrin recorded in her diary entry of April 15, 1938 data given to her by the Red Swastika Society: "From the time they were able to encoffin bodies, i.e. about the middle of January to April 14, their society had buried 1793 bodies found in the city, and of this number about 80% were civilians. Outside the city during this time they have buried 39,589 men, women, and children, and about 2.5% of this number were civilians. These figures do not include Hsia Gwan and Shan Sin Ho which we know were terrible in the loss of life."

In addition, in early 1938, American military intelligence organs intercepted and decoded some Japanese diplomatic telegrams. In a telegram of January 17, 1938 to the Japanese ambassador to the U.S., Foreign Minister Hirota quoted Timperley and included this admonishment: "I have looked into the reports of atrocities committed by the Japanese army in Nanjing and its vicinity in the last few days since my return to Shanghai. Oral records of reliable eyewitnesses and letters by people with irrefutable credibility have provided abundant evidence that the actions of the Japanese army and its continued atrocities have reminded people of Attila and his Huns. At least 300,000 Chinese civilians have been massacred."[51]

The American perspective also includes records of sexual violence by the Japanese army.

Dr. Robert Wilson was a graduate of Princeton and Harvard. To him, the Rape of Nanking was a real-life version of Dante's *Inferno*. Even after performing over a dozen surgeries, Wilson had to make several trips to Ginling Women's College at night to stand duty and protect the women there. Nevertheless, he wrote in a letter of December 18, 1937 that on the previous night, "some Japanese soldiers had climbed over the wall and helped themselves to sixteen women" (Yale Divinity n.d., n.p.). In a letter to his family of January 3, 1938, Wilson wrote: "A women of forty or so came in with the tale of having been taken from one of the refugee camps on December 31, ostensibly for the purpose of washing clothes for some officers. Six women were taken. During the days they washed clothes and during the nights they were raped. Five of them had from ten to twenty visits a night but the sixth was young and good looking, so she had about forty" (Yale Divinity n.d., n.p.).

Vautrin wrote in her diary entry of December 17, 1938: "A stream of weary wild-eyed women were coming in. Said their night had been one of horror; that again and again their homes had been visited by soldiers. (Twelve-year old girls up to sixty-year old women raped. Husbands forced to leave bedroom and pregnant wife at point of bayonet. If only the thoughtful people of Japan knew facts of these days of horror)." That very day several women were dragged off from the College sobbing. Vautrin wrote again on February 7, 1938: "It seems that in several homes out near West Flower Gate the soldiers, failing to find young girls, are using teen age boys."

---

51 *Hirota to Washington*, National Archives II of USA, Maryland. The original is stored in the National Archives II of the U.S. Mr. Ao Wang of the "Society for Maintaining the Truth of the History of the War of Resistance Against Japan" provided us with a digital copy. All parentheses and Chinese characters are contained in the original. Sun Zhaiwei thinks that this telegram "cannot be used as direct evidence that over 300,000 Chinese compatriots were killed during the Rape of Nanking during the Japanese invasion of China. However, the 'special message' of Timperley contained in the telegram is still of great value to our study of Japanese atrocities in China and the Rape of Nanking." Sun goes on to note that Hirota did not "add any comments whatsoever refuting Timperley's contents" (Sun 2005, 272–273). I personally agree with Sun's general opinion of Hirota's telegram. For more research on the "Hirota telegram," see Yang Daqing (1998). See also the letter of Timperley to Bates of March 28, 1938, referring to dispatches sent from British reporter Chancellor to London: "The foreign observer quoted in the first paragraph on that page is Father Jacquinot, who is quite certain that his figure of 300,000 Chinese civilian casualties is correct."

The consequences of rape are severe. Lewis Smythe wrote in "Notes on Present Situation in Nanking" of January 31, 1938: "Jan. 25th, afternoon a Chinese woman came to the University Hospital. She and her husband had moved into the Safety Zone and were living in a straw hut near the Bible Teachers Training School. On December 13th her husband was taken away by the Japanese soldiers and the wife, this woman, was taken to the South City where she has been ever since. She has been raped every day from 7 to 10 times since but usually was given an opportunity to sleep at night. She has developed all three types of venereal disease in their most virulent forms: syphilis, gonorrhea, chancroi" (Zhang 2006b, 211). The Safety Zone Documents include a record of a case of rape that led to death: "The 17-year old daughter of the owner of a tea house was gang raped by seven Japanese soldiers, and died on December 18... In Ping'an Alley, a girl was raped to death by Japanese soldiers" (Zhang 2006b, 296). Many women became pregnant as a result of being raped. Albert N. Steward wrote in his diary: "Accompanying the mass murders there was wholesale rape of many thousands of women in the city... During recent months many of these unfortunate women have come to the University Hospital for help, and Dr.—has relieved a number of them of their unwelcome burden" (Zhang 2005, 299–300). In addition to the obvious physical damage, rape also inflicts long-term suffering from post-traumatic stress disorder (PTSD) on its victims (Zhang 2009).

Third, the American perspective includes records of looting, arson, and other crimes.

The assignment of blame for organized looting and arson is very clear in the American perspective. Bates wrote in a letter passed on to the German embassy in Hankou: "...such looting is now happening under command of high-ranking Japanese officers, and there is organized destruction of shops of a large area" (Zhang 2005, 290). Smythe wrote in a letter to friends of March 8, 1938: "On the 20th of December when Mr. Fitch and I drove around the southern part of the city in the gathering dusk and found the Japanese Army systematically taking the remaining goods out of stores and loading it in Army trucks, then setting fire to the buildings we realized that it was deliberate destruction rather than accidental" (Zhang 2005, 278).

On December 25, 1937, the American government received information that the Japanese army had entered all buildings in the city except those occupied by foreigners, systematically looting both civilian homes and stores, and causing great destruction to Chinese property across the city, in addition to indiscriminate shooting and killing (FRUS IV, 414–415).

Looting and arson resulted in major property losses. A report of the Nanking International Relief Committee titled *War Relief in Nanking (April 30, 1938)* read:

"Here we mention only that 31% of all buildings in Nanking were burned; and a higher percentage of shops; that the direct loss by military destruction and looting in Nanking approached $100,000,000.00 that the farm areas along the main roads near to Nanking were practically stripped, and amid shortage of seed, animals, labor, and tools, they are planting only 10% of the usual rice crop" (Yale Divinity n.d., n.p.).

Fourth, the American perspective revealed the organized sale of drugs by the Japanese army as well as the establishment of "comfort stations."

Bates was the primary reporter on the organized sale of drugs by the Japanese army. In his "An Open Letter: On the Narcotic Problem," he estimated that the Japanese army "takes away from the impoverished population of this region a minimum of $5,000,000 monthly, reducing their buying power for decent goods and their ability to do productive labor of any kind." Bates went on to note the close link between the Japanese army's Special Service Organ and the sale of heroin, sarcastically writing that "the first and greatest achievement of Sino-Japanese co-operation in this important region is the poisoning of the common people" (Zhang 2005, 42–45). Bates was also sensitive to advertisements for comfort stations posted around the city by the Japanese army. In the article "Brothels are Political Tools in 'the New Order in East Asia,'" Bates attached a photograph of an advertisement for a comfort station in Nanjing, advertising "Chinese beauties," authorized by "base camp authorities," located at "No. 4 Hall for friendly relations between Japan and China." Bates continued: "Residents of the occupied areas know that the Japanese Army cannot exist without vice, and plenty of it" (Zhang 2005, 36).

Fifth, the American perspective documented the destruction of the living environment of Nanjing by the Japanese army.

At the time, "the corpses of soldiers and civilians cruelly murdered by the enemy Japanese were everywhere inside and outside the city, raising a horrid stench to the heavens, causing a sanitation hazard and also representing a violation of humanity... After the ravages of war came the ravages of epidemic. No public or private hospitals or clinics have returned to normal, and so the sick have nowhere to seek treatment" (Nanjing Municipal Archives no. 1024-1-34512).[52] Smythe wrote in "Notes on Present Situation" of January 31, 1938: "The ponds are polluted by corpses, which has greatly reduced or rather eliminated the sources of drinking water to the Safety Zone. The danger of this situa-

---

[52] The Red Cross of Nanjing was chaired by John Magee and comprised 10 American members, including Vautrin, Forster, Wilson, Trimmer, McCallum, Bates, Smythe, and Mills. See the list of members of the Red Cross of Nanjing in Zhang (2006b), 272.

tion in the long term is great, particularly in dry times" (Zhang 2006b, 326). Ido Naojiro, a Japanese soldier stationed in Nanjing at the time, confirmed Smythe's observation: "When we were cooking rice in our mess tins at night, we discovered that the water in the small rivers was very red. We had no choice but to use the water to cook our rice, which also became red. We ate it. We only noticed the morning of the next day that the little river was full of dead bodies, and that the water had been dyed red by their blood" (Matsuoka 2002; CN, 244–246).

Sixth, the American perspective recorded the Japanese army's measures to cover up their crimes.

Smythe wrote of the farce put on by the Japanese in his letter to friends of March 8, 1938: "We now better understand Japanese news propaganda... a Japanese news team enacted a farce in which children were given candy and a Japanese doctor gave 20 children a physical. Why are these scenes not reenacted when the cameras are not present!?" (Zhang 2005, 283).

The Japanese army also used the *Sin Shun Pao* newspaper in Shanghai to clean up the image of Nanjing, then currently in the midst of massacre. The Americans in Nanjing made records of this as well, as demonstrated in the translation to English of one article from December 28, 1937, titled "Nanking Nan Ming Chu – Order Recovered – All shops opened for business": "The Nan Ming Chu [Safety Zone] contains more than one hundred thousand refugees who are now beginning to be very kindred with the officers and soldiers clothed in black-yellow uniforms. Now, a great many of shops have been opened and their business is very busy and prosperous... Refugees' children who have never before seen Japanese soldiers crowd to look at the soldiers around" (Yale Divinity n.d., n.p.). Vautrin wrote on January 21, 1938 of another article that appeared in the same newspaper on January 8, titled "Japanese Troops Gently Soothe the Refugees; the Harmonious Atmosphere of Nanking City Develops Enjoyably": "There are 25 sentences in the article, 4 sentences are true, one about the sun, the Drum Tower, military police and the position of the Japanese flag; one is half true, 19 are false, and one is unknown to me."

Seventh, the American perspective provided testimony on the truth of the Rape of Nanking to the Tokyo and Nanjing trials.

The sworn statement provided by Smythe to the Tokyo trials confirmed that during the first six weeks of the Japanese occupation of Nanjing, he and Rabe submitted two letters of protest almost daily to the Japanese embassy detailing abuses of civilians and disarmed Chinese soldiers by the Japanese army. Smythe and Rabe took turns signing the letters, of which they submitted one in person and had the other delivered by courier. Smythe wrote: "In the almost daily conferences that Mr. Rabe and I had with the Japanese Embassy, they at no time denied the accuracy of these reports" (IMTFE no. 306). Fitch wrote in his sworn affidavit: "Many hundreds of innocent civilians are taken out before your eyes to be shot or used for bayonet practice." He continued: "On December 15, I saw approximately 1300 men, all in civilian clothes, just taken from one of our camps near our headquarters, lined up and roped together in groups of about 100 by soldiers with fixed bayonets. In spite of my protests to the commanding officer, they were marched off to be shot." Of December 20 he wrote: "I saw many Japanese army trucks being loaded with the loot which they were taking from the shops before setting fire to them." He wrote that anyone with "callouses on hands or cropped heads" were deemed to be soldiers and executed. He also recounted how ponds, streets, and houses were full of dead bodies, mostly men, some women, but "all dressed in civilian clothes" (IMTFE no. 307). The diary of James McCallum was also submitted to the Tokyo trials as evidence. In it he detailed massacres, rapes, and other atrocities. In his entry of January 1, 1938, he estimated that about 30% of houses between the Gulou Hospital to Zhongzheng Road and Baixia Road were destroyed, and possibly less beyond. He wrote that not many houses were destroyed in the "extreme southern part" of the city, but he estimated 20 to 30% destroyed between the south side of the Drum Tower to the eastern wall, "concentrated in certain areas" (IMFTE No. 309).

Three cases provided in a sworn statement by Lewis Smythe, three by Charles Riggs, and 22 by George Fitch were used as evidence against Tani Hisao in the Nanjing trials (Hu 2006, 79–80). Another two people who were "foreign professors of the University of Nanking" and who worked in the Safety Zone also testified, demonstrating the veracity of their documents and reports on Japanese atrocities (Hu 2006, 352).[53]

5.4 The American Perspective and American Interests

A great deal of emphasis has been placed on the humanitarian contributions made by Americans during the Rape of Nanking, and I do not think they have gone too far. Nevertheless, we must not forget that tangible American interests lay at the foundations of the American perspective.

As noted above, the activities of the Americans during the Rape of Nanking were largely limited to the Safety Zone and its immediate environs. One reason was that American property in Nanjing at the time was largely concentrated in this area, including religious universities, middle schools, primary schools, hos-

---

[53] This document does not give names; we infer it refers to Bates and Smythe.

pitals, the American embassy, the majority of private American residences, commercial organs, and other forms of property. The only reason I have been able to discern that the Britisher Shields was originally a member of the International Committee but did not join in its work, from the many documents available, is that he did not want his name associated with the other Westerners involved. As his factory had not been included within the Safety Zone, Cabot Coville wrote that Shields complained that the Safety Zone's "true goal was to protect the property of Americans, Germans, and rich Chinese" (Zhang 2006b, 82–83). Despite the slanderous nature of his comment, it does reflect the fact that most American property was included within the Safety Zone.

Bates referred to himself in a letter to Timperley of March 3, 1938, as "the most strenuous reporter from the University" (Zhang 2005, 32). His letters are an excellent starting point for understanding the core concerns of the American perspective.

Bates wrote a series of letters of protest detailing atrocities by the Japanese army to the Japanese embassy from December 16 to 27, 1938. In order of time, the letters tell us the following: on the 14th, Japanese soldiers tore down the American flag and notice from the American embassy from the University of Nanking's department of agricultural economics and looted the premises. On the 15th, Japanese soldiers raped or abducted women from the university's library building, with over 100 such cases cited. On the 16th, Japanese soldiers raped more than 30 women in the department of agricultural economics. On the 17th, Japanese soldiers robbed refugees and raped women in the library, physically assaulted American employees and guards, and broke into private residences of American citizens flying American flags with American embassy notices attached to them. On the 18th, Japanese soldiers harmed children, beat employees, raped eight women, and teared down the American flags in the university's attached middle school; soldiers raped six other women on the university grounds and threatened Bates with a gun. On the 21st, Japanese soldiers abducted seven women from the library building; gang raped a woman in front of the entrance to the Japanese embassy at Number 4 Toutiao Alley (author's note: abutting the University of Nanking); broke into and looted Bates' house; beat three and raped one woman before looting Anleli, neighboring the university; raped women at the Gaojia Tavern (author's note: about 500 meters from the university); broke into the University Hospital; abducted girls from Wutaishan (abutting the university and Ginling Women's College); and tore up an American flag at Wutaishan. On the 22nd, Japanese soldiers abducted 11 people from the university library; stabbed the watchman; looted university dormitories; raped women in a group of seven soldiers in the Bible Teachers' Training School; broke indoors at the department of agricultural economics and seized the watchman; and fired three shots into a group of refugees in the sericulture department. On the 25th, Japanese soldiers broke into the university, robbed refugees, and stole vehicles; had raped more than 10 women per day in the sericulture department; beat American colleagues and tore off their arm badges; and completely ignored notices posted by the Japanese embassy. On the 27th, Japanese soldiers stole the American flag from the Rural Teachers' Training School; abducted three women from the campus and raped them, including one girl of 11; abducted several university servants and watchmen; broke into two American private residences, and raped 27 women in the Bible Teachers' Training School. We can see that the majority of cases reported took place in American-owned property, that is in places of American interests. His letters in effect are reminding the Japanese to abide by their promise to "protect foreign property" (The Second Historical Archives of China, no. 718(5)/14).

American property outside of the Safety Zone similarly consumed a great deal of the energies of Americans in Nanjing. Ernest Forster, for example, was extremely busy, participating in the work of both the Red Cross and the Gulou Hospital. His affiliated church, the Episcopalian church, included a residential area located on Baixia Road and a church area on Taiping Road, both outside the Safety Zone. Per his statistics, he made 12 visits to these properties, on December 11, December 14, December 17, December 23, and December 26 of 1937 and January 10, January 15, January 17, January 26, January 27, February 2, and February 3 of 1938, in addition to the "several" times he did not specifically record between January 17 and 26, 1938, and once in February. In a report to the American embassy of March 10, 1938, Forster wrote conclusively: "it is my firm conviction that the damage to our buildings and the looting was done by Japanese and not by Chinese". His report included damages to bicycles, pianos, bathtubs, beds, mattresses, chairs, and so on (Yale Divinity n.d.). It is hard for us today to not feel a sense of imbalance regarding Forster's detailed records of furniture at a time when Chinese people were being massacred wholesale in the city, but this does demonstrate Forster's high degree of concern for American interests.

Church property, of such great concern to the Americans in Nanjing, was an important component of American interests in the city. We should first note that all the Americans in the city felt that using church resources to provide relief to Chinese refugees was worth doing. Bates and Mills write in a joint report titled *Preliminary Report on Christian Work in Nanking:* "The resultant wear and tear upon buildings has been heavy, and repair bills for this item will be large. But repair bills of this sort can perhaps be paid with satisfaction because of the tremendous service which the buildings have rendered to the people at this time of crisis. Never have the buildings been more useful than in these recent months"

(Yale Divinity n.d., n.p.). We should also note that after the massacre, the Americans in Nanjing continued to spread the gospel and build up their flocks as the most important aspects of their work.

In subjective terms, they saw Nanjing's crisis as an opportunity for their religious work. Vautrin wrote on September 18, 1938, about her weighing the pros and cons of staying: "Our greatest investments are in friendly relationships and in cooperation with the members of a young church – to leave at the time when we are most needed seems to me to be missing one of the greatest opportunities for service which comes to us." She goes on to write about the great pride she felt in her decision to stay: "A long expected day has come in my Mission career, when women who are bearing special responsibility are treated as men who are carrying special responsibility – and we are not required to leave at the same time as mothers with children." She also wrote that day of how Smythe criticized the missionaries leaving the city, using the word "running – the word used by Madame Chiang." Bates wrote in a letter to his wife of November 14, 1937: "My teaching is not very interesting under these conditions, but there is plenty of special missionary work at this time" (Yale Divinity n.d., n.p.).

In terms of concrete actions, missionary work was the foundation of the vast majority of documents of the American perspective. Space constraints prevent us from listing all examples, but one needs only to examine Vautrin's diary entries in the month of April 1938, in particular the days of the 3rd to the 6th, the 8th, the 10th to the 18th, the 24th, the 25th, and the 28th, on which days she organized ten separate religious activities. So the humanitarian relief and the religious activities of the Americans in Nanjing were closely linked; this is another important characteristic of American interests represented under the American perspective. If we try to understand them separately, we easily arrive at one of two extreme conclusions: they were believers in fairy tales, or they were on the war path for guilty parties to reproach.

American officials lay identical emphasis on American property as private citizens and church groups. A report from President Roosevelt to the Secretary of State of January 21, 1938, detailing the Allison incident, read: "Few Americans can object to our protection of Americans against an army which is out of the control of its own civilian government at home" (FRUS IV, 396). On February 21, Ambassador Johnson gave orders on handling disputes with the Japanese, citing a memo from Hull and Grew, for which these two gave permission to send a formal copy to the Japanese foreign ministry. The gist of the report was that the Japanese army's behavior made it impossible to deem it a well-controlled military organization, and as for the destruction caused thereby, "full indemnification will be made for losses and damages inflicted" (IMTFE no. 328).

The Japanese government declared multiple times that as it had repeatedly warned Americans to leave the battle zone, it would not bear responsibilities for damages or losses sustained by American organizations or individuals owing to warfare and inability to follow the instructions of the Japanese army. In response, American Ambassador Grew in Japan wrote a hardline letter to Foreign Minister Hirota on February 21, 1938: "American nationals, although advised by American authorities to withdraw from areas in which danger exists, are under no obligation to do so, and in some cases find withdrawal impossible; American property situated in areas which are made or which are about to be made theaters of military operations can in most cases not be removed; this is obviously the case as regards real property... In the light of these facts and considerations, failure on the part of American officials or nationals to have complied with the requests of the Imperial forces under the circumstances affords no excuse for injury which has occurred or which may occur to American nationals or property by Japanese armed forces; and any such injury, as has been stated in my note No. 781 of August 27, 1937, is considered by the American Government as upon the responsibility of the Japanese Government" (Yang 2010, 396–397).

It is noteworthy that the American government demanded not only that Japan respect its interests in China, but also that the Chinese government do so. In a cable from Ambassador Johnson to Secretary of State Hull of August 25, 1937, Johnson detailed that the British government wrote a note to the Chinese government reading "His Majesty's Government must reserve all their rights as regards holding the Chinese Government responsible for damage to or loss of either life or property that may be incurred by subjects of His Majesty as a result of action taken by Chinese forces in the course of the present hostilities in China" and requesting "that the Department instruct me as to whether similar action should be taken by us" (FRUS IV, 281). On January 10, 1938, Johnson, taking Allison's advice, wrote a letter to the Chinese foreign minister, demanding that the Chinese air force take precautions to protect American property in the case it undertook actions there (Yang 2010, 312–313). So there were no differences in treatment of Chinese and Japanese when it came to American interests.

Although both private citizens and government officials laid stress on American interests, there were still some disparities between them, for three reasons. First, the private citizens living in the city referred to themselves as "old citizens of Nanking" (Zhang Kaiyuan 2005, 5). They directly observed and experienced the suffering of Chinese residents there, and hoped for a rapid turnaround in conditions there. Second, the private citizens had observed Sino-Japanese relations from up close for many years, and had profound insights into Japan's expansive ambitions. In a *National Affairs* article on the explosive nature of Sino-Japanese relations and its influence on the rest of the world of October 1936,

Bates wrote: "Every friend of the two nations must still desire reason and time and conciliation. When once the military way is taken, the East can hardly be turned from a fearful series of conflicts running through the decades to the ruin of China and Japan alike. There is also no small danger of the ultimate involvement of Russia and perhaps of other nations with great interests in the Pacific; while the common policies of Japan and Germany make anxious connections with uneasy Europe" (Yale Divinity n.d., n.p.). George Fitch wrote in a diary entry later included in a *Reader's Digest* article of July 1938: "the Japanese army, with no background of Christian idealism, has today become a brutal, destructive force that not only menaces the East but also may menace the West someday" (Zhang 2005, 202). Their hopes were that the American government would intervene before a crisis set in. By comparison, American government officials continued a course of appeasement even after American interests had been infringed upon by Japan. Commander in Chief of the U.S. Asiatic Fleet Yarnell wrote in a letter of December 26, 1937 to the Secretary of State: "I have heard it stated that the real Japanese policy is to drive out of Shanghai all commercial interests except their own. This I cannot believe, since it is directly contrary to the repeated statements of the Japanese Government" (FRUS IV, 416–417). Third, a factor that directly struck the nerves of American private citizens was the presence of an extremely obvious and extremely immoral happening in Nanjing: despite stern rebukes of the brazen acts of the Japanese army by high-ranking American officials, the American government continued to provide essential support for the operations of Japanese war machinery, as noted by Allison in a letter to the Secretary of State of November 18, 1938 (Yang 2010, 471).

Why would the American government act in that way? Strong isolationist forces within the country were the key reason. The Japanese were thoroughly aware of this point. A secret telegram from the Japanese embassy in the U.S. to the Foreign Ministry in Tokyo read: "The attitude of the American public has always been and now still is that the U.S. must avoid becoming embroiled in foreign wars no matter the cost" (Yang 2010, 509).[54] In addition, President Roosevelt even openly questioned whether China could last the winter in a meeting with Chinese Ambassador Hu Shih on October 12, 1937. Hu asked for instructions from Nanjing on this point. Chiang Kai-shek responded that China would keep fighting even if the capital fell, that China would not only last out the winter, but would last into the distant future (FRUS III, 711).

---

[54] Most satirically, this telegram was decoded by the American government, but it was unable to make changes at that time.

On October 13, 1937, Chiang Kai-shek and Soong Mei-ling met with Ambassador Johnson. The following day Johnson wrote in a report to the Secretary of State: "General Chiang asked me to convey to you his firm belief that the decisions of the [Geneva] Conference would be determined by the position taken by the United States. He said it was clear that the British Government for one was waiting to follow the lead of the American Government" (FRUS IV, 75–76). On November 8, Chiang held a press conference where he declared that China's resolve to resist the invaders would remain unabated "until justice is reestablished in this part of the world" (FRUS IV, 166–167). Roosevelt wrote in a letter to Secretary of State Hull of November 30: "I think we should seek in every way possible to avoid helping one side and not the other" (FRUS III, 736).

On the afternoon of December 12, 1937, the USS Panay was sunk near Nanjing in a Japanese air raid. Admiral Yarnell, commander of the U.S. Asiatic Fleet, described the attack as coming "without warning" (Yang 2010, 246–249). Secretary of State Hull wrote in a letter of December 13 that the Japanese even admitted that the bombing had been a "very grave blunder" (FRUS IV, 496). Most unexpectedly, the U.S. took receipt of Japan's indemnification for the bombing of the Panay in the amount of $2,214,007.36 on April 22 (Yang 2010). The handling of the Panay incident and the results of that process demonstrated the hard stance taken by the American government in previous diplomatic correspondence had been empty posturing, that the true American intention was to remain neutral in the fight (of course, some individuals in the American government expressed concerns about the actual support the U.S. was providing to Japan in the form of sales of motorized equipment) (Yang 2010).

The patient forbearance of American officials fueled the aggressiveness of the Japanese army, which was subsequently released on Nanjing. Per a U.S. embassy report, General Amaya, commander of the Japanese garrison at Nanjing, held a meeting with foreign diplomats, in which he expressed the following: "in Nanking interference by foreigners which encouraged continuance of anti-Japanese feeling amongst the local Chinese population, had hindered a return to normal and large numbers of Chinese continued to live in the so-called 'Safety Zone.' He referred particularly to reports and activities of nationals of a 'certain country' which were damaging relations between Japan and that country. (This obviously refers to the United States). The general expressed dislike of the attitude of a judge in a law court taken by the foreigners and warned them that their criticisms and interference between Chinese and Japanese would anger the Japanese troops and might lead to some unpleasant incident" (IMTFE no. 328).

Bates was furious over the tolerance and indulgence of the American government, writing in a November 1937 article for the magazine *Public Affairs:* "It will be possible [for Japan] even to burn with contempt the torn fragments of the Nine-Power Treaty. For Japan counts upon the isolationism of the United States, combined with American willingness to sell essential supplies ('even to the Devil if he pays cash')" (Yale Divinity n.d., n.p.). Forster did not want the U.S. to become embroiled in the conflict, but he wrote in a letter to his family of February 10, 1938: "if England and America had adopted other measures – economic or political pressure, for instance, Japan would never have dared to go as far as she has. The time for such action, should have been in 1931 when Japan was permitted to begin her career of madness that is causing such havoc now" (Yale Divinity, n.d., n.p.). The willingness of American missionaries to negotiate with the Japanese army completely unarmed, to demand an end to atrocities, and to reveal the truth of the Rape of Nanking to the outside world, were all extreme manifestations of "intervention." It is clear that although American private citizens and government officials alike were concerned with American interests, they differed in thinking on exactly how to protect those interests. It is precisely for these reasons that in a report from the Japanese embassy in Washington to Tokyo, the author wrote of the effect of the bombing of the Panay and atrocities in Nanjing on changes in public sentiment in the U.S., that "the influence of American missionaries in China on public thought" was seen as an important reason for "intensified anti-Japan feelings" among the American public" (Yang 2010, 509– 510).

American interests were the point of departure for American actions, but these actions served to restrain the Japanese army and provide support to helpless soldiers and civilians in Nanjing in and around the time of the Rape of Nanking. Looking further, we see that American interests in Nanjing and other parts of China at the time were grounded in the treaty system, logically a negative factor impeding China from achieving full territorial sovereignty and national independence, yet because the U.S. was seen as providing useful assistance in resisting the Japanese invasion of China, that country's presence was viewed as positive, and there were repeated calls for it to take action.[55] So the emphasis on

---

55 In a letter of October 11, 1937 to President Roosevelt, Chinese Ambassador Wang Zhengting (C.T. Wang) highly praises the president's speech in Chicago, writing: "It is my sincere hope that America under your leadership will lead the world in taking active and effective measures to safeguard world peace and democracy" (FRUS III, 595–596). In a letter of December 24, Chiang Kai-shek writes to President Roosevelt: "We are fighting for the liberty of the Chinese nation and against the common menace to the humanity as a whole. We are not only defending ourselves, but also the principle of the sanctity of treaties especially the Nine Power Treaty... On behalf of the Chinese people, I therefore take liberty at this critical moment of urgently appealing to Your Excellency and, through you, the American people to render such effective assistance to China

American interests within the American perspective was subject to very little revile on the part of Chinese, and was rather quite welcomed.

As stated above, the American perspective does not give the entire picture when it comes to estimating the actual scale of the massacre. However, the third-party standpoint it represents had effects even at the time the event was unfolding. Ishii Itaro, former director of the East Asian Affairs Bureau of Japan's Ministry of Foreign Affairs, testified at the Tokyo trials that after Japan had occupied Nanjing, the first telegram sent out by acting Consul-General Fukui Kiyoshi, just arrived from Shanghai, was about atrocities committed by the Japanese army in Nanjing; this telegram was immediately sent to the Japanese Ministry of the Army. The telegram was highly alarming and concerning to then Foreign Minister Hirota, who demanded that these undignified acts be immediately covered up. Later, after Fukui's telegram had been sent out, it was determined that a third party in Nanjing had originally written it in English. Military officials announced that a stern warning had been issued. The atrocities ended only with the arrival of Major General Honma to Nanjing in January the following year. He even heard Foreign Minister Hirota say he had asked Minister of the Army Sugiyama to take major emergency measures regarding conditions in Nanjing (IMTFE no. 3287). When asked if he took international reports on atrocities in Nanjing as true during his cross-examination, Itaro answered: "We considered most of them to be facts" (Yang 2006, 509, 519). The reports of American missionaries were taken as facts, demonstrating that the American perspective caused Japanese officials to "discover" the Rape of Nanking as it was ongoing.

After summer 1938, however, the American perspective made extremely few mentions of the Rape of Nanking. The U.S. "rediscovered" the event after the outbreak of the Pacific War, linking Japanese atrocities in China with the conspiracy to subjugate the U.S. (United States Defense Savings Bonds and Stamps). After the war, it was the U.S. that first revealed the truth behind the Rape of Nanking. All manner of American perspective documents were used in the Tokyo and Nanjing trials, becoming important evidence in clarifying Japan's responsibility for the invasion of China and the subsequent war (Hu 2006, 79–80; IMTFE no. 309; Yang 2006, 41, 77, 110). Thus the American perspective transcends the history of China, and is rather significant at the global level.

After the onset of the Cold War, the U.S. no longer saw revelation of Japanese atrocities in Nanjing as a primary duty. In mainland China, the outbreak of the Korean War completely changed the views of the role played by Westerners dur-

---

as will enable the struggle for the cause of world peace and solidarity to be carried on to a successful conclusion at an early date" (FRUS III, 832–833).

ing the Rape of Nanking, particularly of Americans (Liu Yanjun). The American perspective was again relegated to the dust heap. Since documents of the American perspective were rediscovered by American, Japanese, and Chinese scholars in the 1980s, the history of the Rape of Nanking has grown greatly deeper.[56]

We can thus conclude that like the history of the Rape of Nanking, the American perspective has undergone repeated "discoveries" and "rediscoveries," and has ultimately become a part of humanity's shared memory of war.[57]

---

[56] This "discovery" touched on many more nuanced layers. For example, the battlefield diary of a Japanese soldier was discovered in the U.S. National Archives, in which he writes that he mowed down more than 80 people with machine gun fire "on orders" in the vicinity of Changzhou. This demonstrates that "massacre orders" existed even before the occupation of Nanjing. The document was, however, labeled "unimportant" at the time of its filing. See *Field Diary kept by member of Japanese medical corps*, National Archives II of USA, Maryland.
[57] The contents of this chapter were originally published in *Lishi yanjiu* 5 (2012) under the title "Meiguo wenben jilu de Nanjing da tusha" [The Rape of Nanking in American Records]. Some changes and additions were made for its inclusion in this book.

6 The Rape of Nanking in Japanese Historical Sources

From the announcement of Japan's unconditional surrender on August 15, 1945 to the occupation of Japan by General Douglas MacArthur's forces, the Japanese government systematically burned or disposed of wartime archives at a grand scale, such that at the time of the Tokyo Trials, some records requested by the court with the files related to the Rape of Nanking were among the "missing," owing to their sensitive nature.

Nevertheless, a great quantity of Japanese-related archives survived the purge, and provide us with abundant evidence despite the massive "clean-up" effort. In addition to official documents, we have access to abundant stores of diaries, correspondence, and battle reports of Japanese officers and soldiers, unit histories, reports in Japanese newspapers, memoirs, and so on. More are still being discovered to this day.

A deep reading of these Japanese documents is indispensable to our organization of overt evidence for the Rape of Nanking, for uncovering hidden evidence, and for poking holes in the arguments of the event's deniers.

6.1 Japanese Military Archives

6.1.1 Battle plans and battle orders

The vast majority of Japanese military documents were burned when Japan surrendered in 1945. The majority of documents not destroyed were obtained by the U.S., or went into the possession of former officers or soldiers. After negotiations, the U.S. returned the documents it had obtained to Japan in April 1958, the majority of which are now stored in the library of Japan's National Institute for Defense Studies. The library has also collected some military documents that had been in civilian possession. The library now possesses over 81,000 Imperial Japanese Army documents and 35,000 Imperial Japanese Navy documents. After the war, some military documents on the siege of Nanjing and the Rape of Nanking were compiled into a book, publicly issued in Japan.

The book *Nanjing zhan shi ziliao ji* [Compilation of Nanjing war history materials] compiled and edited by the "Nanjing War History Compilation Commit-

---

Note: Chapter contributed by Wang Weixing

https://doi.org/10.1515/9783110652789-009

tee" and published by Kaikosha (of Japan) in November 1989 is the compilation containing the most Japanese military documents. Kaikosha in December 1993 Kaikosha released an expanded and revised edition with two volumes, the majority of military documents concentrated in the first volume, including documents from the central government documents (the Army Ministry, the Imperial Japanese Army General Staff Office, etc.), the Central China Expeditionary Army, the Shanghai Expeditionary Force (SEF), the 10th Army, and individual divisions, battalions, and companies, as well as detailed battle reports, battlefield orders, and combat diaries. The battle plans and orders contained in them clearly show the evolution of Japanese strategic goals following the August 13 Incident, which started the Battle of Shanghai.

On November 11, 1937, two days after the landing of the Japanese 10th Army at Hangzhou Bay, the Imperial Japanese Army General Staff Office issued "General Staff Office order 138," creating the Central China Area Army, merging the Shanghai Expeditionary Force with the 10th Army, and appointing Matsui Iwane commander of the Central China Area Army (Nanjing War History Editing and Compilation Committee I n.d., 427).

After the Japanese army had occupied Shanghai, the nationalist government issued its "Declaration on Moving the Capital to Chongqing" on November 20, indicating China's continued resolve to carry on fighting. The Japanese advanced in a blitzkrieg-like rush, accomplishing the strategic objectives of the "China Incident," which they prosecuted rapidly. Accordingly the Central China Area Army's general staff headquarters issued "Opinions on Operations in the Central China Area Going Forward" on November 11. The Opinions read: "The Nanjing government has decided to move the capital after suffering a major defeat in the Battle to the East of the Lake,[58] leaving only commanding organs in Nanjing. Their first-line defenders have clearly lost the ability to fight. Enemy resistance on all battlefields is extremely weak. It is hard to determine whether the enemy intends to hold Nanjing. Their forces along the front line from Suzhou to Jiaxing have lost their fighter planes, causing a reinvigoration of their spirits and preparations to restore fighting capacity... We must quickly resolve the incident and with no doubt we must consider opening new battle theaters in the Southwest Area or in Shandong, but despite the considerable value of the influence such a strategy would impose on the Chinese government, the significance of capturing the enemy capital and crushing their hearts would be far greater... If, in the taking of Nanjing, we use crack troops from the Area Army (assembling as many units as necessary) and make full use of railways and waterways, we

---

[58] Battles to the east of Lake Tai.

can guarantee safety in the rear. In addition, once the enemy resistance at Wuxi and Huzhou has been put down, there should not be great losses to our forces, based on our observations of geography and normal installations. We estimate that the objective can be reached within two months." The Opinions reach this conclusion: "The Central China Area Army needs to capture Nanjing while enemy forces are on their back foot in order to quickly resolve the incident" (Nanjing War History Editing and Compilation Committee n.d., 430–431).

On November 24, the Central China Area Army formulated the "Central China Area Army Phase Two Master Battle Plan." The Plan covered six areas, including the overall battle plan, command essentials, battle preparations, unit deployments, coordination between army and navy, and army depots transportation and communications. The Plan read: "The Central China Area Army will coordinate with the China Area Fleet to quickly capture Nanjing… One portion of the Area Army will advance on Nanjing from the rear by the left bank of the Yangtze River from the direction of Wuhu, with primary forces advancing from Danyang along the railway to Jurong, and another force advancing from Huzhou to Yixing to Liyang to Lishui to meet the primary force. These forces will annihilate the enemy's field army outside Nanjing's forts and then capture Nanjing" (Nanjing War History Editing and Compilation Committee n.d., 431).

On December 1, the Japanese Imperial General Headquarters Chief of the Army General Staff issued "Continental Order Number 7," clarifying the battle array of the Central China Area Army. The same body also issued "Continental Order Number 8" that same day, reading: "The Central China Area Army should coordinate with the navy to attack the enemy capital of Nanjing" (Nanjing War History Editing and Compilation Committee n.d., 428). Upon receipt of these orders, Matsui Iwane then issued his own orders to the Central China Area army at 7 p.m., those orders reading:

1. The Central China Area Army plans to coordinate an attack to capture Nanjing with the China Area Fleet.

2. The main force of the Shanghai Expeditionary Force will begin actions around December 5th. They will maintain their thrust in the areas of Danyang and Jurong, defeating enemies before them, and advancing to the area of the western Mopan mountain range.

Another force will attack the enemy in the rear from the left bank of the Yangtze River and will cut off the Tianjin-Pukou Railway and the Grand Canal to the north of the river.

3. The main force of the 10th Army will begin actions around December 3. One section will advance to the rear of Nanjing from the direction of Wuhu, and the main force will annihilate enemies before it and advance to the vicinity of Lishui (Nanjing War History Editing and Compilation Committee n.d., 432).

By December 9, the Japanese army had advanced to outside of the city and surrounded it. On this day the Japanese army dropped "letters exhorting surrender" on the city giving the deadline as noon of the 10th, or else a general assault would be launched.

On December 10, after the deadline passed with no answer from the Chinese, Matsui issued "China Central Area Army battle command number 34": "One, the Chinese army has not accepted our exhortations and is still resisting stubbornly. Two, the Shanghai Expeditionary Army and 10th Army should continue the assault on Nanjing and then sweep the city for remnant forces" (Nanjing War History Editing and Compilation Committee I n.d., 435).

Upon receipt of Matsui's orders, the Shanghai Expeditionary Army and the 10th Army each issued their own orders to enter and sweep the city. At noon on December 13, the 9th Division of the Shanghai Expeditionary Army issued "9th Division Order 131 A," the essentials of which were as follows:

One. The army is to carry out a sweep inside the city of Nanjing.

Two. The Division is responsible for sweeping a sector of the city (see 9th Division Order No. 130). We are to act in accordance with the following in the demarcated combat zone with the 10th Army and the 16th Division. Between the 10th Army and the 9th Division: the line running from Gonghe Gate (Tongji Gate) – Gongyuan Road – Zhongzheng Street – Zhongzheng Road – Hanzhong Road. The Gonghe Gate belongs to the 10th Army; the rest belongs to our division.

Between the 9th Division and the 16th Division: the line running from Zhongbu Bridge (800 meters south of the Zhongshan Gate) – the rivers between the Waiwulong Bridge – the antique depository (800 meters to the west of Zhongshan Gate) – Zhongshan Road (to Zhongshan Wharf). The line belongs to our division, can use Zhongshan Gate and Zhongshan Road.

Three. The right flank is now the city-sweeping unit; this unit should be responsible for the Division's sweep zone in the city per the attached main points. Orders will be given when the opportunity to begin the sweep arises (Nanjing War History Editing and Compilation Committee I n.d., 441).

Upon receipt of the Division's orders, the 6th Infantry Battalion of the 9th Division, serving as right flank, issued "6th Battalion Order 138 A": "One. The right flank is the Division's sweeping unit and should sweep within the Division's zone of responsibility. A light armored vehicle company and an engineering platoon will be dispatched in reinforcement, and the 35th Infantry Regiment (less a battalion) will return to its original unit. Two. The 7th Infantry Regiment [apportioned a tank company (less one platoon), and an engineering company (less one platoon)] is the sweeping unit in the northern sector, responsible for sweeping its zone of responsibility (to be assigned separately). Three. The 35th Infantry Regiment (less one company. Apportioned one light armored vehicle company, the independent 3rd Machine Gun Company, and an engineering platoon) is the sweeping unit in the southern sector, responsible for sweeping its zone of responsibility (see attached instructions)" (Nanjing War History Editing and Compilation Committee n.d., 444).

Upon receipt of the Battalion's orders, the 7th Infantry Regiment of the 9th Division issued "7th Infantry Order No. 105": "One. The right flank is the Division's sweeping unit and is to sweep its zone of responsibility. Two. The Regiment (apportioned a motorized company and an engineering company (less one platoon)] is the sweeping unit in the northern sector, and is to begin sweeping immediately. Three. All battalions (each apportioned an engineering unit) are responsible for sweeping areas indicated in the appendix with two thirds of the troops. Four. The Motorized Company (apportioned two platoons commanded by the engineering platoon leader) are responsible for sweeping areas indicated in the appendix" (Wang, Ye et al. n.d., 120). This Regiment subsequently issued multiple orders to continue the sweep. As the area of responsibility of this Regiment included the International Safety Zone, clearer orders were issued at 8:30 a.m. on December 15: "One. As of today, the 15, searches of prisoners have revealed mostly low-ranking officers and enlisted men, nearly no officers above the grade of lieutenant. Higher-ranking officers seem to have all changed into civilian clothes and slipped into the refugee zone. Two. Tomorrow, the 16, the Regiment will perform a thorough sweep of the refugee zone in full force. Three. Starting tomorrow, the 16, all battalions will perform sweeps of their areas of responsibility, particularly a continued sweep of the refugee zone" (Wang 2007b, 124).

The 16th Division of the Shanghai Expeditionary Force also issued a "sweep" order during the occupation of Nanjing. Upon receipt of the Division's orders, the 30th Infantry Battalion (the Sasaki Detachment) issued a "Right Flank Detachment Order" at 5:35 p.m. on the 13: "One. Enemy forces to be completely annihilated. The Detachment is to occupy the Heping Gate, all gates to the west of that position, and Xiaguan, and completely block all routes to evacuation for enemy forces. Two. Tonight, the Detachment will keep a watch on enemy forces under present conditions and will dispatch a unit to cut off communications in the rear, and enact a sweep" (Nanjing War History Editing and Compilation Committee I n.d., 439).

At 4:50 a.m. on the 14, the 30th Infantry Battalion issued new orders: "One. Although enemy forces have been annihilated, there are people intending to resist wandering in all quarters. Two. The Battalion is to perform a thorough sweep of the city's northern sector and the exterior perimeter of the city today, the 14. Three. The 33rd Infantry Regiment will hold all gates to the west of the Jinchuan

Gate (including this gate), and perform a sweep from Xiaguan to the northernmost corner where it meets the east-west line, and the triangular zone from the city center along roads leading to Shizi Mountain, and should annihilate Chinese soldiers. Four. The 38th Infantry Regiment will hold all gates to the east of the Jinchuan Gate (not including this gate), and the 33rd Infantry Regiment will sweep all parts of the city to the east of this zone, these being the areas to the west of the agroforestry line of Central University's connecting to Heping Gate. All Chinese soldiers to be annihilated. Five. The 2nd Battalion of the 38th Infantry Regiment is to sweep the mountainous zone between Xuanwu Lake and Purple Mountain (including regions lying to the north), and should annihilate Chinese soldiers. Six. No unit, up to the level of the Division, is to take prisoners until instructed to" (Nanjing War History Editing and Compilation Committee I n.d., 439).

The 38th Infantry Regiment of the 30th Infantry Battalion was issued these orders at 9:00 a.m. on the 14: "1. Even though enemy forces have been completely annihilated, there remain some scattered people intending to resist. The Battalion conducted a thorough sweep of the northern part of Nanjing inside and outside the wall today (the 14). The 33rd Infantry Regiment will sweep the region to the west of the fort at Shizi Mountain to Zhongshan Road and the central three-way intersection, as well as Xiaguan. 2. The 38th Infantry Regiment (less the 2nd Batallion) will sweep from Heping Gate to Jinchuan Gate to Zhongshan Road (non inclusive) and the area inside the water sluice at the intersection in the Zhongyang Gate, and will annihilate Chinese soldiers. The 2nd Battalion will sweep the area between Xuanwu Lake eastward to Purple Mountain. 3. The 1st Battalion is the right-side sweeping unit, and the 3rd Battalion is the left-side sweeping unit. The area of their sweep runs between the Model Road to Nanbei Boulevard at the Zhongyang Gate. The line belongs to the left-side battalion. 4. At 10 a.m., the two sweeping battalions will make preparations at the front on Zhongshan Road. Before 10 a.m., the 1st Company will dispatch a unit to occupy the line from Zhongbu Gate (one kilometer to the west of the Zhongyang Gate) – Xuanwu Gate – water gate – northern sluice, and the important location in the vicinity of the three-way intersection of Zhongshan Road and Zhongyang Gate Boulevard" (Nanjing War History Editing and Compilation Committee I n.d., 448).

The 20th Infantry Regiment of the 16th Division issued "Battle Command No. 169" at noon on December 13: "One. The left-flank unit is the current sweeping unit, and is to thoroughly sweep all enemies within the city of Nanjing, in order to reestablish order. Main force to assist the newly arrived Engineering Regiment. Main forces of the Motorized Battalion and Engineering Regiment to assist city sweep of front-line infantry. Two. The 3rd Battalion (less the 10th Company) of the Regiment (apportioned an engineering platoon) will from now begin to sweep enemy soldiers in the city of Nanjing. Three. The 1st Battalion and 2nd Battalion will be given separate orders on the zone of their sweeps, with the time of their sweeps tentatively set as 2 p.m.; orders will be given then" (Wang, Ye et al. n.d., 178–179).

The 10th Army issued "Combat Order No. 4 B" at 8:30 a.m. on December 13: "One. Enemy forces continue to put up strong resistance in Nanjing. Two. We must annihilate enemy forces in Nanjing... Four. Needless to say, in the attack on the city, all units must exhaust all measures to annihilate enemy forces. So if needed, burn the city, and under no circumstances be fooled by tricky behavior of remnant forces. Five. The sweep zone for our group is to the south of the line from Gonghe Gate – Gongyuan Road – Zhongzheng Gate – Zhongzheng Road – Hanzhong Road (inclusive); the Shanghai Expeditionary Force is responsible for the area to the north of this line" (Nanjing War History Editing and Compilation Committee I n.d., 448–449).

The 114th Division of the 10th Army issued a sweep order at 9:30 a.m. on the 13: "One. Enemy resistance in the city remains fierce. The Kunisaki Detachment has arrived at Pukou and cut off the enemy's retreat route. The group's sweep zone is to the south of the line from Gonghe Gate – Gongyuan Road – Zhongzheng Road – Hanzhong Road (inclusive). Two. The Division must continue the offensive and annihilate enemy forces in the city. Three. When both flanks enter the city, they must, needless to say, attack furiously and exhaust all means to annihilate enemy forces. To this end, you can burn areas of the city if needed, and in particular do not be deceived by tricky behavior of remnant forces... Four. Artillery units should incrementally advance near to the front near Zengjiamen and Lijia'ao, and are responsible for destroying the urban area and helping units on both flanks to sweep the city. Five. Cavalry units should continue carrying out previously assigned tasks. Six. The 5th Armored Battalion should enter the city and help units on both flanks carry out their sweep..." (Nanjing War History Editing and Compilation Committee I n.d., 450).

Upon receipt of orders, the 150th Infantry Regiment of the 114th Division's 128th Battalion issued orders to the 1st Battalion under Major Aida: "The Commanding 1st Battalion (less the 2nd and 3rd Companies); the 8th, 5th, 6th, and 7th Companies of the 120th Field Artillery Regiment; the 1st Machine Gun Company and Infantry Company (less the 2nd Company and 1st platoon), will conduct a sweep in the appointed zone beginning at daybreak on the 13... The sweeping units will remain on extremely high alert while aggressively sweeping, beginning at about 7:10 a.m" (Nanjing War History Editing and Compilation Committee I n.d., 578).

The 128th Battalion's 115th Infantry Regiment issued "115th Infantry Regiment Battle Order No. 67" at 10 p.m. on December 12: "One. The division's main force is clustering south of the line from Zhoujia'ao to Yuhuatai, and will send one unit to sweep the city. The main force on the right flank will cluster to the south of this line, and will send one unit to sweep the city. The 150th Infantry Regiment will sweep the area to the east of the railway (including the railway). Two. Beginning tomorrow morning the Regiment will resolutely occupy advantageous positions near the city wall, to prevent counterattacks from enemy forces, setting watches at city gates, and will sweep areas to the west of the railway (including the railway) one by one. The 2nd Battalion will primarily push into the city government complex, and will then sweep the roads to the west of Gonghe Gate and between city walls. The 3rd Battalion will set a unit to guard city gates, and its main force will sweep the nearby area, gradually progressing northward" (Takasaki City Special History Commission n.d., 98).

The 127th Battalion's 66th Infantry Regiment issued "66th Infantry Regiment No. 85 A" in the early morning of the 13: "The Regiment (formation unchanged) will assist the 102nd Infantry Regiment's charge with as many heavy weapons as possible. After the charge, the Regiment will rush in to sweep the following areas: the area to the south of Ximian Boulevard from Xiehe Gate; the area to the east of Beifang Boulevard running from the South Gate; then the area to the west of the line from the eastern side of Zhoujia'ao – Yanghu Alley – Pipa Lake – City Government Social Department – Continental Bank. This is the Regiment's area of responsibility. The 102nd Infantry Regiment's assault unit will be responsible for the western half. The 66th Infantry Regiment will be responsible for the eastern half..." (Nanjing War History Editing and Compilation Committee I n.d., 565).

Upon receipt of the 10th Army's orders to sweep the city, the 6th Division issued these orders on December 13: "The Division is to dispatch a force to continue the assault in the city and in the vicinity of Qingliang Mountain, and its main force is to gradually assemble outside of the South Gate and the West Gate" (Nanjing War History Editing and Compilation Committee I n.d., 452).

At 12:30 p.m. on the 13, the 1st Battalion of the 6th Division's 47th Infantry Regiment issued "Battle Order No. 139": "1. There seems not to be a large quantity of enemy forces on the streets in the city to the north of the Regiment's first line; The 114th Division and 23rd Infantry Regiment will begin to sweep streets in this area. At 12:00, the Regiment's main force is to issue forth from the front at the city wall and will perform a sweep of the city near the "supporting line" in the city's southwest. At 12:00, the 3rd battalion is to issue force from the front at the city wall, sweep the southeast area of the "supporting line" and send platoons to occupy the "supporting line" height. 2. The 1st Battalion is to cover the 3rd Battalion's charge, and will perform a sweep of the area designated on the attached map. 3. The 1st, 2nd, and 4th Companies will perform sweeps of the areas designated on the attached map. 4. All other units are to stand in reserve, and be prepared to lay down cover for sweeping teams from present positions on the city walls" (Nanjing War History Editing and Compilation Committee I n.d., 400).

After the Japanese army had occupied all city gates and Xiaguan on December 13, nearly all divisions issued orders to subordinate units to carry out "sweeps" of the city, surrounding and annihilating all Chinese forces remaining in Nanjing.

So far no documentation of a "massacre order" has been discovered, but detailed battle reports from Japanese army units mention related orders. For example, the 1st Battalion of the 114th Division's 66th Infantry Regiment captured 1,500 prisoners during a sweep of the area outside the Zhonghua Gate. At 2 p.m. on the 13, the 1st Battalion received these orders: "Per Division orders, kill all prisoners. The method is to tie ten or more together and shoot them in batches" (Nanjing War History Editing and Compilation Committee I n.d., 567).

The Shanghai Expeditionary Force's 13th Division's 103rd Battalion (the Yamada Detachment) also captured a large number of prisoners during its attack on the batteries at Wulong Mountain and Mufu Mountain. Battalion commander Yamada Senji wrote in his journal entry of December 14: "It is difficult to deal with the prisoners. We chanced to find a school at Shangyuan Gate, and are keeping them inside the school. There are 14,777 prisoners. With so many, it's difficult both to kill them and to keep them alive." On the 15, Yamada wrote a note to superiors asking how to deal with the prisoners: "Cavalry Second Lieutenant Honma was sent to Nanjing to inquire after how to handle the prisoners and other matters. The orders he received were to kill them all" (Nanjing War History Editing and Compilation Committee I n.d., 331).

Ikehata Masami of the 2nd Battalion of the 16th Division's 33rd Infantry Regiment recalled: "When our unit arrived at the Taiping Gate to perform a sweep, an unbroken stream of evacuating enemy troops flooded in from Zhenjiang. They had already lost the will to fight, and surrendered to us one after another. They probably came here from the mistaken thought that Nanjing was untroubled. They came to the Taiping Gate and were disarmed one by one. With so many prisoners and so many objects turned over, the question of how to deal with these remnant forces became a problem. There were very few men in our unit, fewer than 100, but there were a thousand and a few hundred prisoners. We didn't have enough food for them... We had problems feeding ourselves already. We asked the commanding Division what to do, and the Division ordered us to 'dispose of them'" (Matsuoka 2002 JP, 140). Here "dispose" is a euphemism for "massacre."

We can see from the above historical documents that the massacre of prisoners by Japanese forces occupying Nanjing was carried out on orders from superiors.

6.1.2 Combat reports and battlefield diaries

Japanese army units all wrote "detailed combat reports," "combat summaries," and "battlefield diaries" throughout the war, recording events in detail. Most extant copies of such documents are contained in volume one of the *Compilation of Nanjing War History Materials*. A small quantity have also been published in some Japanese periodicals and books. The library of Japan's National Institute for Defense Studies also possesses some combat reports and battlefield diaries in its archives.

The primary objective of the Shanghai Expeditionary Force's 16th Division was to capture Nanjing's Zhongshan Gate. The Division records the assault on Nanjing in a "combat summary": on December 7 they "entered area to the south of Tangshui Town.[59] Although enemy forces have established positions in a line from the south to the southwest of the town and intend to put up a stubborn resistance, the detachment under Major General Sasaki has arrived in their rear by cutting through the mountainous regions to the north. Also, the main force of the pursuit unit under Major General Kusaba charged into the enemy position near Meitang in broad daylight and took the position in fierce hand-to-hand fighting... Beginning on the 8, the right flank unit of the Division (33rd Infantry Regiment) attacked Purple Mountain and the left flank unit (19th Infantry Battalion) attacked the area along the roads from the Qilin Gate to the Zhongshan Gate. The detachment under Major General Sasaki on the right flank attacked into Xiaguan from the northern side of Purple Mountain, and cut off the enemy soldiers' retreat. On December 10, the right flank unit secured the high ground at point 227 on purple mountain, and expanded their gains to the high ground at point 336 on the east side of the mountain. The left flank unit advanced to near the Central Exercise Facility on the same day. The next day (the 11), the 20th Infantry Regiment charged into an important strong point to the south of Purple mountain – the West Mountain – eliminating stubborn enemy resistance and counterattacks, occupying this position. On the 12, the right flank unit captured a strong enemy position through heroic fighting – the peak of Purple Mountain, destroying all hope for the Chinese defenders of

---

59 Located in Nanjing's eastern suburbs.

Nanjing. The 20th Regiment on the left flank stormed by surprise and captured the enemy position near the Yizu School, pushing right up to the edge of Nanjing in one move. At 3:10 a.m. on the 13, this unit took the lead in capturing Zhongshan Gate. Thereupon all other units of the Division drove back the enemy forces before them, giving us complete control of Nanjing. The detachment on the right flank continued routing strong enemy positions at Yaohua Gate and the crossroads. On the 13 we entered Xiaguan and cut off the enemy's retreat, surrounding and capturing their troops with the combined forces of the Division, achieving devastating battle gains" (Nanjing War History Editing and Compilation Committee I n.d., 473–474).

All regiments of the 16th Division made detailed records of their attacks on Purple Mountain, Xiaguan, Zhongshan Gate, and other locations. The 33rd Infantry Regiment's detailed battle record reads thus: on December 12, "the Regiment was prepared before dawn, in order to rapidly seize the mountain top with artillery support. So we made an artillery attack plan with Division command and the 3rd Field Artillery Battalion. Owing to the geography and difficulty in making observations, the artillery was unable to play the role it should have in supporting our attack. Under these conditions, the commander of the 2nd Battalion planned to quickly push his artillery pieces, his artillery soldiers, and his machine gunners to near the front on the mountain ridge while the 8th Company was offering extreme support to the ongoing attack, calling for close coordination to launch a surprise attack... At around 1:00 a.m., we stormed the enemy position at the southeast of the peak, where there were few pine trees (a circular elevation of curved lines?), and engaged in close combat for a few hours, gradually expanding battle gains... At 5:30 p.m., the 7th Company on the right-side front started climbing the peak, and had completely occupied it by 6:00 p.m. Then the 2nd Battalion entered the saddle to the west of the peak to observe enemy conditions and the geography at the observatory, to prepare an attack at dawn. On the night of the 12, the Regiment, after occupying the peak of Purple Mountain, continued attacking forward. At around 7:30 a.m. on the 13, the 2nd and 3rd Battalions successively occupied the high ground at the observatory. At 9:10 a.m. on the same day, a portion of the 2nd Battalion's forces (the 6th Company, a machine gun platoon, and an engineering platoon) occupied Taiping Gate and flew the Japanese flag high over the gate... At 9:30 a.m., the Regiment received '16th Division Combat Order No. 171 A," and on those orders dispatched a unit to hold the Taiping gate while the main force drove to Xiaguan to cut off the enemy's retreat. We departed at 10:30 a.m., and the 2nd Battalion (less the 2nd Company) served as the fore in the advance from Taiping Gate to Pinghe Gate to the road to Xiaguan. There were countless remnant enemy forces in the villages on either side of the road, so we had to sweep as we advanced. At 2:30 p.m., scouts of the advance unit scouted enemy conditions at Xiaguan, discovering that the Yangtze River was full of boats, rafts, and all manner of floating objects, on which remnant forces were escaping downriver in enormous numbers. The Regiment then moved its advance units and its fast-fire artillery along the side of the river and ferociously attacked enemy forces on the river. It is estimated that at least 2,000 enemy troops were annihilated in two hours" (Ministry of Defense Defense National Institute of Defense Studies [Japan] China Incident – North China no. 333).

The 16th Division's 38th Infantry Regiment's objective was a direct attack on Xiaguan from the north of Purple Mountain through Heping Gate. The Regiment's detailed combat record reads: on December 13, "enemy forces in front of the detachment continue stiff resistance; the right flank unit has captured Purple Mountain since last night. Also, we have received a report that all units continue to press toward Nanjing. Upon receipt of orders (as follows) to attack before dawn the next day, we ordered the Regiment to begin preparing to attack at 3:30 a.m. the following day. At 5:00 a.m. we began actions... Despite fierce resistance being put up by strong enemy units holding Nanjing at Guanghua Gate and other locations, their will to fight was clearly destroyed under our fierce assault. Although they began to retreat toward Xiaguan in waves, our vanguard – the 8th Light Armored Company – launched rapid, fierce attack. By about 1:40 a.m. we had dealt a thorough, heavy blow to the five to six thousand enemy troops crossing the river, annihilating them on the shores and the water. Then we dispatched our main force to move into Xiaguan at about 3:00 p.m. At least 500 enemy soldiers were captured before nightfall in a sweep" (Nanjing War History Editing and Compilation Committee I n.d., 477–479).

As for the 10th Army, its 6th Division writes in a 10-day battle report that all its units were preparing a breakthrough attack on December 12, with the following objectives: 13th Infantry Regiment – Zhonghua Gate; 47th Infantry Regiment – the area between Zhonghua Gate and the city's southwestern corner; 23rd Infantry Regiment – the city's southwestern corner; 45th Infantry Regiment – Shuixi Gate. At the same time "artillerymen under unified command planned to blow open three channels for entry in the southern city wall. Regiment commanders strove to blow open these channels for attack. The result was the blowing open of three large breaches in the southwestern corner, but the results of the right and middle attacks were poor due to insufficient gunpowder and poor angle of attack... Although the artillery onslaught was not thorough, the 47th Infantry Regiment still managed for its 3rd Company to make a stunning attack at 12:30 p.m. on the strength of the Regiment's heavy weaponry. However, difficulty crossing the moat outside the wall and stiff resistance from enemy forces made it difficult to expand battle gains. Also, on the left flank, it was very difficult to break through as a result of the moat and resistance of enemy forces, despite artillery support and two large breaches in the city wall's southwestern corner. With support from combined artillery forces, at 4:45 p.m. the 23rd Infantry Regiment's 1st Battalion finally occupied the city wall, and gradually expanded battle gains into the night... That same night, the 13th Infantry Regiment on the right flank occupied Zhonghua Gate directly in front of it. The cavalry regiment on the left flank encountered about 10,000 enemy troops fleeing southward from Xiaguan at Xinhe Town that evening. After intense fighting, the enemy fled pell-mell to a delta on the opposite shore, leaving behind over 1,000 corpses. It was thus that the 23rd Infantry Regiment's 3rd Battalion occupied Shuixi Gate at 8:30 a.m. on the 13, then dispatching some units to begin a sweep inside the city. At 10:00 a.m. the 47th Infantry Regiment ordered approximately one battalion to begin sweeping the city." The appendix to this report informs us that the Division captured 5,500 prisoners in the course of occupying Nanjing (Ministry of Defense Defense National Institute of Defense Studies [Japan] Library. China Incident – North China no. 128).

The 6th Division's 45th Infantry Regiment outflanked and enveloped Xiaguan from the west of Nanjing starting at noon on December 13. A battlefield diary from the Regiment's 2nd Company reads: "At noon we departed from Xiying Village and advanced toward Xiaguan via Shuixi Gate. Remnant forces to the north of Shuixi Gate threw hand grenades at us; we captured and shot them. By 7:00 p.m. we arrived at Yandi Alley, returned to command of the Regiment, and took up quarters there, being primarily in charge of guard duty to the south and east of the campsite" (Nanjing War History Editing and Compilation Committee I n.d., 389).

The 10th Army's 114th Division's primary objective was the Zhonghua Gate, the city wall to its east, and the Yuhua Gate. A 10-day combat report of the Division tells us: on December 11, "the Division shifted our focus from Zengjiamen onto the southern corner of Nanjing. We continued attacking into the night, breaking through entrenched enemy positions one at a time, entering Zhoujia'ao and Yuhuatai by the afternoon of the 12. Some units finally broke through the Nanjing city wall. The Division began issuing deployments on the evening of the 12. They concentrated our main force to the south of the line from Yuhuatai to Zhoujia'ao, and sent some units in the city to conduct a sweep. But we received orders from the Army on the morning of the 13 to annihilate enemy forces in the city using whatever means necessary. The Division then changed course and used its main force to sweep the city for enemy soldiers. On the evening of the 13, we had basically completed the task of sweeping enemy soldiers in the city. Division command entered the city on the afternoon of the 14" (Ministry of Defense Defense National Institute of Defense Studies [Japan] Library. China Incident – North China no. 223).

The 114th Division's 66th Infantry Regiment conducted its main attack on the Zhonghua Gate and surrounding city walls. We read in a detailed combat report of the Regiment's 1st Battalion: on the night of December 12, "enemy forces shot wildly from the city wall all night. During the first half of the night we were struck multiple times by fire from field artillery and mortars. We suffered no losses, but several shells struck houses near our headquarters." On December 13, "at 7:00 a.m., we began actions at the predesignated time, machine guns opening fire in unison, laying down fire for the Regiment's main force to enter the city and begin sweeping. At 7:40 a.m., as the sun was rising, the entire Army stood at attention and loudly honored the emperor, wishing him a long life, and became engulfed in profound emotions. As the sweep continued, enemy units began to surrender. By around 9:00 a.m., 300 men had already surrendered. We also saw an unbroken stream of shells from our artillery strike inside the city... At 10:00 a.m., we saw from afar the Japanese flag hoisted high atop the southern city wall that had been blown open, and knew that the main force of the Regiment had entered Nanjing. All our soldiers excitedly screamed "*banzai* [long may he live]" three times with the Battalion commander, and performed obeisance to the emperor" (Nanjing War History Editing and Compilation Committee I n.d., 562–566).

The most important of all Japanese military documents recording the massacre of prisoners is probably the battle diary of Nishihara Issaku, First Section Chief of the Shanghai Expeditionary Army's general staff. This "diary" is not a personal diary, but rather is a military document written in Nishihara's capacity as a section chief. Nishihara maintained possession of the diary after the war, and after his death his family gave it to a Japanese library, and published it for the general public. This battle diary records atrocities committed by the Japanese army as it occupied Nanjing as the massacre of prisoners by the 13th Division's 65th Infantry Regiment (the Yamada Detachment):

December 14, sunny

... It is said that the 11th Division's transport corps abducted girls of 12 or 13 and dishonored them as the army marched. Per a military police report, there have been many other similar incidents; this makes us feel the necessity of establishing comfort stations.

......

December 14, sunny

Dispatched someone to look in on the approximately 500 enemy remnant forces located in the valley to the northeast of Tangshui Town. The Yamada Detachment of the 13th Division captured 20,000 prisoners, but very difficult to deal with them due to lack of food.

December 15, sunny

Foreigners in Nanjing are extremely overbearing. Also, representative Chinese people seem to have disappeared into buildings of the Soviet Union and other countries. Lieutenant Colonel Cho[60] has arrived on the scene to handle them.

December 16, sunny

Sweep continued in city.

December 17, sunny and warm

Held ceremony for entry into Nanjing, a scene of historic significance.

On the way back encountered a group of about 2,000 prisoners, including some boys of 14 to 15.

December 18, overcast and cold

Held ceremony to honor the dead. The Yamada Battalion disposed of 15,000 prisoners (□□□□□□□□); one of our soldiers was shot to death along with the prisoners. About a regiment's worth of prisoners put up resistance, attempted to flee, and this soldier was sacrificed in the chaos. Lieutenant Colonel Oba came to take a report and dined with us.

……

December 26, sunny

This morning, Colonel Kato Reisanku came. Otsuki left. At 1:30 p.m. he departed to observe the environs of Nanjing with the Army's commander. Supply to the north of the river should be delivered on boats, landing at Pukou. There is an alarming quantity of dead bodies on Nanjing's shores, also outside the Taiping Gate. We are currently burning them with great persistence. Underground defense works at Yijiang Mountain[61] and Fugui Mountain very well built; Japan is strong in the concept of air defense. Putrid stench emanating from corpses on roads at Yijiang Gate, causing passers-by to hold their noses. Trenches are currently being dug by men with pickaxes. The soldiers cannot rectify their bad habits; they burn houses wherever they can. I think we need to control them more strictly (Nishihara n.d., n.p.).

There are also records of massacred prisoners in the detailed combat reports of units of the Shanghai Expeditionary Army. The 7th Infantry Regiment of that

---

60 Cho Isamu, infantry officer in the general staff of the Shanghai Expeditionary Army.
61 This is how the diary was written. Here he probably refers to Shizi Mountain near the Yijiang Gate.

Army's 9th Division conducted repeated "sweeps" in the International Safety Zone and other areas from the night of December 14 until the 24th. An appendix to the Regiment's detailed combat report titled "Table of Achievements of Sweeps in Nanjing by the 7th Regiment from December 13 to 24" tells us that the Regiment "stabbed or shot to death 6,670 remnant forces" and seized a great quantity of weapons during their sweeps (Nanjing War History Editing and Compilation Committee I n.d., 524).

The main force of the 6th Division's 20th Infantry Regiment entered the city by the Zhongshan Gate on the afternoon of the 13, and conducted a "sweep" along Zhongshan Road. The fifth entry of the "battlefield diary" of the Regiment's 4th Company tells us: on the 14th, the 20th Infantry Regiment conducted a continuous sweep of the city, and the 4th Company of the 1st Battalion alone "shot and buried 328 remnant forces" (Nanjing War History Editing and Compilation Committee I n.d., 505).

The 1st Armored Battalion, then assigned to the Shanghai Expeditionary Force, also participated in sweeps in Nanjing. Per the "Action Records of the 1st Armored Battalion's 1st Company" (Summary), on December 14, this unit helped the 3rd Battalion of the 7th Infantry Regiment perform a sweep: "At 9:30 a.m., actions were commenced per the above orders. The 7th Infantry Regiment swept the northern area, primarily assisted the 3rd Battalion. The day's actions were as follows: captured many prisoners and weapons." The record goes on to note that 250 prisoners were taken that day, and that "about 70 or 80 remnant forces attempting to resist were shot during the sweep" (Nanjing War History Editing and Compilation Committee I n.d., 418).

Detailed combat records from many units of the 10th Army similarly recount the wanton massacre of prisoners. The 1st Battalion of the 114th Division's 66th Infantry Regiment took more than 1,500 prisoners during a sweep outside the Zhonghua Gate on December 12. That night, the prisoners were housed in a Western-style building outside the Zhonghua Gate, with Japanese sentries guarding it. The 1st Battalion received these orders from the 66th Regiment at 2:00 p.m. on December 13: "Per Battalion orders, all prisoners are to be killed. The method is tie them up in groups of ten or more and shoot them in batches." At 3:30 p.m. that day, the 1st Battalion "summoned all company commanders and had them exchange ideas on how to dispose of prisoners. It was ultimately decided that each company (the 1st, 3rd, and 4th) would share the burden, removing 50 men at a time from confinement. The 1st Company took its men to the valley to the south of the campsite, the 3rd Company to a depression to the southwest of the campsite, and the 4th Company to near the valley to the southeast of the campsite, and killed them with bayonets... We paid special attention to stationing strong troop forces to be on alert around the confinement center, but absolutely not allowing prisoners to observe this as they were removed." The bayoneting of prisoners was planned to begin at 5:00 p.m., being basically completed by 7:30 p.m. Also, "the 1st Company changed its initial decision, wanting to burn its prisoners to death in confinement all at once, but this was not successful. Prisoners with no hope for life were fearless. Some stuck their necks out in front of bayonets. Some blithely faced oncoming bayonets. Some, however, sobbed and begged, and in particular sobbing was heard everywhere when the commander came to inspect" (Nanjing War History Editing and Compilation Committee I n.d., 567–568). The Battalion's detailed combat report tells us more: "A thousand and a few hundred prisoners remained of enemy forces holding Nanjing after our Regiment's ferocious attack. At 11:35 a.m. (of the 13) we captured Nanjing's South Gate, and then sent units to sweep designated areas, shooting to death about a hundred enemy soldiers" (Nanjing War History Editing and Compilation Committee I n.d., 568). Japanese units entering the city to conduct sweeps did not encounter organized resistance by Chinese forces; consequently the "shooting to death" of "about a hundred enemy soldiers" was clearly a massacre of Chinese soldiers who had thrown down their arms or of civilians suspected by the Japanese of being soldiers.

6.1.3 Unit histories

Some former Japanese officers and enlisted men formed "comrade clubs" or "unit history publication societies" or other groups with other members of their wartime units. These groups collected and organized historical materials in the possession of former soldiers and officers, and on their basis wrote unit histories. These unit histories recount the attack on Nanjing from different perspectives; some even mention massacres. Some Japanese high-ranking officers along with a few units also compiled war histories or histories of their own units during and after the war, including the *Summary History of the China Incident and Continental War* published by the Imperial Japanese Army General Staff Office; the *Daily Records of the China Incident* issued by the Japanese Ministry of the Army's News Bureau on August 15, 1938; the *Summary of Major Battles in the China Incident* (of the year 1937) published by the Imperial Japanese Army General Staff Office in May 1943; *War History of the Third Division* published by the command staff of the Japanese Ground Self-Defense Force's 10th Division in March 1965; and so on.

Histories written after the war by former soldiers and officers range in unit size from division to regiment to battalion to company, but most are of regiments. As most of these histories were written years after the end of the war from the diaries and memories of former Japanese officers and soldiers, and from other historical materials, there are some errors in their recollections.

The majority of histories written by high-ranking officers view the course of the "China Incident" from a macro perspective, including the process of high-level army decision-making and a summary of the attack on Nanjing. For example, we read this in the *Summary History of the China Incident and Continental War:* "In late November, headquarters found itself in a situation in which the enemy was retreating and we were advancing. As such, and in consideration of various other factors, we resolved to launch a rapid attack on Nanjing with the current strength of the Central China Area Army. On December 1 we ordered that the Central China Area Army coordinate this attack on Nanjing with the navy, and issued instructions that a unit could make battle in the region of the left bank of the Yangtze River to support this mission" (Wang 2010a, vol. 1, 8). The book also includes a report of the attack on Nanjing by the 65th Infantry Regiment of the 13th Division on orders from the Shanghai Expeditionary Force, as well as conditions in Nanjing under occupation of all Japanese units at the time: "To make the attack by the 16th Division's right flank more effective and to cut off the enemy's retreat to the east, the Army's commander ordered the 13th Division, then awaiting orders at Zhenjiang, to dispatch a unit (comprised primarily of the 3rd Infantry Battalion and the 1st Mountain Artillery Battalion, collectively known as the Yamada Detachment) to proceed to the north of Nanjing and occupy the batteries at Wulong Mountain and Mufu Mountain. The Detachment left Zhenjiang on the 12, and occupied Mufu Mountain on the 14, taking about 15,000 prisoners (after occupying Nanjing, this Detachment crossed the Yangtze River and rejoined its Division)... On the morning of the 13, enemy forces evacuated from Nanjing. All divisions, per attack plans designated in advance, dispatched units with infantry regiments serving as their backbone to conduct sweeps in the city of predesignated zones. One unit of the 16th Division fiercely swept the river with gunfire at enemy forces retreating on boats, dealing the enemy a heavy blow. On the 13, the Amaya Detachment continued crossing the river from Zhenjiang, occupied Yangzhou on the 14, and cut off the Grand Canal to the north of the river. On the 15 this Detachment occupied Shaobo Town. The 13th Division followed closely on the heels of the Amaya Detachment, and occupied Chu County on the 20, cutting off the Tianjin-Pukou Railway" (Wang 2010a, vol. 1, 12–13).

In the Shanghai Expeditionary Force, the 9th Division's 7th Infantry Regiment conducted multiple "sweeps" many sections of occupied Nanjing, including the International Safety Zone. After the War, some of its members formed the "7th Infantry Regiment Comrade Club," and the Regiment's commander at the time of the occupation of Nanjing, Isa Kazuo, led the publication of the club's *History of* the *7th Infantry Regiment* in 1967. It tells us: on December 13, "at around 5:00 p.m., we received orders from the Battalion to sweep the city, whereupon the Regiment [apportioned an armored company (less a platoon) and an engineering company (less a platoon)] immediately massed to the west of the airport, where orders were given to all battalions and armored companies to conduct a sweep of area no. 37, as indicated on the attached map. All units had basically finished their sweeps by 3:00 a.m. of the 14, and returned to the Regiment. We were responsible for sweeping area no. 38 on the attached map from the 14 to the 17. The Regiment's area of responsibility included the refugee zone, which contained 100,000 refugees." From the 19 to the 23, the Regiment continued conducting sweeps with a portion of its units. On the 24 the sweeping unit's duty was canceled and handed over to units of the 16th Division" (Isa n.d., 27). Noteworthy here is the "Table of Achievements of Sweeps Conducted in Nanjing from December 13 to 24 by the 7th Infantry Regiment" in the section titled "7th Infantry Regiment Detailed Combat Reports," which clearly indicates that the Regiment in total "killed (bayoneted) 6,670 enemy remnant forces," and obtained a great quantity of weapons and equipment, but not one word is written in the *History* about these achievements.

The 9th Division's 19th Infantry Regiment (also called the Tsuruga Regiment) also participated in sweeps of Nanjing. After the war, former officers and soldiers of this Regiment founded the "Society for Preserving the Historical Events of the Tsuruga Regiment," which in November 1964 published the book *History of the Tsuruga Regiment*. The *History* reads: "At 5:00 a.m. on the 13, the 36th Infantry Regiment completed the occupation of the Guanghua Gate. At 7:00 a.m. the Regiment advanced from Qiweng Bridge to the Air Defense School. At 9:00 a.m., under guidance of the Battalion commander, the Regiment planted a military flag atop the Guanghua Gate. The unit assembled beneath the gate and conducted a ceremony of remotely worshiping the emperor. With the flag flying atop the fallen capital, the officers and men were emotional in the extreme. The Regiment entered the city from the Guanghua Gate at 10:00 a.m. and conducted a sweep of the southeastern section of the city, then mustered to the west of the Tongji Gate and prepared later actions... From December 14 to 24, the Regiment assembled inside the city and was put on guard duty. From the night of the 13 to the 16, the Regiment's main force swept remnant forces near Tangshui Town" (Society for Preservation of the History of the Tsuruga Regiment n.d., 131–133).

The 16th Division's 33rd Infantry Regiment pushed toward Xiaguan after occupying Purple Mountain. In February 1972, the "33rd Infantry Regiment History Publication Society" published *History of the 33rd Infantry Regiment – 50 Years of Glory*, written by a former second lieutenant in the Regiment Shimada Katsumi. One passage reads: On December 13, "The Regiment received orders from the

Division to press toward Xiaguan, to cut off the enemy's retreat route. At 10:30 a.m., after receiving orders directly from the Division, we left the 6th Company to guard the Taiping Gate, and our main force advanced down the mountain from the north of the observatory with the 2nd Battalion as vanguard. We took the route from Taiping Gate to Heping Gate to Xiaguan, sweeping small villages along the way as we rapidly advanced on Xiaguan... The 1st Battalion was put on the right flank, and captured Red Mountain at about 8:30 a.m., and then chased after retreating enemy forces, finally arriving at Xiaguan by the fastest route at 1:00 p.m. Enemy forces attempting to put up a final resistance collapsed under a fierce Japanese attack from the north, east, and south. We left them only one escape route, to the west, the road to the Yangtze River, but they fell into extreme disorder during the rout. If these enemy forces had crossed the Yangtze and escaped toward Xuzhou from Pukou, they could have embarked on a new road of resistance... The main force of the Regiment arrived in Xiaguan first at 2:30 p.m. and joined ranks with the 1st Battalion. Those enemy troops who had not had the time to flee were crossing to the other side of the river on motorized sailboats, little sampans, rafts, and other vessels. The Regiment immediately spread out along the riverbank and began shooting at them with rifles and heavy weapons, in an attempt to wipe them out. Right at that moment one of our gunboats coming upriver turned a flank to them and opened fire. This pursuit battle coordinated between the army and the navy was the closing act in the battle for the capital... Beginning on the 14, the 2nd Battalion conducted sweeps of the northwestern corner of the city, and the 1st and 3rd Battalions of Xiaguan and environs. There had allegedly been 100,000 Chinese soldiers from the defense garrison inside the city, of whom most escaped to the opposite bank of the Yangtze, but a considerable quantity of remnant forces with a small quantity of weapons had concealed themselves throughout the city, making sweeps very difficult. The very last unit of enemy troops putting up stubborn resistance at the permanent military installation on Shizi Mountain in the city's northwestern corner was unable to retreat. When the 2nd Battalion began its sweep, these troops discarded their weapons, donned civilian clothes, and surrendered to us, yielding us 200 to 300 prisoners in a blow. Japanese forces encountered similar mass surrenders all over the city, which made handling such a quantity of prisoners very difficult. As there is no news whatsoever of these surrendered soldiers, this event was later disseminated all over the world as the 'Nanjing Massacre Incident,' which did an extreme amount of damage to the traditional prestige of our army; I feel this is a great pity" (Shimada n.d., 408–411).

The 16th Division's 38th Infantry Regiment (also known as the Nara Regiment) attacked Nanjing from the north of Purple Mountain, arriving in Xiaguan on December 13, and commencing sweeps to the west of the battery at Shizi Mountain,

Zhongshan Road, and the three-way intersection of Zhongyang Road. In May 1963, Yamato Jihosha of Nara published *Combat Records of the Nara Regiment* written by Noguchi Toshio. Handwritten records by 38th Regiment Headquarters Secretary Miyamoto Nobuyoshi are included under the heading "Miscellaneous Battlefield Notes." Miyamoto wrote: "The Sukegawa Unit just changed our deployment to annihilate enemy forces, so we've been consistently chasing at top speed after the 70,000 to 80,000 enemy troops routing toward the north of Nanjing, and we swept up nearly 40,000 enemy soldiers in the area from the north of Purple Mountain to the bank of the Yangtze River. Consequently, the river has been dyed red, and the accumulated bodies stretch downriver two to three *ri*.[62]... After sweeping up remnant forces, we made a rough reckoning of how many enemies we had killed in the general attack on Nanjing, arriving at a figure of about 70,000. We killed about 15,000 in sweeps in the city and at least 12,000 prisoners" (Noguchi n.d., 208–209).

After the 13th Division arrived in Zhenjiang, it dispatched a detachment under command of 103rd Battalion commander Commander Yamada Senji, the "Yamada Detachment" to rush toward Nanjing. To this detachment were assigned the commander of the 103rd Infantry Battalion, the 65th Infantry Regiment, the 17th Cavalry Battalion, and the 3rd Battalion of the 19th Mountain Artillery Regiment. In October 1975, the "19th Mountain Artillery Regiment's 'Regiment History' Commemorative Publication Committee" published *History of the 19th Mountain Artillery Regiment*. One section of the *History* reads: "To reduce the pressure on the 16th Division's right flank attack and cut off the enemy's route of retreat to the east, on December 12 the Detachment departed from Zhenjiang, attacked Wulong Mountain on the 13, and occupied Mufu Mountain on the 14, taking 15,000 prisoners along the way. Owing to the enemy's general retreat from Nanjing on the 13, all units completed sweeps within the city" (Nineteenth Mountain Artillery Regiment's 'Regiment History' Commemorative Publication Committee n.d., 83).

As for the 10th Army, the 6th Division (also known as the Kumamoto Division) was its main force. In April 1965, the *Kumamoto Nichinichi Shimbun* published *Military History of the Kumamoto Corps – China Incident*. It reads: "On the morning of December 13, the 3rd Battalion of the 23rd Infantry Regiment occupied the Shuixi Gate, and sent a unit within the walls. On the 11, the 45th Infantry Regiment, the left flank's front line unit, engaged enemy forces using multiple rivers to put up stiff resistance in desperate combat. By about midnight on the 12, the Regiment captured the Jiangdong Gate. Then, to cut off the enemy's escape route

---

62 In the Japanese system one *ri* is equivalent to 3.924 kilometers (translator's note).

from the city, the Regiment marched toward Xiaguan, arriving at the north side of Shangbaochang by 10:00 a.m. During this time the left flank detachment (the Ozono Company, apportioned an artillery piece) engaged in unusually fierce fighting near the Jiangdong Gate and Shanghe Town. The Company's commander was killed and suffered many casualties... and the 47th Infantry Regiment also entered the city and began sweeps with forces roughly equivalent to a Battalion... The 6th Cavalry Regiment, assigned to the left flank (under command of Lieutenant Colonel Inoki Kintai) fought an encounter battle with about 6,000 enemy forces moving southward from Xiaguan in cotton fields on the morning of the 13. After fierce fighting that left hundreds of enemy bodies on the ground, the enemy routed to a delta on the other side of the river; we annihilated them on the river" (Military History of the Kumamoto Corps Editing and Compilation Committee n.d., 124).

In the pre-dawn hours of December 13, the 6th Cavalry Regiment was not the only unit to encounter Chinese forces near Shanghe Town; the 45th Infantry Regiment had the same experience. In August 1981, the "Committee for Compiling the History of the 45th Infantry Regiment" published *History of the 45th Infantry Regiment*. It reads: on December 12, "the Regiment ordered the 3rd Battalion to take the van in an attack on Shanghe Town about three kilometers to the West of Nanjing's Shuixi Gate, holding the 2nd Battalion in reserve. The 3rd Battalion encountered the enemy at Shanghe Town, both sides putting up a spirited fight until nightfall, but neither taking the upper hand. The Regiment's commander ordered the 3rd Battalion to continue the attack, and ordered the 2nd Battalion to occupy the Jiangdong Gate (between Shanghe Town and the Shuixi Gate). Battalion Commander Shigetomo heard unbroken gunfire from the direction of the 3rd Battalion on the left side, so he had the 7th Company take the lead in an advance along levee roads, with swamps on both sides of the roads. Since only the 7th Company leading the column could engage in battle, it was decided that they should engage. Without meeting any great resistance, they occupied the Jiangdong Gate. From the night of the 12 to the morning of the 13, the Chinese army planned to flee from the city in search of a retreat route. A great number of enemy troops fled from Xiaguan onto the Yangtze River, or clustered in the direction of the Shuixi Gate from Xiaguan. On the morning of the 13, the 2nd Battalion advanced directly on Xiaguan. A heavy fog set in, and lakes and swamps big and small, like the Mochou Lake, surrounded the route. Enemy troops were everywhere between the city and the Yangtze River. Our units routed their forces while pressing southward to Sanchahe (1,500 meters south of Xiaguan). The 3rd Battalion followed close on the heels of the 2nd Battalion. In the thick fog, they engaged enemy units moving from the direction of the Shuixi Gate in a fierce encounter battle. The 2nd Battalion, reaching the southeast of Sanchahe, was at that moment attacking enemy forces putting up stiff resistance from within villages. Once the enemy had left the city, they were obstructed to the rear by the Yangtze River. This was truly a 'fight with one's back to water'.[63] The enemy's resistance was extremely tenacious. At this time the Machine Gun Company and the Battalion's Artillery Platoon, after landing at Shanghai and raced to Nanjing, began to assist the attack. The Rapid Fire Artillery Platoon also helped the Company on the front line in its attack. The enemy finally began a second retreat in the direction of Xiaguan. The enemy put up its final resistance from across the river. Our forces engaged the enemy in fierce fighting on the north and south of a canal 20 meters wide. Despite support from mortars, the enemy retreated leaving behind many bodies. Our forces used these bodies to fill in the 20 meter wide canal at a length of 45 meters… On the morning of the 14, the 2nd Battalion reached Xiaguan without encountering any enemy resistance, capturing more than 30 artillery pieces and a great quantity of rifles and machine guns, in addition to several hundred war horses. They also captured 5,000 to 6,000 prisoners at Xiaguan. At this time, the 16th Division arrived at Xiaguan from the city, and several of our destroyers arrived from downriver. The Battalion received orders from the Regiment at its camp at the Jiangdong Gate to hand over the battlefield to the 16th Division, and then proceeded to the Jiangdong Gate" (Committee for Compiling the History of the 45th Infantry Regiment n.d., 232–234).

In October 1982, *Fighting History of the Kyodo Unit (One)*, written by Senmatsu Takashi, was published by the *Oitagobun Shimbun*. The "Kyodo Unit" referred to is the 6th Division's 47th Infantry Regiment. The book chronicles the Regiment's battle experience from landing at Hangzhou Bay to occupying Nanjing, as well as its disposal of bodies in Nanjing: "After the ceremony for entry into Nanjing had been completed, the divisions occupied positions around the city, and began life on guard. The 47th Regiment was responsible for guarding the southern portion of Nanjing, and the clean-up of battlegrounds in the city for many consecutive days. The smell of gunpowder lingered across the battlefield, and bodies were scattered everywhere. Our primary job was disposal of bodies, as well as searching for military material hidden all throughout the city" (Senmatsu n.d., 413).

---

[63] Euphemism for a fight to the death (translator's note).

6.2 Diaries and Correspondence of Japanese Officers and Soldiers

6.2.1 Diaries of Japanese officers and soldiers

After the war, some diaries of former Japanese officers and soldiers were published in Japan. Some other former officers and soldiers publicized diaries they had long kept secret as a warning to later generations, spurred to do so by their consciences and sense of justice. Some diarists first edited their writings, and most added annotations, without changing the original contents of their diaries. These diaries narrate the truth of the Rape of Nanking from different perspectives, and so are of great historical value.

Diaries of former Japanese officers and soldiers related to the Rape of Nanking and now made public fall into three main categories. The first category is the diaries contained in the *Compilation of Nanjing War History Materials*, such as the "Battlefield Diary of General Matsui Iwane," "Diary of Army General Hata Shunroku," "Diary of Iinuma Mamoru," "Diary of Uemura Toshimichi," and "Diary of Kesago Nakajima," as well as the diaries of low-ranking Japanese officers and soldiers such as "Diary of Kazuo Isa," "Diary of Kisa Kiku," "Diary of Second Lieutenant Yoshihiko Maeda," and "Diary of Ike Mataichi." The second category is contained in the book *Compilation of Materials Related to the Kyoto Division in the Nanjing Incident*, edited by Iguchi Kazuk, Kisaka Junichiro, and Shimozato Masaki, published in December 1989 by Aoki Shoten, containing many diaries kept by officers and enlisted men from the 16th Division. The third category is contained in the book *Records of Imperial Army Soldiers from the Rape of Nanking*, edited by Ono Kenji, Fujiwara Akira, and Honda Katsuichi, published in March 1996 by Otsuki Shoten, containing more than 30 diaries from soldiers in the 13th Division's Yamada Detachment.

Some other diaries of former Japanese officers and soldiers were published individually, such as Our Infantry Unit in Nanjing by Azuma Shiro. A small quantity of diaries were included in unit histories as well, including the diary of the 3rd Independent Mountain Artillery Regiment (of the 10th Army's Kunisaki Detachment) Commander Tsukinoki Masao, included in the book Our Youth – History of the 3rd Independent Mountain Artillery Regiment's 6th Company (published in February 1983 by the Doksan Sanarakukai Editing and Compilation Committee). Some other diaries have been made public but never published, such as Records of Feelings of Battle by Okamura Yasuji.

The above-mentioned diaries record the truth of the Rape of Nanking to differing extents all from different perspectives. General Matsui Iwane, commander of the Central China Area Army, wrote thus in his diary entry of December 20,

1937: "For a time, looting (mostly of furniture, etc.) and raping emerged among a small number of my soldiers, but this is difficult to avoid" (Nanjing War History Editing and Compilation Committee II n.d., 145). On December 21, Matsui made observations at Xiaguan to the north of Nanjing, writing in his diary that day: "Departed at 10:00 a.m. Observed vicinity of Yijiang Gate and Xiaguan. This whole area is still in great disorder, with bodies scattered everywhere. Much time still needs to be spent in clean-up work" (Nanjing War History Editing and Compilation Committee II n.d., 145). Matsui wrote on December 29: "There have been incidents of my soldiers looting cars and other objects from the embassies of various nations in Nanjing; the ignorance of their units and their crude behavior have shocked me immensely" (Nanjing War History Editing and Compilation Committee II n.d., 149). He wrote in his diary entry of February 6 the following year: "Slackened military discipline has still not been fully restored. Unit leaders have adopted lenient attitudes toward some prohibited behaviors to spare bad feelings. As for the propaganda and pacification work the units have undertaken on their own initiative, honestly they've caused more harm than good, and have produced the opposite effects from those desired" (Nanjing War History Editing and Compilation Committee II n.d., 168).

In *Diary Excerpts on the China Incident*, under the heading "Atrocities and Looting Incidents of Our Army," Matsui detailed Japanese atrocities committed in Nanjing: "At the time we repeatedly implored all units to maintain strict military discipline. What we did not expect was that our army committed many atrocities and incidents of looting upon entering the city. These incidents greatly damaged the prestige and image of benevolence and righteousness of the Imperial Army" (Nanjing War History Editing and Compilation Committee II n.d., 185).

In February 1938, the Central China Area Army was officially disbanded, and in its place was created the Central China Expeditionary Army, under command of General Hata Shunroku. Okamura Yasuji was then appointed commander of the 11th Army, subordinate to the Central China Expeditionary Army. Both of these high-ranking officers were aware of atrocities committed by Japanese troops in Nanjing. Hata wrote in his diary entry of January 29, 1938: "As a chapter in the war came to a close, military discipline in the China Expeditionary Army began to break down, and it seems that there were many instances of looting and rape, the kinds of behaviors that military units hold most taboo. It was under these conditions that we recalled conscripted reserve soldiers back to the country and replaced them with active duty soldiers. In addition, General Matsui in Shanghai should be replaced by an active duty officer, and all army and division level commanders should also be replaced by active duty officers in batches" (Nanjing War History Editing and Compilation Committee II n.d., 189).

Okamura wrote in his "reflections" of July 13, 1938: "Upon arrival to the Central China battlefield, it was only after hearing reports from Staff Officer Miyazaki, an advance officer, Major General Harada, chief of the Central China Expeditionary Army's Special Service Organ, and Major Ogihara in the Hangzhou office that I became aware that front line soldiers of the Expeditionary Army had executed large numbers of prisoners, citing supply difficulties as their excuse, and that this had become a habit. During the Battle of Nanjing, as many as 40,000 to 50,000 were massacred, and as many civilians in the city were subjected to looting and rape" (Ministry of Health and Welfare Repatriation Support Bureau n.d., 1).

Iinuma Mamoru, then chief of staff of the Shanghai Expeditionary Force, also wrote about atrocities committed by the Japanese army in Nanjing in his diary. He wrote in the entry of December 14: "The 13th Division's Yamada Detachment swept up over a thousand remnant forces on the way, occupying the battery at Wulong Mountain at 4:30 p.m., capturing over 10 anti-aircraft guns and heavy artillery pieces... I have heard that it was discovered from aboard an airplane that two groups of more than 1,000 prisoners are being transported from the eastern section of Nanjing to Xiaguan... It is claimed that at around 3:00, one company from the Sasaki Detachment captured about 20,000 prisoners in the northeastern section of Nanjing. Per another report, from an airplane it was clearly observed that four columns of prisoners stretching as far as eight kilometers each are being escorted to the northern section of Nanjing" (Nanjing War History Editing and Compilation Committee I n.d., 156–157). He continued on December 19: "A military police report claims that someone set fire to buildings in the Sun Yat-sen Mausoleum on the 18, and that a massive conflagration continues to rage. The report also claimed that officers led their units to force their way into the refugee zone to commit rape (still unverified). There are also reports of similar incidents, as well as requisitioning of trucks from the British and American embassies, and others who wish to requisition more. Items of note have yet to be enforced" (Nanjing War History Editing and Compilation Committee I n.d., 162).

On December 21 Iinuma wrote about the 13th Division's Yamada Detachment's massacre of more than 15,000 prisoners: "According to rumor, when the Yamada Detachment of the Ogisu Unit killed 10,000 plus several thousand prisoners by bayonet in batches, there was a great disturbance among the prisoners as they were all led to the same place. Ultimately our forces mowed them down with machine guns, leading to the deaths of several of our own soldiers and officers" (Nanjing War History Editing and Compilation Committee I n.d., 164). Iinuma also detailed the letters of protest the International Committee wrote to the Japanese embassy, as in his diary entry of December 29: "Just as we were studying how to receive officials from the embassies and consulates of the UK, the U.S., Germany, Italy, and other countries, Secretary Fukui (consul at Nanjing) came. A Chinese in the employ of the American embassy said that Japanese soldiers had looted personal possessions of Chinese citizens from within the embassy on the 23, and had also looted private rooms of embassy personnel, had forced doors with bayonets, had stolen calligraphy paintings from the German embassy, and so on. They left a letter written to the consul by Americans and went on" (Nanjing War History Editing and Compilation Committee I n.d., 171).

Commander of the Shanghai Expeditionary Force's 16th Division Kesago Nakajima's diary is extremely noteworthy, as Kesago detailed all manner of atrocities with no reservations whatsoever. He wrote on December 13: "In the fighting near the observatory, a drillmaster from the enemy's military engineering school, a second lieutenant, was captured, and from him it was learned where mines were buried. After interrogation, he claimed he did not know the locations of all mines, and so he was immediately hacked to death by an infantryman. There's really nothing we can do with these soldiers" (Nanjing War History Editing and Compilation Committee I n.d., 217). On the 13th, Nakajima lent his saber to another soldier to use in the killing of a Chinese prisoner: "Today at noon swordsman Takayama paid me a visit, at which time I happened to have seven prisoners with me, so I told him to test his beheading skills. I even had him use my saber, and he chopped off two heads with unexpected skill" (Nanjing War History Editing and Compilation Committee I n.d., 218). Nakajima writes on the 13th about the disposal of large numbers of prisoners: "Most fleeing enemy troops entered forests or villages in the 16th Division's combat zone, and on the other end a large number fled in from the fort at Zhenjiang. There were prisoners everywhere, in such great numbers it was difficult to deal with them... Our policy was basically to take no prisoners, and we adopted a guiding policy of annihilating them all. However, as they came in groups of 1,000, 5,000, and 10,000, we couldn't even have the time to disarm them. They had, nevertheless, completely lost the will to fight. The walked over in groups and posed no threat to our troops. Despite the inherent safety, the situation could become difficult to control in case of a disturbance. So additional units were dispatched in trucks to be in charge of supervision and guidance... After the fact I found out that Sasaki Detachment alone disposed of about 15,000 of them, and the commander of the company holding Taiping Gate disposed of about 1,300. There were about 7,000 to 8,000 people congregated near the Xianhe Gate. And there was an unbroken chain of men coming forward to surrender... A large trench was needed to dispose of the aforementioned 7,000 to 8,000, but it was difficult to find one. It was determined to split them into small groups of 100 to 200 and lead them to appropriate places for disposal... The 16th Division took charge of the disposal of the majority of these defeated soldiers, so the Division had no spare time to attend to entering the city or setting up camp; they were completely occupied running left and right" (Nanjing War History Editing and Compilation Committee I n.d., 220).

Nakajima also recorded the Japanese army's wanton looting. He wrote in his diary entry of December 19: "Japanese army units are looting everywhere, even in areas under the jurisdiction of other units. They force their way into private residences in these places and loot them to the last. Put succinctly, the more brazen and lacking shame they are, the more they get their hands on. The best example is: soldiers of the 16th Division already swept official residences of the nationalist government on the 13. On the morning of the 14, the management department made a plan for dividing up the housing after observations and hung up signs reading 'Division Command.' The result was that every single room, from the chairman's bedroom down to the smallest bedroom, had been thoroughly looted, all boxes opened and all cabinets overturned. Everything deemed of any value was taken, antiques, display pieces, everything. After entering the city on the 15, I collected all other objects together in a chest and sealed it, but even this wasn't enough. On the third day when I came to check, there wasn't a trace of anything I had put inside. It seems like storing objects anywhere outside of a safe is useless... The most dastardly has been the theft of currency. There are experts in every unit who have been looting bank coffers all over the city, specifically targeting central bank notes. And as compared to U.S. dollars, central bank notes are more valuable than Japanese money, and so it's best to bring them to Shanghai to exchange into Japanese bills. There are not a few such intermediaries among news reporters and automobile drivers, and there are brokers in Shanghai who make their living on the massive gains of such transactions" (Nanjing War History Editing and Compilation Committee I n.d., 226–227).

Sasaki Toichi, commander of the 16th Division's 30th Infantry Battalion also recorded scenes of massacre in his diary. He wrote in his entry of December 13: "At 8:00 a.m., a loud burst of gunfire shot me awake from sleep. Messengers, transport team members, and orderlies were firing, bang bang bang. 'What's going on?' I ran out of the house and asked. 'We just fought them back. A dense mass of enemy troops come down from Purple Mountain.' 'Were they defeated soldiers?' 'Right as we were performing a search, they suddenly attacked down on us from above. They charged in a group at a time, each wave containing at least five to six hundred of them.' 'Did they throw down their guns?' 'You think we had time to have them surrender? We killed them all.'" "Today, in my Detachment's combat zone, the enemy left behind 10,000 and some few thousand more corpses. If we count these together with the soldiers shot on the river by our armored cars and the prisoners taken by all our units, then my Detachment alone has taken care of more than 20,000 of them... Thereafter an unbroken chain of prisoners came forward to surrender, numbering in the thousands. Soldiers in the heat of passion paid no heed at all to the objections of superior officers, killing every last prisoner one by one. Now thinking back on the vast amount of our comrades' blood spilled on the battlefield and these last ten days of difficulties and hardships, it's not just the soldiers, but even I want to say 'kill them all'" (Nanjing War History Editing and Compilation Committee I n.d., 270–272). Sasaki wrote in his diary entry of December 14: "Now I am in complete control of two regiments, which are performing sweeps in and out of the city. The troops are searching out remnant forces hiding everywhere around the city. However, they have already discarded or hidden all their weapons. Big groups of prisoners, numbering from 500 to 1,000, have been brought forward in quick succession... The big moat in front of the Taiping Gate is full of cadavers... The former busy shopping district at Xiaguan has been burned to ashes. Hundreds of vehicles have been abandoned on the roads along the river, and hundreds of bodies lying on the banks have been washed into the river" (Nanjing War History Editing and Compilation Committee I n.d., 272–273).

Sasaki continued on December 16: "We followed orders to sweep the region to the north of Purple Mountain. Although we didn't gain much, the two regiments found several hundred remnant forces, all of whom were shot" (Nanjing War History Editing and Compilation Committee I n.d., 274). Sasaki was still describing massacres of prisoners as late as January 5 1938: "About 2,000 defeated soldiers have been cleared out of the city as of today, and are being held in the former Foreign Ministry. We have also taken wounded and infirm Chinese soldiers as prisoners from the missionaries. Remnants of the routed army persistently engaging in illegal behaviors in the environs of the city have also been gradually rounded up, with several thousand executed at Xiaguan" (Nanjing War History Editing and Compilation Committee I n.d., 276).

Many low-ranking officers and enlisted men also recorded Japanese atrocities in their diaries. Azuma Shiro, a superior private in the 16th Division's 20th Infantry Regiment, wrote thus in his diary:

> The Supreme Court on Zhongshan Road was a gray building, the home of the Ministry of Justice. In front of the court there was a ruined private sedan lying upside down, having been pushed into that position. There was a pond across the street. At this time they pulled over a Chinese person from I-don't-know-where. My comrades were playing with him like children playing with a puppy. Hashimoto then proposed a cruel plan, to put him in a sack, douse it with gasoline, and light it on fire. The crying, screaming Chinese man was put into a mailbag, and they tied it shut with a tight knot. He continued sobbing and screaming inside the bag. My comrades kicked the bag back and forth like a soccer ball,

and then urinated on it as though watering a vegetable garden. Hashimoto retrieved some gasoline from the broken-down car, poured it on the bag, and then tied a long strap to the end of the bag and carried it back and forth for fun.

Everyone with a conscience stood to one side and furrowed their eyebrows at this cruel scene. Everybody without a conscience cheered him on.

Then Hashimoto set it afire. It went up in a second. At this point a scream of terror emitted from inside the bag. The Chinese man jumped with all the energy in his body, and so the bag jumped with him, and then went rolling.

Some comrades found this cruel fire game exhilarating and extremely interesting. Lamentations from hell emitted from within the bag as it rolled on the ground like a fireball. Hashimoto pulled the strap and said: "Hey! If you're that hot, then I'll cool you down!" As he said this, he attached three hand grenades to the strap, and pulled the sack into the pond. The fire was extinguished, and the bag sank. Just as the ripples were disappearing, the grenades exploded underwater. There was a giant spray, and then the water receded, and the game was over (Wang 2005b, 460).

Masuda Rokusuke, also a superior private in the 16th Division's 20th Infantry Regiment, participated in massacres near Xuawu Lake. He wrote in his diary entry of December 14: "Entered the foreign concession[64] and swept up remnant forces mixed in with the refugees. The 4th Company alone pulled out over 500. We shot them all to death next to the Xuanwu Gate. It is said that all units achieved about this number" (Iguchi et al. n.d., 7). Masuda also kept handwritten records, which described the massacre at Xuanwu Lake in much greater detail:

> The next day (the 14), we needed to sweep the refugee zone established by the International Committee.
>
> Tens of thousands of remnant forces swore to resist to their death, but after we had completely surrounded them, not a one ran away, but rather they all escaped into this refugee zone. Today we will find them all out even if we have to push aside every blade of grass to exact vengeance for fallen comrades. We divided into platoons and searched door to door. The men in every house were subjected to our interrogation. A liaison soldier of the 2nd Platoon, Corporal Maehara, found several hundred enemy soldiers in the process of changing into civilian clothes in one large building. So we all rushed over, and lo and behold, all young remnant soldiers in matching uniforms. The rifles, pistols, sabers, and other weapons they had discarded looked like a mountain. Some had just taken off their uniforms, and others were already wearing civilian clothes, and some were wearing uniform pants with traditional Chinese clothes on their upper bodies; these were not dressed in accordance with the season, and looked out of place, so we knew at a glance what was going on.
>
> We pulled them out of the corner and had them strip so we could search them. Then we tied them up with fallen power lines. Corporal Oishi, Corporal Imoto, and some other angry men

---

64 Meaning the International Safety Zone.

beat them fiercely with sticks or power lines while scolding: "I'm only experiencing such hardship because of you! Ah!" Bam, bam – "It's because of you that we lost who-knows-how-many of our comrades! Ah!" Bam, bam –.

"Because of you, who-knows-how-many people are crying. Do you know? Ah!" Bam, bam – bam, bam. "Ah! You devil!" Boom! "You devils!" Boom! They were kicked and beaten mercilessly whether they exposed their heads or their backs. There were at least 300 Chinese there, and somewhat more of us. It was quite difficult for us to finish them off.

Not long afterward we asked a Chinese person wearing an International Committee armband: "You! Are there any Chinese soldiers?" The person pointed at a large building across from us and said: "Many." When we entered the building to look, it was completely full of refugees. We rounded up about 1,000 suspicious ones and packed them into a room, and from these we took out about 300 confirmed soldiers and tied them up... As dusk fell, nearly 600 remnant soldiers were brought near the Xuanwu Gate and all shot to death" (Nanjing War History Editing and Compilation Committee I n.d., 416).

Takashima Shiryo was a soldier in the 16th Division's 33rd Infantry Regiment. He self-published a book titled *Army Records from the Japan-China War – from Battle Diaries*, in February 2001. In his diary entry of December 14, he wrote: "The 1nd Platoon captured more than 200 remnant soldiers. They probably ran here because they hadn't known about Nanjing's fall. I went to ask Adjutant Oshima what to do with these prisoners. He said: 'Whether there are 200 or 500 of them, drag them wherever you want and kill them all!' So we loaded them into an empty train carriage at the station. It was determined that the Platoon would assist the heavy machine gun team in disposing of the prisoners on the shore of the Yangtze River. They were screaming from within the truck. A misty vapor emanated from within the truck. We took them out one by one. They were all naked and had trouble breathing, groaning and pointing to water bottles saying: 'Master, master, water, water.' 'Bastard!' I scolded. They scooped up muddy water accumulated in depressions to drink. We lined the prisoners up into four groups, with their hands up. We pulled 50 of them to the riverside. The danger was extremely small as we placed hand grenades under their feet. There were very few of us in the small unit, with only two junior officers, me and Kondo. We would have lost control if they'd gone into an all-out struggle. Maybe they gave up because they 'had no face.' If anyone had called out 'Help! Save me!' then there would have been applause all around. We dragged them out of the trucks and the warehouse, a total of 1,200 of them, and had them stand facing the river in mud up to just under their knees. When the order was given, the heavy machine gunners hiding in a trench behind them opened fire all together. They fell like dominoes, blood and flesh flying through the air. The few dozen who jumped into the river were all killed by the light machine gunners waiting on the loading pier, their blood staining the water red. Ah! What a brutal sight. Where can you see things like that in the human world? Anyone still squirming was finished off with the rifles we had captured from them. There was a naval vessel floating on the river, and sailors also observed this scene from its deck" (Wang Weixing 2005b, 714).

The 13th Division's Yamada Detachment also massacred more than 15,000 prisoners near the Shangyuan Gate. Many officers and enlisted men of the Yamada Detachment documented this massacre in their diaries; many are included in *Records of Imperial Army Soldiers from the Rape of Nanking*, edited by Ono Kenji, Fujiwara Akira, and Honda Katsuichi. Yamada Senji, commander of the 13th Division's 103rd Infantry Battalion, was author of one of the diaries included.

Yamada's diary exposed the detail that the massacre order was issued by the Army's commander. He wrote in his entry of December 14: "At dawn, shortly after arriving near the battery, I saw innumerable surrendered enemy soldiers, difficult to deal with... prisoners are difficult to deal with. At that time we happened to find a school outside the Shangyuan Gate, so we herded them into the school. There were 14,777 prisoners. With so many prisoners, it was going to be difficult whether we killed them or let them live" (Nanjing War History Editing and Compilation Committee II n.d., 331). He continued on December 15: "I sent Cavalry Second Lieutenant Honma to Nanjing to inquire in the matter of how to deal with prisoners and other matters. Orders came back to kill them all." He continued on the 16th: "I sent Lieutenant Colonel Aida to headquarters[65] to discuss the problem of how to dispose of prisoners and other matters. Guarding prisoners has become the most important task of the Tayama Battalion" (Nanjing War History Editing and Compilation Committee II n.d., 331–332). Yamada continued on December 18: "The unit has spared no effort in its disposal of prisoners. I observed conditions of the disposal from the riverbank." On the 19th, he wrote: "Our departure has been postponed due to disposal of prisoners. This morning we went out in full force to exert great efforts in disposing of prisoners" (Nanjing War History Editing and Compilation Committee II n.d., 332).

Second Lieutenant Miyamoto Shogo of the 65th Infantry Regiment's 4th Company wrote in great detail in his diary entry of December 13: "Attacked Wulong Mountain at nightfall. No enemy troops on battlefield, took many prisoners from routing soldiers and killed some too." He continues on the 14th: "Departed at 5:00 a.m., swept up enemy remnant forces. We still haven't launched an attack. The enemy has no heart for further fighting, and is surrendering. We disarmed several thousand soldiers without firing a shot. We escorted the prisoners to a camp in Nanjing at nightfall; to our amazement, they totaled 10,000. We imme-

---

65 Of the Shanghai Expeditionary Army.

diately went on guard duty. My Company set sentries at eight locations to serve as guards. Some among the prisoners ate vegetables along the road from hunger. And some asked for water to drink as they hadn't eaten in three days; it was heartrending. Nevertheless, on the field of battle one must adopt extreme measures to a certain extent. During the night, the sanitation team escorted another 200 prisoners over. There were more than 200 soldiers on guard duty, including the company commander. As these are all highly seasoned troops, they performed extremely orderly searches of everyone entering and leaving the camp, most interesting" (Ono et al. 1996, 133). On the 16, the Japanese army began to massacre this group of prisoners. Miyamoto wrote: "Just as we were eating lunch a great fire broke out, causing disorder in the extreme, and resulting in the burning of one-third of the camp. At 3:00 p.m., the Battalion decided to enact an extreme measure: to bring about 3,000 prisoners to the bank of the Yangtze River and shoot them. This is the sort of thing you can see only on the field of battle" (Ono et al. 1996, 134). On the 17, the day the Japanese army celebrated its ceremony of entering the city, Miyamoto wrote: "Today the army held the ceremony of entering Nanjing. Most people in the unit participated in the execution of prisoners. I set off at 8:30, leading our men toward Nanjing. In the afternoon we participated in the magnificent city entrance ceremony, and I witnessed with my own eyes this solemn event of historic significance... I returned at nightfall, and immediately departed to take part in the execution of prisoner soldiers. As they had already killed over 20,000, the soldiers went red-eyed with bloodlust, and in consequence unexpectedly fired upon friendly forces, killing and wounding many comrades. My Company also suffered three casualties, one dead and two wounded" (Ono et al. 1996, 134).

Second Lieutenant Sugiyuchi Toshio of the 65th Infantry Regiment's 7th Company wrote in his diary entry of December 14: "The unit departed at 5:00 a.m., direction Nanjing, at rapid march. Took 17,000 enemy prisoners near Mufu Mountain, about six kilometers outside of Nanjing, stripped them of all weapons, and handed them over to custody of the 3rd Battalion" (Ono et al. 1996, 147). Second Lieutenant Endo Takaaki of the 65th Infantry Regiment's 8th Company wrote in great detail about the capturing and massacring of prisoners in his diary:

December 14, sunny

Departed at 5:00 a.m. to attack the fort at Mufu Mountain about four kilometers to the north of Nanjing... Near Taiping Mountain encountered 1st Battalion and the several hundred prisoners it had taken, as well as repeating pistols and horses ridden by Chinese officers. We took the horses and continued our advance mounted, arriving at Mufu Mountain at noon. The enemy had no more will to fight. We captured 450 enemy soldiers and a great quantity of weapons. At nightfall we arranged to spend the night at Shangyuanli. Owing to an insufficient quantity of private residences, each platoon had to quarter in a single house. At dusk we captured another 400 or so prisoners.

December 15, sunny

Arose at 7:00 a.m. At 9:00 a.m., the Xth Platoon received orders to proceed to the east of Mufu Mountain to sweep up remnant forces on the riverbank. We took 360 prisoners. It is said that nearly 10,000 more await being taken into custody.

December 16, sunny

... At 12:30 p.m., orders were given to move out owing to a fire in the prisoner shelter. We returned at 3:00. At the shelter encountered Mr. Yokota, reporter for the *Asahi Shimbun*, and heard from him general conditions. The total number of prisoners was 17,025. At nightfall, one-third of prisoners were taken to the riverbank and shot by the 1st Battalion on orders from Army command.

As noted in the orders that came down, we would need 100 sacks (of grain) to feed them if only twice a day. But at present our soldiers are relying on requisitioned food. So it is impossible to provide them grain. Army headquarters must adopt an appropriate response.

December 17, sunny

Nighttime, five soldiers were dispatched to execute the remaining more than 10,000 prisoners...

December 18

At 1:00 a.m., superior officers ordered us to move out and help in the clean-up as the prisoner executions were not thorough, and some were left alive. We shortly arrived on the scene. A cold wind blew hard, and it began to blizzard at about 3:00, with the cold piercing to our bones. Everyone quietly but fervently longed for the dawn. At 8:30 a.m. the cleanup was completed. The wind had died down, and the weather started turning for the better. The soldiers on guard at Mufu Mountain returned. Six men went to survey Nanjing. Slept about an hour in the morning. An apple was sent down. It's been a long time since I ate an apple. At noon, nine replacement soldiers joined our rank. The Platoon dispatched 25 men to help clean up the more than 10,000 bodies from 2:00 to 7:30 p.m.

December 19, sunny

Sent out 15 soldiers at 8:00 a.m. to continue cleaning up bodies... (Ono et al. 1996, 219-220).

Some Japanese officers and enlisted men recorded the horrible scenes that followed the massacres in their diaries. Yamazaki Masao (Infantry Lieutenant Colonel) was a staff officer in the 10th Army headquarters. He wrote in his diary entry of December 17: "After the celebration, Lieutenant Colonel Hiroshi took us to inspect the city. We first arrived at the Japanese embassy, where Staff Officer Hidaka and embassy officials came out to meet us. He expressed profound thanks to us: only four months had passed since the Japanese flag had been taken down, and now it was again flying high above the roof. This was an extremely emotional event for him. We then proceeded northward on Zhongshan North Road, where we saw the Ministry of War, the Ministry of Communications, the Foreign Ministry, the Ministry of Railways, the Supreme Court, and other buildings of the nationalist government, before proceeding to the Zhongshan Wharf on the Yangtze River. The river is relatively narrow at this point; there were seven or eight navy destroyers moored on the river there. Innumerable bodies had been discarded on the riverbank, all soaking in the water. The bodies were stacked in piles of different heights. Truly it was a scene of innumerable dead bodies all along the Yangtze River's shore. If they were all salvaged from the water onto the land, they could be piled as high as a mountain" (Nanjing War History Editing and Compilation Committee I n.d., 302).

Ueba Buichiro was a medic in the 16th Division's hospital corps. He wrote in his diary entry of December 21: "The army advanced to inspect the aftermath of the intense fighting at the Sun Yat-sen Mausoleum. We saw about 500 bodies cruelly piled on the ground at the entrance from Taiping Gate. These people were truly pitiable! Some of the bodies had their abdomens pierced, or their heads cut off, or their faces smashed. There were gun carriages and traces of fierce fighting everywhere" (Iguchi et al. n.d., 31).

Kitayama Atae was assigned to the 3rd Machine Gun Company of the 16th Division's 20th Infantry Regiment. He wrote in his diary entry of December 27: "We exited from the Hanzhong Gate to requisition vegetables and water buffaloes. The dead were piled into a mountain where we arrived, about 500 of them in all, piled up and killed together. Most of them were soldiers, but some were dressed like civilians. Most of them were prisoners who had been killed en masse. Both sides of the road were piled to capacity with dead Chinese soldiers" (Iguchi et al. n.d., 74).

Makino Nobuo was a superior private in the 16th Division's 20th Infantry Regiment. He wrote in his diary entry of December 27: "Got up at 6:00 a.m. Immediately prepared breakfast. After breakfast, went to requisition vegetables at 8:00 a.m. Corporal Yotsukata led. Went out Hanzhong Gate toward Yangtze River. When exiting Hanzhong Gate, saw 500 to 600 burned bodies in a tight group piled there. Their burned skin had gone yellow, and was horrid to look at. Maybe we had been too far removed from the fighting, so we felt nauseous after seeing them. Wretched bodies like this were scattered everywhere" (Nanjing War History Editing and Compilation Committee I n.d., 408–409).

6.2.2 Correspondences

At present, most wartime correspondence of Japanese officers and soldiers is still held by private citizens in Japan, but some have been included in local history compilations and, thereby, made public. For example, there is the *History of Asaba (Compilation Three: Modern Era)*, compiled and edited by the Asaba Town History Compilation Committee and published in August 1998 by the Town of Asaba, Shizuoka Prefecture. The *History* contains many pieces of wartime correspondence by combat soldiers, but the names of senders and recipients alike are kept anonymous. In addition, other collections of wartime correspondence have been published in individual cases, such as the letters of Superior Private Iwasaki Shoji of the Shanghai Expeditionary Army's 1st Independent Engineering Regiment, edited by his posterity and published in a volume titled *The Orbit of a Battle – Iwasaki Shoji's Wartime Correspondence*, published by Kindai Bungeisha of Japan in June 1995.

Tabata Yasuzo was a member of the 16th Division's 22nd Field Heavy Artillery Regiment. He wrote in a letter home to the village administrative office of Sana Village on December 22: "On the 14 we entered the city of Nanjing. From then until now, we have not stopped sweeping up remnant soldiers inside and outside the city. Many refugees have congregated everywhere inside the city, revealing to us the tragic, pitiable plight of the people of a defeated nation. Not long after fighting ended, the air of Nanjing still reeked of blood. Now my unit has been assigned to guard duty in Nanjing (time undetermined), but I predict we will remain within the city. As another chapter of the war has come to a close, the day of ultimate victory may not be too far off." On January 1, 1938, Tabata wrote another letter, to Mr. Hanatani Matsuzo of the Military Support Association of Sana Village, this time writing: "So far we're still in Nanjing, on guard duty in the city. Conditions are gory. The new battlefield is now being gradually cleaned up through great efforts by all units of the Imperial Army. Most of the bodies of Chinese soldiers, previously piled into mountains, have now been burned. I predict my unit will stay in Nanjing for the time being. The duration of the stay, however, is undetermined" (Mie Prefecture History Compilation Bureau n.d., n.p.).

Okemura Kametaro was a member of an artillery company in the 16th Division's 33rd Infantry Regiment. In a letter home to the village chief of Hanatani Village of January 13, 1938, he wrote: "On November 12 we conducted a landing before the enemy at Wujiang on the right bank of the Yangtze River under cover from the navy. From then until the fall of Nanjing on December 12, I've been killing with my bayonet, both enemy soldiers and rural civilians. All houses and food have been burned. As for camps, I've been dreaming my nightly dreams on grass piled on mud under trees. To cook rice we've been using turbid water from little streams on which bodies float... On the 14 we entered the city via the Yijiang Gate. The once proud capital of Nanjing is now a tragic scene too horrible to look at. From now on I'm to sweep up remnant forces inside and outside the city and to be on guard duty" (Mie Prefecture History Compilation Bureau n.d.).

The *History of Asaba (Compilation Three: Modern Era)* contains letters written by a soldier working in the supply department of the Central China Area Army, all presented in the book as "letter from ____ to B." One such letter reads: "Once arrived in Nanjing, I took a look around, and truly it is the Nanjing so famous around the world. The city walls are five stories high and as wide as five rooms. In fact, this gave our army quite a headache. The city wall three *ri* horizontal and three *ri* vertical separates the city of Nanjing from the outside world. Now there is not a single house fully intact within the city, only ruins leftover from fires, a tragedy... I am stationed outside the city, actually on the Yangtze River. The Bank of China, originally five stories tall, is now only three stories after having been burned. I am assigned to Supply Department Unit B. Our commander Major Aoki is a good person. The Supply Department's job is to distribute grain and such to the various units. All goods shipped up the Yangtze come here. There are so many goods here, but only 50 infantrymen to guard over it all, making the job especially onerous. As of the 31 (of December) of last year, at least 200 captive Chinese soldiers were executed on the shore of the Yangtze every day. They were pushed into the river with their hands bound, or had machine guns opened on them from above, or had their heads cut off with swords. The people of a defeated nation are truly wretched. To me it felt just like killing chickens. During the night of December 27, some people came to rob the supply depot of food. Seven people were caught, and all stabbed to death with bayonets, quite fun. These are all miserable conditions people in Japan will never see" (Asaba Town History Commission n.d., 456).

Iwasaki Shoji was a superior private in the 1st Independent Engineering Regiment of the Shanghai Expeditionary Force who died in combat near Zhengyangguan, Anhui, on June 9, 1938. Prior to his death he wrote many letters to family and friends at home. In a letter of December 17 to Yamaguchi Fumiko, he wrote: "On the evening of December 11, our company also joined the attack on the city of Nanjing. I say the city of Nanjing, but it is five *ri* in circumference, surrounded by walls six meters thick and 10 meters high, with machine gun firing points everywhere. How many of our loyal, brave soldiers fell before these machine guns! We covered them with the bodies of enemies before the walls, and onto that shoveled earth; this is how our comrades were buried. There were also foreigners within the city. There were five or six thousand Chinese bodies in that great river called the Yangtze. We killed more than 300 in one day on the 14. We didn't know if we were killing or what we were doing" (Iwasaki n.d., 71–72).

6.2 Diaries and Correspondence of Japanese Officers and Soldiers — 379

In a letter to his family written at the Xiaguan Railway Station on December 17, Iwasaki described the massacre of prisoners:

On December 12, we received orders to attack the city of Nanjing (I fear that people back home can't imagine what I mean when I use the simple term "city of Nanjing." Its wall is about 35 *shaku* or more high, and its circumference is purported to be four *ri*). We then charged forward to the military engineering school about two kilometers ahead of us... By late in the night of the 12, the military engineering school had fallen completely under the control of us military engineers. One of our number was wounded, but they ran off, leaving behind several dozen weapons. We captured 77 remnant soldiers, and shot them on the spot. These were worthy of being called Chinese regular troops; some died most righteously, and some met their demise standing erect, smiling into the muzzles of our guns. If only a tenth of the men of China are like them, it will be most arduous for Japan to fight with them.

... before dawn on December 13, we circled around the city of Nanjing and seized some passenger boats on the shore of the Yangtze River, as well as 15 automobiles, three tanks, and two motorcycles in the surrounding area. At the time our navy had arrived on the river and was laying down constant fire. Gunfire into the city from the land was also unbroken, a truly awesome scene. The engineering unit seized the Railway Station at Xiaguan before dawn on the 14. Right then we military engineers shot to death about 800 remnant soldiers with our own hands on the bank of the Yangtze. We even had no idea if we were killing people or throwing bamboo into the river to float away.

Today (now 2:30 p.m. on the 17) I spent the entire morning making rounds in the surrounding area, and have been resting this afternoon. After killing Chinese soldiers on the land, we piled their bodies, doused them with oil, and burned them. The bodies of Chinese soldiers were piled two to three high over an area about as big as the plaza of Aikawa Primary School. Today the ceremony for the entrance of Nanjing was held. I did not attend (only one officer and 12 enlisted men of our company went). Consequently, we assembled the about 2,000 Chinese captured in the city last night and killed them all before dawn this morning. There were about 5,000 dead bodies piled in disarray on the banks of the Yangtze alone. A kind of river fish roughly equivalent to "dolphins" kept swimming over and picking at the bodies.

Now the general feeling is greatly relaxed. Looking out from the front windows of the Xiaguan Railway Station, I'm thinking of many people back home I haven't seen in a long time. Outside there is a frequent "bang bang" sound. That's the sound of the shooting of those remnant troops that weren't among the annihilated. The unusual stench from the burning of bodies periodically wafts in... The people of a defeated country are truly pitiable. I've written many times in my letters that I would leave none alive. But why? What would happen if one person were left alive? The Japanese army on the battlefield is in no way like the Japanese army at troop review ceremonies. My subordinates and comrades can be wounded or killed. It's now gone completely crazy. If we so much as see a Chinese, then someone screams "kill him!" and he's doomed. If just one Chinese soldier lives and returns to his ranks, what will the consequences be? The Chinese are deft propagandists. They're being sacrificed for the Imperial Army, for Japan. I'm not the only one who feels this way. It's everyone in my platoon (formerly 16, of whom two are dead and five wounded). No! Everyone in the whole company feels this way. Even if we know they're good people, the feeling is that we have no choice but to kill them. I guess you can understand, right? (Iwasaki n.d., 73–76).

On December 27, Iwasaki wrote a letter from Nanjing to his uncle Ono Minosuke and aunt, writing: "We began participating in the attack on the city of Nanjing on the 10. In the pre-dawn hours of the 11, we launched a wide-scale artillery barrage, with fire concentrated on the city gates, and we quickly seized the city. Our platoon occupied a military engineering school about two kilometers before us. We shot 77 remnant troops, from a feeling of wanting revenge. In the pre-dawn hours of the 14, we completely occupied Nanjing. There were constant cries of "long may he live!" from behind us. Everybody was moved to the point of tears, so happy they simply couldn't stand it, as joyous as little children. The fighting here was easier than elsewhere, and so everyone was quite happy, feeling that the war had already ended. From the 11 to the 14, we ate Nanjing's rice with salted vegetables. There were five or six thousand bodies on the bank of the Yangtze, piled into a mountain. Dogs and cats picked meat from them. One extremely large dog pounced on me. We are now in complete control of Nanjing. There are still many Chinese here" (Iwasaki n.d., 79–80).

6.3 Memoirs of Former Japanese Soldiers and Military Correspondents

6.3.1 Memoirs of Japanese officers and soldiers

After the war, many former Japanese soldiers who had participated in the attack on Nanjing and the Rape of Nanking wrote memoirs or essays on their experiences recounting conditions on the battlefield. The war memoirs of former soldiers published in Japan to date can be grossly divided into the following four categories:

First, compilations of essays recounting war experiences published as books. Most such volumes are published by relevant groups, a few important ones including: *Army Memoirs (the China Incident and the Great Asian War)* volume 1 (August 1970), compiled by the Army Memoir Compilation Committee; *To a Generation that Has Never Known War (53) Kumamoto Edition: The Yangtze River is Crying – Records of Fighting on the Continent by the 6th Division of Kumamoto* (Daisan Bunmeisha, September 1979), compiled by the Soka Gakkai Youth Anti-War Publishing Committee; *The Chinese Continent Dyed Red with Blood – Records of Personal Experiences of the Injurers* (Saisan Bunmeisha, August 1983), compiled by the Soka Gakkai Youth Anti-War Publishing Committee; *The Things We Did in China – Members of the Society for Those Returned from China* (Yokukaze Shuppan, May 2002), edited by Hoshi Toru; *Changjiang Shui · Langtao Tian – Shanghai Dongya Tongwen shuyuan daxue di 34 xueqi xuesheng fanyi congjun ji* [*Water of the Yangtze · Waves in the Sky – Student Translated Military Records of the Shanghai Dongya Tongwen Shuyuan University, 34th Edition*] (Shanghai Friendship Association 34th Student Association, published in April 1993), edited by the Committee for Editing of Translated Military Records; *Nanjing da tusha – xiang Riben ren gaofa* [*The Rape of Nanking – an Accusation Against the People of Japan*] (Dongfang chuban, September 1992), edited by the Nationwide Networking Association for Revealing the Truth of the Rape of Nanking; and so on.

Second, memoirs edited, compiled, and published by editing committees composed of former soldiers from the same unit, and memoirs from some soldiers contained in unit histories, including: *Recollections of the Tsuruga Regiment* (April 1982), edited by the Bureau for Editing and Compiling Recollections of the Tsuruga Regiment; *History of the 36th Infantry Regiment of Sabae* (August 1976), edited by the Committee for Editing the History of the 36th Infantry Regiment of Sabae; *History of the 3rd Cavalry Regiment* (November 1978), edited by the Committee for Compiling the History of the 3rd Cavalry Regiment; *Memoirs of Medics in the 3rd Division* (published by the Committee for Publishing the Memoirs of Medics in the 3rd Division, publication time unknown, noted as 1987 in foreword), edited by the Committee for Editing the Memoirs of Medics in the 3rd Division; *History of the 3rd Company of the 20th Infantry Regiment of Fukuchiyama* (published by the Committee for Publishing the History of the 3rd Company of the 20th Infantry Regiment of Fukuchiyama, November 1982), edited by the Committee for Editing the History of the 3rd Company of the 20th Infantry Regiment of Fukuchiyama; *Hand-written Notes on the China Incident of Comrades in Arms from the 4th Company of the 20th Infantry Regiment (Saka Company)* (date of publication unknown), edited by Ohigashi Shinsuke; and so on. There is also *Battle of Nanjing • Searching for Closed Memories – Testimonies of 102 Former Soldiers* (Shakai Hyoronsha, August 2002), written by Matsuoka Tamaki on the basis of over 100 interviews with former soldiers.

Third, war memoirs written by former soldiers, published as individual volumes. There are many such memoirs in Japan, with some important examples including: *From Ichigayadai to Ichigayadai – Memoir of the Last Deputy Chief of Staff* by Kawabe Torashiro (Jiji Press, November 1962); *Thirty-one Years as a Military Policeman* by Kamisago Shoshichi (Tokyo Raifusha, 1955); *War Memoir* by Watanabe Ushichi (February 1969); *This is How I Fought* by Kodama Yoshio (Tsujido, 1975); *Secret War Memoir of People from Gunma Prefecture – the Road to Defeat* (Asaosha, August 1979); *Hand-written Recollections of a Staff Officer* by Iketa

Nihanjiro (May 1978); *Nanjing – Xuzhou – Wuhan: Recollections of an Advancing Army* by Yamamoto Isamu (Sankuyu Friendship Office, November 1973); *True Records from the Battle Line* by Ishida Giichi (March 1977); *Memoir of a War Horse – Hand-written Records of a Transportation Corps Soldier* by Yoshida Kanoe (Committee for Publishing the "War Horse Memoir," October 1979); *War Memoir of Life* by Ishii Seitaro (IDEA Corporation, April 1991); *True Records of the Japan-China War* by Ito Isamu (Kitaguni Shubbansha, November 1980); *Army Record from the Japan-China Incident – Bursting into Nanjing* by Yokoyama Katsunosuke (December 1999); *Nanjing Massacre and War* by Sone Kazuo (Tairyusha, 1988); and so on.

Fourth, articles written by former Japanese soldiers published in Japanese periodicals. Examples include: "Testimony on the Rape of Nanking – Saying Everything I Want to Say" by Nakamura Misaki (*Numazu Asahi Shimbun*, July 10, 1991); "The Attack on Nanjing and Massacre Incident" by Shimada Katsumi (*Tokushu Jinbutsu Orai*, June 1956); "Participating in the Landing Before the Enemy at Hangzhou Bay – A Soldier Recounts the Japan-China War" by Okamoto Kenzo (*Chugoku*, August 1971); and so on.

Most memoirs on the attack on Nanjing and the Rape of Nanking were written by former soldiers many years after the war, and so there are some disparities in details like times, places, unit numbers, and so on. In addition, some former soldiers were unwilling to attach their names to their memoirs, but rather wrote under pseudonyms. They are, nevertheless, of great value.

Most memoirs written by former high-ranking officers recount the decision-making process behind the attack on Nanjing from a strategic perspective. For example, former chief of the Combat Department of the Army General Staff Headquarters Kawabe Torashiro wrote in his memoir *From Ichigayadai to Ichigayadai – Memoir of the Last Deputy Chief of Staff:* "After remnant enemy forces had been mopped up in the periphery of Shanghai, I obeyed orders to take a trip to discuss battle tasks with commanders of the Area Army stationed nearby... I asked for opinions from the chief of staff and deputy chief of staff of Army Commander Matsui. I also conveyed to them the central ministry's thoughts on expanding the war to Guangdong by diverting a division and a half from Shanghai. After extensive talks, we came to the following conclusions: First, stop the current pursuit of the enemy and allow our units a brief rest and reorganization somewhere between the west of Shanghai and Hangzhou. During the respite, make careful observations of enemy conditions and other conditions in Nanjing and everywhere on the route thereto. Finally, make a new study of whether to launch an attack on Nanjing. The Area Army's commanders did not disagree at all in the diversion of a division and a half worth of forces for other uses. As for personal opinions, General Matsui himself was a hawk who went out of his way to emphasize the necessity of an attack on Nanjing, and to this point he said, categorically and with full self-assurance: We will be victorious in this attack even if a division and a half of forces are diverted away. As for reordering battle lines and allowing the units who had been constantly fighting all-out since August a brief rest and reorganization, he was of the same opinion as his chief of staff, holding that such was extremely necessary... Shortly after my return to Tokyo, Commander Matsui sent a telegram to headquarters saying: 'There have been dramatic changes in battlefield conditions since Colonel Kawabe departed from Shanghai. Enemy forces have been utterly routed. All forts along the Yangtze River between Shanghai and Nanjing have been abandoned. We are preparing to profit from this opportunity to take the fight to the last and drive straight to Nanjing.' The Central Ministry ultimately decided to attack Nanjing based on this telegram" (Kawabe n.d., 144–145).

Hojo Yasuo (pseudonym) was a corporal in the 10th Field Artillery Regiment. He arrived in Nanjing after it had fallen and played a direct role in the Rape of Nanking. He wrote in his memoir:

> After Nanjing had been occupied, we entered the city on the heels of the infantry. We entered Nanjing through the South Gate. Once entered, the first thing that shot into our eyesight were the mountainous piles of bodies everywhere on the battlefield... After entering Nanjing, we were stationed there for a while, and it was just during this time that the Nanjing Massacre Incident occurred. I was a corporal at the time. During this time the behavior of the Japanese army was completely cruel and inhuman. On the one hand, it was my personal ideology that made me think so, and on the other hand, I had achieved the sixth degree in Kendo. I frequently ordered groups of four to five subordinates to massacre enemy soldiers after receiving such orders from superiors. I shudder from terror at the thought of it even now.
>
> One time, we were ordered to burn to death a plainclothes enemy unit. To prevent them from escaping, we tied the prisoners' hands behind their backs and impounded them in an empty private residence. Once they were all in, we doused the house with gasoline and set it on fire. There weren't 10 or 20 prisoners in that house, but hundreds. Once the flames began leaping toward the sky, we heard the screams. Some wanted to open the door to flee, but it had been barred shut from the outside. Some who managed to escape were immediately shot to death by sentries. Hearing their last cries of anguish before being burned to death and watching them roll about in the flames before being burned to death, this was unbearable as a fellow human being, regardless how many times our superiors said: "This is war!" "They are the enemy!"
>
> ...
>
> Similar events constantly reoccurred thereafter... (Hojo n.d., 225–227).

Saito Chujiro belonged to the transportation corps of the 16th Division. He recalled the following scenes in great detail in his memoir:

My company arrived at the strategic location of the Qilin Gate on the afternoon of the 13, I think. ...

The platoon commander said to everyone: "From now we are to begin sweeping up remnant soldiers in the periphery of the camp. These remnant soldiers may be in hiding, and so all small buildings of no value to our army are to be burned without exception." He then gave a box of matches to every soldier.

Our platoon set out under command of Superior Private Nakamura. We walked a stretch of road leading from a crossroads toward the Taiping Gate, from which I saw far away behind some villages to the east two small huts standing side by side looking out into the fields. I approached them and set fire to the rice straw stacked around them. The fire spread quickly. Suddenly a remnant soldier wearing a khaki wool uniform but no helmet burst out.

I screamed "there's someone here!" Three soldiers aside the field held their rifles to their shoulders and began firing in my direction. Maybe because they were flustered and didn't pull the trigger hard enough, no bullets came out. The enemy fled along the ridges in the fields at maximum speed, as though flying. Superior Private Nakamura screamed loudly "What's going on here!?" while pressing his rifle to his shoulder and firing a shot at the enemy soldier. The bullet penetrated his right thigh, and he fell to the ground, and was quickly surrounded by our soldiers. We fished a triangular cloth out of his jacket and used it to bind his wound. Someone asked: "Send him back to regiment headquarters?" Superior Private Nakamura found this bothersome, so he ordered that the soldier be shot to death.

We returned to the shacks overlooking the fields. Just then a young man in sturdy physical condition wearing civilian clothes ran out of the adjacent shack, now also being consumed by a raging fire. He was on fire himself and had been burned so much as to resemble a fire-being, groping forward with both hands. His eyes, nose, mouth, and his whole face had been burned to the color of an earthen wall. He probably had gotten the lay of the land before hiding in the shack, so even though he couldn't see, he darted straight for a pond 20 or 30 meters away and jumped in with a great "kerplunk!"

We stood beside the pond watching.

Someone shouted: "Shoot him!" So we opened fire. Even at only 30 meters, we just couldn't hit our target. Right then Second Lieutenant Nishikawa of regiment headquarters passed by on inspection. He said: "What are you doing? This is how you should shoot!" He stood still and took a single shot with his rifle, killing the man.

......

It seems that Squad Leader Yoshida went to perform a sweep by himself. He ran into a remnant soldier and shot him to death. Maybe because the gunshot had frightened by the gunshot, an enemy soldier suddenly stood up behind him. Yoshida desperately threw down his rifle, turned, and lunged ferociously with his bayonet at the man's abdomen. He told the entire squad: "In went the bayonet, and out came his guts."

......

The next day, I joined the sweeping squad led by Medic Sergeant Ito. This time our sweep proceeded in a different direction: to the left side of the Nanjing-Shanghai Highway. There was a private house built on a height less than 100 meters away. When we went to search it, an old woman came out. There was probably only one way in and out, so she fled in the direction from which we were approaching. Before someone could finish saying "quick, shoot her!" we had opened fire, and didn't stop shooting until she lay motionless on the ground. Sergeant Ito fired the most shots.

The soldiers split up to continue searching, and captured a total of six Chinese. They were all dressed in civilian clothes. One of them was big and tall, of a muscular physique, but he was no more than an innocent child. These six were taken to the side of a pond. Someone said we should let the boy go, but in the end we opened fire on all of them next to the pond, and they all fell into the water.

......

Upon entering the city, we immediately began cleaning up the battlefield, which is to say cleaning up enemy corpses and other things. We loaded them into trucks to be transported elsewhere without expending too much energy, but because there were so many corpses we had to bury the rest of the bodies in nearby air-raid shelters (Saito n.d., 32–41).

One former soldier from the 3rd Battalion of the 13th Division's 19th Mountain Artillery Regiment wrote about massacres near Mufu Mountain, but did not reveal his name:

We were getting closer and closer to Nanjing. The city was right before our eyes, so we summoned all our courage and pressed the attack. Probably on the afternoon of the 14, we saw 50 to 100 captive soldiers clustered together raise a white flag to surrender. Some of these had been wounded by bayonets, rifle shots, and artillery blasts. Upon seeing them I thought to myself: "It's all your fault I'm in this war and have had to endure such hardships!" No matter what, I thought, it's all your fault that I've endured these hardships. At home everyone says I'm a good father, an honest and decent man, but that's all gone on this battlefield. These kinds of thoughts are a matter of course... While camping in some village, we brought all the men into a room and killed them with pistols or rifles. Then we locked the women and children in another room and raped the women at night. Although I didn't do it myself, I think that not a few other soldiers committed rapes like this. The morning of the next day they killed all the women they had raped and their children, and finally set the house on fire, so that even if someone came back they'd have no place to live. This is how we advanced, killing all in our wake. I found this behavior unbelievable, so I asked why they did it. The answer I got was that the anti-Japanese mentality in this region was particularly strong, and our superiors had ordered us to kill everyone here, so the only choice was to kill everyone. In brief, war is replete with arson, looting, rape, murder, and all manner of crimes... By the time we arrived near Nanjing and Mufu Mountain, the number of prisoners taken had gone beyond all counting. The 60th Regiment alone had taken about 20,000 prisoners. Among these prisoners there were boys of 12 and 13 and wrinkly old men with long beards. Absolutely all males had been rounded up... As we neared Nanjing, the prisoners called out "*xiansheng*[66]" and said "give us a smoke, give us some food." But

---

[66] Chinese for "mister" (translator's note).

we had no smokes even for ourselves. We would have had no food if we hadn't requisitioned more every day, so we had not a bit to feed to the prisoners... As there was a large camp below Mufu Mountain, we placed all the prisoners there. We called it a camp, but it was really no more than a big thatched roof supported by about 20 big beams. Nevertheless, the space could accommodate a few tens of thousands of people, so there was room for the 20,000 of them. By the afternoon of the 16, everyone was ordered outside their quarters to line up. I thought: what's going on here? But I went outside and lined up. The resulting orders were that those in the front line would go inspect Nanjing, and those in the rear would sweep up remnant soldiers. I had bad luck that day: I was in the rear... We then advanced to the camp below the battery at Mufu Mountain, the place designated by our superiors. From fear that the prisoners would flee, we stationed about 20 light and heavy machine guns on either side. Not even an ant could have escaped. The commanding officer ordered us to tie up the prisoners, but we had nothing with which to tie them up. So we tore the clothes worn by the Chinese into long strips and tied them up one by one. Once they had been tied, we ordered them to sit abreast in groups of two. When I tell you that it was 5,000 people, you must understand that this was not a small number. There were only a few hundred of us, making their numbers almost impossible to manage. We started at 1:00 p.m. and didn't have all 5,000 of them tied up until the moon had come up. It took a considerable amount of time. Some of our Japanese soldiers did not help tie up prisoners but went to a side to count up the money, watches, and other valuable objects we had stripped from them. We, on the other hand, spent the whole time earnestly tying up prisoners. Some of the prisoners got the gist of what was happening and ran in circles to tie themselves up, but any force applied would immediately loose the bonds; they came free. Nevertheless, since we Japanese soldiers had machine guns, rifles, and bayonets, we figured the prisoners couldn't escape. We aligned the prisoners into two columns and had them advance toward the Yangtze River in great confusion, with armed Japanese soldiers spaced two to three meters apart prodding them forward. On the way a prisoner tripped and fell over I-don't-know-what, and then others began to trip and fall in succession. We had no patience to pick them up, so we stabbed them all to death with our bayonets. The imprisoned soldiers walking in the back were killed. It seemed that we had taken the long way. After walking a *ri* we reached the bank of the Yangtze. On the southern shore there was a barracks or some other building; we couldn't tell. We couldn't see well because it was night. There were soldiers aiming their rifles in the second story windows and downstairs. There were 5,000 prisoners sitting in the plaza, with a stone wall a few meters high on the northern end. Even with the low visibility from darkness, I figured this was a high stone wall, and so they couldn't flee in that direction. The prisoners sat in the courtyard, and the Japanese soldiers among them tested their sabers on them. One dragged out a prisoner and cut off his head. Another bayoneted a prisoner to death. That's how the soldiers did their killing. I had never really cut off a living person's head since joining the war, so I borrowed the sergeant major's saber and took a swing at the paralyzed soldier, but I only cut halfway. Actually it's not easy to cut off a head. I couldn't cut the head off no matter how I tried. As the soldiers were thus engaged, one prisoner loudly shouted "wah!" and everyone got to their feet. The firing shouldn't have started until the machine gun platoon commander ordered "fire!" But because the 5,000 men had all gotten to their feet, we couldn't sit there and do nothing. So before the order to "fire!" had gone out, the machine guns started, da da da, firing from the side. I also wanted to take a shot, or more than one shot, but I figured it was too dangerous, so I stopped after taking one shot. All the same, the

5,000 prisoners fell to the ground one by one under the fire of multiple machine guns. Then an order came down to advance on them with bayonets and stab them, as there may have been survivors among them, so that's what we did. At the time I didn't have a Japanese rifle but a Chinese one, and I couldn't affix a Japanese bayonet to it. With no other option, I borrowed a Japanese rifle from a comrade and slung the Chinese rifle over my back. As I advanced over the prisoners' bodies, I must have stabbed more than 30 of them. The next morning my arms were so sore I couldn't lift them. Then something happened. A member of the machine gun platoon died, and there seemed to have been a prisoner jump over the stone wall. Many hundreds jumped into the Yangtze, escaping on pieces of wood or on broken boards. This is no lie. Per these inferences, the Nanjing Massacre Incident becomes extremely clear. At the time, the prisoners who jumped over the stone wall grabbed hold of soldiers on the sand on the other side holding guns and other emergency necessities and rolled with them into the river. After this sneak attack, once these Japanese soldiers had gulped a few mouthfuls of river water, they let go of their guns and swam to the surface. "Don't let that bastard come up!" a Japanese soldier shouted, then stabbed him to death. We finally started back around 8:00 p.m. and had dinner. The next day was the Nanjing City-Entry Ceremony, in which we participated. I heard that the soldiers who had not swept up remnant forces the day before were ordered to do so that day, and these were quite unlucky. They used hooks made of tree branches to drag all the bodies of prisoners who'd died the day before into the Yangtze. There had been 5,000, but those in the Morozumi Unit spread a rumor that it had been 20,000, so during this time we definitely committed a few massacres of prisoners (Wang 2010d, 243–245).

Akahoshi Yoshio, formerly of the 6th Division, recalls thus: "On December 14 we passed through the city on our way to the shore of the Yangtze... The shore of the Yangtze was like a common dock; it was where boats departed and landed. But while standing there looking at the Yangtze's water, what I saw was an unbelievable sight. There was a number beyond counting of bodies floating across a 2,000-meter wide, no maybe even wider, stretch of the river. Looking out, I could see nothing but bodies. There were bodies on the shore, bodies in the water, and not only soldiers' bodies, but those of ordinary civilians too. There were adults and children, men and women, slowly floating down the river like a big wooden raft. When I looked upstream, I saw bodies piled as high as a mountain. It felt like there was no end to the bodies coming down. I guess that at least there must have been 50,000 or more, most of these being ordinary civilians. The Yangtze had truly become a 'river of cadavers'" (Akahoshi n.d., 28–30).

Kajitani Kenro was the Japanese officer in charge of the second berth at Nanjing. He recalls the scene of massacre he personally witnessed in Nanjing:

Not long after our entry into the capital of Nanjing, on December 15 of the Showa Era, around 2:00 a.m., we heard a loud burst of gunfire that seemed to have come from a heavy machine gun. My bunkmate Corporal Karube Konezou and I felt this couldn't have been an enemy attack, so we held our pistols above our shoulders and rushed out to the Yangtze harbor... Not long afterward, we figured out where the crack of gunfire had come from. We were stunned at the terrifying sight before us. They were in the process of executing enemy soldiers taken prisoner. They had been forced to line up into four horizontal ranks. Their legs were free, but their hands had been tied behind their backs. The ranks extended down the long, winding road. There was a sentry with a bayonet every four to five meters on either side. Anyone who uttered a word or bent slightly at the waste was ruthlessly beaten with a gun. They were forced to march a half step or a step at a time forward. Now let me describe the method of execution. Carrying out the duty were two heavy machine guns. It was the dry season on the Yangtze then. There was a mortar-shaped bottom about 45 meters wide between the shore and the water. They were driven to the water's edge. The two heavy machine guns adjusted their positions slightly and then opened fire. There was about five meters between them. Almost all of were either hopelessly resigned to their impending deaths or tried to run down the slope even against the overwhelming odds they wouldn't make it. I saw eight out of ten fall victim to the heavy machine guns, while the rest struggled in a death-defying effort to open their bonds and run at full sprint to the water. They were already beyond all concern about the bone-cutting cold. The heavy machine guns did not, however, continue firing at them, because there was no time to. Those who jumped into the water swam a great distance before resurfacing, and then continued to swim downstream amid the fierce currents. We could see very clearly because the moon was bright... The bodies gradually multiplied along the bank; I won't forget that scene even unto my dying day. It has remained engraved extremely deeply in my memory. It feels as though it happened yesterday; by no means does it feel like something that happened 44 years ago. Because I was a soldier, I had already prepared myself psychologically for death, so I did my best to stay calm, but I was shocked to stupefaction by that scene... I had not specially intended to count the exact number of prisoners, but their number was far larger than I had expected after I walked 70 or 80 meters behind the unit to take a look. They extended on and on, and I felt more and more overwhelmed. The sound of heavy machine gun fire never stopped during this time... We decided to return to the machine guns by walking around the left side of the column. A sentry holding a bayonet saw our cavalry insignia and marks of our rank as non-commissioned officers and immediately inferred we belonged to another unit. He nodded his head slightly and said in a low voice: "I don't know you, but these were orders from above. Please go somewhere else." This was certainly said to me. I thought this was understandable, so I took a look at him and nodded assent. It would be very hard for a young soldier in the service now to say something like that. He was possibly a drafted soldier, about 30 years old. Being able to say what he did so calmly under such circumstances, he must have fought in every battle between Nanjing and Shanghai, a brave warrior who had risked his life in a hundred battles and come out alive. His wife was probably waiting for him at home. What could this sentry's state of mind have been? I imagine it was quite complicated (Wang 2006b, 106–109).

Okumiya Masatake was a pilot in the Imperial Japanese Navy's 2nd Aviation Company. After the fall of Nanjing he proceeded to the city to retrieve the wreckage of downed Japanese planes and the remains of Japanese pilots. He observed two massacres committed by the Japanese army during this time. He recalled the scenes he witnessed on December 25, 1937 in Nanjing:

> After searching for a while in that area I exited through the Xuanwu Gate, out near the broad Xuanwu Lake. There I saw a scene of unspeakable horror. There were countless bodies of Chinese piled by the lake shore and floating on the lake. I wanted to ask somebody what had led to this, but there was nobody around. This event demonstrates that something odd had taken place in Nanjing, and still was taking place up to that moment. (Note: A record says that on the 13, some units killed fleeing defeated soldiers here, but what I saw was clearly much more than that.)

> ... There was a large train station and a large wharf in Xiaguan. During my inspection there I saw an army unit, as well as what had been expressed in writing – the scene of a massive "massacre" of Chinese people.

> I could see a flat quay along the Yangtze at the most downstream end of the wharf, as well as a group of warehouses occupying a large swath of land. A group of uncovered trucks carrying about 30 Chinese each drove bumper to bumper through the warehouses. I thought this was unbelievable, so I greeted an army sentry on guard and walked up to him to find out what had happened. Perhaps because I was wearing a navy uniform, sporting both my saber and a pistol, and because I had gotten out of a navy vehicle that nobody stopped me. There was also nobody around from news organizations.

> Having walked to the central plaza, I saw a few dozen Chinese with their hands tied behind their backs. They were spaced a few meters apart each and had been dragged to the river bank. They were thrown into the river after having been killed cruelly by saber or bayonet.

> Close to the river bank, the current was so fast that it could be observed by the naked eye, as the river was deep, and the bodies floated quickly downstream. Some, however, were not entirely dead. These struggled into the shallows near the shore, and so the water near the bank became bloody. Those not entirely dead had to be finished off with a final gunshot. The series of executions had been seemingly conducted in assembly-line style, in systematic fashion. Nobody shouted instructions loudly. This point proves allows one to infer, beyond any doubt, that the action had been carried out on orders from army officers (Okumiya n.d., 33–35).

6.3.2 Recollections of military correspondents

As the Central China Area Army advanced on Nanjing, reporters from the Domei Tsushin, the *Tokyo Nichi Nichi Shimbun Company*, the *Osaka Mainichi Shimbun Company*, and other media outlets followed the army and sent reports home from the front. They were present when the army entered Nanjing. After the war, some of these reporters wrote memoirs or essays on their experiences, recording the nature of their reports and their observations of the Japanese army's advance on and capture of Nanjing. Examples include *Shanghai jidai: janarisuto no kaiso* [Shanghai Times: a Journalist's Recollections] (Chuokoron Shinsha, March 1975) by Matsumoto Shigeharu, then Shanghai bureau chief of Domei; *In the Fierce Currents of War* (Zenponsha, March 1982) by Maeda Yuji, Domei war reporter; *Invasion – Testimony of a War Reporter on the China Front* (Gendai Shichu Pankai, 1982); and others. Some Military Correspondents' memoirs have been included in Japanese historical compilations, including *Following the Army on Foot* by *Mainichi Shimbun* photographer Sato Shinju, which will soon be included within the *Compilation of Rape of Nanking Historical Materials* collection. Other recollections have been published in Japanese periodicals, including the article "The Great Massacre in Nanjing City," published in volume one of *Special Compilations – Literary Annals – I Was There (1956)*, by Imai Seigo, special war reporter from Tokyo's *Asahi Shimbun*; and "I Witnessed the 'Nanjing Tragedy,'" published in the magazine *Maru* (November 1971 edition), written by Suzuki Jiro, *Nichi Nichi Shimbun* reporter assigned to the army.

Sato Shinju witnessed the Japanese army's massacre in Nanjing in his capacity as a war photographer for the *Mainichi Shimbun*. He recalled:

After that night, it was morning of December 14.

... A liaison ran over to tell me that it seemed something had happened at the *Lihishe*.

I didn't know what had happened, but I brought my camera along to get to the bottom of it.

When I got there, there was a big door, with sentries on either side. I first took a wide shot of it all.

I took a look inside. It was like a barracks, with a square in front of the buildings. There were a hundred or so people sitting in the square. Their hands were tied behind their backs, and they looked like imprisoned wounded soldiers. In front of them there were two big pits already dug of about five square meters in area and three meters deep.

The Japanese soldier standing in front of the pit on the right was holding a Chinese rifle. He made the Chinese soldiers kneel before the pit, pressed the barrel of the rifle to the backs of their heads, and pulled the trigger. As the gunshot rang out, the Chinese soldier would slump forward and fall into the pit like an acrobat, and then become a dead body. The Japanese soldier before the pit on the left was shirtless and wielded a rifle with a bayonet affixed. He shouted "next," and a seated prisoner would be brought forward and ordered to walk to the front of the pit, and with a ferocious "yah!" he would savagely thrust his bayonet into the back of the Chinese soldier, who then immediately fell into the pit. Occasionally a Chinese soldier on the way to the pit would suddenly turn around and take off running at full clip in an attempt to save his life. The Japanese soldiers observing this unfortunate turn of events would then quickly shoot him down. The shooters stood less than a meter away from me; the bullets whizzed past my ears. That was truly a moment of extreme danger.

The faces of the Japanese soldiers carrying out the executions by rifle and bayonet were twisted. It is hard to imagine that they were normal people. They seemed to be in a state of extreme stimulation, as though they were in the grips of insanity (Nanjing War History Editing and Compilation Committee II n.d., 609–611).

Imai Seigo was a special war reporter from the *Asahi Shimbun* of Tokyo. He recalled:

It was on the slope of a small hill near the sub-office, at dusk. Four to five hundred Chinese men squatted in the darkness on the open ground. On one side there were the remnants of a collapsed black-brick tile wall. Chinese were lined up side-by-side facing the wall, six to a group. Standing 20 to 30 meters behind them were Japanese soldiers wielding rifles, shooting at them. They fell straight forward. As their bodies were about to hit the ground, they were stabbed in the back. Their cries of "ow!" as miserable as the lamentation of the soul-breaker reverberated across the little slope as the sun's last rays shone down. Then it was the turn of the next six.

One group after another was killed. The four to five hundred squatting on the open ground watched with helpless gazes as one group after another fell. What was that helplessness, that nothingness?

A large crowd of women and children surrounding the scene looked on with vacant expressions. If their faces had been carefully scrutinized individually, one would certainly have seen them full of terror and hatred as they watched their fathers, husbands, brothers, and children killed. They were certainly groaning and wailing, but my ears could hear nothing. The only sounds filling my ears were the "bang, bang" of the guns and the screams of "ah." All my eyes could see was the brick wall steadily growing a vivid red in the light of the setting sun (Imai n.d., 157).

Maeda Yuji was a reporter for the Domei News Agency. He recalled in his memoir: "The next day (December 16) I went to the Military Officers' School along with Arai, photographer Haraikawa, and others. I met with them at the site of the 'executions' there. Some prisoners were being held in one corner of the school building. A non-commissioned officer dragged them out to the exercise yard one by one and then escorted them to the air raid trench at the front. Then the unit of soldiers already in place stabbed them in the back with bayonets. After a round of painful screams, the prisoners fell forward into the trench, and the soldiers stabbed them to death from above. This manner of execution was conducted in three places simultaneously... That afternoon, after I'd left the sub-office, I heard a gunshot. So I brought the liaison Nakamura Taroichi to investigate the source of the gunshot. It turned out to have come from beside a pond behind the Bank of Communications, where 'executions' were also taking place. Carrying out these executions were a group of soldiers wielding rifles and handguns. They made the prisoners stand beside the pond and then shot them from behind. Those who fell into the pond but were still breathing were finished off with a supplementary bullet from the bank. These executions were somewhat less cruel than those of the morning. 'Mr. Reporter, would you like to take a try?' The non-commissioned officer in charge of the soldiers handed me a rifle. I retracted my hand in fear and encouraged Nakamura to take the gun, saying, 'how about you?' Nakamura sneered as he took the gun. He pointed the muzzle at the back of a prisoner and pulled the trigger. After the bang, the man fell into the pond with a kerplunk as though his back had been broken, sending ripples across its surface. Just like that, a life ended" (Wang 2007c, 449–451).

Suzuki Jiro was a reporter from the *Tokyo Nichi Nichi Shimbun* covering the army for the journal's society section. After the war, he testified at the International Military Tribunal for the Far East. He recalled the scenes he personally witnessed in Nanjing:

> The next day, the 13, a group of a dozen including the painter Nakagawa Kigen and the now deceased Oya Soichi of the *Osaka Mainichi Shimbun* as well as follow-up reporters and photographers from the *Tokyo Nichi Nichi Shimbun* took an abandoned brick hotel downtown as their headquarter at the front and moved in. I, on the other hand, again returned to the Zhongshan Gate.
>
> There, I witnessed a first cruel, tragic massacre at first time.
>
> The prisoners were lined up single file on the 25-meter wide city wall and were stabbed to death one by one before falling to the outside of the city.
>
> Many Japanese soldiers brandishing bayonets screamed loudly before thrusting their weapons into the chests or abdomens of the prisoners. Fresh blood spurted through the air. It was like hell.
>
> I think it was at this time that I again saw the face of that savage soldier who wanted to stab me to death. Before this cruel scene I stood stupefied for a long time.
>
> ……
>
> When I regained my senses, I left that place. On the way back, I again slipped into the courtyard of the *Lizhishe*. There I saw a large tree I hadn't noticed before with ten or so remnant soldiers tied up with iron wire standing before it.
>
> Their faces were all as white as paper, and they were all topless. Some were sitting, some standing. They looked at me with vacant expressions.

At this time a group of Japanese soldiers entered making a hubbub. Two or three of them were holding pickaxes; this is how I knew they were military engineers.

They didn't cast a single look in my direction. One of them walked up to the tree and said: "so these fellows think they can attack my partners?" With that he swung the pickax into one of the defenseless prisoners.

The shiny pickax tip struck with a "kacha," and then the blood came "gulu gulu" gushing out. Upon seeing this, the others began struggling and squirming, but there was nothing they could do. Then the next soldier came forward to commit a violent act. This was truly a moment of tragedy too horrible to look upon.

Among the prisoners were some wearing military uniforms and wearing belts, but some appeared to be ordinary citizens.

There was nothing I could do to stop it. All I could do was flee.

……

To the north of the city looking across the river at Pukou sits Xiaguan, the major land-water transportation hub. The scene here was even more gory. Thousands of soldiers and civilians with no place to hide were driven here by Japanese soldiers and gunned down by machine guns. Their blood formed rivers, their bodies mountains. Even the yellow waters of the wide Yangtze were stained red, and countless bodies floated down the river.

In this area with its high concentration of warehouses there were countless scenes of soldiers carrying out executions by bayonet. This is now a neighborhood of death that terrifies people to their cores (Wang 2010e, 810 – 812).

Although these military correspondents did not directly participate in the massacre, their recollections provide powerful evidence for the Rape of Nanking perpetrated by their countrymen in arms.

6.3.4 Reports in Major Japanese Newspapers

6.3.4.1 Reports in the Tokyo Nichi Nichi Shimbun

After the Marco Polo Bridge Incident in 1937, the *Tokyo Nichi Nichi Shimbun* and the *Osaka Mainichi Shimbun*, being part of the same news group, jointly dispatched special reporters to report on war conditions in China.

On December 2, the Nichi Nichi Shimbun published this up to date report from the front: "The Imperial Army's attack is accelerating, and strong enemy positions on a line between Jiangyin and Changzhou have fallen into our hands instantaneously... On the morning of the 29, while Changzhou was being completely occupied, the Tashiro, Morozumi, Soeda, and Kurabayashi units sacked the county city of Jiangyin, that afternoon seizing the vital passage to Nanjing, the Changzhou Fort... The forces that occupied Jiangyin have continued to press westward. Their front units have already occupied a corner of Danyang City. The forces advancing westward around the south of Lake Tai through Sanzhoushan passed through XiaSi'an on the afternoon of the 28 and began to enter Anhui province that same day. At dawn on the 30, forces spearheaded by the Nagano and Yamada units broke into Guangde City, and fully occupied it by that afternoon... Forces advancing northward to the west of Lake Tai re-entered Jiangsu Province and joined up with the Fujii and Isa units that had inserted themselves behind enemy lines using boats to pull off a sneak attack... The Yamamoto unit which that had broken through enemy lines at Sanzhoushan by a forced march entered Liyang County City on the morning of the 30. This completed our army's successful attack on the Danyang-Xuancheng (Ningguo) line. On the 30, the Wakisaka unit advanced to within five ri of Jintan, creating an extremely great threat for enemy forces at Jintan and Danyang. On the heels of the occupations of the three strongholds of Jiangyin, Changzhou, and Yixing, our army occupied Guangde and Liyang on the 30. Now our army has put Lake Tai firmly in the rearview mirror in its attack on the Jiangnan region, and has continued advancing west and northwest. Conditions for occupation of Nanjing are now fully in place" (Wang 2010b, 102).

Atrocities never abated as the Japanese army advanced toward Nanjing. The most notorious incident was the so-called "contest to behead 100 people." The *Tokyo Nichi Nichi Shimbun* published the first report on the competition on November 30, 1937:

> [Report filed by special reporters Asakai, Mitsumoto, and Yasuda on the 29] The xx unit which previously crossed the 40 kilometers between Chanshu and Wuxi in only six days and the road from Wuxi to Changzhou, the same distance, in only three days, truly moves at amazing speed. Two officers of the Katagiri unit on the front have launched a "contest to behead a hundred people." It is said that after their departure from Wuxi, one of them quickly cut off 56 heads, and the other 25. One is Second Lieutenant Mukai Toshiaki (26 years old) of the Tomiyama unit, of Kojiro Village, Kuga District, Yamaguchi Prefecture. The other is Second Lieutenant Noda Tsuyoshi (25 years old) of the same unit, of Tashiro Village, Kimotsuki District, Kagoshima Prefecture. Second Lieutenant Mukai, a third-dan Kendo practitioner, carries a "Seki Magoroku" sword at his waist, while Second Lieutenant Noda's sword has no name despite its being a treasured heirloom in his family.
>
> After departing from Wuxi, Second Lieutenant Mukai advanced 26 or 27 kilometers down a railway, and Second Lieutenant Noda advanced along another railway, temporarily separating the two. The morning after their departure, Second Lieutenant Noda beheaded four people in an enemy pillbox at an unnamed village eight kilometers from Wuxi, making him the first to establish prestige. Upon hearing about this, Second Lieutenant Noda became animated. That night he and his troops burst into an enemy position at Henglin Town, where he beheaded 55 enemy soldiers.

Noda subsequently beheaded another nine at Henglin and six at Weiguan Town,[67] followed by another six on the 29 at the Changzhou Railway Station, bringing his total to 25 beheadings. Mukai, for his part, beheaded four in the vicinity of the Changzhou station. Our reporter rushing to the scene happened upon the two men meeting near the train station. Mukai said: "Forget Nanjing. I can probably get my count to 100 at Danyang, and you'll lose. My sword has beheaded 56 so far. There's only one indentation on your sword." Noda responded: "Neither of us kills fleeing men, because we're officers, so the tally hasn't been able to increase. But before we get to Danyang I'll break a big record. You'll see" (Wang 2010b, 95–96).

The *Tokyo Nichi Nichi Shimbun* ran another article on the contest on December 4:

[Report filed by special reporters Asakai and Mitsumoto at Danyang on the 3]. War update. On the march to Nanjing, the young Second Lieutenants Mukai Toshiaki and Noda Tsuyoshi of the Toyama unit within the vanguard Katagiri unit have continued their "contest to behead a hundred people." After numerous hard-fought battles, the count stood at 86 beheadings for Mukai and 65 for Noda as of 6:00 p.m. on the 2, just prior to the entry into Danyang. It's hard to say who will win.

Over the 10 ri from Changzhou to Danyang, Mukai beheaded 30 enemies, and Noda 40. The two second lieutenants' fierce fighting spirit, akin to the war god Asura, is indescribable. On this advance the two brave warriors broke into enemy positions at Benniu Town, Lucheng Town, and Lingkou Town (all to the north of Danyang) as they fought along the Nanjing-Shanghai Railway. Second Lieutenant Mukai was the first to courageously break into the Zhongzheng Gate of Danyang. Second Lieutenant Noda's right wrist has been lightly wounded. Both have made glorious attainments in their contest to behead a hundred people. By the time we reporters caught up with the Toyama unit, which has had not a moment's rest since entering Danyang as it continues to pursue routing enemies, Second Lieutenant Mukai, marching with his unit, jokingly told us: "That Noda is going to catch up to me. I can't let my guard down now. Noda's wound isn't severe, so there's no need to worry. During a beheading in Lingkou Town, one guy's bone chipped my Seki Magoroku. I can still behead another hundred or two with it though. I beseech you Tokyo Nichi Nichi Shimbun and Osaka Mainichi Shimbun reporters to act as referees for me" (Wang 2010b, 112).

The *Tokyo Nichi Nichi Shimbun* ran the third article on the contest on December 6:

[Report filed by special reporters Asakai and Mitsumoto at Jurong on the 5]. The two young officers on their way to Nanjing engaged in the "contest to behead a hundred people," those being Second Lieutenants Mukai Toshiaki and Noda Tsuyoshi of the Katagiri unit, fought at the very fore during the battle to take Jurong. The tally prior to their entry into the city stood at 78 beheaded for Mukai and 89 for Noda. It remains hard to predict a victor (Wang 2010b, 123).

---

67 Likely refers to Qishuyan, a district of Changzhou.

The *Tokyo Nichi Nichi Shimbun* ran the fourth article on the contest on December 13:

> [Report filed by special reporters Asakai and Suzuki at Purple Mountain on the 12] The brave warriors of the Katagiri unit Second Lieutenants Mukai Toshiaki and Noda Tsuyoshi, who began a rarely observed "contest to behead a hundred people" prior to the attack into Nanjing, had set marks of 106 to 105 by the time of the capture of Purple Mountain on the 10. At noon on the 10, the two second lieutenants met, each holding heavily indented Japanese swords. Noda: "Hey, I beheaded 105. How about you?" Mukai: "I got 106!"... Both second lieutenants: "Hahaha!" It was ultimately impossible to determine who had reached 100 beheadings first. "Let's call it a tie then. But, how about we change the bet to 150?" Both quickly agreed. The contest to behead 150 people finally began from the 11. At noon on the 11, Second Lieutenant Mukai, busy sweeping up remnant forces at Purple Mountain overlooking the Sun Yat-sen Mausoleum, discussed the "tie in the hundred beheadings": "Both of us surpassed a hundred without realizing it. This made me truly happy. The reason my Seki Magoroku sword has gotten its blade bent is that I've been cutting steel helmets in half along with the person. I've already promised to donate this Japanese sword to your news agency once the war is over. At 3:00 a.m. on the 11, as friendly forces were "choking" enemy troops out of the Purple Mountain, I was choked out too. As the hail of bullets fell on me I frequently held my sword, stood up, and said "so this is my destiny!" But I wasn't hit by a single bullet. This too is a blessing from my Seki Magoroku sword." Amid whirring enemy bullets, he showed off this Seki Magoroku sword, which had drawn the blood of 106, to the reporters (Wang 2010b, 212).

As the Japanese army attacked Nanjing, the Westerners in the city established the International Committee for the Nanking Safety Zone. The Tokyo Nichi Nichi Shimbun ran an article about this event on November 24: "[Shanghai Domei Agency Nov. 23] Authorities of all countries on the ground have discussed the plan to establish a neutral zone in a portion of the city of Nanjing to isolate it from the ravages of war. Now a Committee for the Nanjing Neutral Zone has been finally established, composed of 15 people from the UK, the U.S., Germany, and Denmark.[68] On the evening of the 23, the American consulate-general in Shanghai presented the plan for the neutral zone to our consulate-general in Shanghai. The plan establishes the neutral zone as the area extending eastward to Shanghai Road, northward to Zhongshan North Road and Shanxi Road, westward to Xikang Road, and southward to Hanzhong Road, located in the northwestern corner of Nanjing. The Chinese are not permitted to erect any military installations or transportation bodies, or to allow any troops to pass through our encamp within the zone. The Japanese must avoid all attacking actions in this

---

[68] This being the International Committee for the Nanking Safety Zone.

area. The plan has also been submitted to Chinese authorities, who are presently discussing it" (Wang 2010b, 61).

On December 9, the *Tokyo Nichi Nichi Shimbun* published a story about the Safety Zone's beginning to admit refugees: "[Shanghai NNS special wire report] (dispatched on the 8) Per reports in Chinese newspapers, military authorities in Nanjing issued formal evacuation orders on the morning of the 8. The International Committee for the Nanking Safety Zone, long in preparation, has just erected Safety Zone markers and is now awaiting a flood of refugees. In an instant the streets were filled with cars and rickshaws packed to capacity with luggage, causing extreme congestion. On this winter day the streets were full of elderly, women, and children, in numbers reported as high as 80,000. The International Committee is doing its utmost to receive them in the buildings, schools, clubs, and other edifices within the Safety Zone, and has established rules for administration, with priority given to sheltering the poor. So far 65,000 have been sheltered indoors. The Red Swastika Society and Red Cross Society are currently doing their utmost to provide cooked food in relief of these refugees" (Wang 2010b, 156).

On December 10, Mastsui Iwane issued orders launching a general attack on Nanjing. On December 11, the Tokyo Nichi Nichi Shimbun published this report: "[Shanghai, Domei Agency, Dec. 10] Supreme Commander Matsui issued a letter exhorting the enemy to surrender, from the spirit and etiquette of Bushido. Tang Shengzhi, on the other hand, has demonstrated a complete lack of etiquette. Not only did he not give any response before the deadline of noon on the 10, but he began a ferocious bombardment of our forces early in the morning on the 10. Thus our army pulled back the curtain of a general attack on Nanjing at 1:30 p.m.... Nanjing is now surrounded on three sides and is like a rat in a bag. The only escape route left is by water on the Yangtze" (Wang 2010b, 190).

On December 13, the *Tokyo Nichi Nichi Shimbun* reported on war conditions in Nanjing: "[Dispatched by NNS special reporter at 1:40 p.m Dec.12. from outside Nanjing] As our forces have pressed the attack inside of Nanjing, the approximately 50,000 remnant forces within are rapidly crumbling and beginning to be beaten back. A general retreat is currently proceeding toward Xiaguan down the central thoroughfare of Zhongshan Road out the Xingzhong Gate (north gate)" (Wang 2010b, 204).

The Japanese army took a great quantity of prisoners while "sweeping" Nanjing. The *Tokyo Nichi Nichi Shimbun* published this report on December 14: "[Domei Agency, Zhongshan East Road, Nanjing, Dec. 13] To avoid detection by the Imperial Army, remnant enemy forces are hiding in the surrounding mountains, but many have still been found and captured, prisoners now totaling approximately 2,000. Chinese Central Army crack troops defeated on the last line of defense have also dug into fastnesses on Purple Mountain, having avoided the line of sight of the Imperial Army. Our army has set fire to the surrounding areas to burn them out. Approximately 500 Chinese soldiers were smoked out of hiding. These were captured one by one by only 50 of our troops lying in wait. An estimated 20,000 Chinese soldiers fled from Zhenjiang toward Nanjing at the time of Zhenjiang's fall, but their number has fallen to 3,000 over the winding course of their retreat. Before dawn on the 13, they appeared near the Qilin Gate behind the Ono, Katagiri, Sukegawa, and Noda units, who easily annihilated them. The bodies of remnant forces in that vicinity have piled as high as a mountain" (Wang 2010b, 222).

Following the Japanese occupation of Nanjing, the Tokyo Nichi Nichi Shimbun reported on "battle achievements" made in Nanjing on December 16: "[Special NNS cable, Nanjing] (dispatched on the 15). As of the 14, remnant enemy forces had been entirely mopped up following sweeping maneuvers in the city. As our army had completely encircled Nanjing prior to launching the general attack, the enemy was entirely without retreat. Other than a few attempting to evacuate before the general attack, the rest were completely annihilated within the city. Now there were as many as 60,000 to 70,000 bodies of enemy soldiers within the city alone. The number of enemy dead totals probably was higher than 100,000 considering the forces annihilated in fighting outside the city as well as those destroyed on the river by our navy and air force" (Wang 2010b, 238).

6.3.4.2 Reports in the *Osaka Mainichi Shimbun*

As the *Tokyo Nichi Nichi Shimbun* and the *Osaka Mainichi Shimbun* were part of the same news group, the two carried many identical or similar articles.

The *Osaka Mainichi Shimbun* published this article on November 16: "[Domei Agency, Shanghai, Nov. 15] After the XX unit landed on the bank of the Yangtze and captured Changshu, Suzhou fell entirely within our army's encirclement. Telegram and telephone service between Nanjing and Suzhou were entirely cut. When a cable announcing the truth that "Suzhou is in imminent danger" arrived at 4:00 p.m. on the 15, Nanjing fell into a state of extreme tumult. City residents who had been preparing to evacuate upstream on the Yangtze since this morning all flooded into Xiaguan, and the roads from Nanjing to Wuhu were completely flooded with an enormous volume of fleeing people" (Wang 2010b, 277–278).

On November 22, the Japanese military delivered the so-called "letter exhorting surrender" to Chiang Kai-shek by air drop. The next day the *Osaka Mainichi*

Shimbun published this article: "[xxXX, OMS special reporter Hayashi] At noon on the 22 a clear-skied winter day was welcomed after 11 days. In Nanjing, sirens again fill the skies over the city after a ten-day hiatus. XX of our fighter planes emblazoned with bright rising suns have arrived in the skies over Nanjing. As enemy anti-aircraft soldiers opened fire into the skies, a plane flying with great ease – a fighter piloted by Nango dropped suddenly like a bird of prey and, in an instant, threw out something odd. This was unlike ordinary bombs. It was a white tube with red and blue streamers five to six *shaku* long affixed. It fell into the Central Party Ministry like an arrow. This was a letter exhorting surrender from Commander Matsui to the defeated Chiang Kai-shek. The letter was full of the spirit of military benevolence addressed 'to Chiang Kai-Shek.' The letter read: 'Oh Chiang Kai-shek, you who have lost Shanghai, who no longer heeds Suzhou, and who has abandoned Wuxi. Put up no more senseless resistance. You have no choice other than reducing your capital to ashes.' Nango's plane continued to fly about at great ease over Nanjing after the dropping the letter to Chiang, and only on this day did it drop no bombs. The enemy also ceased firing when the letter tube was dropped, but rather stood mouths gaping in amazement at the Japanese airplane behaving so differently from the ordinary" (Wang 2010b, 308–309).

On December 5, the *Osaka Mainichi Shimbun* published an article on the Nanjing Safety Zone: "[Domei Agency, Shanghai, Dec. 4] When the Nanjing Shelter Committee[69] founded by foreigners in Nanjing learned of the impending attack by our forces on Nanjing, they accelerated efforts to set up the Nanjing Safety Zone. The committee's chairman John Rabe recently contacted our diplomatic authorities in Shanghai by telegram to inquire about the Japanese attitude and requested a quick response. He also sent a telegram to the chairman of the Shanghai Refugee Zone Father Jacquinot requesting that he meet with ambassador Kawagoe and Counselor Hidaka, and in this also requested a quick response. Father Jacquinot's telegram back to Nanjing expressed clear pessimism. Although the committee still clings to some small hope that our authorities will respond, it is very obvious that this will not happen. In addition, Chinese authorities have accelerated preparation work for the Safety Zone, being unable to await our response owing to the urgency of the situation. It is reported that Chinese authorities have assembled 100,000 in cash and 30,000 sacks of rice for the zone" (Wang 2010b, 370–371).

The *Osaka Mainichi Shimbun* also reported on the "contest to behead a hundred people." An article from December 4 reads:

---

[69] The International Committee for the Nanking Safety Zone.

[Danyang, OMS special reporters Asakai & Mitsumoto, Dec. 3] War update. On the march to Nanjing, the young Second Lieutenants Mukai Toshiaki and Noda Tsuyoshi of the Toyama unit within the vanguard Katagiri unit have continued their "contest to behead a hundred people." After numerous hard-fought battles, the count stood at 86 beheadings for Mukai and 65 for Noda as of 6:00 p.m. on the 2, just prior to the entry into Danyang. It's hard to say who will win. Over the 10 *ri* from Changzhou to Danyang, Mukai beheaded 30 enemies, and Noda 40. The two second lieutenants' fierce fighting spirit, akin to the war god Asura, is indescribable. On this advance the two brave warriors broke into enemy positions at Benniu Town, Lucheng Town, and Lingkou Town (all to the north of Danyang) as they fought along the Nanjing-Shanghai Railway. Second Lieutenant Mukai was the first to courageously break into the Zhongzheng Gate of Danyang. Second Lieutenant Noda's right wrist has been lightly wounded. Both have made glorious attainments in their contest to behead a hundred people. By the time we reporters caught up with the Toyama unit, which has had not a moment's rest since entering Danyang as it continues to pursue routing enemies, Second Lieutenant Mukai, marching with his unit, jokingly told us: "That Noda is going to catch up to me. I can't let my guard down now. Noda's wound isn't severe, so there's no need to worry. During a beheading in Lingkou Town, one guy's bone chipped my Seki Magoroku. I can still behead another hundred or two with it though. I beseech you *Tokyo Nichi Nichi Shimbun* and *Osaka Mainichi Shimbun* reporters to act as referees for me. Haha!" he said while marching briskly (Wang 2010b, 362).

On December 14 the *Mainichi Shimbun* published a report from a war reporter inside Nanjing: "[Nanjing, OMS special reporters Shimura, Wakaume, & Yasuda, Dec. 13] At 3:00 p.m. on the 13, as the Imperial Army entered the city, reporters bearing the flags of the *Osaka Mainichi Shimbun* and the *Tokyo Nichi Nichi Shimbun* along with members of the Sato Photography Company and the Kanbara Motion Pictures Company visited the nationalist government under Imperial Army occupation... A Japanese flag hangs from the gate of the nationalist government, and the words "People's Government" written in bold golden characters glittered under the setting sun. There is a sandbag fortification before the gate, and the government building's iron gate is sealed shut. The gate was not locked, maybe because the enemy fled in haste. In the flagpole above the gate there is still a flag of a white sun in a blue sky. We take this flag down and send up a brand new setting sun flag. Now within the city erupt cries of 'long may he live!' rising to a deafening roar... Seeing how the nationalist government building has become so desolate, we deeply feel the tragedy of the vanquished" (Wang 2010b, 442–443).

The Yamada detachment of the Japanese army's 13th Division captured approximately 20,000 prisoners near Nanjing. The *Mainichi Shimbun* reports on this in an article of December 17: "[Nanjing, OMS special reporter Tanaka, Dec. 16]

The Morozumi Regiment,[70] which attained fame for the lone feat of occupying Jiangyin, captured 20,000 enemy soldiers in the attack on the enemy capital of Nanjing, another outstanding feat. The regiment departed from Jiangyin on the 7 and advanced along the Yangtze 40 *ri* into Zhenjiang. On the 11 the regiment continued westward another 20 *ri* and arrived at the Wulong Mountain battery to the east of Nanjing at noon on the 13. The regiment launched a fierce attack on the enemy troops stationed at the battery, and occupied it within about two hours, capturing 14 240-millimeter cannons and four anti-aircraft guns. Then, in a complete display of our army's might, the regiment took advantage of the victory to advance again to the battery at Mufu Mountain outside Nanjing, also a key location to the defense of Nanjing north gate, by 8:00 a.m. on the 14. Our forces launched a resolute attack on enemy forces putting up a stubborn defense of the battery, and captured the battery by 9:00 a.m. Here our forces captured another dozen or so 240-millimeter cannons as well as a colonel, a lieutenant colonel, a staff officer, and about 200 enlisted men, while also successfully pressing upon the northern edge of Nanjing. During the ensuing general attack by our army on Nanjing, a large enemy force seeking to retreat along the Yangtze encountered the regiment, which, after a great shout of "charge!" by Morozumi's brave warriors, launched a ferocious attack on them. The enemy force, having lost the will to fight, put up little resistance before waving the white flag in surrender. The force in question amazingly numbered as many as 20,000" (Wang 2010b, 463).

On December 18 the *Osaka Mainichi Shimbun* published a report detailing war gains "accurately" down to single digits: "[Shanghai, OMS cable] (Dispatched on the 27). The Shanghai Expeditionary Force made a formal declaration at noon on the 27: After an investigation, the following figures for enemy troops annihilated and spoils of war gained during the attack on Nanjing have been revealed as follows: enemy bodies left on the field, 53,874...." (Wang 2010b, 474).

6.3.4.3 Reports in the *Tokyo Asahi Shimbun*

After the Japanese occupation of Shanghai, the attack toward Nanjing commenced swiftly. The *Tokyo Asahi Shimbun* published an article on this operation on November 13: "[Shanghai, Domei Agency, Nov. 13] Chinese forces defeated in the battle of Dachang Town are now defending Liuhe, Jiading, Nanxiang, Jiangqiao, and other fortified defensive positions at supposedly key locations on the plain in a radius of 70 kilometers between the bank of the Yangtze and Nanjing,

---

[70] Named after Colonel Morozumi Gyosaku, commander of the 13th Division's 65th Regiment.

with troop numbers in excess of 300,000 to meet our forces. To rapidly launch a strong attack on weak enemy positions, the crack troops of the xxXX unit have landed in the enemy's rear to menace him, and are gradually ramping up heavy pressure on the enemy's right flank. The entire enemy line has started to rattle and descend into chaos, and are gradually collapsing from Nanjing outward. The two major positions of Jiangqiao and Nanxiang have also fallen in rapid succession. Enemy forces defending the important left flank position of Jiading have begun to show signs of wavering. So far only three months have passed since the Imperial Army began the war, but all enemy forces defending Shanghai have completely collapsed and begun to retreat... The Battle of Shanghai ended in complete defeat of the Chinese defenders, who did not stint to make a massive sacrifice for their stalwart stand. So now the war is gradually entering its second stage. The true fighting for Nanjing on the line from Kunshan to Taicang has now begun" (Wang 2010c, 6).

On November 18 the *Tokyo Asahi Shimbun* ran an article exaggerating Chinese losses since the beginning of the war: "[Shanghai, Domei Agency, Nov. 17] Dr. Watbeer, representing the International Red Cross Society currently in Changsha, formally announced in Japan that Chinese casualties on the northern and southern fronts total 800,000" (Wang 2010c, 31–32). On November 20, the same newspaper published an estimate of Japanese losses at the hands of the Chinese: "Minister of the Army Sugiyama gave a report on war conditions on the North China front and the Jiangnan front at a cabinet meeting on the 19 of approximately the following contents: On the Jin-Pu line, our army is poised to attack Jinan, and has annihilated enemies on the north shore of the Yellow River. Chinese forces concerned about pursuit from our army blew up the Yellow River bridge and then escaped into Jinan. On the Jiangnan front, our forces are currently launching fierce attacks on the solid defensive positions of Fushan, Changshu, and Suzhou. News has come that we have occupied Changshu, but official cables claim the attack is still under way. Our forces who have been hotly pursuing retreating Chinese troops are continuing their advance toward Suzhou, and are predicted to arrive outside Suzhou on the 19. Since the landing of fresh troops on the north of Hangzhou Bay, great achievements have been made on the Jiangnan front. Under our encirclement and daring pursuits, the enemy has suffered great losses, with the tally of enemy dead on that front standing as high as 81,000, and as many as 300,000 casualties" (Wang 2010c, 44).

The *Tokyo Asahi Shimbun* also published several articles on the Safety Zone in Nanjing. An article of December 6 reads: "[Shanghai, Domei Agency, Dec. 5] The plan to establish a neutral zone in Nanjing was proposed by the International Committee via American authorities in China to our government. It is very difficult for our authorities to assent to the plan for roughly the following reasons:

One, the entirety of Nanjing has become a fortress, and there are no natural features that demarcate the neutral zone from the rest of the city, making it difficult to ascertain. Two, our government holds that the committee has no authority whatsoever, and it will thus be difficult for the committee to prevent Chinese soldiers from penetrating the zone. Nonetheless, our forces will do their utmost to respect the security of the zone, for the sake of the foreigners and innocent masses sheltering therein, given that no military installations are present" (Wang 2010c, 133).

On December 13, the paper ran this article: "[Shanghai, Domei Agency, Dec. 13] Enemy forces within Nanjing, unable to withstand our army's ferocious attack from the south, have retreated on boats on the Yangtze in groups. The enemy's retreat has been entirely cut off, however, as our army units are holding Pukou, across the river from Nanjing, making it impossible for enemy forces to alight at Pukou. Their only choice is to continue their flight upstream. The eastern bank of the Yangtze from Nanjing to Wuhu is now also under our control, so our forces are giving them heavy fire from both banks as they retreat. Enemies aboard these boats are helpless, vainly ducking left and right, but they will soon be completely annihilated by our forces and find themselves in watery graves at the bottom of the river" (Wang 2010c, 212).

Tokyo Asahi Shimbun reporters followed the Japanese occupiers into Nanjing and sent back this report published on December 15: "[Nanjing, special reporter Yokota, Dec. 14] The capital of the Chiang regime – Nanjing, with its population of a million – has finally been occupied. Japanese flags have been flying atop the city walls and above all units since the 13. This was the greatest and most resplendent day for the rising sun flag in our lives. Soldiers have been crying hot tears from over-excitement inside and outside the Zhongshan Gate... A large hole was blown open by our enormous cannons in the wall to the left of the gate near what look like the homes of civilians. The enemy dug a horizontal anti-vehicle trench on the road only a *cho*[71] in front of the gate to prevent our armored vehicles from advancing. Bricks and sand were piled nearly as high as the city wall before the gate; the only possible means of opening the gate was to blast it open. Thus we see how tight were the enemy's defenses. The school for family of deceased soldiers outside the gate concentrated survivors of soldiers under command of Chiang Kai-shek, with Soong Mei-ling, skilled at special education, serving as principle. It has now become a place for the Imperial Army to bask in the sunlight. The four characters *"che di kang ri"* [resist Japan to the last] have now abashedly disappeared from the classrooms... Our

---

71 A Japanese measure of distance equivalent to 109 meters.

forces entered the *Lizhishe* at 3:00 p.m. on the 13, with the Ono unit shouting "long may he live!" as the primary force led on by armored vehicles. Then began the sweeping up of remnant forces... We have also seen the magnificent Chinese-style building that houses the Central Supervision Committee with its glass windows shattered. When we came upon the road before the Central Military Academy, the primary Chinese source of resistance against Japan, remnant forces suddenly opened fire on us from behind sandbag fortifications. We then hurried away after having a quick look at Chiang Kai-shek's residence. There were also sandbag fortifications in front of the massive, modern Central Hospital, with gun muzzles on top seemingly aimed squarely at us. The Construction Committee building, now a barracks for enemy soldiers, contained two hot water bottles, and from the still smoldering fire within, it seems that they only just left. Enemy helmets, rice, alcohol, grenades, and radios that seem to have been commandeered are scattered along one side. One portion of the building seems to have been used to house wounded soldiers; the interior smells strongly of the sick and wounded. The grass and flowers of the spacious Political District Park have all wilted. The streets of Nanjing are like a parasol tree that has dropped all its leaves, having transformed into a wretched lifeless rubble heap" (Wang 2010c, 230–232).

The *Tokyo Asahi Shimbun* published creative reports on the "great discipline" of the Japanese army during its sweeps: "[Nanjing, special reporters Hiramatsu & Fujimoto, Dec. 15] Chiang Kai-shek mobilized his personal crack troops to defend the capital, but their weakness in combat compared to our highly energetic troops should come as a surprise to nobody. It is estimated that 25,000 of these remnant troops have changed into civilian clothes and are hiding in the city. As such our army is sparing no effort to root them out, sorting and arresting anyone suspected of having been a soldier while also protecting the elderly, children, and women. Our army is according special protection to foreign interests, demonstrating the high discipline of the Imperial Army. Our troops are also making efforts to preserve buildings and other properties in the city, having placed sentries at the entrance to every warehouse to prevent any goods from going missing. Some of the warehouses were long ago looted clean by Chinese soldiers, and as such do not require sentries. In many private homes that had been used to house enemy soldiers we have seen pigs cooking over fires but no sign of any people. At the Forbidden Palace airfield, the Fujii unit confiscated two brand new large aircraft and two fighters, all left behind by the enemy, demonstrating the panicked state of the enemy during the evacuation" (Wang 2010c, 241–242).

On December 17, the *Tokyo Asahi Shimbun* ran a report on conditions of Chinese soldiers captured by the Yamada Detachment written by its own military correspondents. The article runs completely contrary to all aforementioned sources:

> [Nanjing, special reporter Yokota, Dec. 16]...
>
> Staff Officer Shen, who walks empty-handed out of the barracks, is a good man, tall, pale of complexion, and only 30 years old. He is wearing a handsome uniform with a collar of otter skin. It is obvious upon first glance that he is one of only very few young officers in the Central Army.
>
> He face is wan and his energy flagging after the Battle of Nanjing. He says: "Victory depends on luck. There's nothing you can do about that. The Japanese army was stronger than we had imagined. I was a staff officer at the Purple Mountain fort. I'm in no position to speak to the entirety of the Battle of Nanjing, but allowing the first line at Jurong to fall was a major defeat. I was born in Fengtian[72] and graduated from the Fengtian Middle School. In the 15th year of China[73] (7th year of the Showa period) I graduated from the Fengtian Army Academy, but I was not involved in the Manchuria Incident. I'll give you more details later, but please don't continue asking me questions before my mood is settled."
>
> His conversational style is very steady. In the end the reporter said: "I hear they will give you food tonight." At this he expressed great gratitude and said, his head still bowed, "If you give me a car and a guard, I'll take you to the basement of the Fugui Mountain battery. There are hundreds of sacks of rice hidden there. That will be enough food not just for us here, but some can go to supply the Japanese army too" (Wang 2010c, 246–247).

Now here is what Second Lieutenant Endo Takaaki, of the 8th Company of the 65th Infantry Regiment recorded in his diary on December 16 about the events described in the article above: "We were ordered to move out at 12:30 p.m. as a fire had broken out in a prisoner shelter, and returned at 3:00 p.m. I met Mr. Yokota of the Asahi News Agency at the shelter and asked him what was going on. There were 17,025 prisoners in total. In the evening a third of the prisoners were brought to the riverside on orders from headquarters and executed by gunshot by the 1st Battalion. If two meals were provided daily as written in the instructions handed down, that would have been a hundred sacks (of grain) per day. But we soldiers have to secure our own food supply by requisitioning. That made provision of food impossible. Headquarters had to take appropriate measures" (Ono et al. n.d., 219). Endo's diary proves that the Asahi Shimbun's Yokota did indeed interview Chinese prisoners on December 16, but these prisoners' ultimate fate demonstrates the mendacity of Yokota's article.

---

72 Now Shenyang.
73 Probably refers to the twenty-first year of the Republic of China.

6.3.4.4 Reports in the *Yomiuri Shimbun*

The Japanese army occupied Shanghai in late November 1937 and then swiftly advanced toward Nanjing. The *Yomiuri Shimbun* published a great quantity of articles on this campaign, wildly lavishing praise on the Japanese Imperial Army for its "bravery," "ferociousness," and "godlike speed."

On November 21, the *Yomiuri Shimbun* published this article: "[Changshu, YS special cable] (Dispatched Nov. 20) With the fall of Jiaxing, Suzhou, the last bastion of the enemy's resistance, has had both of its flanks collapse. In the pre-dawn hours of the 19, Suzhou finally fell at the first blow. The Changshu-Suzhou-Jiaxing line was the last position defending Nanjing to which enemy forces defeated in the Battle of Shanghai clung; as such it was called the "Hindenburg Line." Having broken this line, our army has already sealed Nanjing's fate. To this end, our entire army is in high fighting spirit, carrying on their shoulders the hopes of all 90 million of their compatriots. As it will not be long before the Japanese flag flies from the city wall of Nanjing, our boys are burning with anticipation at spending New Year in Nanjing" (Wang 2010c, 298).

An article of November 17 reads: "[Shanghai, Domei Tsushin urgent cable, Nov. 16] The nationalist government has just resolved to move the capital. All organs of the government have fallen into unprecedented chaos. All important persons of the government are panic-stricken and disoriented as they struggle to organize and arrange for transportation of important files and valuables. All yuan chiefs and ministers have been transported to preordained locations ahead of their staffs. Finance Minister H.H. Kung and Foreign Minister Wang Ch'ung-hui have decided to proceed to Hankou to first handle diplomatic affairs following the move. Communications Minister Yu Feipeng has moved to Changsha to ensure continued operations of the Guangzhou-Hankou Railway and shipping waterways" (Wang 2010c, 286–287).

On December 3, the *Yomiuri Shimbun* ran another article on conditions in Nanjing:

Coordinating with several days of ferocious air raids, the Imperial Army has advanced to within only 100 kilometers of Nanjing. Chaotic conditions in the capital have completely exceeded what we had imagined. Per a reliable report received on December 2, the current population of Nanjing is about 300,000, only a quarter of what it was before the incident. Many civilians will wish to flee in the days to come, but Nanjing's current transit capacity is capable of sending off only 10,000 daily. In addition, city residents have fallen into chaos upon learning that the Japanese army's arrival is imminent, nailing shut windows to their houses, taking all the valuables they can hold, and rushing toward all stations at full speed day and night. With all the shouting and wrangling, the city has fallen into chaos. Other citizens spend the entire day wandering the city looking for food and breaking into homes that may contain some, owing to the great lack of supplies. Disturbances are breaking out everywhere, claiming the lives of many city residents every day (Wang 2010c, 356).

On December 9, the *Yomiuri Shimbun* quoted a December 8 article from the Domei Agency in reporting on a declaration of the Japanese embassy to China regarding the International Safety Zone in Nanjing:

Foreign media agencies have recently reported on the activities of the International Committee for the Nanking Safety Zone as well as refugees swarming into said zone. Unfortunately, as everyone knows, Japanese authorities have been unable to give any guarantees for the establishment of the so-called Safety Zone owing to great practical difficulties. The truth is that Nanjing's geography and defensive conditions make it effectively one large fortress. One must admit that it is a contradiction in terms to designate one area within this fortress as a so-called Safety Zone. As the Imperial Army has declared many times, it goes without saying that lives and property of foreigners are to be spared, and there are no intentions whatsoever to cause the least bit of harm to the common people of China. For the above reasons, our authorities can give no guarantees whatsoever to the so-called Safety Zone in Nanjing. Everyone taking shelter there should understand the danger they may face. We hereby clearly state that if the fighting does spill into this area, we bear no responsibility. Be it hereby declared (Wang 2010c, 395).

The Japanese army entered Nanjing on December 13. The following day the *Yomiuri Shimbun* published this article: "[Purple Mountain, special reporter Kojima, urgent cable, Dec. 13] The Ono unit attacking the Zhongshan Gate continued a ferocious onslaught through the night of the 12, and finally took full control of the gate at 3:00 a.m., upon which the unit charged down Zhongshan Road into the city. On the other side of the city, the Wakisaka unit engaged in fierce urban combat and advancing northward from the Zhonghua Gate[74] also fought its way onto Zhongshan Road early this morning. These two units have continued intense fighting with defenders putting up a stiff resistance around this main thoroughfare of Nanjing. At 11:00 a.m., their vanguards finally occupied the nationalist government and the Central Army Officers' Academy and planted Japanese flags high atop their roofs" (Wang 2010c, 439–440).

On December 16, the *Yomiuri Shimbun* ran another Domei Agency article: "[Shanghai, Domei Tsushin, Dec. 15]. Following our army's occupation of Nanjing, the prisoners taken and enemy soldiers killed inside and outside the city by the Ono, Noda, Sukegawa, and Katagiri units – which attacked from the north –

---

74 Mistake in original. Should be Guanghua Gate.

alone tallied no fewer than 10,000, with estimates ranging as high as 60,000 to 70,000. Our army also obtained countless spoils of war" (Wang 2010c, 456).

The above Japanese historical sources are not entirely false, as they do represent different perspectives, but through comparison they make it possible to clearly view the basic historical truths of the Rape of Nanking, demonstrating the purely fictitious and sophistical nature of the absurd theories proffered by the Japanese right wing of today.

7 Food Issues During the Rape of Nanking. Focusing on the Safety Zone

7.1 Food Supply Conditions and Food Policies in Nanjing before the Fall

7.1.1 Food supply conditions in Nanjing before the fall

Nanjing, at the foot of the Purple Mountain and nestled against the Yangtze River, is known popularly as the capital of 10 dynasties and the golden powder of six kingdoms. After centuries of historical accumulation, Nanjing had already developed markets with goods and foods from all compass points in China well before 1937. At that time, the grain market in Jiangsu Province was divided into southern Jiangsu, central Jiangsu, and northern Jiangsu by natural currents. The southern Jiangsu grain market stretched eastward from Nanjing to the sea, was linked primarily by canals and the Shanghai-Nanjing Railway, and was centered on Wuxi (Jiangsu Province Local History Compilation Committee n.d., 35).

Grains in Nanjing came from two primary sources. The first was the breadbasket to the both sides of the Yangtze, primarily the counties of Anhui abutting the river, such as Anqing, Lujiang, Shucheng, Chaoxian, Hefei, Quanjiao, Hezhou, Hanshan, Chuzhou, and Tianchang in the north of Anhui and Wuhu, Dangtu, Xuancheng, Nanling, and Ningguo in the south of Anhui, but also including Liuhe and Yizheng in northern Jiangsu and a few regions of Jiangxi; most of this grain was shipped to Nanjing on wooden rafts downstream on the Yangtze. The second source was the breadbasket surrounding Nanjing, primarily the grain-producing regions along the Waiqinhuai River, including Jiangning, Jurong, Lishui, Liyang, Jintan, Gaochun, and others; this grain was brought to Nanjing for sale by wooden rafts on the river, or hauled by humans, by beasts of burden, or in wheelbarrows (Nanjing Local History Compilation Committee et al. n.d., 44). This is the origin of the difference in Nanjing between "Waijiang [north of the Yangtze] rice" and "inner river rice" (Nanjing Local History Compilation Committee et al. n.d., 115).

Two major grain markets formed in Nanjing: Zhonghua Gate and Xiaguan. The major grains traded there were unhusked rice, husked rice, and wheat, with some soybeans, corn, sesame, rapeseed, and so on. Most husked rice was sold outside of the city, with grain merchants from Tianjin and Yantai in

Note: Chapter contributed by Qu Shengfei

https://doi.org/10.1515/9783110652789-010

the north and Chaozhou and Shantou in the south, among other places, coming to purchase it; 55% of all husked rice was resold elsewhere. Most wheat was flour coming out of the Datong Mill and the Yangzi Mill, and most of this was sold to Hankou, Tianjin, and other places; only a small portion of wheat was sold via ocean ship to Tianjin and Yantai (Nanjing Local History Compilation Committee et al. n.d., 46). The primary entities undertaking grain transactions were individual resellers, brokers, wholesalers, and shop owners, this latter engaged solely in retail sales (Wu n.d., 136). Statistics demonstrate that from 1921 to 1934, on average 180 million kilograms of grain passed through Nanjing in an average year, and there were 608 registered businesses – factories, shops, wholesalers, brands, warehouses – in the trade. The greatest concentration of grain businesses was found on Yuhua Road, Saozhou Alley, Luxi Alley, and Xijie outside the Zhonghua Gate and between Xianyu Alley and Huimin Bridge at Xiaguan (Nanjing Local History Compilation Committee et al. n.d., 46). In 1935, there were 198 formal businesses in the grain industry with capital of 180,335 yuan and business volume of 4,206,140 yuan. There were 120 flour businesses with total capital of 309,655 yuan and business volume of 1,800,010 yuan. There were also businesses particular to Nanjing, such as the money-and-rice businesses, which were grain traders and money lenders; there were 209 of these with capital of 165,940 yuan and business volume of 3,007,665 yuan (Jing Shenghong et al. 2005b, 90 – 91).

By June 1937, the population of Nanjing stood at "one million fifteen thousand four hundred and fifty" (Jing et al. 2005b, 3).[75] Nanjing's grain demand spiked following dramatic population growth, causing Nanjing to become a classic consumer city, as its surrounding regions could not produce enough grain to meet demand. Consequently most grain transacted in Nanjing's markets was consumed locally, with little being transshipped (Jiangsu Province Local History Compilation Committee n.d., 42). The following table gives production figures of primary crops grown in Nanjing City:

Crop	Number of *mu* planted	Total yield (*piculs*)	Yield per *mu* (*jin*)
Rice	101,750	136,203.80	133
Wheat	96,135	103,606.20	107
Barley	33,270	39,075	117
Buckwheat	100	144	144
Highland barley	1,100	2,800	254
Sorghum	2,050	3,100	151

---

75 Per reports of the Japanese Special Service Organ's Nanjing Pacification Team, the population of Nanjing before the war was approximately 1.08 million (Wang and Lei n.d., 337).

7.1 Food Supply Conditions and Food Policies in Nanjing before the Fall — 411

Continued

Crop	Number of *mu* planted	Total yield (*piculs*)	Yield per *mu* (*jin*)
Corn	27,424	46,478.80	169
Soybeans	32,609	35,188.80	107
Broadbeans	13,510	11,611	85
Peas	8,987	8,185	91
Potatoes	1,160	1,595	137
Sesame	300	216	72

Table 23: Production figures for primary crops grown in Nanjing City (24th Year of the Republic of China.
Source: Nanjing Special Service Organ, 55–56.

By comparing this table's yield figures with Nanjing's population figures in the previous table, we can see how little grain was produced in Nanjing per capita. Faced with massive grain demand, Nanjing had to feed its population by purchasing grain from elsewhere. Per an investigation, in 1935 there were 88,529 *piculs* of grain stored in Nanjing warehouses, with local production of 266,508 *piculs* and inputs of 1,453,729 *piculs*, but no records for outputs. Consumption was 1,730,000 *piculs* and a residual amount of 78,766 *piculs* (Nanjing Special Service Organ: 56). See the following table:

Year	South Gate	Xiaguan	Tongji Gate	Shuixi Gate	Total
1932	499,500	199,168	150,000	18,300	867,700
1933	536,500	178,947	160,900	23,400	899,747
1934	646,530	149,203	137,800	25,100	858,633

Table 24: Quantities of grain transported into Nanjing by waterway, 1932–1934 (unit: *dan*).
Source: Nanjing Local History Compilation Committee et al. (n.d., 117).

The above table indicates only quantities of grain brought into Nanjing by waterway, but it clearly demonstrates the city's enormous demand for grain. With such great quantities of grain consumed in and trans-shipped through Nanjing, there was obviously great demand for warehouses. After the founding of the nationalist government, five new large grain warehouses were built: Shenjiang, Zhongguo, Jiangsu, Chunsheng, and Fuxing. Those on top of existing large warehouses like the Yicang and Hengyu brought the city's grain storage capacity to about 350,000 *dan* (Nanjing Local History Compilation Committee et al. n.d., 141). Grain reserves in these warehouses effectively guaranteed Nanjing's food supply.

The War of Resistance Against Japan erupted in July 1937. During the Battle of Shanghai in August, Nanjing's markets entered a state of insufficient supply for a time. The Nanjing municipal government resolved the problem by transporting grain into the city from far and wide. An article of September 2, 1937 in the *Zhongyang ribao* read: "There have been no great fluctuations in market prices for wheat in Xiaguan these last two weeks. Sales have been sluggish, and there are enormous stocks. With the abundant autumn harvests in the Upper Yangtze, there has been a surge in boats transporting new rice these past few days… Despite these extraordinary times, there is absolutely no problem in grain supply; in fact grain prices have dropped relative to previous years." Grain supply in Nanjing was still sufficient to cover demand through mid-November. Another *Zhongyang ribao* article, of November 17, 1937, read: "Grain stocks in Nanjing have grown more abundant lately. It was planned that over 3,000 *dan* of grain arrive in the city from all points yesterday. The highest price for river rice is 8.3 yuan, while the price for machine-processed rice from north of the Yangtze is a little over six; so the highest price on the retail market is about nine yuan."

However, when the Japanese army pressed near to Nanjing in mid-November, 1937, food supply channels into Nanjing were all cut. Half a month before the fall, on November 28, *Shenbao* ran this article: "The majority of shopfronts in Nanjing are closed. With owners preoccupied, only a few stores selling food remain open. Even open stores are gradually depleting stocks. The only items in abundance are expensive canned foods and foreign alcohols." Conditions worsened when the Japanese surrounded the city. Minnie Vautrin of the Ginling Women's College wrote in her diary entry of December 4, 1937: "No salt or oils can be purchased now."

7.1.2 Food reserves belonging to the International Committee for the Nanking Safety Zone and charitable bodies before the fall

Charitable organizations in China had developed substantially within traditional models in the years leading up to Nanjing's fall. Looking at numbers alone, there were 46 registered charitable organizations of all kinds in Nanjing in October 1935 (Sun 2007, 1–4). As there are no documents directly reporting grain reserves belonging to Nanjing's charitable organizations prior to the fall, our only choice is to indirectly estimate a figure using these organizations' asset declaration statements.

The pamphlet *Nanjing shehui* [Nanjing Society] issued in February 1937 by the Nanjing Bureau of Social Affairs reported registration details on charitable organizations founded in Nanjing in 1936 (Sun 2007, 5–7). After the city fell, many of these were forced to stop operations. For that reason we shall focus

7.1 Food Supply Conditions and Food Policies in Nanjing before the Fall — 413

our observations on those organizations continuing to operate during the Rape of Nanking. In March 1938, the puppet municipal government's secretariat issued survey results of charitable organizations in a document titled "General Municipal Government Conditions in Nanjing in ROC Year 27" (Sun 2007, 7–9). Its authors report on the assets and primary work performed by Nanjing's charitable organizations during the Rape of Nanking per the above registration and investigation information of said organizations. Its results were as follows:

Name	Asset valuation	Primary work
Mingde Cishantang	Approx. 6,000 yuan	Free medicine distribution, healthcare, materials distribution, burials, rice distribution, free rice, school establishment
Zhongzhi Fushantang	Approx. 8,100+ yuan	Free medical treatment, free medicine distribution, materials distribution, burials, winter relief, tea distribution, widow relief, relief to people whose houses have burned
Chongshantang	Approx. 31,130 yuan	Widow relief, infant protection, materials distribution, free medical treatment, free medicine distribution, anti-illiteracy, rice distribution
Sili Public Relief Granary	Approx. 34,300 yuan	Storing grain against famine, winter invigoration, soup kitchen, selling grain at low prices in shortages
Guangfeng Reserve Warehouse	Approx. 35,140+ yuan	Storing grain, selling grain at low prices in shortages, winter relief, distributing congee
Gongshan Nantang		Burial, widow relief, free medicine distribution, funerals, etc.
Red Swastika Society		Congee distribution, rice distribution, materials distribution, anti-illiteracy relief, burial, shelter, medicine
Peishantang		Free medical care, materials distribution, free medicine distribution, widow relief, winter relief

Table 25: Asset valuations and primary work of Nanjing City charitable organizations.

The above table requires some explanations: 1) The "asset valuations" come from the "Excerpted Registrations of Charitable Organizations in Nanjing in 1936 (February 1937)" and "primary work" comes from the "Nanjing Charitable Organizations Survey (March 1938)"; 2) Per the "Nanjing Charitable Organizations Survey (March 1938)," all organizations included in the above table noted which of their activities were currently in progress. Gongshan Nantang, for example, noted that burial work was proceeding but all other services had stopped, and Chongshantang noted that work was proceeding at a reduced scale; and 3) The Guangfeng Reserve Warehouse also noted that it had suspended activities. The Sili Public Relief Granary was occupied by the Japanese army after the fall, and its activities also came to an effective halt. As Guangfeng and Sili were established primarily to provide famine relief, winter relief, and free congee, a great quantity of their assets consisted of rice and other grains. For that reason we included them in the above table even though they had stopped operating during the Rape of Nanking.

Per the above table and grain prices in Nanjing at the end of October 1937[76], the assets of the above-mentioned charitable organizations, converted into grains, were considerable. These assets provided them with the material foundation to continue performing charitable acts during the Rape of Nanking, and also provided sustenance to refugees. Chongshantang Director Zhou Yiyu wrote a letter to the puppet municipal government saying: "Our society has done relief work for years with never a cessation. Our location at Jinshajing in this city cannot continue operations due to military operations, and so we have moved into the refugee zone. We are actively performing relief work as usual, sparing no efforts. Now that the ravages of war are calming down, there is desolation everywhere. Our first task is to organize burial teams to work hard to bury bodies and restore sanitation. At the same time we are distributing food to relieve refugees and maintain a trickle of life in them" (Sun 2007, 144). Major Zhu Qingchuan, vice communications director of the International Red Swastika Society during the Rape of Nanking, recalled: "The Nanjing branch of the Red Swastika Society distributed rice congee every day in the Wutaishan Temple, entirely as a form of alms, not asking for any money. The Nanjing locations at the Shanxi Road intersection and on Huowa Alley also distributed rice congee every day, going through large quantities of rice daily. There was still a stock of dozens of sacks of rice in the Shanxi Road office" (Zhang 2005, 475). Thus we see that the Red Swastika Society also maintained some food reserves during the Rape of Nanking, and provided a degree of food relief to refugees at the time.

The International Committee for the Nanking Safety Zone, which fulfilled the functions of a de facto municipal government after the city's fall, also did a great quantity of work in food supply issues. The International Committee was founded in November 1937, composed of Germans, Americans, and other foreigners, and chaired by a German John Rabe. Members took note of food problems immediately upon the committee's founding. In his diary entry of November 30, Chairman John Rabe listed out a number of problems requiring resolution by the committee. One of these was food. Rabe thought that preparations needed to be made in quantity, storage, and distribution of food (Rabe CN, 91). So Rabe and

---

[76] At the end of October 1937, prices were 1,200 yuan / *dan* for unpolished long-grain rice, 500 yuan / *dan* for wheat, and 390 yuan / sack of top-grade flour (see Nanjing Special Service Organ n.d., 68).

the committee sought food supplies far and wide to be prepared for the coming emergency.

On November 23, Rabe's birthday, a friend of his assistant Han Xianglin gave him two trucks loaded with 100 canisters of gasoline and 200 sacks of flour. Rabe writes joyously of this birthday gift: "We can do something with that, particularly since the committee will have urgent need of food and vehicles" (Rabe EN, 29). Han went to receive the gifts the next day, but Rabe wrote: "One driver has run off, and the second truck along with the gasoline and flour have come under the custody of the 88th Division." With the fortuitous assistance of Dr. Han Li-wuh (Rabe CN, 78), on November 26 Han Xianglin was finally able to retrieve 100 canisters of gasoline and 20 sacks of flour from the Yihetong Brick and Tile Factory (Rabe CN, 83).

The Chinese government cooperated with the International Committee in a range of issues, including food. On December 1, Nanjing Mayor Ma Chaojun promised 30,000 sacks of rice and 10,000 sacks of flour to the committee. That afternoon, Rabe received 20,000 yuan from the commander of the Nanjing garrison, one installment on the 100,000 Chiang Kai-shek had promised (Rabe CN, 93). The International Committee received another 20,000 on December 7, bringing their cash reserve to 40,000, still short of the 100,000 promised (Rabe CN, 111).[77] Over the same period, the International Committee frantically organized labor and vehicles to transport rice and flour before the city's fall. But, according to the Report of the Nanking International Relief Committee (November 1937-April 30, 1939), owing to transportation difficulties, "only 9,067 sacks of rice were able to be transported into this committee's warehouse before the eruption of war. As for flour, only the 1,000 sacks donated by the Datong Mill were received; none of the flour donated by the municipal government was received" (Zhang 2006b, 391). This was thus the actual amount of food in the possession of the International Committee. On November 30, Rabe wrote of a phone call with Committee Secretary Smythe: "Dr. Smythe calls to tell me that we have 60,000 sacks of rice in the city and another 34,000 sacks in Hsiakwan. That may well be enough" (Rabe EN, 42). As we lack supporting evidence, it is impossible to ascertain the actual quantity of stored grain, but it seems that these stores were not under the actual control of the International Committee. The 10,000 sacks of rice and 1,000 sacks of flour under the International Committee's control later became the relief food used to tide refugees in the Safety Zone through

---

[77] George Fitch writes in his diary: "On December 1st Mayor Ma virtually turned over to us the administrative responsibilities for the Zone together with a police force of 450 men, 30,000 piculs (2,000 tons) of rice, 10,000 sacks of flour, and some salt, also a promise of a hundred thousand dollars in cash, 80,000 of which was subsequently received" (Zhang 2005, 97).

the period of hunger. The remaining rice and flour promised to the International Committee but which could not be transported into the Safety Zone before the occupation later became a long-term focus of discussion between committee members and Japanese authorities.

We can see from the above that the reserves of grains and other materials held in the Safety Zone by the International Committee at the time of the city's fall were not abundant. The International Committee even announced via the December 15 edition of the *North China Herald:* "There is not enough food in the Safety Zone" (Zhang 2005, 15). To be able to respond to unpredictable future difficulties, the International Committee announced in early December that "all refugees who have already taken up residence in the Safety Zone must prepare enough food to last for at least a week" and added: "We suggest that merchants specializing in the sale of rice, flour, other foods, and fuels come into the zone and continue business" The Committee further issued a rule about rice and flour allocated by the Nanjing municipal government: "It will be used only once all private commercial grain reserves are exhausted. Once that comes to pass, stored grains will be provided to private merchants bearing permits from the committee for sale" (Rabe CN, 101).

Despite the International Committee's efforts to be prepared, conditions following the city's fall exceeded everybody's imaginings. As refugees thronged in, the Safety Zone, occupying a small area in the city's northwestern corner, swelled in population to 250,000. The document "Memorandum on Relief Conditions" of January 22, 1938 in the Nanking Safety Zone Documents read: "The daily demand is 1,600 sacks (of rice) to feed 250,000 people" (Zhang 2006b, 340). Food shortages emerged quickly in the zone. Consequently, immediately after the city's fall, the International Committee began discussions with Japanese authorities about the food problem. These negotiations ran the entire course of the Rape of Nanking, and were ongoing even as the committee was disbanded.

7.1.3 Supply conditions for the Japanese army and their food policies

The speed of the Japanese army's advance from the occupation of Shanghai to the fall of Nanjing was blinding. Former Japanese soldier Sone Kazuo wrote in his memoir: "During the Battle of Nanjing, we pursued routing troops while advancing. We advanced about 300 kilometers in 13 days, quite an alarming speed" (Wang 2006b, 286). This rapid advance created supply problems for the Japanese army.

Transportation issues exacerbated the army's supply difficulties. A Japanese spy conducted an investigation in Nanjing in October 1937 and produced this report: "Cars traveling between Shanghai and Nanjing generally take the route that runs through Shanghai, Qingpu, Kunshan, Suzhou, Wuxi, Yixing, Jurong, and then Nanjing. It is also possible to take the longer route that passes through Hangzhou. There are many trucks traveling in both directions on the route. The road is badly damaged, but there has been no time to fix it (the worst section running between Qingpu and Wuxi), making vehicle travel difficult" (Ma 2005, 37–38). Chinese authorities also intentionally destroyed these roads to slow the Japanese advance. An article in the *Shenbao* of December 2, 1937 read: "The Chinese army has destroyed by bombing all bridges between Guangde and Wuhu and plans to destroy the roads as well to prevent the Japanese from advancing to Wuhu, and to make it impossible for mechanized units to pass. The Chinese army has also erected many obstacles on the Yangtze River between Wuhu and Zhenjiang" (Ma 2005, 87). The German ambassador to Japan Herbert von Dirksen wrote in a report to the German Foreign Office on January 11, 1938: "What's more, the Chinese have, using an entirely non-Chinese method, completely desolated these undefended places, thereby making it impossible for these places to provide supply to the occupying Japanese army, and have created extraordinary supply difficulties for the Japanese by destroying roads and bridges" (Zhang 2005, 310–311).

Needing both to rapidly advance and to resolve battlefield supply issues, the Japanese army issued orders to "requisition" food and make use of local resources, i.e. to openly steal materials from Chinese residents. The Japanese Army Ministry issued these orders as early as August 5, 1937:

> Under current circumstances, adopt the following measures, which should be obvious:
>
> 1. At times of limitations in the necessity of self-defense, detain, confiscate, destroy, or appropriately dispose of (in the case of detainment of dangerous goods or goods that cannot be stored a long time, appraise the cost of long-term storage and guarding of these items or discard them) chattels and immovable property belonging to hostile Chinese...
>
> 2. In the name of self-defense or the happiness of decent local people, make use of the goods listed in the previous article in emergency conditions with no other options (Wang and Lei n.d., 11).

In truth, the Japanese army advancing toward Nanjing relied almost entirely on local "requisitioning" for its supply. On December 24, 1937, the Japanese 16th Division wrote in a report: "During the present period of combat, provisions for our forces have relied on local materials to adapt to the rapid mobilization" (Wang and Lei n.d., 51). Major Kisa Kiku, staff officer in charge of provisions for the 16th Division, wrote in his diary that on December 1, 1937, his forces requisitioned "800 sacks of rice, 1,000 sacks of wheat, 100 sacks of granulated sugar, two motorboats, and so on" (Wang 2005b, 323). Conditions of other Japanese units were largely similar. A 9th Division report read: "Since our departure from Xinjing Town, resupply has been unable to keep up with the pace of our pursuit. Over the approximately 300 kilometers from Shanghai to Nanjing, almost no rations have been received by our forces. We have been able to maintain the pursuit combat by reliance on resupply from local materials" (Wang and Lei n.d., 116). The 6th Division wrote in its 10-day report: "Nearly all units are adopting methods of requisitioning... Resupply is reliant upon direct requisitioning of rations by all units and rations requisitioned or captured by the Division's quartermaster." The following is a description of the "resupply" conditions of the 6th Division's quartermaster:

1. Jinshan (captured goods)
2. Baiwangmiao (delivered afterward)
3. Xugongqiao Town, Baihegang Town, and Shijibang (delivered afterward)
4. Kunshan (captured goods)
5. Songjiang (captured goods)
6. Jinshan and Songyin Town (obtained by field operations warehouse)
7. Songjing Town (goods surrendered by army depot)
8. Jiashan (goods surrendered by army depot)
9. 9. Shengshe Town (requisitioned goods and army warehouse provisions)
10. Guangde (requisitioned goods, captured goods, and goods delivered afterward)
11. Lukou Town (requisitioned goods, captured goods, and goods delivered afterward)
12. Dongshanqiao (requisitioned goods)
13. Tiexinqiao (requisitioned goods)
14. Xishanqiao (requisitioned goods)
15. Nanjing (requisitioned goods, goods delivered afterward)
16. Wuhu (requisitioned goods, goods delivered afterward) (Wang and Lei n.d., 285–286)

Upon occupying Nanjing, the Japanese army took control of the entire city's grain reserves. The seizure of Nanjing's granaries as discussed above was described in an overbearing manner by a colonel in charge of the Japanese army depot to Zhu Qingchuan, a higher-up within the International Red Swastika Society: "In areas occupied by the great Imperial Japanese Army, all human and material resources are the property of the Imperial Army. On what authority does the Red Swastika Society branch claim that rice in the relief granaries belongs to the Red Swastika Society?" (Zhang 2005, 479–480). Military grain depots in Nanjing were also seized by the Japanese. In a report of January 21,

1938, the Pacification Team wrote: "Materials in Chinese army depots have now all come under management of the Imperial Army" (Jiang et al. n.d., 316).

Following occupation of Nanjing, the Japanese army's "requisitioning" took place hand-in-hand with the massacre. In the "Essential Rules of Sweeps in Nanjing," the Japanese army stipulated that: "During sweeps you must investigate treasuries, weapons stocks, rations, warehouses, and other military-use materials. In accordance with needs, while dispatching soldiers to stand guard over these, also make speedy reports" (Wang and Leiguoshan n.d., 110). After a period of "sweeps" by the Japanese army, Chinese soldiers and civilians could no longer put up a resistance, but the Japanese continued these "sweeps" in order to "requisition" more goods. In a notice to all units under his command, 16th Division Chief of Staff Nakazawa Mitsuo wrote: "All units on garrison duty have completed several successive sweeps in their areas of responsibility, and now no enemy troops seem to be in sight, but from time to time three to five enemy soldiers can still be captured. The sweeps can continue unabated toward the objectives of demonstrating our force, requisitioning, and keeping our troops deployed" (Wang and Leiguoshan n.d., 57). Sone Kazuo wrote in his diary that as the Japanese army attached importance to its so-called "reputation," many lower-ranking officers "killed innocent civilians without any consideration" after so-called "requisitionings" to prevent their units from facing subsequent accusations (Wang 2006b, 220–221).

Female Rape of Nanking survivor Zhang-Yu recalled that her husband was seized by Japanese soldiers and beaten with the butt of a pistol because he could not understand Japanese. The soldiers even unsheathed knives and threatened to cut his throat. Once her family understood what the Japanese wanted, they took the Japanese soldiers to all nearby families who raised chickens in pursuit of eggs. During the egg raid, one Japanese soldier found a pig, which he killed (Matsuoka 2005, 216). Kodera Tadao of the 16th Division's 16th Engineering Regiment recalled that nearly all food consumed by his unit was plundered locally, owing to the long time required to supply food from Japan: "We went to the places inhabited by local Chinese and stole things from them… We collected many things. There were pigs and cows and other food. We stole everything. In any vent after we broke in, we stole everything of any quality. If they resisted, we shot them. So the villagers could not resist" (Matsuoka 2002 CN, 374–375). International Committee treasurer Christian Kröger wrote in a private report of January 13, 1938: "From 14 December on, the situation deteriorated rapidly. Battle-weary Japanese troops, who had been inadequately supplied during their advance, were let loose on the city and behaved in ways no one had thought possible, especially in their treatment of the poorest and most innocent Chinese. They took rice from the refugees, the poorest of the poor, took whatever supplies they could find, warm wool blankets, clothes, watches, bracelets, in short anything that appeared to be of value. Anyone who hesitated to hand something over was immediately slashed with a bayonet, and many people were subjected to such rough treatment for no reason at all. The victims numbered in the thousands, and these brutish soldiers kept coming back to the Zone, its houses packed with refugees, and each time would take what their predecessors had disdained" (Rabe EN, 143).

What were the reasons for the brazen robbery and massacre committed by the Japanese army, despite damage done to their oft-vaunted "prestige and benevolent image of the Imperial Army"? In his "confession," Matsui Iwane cited the following two reasons for the looting and other atrocities:

> 1. Our soldiers were engaged in ruthless, arduous fighting ever since the landing at Shanghai. This fighting led to intense feelings of enmity toward enemy soldiers on the part of our troops.
>
> 2. During the intense, rapid pursuit battle, provisions and other material supplies could not keep up (Wang 2005b, 194).

7.2 Food Negotiations between the International Committee and the Japanese

After the fall of Nanjing, Japanese military authorities were extremely aware of the importance of food; control of the food supply meant control of Nanjing's economic lifeline and civilian lives. They not only used food as a weapon to force Nanjing to submit to Japanese rule, but also attempted to seize the power of administration over refugees from the International Committee, and ultimately force the committee itself to submit, or even disband (Jiang Liangqin et al. n.d., 316). The International Committee, deeply aware of these intentions, steeled themselves for arduous negotiations with Japanese authorities.

7.2.1 Initial negotiations

On December 14, 1937, the next day after the fall of Nanjing, the International Committee drafted a letter in English and Japanese for the commanding officer of the Japanese forces. In the letter, part of the Nanking Safety Zone Documents, the committee wrote that it had "already taken responsibility for resettling Chinese citizens in the Safety Zone and storing rice and flour, as well as temporarily providing relief to refugees and undertaking police work in the Safety Zone." The

7.2 Food Negotiations between the International Committee and the Japanese — 421

letter also raised five requests of the Japanese commanding officer, including: "Allowing the International Committee to sell rice and flour and establish soup kitchens in the Safety Zone. The committee has rice stores in other areas, from which we hope to transport rice freely on trucks" (Zhang 2006b, 270; Rabe CN, 136–137). Committee members located about six Japanese officers, but none of them paid heed to the questions raised by the committee, but rather told them to contact 6th Division commander Tani Hisao, who would arrive two days later (Rabe CN, 137–138). This was the first contact made between the International Committee and the Japanese army, but the attempt ended fruitlessly as nobody truly in charge on the Japanese side could be found.

The following day the International Committee transmitted the letter to the Japanese Special Service Organ via Fukuda Tokoyaso of the Japanese embassy. That afternoon the committee had an answer from the Japanese army in a meeting with an agent of the Special Service Organ, as recorded in the "Memorandum on Meeting with Special Service Organ": "The committee may supply the 10,000 piculs of rice stored in the Safety Zone to refugees, but Japanese soldiers also need rice, and so they may also buy rice in the Safety Zone" (Zhang 2006b, 274).[78] The truth was that the Japanese, now "victors," felt that "buying" grain was beneath them. Rabe wrote in his diary entry of December 14: "Japanese make their way through the city in small groups of 10 to 20, looting stores to the last. I wouldn't believe it if I hadn't seen it myself. They break in doors and windows of shops and steal whatever they want, probably because they lack food" (Rabe CN, 138). Miner Bates of the University of Nanking wrote of the looting in a letter titled "Some Pictures from Nanking" of December 15, 1937: "Food was apparently in first demand, but everything else useful or valuable had its turn. Thousands upon thousands of private homes all through the city, with people living and empty, large and small, Chinese and foreign, have been impartially plundered" (Zhang 2005, 6). The International Committee submitted its first report on atrocities committed by Japanese soldiers in a letter titled "Cases of Disorder by Japanese Soldiers in the Safety Zone" to Fukuda on December 16: "Our Ninghai Road rice shop was visited on December 15th in

---

78 In his diary, Rabe describes the meeting as having taken place with the chief of staff of the Japanese general staff headquarters, and his records differ from those of the agent of the Special Service Organ, but probably he is referring to the same person. See his diary entry for December 14, 1937 at Rabe CN, 143. During a post-war deposition by international prosecutors, Fukuda claimed that the agent of the Special Service Organ in question was surnamed Sakata, though he forgot the given name, and that his rank was major; see Yang and Zhang n.d., 278. We believe the Major Sakata in question is Sakata Shigemori of the "Sakata Organ," but lacking supporting evidence, this remains conjecture.

the afternoon by Japanese soldiers who bought 3 bags of rice (3.75 piculs) and only paid $5.00. The regular price of rice is $9 per picul, so the Imperial Japanese Army owes the International Committee $28.75 for this" (Zhang 2006b, 277). Despite the honorable name of "buying" the Japanese attached to this action, it was no less than robbery.

At 2:00 p.m. on December 21, the combined foreign residents remaining in Nanjing sent a collective letter to the Japanese embassy: "In view of the fact that the looting and burning have brought the business life of the city to a standstill and consequently reduced the whole civilian population to one vast refugee camp, and in view of the fact that the International Committee has reserve food supplies to feed these 200,000 people one week only, we most earnestly beg you to take immediate steps to restore normal conditions of civilian life in order that the food and fuel supply of the city may be replenished" (Rabe CN, 191). The Japanese responded that they were unwilling to discuss the matter with the International Committee and, claiming that their own food supplies were lacking, said they were not concerned with whether the International Committee's reserves were sufficient (Rabe CN, 192). Once again, the committee's attempt to negotiate with Japanese authorities concerning the food situation ended fruitlessly.

Two weeks after the fall of Nanjing, the food problem started becoming apparent. Rabe wrote in his diary entry of December 26: "Dr. Smythe estimates our rice reserves will last another week. I'm not that pessimistic" (Rabe EN, 98). Rabe did, however, conclude that "the best will be to prepare for the unforeseen, and be ready in case refugee food reserves are exhausted and calamity befalls us" (Rabe CN, 228–229). So on December 27 Rabe and Smythe met with Second Class Secretary Fukui Kiyoshi to request aid in transporting food into the Safety Zone. They presented Fukui with a letter providing details on the committee's food and fuel reserves, noting that "private rice reserves of families in the Safety Zone are nearing exhaustion, and there will be a dramatic spike in rice demand," and that the International Committee's "stores will be exhausted in less than a week" if it had to provide food for all refugees, and that "fuel reserves for soup kitchens are sufficient for only a week" (Rabe CN, 236). Fukui promised to discuss the matter with military authorities, but in a letter to his family of December 27, Smythe doubted that Fukui would be effective in discussions with the military (Zhang 2005, 253). Smythe's assumption was again proven right in a meeting with Fukui on December 29, of which Rabe wrote: "Mr. Fukui wants to help explain our situation to the army, but he can't help us, because everything is running through military authorities" (Rabe CN, 244).

The Japanese refused to pay heed to the International Committee's appeals for help with food because they wanted to force the committee to disband. Bates wrote in a letter to friends of January 11, 1938 that "A Japanese Embassy officer told us the generals were angry at having to complete their occupation under the eyes of neutral observers, claiming (ignorantly, of course) that never in the history of the world had that been true before (Zhang 2005, 18). In a letter to family Smythe wrote that when he and Rabe submitted a short letter on Japanese atrocities to the Japanese embassy, Fukuda and Tanaka were speechless for a moment, before Fukuda said: "The army claims that the reason for such insanity is that this is the first time that neutral observers have been present during a military occupation" (Zhang 2005, 265). Rabe wrote in his diary entry of December 26: "Our various petitions to Japanese authorities to let us search the city for more stores of rice and then bring them to the Zone have remained unanswered. The Japanese want the Chinese to leave the Zone and return to their homes" (Rabe EN, 98). In a letter to his wife of January 11, John Magee wrote: "They are trying to put our International Refugee Zone Committee out of business and get control of the food, oil, and funds in our hands" (Zhang 2005, 166). Thus the Japanese continually threw up obstructions to helping the International Committee resolve its food problems.

7.2.2 The International Committee subdues the puppet municipal government in the food issue

On January 1, 1938, the Nanjing Autonomous Committee entered the scene with great pomp. On January 3, the International Committee passed an internal resolution on a top-secret document detailing the problems currently facing the committee, as well as response measures adopted by the International Committee following the founding of the Autonomous Committee and its attitudes. The International Committee agreed to support and acknowledge the Autonomous Committee's restoration of order and public services, but it persisted in maintaining control over distributions of food and other resources, which it refused to hand over. The document stressed: "We must be on alert to not allow anyone to give us work or duties that will exhaust our financial resources, nor any work that will cause us to lose control over these funds" (Rabe CN, 268–269).

Three days after this top-secret document was created, on January 6, Fukuda Tokoyaso informed Rabe that Japanese military authorities had resolved to disband the International Committee, and that the Autonomous Committee would take control of its stocks and funds. Rabe immediately protested, and then convened a meeting of the International Committee, where members discussed what response to make and drafted a letter outlining their vision on the restoration of law and order (Rabe CN, 297). The next day Rabe gave the letter to Fukuda, who expressed his sympathy for the International Committee's positions but told

Rabe that "strict instructions have come from Tokyo stating that order absolutely must be restored in Nanking immediately. At the same time, however, all administrative tasks (including those of Mayor Rabe?) must be handled by the Autonomous Government Committee and not by us Westerners" (Rabe EN, 115).

At the same time Fukuda was telling Rabe that the International Committee was to be dissolved, the committee received notice that it could buy rice and flour from Japanese military authorities. Supplies brought into the Safety Zone by refugees were nearing exhaustion, so the International Committee resolved to purchase 50,000 yuan of rice and flour in addition to 12,000 yuan of coal, despite their high prices (about 13 yuan per sack of rice) (Rabe CN, 296). So on January 6 the International Committee delivered a letter signed by Rabe to Major Ishida of the Japanese army's quartermaster supply officer, detailing the quantities of food and coal required by the committee (Rabe CN, 298–299). After a few days of negotiations, on January 10 the International Committee's treasurer Kröger received Major Ishida's final answer: the Japanese were no longer willing to sell rice and flour to the International committee; they would provide it to the Autonomous Committee only (Rabe CN, 320).

Several other incidents occurring at the same time drove the International Committee to change course, to resolve their needs through the Autonomous Committee. Deputy chairman of the International Committee's housing commission Charles Riggs said that (Jimmy) Wang Chengdian was willing to help the International Committee procure food, but in exchange the International Committee would have to help the Autonomous Committee transport food. Bates said that "Rice is most urgently needed now." In a letter to family of January 5, Smythe noted he was also willing to do anything to cooperate (Zhang 2005, 266). Mills had an idea, which Smythe related in the same letter: "We've long felt that we've been forced to resolve some problems through the Autonomous Committee and not directly through the Japanese embassy. The Japanese urgently wish to weaken the International Committee and hand its functions to the Autonomous Committee. So Mills suggested that we being working clearly on that basis, handing issues to the Autonomous Committee and greatly encourage them to hand demands to the Japanese directly" (Zhang 2005, 326).

In truth, the Autonomous Committee was also negotiating with the Japanese to obtain grains for its own considerations. A January report of the Japanese Special Service Organ's Nanjing office read: "In the transitional period, the Autonomous Committee currently lacks financial resources, so in addition to the money it is earning from grain sales and the planned rickshaw tax (about 1,000 of which are in service), we plan for the Autonomous Committee to directly operate markets selling fish, vegetables, and other goods, to augment its income. In the future a guiding policy of collecting household taxes to pay for operations costs will be adopted" (Jiang et al. n.d., 310). So, as noted by Smythe in a letter of January 9, the puppet Autonomous Committee established a food commission on the model adopted by the International Committee, with (Jimmy) Wang Chengdian appointed as its chairman (Zhang 2005, 270). On January 7, at the second regular session of the Autonomous Committee, it was resolved that Wang and deputy commission chairmen Sun Shurong and Cheng Langbo would proceed to the Japanese embassy to discuss the sale of rice and wheat with the Japanese army via Fukuda (Nanjing Municipal Archives no. 1002–19–8).

In a letter to family of January 9, Smythe wrote that Wang told him that Japanese military authorities planned to distributed 5,000 sacks of rice free of charge outside the Safety Zone to induce the Chinese to return to their ruined homes, and that the Japanese would sell 100,000 sacks of rice to him at the price of five yuan per sack, which he could resell at eight yuan per *dan* (Zhang 2005, 329). A message delivered to Rabe by Autonomous Committee adviser Xu Chuanyin[79] confirmed Wang's proposition. Xu likewise told Rabe that the Japanese were prepared to give away 5,000 sacks of rice to the Autonomous Committee on condition that the rice not be distributed in the Safety Zone, and that this was being done to prompt people in the Safety Zone to return to their residences outside of the zone (Rabe CN, 308). This demonstrates that Japanese military authorities had assented to Wang Chengdian's request related to sales of rice and flour, but came with a condition: no distribution in the Safety Zone, in order to lure refugees out of the Safety Zone and lead to dissolution of the International Committee.

On the morning of January 9, Wang Chengdian had a meeting with relevant members of the International Committee. Wang claimed that the Japanese had planned to force all International Committee rice shops to shut, then thought better of it, but still refused to allow the International Committee to sell rice to refugees (Rabe CN, 316–317). Forcing International Committee rice shops to close would have been yet another means of coercing the International Committee into disbanding the Safety Zone while simultaneously augmenting the status of their puppet Autonomous Committee. The Autonomous Committee itself likewise attempted closing the International Committee's rice shops to take control of all rights to sell grain in the city. The International Committee beat the Japanese and the Autonomous Committee at their own game by agreeing to close their own rice shops. As the International Committee's reserve of rice stood at only 4,000 sacks, and was diminishing at a rate of 250 sacks per day, insufficient for two weeks of supply, and because free distribution of 100 sacks of rice per

---

[79] Known in many sources of the time as Dr. C.Y. Hsü (translator's note).

day would make reserves last 40 days, Smythe told Wang that they wanted to close the shops: "Today we have only one rice shop operating. The rice will be taken away either this afternoon or tomorrow, and so we'll close the shop tomorrow morning" (Zhang 2005, 330).

Early in the morning on January 10, the International Committee ceased rice sales before the Japanese order landed. At 4:00 p.m. that afternoon, the puppet Autonomous Committee set up a rice vending booth near the International Committee's headquarters in the Safety Zone. One reason was that Japanese military authorities had prohibited rice sales inside the Safety Zone, but Bates wrote in a letter of January 10: "Japanese supply departments are beginning to let out for monetary and political reasons a little of the rice confiscated from considerable Chinese Government supplies, though the soldiers burned not small reserves" (Zhang 2005, 17). Another reason was the poor capacity of the puppet Autonomous Committee to transport the food the Japanese army had allocated to it. So Wang Chengdian asked the International Committee to help resolve the food transport problem.

After negotiations, the International Committee dispatched drivers in the committee's own five trucks to transport the 10,000 sacks of rice Japanese military authorities had allocated to the Autonomous Committee. The International Committee charged shipping fees on rice to be sold but not on rice to be distributed free of charge (it was claimed that an additional 1,250 sacks were to be distributed free of charge outside the Safety Zone), according to a "Letter to Allison" of January 10, 1938 (Zhang 2006b, 323).

Despite cooperative attitudes, matters evolved circuitously. It took two days for the International Committee to move 1,250 sacks of rice for the Autonomous Committee, but the driver was notified while picking up an additional 10,000 sacks of rice on January 12 that "a new order has been issued for this time, and per this order 1,000 sacks of rice will be provided every three days" (Rabe CN, 334). Rabe wrote in his diary entry of January 11: "The Japanese have cut off our rice supply today. At noon the transport of rice, which we had undertaken on behalf of the Autonomous Government Committee, was halted" (Rabe EN, 122). This demonstrates that the Autonomous Committee received only 1,250 sacks of rice, and the promise of an additional 10,000 from Japanese military authorities evaporated. The 1,250 sacks of rice were sold out immediately. On January 12, the Japanese began posting notices in the Safety Zone requesting refugees to return to their homes. At this time all rice sales had been halted, and the Japanese did not permit the International Committee to transport any more rice or coal into the Safety Zone (Rabe CN, 326). Japanese authorities' intentions here were crystal clear: force the International Committee to disband the Safety Zone, citing food as a reason, also in order to not have to resort to force to disband the zone, which would further tarnish their image.

7.2.3 The International Committee negotiates with the Japanese to transport rice into the city

American, British, and German diplomats returned to the city between January 6 and 9, 1938. This was a glad happening indeed for the foreigners of the International Committee, who had been fighting all by themselves. Rabe was extremely hopeful the three diplomats returning to the American embassy would support his cause, even not knowing their standpoints (Rabe CN, 297). In a letter to family of January 9, Smythe wrote: "Members of the American legation returned to Nanjing on the 6th, making us feel relieved of a massive burden. They could of course not do anything or become directly involved in the Safety Zone, etc., but we felt that their presence had a certain deterrent effect on the Japanese, that it would be clearly effective... Today British and German diplomats have come ashore, and we feel like we've been given even more relief forces – as though we've been in a siege that has just been lifted" (Zhang 2005, 268).

Members of the International Committee asked the returning diplomats for news from the outside while bending their ears about what had transpired in the city since its fall. They also asked for their help in exerting pressure on the Japanese to stop the atrocities being committed by Japanese soldiers. In a letter to Secretary Third Class Allison of the American embassy of January 10, Smythe detailed conditions of the International Committee and Japanese intentions to requisition their relief materials, finishing by thanking Allison for his concern for the International Committee and its work for the people of Nanjing (Zhang 2006b, 322–324).

On January 13, Rabe suggested dissolving the Committee for the Safety Zone and founding an International Relief Committee, with Japanese representation. Rabe described his thinking in his diary entry of January 13: "This seemed like the only way to coexist with the Japanese on a friendly basis and for us to attain the goal we were seeking, to prevent the refugees from starving and to restore peace and order to the city" (Rabe CN, 327). The other members of the committee voted against Rabe's proposal. Their logic was that the Japanese had already de facto acknowledged the Safety Zone, and they were concerned that if the International Committee were dissolved, they might be completely ignored. Nobody disagreed, however, on the need to maintain good relations with the Japanese.

On January 14, the International Committee sent a letter to Fukuda Tokoyasu, in Rabe's name, detailing the course of negotiations on food and fuel between the International Committee and Japanese authorities since December 21, 1938: "We understand that you registered 160,000 people without including children under 10 years of age, and in some sections without including older women. Therefore, there are probably 250,000 to 300,000 civilians in the city. To feed this population on normal rations of rice would require 2,000 *tan* of rice per day (or 1,600 bags per day). From this it will be clear that the proposed 1,000 bags for every 3 days is less than one-third the amount of rice needed. Up to the present the people have gotten along very largely on their private stores of rice but that is being rapidly used up and the demand for purchasing rice has risen very rapidly since January first. There should immediately be made available for purchase by the people at least 1,000 bags of rice per day and that should be increased to 1,600 bags per day as soon as possible." Toward the end the letter read: "I write therefore to inquire what the state of affairs actually is, and why the arrangements previously made have been canceled? The people must eat and when they are deprived of rice or the fuel with which to cook it, they are reduced to a bitter condition indeed" (Rabe CN, 334). Of course, the International Committee still wished for Fukuda's help to carry out their plans. Like Rabe, their hope was that the "people have enough to eat, no matter how this is managed" (Rabe CN, 335). The Japanese, however, ignored even this most basic of demands.

Right as the International Committee was negotiating with the Japanese to increase the daily grain supply to refugees in the city, glad tidings arrived from Shanghai. On the morning of January 15, the International Committee received a telegram from the International Society of the Red Cross in Shanghai in which C.L. Boynton, secretary of the National Christian Council of China, notified the committee that about 600 tons of food had been prepared for Nanjing in Shanghai. The International Committee immediately wrote to the Japanese embassy requesting that they obtain permission from Japanese military authorities to transport and unload this food to get the shipment loaded on boats and headed toward Nanjing as quickly as possible. The letter stressed the following: "In our discussion with Major Ishida he said the Japanese Army did not have any beans, peanuts or oils, green vegetables or substitute that they could sell to us for civilians in Nanking. If this large population has only rice for many weeks in the winter, there will be more danger of sickness" (Zhang 2006b, 331). As Japanese military authorities had refused their requests to transport grain into the city several times, the International Committee made preparations to respond to another refusal, i.e. exposing the affair to the outside world. Rabe wrote in his diary entry of January 15: "If they do not grant permission to us, we will send a telegram through the British navy to all newspapers in Shanghai to expose this matter to the world" (Rabe CN, 341). The International Committee sent a reply to Boynton, writing: "Today we requested permission to have the

600 tons of food transported to Nanjing," adding "what other kinds of appropriate foods can be purchased in Shanghai?" The International Committee "still lacks reliable channels for purchasing food and fuel to feed 250,000" (Rabe CN, 344).

Two days quickly passed, but no response from the Japanese came. In fact, the International Committee had already sent a letter to the Japanese embassy on January 13, two days after Japanese military authorities had forbidden transport and sales of rice, asking for permission to have rice and flour shipped into the city.[80] The International Committee had purchased this rice and flour from the Shanghai Commercial & Savings Bank, Ltd. prior to the fall of Nanjing, in the following quantities related in a letter of January 13 to Fukuda:

Warehouse One – Sanchahe – 5,000 sacks of wheat and 2,000 sacks of rice
Warehouse Two – Hanxi Gate – 4,000 sacks of wheat
Warehouse Three – Xiaguan – 1,000 sacks of rice (Zhang 2006b, 328–329).

After the fall of Nanjing, these warehouses were searched and sealed off by the supply departments of the Japanese army and navy. The International Committee was of the opinion that this flour and rice was meant to be distributed free of charge and not sold, and that these were private stores, and as such there should be no difficulty in their obtaining permits to distribute these stores. Much to their chagrin, however, their request to distribute these stores met with the same fate as their request of January 14 to sell rice and fuel and their request of January 15 to have food shipped from Shanghai: it was either ignored or outright refused by Japanese military authorities.

So the International Committee took a two-pronged approach beginning on January 17, both continuing to write to the Japanese embassy asking for clear answers to their three requests (Zhang 2006b, 332) and also requesting Allison's help to apply pressure to the Japanese embassy (Zhang 2006b, 333). Smythe and George Fitch paid a visit to the Japanese embassy on January 18; Fukui asked them to meet with Vice-Consul Tanaka, whom they found presently. Tanaka told them that the Japanese army had confiscated the rice and wheat in the warehouses. When Smythe and Fitch reminded him that these stores were private property and not property of the Chinese army, Tanaka noted that it was possible that the Japanese army would use the stores to feed Chinese civilians. This was in

---

[80] There are discrepancies among different sources regarding to whom this letter was addressed. Rabe notes Fukui Kiyoshi as the recipient in his diary (Rabe CN, 368). Xu Shuxi claims the recipient to be Fukuda Tokoyasu in her Documents of the Nanking Safety Zone (Zhang 2006b, 328–329). The contents of the letters in both sources are largely identical, however.

truth a dressed-up refusal to the International Committee's request to access and transport these food stores. As for the International Committee's request to have 3,000 sacks of rice and 600 tons of supplementary foodstuffs shipped from Shanghai, Tanaka refused with a simple "no." He told Smythe and Fitch that no ship would come to transport these foodstuffs. When the two mentioned Japanese ships, Tanaka explained that these were "all being used toward military objectives." When they mentioned British ships, Tanaka did not respond (Rabe CN, 377).

The International Committee then quickly adopted the following response measures.

First, immediately upon their return from the Japanese embassy, Smythe and Fitch wrote a telegram to Boynton in Shanghai signed by Fitch, reading:

> Food question more serious because no regular supply available civilian population. Only twenty-two hundred bags rice and one thousand bags flour released for sale from large stocks on hand to two hundred fifty thousand people since December thirteenth.[81] Population has existed on private family stocks which are now running out. We are feeding fifty thousand daily free rice. Request to truck in rice wheat purchased here and request for necessary passes to ship six hundred tons foodstuffs from Shanghai turned down. Please try negotiations Shanghai. If you can buy Chinese green beans Shanghai get permission and ship one hundred tons as soon as possible. Go ahead raising funds. We will find way to use them. Release. Fitch. January 18, 1938, 3 p.m. (Zhang 2006b, 334).

At the same time, the International Committee wrote letters to Allison in the American embassy, Prideaux-Brune in the British embassy, and Rosen in the German embassy, notifying them of the three major requests the committee had made of the Japanese as well as how negotiations on these three requests had concluded. The International Committee posited that under current conditions it was not advisable for the three diplomats to directly pressure the Japanese into acceding to the food shipment request, but that since Tanaka had claimed the Japanese army would bear responsibility for resolving the food question for Chinese civilians, the three diplomats could informally hint to the Japanese: "let us see you do this!" (Rabe CN, 376–378).

Nevertheless, the International Committee still hoped that the "1,000 pounds of bulk cod liver oil and 200 pounds of surgical gauze could be shipped to the University Hospital by a British gunboat on the 23 (Sunday)" from Shanghai and "urged that the 200,000 units of anti-diphtheria medication ordered by

---

[81] On January 17, the Japanese army allocated 1,000 sacks of rice and 1,000 sacks of flour to the Autonomous Committee, in addition to the 1,200 sacks of rice allocated by the Japanese army to the Autonomous Committee on January 10 (see Rabe CN, 377).

the International Committee on January 10 be included in the shipment by any means possible." The 1,000 pounds of cod liver oil was to be used to strengthen people suffering from lung infections, and the 200,000 units of anti-toxins to combat the spreading epidemic of diphtheria (Rabe CN, 392). Japanese military authorities still refused the request, even though these were to be used to treat refugees. In response, the International Committee "hopes that it may rely on obtaining help from the embassy in short order, or else the heartless refusal of Japanese authorities would soon have to be revealed" (Rabe CN, 393). We thus see that the International Committee was turning to the power of public opinion to force an end to Japanese atrocities.

In truth, the only effective means available to the staffs of the American, British, and German embassies was to turn the matter over to their home offices or ask that their embassies in Tokyo negotiate with Japanese authorities there. In a telegraph to Boynton of January 22, the International Committee noted: "A complete report has gone to the U.S. State Department today. But they cannot act officially until the problem reaches a more dangerous stage – dangers of riots. We are trying to prevent such a situation from developing!" (Rabe CN, 405). As stated in the telegram, on that same day Allison reported the food supply situation in Nanjing to the U.S. State Department, noting that Prideaux-Brune "does not wish to take precipitate action" and that Rosen "who has been taking an extremely strong stand with the Japanese regarding the inhuman activities of their troops, is willing to approach them at once." Allison's opinion was: "Quite apart from the humanitarian aspect of the matter it would appear that the possible danger to American interests ensuing as a result of this slow starvation of thousands of Chinese might be sufficient grounds for this Office to take up the question with the Japanese authorities." He requested instructions from U.S. Ambassador to China Johnson on what actions to take (Yang 2010, 370).

Johnson replied to Allison on January 24, writing: "I see no reason why you should not approach Japanese military with a view to urging that International Committee be permitted to import supplies. I have repeated this telegram to Washington and Tokyo" (Yang 2010, 370). The U.S. State Department sent instructions to Nelson on January 25 reading: "The Department approves your instruction to Allison and suggests that Allison be advised to stress the humanitarian aspect of the matter." The U.S. State Department further instructed its ambassador in Tokyo to engage in direct consultations with the Japanese Ministry of Foreign Affairs owing to the severity of conditions in Nanjing (Yang 2010, 371).

In a letter to his wife of January 24, Ernest Forster wrote: "Allison and the British and German Consuls are not standing for any nonsense. When their protests, etc. are tabled by the J. Embassy officials, they get into direct communication with Tokyo through Washington London and Berlin. This has made the J. awfully mad here... Since Allison communicated directly with Tokyo through Washington the local J. officials here have been more tractible [sic], though still not all they should be" (Zhang 2005, 117). We also observe the progress made in diplomatic negotiations from the telegram of the American ambassador in Tokyo resent by American Consul Gauss at Shanghai to the U.S. State Department: "The Foreign Office informed us today that Okazaki, who is now temporarily in Tokyo, reported that an arrangement had been made by which the International Committee could bring into the safety zone whatever supplies it might have owned prior to the Japanese occupation of Nanking and is authorized to purchase supplies up to Mexican dollars 100,000 granted by the Committee by the Nanking municipality" It went on: "The [Japanese] Foreign Office also stated that it has instructed the Japanese Consul General at Shanghai to submit a full report on the situation at Nanking and to extend in the meantime full cooperation to the International Committee with respect to caring for Chinese refugees" (Yang 2010, 371–372).

Despite these lofty words, concrete actions were lacking. It was during this time, on February 4, that Japanese military authorities announced that they were going to forcibly disband all refugee shelters. It was truly as the American ambassador in Tokyo related to American consul Gauss in Shanghai: "The impression given us at the Foreign Office is that the military authorities at Nanking who have not 'recognized' the International Committee feel that conditions at Nanking do not warrant this Committee assuming continued responsibilities of the care of the Chinese refugees and are anxious to have this work turned over to the local Chinese Autonomous Committee" (Yang 2010, 372). The International Committee now faced new challenges.

7.2.4 Final efforts of the International Committee

After continued fruitless discussions with Japanese authorities, the International Committee had no choice but to borrow the strength of the media. Rabe made several mentions of trying to pressure Japanese authorities through revealing the actions of their troops in the media. On January 24, 1938, the National Christian Council (NCC) in Shanghai made the following radio report on most recent conditions in Shanghai:

> Last week Mr. Fitch cabled asking for $50,000. We have already donated $200,000. We have received about 100 letters from Nanking reporting on alarming circumstances there. There are 250,000 refugees, of whom 30,000 are sheltered in the University of Nanking. Soup

7.2 Food Negotiations between the International Committee and the Japanese — 433

> kitchens are serving congee free of charge to 50,000 daily, although their food stores will soon be exhausted. The Japanese have offered only 2,200 sacks of rice and 1,000 sacks of flour from their expansive reserves to be sold, yet the daily demand is estimated at 1,600 sacks of rice. Nanking has also requested that we ship foodstuffs there from Shanghai, but we have yet to receive approval from the Japanese. All we can do is to ship them some small private goods through Domei. A shipment of codliver oil and surgical gauze has been prepared for shipment to the University (Kulou) Hospital. The Shanghai Committee for Relief to Nanking was founded on Friday afternoon, its members including the honorable John C. Ferguson, W. W. Ren, Di Mingze (transliteration), and W. F. Roberts. The chairmen are P. F. Price and a Chinese (whose name I didn't hear clearly). Also on the committee are four missionaries who previously resided at Nanking (Rabe CN, 409).

Rabe was greatly encouraged to hear this news over the radio, which informed everyone that great amounts of money had been raised in Shanghai to relieve refugees in Nanjing, that the foodstuffs and medicines required in Nanjing had been purchased, and that a committee had been organized to aid in relief efforts. Most attention-worthy was the broadcast's implication that the food crisis in Nanjing had been intentionally caused by the Japanese.

The International Committee sent a telegram to Boynton on January 24 expressing gratitude for his help and asking him to try to obtain permission to ship foodstuffs into the city by negotiating with the Japanese in Shanghai. The International Committee also took actions in Nanjing: continuing to press the Japanese into granting permission to have their food shipped in, and urging the Japanese to increase the quantities of rice, flour, and fuel they were making available (Rabe CN, 410).

On January 27, the *North China Daily News* published a detailed report on current conditions in the Nanjing Safety Zone titled "Nanking Safety Zone Still Filled with Refugees." The report claimed that the International Committee was still functioning as a relief committee, working for the survival of 250,000 Chinese civilians, managing 25 refugee shelters, and providing food free of charge to the penniless. The article sharply contrasted Japanese atrocities with the International Committee's humanitarianism, claiming that the Japanese refused to allow the people to return to their homes. It went on: "The majority of residents (at least 90%) remain in the Safety Zone from fear that they will come to harm at the hands of roving Japanese soldiers in other parts of the city or that their homes have been burned down. Some, having gone home, are returning to the Safety Zone after experiencing the ruthlessness of Japanese soldiers... Those living here have not only not moved out but are demonstrating a wholehearted intention to stay here through winter." The article further claims that Japanese authorities restricted the supply of rice, and that unless resolute actions were taken to provide rice and fuel to the population, severe starvation would be imminent, yet Japanese authorities were obstructing the International Committee's efforts to purchase relief food from around Nanjing and Shanghai. It read: "Widows and orphans constitute another problem preventing a return to normalcy". A survey conducted in Ginling Women's College revealed "420 women who depended on the support of their husbands, those husbands now massacred by the Japanese. Many men in the city met this same fate on suspicion of being 'soldiers in plainclothes.'" The International Committee could do nothing to stop this, but could only turn to Chinese organizations in Shanghai and elsewhere that could help with these problems, which had in turn provided enormous assistance to their compatriots and family members in dire straits in the city. The article finished by praising Wang Chengdian and Charles Riggs, claiming that a moving story should be written about them, because of "their joint efforts to convince the Japanese army to permit them to bring rice, flour, and coal to the city's residents" (Zhang 2005, 154–157).

International Committee treasurer Christian Kröger returned to Shanghai on January 23. On the 28th he notified Rabe by letter that the Japanese still refused to allow the food shipment. Kröger clearly noted: "This problem should be constantly reported on. Have the news agencies stir up public opinion, printing news like 'Japanese forces starving Nanjing residents to death.' News like that has a marked effect on American sentiment... If possible, we should write one news article per day, to ensure that the periodicals are receiving constant news. Otherwise we have nothing with which to counter those ruffians in the army. This band of hooligans is still bragging that they want to bring light back to the East!" (Rabe CN, 500).

The Chinese media quickly became aware of conditions in the city after the fall through various channels. On January 28, the *Dagongbao* in Hankou ran this article: "The administrative office of the Safety Zone in Nanjing is appealing to the outside world. They claim that the 250,000 civilians in the zone feel that food and fuel will soon run out as the Japanese army is preventing authorities in the zone from buying food. There are only two foreign doctors in Nanjing, and this is creating great anxiety in the city. Everyone who has left the zone to return home has fled back to the zone due to intolerable Japanese abuses." That same day, Han Lih-wu, one-time second director of the International Committee who had left Nanjing on orders before its fall, wrote in a telegram to George Fitch: "I have learned, to my consternation, that the committee needs money and food. Please inform quantities of all goods needed other than those being donated from Shanghai and other details" (Rabe CN, 446). This all goes to demonstrate that the food crisis facing the International Committee as well as the impending famine had already received wide traction in the outside world.

The International Committee continued work as usual even as media outside the city reported on the coming food crisis. On January 26, the committee sent letters to the American, British, and German embassies attempting to convince them to help the committee resolve their rice reserve problems (Zhang 2006b, 346–347). These reserves had been given to the International Committee by the former municipal government of Nanjing; the International Committee represented this fact to Japanese authorities many times, but they stalwartly refused to return them. The Japanese authorities consented neither to allow the International Committee to purchase food locally in Nanjing nor to allow a shipment of food from Shanghai. Under these conditions, the only resort left to the International Committee was to repeatedly bring up the food stored in Nanjing that originally belonged to their organization. Rabe wrote in his diary entry of January 26: "We are trying to get the German, American, and British embassies to help us in regard to supplies of rice that we still have stored in warehouses that are now the property of the Japanese. But there is little prospect of success. All three gentlemen shake doubtful heads." He continued: "We can hardly expect the Japanese to hand over these remaining supplies at some point. On the contrary, they will make every effort to prevent us from bringing in any more food. We are in their way, and the Japanese authorities want to be rid of us. With each new day, we make ourselves more unpopular, and are afraid that one fine day they'll simply pack us all off to Shanghai" (Rabe EN, 158).

On January 27, Rabe and Smythe hand-delivered a to Fukui Kiyoshi in the Japanese embassy a letter, in which they renewed their appeals for the Japanese to return the food given them by the former Nanjing municipal government, listing out the quantities in question (Zhang 2006b, 347–348):

	Original quantity	Received by committee	Confiscated by Japanese authorities	Units
Rice	20,009 sacks	9,076 sacks	10,933 sacks	96 kg / sack
Flour	10,000 sacks	0 sacks	10,000 sacks	50 lb / sack

After repeated consultations, Fukui promised to bring the issue up with military authorities once again (Rabe CN, 426).

Rabe then received news that the Japanese planned to disband their refugee shelters by force. The International Committee was obliged to reconsider the issue of "whether to dissolve the International Safety Zone Committee and replace it with a relief committee, and whether to cooperate with the Autonomous Committee, i.e. the new autonomous government" (Rabe CN, 436). On January 28, the International Committee sent a letter to the Autonomous Committee claiming that Fukui had requested that they resolve the food problem through discussions with the Autonomous Committee. The letter also noted that per previous experience with flooding, refugees subsist chiefly on relief rice in March and April, but that the International Committee's rice reserves would be spent around February 15. In the letter the International Committee stressed:

> At present our soup kitchens are serving rice or congee to a fixed number of people, 50,000, free of charge. The amount of rice thus used will increase to double its present quantity by next month. We must take preventative measures to prevent exhaustion and meet the demands of 100,000 people for 10 weeks. To ensure sufficient supply during the crisis period, we need 12,000 sacks of rice to keep 50,000 people alive for 10 weeks, and double that quantity for 100,000 people: 24,000 sacks. You can thus see that the 10,933 sacks of rice and 10,000 sacks of flour mentioned in our letter are sufficient only for distribution during the springtime in Nanjing (Zhang 2006b, 348–349).

On January 30, Rabe and Smythe met with Wang Chengdian to discuss the food question. Wang promised to do his best to convince the Japanese to return confiscated rice and flour reserves. Rabe said: "It is precisely these kinds of efforts that are not guaranteed to yield results, but we must try anyway, because we cannot give up all attempts. We must persist in maintaining our rights" (Rabe CN, 443).

On February 2, Rabe was invited to a lunch with Japanese Embassy Counselor Hidaka Shinrokuro at Rosen's house. Rabe raised the question of a forcible disbanding of the Safety Zone with Hidaka, who explained away Japanese atrocities and denied any safety issues while explaining to Rabe that force was absolutely not going to be used. Hidaka asked Rabe not to tell the Chinese that the Japanese did not wish to forcibly disband the Safety Zone, so as not to cause a stoppage in the work of disbandment (Rabe CN, 455–456). The following day Rabe sent a letter to Hidaka to formally confirm his pledge not to drive refugees from the Safety Zone by force, writing: "I recall with friendly appreciation your assurances of yesterday that refugees will not be forcibly evicted from the present camps, and am sure that this wise policy will obviate any danger of serious difficulties over the problem. You will of course realize the importance of securing the detailed co-operation of the military authorities to this end so that all possibility of misunderstanding may be averted" (Rabe CN, 468).

February 4, the date the Japanese military had announced for the forcible disbandment of the Safety Zone, was fraught with anxiety. Military authorities, however, issued new orders that all shelters must disband by February 8, which caused a commotion among refugees. In reaction to this potentially dangerous situation, on February 5 the International Committee held a directors' meeting to discuss whether to rename the committee to the "Nanking Relief

Committee" to be run by Rabe, Smythe, and International Committee deputy director Hubert Sone, with the results to be announced in the report of the next directors' meeting. On February 6, the International Committee wrote a letter to Allison noting their willingness to cooperate with the Autonomous Committee or to distribute rice in the name of the Autonomous Committee, but expressing that the International Committee could not abandon the model of food distribution upon which it had resolved. The letter stressed: "The Committee must also point out that the attitudes of large sections of foreign opinion both in China and abroad would be unfavorably affected by confiscation of means legally given to the Committee" (Zhang 2006b, 377–378).

The impact of "foreign opinion" stressed in the letter was felt quickly. On February 9, the *Chicago Daily News* published an article by Reginald Sweetland on a report signed by 10 representatives at a rally of American Christian leaders accusing the Japanese army occupying China of attacking and kidnapping girls and women and massacring unarmed civilians. The report praised the humanitarian work being performed by missionaries zealously clinging to their posts and detailed their difficulties and the danger facing them. The article read: "Their second great task is to provide food and housing. They receive very little support from the Japanese army in performing these charitable deeds. Much evidence demonstrates that they are, in fact, being obstructed, and that to date they are still unable to obtain supply of fresh grains and other foodstuffs" (Zhang 2005, 162–164).

On February 13 the *Dagongbao* in Hankou published a letter from former Nanjing mayor Ma Chaojun to the International Committee in which Ma enumerated the inhuman atrocities being committed by the Japanese army in Nanjing and accused the Japanese of restricting food supply to the city. He wrote: "I have furthermore recently learned that the grains, vegetables, and medicine supplying the 200,000 in the Safety Zone have been used up. Your committee has asked for relief from all quarters, yet the Japanese refuse, wishing instead to drive out 200,000 innocent refugees to the brink of starvation. I was severely aggrieved to hear this." Ma entreated the International Committee to solemnly engage the Japanese army in negotiations to bring food and other forms of relief to the Safety Zone, to prevent mass deaths.

Under pressure from all sides, Admiral Hasegawa Kiyoshi, commander of the Imperial Japanese Navy's 3rd Fleet, ultimately acceded to the request to have food shipped from Shanghai to Nanjing. But just as mentioned in the NCC broadcast, the Japanese allowed only a small amount. The Shanghai Committee for Relief to Nanjing then arranged for a shipment of 100 tons of broadbeans to be brought to Nanjing on the Butterfield and Swire Co. steamer Wantung. These beans had been requested by the International Committee to treat the beriberi spreading among refugees.

The International Committee foresaw that Japanese military authorities would throw up obstructions to bringing these beans into Nanjing, and so on February 12 sent a letter to Wang Chengdian requesting that the Autonomous Committee arrange for the shipment to come in its name, and to acquire written permission for doing so. The International Committee pledged to store the beans in its own warehouses to facilitate distribution free of charge to the poor and distressed of Nanjing (Rabe CN, 540). Unexpectedly, Japanese military authorities refused this request from the Autonomous Committee, demanding that the International Committee hand over the shipment of broadbeans to the Autonomous Committee with no conditions, lest permission not be granted. The International Committee refused this counteroffer, and Rabe again tried to press the Japanese to change their minds through Allison and Prideaux-Brune's replacement at the British embassy Jeffrey (Rabe CN, 541). Under pressure, Japanese military authorities finally consented on February 16 to allow the shipment of broadbeans into the city and permitted for these beans to be distributed both inside and outside of the Safety Zone (Rabe CN, 551). The only condition was that the work of distributing the beans was to be handed over to the Autonomous Committee. Japanese military authorities made assurances to the American and British embassies and to the International Committee that "if the beans are distributed by the Autonomous Committee, no restrictions will be imposed on distribution of the beans inside or outside the Safety Zone" (Rabe CN, 553).

In a letter to his wife of February 17, Miner Bates wrote: "We have yielded a great deal in order to get the beans into the refugees and to avoid a fight that would certainly close the door on future shipments for some time. Jimmy Wang, who is working very closely with Sone and Riggs, will receive and store the beans as Food Commissioner of the Self-Government Committee and distribute them according to our order (which the Japs do not know)" (Yale Divinity n.d., n.p.).

The "bean problem" seemed solved, but the International Committee for the Nanking Safety Zone was drawing close to the end of its life. After its directors' meeting of February 5, four more meetings were held over two weeks. At the final meeting on February 18 the members resolved to rename the body the "Nanking International Relief Committee," declaring that the rights claimed by the International Committee to negotiate with the Japanese in food and other issues were to be assumed by the newly formed Relief Committee.

7.2.5 Follow-up work of the Nanking International Relief Committee

On February 23, 1938, Rabe, having lived through the "dance of death"[82] in Nanjing, left the city for Shanghai aboard the British gunboat HMS Bee. Prior to his departure, Bates gave him a press briefing on conditions in Nanjing for newspapers in Shanghai, writing:

> There is one problem that continues whether people are at home or in a Zone: that is food...
>
> We have been very anxious about the food situation and until some of our Shanghai friends very energetically loaded and secured permission for 100 tons of beans to come to Nanking, we did not have any supplementary foods to add to the rice gruel the people fed by soup kitchens were getting. Worse than that we were not able to set up enough kitchens for the people in the camps so we had to give many of them raw rice which they had to cook themselves and many of them could not buy vegetables to add. Consequently, a large part of the 50,000 people on free rice have had very little else since the middle of December, two months.
>
> Beans is beans, but I must add a word or two to that discussion. We do not have the beans yet! That is because we did not have time to negotiate for their landing after it was learned the Army would not accept Admiral Hasegawa's permission for them to be shipped and landed at Nanking. However, they are expected back to Nanking on Saturday and will be received by the Nanking Self-Government Committee and distributed to the poor of the city free by them. We were assured that the Japanese military will place no restrictions on their use either outside or inside the former Safety Zone. That will be an interesting experiment in cooperation. If it works out to the satisfaction of all, we hope it will open the way for shipping in more foodstuffs soon.
>
> In this case, we decided to forego the rights inherent in a shipment consigned to an American mission institution and the rights of a private relief organization to send or receive supplies for the benefit of the needy in any country. This was because we thought that it was more important for the people to have the beans than to stick to the strict observance of these principles at present. But we trust those principles can be faithfully adhered to in the future... (Rabe CN, 580–581).

Bates intended to transmit word on three problems in the city: first, the severity of the food problem in Nanjing and people's worries about it; second, the Japanese army's obstruction of the food relief work being performed by the International Committee; and third, the International Committee's difficult decision to forego its rights to ensure the people received food, and even the renaming of the committee toward the same end.

---

[82] This is Wakely LAIBI's vivid analogy for the Japanese atrocities committed in Nanjing. See Wakely LAIBI, *"rijun zai nanjing de 'siwang wudao'"*, The China Forum 1, no. 5, March 19, 1938 (Zhang 2005, 183–185).

Nevertheless, the International Committee's efforts still ended in failure. On March 2, 1938, the International Relief Committee attempted to restart negotiations with Japanese military authorities to recover the rice and flour the army had confiscated. These efforts were fruitless. Despite multiple meetings with Japanese Consul-General Hanawa Yoshitaka, no substantial progress was made toward recovery of the food reserves (Zhang 2006b, 137).

On May 13, 1938, the International Relief Committee, which had long patiently remained silent, finally published news on the Japanese army's confiscation of its rice and wheat stocks. In the report, the committee wrote: "Chinese authorities, in a humanitarian concession, turned over a large quantity of rice, wheat, and other necessities of smaller demand to this committee." They continued: "The rice and flour were inappropriately confiscated and applied to uses that had no direct relationship to us. This is tantamount to a detainment of important items among the assets of the committee. Consequently, if we did not make efforts through proper demands or ignored these matters, the committee would not only be in breach of responsibility to all contributors but would also be in abrogation of its duties to refugees." The International Relief Committee resolved to issue a declaration on the Japanese army's confiscation of its food stocks and treacherous attacks on its charitable work, noting in the report the Japanese method for dealing with refugees, as well as its attitude toward legal relief provided by large foreign contributions toward humanitarian ends are the same: confiscation (Zhang 2006b, 142–144).

In truth, Japanese military authorities confiscated not only the rice and flour reserves of the International Committee, but also attempted to take a cut out of international donations. An article in the *Dagongbao* of Hankou published on February 16, 1938 recounts the heavy-handed declaration of a spokesperson of the Japanese embassy at a reception: "Donations to relieve refugees in battle zones from all countries, but in particular the one million dollars raised by the American Red Cross Society in response to President Roosevelt's request, will be appropriately allocated in cooperation between charitable bodies and Japanese authorities."

In summary, there was great asymmetry in negotiations between the International Committee and Japanese authorities regarding the food question, with the International Committee consistently relegated to a disadvantageous position. Nevertheless, the course of these negotiations further reveals the International Committee's resistance against Japanese atrocities.

7.3 Food and Living Conditions of Nanjing Residents during the Rape of Nanking

In the wake of the Japanese occupation of Nanjing, the people of the city faced threat of death on a daily basis, in addition to the dearth of food manufactured by the Japanese army. Iris Chang wrote: "Looting and arson made food so scarce that some Chinese refugees ate the Michaelmas daisies and goldenrod growing on the Ginling College campus or subsisted on mushrooms found in the city. Even the zone leaders went hungry from lack of meals. They not only provided free rice to the refugees through soup kitchens but delivered some of it directly to refugee compounds, because many Chinese in the zone were too scared to leave their buildings" (Chang n.d., 155–156). Thus we see that people both inside and outside the city walls lived in an environment of both terror and hunger.

7.3.1 Overview of food sources during the Rape of Nanking

International Committee secretary and University of Nanking professor Lewis Smythe was commissioned by the International Committee to conduct an investigation into war damages within Nanjing and in its outskirts from March to June 1938. On the basis of work performed, Smythe wrote a report titled *War Damage in the Nanking Area, December, 1937 to March, 1938*, which was published in Nanjing in June 1938. He wrote: "Under the economic conditions of March, that was true a fortiori; for the poorer people had practically nothing in the way of vegetables or oils, much less of meat or fruits. Aside from a handful of families that secured flour, all others were dependent upon rice, normally the major cereal of this region" (Jiang et al. n.d., 16). The lack of foods other than rice compelled Smythe to make rice the primary target of his investigation. The report separated out the different sources of grain at the time: Autonomous Committee rice shops, small shops, soup kitchens, and others. The overall conditions uncovered by the investigation are as follows:

> Considering all sections of the city, 17 per cent of the people were getting their rice from food kitchens (free, or at a nominal charge); 64 per cent from small private dealers; 14 per cent from the stores conducted by the Self-Government Committee; 5 per cent from "others," which usually obscured the real source by interposing a friend or a relative.
>
> Outside the wall no people could get food from the kitchens, while at the other extreme were 82 per cent of the people in the refugee camps, plainly among the poorest in the city, on the average.

In the Safety Zone Area, 17 per cent were dependent on the kitchens, and in Cheng Hsi [Chengxi] 12; both districts were adjacent to the kitchens that were in operation (Jiang et al. n.d., 16–17).

The majority of food distributed by the International Committee to refugees came from the store of grain donated by former Mayor Ma Chaojun to the committee to be used for humanitarian assistance, this being the 9,067 sacks of rice and 1,000 sacks of flour under the committee's actual control, as well as 350 bags of salt donated by the municipal government.[83] The International Committee attempted to purchase grains from Shanghai and other areas during the Rape of Nanking, but was obstructed from doing so by the Japanese army. The *Report of the Nanking International Relief Committee (November, 1937 to April 30, 1939)* recounts the food relief activities of the committee during the Rape of Nanking in great detail. Here is an excerpt:

> During the period Dec. 17–31, the International Committee made regular deliveries of rice averaging 84.5 bags per Day among 2 camps, plus 28.5 bags to kitchens, plus 3 to police and sanitary workers, plus 20 among special grants including the Red Swastika Society. Of the regular kitchens there were two in camps conducted by the Committee, two conducted by the Red Swastika Society largely serving persons from the camps, and one by the Red Cross Society entirely serving persons in the camps. The remainder of the rice to the camps was given out dry. Of the camp population averaging 70,750 during this period, 25,150 were fed inside the camps, 8,200 in kitchens adjoining camps. About 5,000 were fed by the special grants. Thus some 38,350 persons were receiving their basic food, some of them their only food, from the Committee. Some groups had private supplies of rice with which they could provide for themselves wholly or in part, and some were able to get supplements of vegetables, oils, or peanuts. Meat was seldom seen in the camps and supplies of green vegetables or of beans were small and costly. The total number of bags of rice given out free or at the nominal charge made by kitchens for those able to pay it, was 2,035.

> All figures for the December half-month and for the following months are on the basis of the full time specified. Actually a larger number of people were fed, but some of them for less than the time specified. It was expected that one bag of rice would feed 300 persons for one day in the form of thick gruel made in a collective kitchen. Where rice was given out dry, the calculation was 250 person-days per bag. In many instances the rice was spread even more thinly, since some people were served from the kitchens only once a day, or re-

---

83 Before the fall of Nanjing, Mayor Ma Chaojun gave the International Committee 30,000 *dan* of rice and 10,000 sacks of flour, but owing to difficult traffic conditions, the International Committee was able to transport only 9,067 sacks of rice into its warehouse. The 1,000 sacks of flour were donated by the Datong Mill. The rest all fell into the hands of the Japanese army. Despite repeated attempts to negotiate with the Japanese for the return of these supplies, they were never returned. See *Report of the Nanking International Relief Committee (November, 1937 to April 30, 1939)* (Zhang 2006b, 391).

ceived relatively small allotments of dry rice. A bag of rice of the lower middle grade which constituted the bulk of the Committee's supplies weighed on the average 212.25 pounds, or nearly 77.5 kilograms; it represented 1.25 *shih tan* by measure.

For January the average of the camp population was 62,500, of whom 25,250 were fed inside the camps by a distribution of 79 bags daily among the 25 camps; there were also given out 4.5 bags daily among police and sanitary workers and other staff not covered in the camps, and 4.5 bags in grants to the Red Cross Hospital and other special interests. Thus about 27,125 persons were largely or wholly maintained by the free rice. In this period the kitchens conducted by the Red Swastika Society did not need to draw considerably upon the International Committee for rice, and that under the Red Cross was moved inside a camp. The total number of bags used by the Committee was 2,721.

In February the camp population was sharply reduced to an average of 36,800, which included, however, many of the poorest people whose private resources were early exhausted. 20,800 were fed in the camps by a daily distribution of 69 bags. The Committee's workers now received maintenance allowances in cash, and all other special grants were stopped. Total 1,935 bags.

For March the average total population of 22 camps was 26,700, of whom 17,300 were fed by the Committee on a daily allowance of 59 bags, totalling 1,821 (Zhang 2006b, 397–398).

The contents of the report reflect the number of people on food relief from the International Committee as well as the quantity of food the committee distributed between December 17, 1937, and March 1938. They also reflect the International Committee's cooperation with the Red Swastika Society and Red Cross Society. On January 28, 1938, the International Committee sent a letter to the Red Cross Society of China, imploring them to: "purchase 100 sacks of rice to be delivered to the Red Cross shelter in the University of Nanking to relieve the penniless refugees there" (Rabe CN, 438). Beginning in January 1938, however, the International Committee's cooperation with the Red Swastika Society began to diminish, as reflected in the statement: "In this period the kitchens conducted by the Red Swastika Society did not need to draw considerably upon the International Committee for rice." Here are the reasons:

First, Japanese military authorities saw the International Committee as a thorn in their side, and thus attempted to disband the committee's camps by hook or by crook. As far as the Japanese were concerned, "the existence of the Safety Zone prevented the Japanese army from establishing a 'new order' in Nanjing" (Zhang 2001, n.p.). So Japanese military authorities resorted to a multitude of ruses to obstruct the International Committee in its attempts to feed refugees.

Second, realizing that Japanese military authorities viewed the International Committee with contempt, the Red Swastika Society had no choice but to rely on itself. Then vice chairman of the Red Swastika Society Chen Guanlin recalled:

"The Nanjing branch of the Red Swastika Society participated in the International Committee's Safety Zone relief work, but once the Japanese army entered the city, refusing to acknowledge this 'international' organization and wantonly engaging in massacre, arson, looting, and rape around the city... we had to rely entirely on our own forces to relieve the people in dire straits" (Zhang 2005, 475).

Third, the puppet Nanjing Municipal Autonomous Committee installed by the Japanese army in 1938 included a considerable number of Red Swastika Society members. Most prominent was Tao Xisan, concurrently chairman of the International Red Swastika Society and chairman of the Autonomous Committee. Red Swastika Society Vice Chairman Xu Chuanyin served as advisor to the Autonomous Committee. Red Swastika Society Communications Director Sun Shurong, previously employed by the Japanese embassy, served as vice chairman of the Autonomous Committee.

Zhu Qingchuan, who served as vice communications director of the International Red Swastika Society during the Rape of Nanking, recalled: "The Nanjing branch of the Red Swastika Society distributed rice congee every day in the Wutaishan Temple, entirely as a form of alms, not asking for any money. The Nanjing locations at the Shanxi Road intersection and on Huowa Alley also distributed rice congee every day, going through large quantities of rice daily. There was still a stock of dozens of sacks of rice in the Shanxi Road office" (Zhang 2005, 475). Faced with the Japanese army's blockade, the Red Swastika Society decided to negotiate with military authorities to transport grain stores from the granary outside the Zhonghua Gate into the city. As Zhu Qingchuan had studied politics and law at Waseda University in Japan and spoke Japanese fluently, he established a good relationship with Buddhist monk Tsukamoto, who was traveling with the army. In early January 1938, Zhu and Xu Chuanyin visited the Japanese army depot at Xinjiekou, escorted by Tsukamoto, to negotiate with Lieutenant Colonel Haba. Haba agreed to return the rice in the Zhonghua Gate granary to the Red Swastika Society and assigned Captain Futagawa Kiyo to handle liaison work. Futagawa signed a double-sheeted bill of lading for the Red Swastika Society, which could thereby retrieve rice using the Society's official stamp. Zhu recalled: "The Red Swastika Society was very fortunate to obtain the allocation of 3,000 sacks with the help of the Japanese monk; they stored this to the south of Hanzhong Road" (Zhang 2005, 479–480).

The Red Swastika Society had obvious advantages in the food issue. First was the good relationship it shared with the Japanese-installed puppet municipal government. Second was the good relationship between its members and the monk Tsukamoto. Third was the donation of over 100,000 tons of rice the Society had made to Japan following the great Tokyo earthquake of 1923 (Zhang 2005, 476). Fourth, the Red Swastika Society had taken up the burden of burying Japanese pilots downed in air raids over the city beginning in August 1937. After the Japanese occupation of Nanjing, Japanese naval officer Shiozawa thanked the Red Swastika Society on behalf of the naval high commander (Zhang 2005, 477–478), laying foundations for a good relationship between the Japanese navy and the Red Swastika Society. Fifth, Zhu Qingchuan's education in Japan played a role in allowing the Society to perform its relief work relatively unhindered.

In addition, other charitable groups, including the Nanjing branch of the Red Cross Society of China, Chongshantang, Mingde Cishantang, Zhongzhi Fushantang and others, provided food to refugees as well. Per the report *Excerpts from the Red Cross of China Nanjing Branch Summary on Refugee Relief Work (July 14, 1938):* "This branch's soup kitchen was established in the Ginling Women's College and served congee twice daily, from 8:00 to 10:00 a.m. and again from 3:00 to 5:00 p.m. This soup kitchen served women and children refugees living on the college campus exclusively, with the most people served in one day being over 8,000. Over six months the total of person-meals served was 864,020, funds expended on rice and coal about 20,000 yuan, and funds expended on personnel and equipment 2,100 yuan. The kitchen is still operating" (Sun 2007, 177). Per the report *Status of Chongshantang Activities such as Burying Bodies*, after its evacuation into the Safety Zone to avoid Japanese soldiers, Chongshantang "served rice to refugees from December 11 of the 26th year, but operated intermittently following May" (Sun 2007, 145). Chongshantang Director Zhou Yiyu said "Now that the ravages of war are calming down, there is desolation everywhere. Our first task is to organize burial teams to work hard to bury bodies and restore sanitation. At the same time we are distributing food to relieve refugees and maintain a trickle of life in them" (Sun 2007, 144). Nevertheless, these charitable bodies were often unable to keep up with demand for their services, their greatest difficulty being insufficient food supply. Zhou Yiyu once borrowed grain from the puppet municipal government, saying: "Our organization currently has no income, making it difficult to respond. Having no choice, I have temporarily borrowed 600 *dan* of rice under these special conditions for allocation, given the extreme urgency of the situation" (Sun 2007, 144).

Objectively speaking, Japanese military authorities did distribute a quantity of food through its puppet regime the Autonomous Committee to be used to "win over" the people. Miner Bates wrote in a report of February 10, 1938: "The Japanese authorities to date have released a total of 5,200 bags of rice and 10,000 bags of flour for civilian use. All of this was for sale through the Self-Government Committee excepting 2,000 bags of rice (included in the above) which was for free distribution to families returning to their homes" (Zhang 2010, vol. 2,

500). He wrote again in the International Committee report *Relief Situation in Nanking* of February 14, 1938: "From December 13th to February 12th, only 5,200 bags of rice (including the 2,000 for free distribution mentioned above) and 10,000 bags of flour had been released" (Bates n.d.). In the press release given to the departing Rabe on February 23, Bates wrote: "…in the two months since their entry into Nanking," Japanese authorities "have released through the Self-Government Committee only 2,000 bags of rice for free distribution. Besides this 8,000 bags of rice and 10,000 bags of flour have been sold by them to the Self-Government Committee for resale to the people" (Rabe CN, 582). In his "Notes on the Present Situation" of March 3, Bates wrote that Japanese military authorities made available to the population of 250,000 to 300,000 only 10,000 bags of rice and 10,000 bags of flour over the two months from their entry into the city on December 13 through February 19, 1938 (Zhang 2010, vol. 2, 533). This relieved only a part of the food problem for refugees.

Liu Enlu submitted this plan for refugee relief to the Autonomous Committee: "We see more refugees in Nanjing every day. During this bitterly cold season, they have nothing with which to feed their families. I entreat that we provide relief, as they truly have no clothes against warmth nor rice against hunger. We can allocate clothes, rice, and flour by the head" (Nanjing Municipal Archives 1002–19–7). The Autonomous Committee then established a dedicated Relief Office, which established sub-offices in the official districts later defined by the Autonomous Committee to be in charge of actual allocations. On February 4, the Autonomous Committee came to a resolution on how to distribute rice allocated to it by the Japanese Special Service Organ: "Four *ge*[84] of rice per adult and half for children. District offices to be in charge of confirming household figures. Allocations for the elderly, infirm, under-clothed, and poor only. This plan is to be enacted via consultations with the Relief Office and all district sub-offices" (Nanjing Municipal Archives 1002–19–8). A report of the first district office of the Autonomous Committee read: "There is extreme crowding at the daily allocations of rice and flour. Subordinates do their best, working with few breaks, to allocate these goods to relieve refugees of the disaster (this month 301 bags, two *dou* and two *sheng* of rice and 23 bags and 28 and a half kilograms of flour have been given away)" (Zhang 2006b, 481).

Conditions began to calm by March 1938 when farmers in the outskirts of Nanjing began to sell grain reserves not looted by the Japanese into the city, although even this was insufficient to meet demand. To address the situation, the Autonomous Committee requested that the Japanese Special Service Organ pur-

---

[84] Chinese unit of dry measure equivalent to a deciliter (translator's note).

chase 100,000 *dan* of rice from Wuhu, of which 30,000 was to go to relief, 10,000 to expenditures and damages, 30,000 for normal operating expenses of the Autonomous Committee for four months, and 30,000 to local banks in Nanjing to establish a "small ticket fund." The quantity to be used for the committee's operating expenses were to be sold by the committee to raise funds. The Autonomous Committee also adopted two measures to drive rice sales: a rice monopoly enforced by the Industrial and Commercial Office, and a removal of obstacles from the river by the Transportation Office to facilitate shipments of rice from agricultural regions to the southeast.

In summary, the people of Nanjing survived the "period of death" on the strength of their stubbornness and vitality despite rigorous controls placed on the food supply by Japanese military authorities. As E.A. Ross writes in *The Changing Chinese:* "…at least a part of the observed toughness of the Chinese is attributable to a *special race vitality* which they have acquired in the course of a longer and severer elimination of the less fit than our North-European ancestors ever experienced in their civilized state" (Ross n.d., 44).

7.3.2 Refugees' conundrum: food, death, or ethics

There are many definitions to the word "famine," but the perspective of Alamuge seems to fit best with what happened during the Rape of Nanking. He says: "An even more unfortunate aspect to the problem of famine is that famines often break out during times of domestic or international political crisis, and famines are partially caused by political crises" (Kane n.d., 12). The crisis in Nanjing was man-made, created intentionally by Japanese military authorities, in fact. Smythe wrote about Japanese "requisitioning" in a letter to his family of December 24, 1937: "The result has been that no merchant is now interested in hoarding, and everybody is busy melting down their belongings. So a famine happens, and there is soon no meat left" (Zhang 2005, 247). The response of the people was to seek out food by hook or by crook, going so far as even sacrificing their own lives. This is what happened in Nanjing.

One violation of international treaties in the Japanese mistreatment of Chinese prisoners-of-war was cutting off their food supply. Yamada Seiichiro of the 2nd Company of the 9th Division's 36th Infantry Regiment recalled: "Actually we were supposed to give prisoners food and let them live in peace in accordance with international treaties, but that was difficult to imagine under the war conditions of the time, because we didn't have enough to eat for ourselves" (Matsuoka 2002 CN, 261). This is actually nothing more than an excuse used by the Japanese to shirk responsibility for their crimes. Tang Guangpu, an orderly in the

Instruction Corps' 3rd Battalion headquarters was imprisoned during the fall of Nanjing and held in what had been a temporary barracks used for bivouac training by the instruction corps at Mufu Mountain. He recalled: "There were seven or eight rows in the temporary barracks, all shacks made of bamboo and concrete, and they were filled to capacity by people captured by the Japs. We were held inside with no food. They gave us water only on the third day. The Japs shot anyone who irritated them in the least. By the fifth day we were so hungry that our bellies stuck to our spines and we were on our last legs. It was obvious that the Japs wanted to starve us to death" (Zhang 2005, 451). Luo Zuowei, veterinarian for the Central Military Academy's Instruction Corps' Cavalry Division, recalled the fate of his comrade: "After daybreak they were led by a race traitor approaching enemy forces waving a white flag. Not far from Yanziji they encountered enemy cavalry. After being disarmed, they were all held in an 'iron can car' with no food for two days. On the third day they were brought to the riverside, lined up in ranks, and mowed down from behind by machine guns before being stabbed with bayonets and finally pushed into the river" (Zhang 2005, 494). Sun Baoxian, commander of the 3rd Battalion of the Instruction Corps' Engineering Division, was luckier. Not long after the Japanese entry into Nanjing, Sun was captured and made into a conscripted laborer. He was lucky because the Japanese gave him food and eventually released him, whereupon he took shelter in the University of Nanking and survived by buying rice from the International Committee with the six or seven yuan on his person (Zhang 2005, 104).

Wounded Chinese soldiers in the hospitals established in the Foreign Ministry and War Ministry buildings had not only to put up with the pain of their wounds, but also the humiliation and starvation tactics of Japanese troops. Japanese forces occupied these two buildings shortly after their entry into Nanjing and forbade entrance to all, including John Magee (Zhang 2005, 148). Kröger spelled it out plainly in a report: "Only rice can enter the hospital. Horses, doctors, and drugs are not allowed inside" (Zhang 2005, 318). Rabe wrote in his diary entry of December 14: "It's simply a mystery to me how the people and wounded soldiers inside the Foreign Ministry are surviving" (Rabe CN, 139).

Neither the Red Cross nor the International Committee had any means of knowing conditions inside the wounded soldiers' hospitals until a Chinese nurse from the Red Cross hospital in the Foreign Ministry building came out on January 20 on pretense of buying supplies to make this report to Magee: "One of the wounded Chinese soldiers complained that he was not getting enough to eat. The daily ration, she says, is just three little bowls of rice broth. The patient was beaten, and when he asked, once the beating was over, if they had beaten him because he was hungry, the Japanese took him out into the courtyard and bayoneted him" (Rabe EN, 142). On January 25, two nurses, one male and one female, made another report on conditions inside the hospital to the International Committee, which compiled their statements in confidential files. Rabe wrote: "Chinese workers are given two meals per day, at 10:00 a.m. and 4:00 p.m., the meals consisting of rice and an extremely small portion of Chinese cabbage... The wounded are also given two meals per day, at the same hours, but are fed only three bowls of very thin gruel" (Rabe CN, 414). Azuma Shiro, a Japanese soldier stationed inside the War Ministry building, recorded the miserable conditions of Chinese wounded soldiers inside the hospital, writing: "Once the congee was pushed out to them, people came with washing basins and empty cans, and some fought to eat directly from the pot. The immobile wounded had to swallow their anger and eat their leavings" (Wang 2005a, 206).

Conditions were just as bad for civilians. Rape of Nanking survivor Zhang Wenying recalled life during the event: "Life was truly hard then. There was nothing to eat, not even weeds or rancid flour. Japanese soldiers once sold red rice stolen from Chinese people to people anxious from lack of food. Because there was no grain to eat in Nanjing, and because only Japanese soldiers were selling it, the only choice was to buy it from them. The lines were long. Japanese soldiers, just the opposite of the Chinese, lived lavishly, eating only the legs and other savory parts of the pigs they stole" (Matsuoka 2005, 227).

Conditions in the Safety Zone were clearly somewhat better. Li Jingde, a 22 year-old bathhouse worker at the time of the fall of Nanjing, took shelter in Jiangwen Girls' Middle School (at least according to the original interview transcript; we suspect he may have been in the Huiwen Girls' Middle School). He recalled that he had some grains stored away, but he did not dare touch them at will. He recalled Americans giving him food: "They gave us three meals of 'old rice congee' per day. It was very thick and cooked in a big pot. It was aid from the Americans. They also gave us a few dried turnips every day" (Center for History of Republican China, Nanjing University, July 2006). Sun Dongcheng, who sheltered in the University of Nanking, recalled: "We had some rice, some vegetables, and a wok to cook in when we first arrived in the Safety Zone. Public reassurances came three days later. Inside the University of Nanking they served congee, very thick, twice a day, at 9:30 in the morning and 4:00 or 5:00 in the afternoon. One copper coin bought a small pot, enough for five or six to eat" (Center for History of Republican China, Nanjing University, July 2006). Chen Jiaying sheltered in Ginling Women's College, remaining indoors at all times from fear of being raped by Japanese soldiers. She recalled: "Here they served two meals of congee per day. Everybody brought their own bowls to the exercise yard to be served, and then returned immediately to their rooms" (Matsuoka 2005, 120).

Many risked their lives for food. The family of Sun Suzhen, who resided in Sisuo Village at Xiaguan during the Rape of Nanking, took refuge in the Dongyang Temple when Japanese soldiers came. She recalled that the soldiers "came to steal our food every day, taking rice and vegetables and what not." One day, when the family had nothing else to eat, Sun's father left the house looking for food despite his wife's protests, and was shot to death by Japanese soldiers who took him for a Chinese soldier (Matsuoka 2005, 74). Survivor Chen Jiashou's experiences are somewhat more legendary in character. Taking refuge in the Dongcai Bridge shelter with no food whatsoever, he journeyed out for food three times. The first time he was captured by Japanese soldiers near Shanghai Road and brought to the Xiaguan Railway Station, where he moved oil drums for the Japanese, who eventually released him. Three days later he again ventured out from hunger, this time being captured near the Wutaishan Primary School. This time he witnessed the massacre of 200 Chinese policemen. Lined up alongside them, Chen was to be shot as well, but upon hearing the discharge he immediately fell to the ground, where the other victims' bodies piled on top of him, narrowly escaping death. Two days into his new life, he still could not resist the urge to venture forth for food. So he and an older man from next door sallied out, and he was again captured by Japanese soldiers, this time near Xinjiekou. He was sure that he was "done for," but instead he was again made into a conscripted laborer. After working a few days in a Japanese army camp, he was again released (Matsuoka 2005, 281–283).

Many faced ethical dilemmas in their struggles for survival. Kito Kyuji of the 1st Battalion of the 16th Division's 33rd Infantry Regiment recalled: "Some women came out of the Safety Zone on their own to trade their bodies for rice" (Matsuoka 2005, 296). Bates wrote about this too in a letter to friends of November 29, 1938:

> There is a good deal of common labor in the military supply and transport services, and a socially unhealthy provision for soldiers' requirements of all sorts. But I am long past blaming a coolie for serving his country's enemy in order to feed his crying children, or a girl from doing anything to avoid starvation, if they don't bring too much injury to others (such as joining in armed extortion rackets, or spreading heroin and opium). For a good deal of comfortable morality can hardly stand against the basic needs of life, and the war has already brought down scores of millions of us in economic and social ruin. Incidentally, we now have large open brothels, advertising in the official newspaper, and an entire new class of brazen girls as waitresses in restaurants, a complete revolution in manners for Nanking (Zhang 2005, 49)

As compared to the common masses, the "upper crust" of Nanjing society had relatively easy access to food; in fact it was available in relative "abundance."

Ginling Women's College dormitory warden Cheng Ruifang helped Minnie Vautrin administer the refugee shelter on campus. She wrote in her diary entry of January 18, 1938: "Yesterday the embassy (note: the American embassy) delivered two chickens and 12 eggs for Ms. Hua (note: Ms. Vautrin). There are only enough eggs on campus for Vautrin and the rest to eat. My little grandson has one per day. The rest are being kept by Wu (note: Wu Jingyi, astronomy teacher in Ginling Women's College who also helped administer the shelter) to hatch new chickens. With these items on hand our conditions are not too bad; we can't be considered real refugees" (Zhang 2005, 36). Cheng continued: "Our plight as refugees isn't too bad. We're several times better off than the other refugees" (Zhang 2005, 36). At least Cheng had meat, which the other refugees could only dream of. Nevertheless, she wrote: "I haven't had meat in a long time. People's faces get round when they see meat. Usually, when there's no meat, their faces are long. Anyone reading this diary should know that everybody wanted to eat well" (Zhang 2005, 35). Cheng was even able to buy some fruits and other foods from Shanghai through her personal connections. She was extremely satisfied to receive a package from Shanghai containing green vegetables, apples, tangerines, and candy. She wrote: "As a refugee with these three things to eat, am I not a special refugee? They're so good. I haven't had tangerines to eat in a long time. This is what I've been lacking" (Zhang 2005, 38).

Choices in food were extremely limited, and vegetables were particularly lacking. Cheng wrote about her shock at high vegetable prices: "I've eaten vegetarian food for two weeks. Now there are some green vegetables for sale, but their 300 to 400 yuan per *jin*. So expensive" (Zhang 2005, 21). The singular nature of food available and lack of nutrition led to the spread of disease among refugees. In a letter to family of January 1, 1938, Smythe wrote about the diarrhea prevalent among many in the University of Nanking and the former Ministry of Communications: "This is the negative consequence of subsisting on congee for a long time. Many people are truly too poor and have no choice but to live on congee" (Zhang 2005, 262). There followed an outbreak of beriberi in the refugee camps, likewise caused by insufficient nutrition. Rabe wrote in his diary entry of January 5: "Today doctors at the Kulou Hospital sent word that two patients having contracted beriberi have been admitted to the hospital. This is no surprise given that the only nutrition they've been consuming comes from rice" (Rabe CN, 487). On recommendations from Dr. Wilson, the International Committee reached out to connections in Shanghai to help purchase beans to resolve the beriberi outbreak spreading among the refugees.

7.3.3 Food supply and living conditions for the "Nanking gang"

The term "Nanking gang" was a name the American missionaries living long-term in Nanjing applied to themselves. Zhang Kaiyuan wrote: "Long ago we noticed that Bates and others referred to themselves frequently as 'old Nankingers' or 'us Chinese,' both during their time in Nanjing and after returning to the U.S. Now we have also discovered that these '*laowai*' also referred to themselves as the 'Nanking gang'" (Zhang 1999, 8). In a letter of November 23, 1942, Mrs. Charles Riggs wrote: "A few days ago Lucile Jones and I invited the 'Nanking gang' for tea, and to have a visit with as many of you as had written lately... It was a pleasant get-together, and not once was the high cost of living mentioned. We lived mostly in the past for those couple hours, with now and then a hopeful peep into the future" (Zhang 1999, 9). In this section we use the term Nanking gang to refer to all foreigners in the city during the Rape of Nanking. The living conditions of the Nanking gang during this time are also noteworthy. An analysis of their food sources as well as the variety of food available to them helps us clearly see the food issue created by the Japanese army's atrocities.

Although the Nanking gang, leaders of the International Committee, were in charge of relief food sources for refugees, their own living conditions were considerably worse than in peacetime, although sometimes friends and family managed to mail some food to them through private channels. As the NCC broadcast declared on January 23, 1938: "All we can do is to ship them some small private goods through Domei" (Rabe CN, 409). In a letter to his wife of December 23, John Magee described their living and eating conditions in detail:

> Every day we eat "Hai Fan" or soft rice as this will make the rice go longer. A great problem is vegetables and meat which are very scarce. The Japanese have stolen almost everything available... We also had a dish of some salt pork which the Fans had brought with them from Hsiakwan when we moved into town, and in addition some cabbage... Over at Schultz-Pantin's when we have a meal (we never eat there together) we fare much better as Ernest's excellent cook is there and also all of our stores (mostly his). The Forsters have a great deal of stuff as their cook put up many jars of fruit and beans last summer...
>
> This evening we had with our soft rice, peanuts, salt cabbage, cooked cabbage, and another cake of dou-fu-lu, or fermented bean curd. It's all right for me who has an occasional foreign meal but hard on the Chinese here who have been for three weeks on a faulty slim diet. But we are thankful to have what we have (Zhang 2005, 158–159).

On that same day, December 23, Vautrin writes in her diary: "Food is getting more and more scarce. For several days now we have had no meat – it is impossible to buy anything on the street now – even eggs and chickens are no longer available." Nevertheless, the gang were happy to get their hands on anything to eat amid the storm of carnage. George Fitch recounted that the gang feasted on roast pork and sweet potatoes at Christmas 1937 (Zhang 2005, 78). Rabe described the scene thus: "The Americans were sitting together quiet and pensive. They didn't have a tree; a couple of red banners beside the fireplace were the only sign that the servants had wanted to give their employers some small joy" (Rabe EN, 96).

Their food stores were gradually used up, however. Smythe wrote in a letter to family of December 31: "Tonight we had our first entirely vegetarian dinner. I feel this is part of the economic regulations that went into effect this morning. We previously always had meat at lunch and dinner, and three cans of fruit per day. Wilson's cook is determined to use everything! Wilson says we have enough fruit to get us through the tough times, but we've been reduced to one can of fruit and one can of fruit juice per day, and then we eat some snacks, like tonight" (Zhang 2005, 258–259). In her diary entry of New Year's Day, Vautrin wrote: "This morning was uneventful save for a surprise breakfast Mrs. Tsen [Cheng Ruifang] gave us – pineapple, a kind of fried cake, and cocoa were added to our regular breakfast, and were a real treat."

There were occasional surprises. On January 15, the Japanese embassy invited some of the foreigners in Nanjing to an informal dinner. In attendance were Rabe, Vautrin, Grace Bauer, Bates, Mills, Smythe, Trimmer, Kröger, and Magee. The victuals were highly appetizing, as Vautrin wrote: "The dinner was as international as the group, being Chinese, Japanese, and western foods." Rabe wrote of the meal in his diary entry of January 24: "The dishes at the dinner were of the first order. There were savory beef, eggs, and glass noodle hot pot in the Chinese style, asparagus in the Western style, along with both red and white wine. We hadn't had these things in a long time, and so enjoyed ourselves quite blissfully" (Rabe CN, 342).

Notwithstanding, a shadow hung over the feast. Vautrin wrote: "We had a pleasant evening and our lips uttered jokes, though often our hearts were heavy" Cheng Ruifang wrote: "Last night the Japanese consul invited people from the International Committee to dinner. Vautrin was invited too. I said he had hired a kitchen god to curry favor with them" (Zhang 2005, 33).

After Rabe received permission to proceed to Shanghai, Vautrin held a farewell tea party for him on February 17. That day she wrote: "We served a salad, opened our first box of chocolates, had oranges. The cake was not bad – kind of fruit cake made with Esther's mince meat, taking the place of fruit." Another important source of food to the gang was the American, British, and German embassies. In her diary entry of February 22, Vautrin wrote: "Embassies have certainly been untiring and seemingly uncomplaining in sending packages of books and food and mail for us."

Before Rabe's departure from Nanjing, Pastor McCallum wrote a choral piece in his honor titled *Nanking Nan Ming*, including the line "We want beans for our breakfast, beans for our lunch, beans at supper time." Rabe wrote: I didn't know the dear old parson, whom the Japanese came close to stabbing to death, had such a sense of humor" (Rabe EN, 201). The song's lyrics reflect the diet of the Westerners in Nanjing at the time.

8 Property Losses of Nanjing Residents during the Rape of Nanking.
An Initial Analysis Based on Extant Materials in China

In recent years, study of the Rape of Nanking has grown deeper across the academic spectrum, but research on property losses, private and public, during the event have been extremely lacking, owing to constraints in factors such as files and materials.[85] The authors of this chapter sought out and compiled records on relevant property losses scattered among The Second Historical Archives of China, Nanjing Municipal Archives, and the Academia Historia Office in Taibei to compose a review of surveys and statistics on property losses of Nanjing residents during and after the War of Resistance from Chinese and foreign sources. We also calculated the quantities of asset losses of 5,865 households[86] in Nanjing during the Rape of Nanking based on post-war surveys and statistics of the na-

---

Note: This chapter was contributed by Jiang Liangqin. It was originally published as an article in *Lishi yanjiu* 2 (2012). It was modified slightly for inclusion in this book.

[85] One academic performed a dedicated study on losses of books and manuscripts during the Rape of Nanking, labeling the damages the "Great Cultural Massacre." For details see Meng, "Dui Riben xuezhe yanjiu lüeduo Nanjing tushu ruogan wenti de bianxi" [Analysis of several issues of Japanese academics' study of the seizing of books from Nanjing], *Jiangsu xingzheng xueyuan xuebao*, no. 3 (2008); Jing, "Qin Hua Rijun dui Nanjing 'wenhua da tusha' shulun" [Commentary on the 'cultural massacre' imposed on Nanjing by the Japanese army invading China], *Jianghai xuekan*, no. 5 (2004); Li, "Nanjing da tusha qijian Riben dui Nanjing wenxian ziyuan zhi lüeduo" [Japanese plundering of Nanjing's literary resources during the Rape of Nanking], *Jiangsu tushuguan xuebao*, no. 4 (1999); Meng, "Qin Hua Rijun dui Nanjing wenhua de cuican" [Destruction of Nanjing's culture by the Japanese army invading China], *Nanjing shehui kexue*, no. 8 (1997); Gao, "Rikou zai Nanjing de wenhua da tusha" [Cultural massacre in Nanjing by Japanese invaders], *Meizhou Huaren dui Ri suopei zhuankan* (1995); Di et al., "Riben qinlüezhe zai Nanjing wenhua lüeduo shimo" [The whole story of cultural plundering of Nanjing by Japanese invaders], *Liaoning shifan daxue xuebao*, no. 5 (1988). Unfortunately, most of the above pieces proceed from the perspective of quantities, with few investigating the perspective of value lost. Merely assessing quantities lost is far from sufficient to reflect the losses suffered in Nanjing at this time.

[86] The area studied in this chapter is limited to the seven administrative districts of the Nanjing municipal government at the time as well as the four suburban areas of Pukou, Xiaolingwei, Yanziji, and Shangxinhe, a total of 11 districts. The time period covered runs from the Japanese entry into Nanjing on December 13, 1937 to March 1938 when atrocities began to slow down.

tionalist government in order to reveal overall conditions of property losses in Nanjing during the period and promote development of comprehensive, credible statistics on overall wartime losses in China.

8.1 Surveys and Statistics Made during the War

Over the three months from the Japanese army entry into Nanjing on December 13, 1937 until March 1938, when Japanese atrocities began to slow down, the people of Nanjing suffered great losses in their bodies and their property. During the War of Resistance, the Nanking International Relief Committee,[87] composed of foreigners in Nanjing, and the Nanjing Municipal Government propped up by the puppet "Reformed Government of the Republic of China", both conducted surveys of property losses endured by the people of Nanjing, but toward different objectives. The real municipal government of Nanjing, which retreated to the interior with the nationalist government, also made some scattered reports on public and private property losses in the city.

8.1.1 Surveys of the International Relief Committee

In mid-February 1938, the International Relief Committee commissioned Dr. Lewis S.C. Smythe, former member of the International Committee and professor of sociology in the University of Nanking, along with over 20 assistants, to conduct a survey on casualties and property losses suffered by the urban and rural population of Nanjing under Japanese atrocities, to have a better understanding of economic conditions of civilians in and around Nanjing to serve as the basis for relief work. The survey work began in early March 1938 and ended in mid-June, a period of over three months, and resulted in the work *War Damage in the Nanking Area, December, 1937 to March, 1938*.

The survey was conducted in two stages: the first in the urban districts of Nanjing, and the second in rural counties surrounding Nanjing. The urban survey was likewise divided into two categories, the "Family Investigation" that studied losses of households remaining in Nanjing by sampling one in 50 of such households, for a total of 949 households studied. The second category

---

[87] The former International Committee for the Nanking Safety Zone reorganized to the "Nanking International Relief Committee" under pressure from the Japanese on February 18, 1938. The new committee's scope of activities was limited to relief work. See Rabe CN, 565.

was the "Building Investigation," which studied damage to real estate, compiling statistics on damage to structures in the city with a sampling ratio of one in 10 structures studied, to estimate the value of total damages.

Smythe gives an estimate of total property losses of 47,450 households remaining in Nanjing in Table 1 of his report, "Families Studied and Estimated Population by Section of City." He likewise estimates the proportions of causality of said damages by different factors.

Item	Total	Cause					Average per family
		Military operations	Fire	Military robbery	Other robbery	Unknown	
Buildings	12,885,600	496,800	12,291,200	78,600	17,700	1,300	271.56
Movable property	26,882,500	177,800	8,398,900	13,024,900	3,750,800	1,530,100	566.55
Grand total	39,768,100	674,600	20,690,100	13,103,500	3,768,500	1,531,400	838.11
Percentage	100.0	1.7	52.0	33.0	9.5	3.8	——

Table 26: Losses of buildings and movable property for 48 families remaining in Nanjing. Unit: *Fabi*[88] yuan.
Source: Tables 9, "Losses of Buildings and Movable Property for Families Remaining in Nanking, By Cause" (Smythe n.d.).

Explanations:
1. All *fabi* figures based on currency values at the time of survey.
2. "Families remaining in Nanjing" refers to households with surviving members in Nanjing at the time of the fall and throughout the period of Japanese atrocities.

Table 26 demonstrates that property losses of families remaining in Nanjing totaled nearly 40 million yuan. Of these, building damages came to around 13 million, or 32.5% of the total. Movable property losses totaled 27 million yuan, or 67.5% of the total. The average loss per family was about 838 yuan, of which 272 was building damage and 567 was loss of movable property. As most Nanjing residents who remained in Nanjing during and after the fall belonged to relative-

---

[88] A fiat currency implemented by the Republic of China government in 1935 to supplant circulation of silver coins, in force on the mainland until 1948 (translator's note).

ly poor households,[89] Smythe notes: "A view of their losses shows most specifically the economic condition of resident Nanking people, though it is highly inadequate to indicate the total economic blow that the city suffered, quantitatively or qualitatively" (Smythe n.d., 11). Based on his building survey, he estimates overall conditions of private property losses of Nanjing residents.

Items	Total	Cause				Average loss per original family
		Military operations	Fire	Military or other robbery	Unknown	
Buildings	102,991,500	2,176,500	97,205,800	3,609,200	--	527.44
Movable property	143,390,400	692,700	67,962,600	71,609,900	3,125,200	734.33
Grand total	246,381,900	2,869,200	165,168,400	75,219,100	3,125,200	1,261.77
Percentage	100	1	67	31	1	--

Table 27: Losses of buildings and property by original Nanjing families. Unit: *Fabi* yuan. Source: Table 13, "Losses of Buildings and Contents, By Item and Cause" (Smythe n.d.).

Explanations:
1. All *fabi* figures based on currency values at the time of survey.
2. "Original Nanjing families" refers to households of which all members resided in Nanjing prior to the Japanese occupation, including households of which members took refuge outside the city during the occupation, those of which some or all members remained in Nanjing, and those of which the entire family perished during the period.

In Table 27 we see that Smythe estimates the total of private losses of Nanjing residents at over 246 million yuan. Of this, building losses totaled about 103 million, or about 41.9% of the total, and movable property over 143 million yuan, or 58.1% of the total; this latter is nearly 10 percentage points lower than the 67.5% of families remaining in Nanjing.

As the survey was conducted in wartime, against a backdrop of massive population changes in the city, many families having taken refuge outside the city, some others all members of which having perished, and as most of those remaining were of the poorest stratum, many potential respondents had great anxieties.

---

[89] Zhang Lianhong writes: "Most Nanjing residents who opted to stay in the city were the poor who lacked the means to move elsewhere" (Zhang 2002, n.d.).

Add to this the restrictions that the Japanese army placed on their lives at the drop of a hat (Smythe n.d., 28), and it became very difficult to avoid statistical data recording and representative errors.[90] The quality of samples taken in the survey was influenced to a certain degree, making it difficult to arrive at an accurate figure for property losses of Nanjing residents based on the survey. We can, moreover, observe the limitations on the International Relief Committee's survey work by comparing loss figures between "families remaining in Nanjing" and "original Nanjing families."

Items			Average loss of families remaining in Nanjing	Average loss of original Nanjing families
Buildings			271.56	527.44
Movable properties	Economic uses	1. Machinery, tools	16.00	72.96
		2. Shop equipment	65.01	79.70
		3. Material for manufacture	19.55	51.22
		4. Stock for sale	186.71	377.08
		5. Rickshaws	3.60	1.40
		Subtotal	**290.87**	**582.36**
	Domestic uses	6. Household furniture, utensils	110.37	44.51
		7. Clothing, bedding	115.43	58.14
		8. Family food and supplies	7.93	8.73
		9. Bicycles	2.59	3.29
		10. Cash, jewelry	9.53	3.60
		11. Others	29.83	33.70
		Subtotal	**275.68**	**151.97**
	Total		566.55	734.33

---

90 Data recording errors, also known as survey errors or working errors, refer to errors arising from subjective and objective factors in the process of data collection. Representative errors occur when the data structure of a sample is insufficient to produce estimations of overall situations. Representative errors happen under the following two conditions: first, when the principle of randomness in data sampling is violated, and second, when the principle of randomness is abided but the samples pulled randomly are not representative.

Continued

Items	Average loss of families remaining in Nanjing	Average loss of original Nanjing families
Grand total	838.11	1261.77

Table 28: Comparison of losses of families remaining in Nanjing with original Nanjing families. Unit: *Fabi* yuan.
Source: Table 9, "Losses of Buildings and Movable Property for Families Remaining in Nanking, By Cause" and Table 13, "Losses of Buildings and Contents, By Item and Cause" (Smythe n.d.).

Explanation: All *fabi* figures based on currency values at the time of survey.

After the Battle of Shanghai broke out, the nationalist government had no detailed plan on how to protect or resettle the residents of its capital in the face of the encroaching Japanese army. Preparations to move the capital were made in secret so as not to alarm the public; the process also seems to have been conducted in great haste.[91] It was extremely difficult for common citizens to leave Nanjing by boat or coach with just the clothes on their back, owing to traffic conditions at the time,[92] let alone carrying any quantity of valuables. Table 28 demonstrates that families remaining in Nanjing for the duration lost a little less than half of original Nanjing families who fled (527 versus 271 yuan on average), while losses of movable properties for economic uses of re-

---

[91] See Jiang, "Cong Songhu dao Nanjing: Jiang Jieshi zheng zhanlüe xuanze zhi shiwu ji qi zhuanxiang" [From Shanghai to Nanjing: errors in the Chiang Kai-shek government's strategic choices and its change in direction], *Nanjing daxue xuebao*, no. 1 (2011). In addition, advisor to the Ministry of the Interior Chen Tun made this declaration when compiling property losses after the war: "The figures in this table are calculated based on values of the national currency at the time of the government's departure from Nanjing in the 26th year. Of the meager property I accumulated through thrift in clothing and food over a 30 year career as a public servant, I took only two suitcases aboard the ship in strict abidance of orders. The rest was destroyed entirely. In this matter I dare not make even the minutest falsification. Be it hereby declared." Director of general affairs for the Jiangsu Coach Company Xu Chonghan writes: "Half a month before the Japanese attacked Nanjing, I retreated to the rear with my entire family. We brought only the clothes on our backs and some bedding. All our other possessions were left in our landlord's house" (Academia Historia Office no. 301–830).

[92] Wang Zhengyuan recalls: "It was already difficult to buy tickets on Nanjing steamboats before the end of November. Once the announcement was made that Nanjing was in a state of war, throngs of people flooded out of the city. Boat ticket prices ballooned to four or five times their original value. Bought on the black market, they were sometimes as much as ten times their original value, having passed through many hands. As the steamers were all moored in the middle of the river, not daring to approach the shore, anyone with a steamer ticket had also to hire a small wooden boat to bring them to the steamer, and these too were charging astronomical prices" (Wang Zhengyuan n.d., 47).

maining families were, on average, exactly half of original families who fled (582 versus 291 yuan). Remaining families' losses of movable properties for domestic uses were nearly half of those of original families who fled, on average (152 yuan versus 276 yuan). We can thus infer that losses indicated in items 6 and 7 were clearly much lower than actual losses.

Despite the statistical shortcomings of Smythe's survey discussed above, his results remain astonishing. Per his calculations, private losses of the average Nanjing resident totaled around 1,262 yuan, of which 527 were building damages and 734 were movable property losses. The looting and arson perpetrated by Japanese soldiers were the primary causes of private property losses at this time.

8.1.2 Surveys of the puppet Nanjing Municipal Government

Nanjing's municipal government organs retreated westward with the central government prior to the fall of the city in winter 1937, leaving Nanjing in a power vacuum for a short period. In order to remedy the so-called "malady of reliance on Europeans and Westerners" and to "establish norms for self-reliance and self-governance" (Liaoning Provincial Archives n.d., n.p.) on January 1, 1938, the Nanjing Municipal Autonomous Committee, a puppet body propped up by the Japanese army, was founded. On March 28, the puppet "Reformed Government of the Republic of China" declared its founding in Nanjing (The Second Historical Archives of China 1997, 43), its subordinate Nanjing Municipal Autonomous Government following suit in April. At this time conditions in Nanjing following the turmoil of war were catastrophic: "Those returning from exile find their houses in ruins. Hunger and cold are rampant. Friends and family all in similar straits... Refugees are everywhere wailing for relief. The primary means for pacification is to give relief" (Nanjing Municipal Government Secretariat n.d., 13, 181). Nanjing was also the capital of the puppet Reformed Government: "The impression is that the city's appearance is horrid." To get a handle on the refugee problem and make "comprehensive relief plans," the puppet Reformed government ordered its Ministry of the Interior to conduct surveys of both refugee numbers and employment conditions for refugees. These surveys were sent down to all local offices to be filled out within a prescribed time limit. In September 1938, the puppet Nanjing Municipal Government submitted a statistical report on conditions of refugees in Nanjing to the Reformed Government Ministry of the Interior. The report estimated the pre-disaster number of households in Nanjing at 164,476 and the post-disaster number at 76,369, meaning that only 46% of original households remained (Nanjing Municipal Archives no. 1002–2–1499). As many whole households had fled Nanjing, and many entire households had been killed, and many refused to accept aid from the puppet government from racial animosity, only a small portion of original Nanjing households applied to the puppet Municipal Government for aid, and most of these were at the lowest social stratum in dire economic straits. All persons applying for aid on behalf of their household needed the chief of their *fang*, *bao*, or *jia*, all newly appointed by the puppet government, to serve as witness to their claims. Afterward their applications required a check and approval by social bureaus. Thus many residents opted to gloss over Japanese atrocities in order to have their applications for aid approved (Nanjing Municipal Archives no. 1002–2–1045). Furthermore, in November the puppet Municipal Government issued a notice that nobody else would be taken into public poorhouses as they were already full (Nanjing Municipal Archives no. 1002–2–1045). Consequently, the statistics on property losses given in the report do not completely reflect actual property losses of Nanjing residents. Nonetheless, the survey conducted by the puppet Municipal Government into the losses of 76,369 households in Nanjing demonstrates that building damages from bombing and other property losses in the city totaled 57.3 million yuan, an average per household loss of 750 yuan (Nanjing Municipal Archives no. 1002–2–1499).

8.1.3 Scattered reports of true Nanjing Municipal Government organs from the rear

During the early period of the War of Resistance, some people with breadth of vision realized the importance of investigating wartime property losses. Member of the People's Political Council Huang Yanpei noted: "By the time the war ended, first, we had to raise the issue of reparations with the enemy. Second, we had to make detailed records of this unprecedented tragedy for the future of our national history, and proclaim it loudly to the entire world and later generations. For all this we needed accurate numbers as our bases" (The Second Historical Archives of China, no. 416(2)/37). After the nationalist government moved the capital to Chongqing, "losses were extremely heavy in public and private material possessions around the country owing to the enemy's invasion." In 1939, Chiang Kai-shek wrote handwritten letters to the Supreme Defense Commission, the Military Affairs Commission Military Advisory Council, and other organs, asking them to quickly compile statistics on direct and indirect losses caused by the war "and always be mindful of advancing this work" (The Second Historical Archives of China, no. 171/156). In July that year, the Executive Yuan created points of attention and templates for reporting on wartime losses based on the document "Second Meeting of the People's Political Council's Recommendations for Quickly Investigating Wartime Public and Private Losses." The Yuan then ordered all its subordinate organs and local governments to conduct surveys and report back, and put the Directorate General of Accounting, Budget, and Statistics (DGABS) in charge of reviewing and compiling an overall report. The DGABS then issued biannual reports based on accumulated data beginning in 1940. In February 1944, the Executive Yuan formally established the War of Resistance Losses Survey Commission.[93] In August that year the new commission issued rules: "losses in fallen areas should be reported by the municipal or county officials with jurisdiction over the fallen area in question within two months of their fall in a 'Report on Loss Conditions in Fallen Areas," which should be submitted to the War of Resistance Losses Survey Commission. So long as these areas remain in enemy hands, at the end of every year all forms of destruction and thievery by the enemy perpetrated in the area should still be thoroughly investigated, losses estimated, and a report made" (The Second Historical Archives of China, no. 2–5390).

On these orders, organs of the true Nanjing Municipal Government investigated and reported upon direct and indirect public and private losses in the city, from the rear. Owing to constraints of wartime and the fact that Nanjing had fallen to the enemy and was the "capital" of the enemy's puppet regime, the task of investigating losses from the rear was extremely difficult for these organs. In a letter to the Military Affairs Commission, DGABS Director Chen Qicai wrote: "There are very many organs which should have reported per the requirements of the Executive Yuan which have not reported… especially local organs of fallen areas" (The Second Historical Archives of China, no. 782–76). Statistics on wartime losses issued by the DGABS indicated that the damage situation in Nanjing as of June 1944 was extremely severe (see Table 29).

Category	Total	Govt. organs	Schools	Industry	Civil aviation	Households
Property loss	62,951,521	55,460,518	5,146,762	2,069,086	228,073	47,080
Percentage	100	88.1	8.2	3.3	0.4	0.1

Table 29: Overview of direct property losses in Nanjing (as of June 1944). Unit: *Fabi* yuan. Source: Table 6, "Direct property losses: by entity and location" (DGABS).

As demonstrated in Table 29, direct public and private property losses in Nanjing from the beginning of the War of Resistance through June 1944 totaled only 62,951,521 yuan, with losses of Nanjing residents totaling only 47,080 yuan,

---

[93] This Commission was later transferred to the Ministry of the Interior in April 1945 (see The Second Historical Archives of China, no. 12 (2) 1393).

only 0.1% of total direct losses. Han Qitong, then director of the Academia Sinica's Institute of Sociology, noted: "This report is far from satisfactory. Other than losses of administrative organs and industrial equipment, it is of little reference value" (Han Qitong n.d., 3). Director of the Executive Yuan's War of Resistance Losses Survey Commission Zhang Lisheng noted: "There have been very few reports on private property losses. Lacking reports, we have not concocted any figures" (Academia Historia Office no. 129–212).

After the Japanese army's occupation of Nanjing, the houses and movable assets of many foreigners in the city were looted. Three months after the city's fall, on March 14,1938, in order to compile figures on public and private losses in the city to present to the Japanese government in a demand for reparations, the American consul-general in Shanghai Gauss sent a letter to the Japanese embassy in Nanjing asking that the Japanese army "lessen restrictions against return of American missionaries and business men who have important interest there." Gauss cites a letter from the "Nanking American community" saying that "their return is needed in order to assess properly the damages to American property recently occasioned by Japanese soldiers. Only the various owners or persons responsible for such property can file satisfactory statements in regard thereto" (Yang 2010, 441). Third Secretary Allison of the American embassy in Nanjing sent a letter to the State Department on March 15 stating that Japanese officials refused the return of Americans for two reasons: "First, the local military authorities are very sensitive to criticism... second, from a purely military viewpoint it is believed that conditions are not yet such as to permit... foreigners returning" (Yang 2010, 442). With such obstructions to the return of neutral Americans to the city, the nationalist government had "no choice but to wait until after [the city] is restored" to formally begin compiling statistics on wartime losses (Qin n.d., 11–12).

8.2 Surveys and Statistics from after the War

Movements to demand reparations from Japan cropped up in all Allied countries after their victory in the war. Such a demand from the Chinese government also made its way onto the agenda: "China suffered Japan's ravaging for the longest time, over the largest area, resulting in the greatest public and private property losses and the greatest amount of casualties. As such, priority should be given to our demands for all forms of reparation from Japan" (Qin n.d., 25)./ The nationalist government resolved to conduct surveys of wartime losses across the country to facilitate the work of demanding reparations from Japan and trying war criminals. The War of Resistance Losses Survey Commission formulated nine main points to be investigated, created branch offices in every province and prefecture, and quickly got to work (The Second Historical Archives of China, no. 12 (2)-1234). In late October 1945, officials in the Ministry of Foreign Affairs learned that U.S. war reparations specialist James Bauley was about to visit China to discuss matters related to Japanese reparations. On November 13, gathered by the Ministry of Foreign Affairs, representatives from the Ministry of War, the Ministry of Foreign Affairs, the Ministry of Economy, the Ministry of Justice, the Commission on Overseas Chinese, the Ministry of Finance, the Ministry of the Interior, the Ministry of Education, and the Ministry of Agriculture and Forestry met to discuss basic principles in demanding reparations, demanding that all relevant organs produce numbers and other related materials as quickly as possible. At the meeting it was resolved to change the name of the Ministry of the Interior's War of Resistance Losses Survey Commission to the "Reparations Investigation Commission" (with membership of said commission unchanged), to return its jurisdiction to the Executive Yuan, and to demand that the commission produce a complete report on public and private losses during the War of Resistance before August 20, 1946 (Academia Historia Office no. 3–780.6/6). We must note that in the surveying and statistical work that followed, the original and the new name of the commission were frequently intermingled, because the staffs of the two commissions were identical.

On December 10, 1945, the Nanjing Municipal War of Resistance Losses Investigation Commission was formally established and convened its first meeting, discussing and then passing the "Organizational Rules of the Nanjing Municipal War of Resistance Losses Investigation Commission." The commission included representatives from the municipal government, the municipal party committee, capital police force, Central Bureau of Investigation and Statistics, the Military Affairs Commission Bureau of Investigation and Statistics, the Bureau of Social Affairs, the Bureau of Public Works, the Bureau of Finance, the Land Administration Bureau, the Bureau of Health, the Federation of Trade Unions, the Chamber of Commerce, and the Peasant Association. Immediately upon its inception, the commission printed 60,000 questionnaires on injuries and deaths and property losses, which it distributed to all organs and district offices, police departments, and corporations in the city to be filled out (Nanjing Municipal Archives no. 1003–17–9). With this, the commission's study on injuries, deaths, and property losses during the War of Resistance was formally launched.

During the ensuing general investigation, organs of the commission and all relevant local government organs conducted a large quantity of information dissemination and mobilization work. Beginning on December 23, 1945, the commission began running large advertisements in prominent positions in the *Zhongyang ribao*, the *Heping ribao*, and other major newspapers: "Because of the enormous public and private losses suffered in this city during eight years under enemy control, we are in urgent need of detailed reports to prepare demands of reparation to the enemy... All residents of this city... injured in body or property by the enemy during the War of Resistance should come forward to make honest reports to this commission or their local district offices or police stations." The advertisement further asked that all reports be made before January 31, 1946, for "processing by this commission" (Nanjing Municipal Archives no. 1003–17–1). The municipal government posted notices ubiquitously calling on the public to proactively come forward and make reports. The temporary Municipal Representative Committee's secretariat also had seven copies made of a slide show which the Bureau of Social Affairs distributed to cinemas around the city to play before every showing of a film. An article in the *Minguo ribao* of December 21, 1945 reports that in an inspection of Nanjing in December 1945, Chiang Kai-shek publicly pronounced that city residents should do their best to report on damage to their persons and their property suffered at the hand of the enemy. Yet "there was no great enthusiasm among city residents to make reports," as many were unclear on the situation and even did not know where to pick up official forms. By April 10, 1946, the Nanjing Municipal War of Resistance Losses Investigation Commission had collected 9,378 forms submitted through all channels, and of these 8,186 were reports on property losses. After more than three months, city residents had filled in fewer than one-sixth of the forms prepared by the commission: "There are still many people who moved to the interior and have yet to return home. Their losses have naturally not been reported upon. So based on numbers presently in our possession, we can see only an outline of overall losses sustained in Nanjing during the War of Resistance" (Nanjing Municipal Archives no. 1003–13–44). The commission had no choice but to extend the deadline. Nonetheless, fewer than 20,000 households had filled in forms by the end of August 1946: "Yet this should not be the entire number of Nanjing residents who suffered losses during the War of Resistance." The Nanjing Municipal Government resolved to extend the deadline a few days more to encourage residents to head directly to the statistics office in city hall to fill in forms, even offering to fill in forms on behalf of the illiterate. The government further announced that these reports on public and private losses were important because of the "specially-appointed Far East Commission on Reparations is calling for reparations from Japan. The Executive Yuan's Commission for Wartime Losses of the People will soon consolidate reports on public and private losses from all provinces and prefectures and submit them to the Far East Commission on Reparations" (Nanjing Municipal Archives no. 1003–17–1). The government hoped to thereby spur a more active response in making reports among the populace.

A further 1,268 reports on losses were filed after the final extension by September 10, 1946. For details on the overall property loss conditions compiled by the municipal commission, see Table 30.

Items	Units lost	Value (ROC yuan)	
		Total value at time of purchase	Total value at time of loss
Buildings	789 whole buildings and 31,343 rooms		
Clothing	5,920 boxes and 5,914,725 pieces		
Gold, silver, and jewelry	14,222 *liang* and 6,345 pieces		
Calligraphy paintings	28,482 pieces		
Antiques	7,321 pieces	231,785,358,222	34,757,290,323
Livestock	6,277 head		
Utensils	2,406 sets and 309,223 pieces		
Cash	447,958 yuan		
Books	1,815 boxes, 2,859 collections, and 148,619 volumes		
Vehicles	956		
Grain	12,087,975 *dan*		

Table 30: Overview of property losses by Nanjing residents during the War of Resistance. Source: Nanjing Municipal Archives no. 1003–17–9.

Owing to the long duration of the war and dramatic price fluctuations, any quantified statistics compiled on property losses during the period were inevitably going to touch on questions of how to calculate value; this turned out to be the greatest problem encountered by compilers of such statistics both during and after the war. During the war, the nationalist government demanded that local governments report property losses based on "market prices" denominated in *fabi*, but the reports they received were calculated using a vast array of different methods. Owing to "discrepancies in methods employed in investigations among various organs," in May 1941 the nationalist government's DGABS created the "Standardized Methods for Calculating Depreciation on Wartime Property Losses, for Appraising Values of Lost Property, and for Appraising Losses to Annual Revenue" One rule therein called for values at the time of purchase or construction to be inserted, and lacking such, that the market price at the time of loss should be substituted (Supreme War Council no. 782–76). As the DGABS provided no clear methods for reconciling original prices with market prices, it was still difficult for local government organs to report on losses based on the new methods. The Executive Yuan's War of Resistance Losses Investigation Commission clearly specified in the "Essentials on Amendments to War of Resistance Loss Reports" of August 11, 1944 that values at the time of loss should be employed in reporting, but that original purchase prices should also be listed out in cases where they are available (Executive Yuan no. 2–5390). On October 12, 1945, Jiang Menglin employed a method of currency valuation conversion based on the *Fabi* value in August 1945 in a survey report on public and private wartime losses to Chiang Kai-shek; his conversion formula was to take the mean of Chongqing wholesale price indices in all years from 1938 to 1945 (divided by 100), then multiply that by the converted currency value to obtain a corrected value.[94] On August 5, 1946, the War of Resistance Losses Investigation Commission summoned representatives from the DGABS, the Ministry of Foreign Affairs, and the Ministry of Finance to a meeting to discuss a value conversion method for reporting on wartime losses; they reached this consensus: take the mean of Chongqing wholesale price indices from September of every year of the war, divide that by the value of losses reported over all years of the war, and obtain a value denominated in *Fabi* of July 1937, then convert that into a USD value at the exchange rate of the time (1:3.39) (Executive Yuan no. 2(2)-2652). By February 1947, the Executive Yuan's Reparations Commission had finally compiled complete statistics on China's wartime losses per reports from all localities, with nationwide public and private direct losses totaling USD \$31,130,136,000 (The Second Historical Archives of China 2000a, 231–232), equivalent to 105,531,161,040 yuan denominated in *Fabi* of July 1937. Table 30 lists the "value at the time of loss" of Nanjing residents' total property losses as 34,757,290,323 *Fabi* yuan, but unfortunately does not indicate the year of *Fabi* value. The figure for total losses in Nanjing given in Table 30 represents 33% of total nationwide losses as reported in February 1947. As this seems unreasonable, we assume that these losses were not denominated in July 1937 *Fabi*. We further extrapolate that since the War of Resistance Losses Commission established the conversion method based on July 1937 *Fabi* values only on August 5, 1946, the Nanjing commission, which submitted its final figures in September that year, did not have time to make the proper conversions, but rather simply totaled losses reported by city residents over the years in values at the time of loss. In truth, the Executive Yuan's Reparations Commission did notice this problem, and noted in their instructions to all provincial and prefectural governments of January 31, 1947: "There have been great price fluctuations over the years. Consequently, values of losses must be calculated using this commission's standard, based in price in-

---

94 Conversion formula = (135+259+725+1865+5465+17783+51122+196888)/8×1%=34280×1% =342.8=343 (round to nearest whole number) (see Qin Xiaoyi: 11–16).

dices over the years, in order to arrive at a unified calculation. To date all local governments have already published figures. If the results of their calculations are subsequently found to have discrepancies with this commission's assessment, then adjustments will be made. This will require an enormous fuss and will be cause for gossip abroad, and will most likely impact our foreign negotiations… It is imperative that all provincial and prefectural governments send the results of their calculations on wartime losses along with original documents for approval of this commission before publishing those results." The Nanjing Municipal Government responded: "Wartime loss figures collected by this government have never been published. Hereafter we will, naturally, comply with instructions and proceed carefully in this matter."

What's more, the figures listed in Table 30 were based on property loss reports submitted to the Nanjing Municipal War of Resistance Losses Investigation Commission as of September 10, 1946. "Owing to the large number of people who suffered losses and the great variety of items subject to damage, it was difficult to avoid many gaps in the reporting" (Nanjing Municipal Archives no. 1003–17–9): "This investigation is still ongoing." (Nanjing Municipal Archives no. 1003–17–1). As such, the figures in this table only partially reflect total public and private losses suffered in Nanjing during the War of Resistance. Even after the final deadline extension had passed, many city residents continued to file reports with the municipal government. On January 28, 1947, the Nanjing Municipal Representative Assembly's first meeting discussed and passed into law the suggestion of city resident Tang Renjie, extending the deadline for reporting based on the method adopted by officials in Shanghai. On February 13, the municipal government announced: "Public and private property losses were great in the extreme during the War of Resistance as our city is the capital. Reports made to this government by all public and private bodies as well as individual city residents on orders from this government have been compiled into a tentative final report. We only fear that some residents were unaware and have not yet come forward to make their reports." The government then gives instructions for all city government organs to "extend the deadline for reporting to the end of May this year," at which point it would send a final report to the Executive Yuan (Nanjing Municipal Archives no. 1003–17–9). On April 22, the municipal government again "extended until the end of August this year" the deadline for reporting on losses, per the Executive Yuan's "Order No. 13665," again asking city residents "who suffered losses during the War of Resistance but have yet to make reports to come to the government hall to make reports," in order to finish the collection of data (Nanjing Municipal Archives no. 1003–17–1). When that deadline expired, the municipal government's Bureau of Statistics issued an additional 100 wartime loss forms to all organs and units in the city out of consideration that "we understand that many" city residents "have yet to file reports on losses suffered during the war," further indicating that "we hope that any applicable losses not reported will be filed in reports with this bureau before September 6" (Nanjing Municipal Archives no. 1003–13–44). Judging from the time it took residents to submit forms on property losses, the work of collecting these reports continued approximately until the end of 1947. This work came to its ultimate conclusion shortly thereafter as a result of the nationalist-communist civil war and the lack of spare time on the government's part to tend to this matter.

During the War of Resistance, Han Qitong, director of the Academia Sinica's Institute of Sociology, divided wartime losses into two categories based on the experience of Western academics, direct war losses and indirect war losses, calling the former "war damages" and the latter "war effects." (Han n.d., 1). Only by combining statistics from these two areas can we obtain a relatively complete picture. We see from the methods of investigation that in order to compile accurate figures on damages, the method of a general investigation must be adopted. Errors that may arise from a sampling method must be particularly avoided when reparations are involved. As noted above, the Nanjing Municipal War of Resistance Losses Investigation Committee urged reporting through the government and adopted a method of general investigation for city residents to report on property losses suffered during the war. There were discrepancies in reporting during this process owing to differing levels of education among city residents. Problems in the forms they filled out were concentrated in the area of values of property lost, including: filling in only values at the time of purchase or at the time of loss; some values were not included as they were impossible to appraise; some people living outside the city had others fill in forms on their behalf, but these agents, not knowing the values involved, listed only descriptions and quantities; having to rely on memory of possessions and their values owing to the haste with which many left the city, leaving no time for a detailed accounting; filling in forms with currencies other than *Fabi*; not filling in forms with 1937 pre-war *Fabi* values, but rather at more recent values; and so on. Other reasons include the difficulty of reporting on property losses incurred by families of which all members had died or not returned from the interior; some residents were unwilling to fill in the forms owing to the surfeit of trivial details involved in reporting[95]; high illiteracy rates among city residents, requiring commission

---

95 The Ministry of the Interior Wartime Losses Investigation Commission formally issued the "Points for Attention in Reporting Wartime Losses" at its first meeting on September 21, 1945. The document indicates: "When reporting on property losses, attach identification papers to reports in all cases possible; these should be checked, stamped, and returned by county, city, town, and township governments; also note all important identification papers on the original

employees to help individual households fill in their forms, greatly influenced working efficiency[96]; a skew toward reporting direct property losses and not reporting indirect property losses; and massive funding gaps in the Nanjing Municipal War of Resistance Losses Investigation Commission (Nanjing Municipal Archives: 1003–17–1). All these issues led to shortcomings in the work of investigating property losses during the War of Resistance. There were even problems with the data produced in September 1946, particularly in the conversion rate for currency values reported, as the forms lacked detailed explanations. The work of compiling statistics, however, continued on, and so the data released by the commission did not entirely reflect property losses incurred by Nanjing residents during the war. So far nobody has discovered any more recent statistics issued by the commission.

We must note that despite all the above-mentioned shortcomings, the work of compiling these statistics was done at an enormous scale, and did yield considerable results. The work spanned more than two years from 1945 through 1947, and yielded a great quantity of precious first-hand sources, particularly the great quantity of survey forms on property losses incurred by residents of Nanjing during the Rape of Nanking. From the perspective of a researcher, it seems that we could reduce errors through more sophisticated technical methods and reassess this massive quantity of survey materials.

8.3 Calculating Property Losses of Nanjing Residents during the Rape of Nanking

The most reliable and accurate method for calculating property losses incurred by Nanjing residents during the Rape of Nanking is to pool the resources collected during the general investigation. As stated above, the Nanjing Municipal War of Resistance Losses Investigation Commission accumulated a vast quantity of survey forms on losses incurred as a result of Japanese atrocities committed during the Rape of Nanking, but not all these files have survived to present day. Chi Jingde, researcher in Taibei's Academia Historia Office, points out: "Although many of the files and materials of all sorts related to losses incurred during the War of Resistance have survived to present day, there are many gaps, and the record is far from complete." After the KMT's defeat on the mainland, "it

---

form, to facilitate their sending to this commission" (Ministry of the Interior Archives no. 12 (2)-1234).
96 Per a social survey conducted in 1936, the illiteracy rate of permanent residents of Nanjing was 53.36% (see Nanjing Municipal Committee for Population Statistics n.d., 56).

was difficult to avoid some losses of these files during the circuitous movement of the government." The portion of these records that made it to Taibei "has passed through many hands, and were twice immersed in water as a result of typhoons. They were originally stored with the Ministry of Economics but later transferred to the Academia Historia Office... In disarray and shabby with age, some of the original documents have decayed" (Chi Jingde n.d., 261, 4). Nor have the conditions for storage of the portion of these documents on the mainland been ideal.[97] It is now very difficult to find the entirety of these forms on property losses. Several decades after the end of the war, it is now impossible to perform a new investigation into property losses inflicted during the war. Consequently, a general pooling of materials collected in the general investigation is no longer an operable method.

I subsequently calculated figures for property losses of a portion of Nanjing residents during the Rape of Nanking via a broad search for original forms on property losses still extant and revision of statistics and figures expressed therein. Considering current conditions, this seemed like a viable method for glimpsing the overall picture of property losses incurred in Nanjing during the incident. Explanations:

1. The data in Table 31 was compiled from property loss reporting forms from 5,865 Nanjing households detailing losses incurred during the Rape of Nanking found over the course of nearly 10 years in Taibei's Academia Historia Office and the Nanjing Municipal Archives. Although these figures represent only a portion of such forms filled out by Nanjing residents after the war, they are rather representative, as geographically they cover all 11 districts of the city and in terms of resident careers, those filling in reports include public servants, teachers, farmers, service workers, and people employed in industry and commerce.

2. I classified estimated values of losses on the forms by date filed, and then proceeded to analysis. In cases where values of losses at the time of loss were left blank, I employed the value at the time of purchase. In cases where both values were left blank, the form was not included in my calculations.[98]

---

[97] During my visit to The Second Historical Archives of China to find materials related to this topic, a worker there told me that the Archives had in 1980 destroyed some original forms on wartime property losses produced by the nationalist government after the war owing to insufficient storage space and poor storage of some materials. As such, only a small amount of important statistical materials on the topic remained.

[98] For example, we did not include any figures from the form filled out by Nanjing resident Liu Zhuqiao, who did not fill any values.
Property Loss Report (Form 2)
Date of filing: 35th year, March __

8.3 Calculating Property Losses of Nanjing Residents — 473

Item		Currency unit	Amounts	Subtotal	Total
Value at time of loss	Reported in value of 1937 time of loss	Fabi yuan	About 158,510,000	About 158,510,000, roughly equivalent to 167 million Fabi yuan at pre-war (June 1937) value	Roughly equivalent to 167 million Fabi yuan at pre-war (June 1937) value
		Other USD units	About 56,000	Approx. 1.41 million Fabi yuan after conversion	
		Silver coins	About 1.13 million		
		Silver	64,350 liang		
		Gold	7 liang		
	Reported in value at time of reporting (1945–1947)	Fabi yuan	28.653 million (1945.10); 223.72 million (1945.11); 117,346.5 million (1945.12); 8.49329 billion (1946.1); 646.003 million (1946.2); 508.583 million (1946.3); 205.423 million (1946.4); 18.893 million (1946.5); 208.935 million (1946.6); 1.456696 billion (1946.7); 82.82 million (1946.9); 472.39 million (1946.11); 590.00 million (1946.12); 1.47106 billion (1947.2); 3.871046 billion (1947.3); 1.672725 billion (1947.4); 770.193 million (1947.5); 197.96 million (1947.6); 2.942267 billion (1947.7); 4.790712 billion (1947.8); 18.50868 billion (1947.9); 1.55 million (1947.10); 29.50339 billion (1947.12)	Equivalent to approx. 7.3 million Fabi yuan converted to 1937 values	

Table 31: Property losses of 5,865 Nanjing families during the Rape of Nanking (December 1937 – March 1938).
Source: Academia Historia Office (Taibei) records: 301–261; 301–461; 301–816; 301–818; 301–819(1); 301–819(2); 301–820(1); 301–820(2); 301–821; 301–822(1); 301–822(2); 301–823; 301–824; 301–825(1); 301–826(1); 301–827; 301–828; 301–829; 301–830(1); 301–830(2); 301–831; 301–832; 301–835; 301–836; 301–837; 301–838; 301–840; 301–848; 301–849; 301–850; 301–853; 301–854; 301–855; 301–858; 301–860; 301–861; 301–896; 301–897; 301–902; 301–913; Nanjing Municipal Archives Records of the Nanjing Municipal War of Resistance Losses Commission: 1003–13–44; 1003–17–31; 1003–17–32; 1003–17–34; 1003–17–35Z1; 1003–17–35Z2; 1003–17–36; 1003–17–37; 1003–17–38; 1003–17–39; 1003–17–40; 1003–17–41; 1003–17–42; 1003–17–43; 1003–17–44; 1004–1–110.

3. As many respondents did not adhere to the instructions on the forms, some filling in pre-war 1937 values and some filling in post-war (1945–1947) values, I divided the table into these two sections.

4. The form's instructions asked respondents to fill in property loss values denominated in *Guobi* yuan, but many filled in values denominated in USD, silver coins, silver, and other forms of currency, and as such I have further broken the table into these categories.

Figures for property losses of city residents were divided into those valued in 1937 *Fabi*, those valued in post-war *Fabi*, and those valued in other currencies, because respondents did not follow instructions. Han Qitong began studying property losses incurred as a result of the war while it was still ongoing, and he early noticed that different statistical methods yielded different results. He proposed two remedies. The first was the "foreign currency conversion method," by which the original reported value was multiplied by the Chinese exchange rate and converted into a foreign currency value. The second was the "pre-war *Fabi* value conversion method," under which a price index (the last year before the war being the base period) was divided by the reported value to convert the loss figure into a pre-war *Fabi* value. The ultimate goal of both methods was to "eliminate currency fluctuation factors from reported values... Because an artificial monopoly on foreign exchange was imposed in China during the war, no official prices or black market prices can reflect natural levels. There were, furthermore, great fluctuations in the currencies of all other countries during the war, and so it's nearly impossible to arrive at a stable base using values denominated in foreign currencies." As such, "our only choice is to use the pre-war *Fabi* value conversion method" (Han Qitong n.d., 4). To make compiling of the statistics more convenient and eliminate pointless data accumulation, I employed the "pre-war *Fabi* conversion method," meaning that I converted all values reported in post-war currency into pre-war 1937 *Fabi* values. As residents reported losses over a span of approximately September 1945 through the end of 1947, and as the

---

Date of loss; place of loss; date of purchase; units quantity; value (*Guobi* yuan); identification; value at time of purchase; value at time of loss; On the 13th day of the 11th month of the lunar calendar in the 26th year, from number 1 Xiaojiao Alley were stolen 14 tables and chairs; 36 items of clothing; 28 copper, tin, and ceramic utensils and candlesticks; a wall clock; a calligraphy painting by a famous artist; a set of hanging scrolls. Direct-reporting unit, school, group, or enterprise. Person incurring loss: Liu Zhuqiao. Place of service or career: merchant.

Report filer: Liu Zhuqiao. Seal: Relation to person incurring loss: Mailing address: 15 Wujianting. Seal: [seal].

(Executive Yuan Reparations Commission, 301–897).

Fabi was subject to great inflation during this period, I have listed out retail price indices for the entire nation and for Nanjing over the aforementioned period based on a price index for January to June 1937 equal to 1. For details see Table 32.

Date	Nationwide	Nanjing	Date	Nationwide	Nanjing
September 1945	2063.06		November 1946	6601.61	6976.00
October	2120.08		December	7182.74	7459.67
November	2443.21		January 1947	8465.45	8909.20
December	2564.95		February	12207.60	13452.40
January 1946	2056.90	1792.10	March	13246.50	14089.35
February	2643.60	2683.17	April	14765.50	16528.85
March	3207.60	3461.20	May	20980.70	24837.06
April	3417.10	3670.71	June	26446.10	29443.33
May	3844.60	4246.10	July	33221.00	34729.17
June	4229.02	4977.71	August	36506.00	36708.18
July	4633.83	4852.56	September	43257.00	43967.32
August	4856.68	4971.44	October	62703.00	68757.49
September	5420.26	5667.50	November	78376.00	81273.70
August	6193.84	6789.83	December	105460.00	100505.53

Table 32: Retail price indices September 1945 to December 1947 (January through June 1937 = 1).
Source: compiled from data in "Nationwide retail price indicators" (The Second Historical Archives of China 2000b, 441–446) and "Retail price indicators in all important cities" (*Tongji yuebao* [Monthly statistical reports] No. 125–126 for January and February 1948, 55–57).

The retail price indices listed in Table 32 reflect a basket of 50 commodities selected by the nationalist government's DGBAS for their inherent character and their importance to life, "and allocated proportionally in accordance with their degree of importance" (The Second Historical Archives of China 2000b, 431). This conforms relatively well with the articles reported as lost property by city residents, and so I have used them as the basis for price conversions. Retail price indices for the entire nation and for Nanjing increased every month from September 1945 until December 1947, except in January 1946 when "people were excited during the period following victory, and people in cities returned to the countryside. Urban markets slashed prices and sold at losses, and the people put off buying, preferring instead to save Fabi, causing a drop in the Fabi inflation rate and sagging prices for all goods, leading to a great drop in indices" (The Second Historical Archives of China 2000b, 433). Using the post-war nationwide and Nanjing retail price indices listed in Table 32 and method of converting losses reported in post-war currency values, I arrived at a pre-war Fabi value of

7.30 million yuan in property losses.[99] Based on the listed selling price posted by HSBC in July 1937, 100 *Fabi* yuan was equivalent to 29.250 USD (Shanghai Foreign Exchange Data (1926–1937): 1606). This gives us an exchange rate of 1:3.42. The USD $56,000 value at time of loss figure in Table 31 converts to about 190,000 *Fabi* yuan. Per the nationalist Ministry of Finance's 1933 proclamation of "abolishing the *liang* and reforming the yuan," the standard conversion for silver and silver coins was to first divide the number of *liang* of silver by 0.98 to convert them into regulation yuan and then convert regulation yuan into silver coins at a rate of 7.15 regulation yuan to one silver coin. On November 3, 1935, the Ministry of Finance implemented the *Fabi* policy, requiring that all silver coins be converted at a one-to-one ratio into *Fabi* beginning on November 4 (People's Bank of China Office of the Head Adviser: 94; 181). A conservative estimate based on these two policies give us a total of property losses in Nanjing given in values at the time of loss denominated in silver and silver coins that converts to approximately 1.22 million *Fabi* yuan. Consequently, the total of property losses incurred by 5,865 Nanjing households during the Rape of Nanking, based on my conservative calculations using data filed by the residents themselves, comes to not less than 167 million yuan, an average loss of 28,474 yuan per household.[100] It must furthermore be noted that these figures reflect only the direct property losses incurred by these residents. As almost nobody filled in figures for indirect property losses, these have proven difficult to calculate.

Smythe estimated daily average earnings for city residents prior to the war at about 1.01 yuan, and daily average family income at 1.23 yuan (Smythe n.d., 9). The population of Nanjing in June 1937 was estimated at 200,160 households and 1,015,450 people (The Second Historical Archives of China and Nanjing Municipal Archives n.d., 916). The total property loss figure at which we have arrived here is thus equivalent to 678 working days (nearly two years) of income for all pre-war Nanjing households.

---

99 For example, we did not include any figures from the form filled out by Nanjing resident Liu Zhuqiao, who did not fill any values. Direct-reporting unit, school, group, or enterprise: person incurring loss: Liu Zhuqiao. Place of service or career: merchant. Report filer: Liu Zhuqiao. Seal: relation to person incurring loss: Owner. Mailing address: 15 Wujianting.Seal: [seal] (Executive Yuan Reparations Commission, 301–897).
100 This figure for losses per family is about 23 times the figure given by Smythe. It must be noted that the primary reason for this massive discrepancy is that our study of 5,865 families was not based on a sampling survey, but rather on reports filed by residents themselves, and as such this figure cannot be used as the basis for extrapolating losses of the entire city of any sociological value. Nevertheless, this figure reflects the limitations of Smythe's wartime survey, this coming from the degree of destruction to the society and the economy of Nanjing at the time, which led him to an undervaluation.

8.3 Calculating Property Losses of Nanjing Residents — 477

As stressed above, the figures we have derived do not represent the entirety of property losses incurred by Nanjing residents; they are but the results of my calculations based on the loss report forms I have been able to get my hands on. After the national government made Nanjing the capital, the city became the country's political and cultural center soon, and the city was built up at great speed, yet not as fast as population growth. Before total war broke out between China and Japan, Nanjing's population stood at over a million. The number of households that incurred losses at the hands of the Japanese during the Rape of Nanking was far greater than 5,865. Not long after the city's fall, American ambassador to China Nelson T. Johnson wrote the following telegram to U.S. Secretary of State Cordell Hull on December 25, 1937, detailing Japanese atrocities in the city:

> Information received from foreign correspondents who left Nanking after Japanese entry into the city and from Doctor Bates indicates that Japanese troops entered practically every building in Nanking except those occupied by foreigners and systematically looted residences and shops. There was wholesale plundering of the Chinese who remained in the city including those in the refugee zone and much indiscriminate shooting and killing (Yang Xiaming 2010, 299).

The Japanese looted not only Chinese residences, but likewise did not spare the property of American, British, German, and other foreign residents in the city. Reuters reporter L.C. Smith, who left Nanjing on December 15, describes the first three days of the Japanese occupation this way: "They have looted the entire city, systematically, leaving nothing behind. Per my own observations and those of other foreigners, all Chinese residences without exception and the vast majority of foreign-owned residences have been looted clean by the Japanese" (Chen Qianping et al. 2007, 72). On December 22, International Committee deputy chairman W. Plumer Mills wrote a letter to the Japanese embassy detailing the Japanese army's infringements on American property: "Nearly all American residences in Nanking have been broken into and had items stolen by Japanese soldiers. What's more, someone dared to break into the embassy residence and tried several times to steal vehicles from the compound courtyard or garage. One embassy policeman was beaten by a Japanese soldier. Just last night, a car was stolen from the embassy garage. A great quantity of American property in the city has been damaged by Japanese soldiers, some of whom are setting fires as they go. At least eight American flags have been torn down or ripped to shreds by Japanese soldiers. They coerce servants to lower the flags by force, and threaten anyone who dares to raise one in its place" (Zhang 2005, 218–219). Some Japanese diplomats in Nanjing attempted to stop their soldiers from infringing on the rights of third-party countries. Smythe wrote in a letter to family of December

24, 1937: "Tanaka is extremely concerned with this matter. He will set a sentry" (Zhang 2005, 246). Even Central China Area Army Supreme Commander Matsui Iwane was greatly concerned with these happenings:

> There have been more incidents of soldiers looting cars and other goods from foreign embassies in Nanjing. I am quite enraged by the stupid and crude actions of these soldiers. The prestige of the Imperial Army will be destroyed by such incidents. This is extremely regrettable. So I immediately dispatched Staff Officer Nakayama (Central China Area Army staff officer and Imperial Air Force major Nakayama Yasuto, student in the 33rd class of the Imperial Japanese Army Academy) to Nanjing, ordering him to not only take urgent measures to address the matter but also to punish those responsible and discipline their commanding officers. I plan to be particularly harsh in punishing members of the Shanghai Expeditionary Army, as it is commanded by His Highness, and these matters touch on His magnanimity (Wang 2005b, 156-157).

The reason the Japanese attached such importance to preventing these incidents is that they were aware that such could easily incite antagonism and blame of their country by the peoples of third-party countries. In the name of defending Japan's interests and preventing diplomatic conflicts between Japan and Western countries, they hoped that no incidents infringing on the interests of third-party countries perpetrated by Japanese soldiers would occur. As for infringement of Chinese rights and property, they looked the other way.

All residents of Nanjing, rich and poor, incurred great losses during the Rape of Nanking, as indicated on the following two property loss forms submitted after the war.

8.3 Calculating Property Losses of Nanjing Residents — 479

Date of loss	Incident	Location	Items lost	Value (*Guobi* yuan) Value at time of purchase	Value at time of loss	Documentation
December 1937	Attack and burning by Japanese army	Number 56 Taiping Road; Numbers 152 and 280 Zhongshan East Road; Residence Number 1 at Number 6 Qingshi Street, Guofu Road	Newly constructed steel-frame house, two newly constructed foreign-style houses, one old-style single-story house	Unknown	94,000	Complete
			Iron and copper beds, various sizes	Unknown	540	
			All manner of mirrored cabinets; wooden tables, chairs, and benches of various sizes and styles	Unknown	690	
			Leather cases	Unknown	620	
			Clothing	Unknown	5,400	
			Household utensils	Unknown	Approx. 10,000	
			Ancient ceramics	Unknown	Approx. 50,000	
			Books	Unknown	Approx. 30,000	
			Calligraphy paintings by famous artists	Unknown	Approx. 100,000	
			Various and sundry	Unknown	Approx. 100,000	

Table 33: Property losses form submitted by Nanjing resident Wang Yifeng (January 24, 1946).
Source: Executive Yuan no. 301–826 (1).

Date of loss	Incident	Location	Items lost	Value (*Guobi* yuan)		Documentation
				Value at time of purchase	Value at time of loss	
December 1937	Attack of Japanese army	Bao #7, Fangjiaying, Xiaguan, Nanjing	Thatched cottage	210		
			Square table	10		
			Long narrow table	10		
			Table and chairs	2		
			Boxes	10		
			Pots, dishes, etc.	10		
			Clock	5		

Table 34: Property losses form submitted by Nanjing resident Guo Wenxian (January 11, 1946). Source: Executive Yuan no. 301–822 (1).

Tables 33 and 34 demonstrate that both the rich like Wang Yifeng (estimated losses of 200,000 yuan) and the poor like Guo Wenxian (estimated losses of 257 yuan) incurred losses as a result of the indiscriminate burning and looting of Japanese soldiers in Nanjing. Absolutely everything – foreign-style houses, Chinese single-story houses, thatched cottages, antiques, calligraphy paintings, tables, chairs, pots, dishes – was subject to their licentious destruction. Smythe wrote in a letter of April 17, 1938: "In Nanjing, 31% of buildings have been completely destroyed, 46% thoroughly looted, and 23% lightly looted" (Zhang 2010, vol. 2, 577). The puppet municipal government's report gives this estimate: "The proportions of buildings destroyed, farm implements damaged, seed missing, and plow oxen lacking all stand at over 90%" (Nanjing Municipal Archives no. 1002–2–1499). Per my conservative reckoning based on the International Committee's report, if we ignore the 23% only lightly damaged, then the proportion of households in Nanjing suffering property losses stands at 77%. Considering that many Nanjing residents began to flee from the city after the August 13 Incident [beginning of the Battle of Shanghai], and especially after Japanese air raids on the city began on August 15, my conservative figure for the number of households in Nanjing prior to the fall is the one given in the puppet municipal government report: 164,476 (Nanjing Municipal Archives no. 1002–2–1499).[101] Thus a reasonable, conservative estimate for the total of households suffering property losses during the Rape of Nanking is somewhere over 120,000.

8.4 Epilogue: Impact of Nanjing Residents' Property Losses

After the Rape of Nanking, the Westerners in Nanjing performing relief work, the puppet municipal government under the Reformed Government of the Republic of China, and organs of the true city government retreated to the rear and performed surveys on public and private property losses sustained in the city from different perspectives. After the war, the Nanjing Municipal War of Resistance Losses Investigation Commission also performed an investigation. These investigations, though thorough, resulted in extremely different figures, owing to the wartime and post-war environment, differing objectives, and different statistical methods.

The International Relief Committee's survey was sample-based. Smythe wrote: "In March many entrances were barred, and there was some little difficulty in determining which houses were inhabited. Consequently, some may have been passed over." The majority of residents who remained in the city after the fall were of the poorest stratum; their losses were not representative of the losses of residents on the whole. Smythe continued: "For the purpose a house number was considered a "building", though in some cases it included more than one structure... Estimates on loss of contents in uninhabited buildings had to be based on the nature of the building and inquiries from neighbors" (Smythe n.d., 1). It was impossible to avoid both data recording and representative errors in his statistical method, and as such the figures of his survey were far lower than actual losses. Miner Bates wrote in the foreword to Smythe's report: "[W]e venture merely to point out that losses to life and property from actual warfare are shown by these surveys to be one or two per cent of the total." (Smythe n.d., II). The figures reported by the puppet municipal government were, for their part, aggregated from resident reports. The people filing those reports, however, were most interested in receiving relief from the new government, and thus used veiled language owing to the political and social conditions at the time, making it difficult for these reports to reflect actual conditions. For example, one resident claiming to be "of the clans Wang and Xie" wrote "We

---

101 This is an estimate. After the August 13 Incident, some Nanjing families left the city, but they could not bring their houses or other immovable property with them.

have disastrously encountered the God of Fire since the catastrophe began. Nothing is left. My husband was taken to be a conscripted laborer and has not been seen since. Now I pitiably care for my young son and young daughter on my own. I have nothing, and have no one to turn to. They wail from hunger all morning, and have been in a tragic state for a long time. I have just heard that your bureau is offering relief to refugees, taking pity on the humble. I humbly request that you bestow your great virtue upon us and take us into a relief shelter soon, to prevent us from wandering about with no home and restore our life vitality. Being bathed in this benevolence, we mother and children will be deeply grateful and never forget" (Nanjing Municipal Archives no. 1002–2–1044). It is clear from both the Rape of Nanking's occurrence and the background to this survey that conditions for a rapid, effective survey did not exist in Japanese-occupied areas immediately in the period when atrocities abated. It is thus no surprise that the results of this investigation also deviated greatly from actual losses. The aforementioned investigations made during the war thus are only of reference value, and cannot be constituted as grounds for an argument.

Although the Nanjing Municipal War of Resistance Losses Investigation Commission's investigation began eight years after the Rape of Nanking, it too is far from satisfactory. Nevertheless, it reflected an enormous amount of investigatory and statistical work and a great measure of results on the part of the nationalist government and municipal government organizations. These bodies established rigorous protocols for their investigation. Forms on property losses were generally filled in with conditions of property losses, the filer's name, their occupation and mailing addresses, their relationships with victims, and other information, making them stand as firmer evidence. The filers then impressed their seal or made their mark on the form to increase its legal effectiveness. At the end of the investigation, the Executive Yuan's Reparations Commission drafted the "Property Losses Reexamination Measures" to check and verify the contents of property loss forms submitted by city residents: "Strive to confirm accuracy of property loss numbers in order that they may be submitted to the Reparations Commission" (*Zhongyang ribao*, January 28, 1947). A large quantity of extant forms filled out by Nanjing residents on their property losses during the Rape of Nanking have revealed the academic foundations for calculating the actual figure of property losses in the city during the period. Property loss figures for 5,865 Nanjing families have been obtained through classification analysis and statistical study of survey forms on resident property losses during the Rape of Nanking, making use of the fields of statistics and numismatics, and via technical processing of some figures obtained from said methods. Although the figures thereby produced are much lower than actual loss figures of Nanjing residents – the number of households that incurred property losses as a result of the Rape of Nanking was surely over 120,000 – they are sufficient to demonstrate the severity of the crimes committed by the Japanese army in Nanjing.

If we shift our perspective from the flat world of literature into the three-dimensional field of real life, we see how immensely difficult it is to use words to describe the pain and suffering endured by the residents of Nanjing as a result of the destruction and plundering of the Japanese army. Bates summed it up in a letter to friends of January 10, 1938: "It is hardly necessary to say that this letter is not written to stir up animosity against the Japanese people… To me the big thing is the unmeasured misery from this war of conquest, misery multiplied by license and stupidity, and projected far into a gloomy future" (Zhang Kaiyuan 2005, 20).

After the fall of Nanjing, the property of its residents was nearly entirely wiped out. In particular, means of living were stolen and destroyed, and houses burned, razed, and forcibly occupied, causing a precipitous drop in standards of living and driving throngs of people into the streets to wander aimlessly in hardship. The family of resident Li Boqian had lived at number 22 Xinqiaochuanban Alley for generations. His father Li Baoru had worked in silks and satins for over thirty years, and his mother, of the Wu clan, was talented at curing and drying raw silk. The front of their house had been a veritable silk market prior to the war. Upon the Japanese occupation, however, his mother was killed by the Japanese, his "property wantonly plundered in entirety by the Japanese invaders," and his "venerable father, driven to mental derangement from excessive exasperation, suffered from 'liver wind.'" The three Li brothers, "after lamenting their hunger and cold, and after suffering from separation and loss, ended deprived of both an education and a livelihood." They lamented: "We're at our wits' end. We have no art to make a living and have nowhere to shelter in this vast land. Truly we are enduring the hardship of barely staying alive yet not being able to die" (Nanjing Municipal Archives no. 1003–17–9). The two lumber companies *Chengtaiji* and *Chengcaiji* located outside the Shuixi Gate not only had their shops "entirely burned out" by the Japanese army, but "all our lumber stocks on the beach and under the river were loaded into trucks and taken away by the military in waves beginning on February 7 of this year. Now they've taken away everything, leaving not a farthing's worth… We reckon that the lumber stolen from *Chengtaiji* was worth about 7,000 or 8,000 yuan, and the lumber stolen from *Chengcaiji* was worth somewhere in the neighborhood of 5,000 to 6,000." These figures were backed by accounting books. A report written by the puppet municipal government reads: "*Chengtaiji* and *Chengcaiji* are run by two brothers, of great standing in the community. Now it has become very difficult to keep alive the 50 to 60 members of their combined families. Those who witness their plight are greatly heartbroken" (Nanjing Municipal Archives no. 1002–2–1796). Even the plight of Tao Xisan, chairman of the puppet Autonomous Committee, was ignored by the Japanese. His house was looted clean by the Japanese just like everyone else's, as Tao wrote in his official report: "The soldiers previously inhabiting the residence at number 27 Shifu Road have moved out. An inspection upon entering revealed that all the mahogany furniture, trunks, ceramic and copper utensils, and all other utensils, valued at approximately 4,000 to 5,000 yuan, have been completely cleaned out, but this is not the cause for grievance. The house also contained a Buddhist sanctuary, with paintings of elders for worship as well as idols and images of the Buddha, memorial tablets of generations of deceased ancestors, a picture of the deceased mother, copies of *Taiyi beiji zhenjing*, *Wuji zhengjing*, and *Weiji jingsui* given by a Daoist monastery along with many other classics, all of these items having been used for 16 years in the pursuit of self-cultivation in body, mind, and spirit and daily worship of ancestors with incense. These items have all been stolen. To think of it makes me sad to the point of tears, tears of misery falling for my deceased mother and father. I am devastated by the grief" (Guo Biqiang et al. 2010, 197). Tao requested that the Japanese Special Service Organ rectify the situation, but his request was ignored.

The Japanese army not only inflicted great damage on the people of Nanjing, but the city itself was also severely damaged. Dr. Robert O. Wilson of the Kulou Hospital wrote in a letter of December 18: "As I left the hospital for supper after finishing my rounds on the 150 cases now under my care, the full moon was rising over Purple Mountain and was indescribably beautiful and yet it looked down on a Nanking that was more desolate than it has been since the Tai Ping Rebellion. Nine-tenths of the city are totally deserted by Chinese and contain only roving bands of plundering Japanese. The remaining tenth contains almost two hundred thousand terrified citizens" (Zhang Sheng 2010, 71). The wide-scale arson of Japanese soldiers erased the construction of Nanjing that had been going on since 1920 practically overnight. Lead accountant of the Nanjing Bank of Communications Huang Yu wrote in a report on his visit to the city: "Since the invading army entered the city, through early February of this year, only two months have passed, but the fires are still smoldering, and a tremendous quantity of private dwellings on all streets have been destroyed" (The Second Historical Archives of China, no. 398(2)-1439). The plan for cleaning all the city's roads issued by the Nanjing Autonomous Committee in March 1938 described conditions in Nanjing after the disaster: "Everywhere in the city shops, stalls, and houses have been burned or razed... The remains from burned buildings from large streets down to small alleys, vestiges of wood, smashed tiles, broken bricks, dust from destroyed walls, mangled iron, and some broken power poles and power lines are scattered at random, clogging the streets" (The Second

Historical Archives of China and Nanjing Municipal Archives n.d., 485). A great quantity of buildings with deep historical legacies were also burned by the Japanese. One was the *Banmuyuan* [half-*mu* garden], with a history running back more than 300 years to the late Ming Dynasty, and former residence of painter Gong Xian; this was burned when the Japanese soldiers living within lost control of their cooking fire (Zhang et al. 2006, 200). Robbery and destruction of goods for economic and domestic use by Japanese soldiers flung the local economy into depression, making it extremely difficult for many to earn their livings, thereby negatively affecting the city's economic development, making reconstruction an enormous challenge. The puppet Autonomous Government noted in its plan for setting up local government enterprises: "All industries in this city are in decline. It will be particularly difficult to restore them in a short time" (Nanjing Municipal Archives no. 1002–19–9). The Japanese Special Service Organ's Nanjing Pacification Team admitted as much in a report: "After the disbandment of the Safety Zone, the difficulty in resettling refugees returning to their original dwellings was enormous, particularly in finding them work. The situation was accompanied by an insufficiency in material supplies. Our lack of capital and financing channels today has obstructed the commercial resurgence of merchants in the city" (Liaoning Provincial Archives). John Magee wrote pessimistically in a letter to his wife of December 30, 1937: "It's hard to imagine what Nanking will be like in the future, but one thing is sure: it will take many years for Nanking to revive its vitality" (Zhang Kaiyuan 2005, 160). After 10 years of construction, the capital of nationalist China was on the verge of becoming a major international metropolis, in accordance with normal development plans and speed. The Japanese army's invasion and subsequent destruction of the constituent elements of the city – the massacre of its residents, the plundering of its wealth, the damage to its infrastructure – cut short the city's development. Three months after the victorious nationalist government returned to its capital, Nanjing was "still desolation as far as the eye could see; it is truly massively damaged and deeply in pain" (Executive Yuan no. 21(2)-601).

9 Initial Study of PTSD Among Rape of Nanking Victims

Past studies of the Rape of Nanking have concentrated on the murder, rape, arson, looting, and other "overt" crimes perpetrated by Japanese soldiers. Gradually researchers have expanded the field of study to the victims, particularly the "psychological trauma" suffered by female victims, thereby bringing into focus a level of the tragedy hitherto relatively "hidden" from view.

In fact, the world began paying attention to the hidden trauma of war as early as during the Second World War. As the fields of medicine and psychology advanced, it was discovered that "covert" trauma affects a broader swath of the population and lasts longer than physical trauma, and yet such trauma is not limited to psychological problems. In the study of the Rape of Nanking, we are gradually discovering the tip of an iceberg of hidden trauma revealed in a great quantity of stories and livid accusations buried in the documents and survivors' testimonies. We are coming to understand the event at a much deeper level as a result of deeply assessing the statements of witnesses to terror and violence and the comprehensive symptoms of survivors and victims.

This chapter intends to introduce PTSD research into the study of the Rape of Nanking, so as to view the history events in a new light by using an interdisciplinary approach.

9.1 Introduction of the PTSD Concept

The American Psychiatric Association defined PTSD (post-traumatic stress disorder) for the first time in 1980. The consensus reached after many years of research is that it is caused by helplessness in the face of great threats, extreme terror, or violence. Sufferers frequently relive aspects of the event in their conscious thought or in nightmares, and frequently experience severe anxiety, insomnia, uncontrollable emotions, depression, memory loss, and other symptoms. Those with severe cases frequently resort to suicide. Children with PTSD are more likely to experience post-traumatic stress if they are traumatized again as adults (Myers n.d., 584). There is a biological basis for physical symptoms experienced by PTSD patients; for instance, it has already been discovered that PTSD sufferers in general have heightened levels of catecholamines and thyroid hormones in their blood, and that they have heightened activity in their adrenoreceptors. Both positron emission tomography (PET) scans and magnetic resonance imaging (MRI) scans have indicated that functional changes take place in two important structures of the brains of PTSD sufferers, the cerebellar tonsils and the hippocampus, two areas of the brain related to the fight-or-flight response (Yang and Zhang n.d.).

PTSD research abroad has developed rapidly in recent years. The U.S.-based National Center for Biotechnology Information has received more than 14,800 papers on the subject from around the world. Karatzias, Power, Brown, and McGoldrick discuss the role of PTSD on depression. Wilcox, Storr, and Breslau studied suicidal attempts by teenage PTSD-sufferers. Kubzansk, Koenen, Jones, and Eaton studied the effects of PTSD on heart disease in women. Moore studied cognitive abnormalities in PTSD-sufferers. Giosan, Malta, Jayasinghe, Spielman, and Difede studied PTSD among 9–11 survivors, including clean-up workers, and their memory problems. Thompson and Waltz studied the self-pitying of PTSD patients. Klari, Franciskovi, Klari, Kresi, Grkovi, Lisica, and Stevanovi studied PTSD symptoms among Bosnian women and their social support. Dignam studied the psychiatric disorders of PTSD patients who were tortured as children. It is thus clear that PTSD research abroad has developed into many different facets of the disorder, exposing the "soft" and "hidden" aspects of its sufferers, and demonstrating the great prospect for development of research of PTSD in historical sources.

Chinese academics became aware of PTSD research abroad a little over 10 years ago, and have of late begun their own studies, making some progress. Wang Huanlin et al. studied PTSD among Chinese soldiers (Wang et al. n.d.); Zhang et al. studied PTSD in orphans of the Great Tangshan Earthquake (Zhang et al. n.d.); Xu et al. studied PTSD among survivors of explosions (Xu et al); Ma et al. studied the susceptibility of inheriting PTSD (Ma et al. n.d.); Zhang et al. studied PTSD among SARS survivors (Zhang et al. n.d.); Cheng et al. studied prevention and treatment of PTSD (Cheng et al. n.d.); Huang Jing et al. studied PTSD among youth survivors of the Wenchuan earthquake (Huang et al. n.d.); Wang Yao studied PTSD in rape victims (Wang et al. n.d.); and Yang studied PTSD in university students (Yang et al. n.d.). More works on PTSD have been written in the field of medicine in China than in the field of psychology, but almost none have been written combining PTSD research with historiography.

War can illicit darkness and violence stored deep in the hearts of some people, and innocents are powerless to change this reality, which is why so many of them come to suffer from PTSD. One month after the "9–11" incident, for example, 8.5% of Manhattan residents were diagnosed with PTSD (Galea et al. 2002). Another study revealed that nearly 20% of people residing near the World Trade Center experienced symptoms including fear, anxiety, and agoraphobia, and that nearly 400,000 New Yorkers experienced symptoms of PTSD (Susser et al. 2002).

Another study suggests that about 4% of people who live through natural disasters will suffer from PTSD, but the rate climbs to 50% for people who experience kidnapping, being taken prisoner, and being raped (Brewin et al. 2000; Brody 2000; Kessler 2000).

As opposed to New York following the "9–11" incident, Nanjing, in the wake of the Rape of Nanking, was far more universally engulfed in terror. The incident's duration was long, its climax lasting six weeks, and its perpetrators, the Japanese army, remained in direct contact with city residents. The sound of gunshots never stopped; great fires raged for long durations; and bodies of victims littered the streets. In addition, the evidence indicates that the Japanese army intentionally created an atmosphere of terror via the methods of harm they adopted, destroying the will to resist of the Chinese in Nanjing. International Committee Chairman John Rabe wrote in his diary entry of February 3, 1938: "You can't breathe for sheer revulsion when you keep finding the bodies of women with bamboo poles thrust up their vaginas" (Rabe EN, 172). Secretary Georg Rosen of the German embassy in Nanjing wrote in a report: "On 12 January, my English colleague, Consul Prideaux-Brune, the English military attaché Lovat-Fraser, and the English air-force attaché Commander Walser visited the house of Mr. Parsons of the British-American Tobacco Company and discovered there the body of a Chinese woman into whose vagina an entire golf club had been forced" (Rabe EN, 121). Military doctor Jiang Gonggu, who hid in the American embassy during the Rape of Nanking, wrote in his diary: "Nothing was more brutal than being buried alive. The miserable wailing – the shrill, hopeless scream of a life's final struggle – reverberated in the undulating air, and even several *li* distant we could still faintly hear it" (Zhang Lianhong 2005, 64).

Particularly deplorable was the oft-employed practice among Japanese soldiers of forcing husbands and family members to witness their rapes. Rosen wrote in another report to the German Foreign Office: "Every night Japanese soldiers burst into the refugee camp in the University of Nanking, to either carry women off to rape them or rape them right there in front of everybody, including their victims' families, slaking their evil lust. There are frequent cases of accomplices detaining the victims' husband or fathers and forcing them to witness the degradation of their family's honor" (Zhang Sheng 2005, 327). Commander of the Nanjing Instruction Corps Impedimentia Battalion Guo Qi, who hid in the Italian embassy during the event, wrote:

> That day a few dozen Jap soldiers came before the door to the foreign-style building next door, wearing black and yellow collar badges, but without serial numbers and without commanding officers. They first drove every man out of the large parlor. Then they assembled all the women past their prime, and right there in the parlor, in front of the children, in

broad daylight, as brazenly as possible, they stripped these older women naked and performed their collective farce, three-on-one, five-on-one, over and over without end. How many children witness such terrifying scenes? They were all scared to the point of crying. Outside the parlor, inside the courtyard, the husbands of those women were all completely dejected, bearing red faces and ears. Some cowered on the walls and wailed in lamentation. Some covered their heads with their hands and stood completely immobile. Once their bestial desires had been satisfied, the Jap soldiers, who still hadn't fastened their pants, walked out onto the road, where they came across another group of Jap soldiers, again numbering in the dozens. This second group burst right back into the house their comrades had just left... (Zhang Lianhong 2005, 167–168).

The interminable violence was indescribably tortuous for Nanjing residents. Rabe wrote on December 28: "You feel like a seriously ill patient fearfully watching the hour hand inch forward" (Rabe EN, 101). "Time moved too slowly. It was as though the day had 100 hours and not 24, and nobody knew when normalcy would be restored" (Rabe CN, 240). Not only the Chinese, direct targets of the violence, felt the terror. Neutral Westerners, witnesses to the violence, felt the same. On December 17, 1937, Japanese soldiers burst into the refugee camp at Ginling Women's College, claiming to be searching for Chinese soldiers. Minnie Vautrin, in charge of the camp, wrote about the experience in her diary entry of that day: "We later realized their trick – to keep responsible people at front gate with three or four of their soldiers carrying on this mock trial and search for Chinese soldiers while the rest of the men were in the buildings selecting women. We later learned they selected twelve and took them out at a side gate... Never shall I forget that scene – the people kneeling at side of road, Mary, Mrs. Tsen and I standing, the dried leaves rattling, the moaning of the wind, the cry of women being led out... For what seemed an eternity we dared not move for fear of being shot."

The atmosphere of terror and the physical and mental conditions it imposed on the people of Nanjing made PTSD the "norm."

9.2 PTSD Symptoms Among Rape of Nanking Victims

9.2.1 Loss of ability to react in the face of extreme terror

We often hear questions like this: why were the victims dumbstruck and incapable of action in the face of catastrophe? PTSD research tells us that a loss of the ability to react is a common occurrence under conditions of extreme terror. Huang Xuewen, resident of Pukou Village in Nanjing, was one of the "lucky ones." Japanese soldiers arrived in his village on December 15, 1937, and assembled several dozen people together to check them for calluses or other signs that they were soldiers. In the end they led off five men. One was a cripple and released. Huang was another. His parents and wife clung to the thighs of the Japanese soldiers begging them for mercy, and Huang was released. Nobody pleaded for the lives of the other three, as they were *paofan* (dialect for people who run from home to flee the ravages of war). All three were shot. The weather was pleasant that afternoon. "The sun was dazzling." Over the course of his simple, poor, rural life, when had Huang Xuewen ever had the chance to see people killed? The PTSD he experienced exceeded even expert descriptions: "I was so scared that everything went black. I couldn't see a thing. The middle of the day was just like night... All I could hear was gunshots." Of course he had no idea what PTSD is. Sixty-nine years after the event, the only word he could muster when discussing Japanese soldiers were *"haipa"* [scared] (Zhang Sheng et al. 2007, vol. 2, 1369).

Because of the extreme terror, the people of Nanjing huddled together in fear like lambs awaiting slaughter. Rabe notes the miserable conditions in an alley near his house on January 16: "We open the main gate and walk after them a little distance until they vanish in dark narrow streets, where assorted bodies have been lying in the gutter for three days now. Makes you shudder in revulsion. All the women and children, their eyes big with terror, are sitting on the grass in the garden, pressed closely together, in part to keep warm, in part to give each other courage. Their one hope is that I, the 'foreign devil,' will drive these evil spirits away" (Rabe EN, 77).

Having lost the ability to respond, very few Nanjing residents put up any resistance. As Rabe noted in his diary entry of January 25: "The Chinese are far too downtrodden, and they patiently submitted to their fate long ago... If every case of rape were revenged with murder, a good portion of the occupying troops would have been wiped out by now" (Rabe EN, 154).

After this had gone on a long time, the people of Nanjing became extremely calm in the face of apparent danger. This was the case for the refugees sheltering at John Rabe's house, as Rabe recalled in his diary entry of February 6: "After all the misery the Japanese soldiers have brought us, people have become fully indifferent to the dangers of air raids. The crowd of refugees stands in my garden, silently staring up at the airplanes. A few people don't pay any heed at all, but calmly go about their daily business inside the straw huts" (Rabe EN, 177). Citizens of the UK, Germany, and Japan all had similar experiences during the Second World War (Myers n.d., 585).

What's worse, some Nanjing residents lost their personalities and most basic self-esteem after long exposure to violence and terror. On January 2, 1938, a few members of the Japan Women's Defense Association visited Nanjing to put on a show of peace; Vautrin played tour guide for them. Cheng Ruifang, dormitory warden at Ginling Women's College, wrote in her diary: "When they were about to leave, those three she-Japs held out some moldy apples and a little candy. Those middle-aged refugees surrounded them and struggled to get their hands on it. They held out a few copper coins in their hands for the women to fight for, completely destroying all face for the Chinese" (Zhang 2005, 27). These women completely forgot about the rape, robbery, and massacre that was still happening periodically in their camp; this comes close to Stockholm Syndrome.

9.2.2 Mental fatigue and memory loss

George Fitch was secretary of the Nanjing YMCA and an official in the Safety Zone. In spring 1938 he returned to the U.S. with John Magee's film to give a lecture tour on the Rape of Nanking. During the tour he experienced inexplicable memory loss. "During the speech my mind went completely blank. I couldn't remember anything. Where am I? What am I going to say next? Thankfully I remembered the film I had brought. I thought that if I played the film, I'd be able to speak. This went over smoothly enough, but there was another problem at the end: how do I get back to my wife's apartment in Pasadena?" Fitch experienced the same problem during another lecture, but this time since he had not brought the film with him, all he could do was "stammeringly declare that the lecture had ended." An x-ray scan revealed no problems with his brain, and so Fitch came to this self-diagnosis: "The terrible memories of every day in Nanjing are probably somewhat related to this mental fatigue" (Zhang 2006b, 187–188).

9.2.3 Hysteria

Chicago Daily News reporter A.T. Steele, witness to the Rape of Nanking, reported on unusual behavior of Chinese soldiers when calamity befell them:

> As Japanese searches intensified, some soldiers experienced mental disorders resulting from prolonged terror. I once saw a soldier steal a bicycle with brute force and then recklessly rush into a detachment of Japanese army, who was hundreds of yards ahead. After pedestrians on the street had told him this was dangerous, he suddenly turned around and charged in the opposite direction. He then suddenly leapt off the bicycle and ran into a civilian. Finally, I saw him taking off his uniform and attempting to strip the citizen's clothes. Some soldiers ride horses aimlessly around the city streets firing their guns wildly

into the air. One of the few remaining foreigners in the city, a burly German, decided to teach him a lesson, so he pulled the man down from his horse, took away his pistol, and punched him in the face. He took the blow without making a sound (Zhang 2005, 294).

Civilians in the city were even more terrified. Dr. Robert Wilson writes about the aftermath of Japanese looting in a letter to his family of December 19, 1937: "All the food is being stolen from the poor people and they are in a state of terror-stricken, hysterical panic" (Yale Divinity n.d., n.p.). Chancellor Scharffenberg of the German embassy in Nanjing wrote in a memorandum to Ambassador Trautmann in Hankou of February 23, 1938: "Unfortunately the troops occupying Nanjing have been switched out again, with fresh young troops replacing all the old troops. The problem is that many instances of looting, rape, and cases of murder related to those two are still occurring. A mentally deranged mother lives near the house at number 19. We cannot open the window facing in that direction, because she's always screaming loudly 'Nun Yang, small child!' It's unbearable to listen to" (Zhang 2005, 405). The *Ta Kung Pao* of March 28, 1938, newspaper quoted the English newspaper *The Daily Telegraph:* "Refugees are all experiencing psychic horror."

9.2.4 Emotional excitement and loss of control from mention of past events

Encountering extreme terror in childhood can more easily lead to PTSD. The trauma can be relived if the memories are brought up again in adulthood. Zhang Xiuhong, one of the victims of sexual violence in the Nanjing Massacre, was only 12 years old when she was raped by the Japanese soldiers. Below is a newspaper interview with Zhang on her experience reproduced in entirety:

> [Testimony] My family lived near Shazhouwei and Shuangzha in that year (1937). My parents fled with my sister to avoid Japanese soldiers. I stayed behind with my grandfather. Japanese soldiers burned our house. My grandfather and I had no choice but to *paofan* [flee from the ravages of war]. We lived in the fields day and night. We brought some rice to cook and kept it in a bag once it was done. We ate some whenever we were hungry. When we heard that Japanese troops were killing people left and right, we dared not return home.
>
> [Aside] At this point the elderly Zhang was overcome by grief and began sobbing in great distress for the first time.
>
> [Testimony] After hiding for ten or so days, my grandfather brought me home. There were bodies everywhere. Japanese soldiers were grabbing girls everywhere. They had no choice. Some girls blackened their faces with ashes from cooking fires. Some families hid their girls in a haystack. But Japanese soldiers used a bayonet to prick. Some girls were stabbed and experienced unendurable pain, so they ran out. These girls were caught

up by Japanese soldiers, who threw them on the haystack and set it on fire. Many girls were burned to death. So tragic!

Even more girls were hidden in reed marshes by their families. I was hidden in one. I took a look inside. There were 40 or 50 girls there. The Japanese didn't find us at first, but after a few days we were discovered. Those despicable Japanese soldiers lit a fire, and the girls cried out loudly. I jumped into the water with two other girls to get away. It was winter, and the water was freezing! It was tragic. Those girls were all burned to death.

[Aside] Here Zhang again is overcome by sobs, the tears socking her face. The Japanese-language translator at her side also chokes up.

"If I hadn't gone, my grandfather and I would both have died."

[Testimony] I ran back home again to be with my grandfather. A few Japanese soldiers arrived shortly afterward. They wanted to take me away, saying they wanted "saihu, saihu." My grandfather implored: this child is too small, don't hurt her. The Japanese ignored his request and stabbed him with a bayonet. His blood spurted straight out... Sobbing I got to my knees and told my grandfather that if I didn't go, then we'd both be dead. I said it wasn't a big deal if I died, but I couldn't let him die with me... Then I was dragged into the neighbor's house and flung on the bed... It hurt so much I fainted. After the Japanese had left, my grandfather ran over and picked me up, saying: "Hongzi, you saved me! You've suffered!"

There were no doctors or medicine. My grandfather could only wrap up my legs tightly with rope to help my wounds heal. But then more Japanese soldiers came shortly afterward. For my grandfather, I had no choice.

[Aside] The worst experience of her life came when she was only 12! At this point, tears streaming down her face, Zhang suddenly threw her head back and her arms in the air and grieved painfully.

They took pretty girls away for "saihu saihu"...

[Testimony] Later a neighbor came up with the idea to shave my head and dress me up as a boy... After my head was shaved I often sat at the entrance to our house and watched as the Japanese soldiers brought over dozens of girls. They'd bring basins of water and force the girls to wash the ashes and marl off their faces one by one. Then they picked the prettiest ones and took them off for "saihu saihu." The ones who refused were either stabbed with bayonets or dragged off, but some were also killed. The not pretty ones were "ta ta ta" shot dead by the Japanese with machine guns. I saw this happen several times! Many girls died this way.

The adults endured hardships, but so did the children. I saw with my own eyes a Japanese soldier pick up a child. It was only this big (she gestures the height of the child, not more than two feet tall, undoubtedly a baby) and carry it around on the end of his gun. The child was in such pain it cried out loudly, but that pack of animals said he was laughing.

[Aside] Here she again breaks down sobbing. The interpreter also stopped and helped her wipe her tears. Zhang continues: "Those Japs really aren't human! I hate them to death!" Everybody in attendance deeply feels the pain carved into her bones expressed in this sentence.

"It took me three days and three nights to give birth to my son. That was painful!"

[Testimony] Not long after I shaved my head to look like a boy, I was taken off by Japanese soldiers to work, hauling earth, hauling water, hauling stones. I was a girl, and only 12! When I couldn't lift a load, Japanese soldiers poked me in the back with their bayonets or beat me with the butts of their rifles. The top of my left leg hurts to this day.

I was lucky to survive, but those Japanese soldiers left me enormously wounded. It took me three days and three nights to give birth to my son. That was painful! I still wanted children after that but I couldn't have any more.

[Aside] The pain those Japanese soldiers inflicted on this 12-year old girl lasted her entire lifetime. When Zhang was done with her speech, she could barely stand up. Her daughter in law Jiang Jinlan explained that Zhang's life had been very hard, that the Japanese attacks had caused a uterine prolapse, and that it was extremely painful on overcast days even to the present. The attack also damaged her hipbone, making it very painful for her to sit or stand for a long time (China.com n.d., n.p.).

9.2.5 Suicide

Suicide is an extreme reaction to PTSD turned to by some individuals. Studies indicate that victims often give hints of their intention to friends and family before committing suicide, or even openly discuss suicide. Some give all their assets away. The suicide rate for long-term pessimists is five times that of normal people. Suicide is not entirely a form of resistance or revenge. To the contrary, it is often a means of ending unbearable suffering (Bostwiek and Pankratz 2000; Myers n.d., 591).

Evangelist Lu Xiaoting, who had been working in the area of Tangshan in Nanjing prior to the Japanese occupation, had already been a pessimist for a long time. He displayed "a very fine spirit and has been so unselfish and helpful during these trying days," wrote Magee in a letter of December 31. Lu seems to be a clear case of a PTSD victim killing himself to relieve his agony. He told Forster he was going to kill himself "in protest against intolerable conditions." Forster told him "the Christian idea was to live and not to die," but on the morning of December 31, Lu "went off very early... long before daylight, leaving a note for Ernest and also a little poem and his purse." In his letter he wrote "that he did not believe God would hold this act as a sin" (Zhang 2005, 160–161).

This was not an isolated case. Many rape victims chose suicide to alleviate their pain. The story of one 15-year old girl forced to become a "comfort woman" by Japanese soldiers, captured in John Magee's documentary, is a testament to this point: "A girl she knew who had been captured in Wuhu at the same time killed herself. She also heard that others had killed themselves" (Zhang 2005, 190).

9.3 The Case of Minnie Vautrin

As discussed earlier, PTSD symptoms did not emerge only in direct victims of Japanese violence. The truth is that even witnesses to atrocities can suffer extreme duress, leading to serious consequences. This fact has pushed us to expand the scope of "victims" of the Rape of Nanking.

To understand Vautrin's pathology, we must go back 10 years before the Rape of Nanking to the "Nanking Incident," which Vautrin discussed in her diary entry of March 24, 1938:

> How filled is this day with vivid memories! Hour by hour I seem to remember the events of that day just 11 years ago. The joy with which we greeted the new day and the news that the northern troops were retreating quietly, the revolutionary troops were already entering; there the tragic news of Dr. William's death and the fierce anti-foreign attitude of the new soldiers, the anxious waiting; the black figures of the people on the hills around us; our retreat to the University. About this time that evening John Reisner, and I looked out over the city lying in darkness save for the flare of flames from burning foreign buildings. I wander what March 24, 1949 will be like in Nanking.

Memories like this appear cyclically in Vautrin's diary, demonstrating the severe psychological impact of the events of 1927 on her. Her trauma largely calmed down over the 10 peaceful years from 1927 to 1937, but the Rape of Nanking turned out to be even more traumatizing. She saved many Chinese women being raped by Japanese soldiers, and lived day and night with their appeals for succor. She saw many horribly brutalized bodies of victims as well. From today's perspective we can see that her efforts were heroic actions requiring great courage and humanitarian spirit, but she endured an extreme feeling of helplessness from not being able to resolve the hardships of all the Chinese around her, for which she blamed herself. Her PTSD symptoms grew more severe by the day as old trauma mingled with the new.

PTSD is a disease. Today there are medical interventions and treatments for it, including the following:
1. Exposure therapy: helping victims face painful memories and feelings to alleviate their pain.
2. Cognitive therapy: helping victims find the nature of their painful issues to restore their self-confidence and allow for healing.
3. Biofeedback therapy: processing and enlarging of information collected from organs through sensors and promptly converting them into familiar visual and auditory signals displayed to the patient. The society controls for randomness in organ activity to a certain degree through study and training,

and corrects for organ activity deviating from the norm to restore stability in the inner environment.
4. Drug therapy: a large volume of treatment results indicate that SSRIs and SNRIs are effective at treating PTSD, and old anti-depression drugs may be particularly effective at treating PTSD caused by wartime experiences (Yang Xianju and Zhang Yang n.d.).

But at the time, people had not fully realized the problem of PTSD at the scientific level, let alone the treatment. Vautrin, a missionary who had received higher education, knew that she had to overcome her adversity, and her chosen means for doing so was to turn to her familiar God.

On December 11, 1937, Vautrin had already determined the role her religion would play: "Our fellowship service this morning was real. Religion is made for times like these." She had no means of predicting, however, that the Japanese were going to make Nanjing into a hell on earth. At her most helpless, she wrote most despairingly on December 16: "Oh, God, control the cruel beastliness of the soldiers in Nanking tonight, comfort the heartbroken mothers and fathers whose innocent sons have been shot today, and guard the young women and girls through the long agonizing hours of this night. Speed the day when wars shall be no more, when Thy kingdom will come, Thy will be done on earth as it is in heaven." She wrote on December 17 that after the recovery of her assistants Mr. Chen and Miss Lo, they celebrated a "little meeting of thanksgiving. Never have I heard such prayers."

God, however, did not always respond to her prayers. Being able to "see no future," she wrote on December 21: "The once energetic, hopeful capital is now an empty shell – pitiful, heartrending." Reality continually imposed itself into her field of vision. On Christmas Day 1937, she sent up another heartfelt prayer to God. When more than 20 women were released by Japanese officials because their mothers or others vouched for them on December 31, she wrote: "Once in a while I can 'count a blessing.'"

We have no choice but to stand in admiration of Vautrin's kindheartedness. As a PTSD sufferer, she made her condition for extricating herself from Nanking that city residents be saved first. On January 7, 1938, she sent up a heartfelt prayer: "God pity the poor! May they be spared our ten days reign of terror!" She sincerely believed that the suffering of the victims could be reduced through religious services. She wrote of such a service on January 19: "it is a wonderful time for such meetings for everybody is hungry for comfort." Vautrin wrote increasingly more about religious services in her diary in the months following the New Year.

Vautrin did write of a few heartening signs. On January 22 she wrote that the wife of one English-speaking Japanese soldier was a Christian: "His first statement was that they were very sorry for the things that had happened in Nanking and they hoped conditions would soon be better." On January 23 she wrote of a "Miss Wu," a Presbyterian evangelistic worker who "told the wonderful story of her escape at the Women's Meeting this afternoon" and whose "voice... sang out so lustily that afternoon" in the meeting, despite having been forced to strip naked by Japanese soldiers on her entry into the city. On October 16, 1938, she wrote about five girls who converted their beliefs, one of them saying "how the Psalms had become a source of comfort to her." The number of women attending services sometimes significantly increased, and there were great increases in religious fervor among those whose lives were under constant threat.

Unfortunately, however, Vautrin could not redeem herself. On March 30, 1938, she wrote about how she is not entirely a "common individual" but rather a foreigner whose presence affects the lives and safety of many Nanjing residents. This onerous feeling of responsibility became enmeshed with her powerlessness to constantly torture her sensitive heart. Some events completely out of her control led her to heedlessly reproach herself. In one instance, Vautrin convinced a 27-year old woman to leave the camp to return to her husband, the result being that she was raped by three Japanese soldiers less than three hours after leaving. She needed God to give her the wisdom to cast off the suffering of her life, but every day she was crushed under an onerous burden, writing on April 12: "Oppressed by the many tasks to be done each day, and the even greater number that I never seem to get to... my office is constantly besieged by persons asking me for help of various kinds." Vautrin's diary is replete with phrases like "too tired," "exhausted," "no energy whatsoever," and so on. We now know she was losing the opportunity to defeat PTSD.

To doctors, Vautrin's diary reads like the autobiography of a PTSD sufferer. We shall not enumerate all relevant instances here for brevity's sake. Vautrin wrote on June 24, 1938: "Always in the background of my mind are sad pictures – pictures of our refugees." Although she employed numerous techniques to divert her mind from depression, she was constantly reminded of her hardships by countless cases of innocents murdered by Japanese soldiers, the head of a little baby brought to her by her dog Laddie, the ubiquitous stench of decomposing bodies, the entreaties of raped Chinese women, rampant traitors, and tragic accounts from around the city circulating between Western missionaries. Moonlight slowly becomes an indicator of the disease's progression in her diary. Starting in the second half of 1938, bright moonlight becomes a trigger for her misery. The word "lunatic" in English derives from the root "luna," meaning moon, because ancient Westerners conjectured that mental illness was caused by the moon. Vautrin's symptoms coincided very well with this observation. Her writings on exhaustion and anxiety gradually became longer in the diary, and the presence of Japanese soldiers at all levels triggered feelings of "hatred" in her. Although her disposition had been generally pleasant, she quarreled with increasing frequency with her colleagues once her feelings entered a downward spiral. After the outbreak of war in Europe in September 1939, Vautrin wept deeply for the interminable nightmare of war being inflicted on all of humanity. Any day of any significance at all made her recall all her experiences during the Rape of Nanking.

With no other recourse, Vautrin turned more and more fervently to God. Despite her utter exhaustion, she continued to expand the size of her religious study classes. She participated fervently in the services held by Bates, Magee, and others, savoring them repeatedly and being constantly moved. She earnestly recorded the admonition of Plumer Mills on September 11, 1938: "If we have faith in God, in the message of the Cross, in the Kingdom of Heaven and in eternal life, we know that the present chaos will not be permanent." On October 2 she wrote of the Munich Conference: "What a relief to know that a holocaust in Europe may be averted. I believe it was wrought by prayer for very few really want war." On the anniversary of what was for her the most horrifying day of the Rape of Nanking – December 17 – she thanked God for his protection and prayed for the leaders of Japan and for Japanese Christians. She made frequent reference to encouraging phrases from the bible heard at services, such as those from Deuteronomy 31:6: "Be strong and courageous. Do not be afraid or terrified because of them, for the Lord your God goes with you; he will never leave you nor forsake you." Reality, however caused periodic sluggishness in her religious activities. On "Founders' Day" in 1938, November 13, she admitted that "there is little heart for festivities these days," and so a "simple program" was decided upon. On November 20, Vautrin, who never liked to sing her own praises, wrote with dissatisfaction that Bishop Ward "did not commend us on our bravery of last winter" in a service. On March 9 Searle Bates called a group of people together to discuss what he had learned at the Madras Conference. Vautrin wrote: "In general the picture painted by Searle was dark. There is more organized opposition to Christianity at the present time than at any other period in the last 100 years; more non-Christians in the world than in the last 10 years." This further dispirited her.

Vautrin's diary entries began to show signs of desperation on March 1, 1940. She became engulfed in agitation, low spirits, and hopelessness. John Galsworthy's poem *The Valley of the Shadow*, somber and full of deathly tones, had appeared in her diary on November 16, 1939, reflecting her feeling of hopelessness:

> God, I am travelling out to death's sea,
> I, who exulted in sunshine and laughter
> Thought not of dying – death is such waste of me;
> Grant me one comfort; Leave not the hereafter
> Of humanity as a whole to war, as though I had died not –

In the end, God could not save Minnie Vautrin, who committed suicide in the U.S. on May 14, 1941. We do, however, see this more joyous impression that she left behind in her diary on March 29, 1938:

> Early Spiraea is blooming now, and the wild daphne. Double daffodils are just opening. Spring birds are numerous in our trees down here at the Practice School. Our weeping willows are just in the height of their dainty gracefulness, and with kingfishers darting in and out among the long saving branches the picture is a lovely one.

Vautrin had not lost her enthusiasm for life even after the apex of the atrocities, but she was ultimately ruined by PTSD. She was the American victim of the Rape of Nanking.

In November 2004 Iris Chang, American author of *The Rape of Nanking: The Forgotten Holocaust of World War II*, killed herself. Although there are many theories about the cause of her suicide, the gory historical materials on the incident were clearly the most important cause. She writes in the introduction to the book about her first time viewing photographs taken during the event: "In a single blinding moment I recognized the fragility of not just life but the human experience itself" (Chang n.d., 7). Her grief over the lives lost and harm done to human dignity and her anger over the direct and indirect denials of the Rape of Nanking by right wing forces in Japan became Chang's driving obsession. "out shopping or taking walks in the park, images of the Rape of Nanking would flash before my eyes with no warning. I had no desire for these events to destroy the rest of my life" (China News 2007, n.p.). Chang wrote this warning to herself in a letter to her friends, but PTSD put her on the same path as Vautrin. We see how dangerous this foe they call PTSD is.

Initial studies indicate that PTSD was widespread among Rape of Nanking survivors. Not only direct victims of Japanese violence suffered, but also those who witnessed atrocities. The affected came from Nanjing, from China at large, and even from abroad. The time of their sufferings was not limited to the event itself, but has continued to the present day. As such, the Rape of Nanking should be taken seriously by the entire world, as it is a component of the shared history of humanity as a whole.[102]

---

[102] This piece was first published in *Kangri zhanzheng yanjiu* 4 (2009). It was revised before inclusion in this book.

10 The Nanjing Trials

In addition to the Military Tribunal for the Far East established in Tokyo, the Allies established military tribunals in all affected countries to try Japanese war criminals. These tribunals were an important component of the Allies' policies for disposing of war criminals, but they were also somewhat more independent in nature than the tribunal in Tokyo.

The Nanjing Trials were only one set of trials held in post-war China, but they were charged with trying those responsible for the Rape of Nanking. Their verdicts were acknowledged by Japan in the Treaty of San Francisco and other documents.

10.1 Establishment of the Nanjing Military Tribunal

10.1.1 Allies' policies for handling war criminals

Discussions on how to treat war criminals had begun in many arenas among the Allies before the war had even ended. Primary principles and concrete policies were established through several important international conferences, and were ultimately codified in concentrated form in the Charter of the International Military Tribunal (Nuremberg) and the Charter of the International Military Tribunal for the Far East.

As early as December 4, 1941, the Soviet Union published a declaration signed by Stalin, the first of its kind, calling for severe punishments for the war crimes of Hitler and his cohort after the conclusion of the war (Raginsky et al. n.d., 19). In late 1941 British Prime Minister Churchill declared: "Retribution for these crimes must henceforth take its place among the major purposes of the war" (Shekhovtsov n.d., 837). On January 13, 1942, the governments in exile of the nine countries invaded by Germany – France, Belgium, Czechoslovakia, Poland, and Norway to name a few – held a meeting in London, where they signed "Punishment for War Crimes, The Inter-Allied Declaration signed at St. James's Palace London". The declaration called for the Allies to "place among their principal war aims the punishment, through the channel of organised justice, of those guilty of or responsible for these crimes, whether they have ordered them, perpetrated them, or participated in them" (Raginsky et al. n.d., 20).

Note: Chapter contributed by Yan Haijian.

When the Allies began their counterattack on Japan in 1943, Japan's defeat became imminent. As a result, China and its allies began considering prosecuting those who had instigated the war of invasion and started preparations for those trials. In October 1943, the Allies met in London at the urging of the UK and U.S. to discuss the formal establishment of the United Nations Commission for the Investigation of War Crimes (later renamed the United Nations War Crimes Commission, UNWCC) to begin investigating the war crimes of the fascist powers Germany, Italy, and Japan. On November 3, at the close of the Moscow Conference between the Soviet Union, the U.S., and the UK, delegates released the Moscow Declarations, which, in addition to reaffirming the necessity of severely punishing war criminals, also called for escorting war criminals who committed atrocities to the country where their crimes were committed to try them for their crimes based on the laws established by their liberated governments. The Declarations also called for: "The above declaration is without prejudice to the case of German criminals whose offenses have no particular geographical localization and who will be punished by joint decision of the government of the Allies" (Wang Shengzu 1983, 14). The declaration determined that the Allies would try war criminals in international tribunals while also giving victim countries the right to try war criminals in their own courts.

Although no detailed discussions on punishing war criminals were held during the Cairo Conference in November 1943, the resulting Cairo Declaration reads: "The three great Allies are fighting this war to restrain and punish the aggression of Japan" (International Treaties (1934–1944), 407). In 1944, the Allies founded the War Crimes Commission and drafted the *Convention on International War Crimes Courts* and the *United Nations Convention on Extradition of War Criminals*. On July 26, 1945, the U.S., the UK, and China issued the Potsdam Declaration, urging Japan's immediate, unconditional surrender. The Declaration read: "There must be eliminated for all time the authority and influence of those who have deceived and misled the people of Japan into embarking on world conquest, for we insist that a new order of peace, security and justice will be impossible until irresponsible militarism is driven from the world." It continued: "We do not intend that the Japanese shall be enslaved as a race or destroyed as a nation, but stern justice shall be meted out to all war criminals, including those who have visited cruelties upon our prisoners" (International Treaties (1945–1947), 77). This was the first time the Allies clearly indicated their intention to punish Japanese war criminals. The aforementioned declarations of the Allies, particularly the Potsdam Declaration, became important legal bases for the subsequently founded International Military Tribunal for the Far East.

On September 2, 1945, Japan submitted its formal declaration of surrender, signed by Foreign Minister Shigemitsu Mamoru and Chief of the Army General

Staff General Umezu Yoshijiro, and accepting the clauses of the Potsdam Declaration, to General Douglas MacArthur, who received it on behalf of all nine of the Allies. On December 27, 1945, the Soviet, American, and British foreign ministers resolved in conference to establish the Far Eastern Commission and the Allied Council for Japan as replacements to the previously-established plan for a Far Eastern Advisory Commission, to be in charge of disposing with post-war Japan (Compilation of documents on Japanese issues vol. 1, 10). The commission was nominally an organization established by multiple countries to formulate Japanese policies, but in reality was of limited use. Real power to determine Japan's direction was held by the General Headquarters in Japan headed by MacArthur.

On January 19, 1946, MacArthur formally issued the Special Proclamation on the International Military Tribunal for the Far East and the Charter of the International Military Tribunal for the Far East, both based on prior resolutions of the Supreme Commander for the Allis Powers. On February 18, 1946, MacArthur formally appointed Sir William Webb, chief justice of the Supreme Court of Queensland (Australia), to lead the panel of 11 judges hailing from Australia, China, the Soviet Union, the U.S., the UK, France, the Netherlands, the Philippines, Canada, New Zealand, and British India. On the same day he also appointed Joseph Keenan chief prosecutor over a team of 30 prosecutors. The allies determined 70 "Class A" suspects per the Charter, and later resolved to try these 70 in two or three rounds owing to the enormity and complexity of their cases. In the first round, trials were to be held for 28 Class A suspects, of whom three were not tried for their war crimes because they died of illness or were gravely ill, but trials were held for the remaining 25. The Tokyo Trials lasted nearly two years and seven months from their convening in May 1946 until their declared conclusion in November 1948. A total of 818 court sessions produced more than 48,000 pages of court records. The trials called a total of 419 witnesses and produced more than 4,000 pieces of evidence. The longest verdict was 1,213 pages. The scale of the trials exceeded that of the Nuremberg Trials, and can legitimately be considered the largest international tribunal in human history, as well as one of the greatest political events to follow in the wake of the Second World War.

In addition to the trials for Class A suspects held in Tokyo, the Allies also held tribunals in Manila, Singapore, Yangon, Saigon, Khabarovsk, and elsewhere to try Class B and Class C suspects. Class B was reserved for conventional war crimes, and Class C for crimes against humanity. A total of 5,423 Japanese war criminals were indicted by the Allies, of whom 4,226 were tried and 941 were executed for their crimes (Li n.d.).

The relationship between the International Military Tribunal for the Far East (hereafter IMTFE) and the domestic courts of the Allies. The Supreme Commander for the Allies Powers MacArthur noted in his Special Proclamation of January 19, 1946, that the founding of the IMTFE did not "prejudice the jurisdiction of any other international, national or occupation court, commission or other tribunal established or to be established in Japan or in any territory of a United Nation with which Japan has been at war, for the trial of war criminals" (Yang 2006, 5–6).

The IMTFE Charter also issued on January 19 stipulated that the tribunal was "established for the just and prompt trial and punishment of the major war criminals in the Far East." Here "major war criminals" referred to criminals defined by the charter who committed "Crimes against Peace." The charter further stipulated that those charged with "Conventional War Crimes" or "Crimes against Humanity" were to be tried in military tribunals established in the country or location where the offense was committed, in accordance with international precedent (Yang 2006, 6–7). This was done not only because offenders were generally of low rank and the facts of their crimes relatively simple, obviating the need for an internationally organized tribunal, but also because there were two great advantages to extraditing those charged with these two classes of crimes to the countries where their alleged crimes were committed. First, since their crimes were committed in a specific place, then trying them for these crimes in that place not only adheres to the criminal law principle of "territorial jurisdiction" but also makes the collection of evidence, calling of witnesses, and investigation of crime scenes more convenient. Second, the trying of these war criminals in the national or local courts in the place where their crimes were committed, and the doling out of legal punishment to these criminals in those places, allowed for psychological and spiritual satisfaction on the part of the local peoples for whom the memory of their atrocities remained fresh (Mei n.d., 37).

10.1.2 The nationalist government's War Criminals Commission

China was one of the primary Allies in the Asian theater of World War Two; so the handling of a series of issues related to Japan's post-war treatment, including trying of war criminals, had to be conducted in accordance with the spirit of allied countries, and any actions committed in this area were limited by the Allies to a certain extent. After consensus was reached in the handling of war criminals among the leaders of the Allies, they founded the Committee on Facts and Evidence and drafted *the Convention for United Nations War Crimes Court* and *the*

Transfer of War Criminals Convention in 1944. On May 16, 1944, the UNWCC General Commission in London resolved to establish a Far Eastern and Pacific Sub-Commission as China had "fought the longest war of resistance" and suffered most deeply from the calamity, in order to facilitate processing of war criminals. The Chinese government was appointed to chair this sub-commission. On November 29, the UNWCC Far Eastern and Pacific Sub-Commission was formally established in Chonqing, chaired by Wang Chonghui. Delegates from more than 10 countries, including the U.S., Australia, Belgium, the UK, France, India, and the Netherlands participated in the sub-commission's meetings as advisers and facilitators of criminal investigations (Qin n.d., 423). The sub-commission released 26 batches of names of Japanese war criminals, for a total of 2,992 names, 2,368 of which were put forward by the Chinese government.

The Chinese government expressed approbation and support for the idea of founding an international tribunal to try war criminals proposed in the November 1944 Moscow Declaration. At the Cairo Conference convened that month it was proposed that "Basic principles for the handling of Japan and measures for punishing chief Japanese war criminals and those responsible for atrocities will be decided upon by China, the UK, and the U.S., just like the measures decided upon for punishing Italy and Germany decided upon at the Moscow Conference" (Liang n.d., 110). On July 26, 1945, China, the U.S., and the UK jointly issued the Potsdam Declaration (or the Proclamation Defining Terms for Japanese Surrender Issued at Potsdam), defining their united stance on punishing Japanese war criminals: "We do not intend that the Japanese shall be enslaved as a race or destroyed as a nation, but stern justice shall be meted out to all war criminals, including those who have visited cruelties upon our prisoners" (International Treaties (1945–1947), 77). The Allies later issued more concrete regulations on treatment of war criminals, that being the IMTFE Charter issued on January 19, 1946. These documents established principles for the trying of war criminals in China and became important bases for the formation of KMT policies.

After Japan's surrender, Nationalist Government chairman Chiang Kai-shek issued a radio address in which he announced that lenient policies "not dwelling on past evils" would be adopted toward post-war Japan. On this basis the nationalist government drafted the basic spirit for the treatment of Japanese war criminals: "All Japanese war criminals extradited internationally or captured in the Chinese military theater will be tried according to law and punished accordingly. Conventional war criminals from among them will be treated leniently, and during their trials they will be made to feel the following main points with stress on punishment regulations replete with educational significance: (1) The error of the militarism and aggression of Japanese warlords; (2) the responsibility for this war that should be borne by Japanese warlords; (3) that the Allies fought for justice and peace; (4) the greatness of the Three Principles of the People; (5) The United Nations Charter and ideology of democratic governance; (6) exposure as false of the history of Japan's divine right to rule and its replacement by true history, that all countries request not to be treated unjustly or trampled upon, and that foundations for eternal peace between China and Japan and for the entire world should be established in accordance with the self-evident truth of justice and friendly feelings between the nations" (Qin 1982, 393). The KMT government then proceeded to establish dedicated bodies for the handling of war criminals in accordance with that general spirit.

On December 6, 1945, the nationalist government established the War Criminals Commission, composed of the Board of Military Operations, the Ministry of Military Affairs, the Ministry of Foreign Affairs, the Ministry of Justice, the secretariat of the Executive Yuan, and the UNWCC Far Eastern and Pacific Sub-Commission, tasked with prosecuting war criminals and presided over by the General Staff Headquarters. Its primary duties were to investigate cases, screen them, produce lists of war criminals for prosecution, issue orders for the arrest of war criminals, review conditions of the execution of verdicts, have war criminals extradited, and review lists of war criminals. At its inception the commission was chaired by Deputy Chief of the General Staff Liu Fei. Later "organizational rules" were established to increase the commission's working efficiency, and its leadership was shaken up in January 1947, at which point Deputy Defense Minister Qin Dechun was appointed chief commissioner, and the commission's work was strengthened.

There was a clear division of labor among the departments that made up the commission: "(1) The second bureau of the Ministry of Defense is responsible for the issuance of all general policies, plans, and orders for the arrest of war criminals, as well as all comprehensive tasks of this commission. (2) The Ministry of Justice is responsible for all investigations, screening of cases, and production of lists of war criminals. (3) The Ministry of Defense's Military Law Enforcement Office is responsible for reviews of war criminal sentences. (4) The Ministry of Foreign Affairs is responsible for translating lists of extradited war criminals. (5) The Far Eastern and Pacific Sub-Commission is responsible for reviewing lists... and for dispatching agents to Shanghai, Guangzhou, Guilin, Hengyang, Pinghan, Taiwan, the Northeast, and other areas to investigate and supervise the promotion of the task of prosecuting war criminals" (Qin 1982, 450). In addition, war criminal organizations were established in the Ministry of Justice and the Ministry of Defense's Bureau of Military Law, the latter of which was dedicated to reviewing the verdicts of military tribunals around the country.

Later the commission established three sub-groups to increase working efficiency. The first group was composed of personnel from the Foreign Ministry to serve as liaisons between the commission, allies such as the U.S., the UK, France, and the Soviet Union, and the International Military Tribunal for the Far East in Tokyo, and to be in charge of extraditions of war criminals; this group was located in the Ministry of Foreign Affairs in Nanjing. The second group was composed of personnel from the Ministry of Justice and was headed by Dr. Tang Zhaolong, director of the ministry's Criminal Division, and was composed of a total of ten members including Li Xiangjun and Tan Yugan. This group was located in the hall of the Ministry of Justice on either side of Zhongshan Road in Nanjing. Its primary task was to collect "Criminal Investigation Forms for Japanese War Criminals," determine the crimes of given war criminals in accordance with the "Regulations of the Republic of China on Punishing Japanese War Crimes" and relevant international law, and to submit "Initial Suggestions on Severity of Crime" along with "Criminal Investigation Forms" to the third group. All such forms not related to war criminals remained in the second group's offices and were later transferred to the archives of the Criminal Division of the Ministry of Justice in specially-made long wooden boxes for use at any time by a third group. This third group was composed of personnel from the Ministry of Defense. It was outwardly not known as the "third group" but as the "Army General Staff Military Tribunal," a name later changed to "Ministry of Defense Military Tribunal." This group was tasked with trying and sentencing war criminals per war trials regulations (Tan Yugan 1995, n.d.).

The nationalist government's consideration was: "Our country's treatment of war criminals is a pioneering effort. We have extremely few judges who have studied international law, and so we lack expertise in the procedures and all other related measures of trying war criminals. If these cases are handled inappropriately in the least, we will be criticized internationally. To bring about consistency in trials of war criminals among all courts, we must establish guiding principles for the handling of war criminals to provide a basis for courts at all levels" (Republic of China Diplomatic Issues Research Association n.d., 458). To this end, in February 1946, the nationalist government's Military Affairs Commission deliberated on and passed the "Measures on War Criminal Trials," "Measures on War Criminal Handling," and "Detailed Rules on the Implementation of the Measures on War Criminal Trials," with participation of experts from China and abroad to deliberate on and create detailed, concrete stipulations on war criminal behaviors, reporting, arrests, sentencing, and carrying out of sentences.

On October 25, 1946, the War Criminals Commission convened a meeting on policies for handling Japanese war criminals, at which it was resolved: "We should adopt farsighted measures toward Japan, and we should look to the big picture in the handling of war criminals. There is no need to get caught on small details. We should quickly conclude the task of handling war criminals." The meeting further resolved in accordance with these principles: (1) leniency and promptness should be the guiding principles in the handling of conventional war criminals. All war criminals currently in custody must be tried by the end of this year. Those for whom no evidence of major crimes can be produced should not be charged but should be released back to Japan. War criminals already sentenced should be returned to Japan for their sentences to be carried out there. All other war crimes trials should be concluded by the end of 1947; (2) Japanese war criminals whose cases are reviewed by the UNWCC Far Eastern and Pacific Sub-commission should be promptly arrested. The Allied Supreme Command should be contacted to extradite all those already returned to Japan; (3) major war crimes related to the great massacre in Nanjing and all subordinate regions should be dealt with severely; (4) we will not ask for extradition of war criminals sentenced by the IMTFE whose cases touch on China at this moment; (5) as related to the surrender, the handling of Japanese military officers of great responsibility and suspected of war crimes will be decided upon after the close of the first session of the Tokyo Trials; and (6) all suspected war criminals for whom no evidence of crimes can be produced should be returned to their home countries with all haste (Republic of China Diplomatic Issues Research Association n.d., 458–459). The reporting of Japanese war criminals ended on October 15, 1947, in accordance with this policy.

The War Criminals Commission received 171,152 reports of war crimes and arrested 2,453 suspected war criminals by October 1946 (Republic of China Diplomatic Issues Research Association n.d., 469). All Japanese soldiers encircled by the nationalist government or reported by civilians – after being disarmed and assembled per regulations – were required to fill in ROC-printed "experience forms" to be officially reviewed. In the case that one was suspected of war crimes, "the General Staff Headquarters should deliberate on the actual situation and make recommendations to the chief commissioner of the Military Affairs Commission to produce orders for arrest at his discretion" (Qin 1981, 398). The nationalist government arrested a total of 1,111 suspected war criminals (of which 82 appeared on government-produced lists, and 1,029 were processed by military tribunals after being reported by the people). There were not only Japanese among the arrested, but also 41 North Koreans, 52 Taiwanese, one Ryukyuan, two Germans, and five Italians (Qin 1981, 422).

On July 16, 1947, the War Criminals Commission established a Ministry of Defense War Criminals Administration Office in Jiangwan Town, Shanghai, to directly administer suspected war criminals in the Central China region. The War Criminals Commission had originally planned to hand sentenced war criminals to Japan to have their sentences carried out there, but later it was determined that "since China has no troops stationed in Japan and therefore no ability to oversee these sentences, and it has been ascertained through back channels that the Supreme Allied Command there has not expressed consent. At the same time, owing to differences in the nature of the languages of these war criminals, it seems we should build a dedicated prison to keep them in concentrated custody. It is resolved at the 67th regular session of this commission that a Ministry of Defense war criminals prison should be established at the site of the former Shanghai detention center... War criminals sentenced anywhere in the country should be escorted to Shanghai for concentrated execution of sentences" (Qin 1981, 451).

A document released by the War Criminals Commission in January 1948 gives us these statistics: "Thirteen war criminals have been extradited to China from Japan at this commission's request, and requests have been put in for four more who have yet to be extradited to China. Plans were made for applications for 71 war criminals to be extradited here, of which eight were filed by bodies other than this commission. The Ministry of Defense has had 64 prisoners extradited directly by the Allied Command, and this commission has arranged for the extradition of seven prisoners from China to other countries." Military tribunals around the country tried most suspected war criminals already in custody in 1946 and 1947. All military tribunals in China were disbanded at the end of 1947, leaving only the Ministry of Defense Military Tribunal in Nanjing to try lingering cases. By that time "all military tribunals around the country processed a total of 1,523 cases, with 1,045 resolved and 478 unresolved. One hundred and ten were sentenced to death, 41 to lifelong imprisonment, and 167 to prison terms. Two hundred and eighty-three were found not guilty; charges were dropped against 661; 30 were never charged. Eight hundred and seventy-eight non-war criminals were returned to Japan. The remaining 218 await trials" (Republic of China Diplomatic Issues Research Association n.d., 468). In July 1948 the War Criminals Commission was disbanded, and the Ministry of Defense Military Tribunal followed suit in April 1949. The nationalist government heard a total of 2,200 war crimes cases, sentenced 145 to death and more than 400 to prison terms, the rest being found not guilty and returned to Japan (*Shenbao*, January 27, 1949).

10.1.3 Establishment of the Nanjing Military Tribunal for trying war criminals

Per a decision of the War Criminals Commission, military tribunals for trying war criminals were established in Nanjing, Shanghai, Beiping, Hankou, Guangzhou, Shenyang, Xuzhou, Jinan, Taiyuan, and Taibei in mid-December 1945. The tribunal in Nanjing was under jurisdiction of the Ministry of Defense, but the rest were under jurisdiction of their local pacified region governments, and all tried cases of war crimes occurring in their area of responsibility.

On February 15, 1946, the Nanjing Military Tribunal for Trying War Criminals was founded under the name "Chinese Army General Staff Headquarters Military Tribunal," but with the founding of the Ministry of Defense in July, the tribunal was put under the ministry's jurisdiction and renamed "Ministry of Defense Military Tribunal for Trying War Criminals." On August 15, 1947, this tribunal was merged with the tribunal in Shanghai, at which point the Nanjing tribunal dispatched some its personnel to Shanghai to process cases there. When military tribunals for trying war criminals were disbanded at the end of 1947, only the tribunal in Nanjing was retained to try lingering cases. This tribunal was itself finally disbanded on April 30, 1949.

Per regulations for trying war criminals, the Ministry of Defense tribunal was composed of personnel from both the Military Law Bureau of the Ministry of Defense and from the Ministry of Justice. Its staff composition was one chief judge, five ordinary judges, two prosecutors, one secretary-general, seven secretaries, two interpreters, one quartermaster, one aide, and three clerks (Hu 2006, 48–49). In August 1947, the staff grew to 35 as a result of the merger with the Shanghai tribunal, with a portion now working in the Shanghai office. As most of the tribunal's work was completed by the end of September 1948, the staff was then reduced to 16.

The War Criminals Commission appointed Shi Meiyu as the Nanjing tribunal's chief judge; Wang Jiamei as chief prosecutor; Chen Guangyu, Li Bo, Xu Jikun, Gao Shuoren, and Shi Yong as prosecutors; and Lu Qi, Li Yuanqing, Lin Jianpeng, Ye Zaizeng, Sun Jianzhong, Long Zhonghuang, Zhang Tikun as judges. This tribunal was responsible for trying all Japanese suspects extradited from Japan by the Chinese delegation there as well as important Japanese war criminals handed over by other tribunals around the country.

Most judges and prosecutors appointed came from higher courts located in the jurisdiction of the tribunal. As trials for traitors were held immediately after victory in the war, therefore before trials for war criminals, most judges and prosecutors chosen for this tribunal had participated in trials for traitors. These selections were expedient in having trials conducted speedily, but very few judges and prosecutors chosen had any experience in international law.

The Nanjing tribunal was directly subordinate to the Ministry of Defense. Most of the suspected war criminals it tried had been handed over by the Ministry of Defense or Ministry of Justice, from tribunals elsewhere in China, or from the War Criminals Administration Office, or otherwise had been extradited from Japan via the Chinese delegation there. Initial statistics indicate that from its founding on February 15, 1946 through to December 25, 1947, the Nanjing tribunal tried 102 suspects, sentenced six to death, sentenced 10 to life in prison, and gave fixed prison terms to 12 (Republic of China Diplomatic Issues Research Association n.d., 469). Four of its trials were of mid to high-ranking Japanese officers: Tani Hisao, Sakai Takashi, Isogai Rensuke, and Takahashi Tan. Also among those tried were lower-ranking officers who had participated in the Rape of Nanking: Tanaka Gunkichi, Noda Tsuyoshi, and Mukai Toshiaki.

10.2 Organization and Structure of the Military Tribunal

The Ministry of Defense Military Tribunal at Nanjing was the highest tribunal for trying Japanese war criminals in China, and there was consequently a great gulf between it and military tribunals established elsewhere in the country. Relatively speaking, the Nanjing tribunal's organization was rigorous, and the legal bases for its jurisdiction very complete. Its structure was also much more standardized than military tribunals elsewhere that reported to local governments. Also, most cases tried in Nanjing were of important war criminals, and so great attention was paid to it. Previous studies often focus only on the proceedings and results of the Nanjing Trials while overlooking its foundations in legal theory and statutory procedures. The truth is that its foundation in legal theory and its statutory procedures directly influenced both the verdicts it produced and the international effects of those verdicts. As such, it is necessary to consider these two areas in great detail.

10.2.1 Applicable law

At the close of World War I, the countries and peoples devastated by the war were not satisfied with victory alone, but wanted to try those responsible for war crimes in international courts. Part VII of the Treaty of Versailles ("Penalties") begins: "The Allied and Associated Powers publicly arraign William II of Hohenzollern, formerly German Emperor, for a supreme offence against international morality and the sanctity of treaties." It continues in Article 228: "The German Government recognises the right of the Allied and Associated Powers to bring before military tribunals persons accused of having committed acts in violation of the laws and customs of war. Such persons shall, if found guilty, be sentenced to punishments laid down by law." And finally: "The German Government shall hand over to the Allied and Associated Powers, or to such one of them as shall so request, all persons accused of having committed an act in violation of the laws and customs of war, who are specified either by name or by the rank, office or employment which they held under the German authorities" (International Treaties (1917–1923), 157–158). These plans were ultimately never put into practice for various reasons, but they did provide a new way of thinking about how to resolve the issue of war crimes and gave rise to a new concept: that leaders should be punished for the criminal policies they are responsible for enacting.

The outbreak of World War II and all the devastation it wrought incited the leaders of all Allied nations to fervently demand punishment of war crimes and gradually led to the formation of a new idea: that war criminals should be tried in international tribunals. After the war's end, the Allies established two such tribunals, the one at Nuremberg, and the IMTFE at Tokyo, respectively charged with trying German and Japanese war criminals. The Charter of the International Military Tribunal (Nuremberg) defines three kinds of war crimes, "crimes against peace," "war crimes," and "crimes against humanity," as follows: "(a) Crimes against peace: namely, planning, preparation, initiation or waging of a war of aggression, or a war in violation of international treaties, agreements or assurances, or participation in a common plan or conspiracy for the accomplishment of any of the foregoing. (b) War Crimes: namely, violations of the laws or customs of war. Such violations shall include, but not be limited to, murder, ill-treatment or deportation to slave labor or for any other purpose of civilian population of or in occupied territory, murder or ill-treatment of prisoners of war or persons on the seas, killing of hostages, plunder of public or private property, wanton destruction of cities, towns or villages, or devastation not justified by military necessity. (c) Crimes against humanity: namely, murder, extermination, enslavement, deportation, and other inhumane acts committed against any civilian population, before or during the war; or persecutions on political, racial or religious grounds in execution of or in connection with any crime within the jurisdiction of the Tribunal, whether or not in violation of the domestic law of the country where perpetrated." The International Tribunal at Nuremberg basically followed the principles laid out in the Charter, but many legal advances were also made, leading to the development of modern international law and law of war.[103]

---

[103] For more details on the historical progress of international law and its relationship to the Charters of the International Military Tribunal of Nuremberg and the International Military Tribunal for the Far East, see He, Zhu, and Ma, "Niulunbao shenpan yu xiandai guojifa de fazhan" [The Nuremberg trials and the development of international law], *Jianghai xuekan* 4 (2006); and chapter 1 article 5 on jurisdiction of the IMTFE in Mei n.d.

The trials of Japanese war criminals held in China were conducted on the basis of the Potsdam Declaration, the IMTFE Charter, and relevant Chinese law. The IMTFE in Tokyo tried Class A suspects, i.e. those suspected of "crimes against peace." Tribunals established in Allied countries primarily tried those suspected of "conventional war crimes," violations of the rules and standard practices of war, and "crimes against humanity." This was the first large-scale trying of war crimes cases in China, and as such there were no precedents to follow. As the Tokyo Trials and the trials held in military tribunals in the various Allied countries, including China, were the two major components of procedures for punishing Japanese war criminals, there was an organic relationship between the Tokyo Trials and those held in the various tribunals. China employed the basic principles set in the Tokyo Trials to the greatest extent possible, creating special decrees and regulations specifically related to war crimes trials to guide the work of trying war criminals.

In February 1946, the nationalist government's Military Affairs Commission deliberated on and passed the "Measures on War Criminal Trials," "Measures on War Criminal Handling," and "Detailed Rules on the Implementation of the Measures on War Criminal Trials," with participation of experts from China and abroad to deliberate on and create detailed, concrete stipulations on war criminal behaviors, reporting, arrest, sentencing, and carrying out of sentences. All three of these documents were employed in military tribunals around China beginning from the time they went into force.

Since, however, China lacked experience in such trials and had no existing applicable laws on its books, and since the documents were composed in haste, some problems emerged when the various tribunals around the country attempted to implement them. The documents were very clear in principles but not clear in some concrete concepts and procedures and also lacked norms; this created a degree of difficulty in the work of conducting these trials. In response, the Ministry of Defense urgently held consultations with the Ministry of Justice, the Ministry of Foreign Affairs, and the Executive Yuan Secretariat to revise the documents, resulting in "Draft Revisions to the Measures for War Criminal Trials" in August of that year. After review by legal experts, the draft was submitted to the Supreme Defense Commission and the Legislative Yuan, which deliberated on and ultimately passed the document into law. The document was subsequently renamed "Law Governing the Trial of War Criminals" and promulgated and entered into force on October 23 (further revisions were made to Articles 25 and 32 in July 1947) in the form of a government decree. The Regulations were much tighter and more operable than their predecessors, and were ultimately made into the official code for war crimes trials.

The revised Regulations did away with the provisions of its three predecessors to apply the "Criminal Code of the Army, Navy, and Air Force" in war crimes trials. Said code was a rigorous military code, and if it had been widely applied, then an enormous amount of Japanese officers and soldiers in the invading army would have been sentenced to capital punishment.

In its place China chose to apply principles of international law to war crimes trials. The Regulations stipulate: "In the trial and punishment of war criminals, where international law is not applicable, then the stipulations of these Regulations are to be applied. In places where there are no relevant stipulations under these Regulations, then relevant provisions of the Republic of China Criminal Code are to be applied. When the Republic of China Criminal Code is applicable, its special provisions are to be applied with priority (and common provisions where special provisions are not applicable), regardless of the identity of the suspected war criminal" (Hu 2006, 30). Domestic law here mostly referred to the criminal code, but international law applied to these trials included primarily the following: the Hague Convention on Respecting the Laws and Customs of War on Land, the Hague Convention on Bombardment by Naval Forces in Time of War, the 1922 Treaty on Submarines and Noxious Gases, the Geneva Conventions, the Convention Relative to the Treatment of Prisoners of War, the International Opium Convention, and other international treaties related to war (Hu 2006, 12–15). There were also international treaties on crimes against peace, precedents in international law, the Covenant of the League of Nations, the Nine-Power Treaty, the Kellogg-Briand Pact, the 1907 Convention on the Pacific Settlement of International Disputes signed in the Hague, the 1907 Hague Convention Relative to the Legal Position of Enemy Merchant Ships at the Start of Hostilities, and others (Hu 2006, 15–18). All of the preceding were cited in Chinese trials of war criminals.

On the whole, the majority of the bases in legal theory employed during the nationalist government's trials of Japanese war criminals came from existing international law, but the principles established in the Nuremberg and IMTFE charters were not entirely absorbed. The reason was that the Nanjing Trials were held at roughly the same time as the Nuremberg and Tokyo Trials, and so the nationalist government was unable to immediately adopt legal precedents laid down in those two cities. In particular, some war crimes of World War Two tried at Nuremberg were unprecedented, and as such there were no applicable provisions in international law. The issues were also clearly related to the different jurisdictions of domestic courts located in the Allied countries, with international tribunals prosecuting Class A suspects and domestic courts prosecuting Class B and C suspects. This invariably led to differences in emphasis on international law precedents cited.

10.2.2 Regulations, organization, and procedures

To provide legal bases for verdicts in war criminal trials, the nationalist government first produced "Measures on War Criminal Trials," "Measures on War Criminal Handling," and "Detailed Rules on the Implementation of the Measures on War Criminal Trials," later revised and combined into a single document, "Regulations on War Crimes Trials," which laid out in detail the jurisdictional scope, organization of courts, trial procedures, and applicable law in war crimes trials, providing a tight and operable set of rules for running said trials.

The following are the primary characteristics and contents of the revised rules (Hu 2006, 30–45):

One. Clarification on the definition of a war criminal. Anyone found guilty of any of the following four was to be considered a war criminal:

(1) Violation of international law: anyone who participated in the launch of the invasion of the Republic of China or supported said invasion, or of any other illegal war; (2) violation of the laws and customs of war: anyone who directly or indirectly enacted atrocities; (3) anyone who engaged in "killing, starving, annihilating, enslaving, or exiling; indulging in the thinking of drugging or dominating; spreading strong narcotics; forcing people to use or injecting them with narcotics or eliminating their reproductive capabilities; oppressing or maltreating for political, ethnic, or religious reasons; or any other acts against humanity" to enslave, devastate, or exterminate the Chinese people; and (4) those not guilty of the above three but are otherwise punishable under the Republic of China Criminal Code. The clarification of the definition of "war criminal" gave courts trying these cases operable legal bases on which to argue, both increasing efficiency and enhancing the precision of trying these cases.

Two. Concrete rules on the arrest of war criminals:

(1) After Japan's surrender, to arrest war criminals, the Army General Staff Headquarters sent a request to the Military Affairs Commission, which then issued the order to proceed; (2) once proof of a crime was reported or once war crimes reported by the public were found to be truthful, arrests were immediately carried out by a commander in the war zone; (3) to arrest war criminals from the Japanese government system, the War Criminals Commission sent a request to the Supreme Command in occupied Japan, which arrested them and turned them over to China. For War Criminals in the Northeast, the request was sent to the Soviet Red Army's Far East Command to carry this out; and (4) for war criminals on the run, the Army General Staff Headquarters issued an order for arrest. If the criminal had escaped abroad, the Ministry of Foreign Affairs negotiated for their arrest.

Three. Clear rules on sentencing war criminals, including in jurisdiction of courts and composition and functions of courts. Relatively concrete rules were made for recommendations and appointments of military judges and prosecutors, the powers of military prosecutors, the right to a defense by defendants, courts' rights of search and seizure, and publication of court sentences: (1) all Japanese war criminals except those sentenced by the special tribunal at Tokyo were to be sentenced per the Regulations; (2) Japanese war criminals were to be sentenced by military tribunals established by the Army General Staff Headquarters or by commanders in the war zone; (3) military judges (five) and military prosecutors (one) for each military tribunal were appointed by, respectively, the presiding military organ and the provincial or regional supreme court, and reporting to, respectively, the Ministry of War and the Ministry of Justice. Appointments were first submitted to the War Crimes Commission, which then handed them over to the Military Affairs Commission Chief Commissioner for final appointment; (4) military organs or provincial or regional high courts were to prepare appropriate selections for replacements in the case a judge or prosecutor had to be absent for various reasons; (5) rules applying to the official powers of prosecutors under the applicable code of criminal procedure were applicable in the performance of duties by military prosecutors; (6) defendants needed to appoint attorneys to appear in court as their defense per the Chinese attorney law. Those not appointing attorneys had public defenders appointed for them from the local area by the court. In case of a lack of public defender, the chief judge appointed an attorney to fill the gap; (7) all indictments in war crimes cases were to be raised by military prosecutors; (8) all arguments in court and pronouncements of sentences were to be made public; (9) teams from organs or local civilians could give statements of their views through representatives at the time of a trial; and (10) in cases of necessity, military tribunals could dispatch three judges and a prosecutor to the scene of a war crime to hold trial there.

Four. The Regulations gave detailed rules on regulations and conventions for ordinary war criminals, that is those in violation of the laws of warfare, and on criminals whose actions directly or indirectly constituted atrocities. The Regulations broke down these criminal behaviors into 38 articles, making determination of criminal behavior determinable, operable, and precise. The Regulations stipulated that any of the following actions constituted a violation of the laws and conventions of war: (1) planned slaughter, murder or other terrorist action; (2) robbing; (3) rape; (4) employment of inhuman weapons.; (5) kidnapping children; (6) torturing of prisoners or wounded; (7) deliberate bombing of non-defended areas and hospitals; (8) destroying freighters or passenger boats without previous warning and without regard to the safety of passengers and crew; (9)

ordering wholesale slaughter; (10) plundering of historical, artistic or other cultural treasures.; etc.

Five. Clear rules were made for time period of prosecution of war crimes. The Regulations stipulated that the time for occurrence of prosecutable war crimes was after September 18, 1931 and before September 2, 1945. But per Clauses 1 and 3 (behaviors similar to crimes against humanity) of Article 2 (similar to crimes against peace), even crimes occurring before September 18, 1931 could be prosecuted.

Six. Rules on items of criminal liability not subject to exemption. The Regulations stipulated that war criminals could not be exempted from criminal liability for the following:

(1) Crimes committed on orders from superiors; (2) crimes committed as result of carrying out one's duty; (3) crimes committed carrying out government-established national policy; (4) crimes committed as political acts. These rules were extremely important. Without them, all criminals would claim innocence on pretense of acting on orders, pushing blame up the chain of command and escaping punishment.

Seven. Punishment of culpable commanders. The Regulations stipulated that anyone in a supervisory or commanding role "who did not do the utmost possible to prevent the occurrence of war crimes shall be considered accessory to a war crime.".

Eight. Sentencing standards. Sentencing standards from seven years in prison to the death penalty were established based on the severity of crimes committed.

Nine. Reviews of verdicts were strengthened. The Regulations stipulated that in any case in which a court found the suspect guilty, it must first submit the case to the Ministry of Defense for review before carrying out the sentence. In cases of sentences of death or life imprisonment, the Ministry of Defense had to in turn ask the chairman of the Nationalist Government to review the case before execution of sentence. In cases where the chairman determined that a verdict had violated the law or been inappropriate, he sent the case back for retrial. In cases where he found the penalty excessively severe, he reduced it.

The Regulations grant us a general understanding of ordinary procedures in war crimes trials, which were: the court received a case; the chief clerk then handed the case to a prosecutor for investigation; in cases where the prosecutor determined there was sufficient evidence to try a suspect, he filed an indictment; the chief clerk then handed this to the judge in charge, who investigated the case; then this judge handed his findings to the chief judge, who determined a trial date. In cases where the prosecutor chose not to indict a suspect, the suspect was handed over to the Port Command for assembly and concentrated repatriation. All decisions, guilty, not guilty, and a decision not to indict, were subject to review by the Ministry of Defense. Some had their sentences carried out in the war criminals prison, and some were repatriated. All important cases were subject to review by the chairman of the Nationalist Government. Final decision-making authority in all cases rested with the Ministry of Defense. The courts merely tried the cases in accordance with the stipulations of the Regulations and the code of criminal procedure.

Rigorous trial procedures ensured orderly trials, but we should note some degree of deficiency in the Regulations on War Crimes Trials, particularly the lack of a Ministry of Defense charter for war crimes military tribunals. As compared to the IMTFE, which had a charter, the nationalist government did not establish a rigorous tribunal charter with detailed stipulations in trial procedures, authorities, collection of evidence and recognizance by the court, defendants' rights, and so on. There was also a problem of overlapping jurisdiction with the IMTFE, with no clear delineations regarding jurisdiction of the IMTFE and war criminal courts in various victim countries. As a result, the people and relevant organs of China frequently petitioned to have Class A suspects extradited to China for trial throughout reporting procedures.

10.2.3 Prosecutors, defendants, and judges

The legal factors of the Regulations on War Crimes Trials were complete. Its factors of court composition were complete, including the war criminal as defendant, the indicting prosecutor as accuser, and the judge serving on behalf of the court. The war criminal was the defendant and, as the crimes were committed in China and the Chinese people were the victims of their wartime atrocities, the Chinese people were therefore the accusers. Specially appointed prosecutors generally raised indictments to the court on behalf of the accuser, the Chinese people, and the case was tried in a military court. The judges reached verdicts per relevant tenets of international and domestic law. The courts operated on the collegiate system, whereby all judges in a case had to come to a unanimous decision to arrive at a verdict.

The Regulations legally defined defendants as persons suspected of having committed one of four kinds of crimes considered war crimes. Suspected war criminals were generally reported by the people to prosecutors, who, upon determining sufficient cause, sent an indictment to the court to start a trial procedure. The defendants had legal rights: they could request an appeal, defend themselves, or have an attorney defend them. The selection of defense attorneys for defendants in the Nanjing military tribunal was stipulated in the Regulations:

the defendant must appoint an attorney as his defense counsel to appear in court in his defense per the Chinese attorney law; those not appointing attorneys would have a public defender appointed by the court from the local area; in cases where no public defender was available, the judge would appoint an attorney to fill the role. This process was fair and equal in legal terms (Hu 2006, 35).

Per the Regulations, military tribunals for trying war criminals were composed of military judges and military prosecutors. Trials were constituted of three to five judges and one prosecutor, but personnel could be added in relatively complex cases. There were always one chief judge and one chief prosecutor. Military prosecutors raised indictments in war crimes cases, and military judges presided over court proceedings and delivered sentences.

In all war crimes cases military prosecutors raised indictments and served as prosecutors on behalf of the public. There were two primary categories of cases in which they raised indictments. The first was in the case of suspected war criminals determined to be so through nationalist government investigations; in these cases the government issued lists which were the primary source of suspects in such cases. The second was reporting and allegations from the people and all manner of social groups, for example the many reports and allegations from the people and social groups received by Rape of Nanking Enemy Crimes Investigation Commission, which were handed over to military prosecutors. Prosecutors, acting on the public's behalf, had to serve the functions of accuser, meaning that they raised indictments, used their powers of investigation, collected evidence on crimes committed, and submitted all relevant witness statements and material evidence on war crimes to the tribunal. They also engaged in arguments with suspects' defense counsels during trial proceedings.

Every military tribunal had one chief judge and a total of three to five judges to hear cases. In general, these judges reached verdicts and passed sentences in accordance with relevant international and domestic laws based on evidence produced by prosecutors and the defense of defendants. Judges could also conduct their own investigations in the course of trials to determine the facts of alleged crimes, as well as on-site investigations in the places where alleged cries happened.

Per the stipulations of the Detailed Implementation Rules of the Measures on War Criminal Trials, military judges and military prosecutors were appointed by, respectively, the presiding military organ and the provincial or regional supreme court, reporting to, respectively, the Ministry of War and the Ministry of Justice.

10.3 Building Cases for the Rape of Nanking

10.3.1 Preliminary case-filing and trial work

After the war, the nationalist government attached extreme importance to the processing of Rape of Nanking criminal cases. The War Criminals Commission handled these cases with a maximum of rigor (Hu 2006, 54), strengthening on-the-ground investigations of Japanese atrocities during the event, laying solid foundations for the trials that came later.

Shortly after the beginning of the War of Resistance, the nationalist government and private groups began collecting evidence on war crimes committed by the Japanese army. In 1937, once the full-on Japanese invasion of China had begun, most investigations into Japanese war crimes were conducted by the Ministry of Foreign Affairs. In June 1943 the nationalist government resolved to establish the Enemy Crimes Investigation Commission, directly subordinate to the Executive Yuan, charged with investigations of all Japanese crimes in China. The nationalist government directed the Ministry of Justice to draft the "Organizational Rules of the Enemy Crimes Investigation Commission" with the Ministry of Foreign Affairs and the Ministry of War. The Enemy Crimes Investigation Commission was formally founded in Chongqing on February 23, 1944 (Hu 1988). After its founding, the commission established 13 concrete investigation programs to investigate Japanese violations of the laws and customs of war in China. On March 5, 1945, this commission was merged with the War of Resistance Losses Investigation Commission, and put under control of the Ministry of the Interior.

Japan surrendered unconditionally on August 15, 1945. Putting Japanese war criminals on trial was placed on the agenda; this spurred on the work of investigating Japanese war crimes. On September 14, the Executive Yuan issued the "Enemy Crimes Investigations Measures (Revised Version)," further normalizing investigative work. After more than a year of efforts, results began to be achieved from these investigations. Per a report on the War Criminals Commission from Minister of Justice Xie Guansheng, his ministry had processed 171,152 cases of Japanese war crimes (Republic of China Diplomatic Issues Research Association n.d., 457), laying the foundation for later trial work.

Chinese investigators of Japanese war crimes maintained close contact and cooperation with war crimes investigations bodies of other Allies. In January 1944, the UNWCC was formally established in London. In May the UNWCC Far Eastern and Pacific Sub-committee was founded in Chongqing at China's request, responsible primarily for investigating Japanese war crimes, and was composed of representatives from 11 countries, including China, the UK, the U.S.,

France, Australia, and the Netherlands. Former chief judge of the international court, Dr. Wang Chonghui, served as chairman. As China was the greatest victim of Japanese aggression and as there was a relatively great volume of evidence on Japanese war crimes in China, China naturally played the main role in this sub-commission. Many Chinese materials on war crimes investigations were given to the sub-commission by the Chinese Ministry of Foreign Affairs; in fact 90 % of all cases processed by the sub-commission were filed by China.

In October 1945, the War Criminals Commission was established, and all investigative bodies were merged into it, giving it further control of all investigations of war crimes. To advance the work of war criminals processing, the commission established a guiding working principle of government investigation and reporting by the people on the one hand and requested funding support from the government on the other. In 1947 the Executive Yuan allocated 300 million yuan to be used for investigating war criminals, allowing for the commission's work to proceed smoothly (Republic of China Diplomatic Issues Research Association n.d., 445).

The nationalist government adopted many forms in its work of investigating Japanese war crimes. In addition to previous methods, in July 1947 the method of listing out important war criminals was promulgated in an attempt to collect evidence. The national government also ordered local governments to further advance the work of investigating war crimes. The list of important war criminals included 261 names, with ranks, duties, and primary evidence of crimes committed (List of Important Japanese War Criminals 1991).

The Rape of Nanking was one of the events to which the post-war nationalist government attached the most importance. After the Japanese surrender, over a period spanning the end of 1945 to the beginning of 1947, the Capital Police Department, the Nanjing Enemy Crimes Investigation Commission, the Nanjing Municipal War of Resistance Losses Investigation Commission, the Rape of Nanking Enemy Crimes Investigation Commission, and the Ministry of Defense Military Tribunal all conducted social investigations into the Rape of Nanking from different perspectives. The focus of investigative work at first was on wartime losses and the victimization of the people. The focus later shifted onto atrocities committed in Nanjing by the Japanese army during the event. The Rape of Nanking Enemy Crimes Investigation Commission, presided over by the provisional Nanjing Municipal Representative Assembly, was founded specifically to facilitate trials for the event for the IMTFE. With great support from relevant organs, groups, the people of Nanjing, and foreigners, case materials were collected and compiled by district and by industry. After authentication, discussions were held in a plenary conference of the commission. Once confirmed, the commission turned the case over to the capital (Nanjing) local courts for them to forward it to the Ministry of Justice for further processing. Investigative forms were highly professional in the detailed records required for victims, witnesses, and investigators. There was legal significance to investigative procedures, design of forms, witness testimony, and so on. In less than five months, the commission compiled 2,784 cases on Japanese crimes during the Rape of Nanking, providing a large amount of valid original materials in a timely manner to the Nanjing tribunal and the IMTFE.

Far back on January 29, 1946, the War Criminals Commission passed a resolution on the processing of materials related to the Rape of Nanking perpetrated by the Japanese army invading China: "Materials on the Rape of Nanking and cities massacred by the Japanese army invading China collected by relevant units of the Army General Command are to be provided to the Ministry of Justice. These are to be sent by cable to Army Headquarters, which will then conduct a thorough investigation into the Japanese massacre of Nanjing and compile a list of Japanese war criminals. The Ministry of Foreign affairs will collect data on the Rape of Nanking and hand these to the Ministry of Justice for processing" (Hu 2006, 50). The War Criminals Commission resolved at a regular session on December 25, 1946 to file cases on the foundation of the investigations into crimes committed during the Rape of Nanking. The commission then compiled data on the crimes and released a list of 83 Japanese war criminals, and 59 of confirmed name, rank, and unit. There were 12 division commanders on the list; the rest were commanding officers of smaller units (Hu 2006).

Thereafter discussions began on the arrest or extradition of relevant criminals. Among major war criminals arrested in or extradited to China were Tani Hisao, Tanaka Gunkichi, Mukai Toshiaki, Noda Tsuyoshi, and others. Very few of the people listed by the commission were arrested or extradited. The nationalist government had consistently made active demands to extradite those war criminals connected to the Rape of Nanking. As early as July 1946, Shi Meiyu, chief judge of the Ministry of Defense Military Tribunal for Trying War Criminals, had expressed: "The primary war criminals will, I fear, have to be extradited from Japan to China. For example, our government has requested that the International Military Tribunal for the Far East extradite Matsui Iwane, the principle criminal behind the Rape of Nanking. If our government is not satisfied with the International Military Tribunal for the Far East's sentencing of him for his war crimes in invading China, we can demand that he be extradited to China for trial here" (Hu 2006, 46). During the trial of Tani Hisao, the War Criminals Commission asked the Allied Command to extradite all war criminals related to the Rape of Nanking to China: "The list is to include the supreme commander of the Japanese army's attack on Nanjing Matsui Iwane as well as Commanders Yanagawa and Nakajima. We have also pleaded many times in writing that Tani Hisao's accomplices, including Shimono, Tanabe, and others, be extradited to China" (Hu 2006, 57). We thus see that the nationalist government worked actively to have relevant war criminals extradited to China, but in this they needed cooperation from the Allied Supreme Command, and that was difficult to obtain in practice. Therefore, only a very small portion of relevant war criminals ended up being extradited.

10.3.2 The trial of Tani Hisao

Only one of the division commanders listed as primary war criminals in the Rape of Nanking was actually extradited to China for trial: Tani Hasao, former commander of the 6th Division. Prince Asaka Yasuhiko, commander of the Shanghai Expeditionary Army at the time of the event, was exempted from pursuit of justice as part of the royal family. Matsui Iwane was a Class A suspect and therefore tried in Tokyo at the IMTFE. Yanagawa Heisuke, commander of the 10th Army during the event, and Nakajima Kesago, commander of the Nanjing Garrison during the event, died of illness on January 1 and 10, respectively, 1945. So Tani Hisao was the only major war criminal involved with the Rape of Nanking extradited to China. His trial became an important basis for other conclusions reached about the Rape of Nanking.

The war criminal Tani Hisao was born in Tokyo in 1882 and later graduated from the Japanese Army Officer Academy and the Army University. In 1928 he was involved with the Jinan Incident, in which Chinese diplomats were massacred. In August 1937 he led the 6th Division in its invasion of North China and elsewhere. As it was needed for the invasions of Shanghai and Nanjing, the 6th Division was rerouted to East China. It slaughtered its way across China to Nanjing, where it was one of the chief culprits of the Rape of Nanking. On February 2, 1946, Tani was arrested by the Allied Supreme Command and held in Sugamo Prison in Tokyo. In August 1946 he was extradited to China and initially detained in Shanghai. The Ministry of Defense Military Tribunal for Trying War Criminals found him to "be the most forceful important war criminal in the invasion of China," "a primary important criminal in the Rape of Nanking, and so to expedite investigation and interrogation," it was necessary that he be handed to the Ministry of Defense Military Tribunal for trial (Hu 2006, 61). The military tribunal under the commander of the First Suijing District received orders to dispatch deputy judge of the tribunal Liu Shan to lead the chief of the special affairs battalion and six soldiers to escort Tani from Shanghai to Nanjing, where he was held in the Xiaoying War Criminals Detention Center of the Ministry of Defense.

A public trial was held for Tani in the *Lizhishe* great hall from February 6 to 8, 1947.

Of all trials related to the Rape of Nanking, Tani's was the longest and most thorough. His was also the most important as he was the primary perpetrator of the Rape of Nanking.

10.3.2.1 Investigation and indictment of Tani

Tani was arrested by the Allied Supreme Command in Japan and extradited to China at the Chinese government's request. His trial was initially slated to be held in the Shanghai tribunal, but he was moved to Nanjing on October 3, 1946, and the Ministry of Defense Tribunal tried his case.

On October 19, 1946, Chen Guangyu, prosecutor for the Ministry of Defense tribunal, began interrogating Tani in the Xiaoying Detention Center. Testimony was given by three people recommended by the Municipal Assembly, Bai Hong'en, Yin Youyu, and Li Xiuying: "Also there was Liang Tingfang, head of the Ministry of War hospital stretcher team and Bai Zengrong, head of nursing, both of whom had remained in Nanjing and witnessed the crimes of the enemy invaders, who came forward voluntarily to testify" (Hu 2006, 320).

Over the following several months, Tani was brought into court several times, yet he adamantly denied any massacres had taken place in Nanjing. During interviews with the media he kept his lips sealed about the event, and consistently claimed he had known nothing about atrocities committed in Nanjing.

On December 18, Tani submitted a document titled "Statement on the Situation of My Forces in the Battle of Nanjiing at the end of the 12th Year of the Showa Era" from his detention center, offering the following defense against his alleged crimes: (1) all residents had left the area where the 6th Division had encamped, in the vicinity of the Zhonghua Gate: "The center of the unfortunate incident in Nanjing was to the north of the middle of the city, on the banks of the Yangtzi River near Xiaguan and around Purple Mountain. The main units in these areas were the 16th, 9th, 110th, 13th, and 3rd Divisions, as well as the Shigeto Detachment (Battalion); none of these was related to my 6th Division"; (2) by December 21, 1937, the 6th Division had basically based itself at Wuhu, and thus could not have had any connection with the Rape of Nanking; and (3) Tani claimed that his demands of his troops were rigorous, that he never would have allowed any criminal behaviors of them, and that he firmly believed they had not engaged in criminal behavior. In his statement, Tani admitted that the Rape of Nanking had truly happened, but he denied any connection between the 6th Division under his command and the event, claiming that it must have been perpetrated by other units (Hu 2006, 461–462).

On December 31, the Ministry of Defense Tribunal for Trying War Criminals indicted Tani and requested that the Ministry of Defense Military Tribunal try the case. The indictment's primary contents were the primary conditions of the defendant, the facts of his crimes, the reason for the indictment, evidence collected, laws broken, measurement of penalty and appendices of evidence on concrete atrocities committed. The appendices contained detailed lists of murders, rapes, looting, and intentional destruction of property (Hu 2006, 324–346). Among the reasons for his indictment were: that Tani had been a radical supporter of the Japanese movement to invade China, that he had participated in the conspiracy to invade China and had supported and driven invasion actions; that Tani's forces had stolen property from Chinese civilians while encamped at Baoding, Hebei; and that Tani's troops participated in murder, rape, and looting in Nanjing after it had fallen to Japanese forces.

On January 15, 1947, Tani submitted a written defense to in response to the prosecutors' indictment. In his defense Tani denies any involvement in any atrocities by his troops. Tani writes of atrocities: "Since I never saw or heard of them, nor tacitly allowed or tacitly acknowledged them, I much less did not issue any related orders and did not receive any related reports. Furthermore, I likewise never received any complaints or allegations from residents as related to the aforementioned two charges." He also points out the stern and rigorous behaviors of his 6th Division, which could not allow for any infraction of discipline. Tani continues in his defense: (1) the 6th Division, under my command, encamped at Zhonghua Gate during the attack on Nanjing, and then moved in entirety to Wuhu on December 21, 1937. There was intense fighting in the area of Zhonghua Gate at the time. All residents vacated the area. Thus there was no object of massacre. Furthermore, no victims have been able to produce evidence on the unit numbers of Japanese soldiers committing atrocities; therefore the "Nakajima" unit, the "Suematsu" unit, and other units should be held responsible for the massacre incident. (2) The place and time of encampment of the unit under my command in Nanjing do not match with the time or the scope of atrocities in Nanjing. Furthermore, the unit under my command rigorously abided by military discipline. I can guarantee that they did not kill a single person. I learned of the Nanjing massacre incident only after the war had ended. Thus you see that I was completely unaware of the atrocities in Nanjing, and I believe firmly that my unit did not commit any criminal acts; therefore I do not bear any responsibility. (3) I have always advocated for friendship between China and Japan, and my thinking has always been stable. My position has always been: "Our key purpose toward our brother country China is that we should treat its residents as our own flesh and blood, that we should show tender care for them in all cases except when fighting necessitates otherwise, that we should treat prisoners well, and strictly forbid the mistake of looting and atrocities." Tani fervently denied being a radical militarist (Hu 2006, 463–472). In his defense Tani denied involvement in the Rape of Nanking and the veracity of evidence proffered by prosecutors.

In response to Tani's defense, the Ministry of Defense Tribunal conducted a provisional investigative session of the court outside the Zhonghua Gate, beginning on January 19, to investigate Tani's crimes, to strengthen collection of evidence on the crimes committed by Tani's forces. More than 600 people had reported crimes committed there by January 28. During the period "A mass grave of executed people was unearthed, and the bodies were examined. Also the China Film Studio, the Central Ministry of Propaganda Central Film Studio, and the International Propaganda Office were asked to dispatch personnel to take films to serve as conclusive evidence of this criminal's tacitly allowing the massacre of innocent civilians. Three to four such places were unearthed" (Hu 2006, 353). The military tribunal dispatched prosecutors to investigate the unearthed bodies of victims and had written appraisals made confirming that these people had died from stabbing, shooting, burning, and other external injuries.

10.3.2.2 The trial of war criminal Tani Hisao

On February 6, 1947, the Ministry of Defense Military Tribunal for Trying War Criminals convened the trial of Tani Hisao in the great hall of the *Lizhishe*. The public trial lasted three days. The first two days were mostly occupied by witness interrogation. The closed session for arguments began on February 9. In attendance were Chief Judge Shi Meiyu; deputy judges Song Shutong, Li Yuanqing, Ge Zhaotang, and Ye Zaizeng; prosecutor Chen Guangyu; defense attorneys Mei Zufang and Zhang Rende; as well as all important witnesses and English and Japanese interpreters.

The public trial began with Chief Judge Shi Meiyu asking the defendant's name, age, and birthplace. Then the accuser Chen Guangyu solemnly read the indictment into evidence, followed by a reading of its Japanese translation. As Tani's defense claimed that his troops were encamped and active only in the area around Zhonghua Gate, the indictment read at the public trial raised only evidence of atrocities committed in that area.

The indictment mentioned four classes of atrocities committed by the Japanese army: (1) damage of civilian property and arson; (2) willful looting of civilian property at all times and in all places; (3) raping of women, and gang rapes with a single woman being raped more than 30 times, and the bayoneting of all who resisted; and (4) massacre. The Japanese army conducted mass executions of innocent civilians in Xiaguan, Hanzhong Gate, and other places, first by sweeping with machine guns, then by bayonet charges, and finishing the job with fire. It was estimated that at least 400,000 Nanjing residents were killed in this massacre (Hu 2006, 375–376).

After the prosecutor had read his indictment into the record, Shi Meiyu declared that the defendant was charged with crimes against humanity and the crime of violating peace, per the descriptions of the indictment. Then the judges began asking the defendant questions regarding the Rape of Nanking, and asking for evidence of all of Tani's primary crimes.

When the judges asked Tani about his family background and the posts he had held, Tani answered: "I graduated from the Imperial Japanese Army Academy. I have served as an instructor in the Army University, a member of the General Staff Office, a military attaché to the Japanese embassy in the UK, chief of staff of the 3rd Division, and a participant in the Russo-Japanese War. At that time I was a platoon commander. I have been a military man my whole life, ultimately achieving the rank of Lieutenant General." The judges then asked: "In the opinion of the defendant, a high-ranking army officer and former military instructor, who should be held responsible for the war of invasion?" Tani answered: "I had nothing to do with the invasion movement. At the time, I was working in the General Staff Office, in charge of investigating conditions in Europe. During my time at the Army University, my efforts were concentrated on the study of the history of the Russo-Japanese War. I took no part whatsoever in national policy or invasion plans. As for China, my opinion is that China and Japan should be friendly. Both times I came to China were on orders. As a soldier, I had no choice but to obey orders. In the 17th year of the ROC, I led troops to defend our expatriates in Shandong. I think China and Japan are like brothers, and that it wasn't necessary to mobilize troops. During fierce combat, it is very difficult to avoid harm to civilians."

The judges asked: "How can the defendant guarantee that the troops under his command did not massacre civilians?" Tani answered: "I assert categorically that they did not." The judges gave a report on the number of bodies buried by the Nanjing Municipal Assembly to Tani for his inspection. Then the judges displayed on the rostrum eight photographs of bodies unearthed at Yuhuatai, determined by medical experts to have been women and children who had been shot, stabbed, and beaten. Tani said: "It is difficult to avoid casualties among civilians among fierce fighting. All the records on the Red Swastika Society report were of events that happened after my unit left Nanjing. As such there is no conclusive evidence, and the defendant cannot acknowledge these" (Hu 2006, 374–375).

Tani's trial continued on February 7. Chief Judge Shi Meiyu continued his interrogation of the defendant: "On what date did you lead your unit into the city? Was the wanton massacre an act of revenge for the fierce resistance put up by Chinese defenders?" Tani responded: "My unit formally entered the city on the 13. My troops began leaving Nanjing in waves on the 15, the 16, and the 17. On the 21 the defendant led the remaining small number of troops to Wuhu. Fighting was fierce in the outskirts of the city on the 12 and 13. There were no traces of habitation at Yuhuatai and Zhonghua Gate. The alleged wanton massacre at the time of our entry into the city was truly not possible and did not happen." Tani continued: "The unit I led stayed in Nanjing for a week. On the 17 we participated in the city entry ceremony. On the 18 I participated in the memorial to pacify the dead. I saw no bodies anywhere I went, and I am truly not lying. Other unit commanders can testify to this point." The judges asked: "The defendant once admitted that the Europeans and Americans in Nanjing had raised a protest with Commander Matsui, but the defendant does not admit that any massacre took place. If that's the case, what matter was raised in the protest lodged by the Europeans and Americans?" Tani responded: "This happened when I was detained in Sugamo Prison. Commander Matsui did tell me that Europeans and Americans had raised a protest due to their dissatisfaction with the behavior of the Japanese army, but he did not mention the behaviors of my unit" (Hu 2006, 376–377).

Then the judges asked former deputy speaker of the Nanjing Temporary Municipal Assembly Chen Yaodong to read a report on the course of the massacre. He read: "After its founding last year, the Nanjing Temporary Municipal Assembly received reports from the people on the great massacre that had taken place in Nanjing, and has calculated about 400,000 victims thereof... The area around Zhonghua Gate accounts for about one-third of these victims, that being more than 100,000. This was the area where the defendant's unit was stationed. This massacre was perpetrated by the defendant's unit. As such, our assembly asked the government, on behalf of the people, to have the defendant extradited to China to be punished in accordance with the law" (Hu 2006, 372).

Witness interrogations began next. One witness was Zhao Yongshun, whose head had suffered 11 knife strokes, who had had a finger cut off of his left hand, and whose neck had been repeatedly stabbed. Another was He Rongfu, who had been stabbed seven times and shot twice. Both had narrowly survived, and were direct victims of atrocities perpetrated by the Japanese army in Nanjing. Another witness was Cheng Jie, a nurse in the Kulou Hospital during the event, who also testified to atrocities she had witnessed committed by Japanese soldiers.

On February 8, arguments began. Tani asked to be allowed to make a statement, which he did: the descriptions given by witnesses these last days are mostly of crimes that happened in the area of the Zhonghua Gate. In truth, during the fierce fighting on the two days of the 12th and the 13th, that area was devoid of civilians. If there had been any residents left, the defendant would absolutely not have allowed for them to come to harm. The defendant has discovered that many of the crimes in investigation documents were committed by the Nakajima unit, and did not happen within his garrison area. I request that the court take note of this.

The judges then enumerated three incidents of concentrated massacre: (1) on December 16 of the twenty-sixth year of the ROC, 57,000 captured Chinese soldiers and refugees were driven by Japanese soldiers from Mufushan to the riverbank at Xiaguan, where they were mowed down with machine guns and then bayoneted before having their bodies thrown into the river. This was the massacre of the largest amount of people at one time; (2) on the 25th another 9,000-plus refugees were also killed at Xiaguan; (3) on the night of the 16th, more than 5,000 refugees were taken from the Overseas Chinese Hotel to the Zhonshan Wharf at Xiaguan, where they were mowed down by machine gun and thrown into the river. Survivors of all three events gave testimony. Also given into evidence were the *Tokyo Nichi Nichi Shimbun* articles on the contest between two soldiers to behead 100 people, with one having killed 105 and one having killed 106 within three days. The defendant was asked if he had heard of this event. Tani responded: this is the first time I have heard about what the judges have described. The concentrated massacres at Xiaguan were perpetrated by the navy or other units, and had nothing to do with me. My garrison area was devoid of people. I swear to the gods that nothing like that happened there. The judges are mistaken in their belief that I am a primary perpetrator of the great massacre. If the supreme commander of that time could be brought to this court for interrogation, there would be an explanation on the massacre and atrocities.

More witnesses were called. Victims of Japanese atrocities including Lian Tengfang, Xiang Zhenrong, Chen Fubao, Liu Zhenhan, Ding Hui, and others testified to their experiences. Tani claimed that those responsible were plainclothes Chinese soldiers and traitors who had taken advantage of circumstances to engage in looting, and that his unit was not responsible.

When it was mentioned that the defendant had allowed his units to steal clothes and antiques from resident Chen Sizhe and had forced women to offer services with their bodies while his troops were in Shijiazhuang and Baoding, Tani responded: at that time I was busy preparing to head south under orders from Commander Katsuki. Looting was not possible as we were on the march, and nor did it happen. The details on these allegations are fuzzy, and I have never heard of them before.

The trial for arguments began after the court investigations and interrogations were finished. First Prosecutor Chen Guangyu stood and described the facts of Tani's crimes to the court: "This prosecutor has shown how the killing, raping, burning, and looting in the case of the Rape of Nanking have been attested to by witnesses both Chinese and foreign, and how all forms of atrocities were committed in the defendant's garrison area… Although the defendant was encamped at the Zhonghua Gate for only a short time, 2,784 cases have been confirmed by the Temporary Municipal Assembly as having been his responsibility. The Rape of Nanking was a deliberate action on the part of the Japanese army. Nanjing is our country's capital, the seat of the greatest emotions in the War of Resistance. The Rape of Nanking was perpetrated by the Japanese army in an attempt to reduce our national spirit. Although the Rape of Nanking was large in entirety, the defendant was a participator therein, and thus should bear responsibility. The massacres perpetrated on the 12 and 13 were the most intense. At that time only the defendant's unit was present in Nanjing. There were no other units. As such, the defendant is the chief culprit for the massacre. We absolutely cannot allow him to shirk guilt. As for the evidential problems raised by the defendant, the cases investigated by the Temporary Municipal Assembly are all backed by evidence. The body-burying reports of the Red Swastika Society and Chongshantang, as well as pictures, films, and so on, are all conclusive proof and beyond any reproach. This mass of evidence is irrefutable and do not allow for shifting of blame or dressing up. We request that the court impose capital punishment in accordance with the law" (Hu 2006, 375–376).

Tani's defense began with this claim: the prosecutor's conclusions are entirely mistaken, as his initial assumption is my responsibility for crimes committed in the area of the Zhonghua Gate. He has intentionally fabricated records of factual basis. His charge that I perpetrated criminal acts of the great massacre is careless. I cannot acknowledge reports made incorrectly or one-sidedly. Tani claimed that many civilians who had been harmed by soldiers in other Japanese units were making use of this rare opportunity to claim their revenge, putting the guilt for crimes committed onto him. All the crimes testified to by witnesses over the preceding two days, he said, had not been committed by his unit. Tani went on: the court is basing its charges on conjecture, conjecture that cannot be construed as criminal conditions, and that such a trial was truly unprecedented in worldwide legal history. Only by subpoenaing victims and those who allegedly harmed them at the same time could any conclusions of guilt be made, and one-sided statements could not be construed as evidence for wrongdoing. He said he hoped he would receive a just sentence free from error (Hu 2006, 378–380).

The court briefly adjourned after Tani's trial ended on February 9 to continue investigating questions that had come up during the trial and collect more evidence. The argumentation trial was reconvened on February 25.

Many items of evidence were introduced to fill gaps after the reconvening on February 25. Military officer Guo Qi, witness to Japanese atrocities, and Ouyang Changlin, who had been responsible for the Red Swastika Society's body-burying activities, both came forward to testify. Also at Tani's request, the Japanese liaison officer Ogasawara Kiyoshi was called to testify in his defense. However the court refused Tani's request to call Staff Officer Shimono and Battalion Commander Sakai formerly under his command per Article 27 of the code of criminal procedure, as these two were suspected to be his accomplices in the crimes committed.

Ogasawara did testify. When asked by the judges if he had participated in the attack on Nanjing, Ogasawara said he had not. The judges asked: what post was the witness filling at the time of the attack on Nanjing? Ogasawara responded: I was a student in the Army University. The judges asked: How do you know about conditions in the Battle of Nanjing? Ogasawara responded: I studied about the history of the Battle of Nanjing in university, and learned even more after coming to China to serve as a staff officer. The judges asked: did Tani's unit enter the city on the 12th? Ogaswara responded: "There was fierce fighting on the city walls on the 12th. The city was entered on the 13th. The judges asked: was Tani's unit the first to enter the city? Ogasawara responded: per my personal research, the unit outside the Zhongshan Gate was the first to break into the city, at the Zhongshan Gate, on the 12th."

At this point Tani requested to make a statement, saying, more or less: "Those who participated in the fighting at that time can attest to whether my descriptions were true or not. Although Chinese witnesses have enumerated facts, they have not been able to identify a perpetrator. How can a just verdict thus be reached? Thus I hope that witnesses can be called from Tokyo." His request was refused by the chief judge: "The defendant has produced no beneficial evidence in the several months since his extradition to China. The witnesses the defendant wishes to call are all accomplices and suspects, and thus not qualified to testify" (Hu 2006, 382).

The court then called Guo Qi to testify on the atrocities he had witnessed in Nanjing at the time. Tani claimed that Guo had fabricated these events and was not credible.

Photographs documenting Japanese atrocities and letters of protest submitted by the International Committee to the Japanese embassy were entered into evidence. Tani claimed that the atrocities had been committed by main units, and that because his unit was stationed in Nanjing only for a few days and then left for Wuhu, they had no time to commit any atrocities, and said that he would say the same before all the gods of heaven and earth.

Tani later read a handwritten defense to the court, reading, more or less: "At the time we were at the Zhonghua Gate, the supreme commander of Japanese forces there was Yanagawa. In addition there were also the 114th Division and the 18th Division. The atrocities alleged here cannot have been committed by my unit, because I always kept my troops in check with rigorous military discipline. No incidents at all occurred in Wuhu, and our troops were on friendly terms with the locals. The Chinese witnesses who have testified in this trial harbor grudges against Japan and have thus pushed guilt for all incidents onto me. I was one of many unit commanders, and thus I should not bear guilt for all incidents. Furthermore, the evidence has been inconclusive, and no concrete facts have been demonstrated. They have gone so far as to shift events that happened in the Safety Zone to outside of the Zhonghua Gate. These are particularly not worthy of believing. I still hope that the court will subpoena those culpable for these injuries. I trust that Japanese soldiers will certainly make truthful representations. Without a meticulous investigation, the unfairness of this trial, based on unlawful and one-sided materials, is manifest. This will have been an unreasonable judgment unprecedented in world history. Most events testified to by witnesses in this trial happened outside the scope of my unit's garrison area. All those alleged to have happened in my garrison area were fabricated whole cloth. The court has made only hasty and rash investigations of evidence presented here; this trial has been a course of question and answers between the court and victims, and no more. If you truly wish to set a new precedent in the world for judgments, then I refuse to submit from the bottom of my heart. The only means to a just verdict would be for the court to call my witnesses to the stand before coming to conclusions. The prosecutor's claim that I bear full responsibility for the massacre is truly inappropriate. As I was only one of many unit commanders, how could I bear such great guilt?" (Hu 2006, 382–383).

The court allowed Tani to rest after he had read his statement. Then his defense attorney Mei Zufang began arguments: "In the indictment, the prosecutor seems to have leveled charges of crimes against peace and crimes against humanity, but the defendant is merely a lieutenant general, unqualified to participate in strategic planning. As for his coming to China as a soldier to fight, he did so on orders. This cannot constitute crimes against peace. The Rape of Nanking is an irrefutable fact. The question at present is whom to blame. Legal judgments should not be partial to popular sentiment. As such, the court should truly subpoena Shimono, Sakai, and the commander of the 114th Division to make a thorough investigation and get to the bottom of responsibility in this case" (Hu 2006, 383).

Prosecutor Chen Guangyu refuted the defense item by item, reminding the defendant that despite his support for China-Japan friendship, he had never spoken, written, or acted against the invasion of China. Furthermore, Cai Gongshi had been killed by Japanese soldiers in the Jinan incident. As for the defendant's brag about rigorous military discipline, everyone knew about the crimes perpetrated by the "Imperial Army," and the facts were beyond denying. Yes, soldiers do have to obey orders, but they should not accept erroneous orders. Chen found the defense to be entirely baseless and maintained charges of war crimes, against peace and against humanity, and upheld his call for capital punishment. The court ordered a recess and reconvened at 2:00 p.m. on March 3.

Arguments continued on March 3. Tani still denied all allegations. His defense claimed he witnessed Nanjing witnesses fleeing at the time. There was fierce fighting for two days in the area running from Yuhuatai to Zhonghua Gate. After the defendant led his troops in a landing at Hangzhou Bay, they found nine of ten houses unoccupied. His troops took shelter only in unoccupied houses and public buildings like schools and government organs. After arriving in Nanjing, the defendant visited all areas of Nanjing for inspections on the 17th, the day of the city entry ceremony, and the 18th, the day of memorials for the dead, and saw no residents. All stories of mass killings, raping of women, and arson were entirely fabricated. The defendant received no orders to keep the peace while in Nanjing, but rather received an order to move out to Wuhu. Guilt for atrocities should, ethically and legally speaking, be assigned to the garrison commander in charge of maintaining peace in the city on those days. The Chinese were basing their trial on erroneous facts denied in toto by the defendant. The defense again asked the court to summon Japanese witnesses proposed by the defendant, Supreme Commander Yangawa, as well as the staff officer and battalion commander, and other unit commanders for questioning, and only then could a fair trial take place. The defense also asked that the erroneous indictment be rescinded.

The defense went on: the defendant would not be genuinely convinced by a one-sided judgment. He hoped for a just judgment and that the sacred duty of trying war criminals would not be besmirched, lest the defendant be sacrificed for baseless allegations. In the future when those truly guilty are found out, it will be too late to regret, and another cloud will hang over prospects for China-Japan friendship. The defense continued: obeying orders is a soldier's lot. He had not come to China those two times because he wanted to. The dispatching of soldiers to Shandong had not prevented China's unification. The killing of Cai Gongshi by the defendant should not be judged as a crime against humanity, but an action ignoring humanity. To hold atrocities and non-atrocities at a par would be unprecedented in worldwide legal history.

At 5:30 p.m., Prosecutor Chen Guangyu stood and refuted Tani's defense, claiming that the defendant had repeatedly shirked guilt with empty diction. If Tani truly wanted China-Japan friendship, why had he led soldiers in an invasive war in China at the age when he could have retired? Why was there no paper order or other form of evidence confirming his so-called military discipline? As for his claim that all the evidence presented in court was fabricated, did he mean to claim that the investigations of the Temporary Municipal Assembly, the records of the foreigners in the Safety Zone, the articles about the murderous contest of the two officers in the *Tokyo Nichi Nichi Shimbun*, and the film taken during the Japanese occupation of the city were all fabricated? The evidence against the defendant was overwhelming, and there was no space for any defense of his willful crimes of the most extreme nature. He had insulted the court of the ROC and merited the death penalty. As the two Japanese witnesses he wished subpoenaed were all suspected accomplices, the request should be denied per the law (Hu 2006, 384–385).

After hearing Chen's arguments, Tani immediately refuted them: both of my trips to China were made on orders, not because I wanted to come, and as such I should not be charged with violating peace and with supporting the policy of invasion. The massacre was perpetrated by the main forces, and so the defendant should not be held liable for that either. As for the prosecutor's claim that the Chinese people in Nanjing were unwilling to leave their homes, this was particularly ludicrous in light of the hail of bullets falling on those homes at the time. The erroneous claims of the indictment laid crimes committed by other units onto Tani's head, and this was most regrettable. The prosecutor's claim that he had been an accomplice to atrocities was spurious per both the law and basic common sense. As for those who committed atrocities, such as those who broke into houses and murdered their occupants, the murderers themselves should be found, and their guilt should not be foisted onto any other person.

Chen went on to refute these claims as well, holding that it was a fact that the defendant had been a supporter of the invasion, and that if he had truly called for friendship between China and Japan, why had he not retired from the army? The Great Massacre, he claimed, was a joint effort, making Tani an accomplice. All evidence had been collected long before the defendant had been interrogated and was absolutely not fabricated. There had even been testimony of foreign witnesses, and that certainly was not one-sided evidence. As the witnesses the defendant wanted subpoenaed were suspected accomplices, they were not qualified to testify. After Chen had finished, Tani spoke again in his defense, again assigning guilt to other units and that if the courtroom conditions of that day were reported in Japan, the true criminals would certainly turn themselves in.

Tani's defense attorney spoke in his defense, asking that the court carefully investigate and process the positive and negative crimes raised in the indictment and in the prosecutor's judgment of the facts. Defense attorney Zhang Rende said: "The defendant is accused of participating in the invasion plot and in allowing troops under his command to engage in massacre, rape, and looting. We beseech the court to deliberate circumspectly and get to the bottom of the matter: were there other units at the time the Zhonghua Gate was entered? If the supreme responsible person and all those jointly responsible are not found out, but rather if the defendant takes the fall for them, this will be particularly inappropriate. Thus we continue to beseech the court to forcefully uphold justice, to avoid partiality, and to cautiously make the truth clear." The prosecutor again refuted this defense line by line, claiming that support of the invasion had already been established as a charge, and that the defendant's testimony had changed many times, demonstrating his guilty conscience and confirming that only the defendant's unit had entered the Zhonghua Gate.

In Tani's final defense, he stressed the following: (1) he could not disobey orders in his position; (2) there was a sharp distinction between his unit and Nakajima's, and his unit had not jointly engaged in massacre; (3) the conclusion about a premeditated massacre at Zhonghua Gate was incorrect; and (4) all those people harmed were harmed by other units.

At this point Chief Judge Shi Meiyu declared arguments closed and declared that a verdict would be read at 3:00 p.m. on March 10. Upon hearing the judge's motion to end the trial, Tani objected, saying that such a speedy verdict reached without calling more witnesses to lay factual foundations would be hard to believe (Hu 2006).

The entire process surrounding Tani's trial lasted about five months. The court collected over 4,000 pieces of evidence, took depositions from more than 500 witnesses, and had more than 80 witnesses testify in court, including victims and witnesses of atrocities, such as Commander of the Nanjing Instruction Corps Impedimentia Battalion Guo Qi, Director of the Nanjing Red Cross Society Dr. Xu Chuanyin, victim Li Xiuying, Cheng Jie of the Kulou Hospital, and other survivors like Zhao Yongshun. There were also foreign witnesses called, including Smythe and Bates of the International Committee and Ogasawara, the liaison officer called at Tani's request. Among evidence presented were the reports of crimes committed compiled by the Temporary Municipal Assembly, reports on bodies buried by the Red Cross Society, the bodies of victims unearthed near Zhonghua Gate and examined by court doctors, the documentary film recording Japanese atrocities and Chinese victims taken by John Magee, and films taken by Japanese soldiers themselves for later bragging rights at the site of the Xinjiekou massacre.

10.3.2.3 Judgment, sentencing, and execution of Tani Hisao

On March 10, 1947, the court issued a final verdict: "Tani Hisao is convicted of allowing subordinate troops to massacre prisoners and non-combatants, as well as engaging in rape, looting, and destruction of property during combat operations. He is sentenced to death" (Hu 2006, 388).

In format and contents the verdict read largely like the indictment, the only difference being clarification on some facts, particularly enhanced descriptions of the facts and evidence of crimes committed by Tani's unit in the area of the Zhonghua Gate, its area of responsibility. The verdict's main points include: (1) war crime facts: confirmation that the Rape of Nanking had been a premeditated massacre; enumeration of the times, places, and numbers killed in the primary concentrated massacres perpetrated by the Japanese army invading China; and enumerating the primary facts behind scattered atrocities committed by Tani's unit in its area of responsibility around the Zhonghua Gate; and (2) grounds of judgment: thoroughly listing facts of war crimes and legal bases for the court's judgment; confirming that the court had sufficient evidence to prove that the defendant Tani Hisao and all high-ranking officers leading the attack on Nanjing were jointly responsible for the commission of atrocities. The verdict reads: "This verdict is hereby made on the basis of the first part of Article 291 of the Code of Criminal Procedure; Article 4 Clause 2, Article 23 Clauses 3 and 7, Article 7, Article 28, Article 46, and Article 47 of the Hague Convention with Respect to Laws and Customs of War on Land; Article 2 and Article 3 of the Convention Relative to the Treatment of Prisoners of War; Article 1, Article 2 Clause 2, Article 3 Clauses 1, 4, 24, and 27, and Article 211 of the Regulations for the Trying of War Criminals; and Article 28, Article 55, the first part of Article 56, and Article 57 of the Criminal Code" (Hu 2006, 395).

The majority of evidence presented in the trial of Tani Hisao as well as the evidence cited in his verdict go to demonstrate that the Rape of Nanking perpetrated by the Japanese army invading China is a fact. The court also presented a great deal of evidence proving that war crimes had been committed near the Zhonghua Gate, truly confirming that egregious atrocities were committed in that area. There were, however, some problems in the court's evidence from the perspective of the overall chain of evidence, including the limitation of the court's investigation into atrocities committed by the 6th Division to the area near the Zhonghua Gate, when the truth is that the 6th Division also participated in the mass executions carried out on the shore of the Yangtze River. We clearly see from the evidence provided that Tani was lying when he claimed to have no knowledge of the Rape of Nanking and that his claim of issuing stern orders to his troops to commit no crimes had no legs to stand on. Tani Hisao bore irrefutable guilt for atrocities committed by the Japanese army in the attack and occupation of Nanjing, as he was one of the leaders of that attack.

The collection of evidence in Tani's trial presented certain difficulties to the court. Different from trials of Class A suspects, Class B and Class C crimes, "conventional war crimes," legally required that victims be able to identify those responsible for their injuries, but in practice this was very difficult to accomplish. On the basis of evidence collected, however, it was at least possible to confirm Tani's guilt for the war by negative omission.

On March 18, 1947, the Nanjing Military Tribunal sent copies of the verdict and the "application" from Tani's trial to the nationalist government chairman and the army chief of staff for their approval. Tani did not accept the verdict and submitted an appeal on March 18 and a follow-up appeal on March 24, writing his reasons for requesting a retrial. He made particular note of the fact that the verdict in his case "will cast a large shadow over future peace in the Eastern Sea and even on the more important friendship between China and Japan" (Hu 2006, 481).

On April 25, the Nanjing Military Tribunal received a response from the nationalist government: "In light of the fact that evidence has clearly proven that the defendant Tani Hisao allowed his troops to massacre prisoners and non-combatants, as well as to engage in rape, looting, and property destruction, we find no fault with the original verdict and its lawful imposition of the death penalty, and hereby grant the court's request. We reject the defendant's appeal for a retrial, as his reasons cited do not conform to the stipulations under Article 45 of the Army, Navy, and Air Force Trial Law. We hope that the sentence be carried out immediately" (Hu 2006, 455). The Nanjing Military Tribunal later posted this notice in the city: "As war criminal Tani Hisao... has been sentenced to death... at 10:00 a.m. on the 26 of this month, the prosecutor of this court will read out the name of the criminal Tani Hisao, verify his identity, and escort him to the execution ground at Yuhuatai, where the death penalty will be carried out in accordance with the law. In addition to closed reports, this fact is being urgently proclaimed for public knowledge. Be it proclaimed" (Hu 2006, 456). With the citizenry of the city waiting to witness his execution, on April 26 Tani Hisao was led out of the Ministry of Defense detention center and escorted to the execution ground at Yuhuatai. Ye Zaizeng recalls what happened next: "The authorization came down on April 25. Fearing that a long delay could lead to hitches, we posted notices that night and notified news agencies. The next day his sentence of execution by firing squad was carried out at Yuhuatai. City residents turned out en masse and were elated" (*Wuhan wanbao* August 20, 1994).

Judicial police escorted Tani to the execution ground at Yuhuatai, where the judge confirmed his identity and a prosecutor read out the order to carry out his sentence. Per custom and in accordance with the law, he was given the opportunity to speak his last words. He asked that a small bag containing his hair, fingernails, and a poem be delivered to his family in Tokyo. In the spirit of humanitarianism, the prosecutor acceded to this request. Then Tani signed the court record. With procedures for the execution out of the way, Chief Judge Shi Meiyu gave the order to carry out the sentence, and military police opened fire upon Tani.

10.3.3 The Trials of Mukai Toshiaki, Noda Tsuyoshi, and Tanaka Gunkichi

Mukai Toshiaki, Noda Tsuyoshi, and Tanaka Gunkichi were low-ranking Japanese officers who had directly participated in mass executions of prisoners and non-combatants during the Rape of Nanking. We have combined their trials together as the details thereof were highly similar.

Tanaka Gunkichi was born in Tokyo in 1905 and graduated from the Imperial Japanese Army Academy. In August 1937 he was with the Japanese army during its invasion of North China as a company commander in the 6th Division's 45th Regiment. During the Rape of Nanking, he was a Captain in Tani Hisao's division, and he used his saber "Sukehiro" to kill more than 300 civilians. Tanaka was not among those on the list of war criminals responsible for the Rape of Nanking, but in April 1947 the War Criminals Commission received a request from the Chinese delegation in Japan to extradite Tanaka to China as a war criminal. On May 14 the request to add him to the list of those to be tried in connection with the Rape of Nanking was approved. On May 18 he was extradited to Shanghai and held in the war criminals detention center before being moved to Nanjing on May 22. On December 12, the Nanjing War Crimes Tribunal began Tanaka's public trial for war crimes. On December 18, the Ministry of Defense Military Tribunal combined Tanaka's case with that of the two officers of the "contest to behead 100 people."

Mukai Toshiaki and Noda Tsuyoshi were responsible for the "contest to behead 100 people." Mukai, born in Yamaguchi Prefecture, was an artillery platoon leader in the Toyama Battalion of the Katagiri Regiment in the 6th Division in 1937. Noda Tsuyoshi, born in Kagoshima, was a platoon adjutant, likewise in the Toyama Battalion of the Katagiri Regiment in the 6th Division. During the attack on Nanjing in December 1937, the men had entered a murdering contest to see who could get to 150 kills first. The contest ended with a tally of 106 kills for Mukai and 105 kills for Noda. Their contest was reported on in the *Tokyo Nichi*

Nichi Shimbun, with pictures under the title "contest to behead 100 people." In October 1947, the two were extradited to Shanghai and held in the war criminals detention center before being moved to Nanjing on November 5. Their public trial began on December 18.

On December 18, 1947, the Nanjing War Crimes Tribunal publicly tried Noda, Mukai, and Tanaka. The chief judge was Shi Meiyu, with the other judges Li Yuanqing, Sun Jianzhong, Long Zhonghuang, and Zhang Kun. The prosecutor was Li Xuan. The first secretary was Shi Yong, and the defense attorneys were Cui Peijun, Xue Songqi, and Chen Siqing (Hu 2006, 494).

After the chief judge had asked and ascertained the ages and hometowns of the defendants, Prosecutor Li Xuan read the indictments for all three into the record. That done, the chief judge ordered Noda and Mukai to leave the court so that Tanaka could be questioned first. The chief judge asked: were you a part of Tani Hisao's unit during the attack on Nanjing in the 26th year of the ROC? Tanaka responded: yes. The chief judge continued: during the investigatory trial begun on October 28, you testified that you fought in the outskirts of Nanjing. Did you carry a sword named "Sukehiro" with you in that fighting (a picture was displayed to the court)? Tanaka responded: during the attack on Nanjing on December 12, I did carry this sword in fighting four kilometers southeast from the city. The chief judge asked: in the book *Imperial Soldiers*, author Yamanaka Minetaro wrote that you killed more than 300 people with your "beloved sword Sukehiro." The book also includes a photo of you in Nanjing from 10 years ago and another photo of you cutting off the head of a civilian with this sword. Were these 300 people killed inside or outside of the city? Tanaka responded: the book *Imperial Soldiers* was propaganda intended to paint me as a heroic fighter. The killing of 300 people was not a fact; it was imagined up by the author. It was not a fact. The photo you have just displayed contains bare feet, short-sleeved shirts, and straw hats. That demonstrates it was taken in summer and had nothing to do with the attack on Nanjing. Yes, I was part of Tani Hisao's unit, but you can ask all the gods of heaven and earth, and they will attest that I had nothing to do with the Rape of Nanking. The chief judge asked: so where was the victim in the photo killed? Tanaka responded: in Tongcheng, Hubei. I was carrying out orders of the regiment commander. The person being executed had destroyed Japanese equipment several times. After his arrest, he was sentenced to death and executed in accordance with the law (Hu 2006, 500).

Then Mukai and Noda were brought back for questioning. The chief judge first questioned Mukai: during the attack on Nanjing of December 12 of the 26th year of the ROC, you were serving as a captain in the Nakajima unit, correct? Mukai responded: I was an artillery platoon commander with the rank of Captain in the Nakajima unit at that time. The chief judge continued: at the foot of Purple Mountain you and Noda Tsuyoshi entered a murdering contest, with you killing 106 and Noda killing 105, correct? Mukai responded: it's not true. The chief judge asked: the *Tokyo Nichi Nichi Shimbun* published an article about murders as entertainment with photographs. This piece of evidence was mailed to this court by the International Military Tribunal in Tokyo. Do you dare to deny it? After taking a look at the evidence provided by the court, Mukai opened a map he had brought with him and responded: I had not been to Nanjing, nor to Jurong. I made it only as far as Wuxi, but then I was injured in combat at Danyang. In Wuxi I encountered a war reporter who spoke to me in a joking manner about describing my heroics in an extreme way in order to help me find a wife. I was interrogated by the International Military Tribunal last year about this very article, but they found it to be baseless and released me three days later. The *Tokyo Nichi Nichi Shimbun* article was entirely fictional and not based in fact. The judges then had the portion of H.J. Timperley's book *What War Means* about the contest. The defendant responded: I didn't hear about the article in the *Nichi Nichi Shimbun* until half a year after the fact (Hu 2006, 500–501).

Then the questioning of Noda began, with Noda denying that he had been to Nanjing or Jurong, claiming that he and Mukai had parted ways in Danyang and never saw each other again, and that the article in the *Tokyo Nichi Nichi Shimbun* was not factual.

After questioning had finished, the prosecutor stood and enumerated the facts about the killing of civilians by the three war criminals, asking the court to sentence them per the indictment. Then arguments began. Tanaka's defense regarding the photos of himself and his sword "Sukehiro" in the book *Imperial Soldiers* was that the people in the photo were wearing short-sleeves, meaning that it could not have been taken during the Rape of Nanking, which happened in winter. The prosecutor answered that it was entirely possible to remove one's jacket in the commission of brutal acts. Noda and Mukai both claimed that the article in the *Tokyo Nichi Nichi Shimbun* had been fictitious, that its author Asami had extolled their martial valor to win admiration among the women of Japan in the hopes that they would find wives. As such, the article's claims were not to be believed. Then Prosecutor Long Zhonghuang exhibited an article from December 1937 in the *Shanghai Evening Post and Mercury* also about the contest to behead 100 people and refuted their claims with reason: "During the Japanese War of Invasion, Japanese authorities were extremely concerned with control and censorship of all military news. The *Tokyo Nichi Nichi Shimbun* was an important media outlet in Japan. If there was no factual basis for the contest to behead 100 people reported in this paper, there would have been no reason to popularize the story about the two defendants using a gigantic headline all based on fiction. What's more, this court has proven the veracity of the news story published on the basis of the evidence already produced. It is not comparable to ordinary hearsay. This should naturally constitute the basis for a verdict. As for using the cruel, bestial act of a murder contest as an advertisement for wives, to win over the hearts of women, this is even more unprecedented in modern human history. Not one part of their defense is believable" (Hu 2006, 496–497). The defense attorney asked the court to subpoena the war reporter in order for fair judgment to be made.

We see from evidence provided by the accuser that primary evidence against the three war criminals had already been collected at the time their case was filed, and so not much supplementary investigative work was performed. Also, the core evidence against them came from Japanese publications. Although the three firmly denied the objectivity of the evidence against them, they were unable to produce any effective evidence in their defense or good cause for overturning the evidence against them. Even if the publications had been exaggerated, their basic truths were undeniable.

The court's final verdict was that Tanaka Gunkichi, Mukai Toshiaki, and Noda Tsuyoshi successively massacred prisoners and non-combatants during the war, with all sentenced to death. The written verdict contained facts of the war crimes committed, reasons for the verdict, and the laws upon which the verdict had been based.

The Nanjing War Crimes Tribunal then sent the verdict along with their written defense to the nationalist government for approval. On January 26, 1948, the nationalist chairman approved, writing: "The defendants Mukai Toshiaki, Noda Tsuyoshi, and Tanaka Gunkichi, committed joint successive massacres during the war; this is unequivocally demonstrated in their interrogations. Their original sentence of the death penalty is appropriate, and I approve it. As for the defendants' request for a retrial, the reason they cite does not conform to the stipulations made in all clauses of Article 45 of the Navy and Army Trial Law, and so their request is denied. Notify them in order. Prepare a report on the date of execution of their sentence for reference. Enclosed are the original verdict and defenses sent here" (Hu 2006, 502).

On January 27, 1948, large notices were posted at all intersections of major Nanjing thoroughfares, and Nanjing residents flocked to read them: "In light of the fact that the war criminals Mukai Toshiaki, Noda Tsuyoshi, and Tanaka Gunkichi committed joint, successive acts of massacring prisoners and non-combatants during the war, proven by conclusive evidence, they have been lawfully sentenced by this court to death. The verdict was sent to the Ministry of Defense Chief of the General Staff Chen and to the government chairman, who have approved the immediate carrying out of their sentences. So at noon on the 28 of this month, the prosecutor will retrieve the war criminals Mukai Toshiaki, Noda Tsuyoshi, and Tanaka Gunkichi, read their charges, identify them, and escort them to the execution ground at Yuhuatai for execution of their sentences, to serve as a clear warning to the world. In addition to submitting this report, the chairman wishes for this to be made public knowledge. Be it proclaimed" (Hu 2006, 503). On January 28 Mukai, Noda, and Tanaka were brought to the execution ground at Yuhuatai and killed by firing squad.

The "contest to behead 100 people" was a murdering competition between two Japanese soldiers that took place between Shanghai and Nanjing. The two "competitors" were executed for their game by the Nanjing War Crimes Tribunal after the war. Many in Japan have expressed that their trial was unjust, including their family members and members of the Japanese political right wing. Right-wingers think that the contest was fabricated by wartime media outlets and was not based in fact. Suzuki Akira's book *The Illusion of the Nanjing Massacre* is representative of the right-wing position. Cheng Zhaoqi wrote of their position: the so-called "evidence" produced by the right wing has not come close to shaking the facts of the "contest to behead 100 people." (Cheng Zhaoqi 2002b, n.p.).

In addition, in 2003, three family members of Sakai and Noda including Sakai Chie filed a defamation lawsuit in a Tokyo court against the *Asahi Shimbun*, the *Mainichi Shimbun*, and Honda Katsuichi of the Kashiwa Shobo publishing company, claiming that the articles had damaged the reputations of the deceased and their families. They demanded an apology, a halt to copyright infringements, and reparations. In August 2005, a local Tokyo court denied their request. One reason cited in the verdict was that the criminals themselves had admitted to the truth of the contest themselves. The family members then appealed their case to a higher court. In May 2006 the High Court of Tokyo denied their appeal and upheld the original verdict.

Outside of the Ministry of Defense War Crimes Tribunal in Nanjing, local tribunals around the country also tried a great quantity of cases. The nationalist government processed 2,200 war crimes cases, sentencing 145 to death and more than 400 to prison, the rest being found not guilty and returning home.

10.4 Public Participation in the Trials

The trials related to the Rape of Nanking received widespread attention after the war, and the public actively participated in all aspects, from reporting war criminals to helping collect evidence to the trials and executions of sentences. The social influence of these trials was expanded through media reports, public trials, and public showing of films on the trials. It is not difficult to surmise the real effect of reports in the media and court records on every level of the public. The trials allowed individual victims to heal wounds in their memories and also spread this effect widely, creating early collective memories about Japanese atrocities in Nanjing. Owing to the ideological influences of the Chinese Civil War and the Cold War, the social effects of the trials over the Rape of Nanking, particularly the relationship between the trials and collective memory, were either ignored or faded from memory. This has created a cognitive gap in the social effects of the Nanjing trials.

10.4.1 Collection of evidence and public participation

The trials of cases related to the Rape of Nanking by the Ministry of Defense War Crimes Tribunal in Nanjing were of greater significance locally – Nanjing being the site of the event – than the trials of other major Japanese war criminals like Sakai Takashi, Isogai Rensuke, and Takahashi Tan. The trying of cases related to the Rape of Nanking naturally resulted in more widespread public attention, making it very easy for the court to mobilize active public participation. This increased the efficiency of the work behind the trials and also greatly be expanded their social influence.

During the War the nationalist government had already established the War of Resistance Losses Investigation Commission and bodies for investigating Japanese crimes. Work in these areas was strengthened after the war to facilitate the trying of war criminals. Post-war evidence collection first began under the guidance of the Nanjing Municipal Enemy Crimes Investigation Commission. This commission, founded on November 7, 1945, was composed of 14 organs and groups, including: the Nanjing Municipal Government, the Capital Police Department, the KMT Nanjing Party Headquarters, the Nanjing Urban Military Police Command, the Military Commission Investigation and Statistics Bureau, the KMT Central Bureau of Investigation and Statistics, the Nanjing Branch of the Third Youth League, the Nanjing Trade Union, the Peasant Association, the Red Cross Society, the Chamber of Commerce, the Capital District Court, the Capital Medical Association, and the Bar Association. Chen Guangyu, the tribunal's lead prosecutor, was its convener (Biqiang and Liangqin 2006b, 1722). We see from its composition that the commission garnered widespread public participation. Its goal was to mobilize the greatest possible extent of governmental and public participation. The commission then began to investigate different aspects of crimes committed in Nanjing by the invading Japanese army per the different natures of its constituent members. For example, the Trade Union conducted investigations in factories, and the Chamber of Commerce investigated local businesses. All materials collected were compiled and sent to the commission for initial review, and then sent to the Capital Court for legal processing. The commission established the Rape of Nanking as a dedicated topic for the collection, compiling, and study of evidence.

On June 23, 1946, the Nanjing Temporary Municipal Assembly established the Rape of Nanking Enemy Crimes Investigation Commission to facilitate the work of trying Japanese war criminals being done by the IMTFE and the Ministry of Defense War Crimes Tribunal. This new commission was chaired by Temporary Municipal Assembly President Chen Yuguang, and all other assembly members were ex-officio members of the commission as well. The commission included a broad swath of society, with members also coming from the Military Police Command, the Red Cross Society, the Institute of International Studies, the Nanjing Muslim Association, the University of Nanking, refugee shelters, and other social groups, as well as some people who had stayed in Nanjing throughout the event. Managers of relevant organs and other prestigious persons were made advisers. The commission had a director and a deputy director to take charge of overall work, along with a secretary-general in charge of quotidian affairs. It also comprised groups for investigations, accounting, and compiling and writing. After its founding, the commission issued a notice to city residents asking for their support and cooperation in investigating war crimes (The Second Historical Archives of China and Nanjing Historical Archives 1981). The subjects of its investigations were primarily criminals, victims, facts of crimes, evidence, and so on related to the Rape of Nanking. This facilitated both the work performed by investigators and recollections of victims' families and conformed to the military tribunal's investigative rules on war crimes investigations. The commission established investigative groups in all administrative districts. The commission as a whole or sub-groups divided by industry collected evidence on crimes committed by the Japanese army during the Rape of Nanking. These were passed onto a review panel, which then passed materials it approved to the entire body of the assembly for final approval. The evidence was then passed to prosecutors in the Capital Court, who passed it on to the Ministry of Justice for processing. The commission issued "Questionnaire on Types of Crimes Committed by the Enemy in the Rape of Nanking," "Names and Addresses of Victims of the Rape of Nanking Who Can Testify," and "Casualty Figures for the Rape of Nanking, by Gender." The commission also collected a large quantity of photographs, newspapers, and other forms of evidence of Japanese atrocities. On November 11, 1946, the Rape of Nanking Enemy Crimes Investigation Commission handed its work over to the Nanjing Temporary Municipal Assembly. From its founding until the work hand-off, the commission filed 2,784 cases of enemy crimes, providing a great quantity of original materials and forceful evidence to both the IMTFE in Tokyo and the Nanjing War Crimes Tribunal (Hu 2006, 372).

In the investigative work of these cases, the commission organized and the municipal government pushed investigations at the level of every district, township, town, lane, *bao*, and *jia*, and police and grassroots government organs also cooperated at all levels. The commission established district investigation commissions in all 13 districts of Nanjing to be comprehensively responsible for collection, review, compiling statistics, and writing reports on all crimes committed by the invading Japanese army. District chiefs were in charge of directing these efforts, with overseers also dispatched by the commission. This was an instance of investigative work of large scale with scientific norms, legal significance, and participation from the whole people.

During the process, the degree of public participation in regions severely victimized was relatively high. For example, the 11th District, encompassing the area of the Zhonghua Gate, where Tani Hisao's unit had been stationed, was given great importance by the Ministry of Defense War Crimes Tribunal. District Chief Wu Xiaoqing headed the daily work of the district investigative commission, and the overseer from the overall commission was Shen Jiuxiang. There were 27 members of the district commission, divided into groups for investigations. Members included the chief and deputy chief of every town and township, the district representative, the district police chief, the chief of the district party group, the director of the district Three People's Principles Youth League, and the chief of the local military police battalion. After over a month of investigations, over 800 victims in the district were identified, from the towns and townships of Yuhua, Xijie, Tongji, Haixin, Fengtai, and Shande; we thus see the depth of investigations and the high degree of public participation (Biqiang and Liangqin 2006b, 1683–1685). As conditions in different districts and townships differed, as did the degree of population fluctuations and the degree to which a given area was damaged, the degree of enthusiasm for public participation and investigation results also differed. For example, very few investigative materials were produced in District 8, at Pukou, but a relatively larger quantity of materials was collected in the Tangshan District and District 7 at Xiaguan. This demonstrates that investigative conditions and conditions of social participation can roughly, objectively, reflect the degree to which a district suffered.

The work of reporting war criminals proceeded in tandem with evidence collection. Relevant organs of the nationalist government made multiple calls on the people of Nanjing to report war criminals, for example in this notice issued by Chiang Kai-shek on December 21, 1945 in his name as chairman: "To all my compatriots, all those who experienced the horrible disaster of the great massacre or violent oppression at the hands of the enemy puppet regime or any kind of injustice, I desire to know about all these matters in detail as well as the chief instigators of the massacre and oppression. I will be most happy to receive all reports from those who report what they witnessed from a responsibility stemming from a sense of justice" (Zhang, Biqiang, and Liangqin 2006, 2). An article in the *Shenbao* of January 6, 1946, declared that Chiang received 1,036 reports during his inspection of Nanjing. General Okamura Yasuji recalls: "After eight years of the chaos of war, those local civilians who had been ravaged by the Japanese army all came forward to report on the tyrannies of Japanese soldiers, and the number of those arrested grew by the day." The nationalist government originally reduced the scope of war crimes to the minimum possible, intending to punish only chief criminals, but the numbers of those arrested for war crimes grew quickly as people around the country filed reports. By May 1946, nearly 3,000 had been arrested (Inaba 1981, 136, 154). We thus see the high degree of public participation in the work of reporting war criminals.

In addition to preliminary evidence collection and reporting, the military tribunal also established investigative courts in areas that had suffered particularly badly to collect evidence and testimony from locals on the ground. On January 19, 1947, the military tribunal established such an investigative court in the district office outside the Zhonghua Gate to facilitate collection of evidence of war crimes committed by Tani Hisao's unit in that vicinity. The court called for people in that area who had experienced or witnessed Japanese killing, burning, raping, or looting or who were family members of deceased victims to make detailed reports to the court for further investigation. The social impact of this method was also pronounced. On the single day of January 28, 1947, more than 180 came forward to make reports to the court, which garnered more than 600 reports in total, providing a great deal of forceful evidence to the court (*Zhongyang ribao*, January 25, 1947).

In summary, active participation in the trial work of the military tribunal by social groups and individuals, particularly in the reporting of criminals and collection of evidence, increased the efficiency of the court's preliminary work. The active participation in this process by the public also demonstrated the high degree of public concern about cases related to the Rape of Nanking, and reflected the widespread social impact of the trials. More importantly, investigations of Japanese war crimes reawakened memories of Japanese atrocities among victims' families and survivors and gave the people of Nanjing an opportunity to denounce the Japanese army for atrocities committed in their city, giving them great emotional solace and satisfaction in the pursuit of justice.

10.4.2 Public attention and social propagation of the trials

The post-war trials of Japanese war criminals received widespread attention in China. The tribunals trying them strove for transparency and openness in their trials. There were many detailed reports on the trials in newspapers, on the radio, and in other forms of mass media. As information about the trials was disseminated, their social impact grew.

Media reports on the trials covered every aspect of the trials, especially those trials related to the Rape of Nanking. Major newspapers at the time including the *Zhongyang ribao*, the *Dagongbao*, the *Shenbao*, the *Xinwenbao*, and the *Jing wanbao* all ran detailed articles on the trials. The *Zhongyang ribao* alone published more than 30 articles on the trial of Tani Hisao, covering absolutely every aspect, including his being brought to Nanjing, his interrogation, his trial, his sentencing, and his execution; the articles came in all forms, from news reports to social commentary and special interviews. In addition to newspapers, the nationalist government made use of all forms of media to get the word out about the trials related to the Rape of Nanking. For example, in July 1946, the Nanjing Municipal Bureau of Social Affairs created seven slideshows on the Rape of Nanking to drive up public attention to the ongoing processes of investigation and trials. An order was given for the Nanjing Film and Drama Commercial Trade Union to play them in all movie theaters before every film being shown, to help get the message out (Biqiang and Liangqin 2006b, 1532).

The nationalist government ordered that all court arguments and sentencing be performed publicly, and this too helped expand the social impact of the trials. The tribunal expressly held public trials in the great hall of the *Lizhishe*, which could seat many, to allow a maximum of city residents to sit in. Nevertheless, seating was still not unlimited, and so the court installed a large loudspeaker outside the building to allow people gathered outside to hear what was happening on the inside. This allowed more people to clearly understand the nature of war crimes committed and to participate in the trials of these war criminals, thereby satisfying the emotional need of the masses to see justice done.

The impact of the public trials was enormous. Okamura Yasuji writes: "The public trial today is being made in consideration of its impact on the masses domestically and abroad. It is a large public exhibition" (Inaba 1981, 136). The trial of Tani Hisao attracted many foreign and domestic media outlets. Its effects were not limited to China alone, as it was paid great attention in both Japan and in the Allied countries. Not long after the trial, the Ministry of Defense War Crimes Tribunal asked the Central Film Company to make a newsreel out of Tani's case. The public exhibition of this film all over the country likewise greatly increased the social impact of the public trial (Hu 2006).

Public executions also received great attention. On March 18, 1947, the nationalist government approved the Nanjing War Crimes Tribunal's sentence of Tani Hisao. First, the tribunal posted this sign all over town: "As war criminal Tani Hisao... has been sentenced to death... at 10:00 a.m. on the 26 of this month, the prosecutor of this court will read out the name of the criminal Tani Hisao, verify his identity, and escort him to the execution ground at Yuhuatai, where the death penalty will be carried out in accordance with the law. In addition to closed reports, this fact is being urgently proclaimed for public knowledge. Be it proclaimed" (Hu 2006, 456). On April 26 at 10:00 a.m., the prosecutor escorted Tani from the tribunal's detention center, identified him, escorted him to the execution grounds at Yuhuatai, and supervised his lawful execution by firing squad. An article in the *Zhongyang ribao* of April 26, 1947, reads: "Oceans of city residents hearing the news thronged to the site, and 10,000 heads nodded approval. The sound of applause and jubilant screams exploded like fireworks and lingered in one's ears." We thus see how great the social impact of the public execution was, as well as the high degree of public participation in the event.

Of course, in historical retrospect we can see that many subjective factors limited the public influence of the trials related to the Rape of Nanking. On the one hand, owing to both the overall policy of leniency toward Japan and insufficient funding, on October 25, 1946, the War Criminals Commission resolved in a meeting to adopt a policy "generally of leniency and expediency" toward ordinary Japanese war criminals, excluding major criminals in places like Nanjing. The commission demanded that all criminals in custody be tried before the end of 1946: "Those without major crimes will not be indicted but will be released back to Japan" (Biqiang and Liangqin 2006a, 28–29). This policy imposed limitations on both trial operations and their results. On the other hand, from the perspective of the people, their difficulty in merely surviving affected the degree to which they could pay attention to the trials. One city resident from the time writes in an article in the *Shenbao* of January 6, 1946: "All letters from the people add up to 1,063... Most of these were asking for aid or for workers to be dispatched." On October 19, 1946, when the court inquired about Li Xiuying's written records, she asked that "the court apply for relief funds on our behalf, and also to Japan for reparations" (Jurong 2006, 221). So we see that ordinary citizens were more urgently concerned with resolving the difficulties in their lives than with seeing justice done to war criminals.

Nevertheless, we cannot write off the social impact of the trials related to the Rape of Nanking either. We see from sources at the time that the trials permeated deeply into the lives of some city residents. The practical difficulties faced by others did not completely erase the memories of harm done to them during the war, and they too paid attention to the trials.

10.4.3 Conflicts between popular sentiment and legal principles, and adjustments made

The Ministry of Defense War Crimes Tribunal tried Japanese war criminals in the very city where they had committed atrocities. Mei Ru'ao,[104] Chinese judicial delegate to the IMTFE in Tokyo, said the significance of trying Japanese war criminals in the countries where they had committed their crimes was: "By making this class of war criminal receive punishment locally, we can offer psychological and spiritual solace to locals for whom the memories of atrocities remain fresh" (Ru'ao 2005, 37). For the Chinese people who had suffered during the war, the trials of perpetrators of atrocities in Nanjing was a means of healing wounds suffered in the war. The trials were not, however, unprincipled venting of popular sentiment. During the trials attention had to be paid to both popular sentiment and legal principles, yet at times there were differences between government policy and popular sentiment. We can perceive the many aspects of popular sentiment at the time through both newspaper articles and legal records of the time, and going further we can understand the actual impact of the trials on society by studying popular perceptions of the trials.

Upon hearing the news of the Japanese surrender, people were immediately divided between the ecstasy of victory and their bitter memories: "Over the eight years of the War of Resistance, the hundreds of millions of Chinese people suffered so much and endured so many hardships. Everyone had a bloody score to settle with the invaders" (Zhang Yan 1995). This sentiment was shared by most people in the country. Nevertheless, the nationalist government's treatment of Japan after the war mostly abided by the principles announced in a radio address by Chiang Kai-shek: "not recalling past grievances," "broad love for humanity," and "repaying enmity with virtue." Chiang's hope was to establish foundations for eternal peace between China and Japan, and so he adopted a policy of leniency toward Japanese war criminals and not being a stickler for minor details, in order to finish the work of dealing with war criminals as quickly as possible (Qin 1982, 449). The people, however, were extremely proactive in reporting war criminals, and calls for punishing these criminals were loud and ubiquitous. Nearly 3,000 had been arrested as suspected war criminals by May

---

104 Known at the time as Mei Ju-ao (translator's note).

1946, and this goes to demonstrate the disparity between government policy and popular sentiment. It is easy to conclude that the nationalist government was under enormous pressure from public opinion in the issue of how to deal with war criminals.

One example is the government's request to extradite Matsui Iwane, the commander of the Central China Area Army during the Rape of Nanking and bearer of primary guilt for the event. His extradition became a focus of popular attention at the time. On July 26, 1946, the Nanjing Municipal Assembly's Rape of Nanking Crimes Investigation Commission resolved to ask the government to submit a written request to the IMTFE to extradite Matsui and other chief culprits of the Rape of Nanking to Nanjing for trial.

On July 29, 1946, the *Zhongyang ribao* published an article on the process of having Matsui and others extradited for trial in Nanjing. The commentary read, regarding the blood debt owed for the Rape of Nanking: "If we do not settle the score, or if the score is settled by the war crimes tribunal in Tokyo alone, and war criminals are not brought to Nanjing for trial, then there will be no way to resolve the anger of the dead for the injustice done to them." Despite the Japanese surrender, "we cannot go without a symbolic method for settling the score." The article posited that the best means for settling the score was to publicly try the chief culprits in the country where they had done harm, and to punish them openly. The article cites the following as its primary reasons: first, if the principal culprits of the Rape of Nanking were not punished before the residents of Nanjing, not only would it be impossible to placate the souls of the more than 250,000 people who died cruelly before their time was up, but the anger of their living relatives would also go unabated. Second, if the chief culprits were not tried in China by Chinese judges, then many soldiers and civilians would feel that China had not won any glory in the War of Resistance. Third, not every blood debt needed to be settled, but at least a symbolic means of reparation must be adopted: "If Matsui Iwane does not pay back the blood debt he incurred during the Rape of Nanking, then we will lack even a symbolic repayment of his debt. Without even a symbolic repayment, would we not be asking for even greater losses when other foreign countries see us as weak and do not fear us?" The article goes on: "The punishment of those chief criminals who committed crimes heinous before heaven will demonstrate that we are absolutely not a people who gladly suffer massacre at the hands of other peoples, and symbolize that we are absolutely not a state that does not directly punish key criminals."

As Matsui was a Class A suspect per the IMTFE Charter charged with having committed crimes against peace, he was supposed to be tried by the IMTFE itself, and it would have been inappropriate to extradite him to China for trial. Of course, the actual international impact of trying a major criminal like Matsui in Tokyo was going to be much greater than if he had been tried in China. The fervent calls from Nanjing social groups to have him extradited to China for trial were unreasonable and overly emotional to a certain extent, and the government of China was limited by the international framework in place, making it impossible for them to appease the people.

We can also glean some information about popular sentiment from the evidence collection and arguments of the trial of Tani Hisao. Most in the general public thought Tani deserved punishment for his crimes. One newspaper article from the *Shenbao* of February 12, 1947, reads: "Today the Ministry of Defense War Crimes Tribunal is going to try this great butcher, and the people of Nanjing should be elated with pride. Yet even if we hacked 10,000 Tani Hisaos to pieces, this would not suffice to redress his crimes." During his trial, the appeals raised by victims were most effective at demonstrating the true feelings of the people. For example, per a *Shenbao* article of February 8, 1947, when the chief judge asked a woman surnamed Zhang where her murdered husband was injured, her answer was: "You think I had a chance to see?" She continued: "I have great enmity for the Japs! I couldn't finish describing its depth if I talked for three days straight. My loss was too great." She went on to say that she had been raped by enemy soldiers and that she had seen her sister-in-law and a neighbor raped at the same time, both of them becoming ill as a result. Her tone of speech was heavy and pained, causing all in attendance to bristle with rage. We thus see that there was a certain degree of release for popular sentiment during the trial of Tani Hisao, and the government wanted to claim some victory for justice on this account to quell popular rage.

The execution of sentences passed against war criminals in the places where they had committed their crimes also provided great satisfaction to the people, and popular enthusiasm for participation was particularly high. Tribunals in some places paraded criminals through the streets on their way to execution to satisfy the local masses. Although this was extremely satisfying psychologically and spiritually to the gathered crowds, it was a clear deviation from national policies and legal principles regarding the treatment of war criminals. To this end, the Ministry of Defense sent this cable to all war crimes tribunals, reproduced in a *Shenbao* article of July 1, 1947: "The goal of punishing war criminals is to uphold principles of humanitarianism and justice and to maintain the prestige of international law, not to exact revenge... Thus it is henceforth forbidden for military tribunals anywhere in the country to parade war criminals before the masses prior to their execution by shooting. It is furthermore not permitted to use phrases related to revenge in any public pronouncements. For example it is inappropriate to use wording such as 'to bring satisfaction to people's hearts.'"

We thus see that there was a certain degree of disparity between popular sentiment and legal principles.

On the whole, most people in China did pay attention to the trials, but some civilians and victims remained aloof, lacking enthusiasm for participation. One the one hand this may have been the result of insufficient understanding of the significance of war crimes trials, and on the other hand, some people may have been more concerned with whether they could improve their plights or other practical matters. One report made by the Nanjing Municipal Assembly explains that since eight years had passed since the commission of Japanese atrocities: "There are many on whose behalf no explanations are given, because they died as victims, or their family members have moved on. For others, circumstances are different, and their enmity has abated, and they are not willing to reopen old wounds. For example, women belonging to higher-status families who were raped generally did not report on the rapes, but rather on killings only. Some other victims, not knowing the unit numbers of their aggressors, or because of great difficulties surviving, or because they knew that filling out survey forms would be of no avail in satisfying their appetite, adopted unconcerned attitudes and ignored visits by investigators" (The Second Historical Archives of China and Nanjing Historical Archives 1981, 556). Of course, there were other reasons, such as the need to keep wartime injuries buried in the past or the Chinese traditional view of accepting fate, for which victims often chose to avoid any issues related to atrocities that had occurred in wartime.

10.4.4 War crimes trials and formation of public memories

The entire course of war crimes trials related to the Rape of Nanking received wide attention across society. The trials allowed for the wounded memories of individuals to be addressed and served as the vehicle for wide-scale propagation of information on the event. This allowed for the wounded memories of victims to exceed the limitations of individual memories and become public memories, and this turned out to be one of the least visible but most profound social effects of these trials.[105] In recent years, study of public memories of wartime atrocities

---

[105] Maurice Halbwachs helps us differentiate between collective memory and social memory, holding that collective memory is contained to a particular group, and cannot be simply equated to a fixed social memory (see (Halbwachs n.d., 235). Paul Connerton writes: "To the extent that their memories of a society's past diverge, to that extent its members can share neither experiences nor assumptions" (Connerton n.d., 3). So when we analyze memories of the Rape of Nank-

has become a focus topic in academia.[106] However, most studies to date have focused on the wounded memories of survivors and on the public memories of the atrocities held by the following generation. Few studies have focused on the formation of public memories of wartime atrocities.

One researcher writes about the formation and arousal of public memories: "After the Rape of Nanking, the wounded memories of Nanjing residents, formed under the high pressure and terror of the rule of the Japanese army, were buried deep in their hearts. However, every year on Tomb Sweeping Day or on the memorial of the massacre, they recalled those unforgettable wounds in the simplest and most concealed manner. On August 15, 1945, when the surrender of Japan was announced, the long-repressed memories of wounds of Nanjing residents were finally released, and the people participated in the entire course of investigation and trials of criminals responsible for the Rape of Nanking with the greatest enthusiasm" (Zhang 2003, n.p.). We thus see that the post-war war crimes trials aroused the wounded memories of victims and provided all manner of conditions for wide dissemination of information about the event. The public investigations, reports submitted by city residents, and the reporting of criminals and provision of evidence all included descriptions of memories wounded by wartime atrocities. The wide-scale, simultaneous expression of similar memories allowed for the formation of public memories about the Rape of Nanking.

With the eruption of the civil war, however, as well as the subsequent fall of the KMT regime, New China did not preserve propagation of or education about the historical significance of the Nanjing trials. The new regime rebuilt public memories in line with its own political values: "The behavior of building public memories was accompanied at the same time by the behavior of forgetting" (Donglan 2004, 173). After the People's Republic of China was founded, memories of the Rape of Nanking were suppressed in the extreme under the theme of China-Japan friendship espoused by the new government and under the influence of extreme "leftist" thinking in the 1950s and 1960s, leading to fissures in public memories. Such fissures "damaged the framework formed by a sense of history, and obstructed the rebuilding of a new framework to serve the functions of the framework just destroyed" (Rüsen 2002, n.p.). It was only with the distortions of the event by the Japanese right wing in the 1980s that public memories of the Rape of Nanking were reawakened.

---

ing, we should recall that wounded memories are more the collective memories of victims, different from fixed social memories.
106 For more information from the primary studies done in this field, see Zhang (2003), Nie, chapter 10, "On Memory", in Sun and Liu (2005).

At the same time, it was only in the 1980s that academics began to focus on the post-war trials of Japanese war criminals by the nationalist government. There is a missing layer in public memories between these two times. The relationship between the Nanjing trials and the formation of public memories related to the Rape of Nanking was forgotten or overlooked, thereby creating a discrepancy in the understanding of the actual effects of the trials between people of that time and people who came later. So it is only through deeply studying the past that we today can see the effects of the trials related to the Rape of Nanking on society at the time and this important step in the formation of early memories about the event among the people of Nanjing.

10.5 Reflections on the Post-War Trials of Rape of Nanking Criminals

Of all Japanese war crimes cases tried in post-war China, those related to the Rape of Nanking were of the greatest historical significance. The Rape of Nanking was an important symbol of overall hardships and wounds suffered by the Chinese people, and is an outstanding case demonstrating the link between history and the present. Many works have been done on the positive significance of the Nanjing trials, and we agree with their essential points, but in this work we will reflect on the trials from a different angle, in an attempt to discover their shortcomings and the lessons they teach us today.

First, as discussed above, there were some shortcomings in the legal basis for the trying of war criminals by the nationalist government, that being the Regulations on Trying War Criminals. In particular, the lack of a charter for the Chinese tribunals affected the independence of their operations and their authoritativeness. These tribunals became the real platforms of Chiang Kai-shek's policy of "repaying enmity with virtue."

Second, there were some problems in the real operations of these tribunals. Okamura Yasuji recalls: "We weren't allowed to use Japanese lawyers, yet connections between officially-appointed layers and those detained were not close, leading to sloppy work and unfair judgments" (Inaba 1981, 136). In his request for appeal, Tani Hisao writes: "I hope that leaders of all units related to this case and witnesses from China and Japan be called, that a rigorous investigation be conducted, and that the truth be grasped, so that a new trial can be conducted on the basis of truth" (Yang 2006, 607–608). In their opinion, the trials were conducted on the basis of Chinese witnesses and Chinese-provided evidence alone, while witnesses and evidence proffered by defendants were ignored. The appointment of Chinese counsel for the defendants also greatly weakened their position, affecting the public image of guilty verdicts and the fairness of the tribunals. All historical materials testify to the guilt of both Okamura and Tani, but their verdicts of guilty needed to be founded on tight trial procedures and solid evidence. At the time in the Republic of China, however, there was a lack of understanding of such matters, and so these principles were not put fully into practice.

Third, the Ministry of Defense War Crimes Tribunal's trials of cases related to the Rape of Nanking were not complete. More than 83 Japanese were charged with crimes related to the event, of whom the tribunal could confirm the name, rank, and unit of 59. Twelve were division commanders or higher (Hu 2006, 54–57), but only one of these 12, Tani Hisao, was actually tried. In particular many responsible for atrocities committed in the primary urban area were never tried. Some, like Nakajima Kesago and Yanagawa Heisuke had died, and others were impossible to extradite, but these were not even tried in absentia in accordance with international precedent to determine their guilt in the war.

Fourth, as compared with abundant preparations made in establishing cases, the preparations made for concluding these cases were weak at every stage of the trials. The IMTFE gave separate verdicts in the case of chief culprit Matsui Iwane, the verdict titled "Nanjing Atrocities" being made independently of the guilty verdict for crimes against peace and giving specifics on the time and geographic scope of the Rape of Nanking, as well as the composition of the body of aggressors and the numbers of victims (Yang 2006, 607–608). The Ministry of Defense War Crimes Tribunal in Nanjing did not produce independent verdicts for the Rape of Nanking, but rather included it in entirety within Tani Hisao's overall verdict, which lacked rigorous differentiation between Tani's guilt for the Rape of Nanking and overall guilt for the event.

Why was this the case? The greatest inhibiting factors were probably the nationalist government's understanding of the trials related to the Rape of Nanking as well as their basic attitudes. Although the nationalist government attached great importance to the work of these trials, the highly political character of these trials negatively influenced their legal connotations. Few in the decision-making stratum of the Nationalist Government realized that these trials required norms and rigorous laws to establish their lawfulness. Ni Zhengyu recalls that the nationalist government "lacked true understanding and appraisals, thinking that the Japanese militarist invasion of China was manifestly true, and that the trials were nothing more than a formality. The victimized country did not need to produce clear evidence but could simply declare the guilt of war criminals" (Ru'ao 2005, 1). We thus see that the nationalist government did not attach sufficient importance to the trials and lacked initiative, leading to insufficient estimation of the complexity of the trials. Of course, there were also many practical difficulties to overcome. For example, there were very few judges in the country who deeply understood relevant laws, and collection of evidence and other materials was far from thorough. The most fundamental reason, however, was that the nationalist government viewed the trials as only one aspect of the handling of post-war Japan. They paid attention to only the domestic impact of the trials, and very little attention to the effects the trials would have on the aggressor nation of Japan. They blindly proclaimed their overall policy of leniency while ignoring problems in practical operations, in an attempt to be done with the trials as quickly as possible. All these factors prevented the trials related to the Rape of Nanking from achieving many goals.

When the nationalist government requested that the Allied Supreme Command extradite Japanese war criminals to China, the head of the Supreme Command Legal Section, Colonel Carpenter, had doubts about "whether Chinese courts could give Tani Hisao a fair trial, or even make it seem like a fair trial" (Ru'ao 2005, 301). Regardless of whether Carpenter was biased, his suspicion demonstrates that there were questions about the rigorousness of Chinese legal procedures and the fairness of trials conducted in China. There is a direct relationship between this issue and the lack of importance attached by the nationalist government to the early IMTFE trials of important criminals and subsequent exposure of this deficiency. The nationalist government later became aware of both shortcomings at the government level and some mishandling of affairs that consequently would lead to criticisms at the international level, and so remedial measures were taken, yet to little avail.

The Nationalist Government naturally realized that the deposition of witnesses in Japan, the extradition of war criminals from Japan, and all evidence collection in Japan would require cooperation from the Allied Supreme Command. Per general principles of international law and a resolution of the Far East Commission on the handling of Japanese war criminals, the Allied Supreme Command could not refuse any request for extradition of Class B and Class C suspects if requested by victim countries. Nevertheless, the Allied Supreme Command always had its own considerations in handling such affairs, and the nationalist government was not always given everything it asked for. Throughout the trials related to the Rape of Nanking, for example, a great number of requests for extradition were not carried out, the notable exception being that for Tani Hisao.

The pursuit of war guilt of Nazis by Jews and other victimized groups in Europe was never subjected to any "time limits" or conducted entirely through the government of Germany or any other country. The rule there was that once any Nazi having committed crimes against Jews was discovered, unless he had already been tried or extradited from his country of residence, special agents or even soldiers were dispatched to arrest him and bring him to Israel for trial. For example, the famous Nazi war criminal Otto Eichmann was arrested in Argentina by Israeli special agents and repatriated for trial (Xin 2006). The nationalist government subjectively lacked such a proactive mentality of seeking out criminals, as compared to European Jews and the subsequently founded state of Israel. Furthermore, the nationalist government lacked the practical conditions for pursuing war criminals owing to some of the aforementioned restrictive factors.

Renowned professor of peace studies Andrew Rigby writes: "After violence takes place, we enter a long process of conflict mitigation, at the end of which comes reconciliation, but reconciliation is not without its principles. There are two stages that come in between: justice and forgiveness. Justice must be established, and the ins and outs of what happened must be determined to explain the truth behind the violence. The perpetrator of violence must be shaken in his soul and sincerely repent. Only on this foundation can victims forgive the other party and bring about reconciliation." Forgiveness is not everything, however: "If forgiveness is stubbornly emphasized with no distinction made of facts, then the perpetrator of violence cannot receive a deserved punishment, and his soul will not be shaken at all, and thus justice cannot be established. If punishment is stubbornly emphasized, and enmity repaid with enmity, then we descend into a vicious cycle of hatred and revenge being taken on both sides" (Rigby 2003, 238).

Under the guiding principles of "repaying enmity with virtue" and "leniency and expediency" established for the trials by the nationalist government, the vast majority of war criminals – other than a handful given capital punishment for particularly heinous crimes – were given leniency without any principles being discussed or the truth of their cases explored. While establishing those guiding principles, the nationalist government also proposed: "Drafting punishment regulations that carry educational meaning, by changing the erroneous ideas and thinking of war criminals during their trials." The government also enumerated the essential points of this program of reeducation of Japanese war criminals: "(One) The erroneous nature of Japanese militarism. (Two) The guilt of Japanese militarists for inciting this war. (Three) That the Allies fought for justice and peace. (Four) The greatness of the Three Principles of the People and Chinese leaders. (Five) The United Nations Charter and democratic governing principles. (Six) Exposure of the fake concept of Japanese rule by divine right, to be replaced by true historical facts and the establishment of foundations for eternal peace between China and Japan and in the entire world achieved by planning for and attending to the self-evident truth of justice and friendly feelings between the peoples" (Qin 1981, 449). All of this big talk never got off of the written page, however, and none of it was put into practice. No Japanese war criminals were successfully reeducated, either in pre-trial detention or in prison. In the end, most detained war crimes suspects were handed to American military authorities in Japan on formality, and in 1950 most of these were released unconditionally, at which point the process of dealing with war criminals ended abruptly.

By comparison, the Communist Party of China's handling of Japanese war criminals after the founding of New China was much more successful. This process was composed of a combination of trials and reeducation, with emphasis on reeducation and trials as a secondary component; this balanced the relationship between justice and forgiveness and the relationship between aggressors and victims. The Fushun War Criminals Administrative Center is a typical case in war criminal reeducation. The war criminal reeducation program in New China gave Japanese war criminals more opportunities for participation and viewed Japanese war criminals as a positive entity in the process of reeducation, and not a passive object to be remade. The program laid particular emphasis on pushing Japanese war criminals to reflect on their crimes and making them aware of the criminal nature of their acts, so that they would be punished in their consciences. After a long process of reform, those war criminals who had acknowledged their crimes publicly declared their guilt on their own initiative at trials in Shenyang and Taiyuan in June 1956, and willingly accepted the courts' verdicts. All sentenced war criminals were released upon the end of their sentences by March 1964. These war criminals had basically all achieved deliverance by clearly separating their selves in the present from their selves with criminal histories, and many became staunch supporters of China-Japan friendship upon returning home.[107]

---

[107] For a detailed exploration of the CPC reformation of Japanese war criminals, see Zhang (n.d.).

11 The Rape of Nanking Cases in the International Military Tribunal for the Far East Trial Arguments and Their "Legacy". Based in a Study of Cross-examinations

In early 1938, American intelligence agencies deciphered a coded telegram sent by Japanese Foreign Minister Hirota Koki citing H.J. Timperley to Japanese diplomats in the U.S. The telegram mentioned atrocities committed by the Japanese army in Nanjing and its environs along with their scale: "Since return (to) Shanghai (a) few days ago I investigated reported atrocities committed by Japanese Army in Nanking and elsewhere. Verbal accounts (of) reliable eye-witnesses and letters from individuals whose credibility (is) beyond question afford convincing proof (that) Japanese Army behaved and (is) continuing (to) behave in (a) fashion reminiscent (of) Attila (and) his Huns. (Not) less than three hundred thousand Chinese civilians slaughtered, many cases (in) cold blood."[108] We thus see that the Rape of Nanking was not a secret at the time.

Eight years later, the United Nations International Military Tribunal for the Far East (IMTFE) tried 28 Class A Japanese war crimes suspects between May 1946 and November 1948, in what have become known to history as the "Tokyo trials." Owing to the importance of cases related to the Rape of Nanking, the IMTFE separated them into their own category. In the end, commander of the

---

[108] The original is stored in the National Archives II of the U.S. Mr. Ao Wang of the "Society for Maintaining the Truth of the History of the War of Resistance Against Japan" provided us with a digital copy. All parentheses and Chinese characters are contained in the original. All documents from the U.S. National Archives referenced in this chapter were personally reviewed by Professor Yang Xiaming and myself in the U.S. We used English language document numbers and search terms in our notes to facilitate follow-up research. Sun Zhaiwei thinks that this telegram "cannot be used as direct evidence that over 300,000 Chinese compatriots were killed during the Rape of Nanking during the Japanese invasion of China". However, the "special message" of Timperley contained in the telegram is still of great value to our study of Japanese atrocities in China and the Rape of Nanking. Sun goes on to note that Hirota did not "add any comments whatsoever refuting Timperley's contents" (Sun 2005, 272–273). I personally agree with Sun's general opinion of Hirota's telegram. For more research on the "Hirota telegram," see Yang (1998). We agree with Sun's assessment of the telegram. See also the letter of Timperley to Bates of March 28, 1938, referring to dispatches sent from British reporter Chancellor to London: "The foreign observer quoted in the first paragraph on that page is Father Jacquinot, who is quite certain that his figure of 300,000 Chinese civilian casualties is correct." *Timperley to Bates (March 28,1938)*, Rg 10, Box 4, Folder 65, Yale University Divinity School Library Special Collections.

Shanghai Expeditionary Army and the Central China Area Army General Matsui Iwane, who directly commanded the attack on Nanjing, was hanged for "dereliction of duty" during the Rape of Nanking. Japanese Foreign Minister Hirota Koki was also sentenced to death for crimes against peace and crimes related to the Rape of Nanking, but in this latter issue he was only found guilty by association. Muto Akira, chief of staff of the Shanghai Expeditionary Army at the time of the event, was also sentenced to death, but he was proclaimed not guilty of charges related to the Rape of Nanking. Hata Shunroku, who took up command of the Central China Area Army after Matsui had been relieved of his duties, was sentenced to life in prison for his crimes.

The Tokyo trials were not "one-sided trials by the victors." IMTFE trials were arranged based on the U.S. court system. Each defendant had one Japanese and one American defense attorney. Both prosecutors and the defense had the right to produce witnesses and evidence and to cross-examine the other's witnesses and make arguments against the other's evidence. As Mei Ru'ao, one of the 11 judges at the IMTFE and China's representative there, writes in the article "On the Trials of Tani Hisao and Matsui Iwane," both sides had completely equal rights and duties in the eyes of the court (Yang 2006, 622). From their beginning on February 24, 1947 until January 12, 1948, defense attorneys spent 187 days on arguments, 45% of which was used to defend their clients (Historical Research Association 1997, 381). Defendants and their defense attorneys employed all their skill to establish a chain of evidence related to the Rape of Nanking and come to conclusions regarding the event to influence the court's final verdict. Their efforts did not go entirely unrewarded, but they were unable to overturn the cases against them. Matsui's plea of not guilty never had a chance.

What defense was mounted in cases related to the Rape of Nanking? How did they confront witnesses and evidence put up by prosecutors? What do the witnesses they called and their own statements have to tell us? How did prosecutors reveal the mendacious nature of their statements? How effective was the self-defense of Matsui and others? These were the key factors in determining ultimate verdicts in the Tokyo trials. Answering these questions is one of our primary goals in this chapter.

The Japanese government acknowledged the rights of the Allies to put war criminals on trial once it unconditionally surrendered, accepting the terms of the Potsdam Declaration. It also recognized the verdicts of the Tokyo trials and other organizations of victorious nations in the Treaty of San Francisco. From the legal perspective, the cases related to the Rape of Nanking are final and binding. Since the 1970s and 1980s, right wing extremists[109] in Japan began denying and distorting the history of the Rape of Nanking in the 1980s, attempting to prove the unfounded nature of the Tokyo trials and the innocence of Matsui Iwane by dissecting the verdict in his case. In their attempt to overturn the "historical perspective of the Tokyo trials," they mean to undermine the entire history of the Rape of Nanking.

The Japanese right wing's postures are constantly changing, so much as to be alarming. Yet upon thorough investigation we see that the basic framework upon which they base their arguments is sophistry and shameless trickery. These people are cut from the same cloth as Matsui Iwane, other Japanese war criminals, and their defense attorneys. In fact, it is not an overstatement to claim that the defenses put up in the Tokyo trials are the fountainheads of Japanese right wing thought. So we must trace the issue to its source and deeply analyze defenses made in the Tokyo trials to refute guilt in the Rape of Nanking in order to destroy the bases upon which the Japanese right wing mounts its arguments, drastic measures but necessary in this case to reach our objectives. This is the other major goal of this chapter.

11.1 Cross-examination and Calling into Question Witnesses and Sworn Statements of the Prosecution

In cases related to the Rape of Nanking, the prosecution produced official documents from American, German, British, and Japanese governments, the documents of the Nanking Safety Zone, documents published during or shortly after the Rape of Nanking, diaries and correspondence of Westerners who lived through the event, Chinese documents – particularly those produced during the Nanjing trials – sworn statements from Chinese and foreign witnesses, depositions of Matsui Iwane, Muto Akira, and other defendants, and so on. The defense focused its attention on witnesses called by the prosecution and sworn statements read into evidence.

Witnesses called by the prosecution included: Dr. Robert O. Wilson of the Kulou Hospital in Nanjing, the only foreign surgeon in the city during the event and a member of the Nanjing branch of the International Red Cross Society; Professor Miner Searle Bates of the University of Nanking, American, chair-

---

[109] The Japanese "right wing" in the broad sense encompasses many groups, modes of thinking, and targets of attention. In this chapter we refer to the "Japanese right wing" as it is conventionally understood in China, particularly to refer to those groups that deny the Rape of Nanking either directly or in disguised form.

man of the University of Nanking Emergency Committee and member of the International Committee for the Nanking Safety Zone; and Pastor John G. Magee, American, chairman of the Nanjing branch of the International Red Cross Society during the event, and member of the International Committee. Chinese witnesses included Xu Chuanyin, Shang Deyi, Wu Changde, Chen Fubao, and Liang Tingfang. Japanese witnesses included Tada Hayao, Hashimoto Kingoro, Ito Nobufumi, and Tanaka Ryukichi.

During cross-examination of Robert Wilson, Okamoto Shoichi, defense attorney for Muta Akira, brought up the question of the population of Nanjing when it fell, which Wilson had addressed in his sworn statement (IMTFE no. 204). Wilson responded that the population had been over a million before the war, but that it fell precipitously to "less than half a million" when the Japanese took the city. When asked when this great drop in population had occurred, Wilson responded: "during the month of November and the first two weeks of December." The defense planned to make a breakthrough in the population issue, but Wilson's responses were airtight. Matsui's defense attorney Ito Kiyoshi changed tact, asking Wilson about a case he described in his statement, that of a Chinese woman raped by a Japanese soldier who exhibited symptoms of the second stage syphilis two months later. Ito said: "According to my observations – of course I am an amateur so they may not be correct – manifestations of the second stage of syphilis are not usually until after over three months have passed after infection. But is that correct?" Wilson, graduate of Princeton and Harvard Medical School, responded: "My observations are that any time from six weeks to three months the secondary rash may appear." Ito kept up: "Well, anyway, according to this book I cannot but conclude that since it takes over three months for the second stage to appear, that this woman could not have been infected by a Japanese soldier two months previously." Ito's strategy was to prove that if Wilson's testimony was wrong in part, it must also be wrong in entirety. Such tactics were prevalent throughout the defenses. Wilson, however, did not stand down when his opinions were questioned (Yang 2006, 51–53).

Chinese laws and courts during the republican era were very different from their American and British counterparts. The ensuing Chinese Civil War occupied the greater part of the energies of Chinese officials and civilians. Prosecution witnesses at the IMTFE, particularly Chinese witnesses, were not sufficiently prepared to give testimony. Defense attorneys, on the other hand, were well versed in the law, and had deeply coordinated their defense strategies prior to the trials, particularly by making thorough studies of American legal procedures and defense tricks. The traps they laid ended up causing great difficulties for prosecution witnesses.

Dr. Xu Chuanyin had received his PhD at the University of Illinois in the U.S., making his the highest level of education among all witnesses called. During the Rape of Nanking, Xu was on extremely close terms with the International Committee and the Red Cross. Like the foreign members of those committees, he also kept a great quantity of records on Japanese atrocities committed there. It was clear, however, that he was not prepared for cross-examination. Russia had an embassy in Nanjing located near the Drum Tower in the city center prior to the city's fall, but it was burned on January 1, 1938. There was another building, belonging to the Russian Legation, located at the Tianwang Temple in the outskirts of the city. Kanzaki Masayushi, defense attorney for Hata Shunroku, discovered that Xu had mistakenly called the embassy the office of the legation in his deposition (IMTFE no. 205), and asked Xu to describe the conditions of the fire at the "Russian Legation." After Xu had described in painstaking detail how Japanese soldiers had poured kerosene on the building and burned it, Kanzaki suddenly interrupted: "But, Mr. Witness, this Russian Legation was not burned. Are you dreaming in regard to this, or are you telling a lie?" This is when Xu realized his error and asked: "I wonder whether we are talking [about] the same thing. I am talking [about] the burning on January 1 of 1938... That Russian Legation were at the back, or near the lake but inside of the city." At this point Xu clarified both the time of the burning and the location of the building burned (Yang 2006, 64–66).

Court President Webb ordered that no more time be wasted on the matter, but by then Matsui's attorney Ito had realized how easily Xu could be lured into a trap. So he set a trap of his own, asking Xu: "Do you know that when the Chinese troops capture a city or flee from a city they usually cause wanton destruction, pillage and set fires." Xu responded: "And the Chinese soldiers were in the city before the Japanese came in and we all lived peacefully and quietly and no atrocities have been reported on such a large scale." He proceeded to say that large scale atrocities did happen under Japanese occupation. This is where Ito set his trap, citing the "Nanjing Incident" of 1927, very well known among the British and Americans, meaning it was not a random example. Ito said that Chinese soldiers at the time assaulted foreigners and also engaged in pillage and rape. Xu said he was aware that Chinese soldiers had committed misdeeds in Nanjing, but that no atrocities had occurred in the city before the Japanese occupation of late. He went on: "Then, after the Japanese came into the city and took the city, the Japanese did all those atrocities and the Japanese authorities did not try to stop them although the city was taken after a few days and several weeks... Also we in the International Committee, and also the Chinese, repeatedly complained to your consulate, to the head of the Special Service... but not a single proclamation has been made prohibiting the Japanese from raping, looting and killing, and also doing all sorts of things." Xu was clearly very worked up when responding to Ito's questions, because Webb had to issue him a warning, but his emotions did not prevent him from evading Ito's trap. Ito said that many fleeing Chinese soldiers disguised themselves as civilians or became plainclothes soldiers. Webb called this question a "trifle," but it is a matter of great importance to the Japanese right wing today. Xu answered: "we consider them as civilians before they gather themselves together in open resistance. If they are not, they are civilians same as we are here now." Ito finished saying: "As far as my competency is concerned, I cannot get the facts or the truth from this witness, and so I regret that I'll have to terminate here" (Yang 2006, 68–69).

Here we must address the looting by Chinese soldiers brought up by Ito. The truth is that some fleeing Chinese soldiers did steal clothes and other goods from civilians shortly before the city's fall to disguise themselves in case of the worst case scenario. American reporter Archibald T. Steel wrote about this (Zhang 2005, 294). During the attack on and fall of Nanjing, however, Chinese soldiers were fully occupied just staying alive. Western witnesses all attest that it was the Japanese army, who later claimed to possess rigorous discipline, that did the looting. Christian Kröger writes in a special report as treasurer of the International Committee: "Children's wagons were used, wheelbarrows, asses, mules, in short, anything that could be found. This organized robbery lasted for over two weeks, and even now no house is safe from some group on a 'commandeering expedition'" (Rabe EN, 144). Mention was also made of how "The refugee centers are hardest hit, because the endless stream of pillaging units think that they can extract more goods from them just by using force or violence" (Sheng 2005, 319–320). International Committee Chairman John Rabe writes: "Not a single shop in the city has escaped looting by the Japanese." Not even the property of citizens of Germany, Japan's ally, was safe. Rabe writes that 38 German-owned houses were either entirely or partially looted by Japanese soldiers. One Japanese soldier even presented Rabe with a receipt after stealing goods (Rabe CN, 313, 212–215, 157). *New York Times* reporter Tillman Durdin described the city this way: "Looting by the Japanese army has grown to the level of cleaning out the entire city. Nearly all properties have been entered by Japanese soldiers, who often steal whatever their hearts desire even under the eyes of their officers. Japanese soldiers even coerce Chinese to carry the goods that are being stolen." Durdin clearly notes that the Japanese conducted wide-scale searches of refugee camps, looting their property to the last. The property of Americans and nurses in the hospital was not spared either (Sheng 2005, 112). Most important of all, Japanese officers began assigning the bulk of blame for looting on Chinese soldiers right at the outset, yet Western witnesses refute their claim. Rabe writes in his diary entry of January 8, 1938: "We have not seen any 'looting Chinese.' Maybe there were a few on the nights of December 12 and 13, but the Chinese have simply been angels as compared with the looting of the Japanese soldiers beginning on December 13" (Rabe CN, 313). After performing an on-the-ground investigation, Kröger no longer suspected Chinese soldiers of looting. He notes in a letter to the German embassy of January 11, 1938 that German houses "were located on the route of retreat of Chinese forces, which retreated in a hurry down major thoroughfares on the nights of the 12 and 13. I once suspected that German houses had been damaged by Chinese soldiers during their retreat. But when I went to check them on the afternoon of December 13, I found that they were all perfectly undamaged, and that the Chinese forces had maintained excellent discipline" (Sheng 2005, 390). Of course, after Japanese soldiers had stolen the most valuable goods, some Chinese civilians took to looting. Scharffenberg of the German embassy writes in a report of January 28, 1938: "More and more Chinese are risking leaving the Safety Zone, but only during the day. Mostly it's just aged women and children, who happily loot while the Japanese watch. My impression is that the Japanese encourage this in order to shift the blame away from themselves" (Rabe EN, 161).

The sworn affidavits of Shang Deyi and Wu Changde (IMTFE nos. 206 and 207) were succinct and clear; attorneys for the defense chose not to cross-examine them. Chen Fubao went so far as to point out unit numbers and names of individual Japanese soldiers, but Ito seized on some problems in his grammar. Chen said: "On the second day the Japanese were in Nanking, 14 December, they took thirty-nine from the Refugee Area. They were civilian men. They examined them, and those that had a hat mark on the forehead, or a callous spot on hands caused by handling a gun, were brought to a little pond, and taken out on the other side. I and another were put to one side, and the Japanese used light machine guns to kill the rest. There were thirty-seven who were killed in this way, and I saw this. Most of the people were civilians. I am a resident of Nanking and knew a number of these people to be civilians in Nanking. I know one in particular was a policeman in Nanking." Ito asked: "In the third line of the Japanese text you say that thirty-nine men were dragged out and you say that they were all civilians. Then in the tenth line of the Japanese text you say that most of the people were civilians and then in the eleventh line you say that 'I know that a number of these people were civilians.' ... And then in the following line you say: 'I know one in particular was a policeman in Nanking.' In this way, concerning whether all these people were civilians or not, you have made four different statements. Which of these is true?" Chen answered: "They were all civilians in the refugees, all of these people." When Ito tried to continue the same line, Webb cut him off: "The answer is plain. He said they were all civilians. You must accept it." The stubborn Ito still planned to exploit Chen's low level of education, however. He asked most insidiously: "In the middle of your affidavit you say 'This was translated to me by Colonel Tu of the Chinese army and is correct.'" Ito was trying to imply that Chen's testimony had been guided by the Chinese interpreter Colonel Tu Yingguang, but what he had not expected was that Tu had done this intentionally, and that there was no problem with the grammar. He furthermore had not counted on Chen's memory being as sharp as it was: "As I told you, when I was relating the story to Colonel Morrow, this Colonel Tu was interpreting for us. That statement, dated 7th of April, is in the office. You can look into that statement" (Yang 2006, 76–77).

Defense attorneys were given fits by the testimony of Professor Bates, but they had no choice but to cross-examine him. Bates, having been educated in history at both Oxford and Yale, realized the significance of the Rape of Nanking as it was happening and began to document it. He expended great energy meticulously documenting Japanese atrocities and conditions in the city under Japanese occupation, even as he worked to provide relief to refugees. He sent reports to the American government and to friends in all walks of life. Bates's precisely worded answers to the questions of the prosecutor Sutton became a complete summary for the entire Rape of Nanking. In many subsequent IMTFE trials, his testimony was quoted, including his reference to Rabe's calculation that 20,000 cases of rape had occurred in the city during the first month of Japanese occupation. Even after defense attorneys Logan and Kleiman had come up empty-handed in their cross-examination of Bates, Koiso Kuniaki's defense attorney Shohei Sammoji Shohei had no choice but to question Bates on his accusations of murder, arson, rape, and looting leveled at Japanese soldiers. He attempted to pry a wedge of doubt into Bates's testimony about Chinese people being induced to use opium, heroin, and other narcotics by Japanese soldiers.

Shohei Sammoji's logic was that China was already the world's largest consumer of opium and heroin before the war, implying that substance abuse after the city's fall was nothing more than reemergence of an old disorder in China, and not at all the Japanese army's fault. Shohei Sammoji repeatedly plied Bates with questions about the opium problem at the global scale, trying to trick Bates into taking up his line of discourse. Bates did not take the bait. He said wisely and modestly: "I am willing to start on what little I know on this, but I have in no way posed as an historian of opium on a worldwide scale." Webb ruled: "The witness merely testified as to conditions in and about Nanking," and forbade Shohei Sammoji from asking about questions outside of that scope. Then Shohei Sammoji made a mistake he must have regretted immediately, asking: "Mr. Witness, you said earlier that after the Japanese Army entered Nanking in 1937 the Japanese sold opium officially. Was not this selling of opium officially to supervise the illicit trade in opium and also to treat opium patients?" This question was tantamount to an admission that Japan had openly sold opium; his point was to force Bates to admit that there were advantages to this practice. The court monitor immediately interjected that Bates's prior statement was "opium was sold in open market," and not "Japanese sold opium." Shohei Sammoji had made an unforced confession.

Today we can practically envision the tantalizing contrast between the cool-headed and brilliant Bates and Shohei Sammoji. Bates responded: "There was no remedial action of any kind in hospitals or treatment of addicts which I ever saw on the part of the public system in Nanking after the entry of the Japanese." He went on: "Not only in the general situation of the few years before 1937, but in the first few weeks and months after the Japanese came in, there was no apparent trade and no widespread consumption of opium. Then within a period of a few months the large system of public supply and sales, which I described, was built up." Bates's rigorous logic forced Shohei Sammoji to speak incoherently, asking: "Do you not know that in all Chinese families above the middle class they have medical dispensary for opium drinking? Do you not know that in all Chinese families above the middle class they have a room which is suitable for drinking opium – smoking opium?" Bates responded: "I do not know that. It is quite contrary to my experience and acquaintance of twenty-five years in Nanking." When Shohei Sammoji wanted to press the issue further, Webb cut him off: "That type of cross-examination is useless" (Yang 2006, 96–100).

The Japanese right wing of today attaches extreme importance to the cross-examination of Pastor John Magee by American defense attorney Brooks. Magee took the only known documentary film of the Rape of Nanking, displaying the horrors of the event that words cannot describe. As a member of the International Committee, he also took many records of atrocities committed against Chinese people in the Safety Zone. During his direct examination by prosecutor Sutton, he recalled Japanese atrocities committed in Nanjing in great detail, but for reasons we do not know, he did not show his film in court. During his cross-examination by Brooks, he honestly answered that he had "personally witnessed" only one person killed by the Japanese and only one person being raped. In the two other cases he mentioned in his direct examination, "the other two men were on the bed with the girl and ran off, and their father said they raped her before we got there." As for robbery, Magee again said he had personally witnessed only one instance. Brooks laid particular emphasis on whether Magee had personally witnessed these acts to highlight that he could not identify the identity of the perpetrators of these acts, and as such the Japanese embassy had no means of punishing those responsible despite the great volume of protests lodged.

Magee discussed an instance in which he, the Russian Podshivaloff, and Forster stopped a Japanese soldier from threatening a Chinese woman with a bayonet and ended up taking his bayonet. Brooks repeatedly asked Magee if he could identify the bayonet's owner or if he could identify the perpetrators of any of the acts he had described. Webb interjected to ask Brooks for the meaning of this line of questioning. Brooks answered: "If the Court please, I wanted to show that there was a difficulty for an investigator. If there was any punishment attempted it would be difficult to identify anyone. They just couldn't pick out any soldier and shoot him because someone else had committed an act, and this is what I was trying to bring out by his testimony." Clearly, Brooks had a duty to look after the interests of the defendants, but in his questioning he had not considered that Nanjing had been entirely overrun by the "bestial machinery" of the Japanese army at the time, that Magee and the other Westerners in the city at the time had to spend most of their time in relief work, and that investigations under those circumstances could obviously not proceed as they would in peacetime. Magee responded: "In your former question, there is no question but that the Japanese could have found out who those people were. We couldn't, but if they had their own men around the city they had their own means of identification. If there was any real desire to stop this thing they could have stopped it." Webb again intervened: "The further the cross-examination goes the less favorable it becomes for the defense" (Yang 2006, 125–131). Brooks had no way of knowing then that his unsuccessful cross-examination would be shamelessly exploited by the Japanese right wing of today.

Defense attorneys were extremely deft at cross-examinations of Japanese witnesses called by the prosecution; there was a great degree of "tacit agreement" between questions and answers. Tojo Hideki's defense attorney Kiyose Ichiro[110] was the first to cross-examine Tada Hayao, vice chief of the Japanese Army General Staff during the Rape of Nanking: "you state that you made plans for the campaign of Japanese armed forces capturing Shanghai, Nanking, and Hankow. May I understand that there was no single overall plan for the three campaigns?" Kiyose was implying that there was a great deal of randomness in the enormous campaign. Tada immediately confirmed: "There was no single overall plan. Each plan was made according to circumstances as they arose." Kiyose asked if the incidents that had happened in North China were the same, and Tada continued helping advance his logic: "The China Incident broke out unexpectedly and therefore there were no plans for it." After two objections from prosecutors, Webb ordered that questioning focus on fighting be-

---

110 Kiyose later served as speaker of the Japanese House of Representatives.

tween Shanghai and Nanjing. Tada said: "Nanking was made an object of occupation according to the plan that once the city was occupied a stage for peace negotiations could be commenced upon." Once Kiyose had induced Tada to declare that the occupation of Nanjing had been pursued toward the end of ultimate peace, he abruptly ended his questioning. Thereupon Hata Shunroku's attorney Kanzaki took up his cross, asking: "Were the duties of the Central China Expeditionary Forces the preservation of peace in the triangular area between Shanghai, Nanking, and Hangchou?" Hashimoto Kingoro's attorney Hayashi Itsuro got Tada to testify that the plan for the attacks on Shanghai, Nanjing, and Hankou had nothing to do with the Greater East Asia War (Yang 2006, 103–106).

Of course, not all Japanese witnesses called by the prosecution were of interest to the defense. Hashimoto Kingoro was a primary culprit in the sinking of the USS Panay and the damaging of the HMS Cricket, but he testified that these actions were carried out on orders from 10th Army Commander Yanagawa Heisuke. By then Yangawa had already died and therefore could not defend himself, a fact that made Hashimoto's defense attorneys giddy (Yang 2006, 106–107). Ito Nobufumi, a prosecution witness, had previously served as a Japanese "Minister-at-large" in China. He testified: "I received reports from members of the diplomatic corps and from press men that the Japanese Army at Nanking had committed various atrocities at this time." He further testified that he had reported this fact to the Japanese Ministry of Foreign Affairs. This testimony that the Japanese government was aware of the Rape of Nanking but did nothing to stop it became a target for attack in cross-examination. Matsui Iwane's defense attorney Ito Kiyoshi mistook Ito Nobufumi's statement of having been at Shanghai as having been at Nanjing. When Webb pointed out that his questioning was taking too long, and that he needed to reorder himself, Ito Kiyoshi lost control of his emotions and abruptly ended his examination. Webb called this a "senseless attitude" (Yang 2006, 109–110).

In summary, defense attorneys in these cases were able to get their way with trickery with some witnesses and in some testimony, but they were unable to overturn the main body of the prosecution's case (atrocities committed by the Japanese army in Nanjing), or to even create any substantial doubt against the mountain of evidence proffered by the prosecution (a thorough analysis of which is fodder for another essay). For example, after Kanzaki harped on about Xu Chuanyin's mistake in claiming that the Russian Legation had burned, the prosecution read a secret telegram from German Ambassador Trautmann to the German Foreign Office: "January 1, 1938, the temporary autonomous government has been established and raised a five-colored flag atop the ancient drum tower. At the same time, the Russian Embassy is a towering inferno" (Yang 2006, 355).

As the defense had no chance at "breaking" the prosecution's case, their only hope was to "establish" their own version of facts, by calling their own witnesses to prove that Matsui and the others had had nothing to do with the "alleged" Rape of Nanking.

11.2 Witnesses and Sworn Affidavits of the Defense, and Cross-examination by the Prosecution

Naturally, among defense witnesses there were: Nakayama Yasuto, Hidaka Shinrokuro, Tsukamoto Tokoji, Wakisaka Jiro, Nakazawa Mitsuo, Iinuma Mamoru, Sakakibara Kazue, Shimonaka Yasaburo, Nakatani Takeyo, Okada Takashi, Ishii Itaro, Aoki Takeshi, Tange Kunji, Mitsunami Teizo, Obata Minoya, Ouchi Yoshihide, Nishijima Takashi, Ogawa Sekijiro, Kokubu Shinhachiro, and others. Wakizaka Jiro and others were not cross-examined.

The defense hoped that the witnesses it called and the sworn affidavits it provided would demonstrate to the tribunal that the Japanese army units that attacked Nanjing had adhered to rigorous military discipline, that Matsui and his subordinates had ably commanded their forces, and that no such thing as the Rape of Nanking ever occurred. Nevertheless, not all defense witnesses helped advance this strategy. Some praised the Japanese army so excessively that their testimony was not worth refuting. Some others gave testimony full of holes, despite their best abilities to cover up the truth. There are mountains of materials that expose their lies, but here we opt against using any Chinese materials, only third-party and Japanese sources, particularly the diaries of Japanese soldiers who were on the ground during the event, to give no wiggle room to the Japanese right wing.

A great quantity of documents prove that the 16th Division was one of the primary units responsible for the Rape of Nanking, but its commander Nakajima Kesago died mysteriously not long after the war ended. Nakasawa Mitsuo was the division's chief of staff during the attack on and occupation of Nanjing. His affidavit artfully introduced some seeming "facts" to undermine the prosecution's case and confuse public opinion. The following is a summary of Nakasawa's affidavit: on December 8, 1937, right as Japanese forces were about to launch their attack on the city, he received orders from superiors to cease all actions. The orders noted that as Nanjing was China's capital, it should not be damaged during the victorious entry therein. The order was "to placate and treat the citizen kindly and to maintain order." Japanese units intentionally avoided using heavy weapons during fighting near the Sun Yat-sen Mausoleum and Ming Tombs to avoid damaging these relics. The Safety Zone fell within the 16th Division's garrison area, and was protected rigorously: "Not even officers could enter without special permission." Those Chinese soldiers identified "one by one through questioning and investigations" via the Japan-China Joint Commission were not massacred, but rather delivered to Japanese army headquarters. All the buildings burned outside of Nanjing were put to the torch by Chinese forces under a scorched earth policy. "It is rumored" that Chinese soldiers burned the houses inside the city. The Japanese army was extremely worried about fires, and frequently arrested young Chinese girls with "good citizen certificates" trying to set fires. There were some reports of looting by Japanese soldiers made to military police, but most looting was done by Chinese soldiers and refugees trying to squeeze into the Safety Zone. Matsui ordered that foreign interests and cultural organs be protected, but there were "all kinds of complications" when the Japanese army attacked areas they considered dangerous. There were absolutely no cases of organized rape, only "a few scattered offenses concerning discipline." The mass grave discovered by the Chinese near Zhongshan Gate and the Maqun neighborhood was a place where both sides incurred great casualties (IMTFE no. 3398).

Since the prosecution had already made a detailed description of the Rape of Nanking in its indictment, the strategy adopted by prosecution attorney Nolan in his cross-examination of Nakasawa was to expose key facts in the obviously evasive portions of his testimony. As expected, Nakasawa admitted that the Japanese army had stolen food and other daily consumption items. Naksaw had personally witnessed the burning of the Russian embassy on January 1, 1938. The "all kinds of complications" in his affidavit were exposed to be Japanese soldiers willfully violating foreign interests, and not Chinese hiding under protection of foreign flags. The "few scattered offenses concerning discipline" were exposed to be "attempts to enter refugee areas, attempts to cohabit with Chinese women" (Yang 2006, 453–545). All of this demonstrates that his prior statement about the Safety Zone receiving special protection was a lie.

Of course, owing to the constraints of the time, Nolan was unaware of the broader scope of crimes committed by the 16th Division. Its commander Nakajima Kesago writes in his diary: "We have basically not carried out a policy of taking prisoners, but have adopted the guiding policy of complete extermination. But since we're dealing with groups numbering in the thousands, the five thousands, and the tens of thousands, not even our arms are sufficient for timely removal... After the fact I learned that Sasaki's troops alone took care of nearly 15,000 people, and a single battalion leader holding Taiping Gate had taken care of 1,300. Another seven or eight thousand had been collectively finished near Xianhe

Gate... A large trench was necessary to handle the aforementioned seven or eight thousand, but it was hard to locate one. We've been scheduled to divide them into groups of one or two hundred to carry to appropriate places for disposal" (Wang 2005b, 280). Nakasawa's monstrous lie about "scattered offenses concerning discipline" was not pressed nearly hard enough on cross-examination, leaving great maneuvering room for the sophistry of the Japanese right wing of today.

If Nakasawa's affidavit and testimony revealed a few glimmers of truth about the Rape of Nanking, that of Artillery Second Lieutenant Osui Hiroshi created a previously unheard of rendition of events through a latticework of out and out lies. The following is a summary of his affidavit: on the night of December 13, 1937, he entered Nanjing through the south gate and saw the body of a Japanese soldier, full of bullet holes, tied to a tree. "At a glance I knew he was taken prisoner by Chinese soldiers and killed." As for Nanjing, "on the whole, this city was preserved entirely intact. I never saw a trace of burning." Osui said that a soldier from one company was arrested by military police, but when he went with the company commander to retrieve the soldier, the military police refused on orders from General Matsui because he had committed rape (IMTFE no. 3393). Osui's obviously mendacious testimony was intended to protect Matsui, yet Matsui had written, albeit circuitously, in his own diary entry of December 20, 1937: "For a time, looting and raping emerged among a small number of my soldiers, but this is difficult to avoid" (Wang 2005b, 153). Nolan did not bother to cross-examine Osui.

Refusing cross-examination is a courtroom technique used when a witness's statements violate common sense, intentionally distort the truth, or are disproven by a mountain of evidence, in the hope that the judge will exercise discretion and ignore the witness's testimony. Of course, a more decisive influence would have been made on the court if the prosecution had torn Osui's lies to pieces on cross-examination. We will now demonstrate the power of a good cross-examination.

Iinuma Mamoru was the chief of staff of the Shanghai Expeditionary Army during the attack on Nanjing. He knew exactly what happened there, but his affidavit was a dissertation on the highly disciplined nature of the Japanese army and Matsui's deep compassion and benevolence. The following is a summary of his affidavit: on entering the city, he obeyed Matsui's command to order all units except the 16th Division out to the east of the city and called for strict military discipline. He inspected Nanjing on the 16, 20, and 31 of December. Other than a few soldiers' bodies at Xiaguan, "I never saw anything like the alleged tens of thousands of massacred bodies, not even in my dreams." He confirms that there were fires, but none set intentionally. Someone reported "cases of looting and rape" to Matsui, but at the same time as Matsui apologized for this, he ordered that all such behaviors be prevented going forward: "All offenders were punished." The punishments were so harsh that the 16th Division lodged a protest about the legal division's procedures. As for the Safety Zone, he gave orders to the 16th Division, guarding it to "allow only passholders and military police in and out of the area." He had "no knowledge whatsoever" of the protests of the International Committee, and never sent any such reports to Matsui (IMTFE no. 3399. In his cross-examination, Nolan confirmed some of the truth about the rape and looting committed by the Japanese army (Yang 2006, 453–454). Iinuma's own diary revealed the rest of his testimony to be lies. Here we raise only a few examples for brevity's sake. In his diary entry of December 21, 1937, Iinuma writes: "When the Yamada Detachment of the Ogisu Unit killed 10,000 plus several thousand prisoners by bayonet in batches, there was a great disturbance among the prisoners as they were all led to the same place. Ultimately our forces mowed them down with machine guns, leading to the deaths of several of our own soldiers and officers" (Wang 2005b, 212–213). On December 30 he writes that Prince Asaka Yasuhiko, having taken command of the Shanghai Expeditionary Army, "assembled adjutants from all units encamped in Nanjing and the surrounding area and demanded that they make enforcement of military discipline stricter, particularly with regard to illegal behaviors toward foreign residences, and that Major General Sasaki (the garrison commander) raised his own requirements and items to pay attention to. Area Army Chief of Staff Nakayama came. I expressed regret to him and him alone for what happened to the foreign embassy and other behaviors in violation of discipline. The regret is truly difficult to bear" (Wang 2005b, 221–222). Iinuma, once finding the "regret difficult to bear," now categorically declared that the Japanese army had had nothing to do with the burning of the Soviet embassy. A later entry in his diary reads: "Major Oka (of the Special Service Organ) said that when he went to the Soviet Union, a corporal and two others of the Sasazawa Unit were inside requisitioning food." On the stand, Iinuma claimed ignorance of the protests lodged by foreigners living in Nanjing, but he writes in his diary entry of January 21, 1938 that the deputy chief of staff of the Japanese Army General Headquarters sent a cable reporting on Japanese soldiers abducting women from American property, stealing pianos from the University of Nanking, and other matters. The cable said that the Japanese Ministry of Foreign Affairs was unable to stop these behaviors, and that the occupying army was likewise incapable of restraining its troops, and that a military policeman escorting a secretary of the American embassy had arrested Japanese soldiers in the process of looting (Wang 2005b, 232–233). His diary entry of January 26 is even more shocking: "Report from Major Hongo tonight. At around 11:00 p.m. on the 24, Japanese soldiers went to a farming implements store operated by Americans, threatened its caretakers, and abducted two women, whom they raped. They left after about two hours. When he went to the building where the women claimed to have been raped, two Americans wished to enter the building to conduct an investigation, but it was where Company Commander Amano and several dozen soldiers were quartering. Amano had his men gather to beat up and drive off the Americans. Upon receiving report of the incident, Hongo rushed to the scene, but it was difficult to enter the company commander's room. There were three or four Chinese women in the abutting room. When he forced his way into Amano's room, he appeared to have been sleeping with a woman. A woman got up from the bed" (Wang 2005b, 235).

Iinuma and others put up persistent defenses, claiming that Matsui had called for rigorous discipline in the ranks. Their claims, however, hold no water whatsoever in consideration of the mountain of contradicting evidence, particularly from third parties and from Japanese soldiers and officials themselves. We have seen glimpses thus far, but there is much more. We have noticed that some defense witnesses flip the perspective to make Japanese war crimes "understandable." Sakakibara Kazue, in charge of logistics for the Shanghai Expeditionary Army, took a different tact. He testified that the Japanese army had indeed requisitioned food locally on its advance from Shanghai to Nanjing, because the Japanese army had no residents or authorities come forward to negotiate with them: "In such cases we had inevitably to use the commodities to be requisitioned without personal consent of the possessors, and we used to put up a poster on which the kind and amount of the goods requisitioned were described so that the possessors might be informed of the fact and come to the headquarters to receive their compensation." He never heard of any cases of food requisitioning in the Safety Zone. There were fires, but this was because: "Both troops of Chinese and Japanese practiced incendiarism in the front as a tactical method... There had been fires before our occupation of Nanking, but no conflagration after the fall of the city." As for "the wounded and the sick Chinese" in the Foreign Ministry building and other places, "we gave them rice and medical supplies" (IMTFE no. 3402). Despite the "novelty" of Sakakibara's testimony, he had difficulty glossing over the facts. Staff Offier Kisa Kiku, in charge of logistics for the 16th division, writes in his diary entry of December 1, 1937 about requisitioning in Benniu Town, Changzhou: "We looked everywhere in the villages for needed materials to requisition. We requisitioned 800 sacks of rice, 1,000 sacks of wheat, 100 sacks of granulated sugar, and two motorboats. We were extremely happy." He makes no mention of leaving any posters or any compensations of any kind (Wang 2005b, 323–324). In a letter to the American embassy of January 22, 1938, International Committee Secretary Smythe writes that the 15,000 sacks of rice and 19,000 sacks of flour the committee had prepared for refugee relief were all confiscated by the Japanese (Rabe CN, 404). As for fires, there is an overabundance of records documenting them. Rabe's diary entry of January 17, 1938 is just one example: "I'm afraid I grossly miscalculated when I wrote that a third of the city had been put to the torch by the Japanese. If the East City, which I've not visited to any extent, was dealt with in the same fashion, then more than half the city lies in ruins" (Rabe EN, 135). As for conditions in the hospitals, they had originally been under supervision of the Red Cross, but "we and the Red Cross were immediately prohibited from entering these hospitals once the city fell" (Rabe CN, 270). This demonstrates why more than half of the wounded in them died. Nolan chose not to cross-examine Sakakibara (Yang 2006, 469–470).

Okada Takashi, whose father was a friend of Matsui Iwane, served as a *shokutaku*[111] to the commander of the Shanghai Expeditionary Army, primarily in charge of using traitors and so-called "peace work." Clearly, he was called as a witness so to make use of his long-term "understanding" of Matsui's character. He recalled affectionately Matsui's great regret for the war and his extreme longing for peace, going out of his way to note one detail: "In compliance with the above request of the General, I went to Tachangchen and got a handful of soil from beneath the remains of a Chinese and a Japanese soldier and sent it to the General by airmail. Using the earth, he got a statue of Bodhisattva made, whose noble and beautiful figure can be seen today on the top of a hill near his house at Izusan, Atami. Furthermore, he had a temple built for the statue and dedicated the same temple to the souls of Chinese and Japanese war dead, and every morning, fine or foul, he climbed the hill to the sacred temple and offered prayers for the repose of the soldiers' souls and for eternal peace of Asia" (IMTFE no. 3409). Truly, Matsui long spoke of friendship between Japan and China, but this was a veneer intended to cover up his inherent bellicosity. At the outset of hostilities, Matsui wrote in his diary: "Japan-China relations are growing worse by the day. As I've written before, recent conditions have forced me to realize with great pain that we seem to have no choice but to force Chinese authorities to reflect by raising an iron hammer" (Wang 2005b, 22). Once appointed to command the Shanghai Expeditionary Army and the Central China Area Army, he strained his imagination to create a battle plan that meshed with the guiding plan issued to him from Tokyo: "Coordinate with the navy to crush the enemy's will to fight, and annihilate all enemy forces in the vicinity of Shanghai to seek an opportunity to end the war." His solution was to push the fight to Nanjing. Even after the capital was occupied, however, Mat-

---

[111] Japanese military office similar to chargé d'affaires (translator's note).

sui continued to push for an expansion of the war. His diary entry of February 4, 1938 discusses how he fervently advocated for an expansion of occupied areas in Zhejiang and Anhui (Wang 2005b, 175). All of Matsui's actions were thoroughly exposed by the prosecution. Okada's description of Matsui's dual personality did not, however, interest Nolan enough to explore. He declined any cross-examination. Nevertheless, the benevolent picture he painted of Matsui has become an important basis of arguments made by the Japanese right wing to this day.

Nakayama Yasuto was a staff officer in the Central China Area Army. In addition to reaffirming Matsui's orders for strict adherence to military discipline and no violations of the Safety Zone, he added a special twist. He realized that the prosecution had produced a great quantity of evidence in the form of correspondence recounting Japanese atrocities from foreigners in Nanjing to Japanese authorities; his tact was to claim that Matsui was completely unaware of atrocities committed by Japanese soldiers in the Safety Zone. He testified: "Later, we heard that the committee had protested against the atrocities committed by the Japanese soldiers within these quarters. However, their protest did not reach the Central China Area Army Headquarters. Even granting that there were such illegal acts there, protests had to be offered to the Japanese Consulate which was to establish communication with the Special Service Organs, and the Shanghai Expeditionary Army Headquarters which had had direct responsibility for guarding Nanking. Despite this, there were no informations form the Shanghai Expeditionary Army to the Central China Area Army and therefore neither Commander Matsui nor the Staff Department know the above-mentioned protests. Unlawful acts by the Japanese soldiers, if any, had to be investigated and court-martialed and only the results were to be reported to the Central China Area Army Headquarters" (IMTFE no. 2577). Nakayama's claims, which matched exceedingly well with those of Matsui himself, are now highly cherished by the Japanese right wing, yet they were immediately torn to shreds by a deft cross-examination.

During his cross, prosecution attorney Sutton first confirmed that Chinese forces had ceased to put up resistance on the morning of December 13, that Matsui entered the city on December 17 and stayed for a week, and that his headquarters was located only 1.5 kilometers from the nearest refugee camp. Sutton meant to imply that there was no way Matsui was unaware of atrocities being committed by his troops. Nakayama, taking the bait, admitted that Matsui's "first report was received immediately after the entry into Nanking. He went on to say that in addition to reports from the military police, Matsui received reports "from commanders and division commanders under General Matsui's command as well as from diplomatic organs." After giving some truthful answers, Nakayama began to prevaricate, claiming that reports of atrocities made by foreigners in Nanjing to Japanese diplomatic organs never made it to the Central China Area Army. Sutton interrupted to note that Matsui himself had already admitted to receiving such reports, from nowhere other than Japanese diplomatic organs in the city. Nakayama had no choice but to answer that he had not always been at Matsui's side. This was not the end of Nakayama's predicament, however. Sutton turned his questioning to the subject of Muto Akira, asking if Nakyama had ever heard from Muto about infringement of foreign interests by Japanese soldiers. Nakayama said no, but Sutton reminded him that Muto himself had already admitted that Central China Area Army Chief of Staff Tsukada Osamu had reported atrocities committed by Japanese soldiers to him. Nakayama had no choice but to repudiate the claim, saying he had heard of looting and rape, but no murder. Sutton immediately reminded Nakayama of his previous statement: "Later, we heard that the committee had protested against the atrocities committed by the Japanese soldiers within these quarters." This demonstrated that Nakayama's claim about rigorously protecting the Safety Zone was nothing but a lie. Nakayama had no choice but to admit one point: "one month after the fall of Nanking Major General Homma was sent to the Central China Expeditionary Forces, and I believe he complained to the Chief of Staff on whether military discipline had not been somewhat lax." He went on to say that the complaint "had nothing to do with such things as massacre or looting." Sutton clearly realized the impression that the judges would have of these explanations coming from Nakayama. Relevant sources claimed that more than 30,000 bodies of Chinese soldiers had been buried along the bank of the Yangtze, but Nakayama had claimed that 5,000 prisoners were released on the other side of the river. Sutton proceeded to ask Nakayama how many Chinese soldiers were "court-martialed before they were shot?" Nakayama said: "I do not remember the number." Sutton responded with acerbic wit: "Were not the only prisoners who ever reached the other side of the Yangtze the dead bodies of Chinese soldiers which drifted there after they had been shot by Japanese soldiers on the southern bank of that river?" Nakayama responded in a muddled fashion, saying that he firmly believed that all such prisoner releases were conducted "in line with this policy that all prisoners of war were released to the north side of the Yangtze River." Nakayama eventually said: "I believe that only history can give a fair appraisal of to what extent military discipline in the Japanese Army had been relaxed." Sutton's brilliant cross stirred Tribunal President Webb to ask Nakayama: "Well, you said this morning that some Chinese soldiers who hid in the safety zone were executed after a court-martial. What was the offense?" Webb then asked: "Was Matsui replaced by Hata as a punishment for the rape of Nanking?" (Yang 2006, 494–507). These questions seem to connote an initial judgment that was forming in the judge's mind. Clearly, these cross examinations deeply influenced the tribunal's decisions.

Prosecution cross-examinations ruthlessly exposed the lies of Nakayama and other defense witnesses. We see in them the great power of facts and logical argumentation; these cross-examinations are the fundamental reason that the Japanese right wing has made no substantial breakthrough against the results of the Tokyo trials despite decades of effort. What we wish to highlight here is that as the Westerners in the city were submitting great volumes of protests on atrocities to Japanese diplomatic organs, Matsui was in the city! In his diary entry of December 21, 1937, Rabe talks of meeting Matsui and shaking his hand:

> At 2 this afternoon all the Germans and Americans, etc., meaning the entire foreign colony, assemble outside Kulou Hospital and march in closed ranks to the Japanese embassy. There were 14 Americans, five Germans, two White Russians, and an Austrian. We presented a letter to the Japanese embassy, asking, for humanitarian reasons, that
>
> 1. the burning of large parts of the city be stopped;
> 2. an end be put at once to the disorderly conduct of the Japanese troops; and
> 3. whatever steps necessary be taken to restore law and order, so that our food and coal supplies can be replenished.
>
> All those demonstrating signed the letter. **We are introduced to Commandant Matsui, who shakes hands all round.**[112] I assume the role of spokesman at the Japanese embassy and explain to Mr. Tanaka that we infer that the city is to be burned down. Tanaka denies this with a smile, promises however to discuss the first two points in our letter with the military authorities. As to point 3, he refuses even to discuss it. The Japanese themselves are short on rations and are not interested in whether or not we can make do with our supplies (Rabe EN, 85).

Unlike Nakayama, Ishii Itaro, former director of the Japanese Bureau of East Asian Affairs, did not deny that atrocities had taken place in Nanjing. The key point of his testimony was that Japanese government and military officials took strong measures once they had been made aware of such. Ishii testified that he had received a report on atrocities committed by Japanese forces in Nanjing from acting Consul-General Fukui Makoto in Nanjing: "This telegraphic report was transmitted without delay to the Director of the Bureau of Military Affairs, War Office." The Foreign Minister was "alarmed and worried about the matter." A liaison conference was quickly held between the War Office, the Ministry of the Navy, and the Foreign Office. Ishii goes on: "I brought forward the

---

112 My bolding, to highlight what the author means to capture from this passage: that Matsui was there (translator's note).

problem of atrocities, reminded the Chief of the First Section, Bureau of Military Affairs, War Office, of the high ideal of 'Holy War' and the glorious name of 'Imperial Army', and demanded to take strict measures to stop them immediately. The military delegate shared my feelings and acceded to my demand. Shortly after that, a written report of the acting Consul-General at Nanking reached the Foreign Office. It was a detailed account, typewritten in English, of the atrocities of our troops, drawn up by an international security committee consisting of representatives of the residents of the third Powers in Nanking... I showed the report in question to the Chief of the First Section, Bureau of Military Affairs, War Office, and repeated my demand, in compliance with the will of the Foreign Minister. The military delegate told me in answer that a strict warning had already been given to the Nanking Occupation Force. From that time onward the cases of atrocities grew less. About the end of January of the following year, if I remember right, the central leaders of the Japanese Army sent a special envoy to the Occupation Force at Nanking. We learned afterwards that the envoy was Major-General Homma. After that, the atrocities in Nanking were exterminated... Foreign Minister Hirota, as I was told, requested War Minister Sugiyama to take strict measures promptly with regard to the case of Nanking atrocities. I was informed of the fact by Foreign Minister Hirota at that time. At the same time I made the same request to the competent authorities of the War Office" (IMTFE no. 3287).

Although he was a defense witness, Ishii's testimony exposed the mendacity of the testimony of many other defense witnesses. Matsui's defense attorney Ito took the first opportunity to attack Ishii's statements, claiming "in the War Office there is no such thing as First and Second Sections of the Military Affair's Bureau." Ishii responded: "It may have been a mistake on my part to use the words 'First Section,' but I remember the name and the person who held the office." Ishii then identified the person as Colonel Shibayama Kaneshiro. Ito's resorting to the tactic of "attacking a single point to crumble the entirety" of defense witnesses only demonstrates his panic.

Comyns Carr of the prosecution, not satisfied with Ishii's partial exposure of the truth, highlighted a key fact buttressing his testimony, noting that despite warnings to Japanese forces in Nanjing, "they [atrocities] continued as bad as ever down to the end of the first week in February, 1938." At this point the cross-examination hit crescendo. Carr asked Ishii if he had not received word from the Information Bureau that "the press of the world was full of denunciations of the rape of Nanking?" Ishii eventually answered: "Yes, I received reports each time such references were made." Ishii also eventually confirmed that these reports were circulated to members of the cabinet, including the foreign minister and vice foreign minister. He also testified that the foreign minister and army minister discussed the matter, but he heard of nobody punished for these atrocities.

Once his own witness had testified to the existence of the Rape of Nanking, Matsui's attorney Ito had no choice but to again start asking deeply obscure questions in an attempt to turn the court's attention: "I should like to found out from this witness the attitude which Foreign Minister Hirota actually took; whether he made this protest to the War Minister from his own independent position or merely because protests were received from foreign governments." Webb judged the line of question to be useless, and Ito did not continue. Then defense attorney Yamaoka began questioning Ishii: "when you received these reports from Nanking, did you and the Foreign Office accept them at face value?" Ishii said: "We considered most of them to be facts... although there were many points of duplication between reports received from foreign sources, which also included reports from the Chinese, and we believed that there may have been, or there may be, duplication in the reports received from both foreign sources and from Chinese sources. But we generally took these at face value." After a series of objections by Carr were sustained, Yamaoka, now flustered, tried a desperate gambit, asking: "Why could you not take any further steps than you did?" Ishii answered: "The Foreign Office could not do more than that from the standpoint of the authority in its possession" (Yang 2006, 509–520).

Defense witness Aoki Takeshi testified about the bombing of the USS Panay shortly before the Rape of Nanking, and shortly thereafter Mitsunami Teizo testified on the same matter. The incident spoke to the aggressiveness of the Japanese military, but it had been resolved long before these trials through diplomatic channels between Japan and the U.S. As such, the prosecution merely enumerated relevant investigation documents before terminating cross-examination. Obata Minoru was a former artillery captain under Admiral Hashimoto Kingoro and the person directly responsible for opening fire on the HMS Cricket. He was ridiculed by the prosecution for testifying that he could see a waving handkerchief 2,000 meters away but could not see an enormous ship on the horizon. His testimony had nothing to do with the Rape of Nanking, however (Yang 2006, 549). Tange Kunji testified on the "January 28 Incident." He was cross-examined, but his testimony did not touch on the Rape of Nanking.

Tsukamoto Koji (also known as Tsukamoto Hirotsugu), was a judiciary officer in the Shanghai Expeditionary Army and the 10th Army. As his title implied, he was in charge of handling disciplinary infractions and criminal behaviors within the ranks. He had clearly been well educated, but the grammatical mistakes of his testimony are on a par with those of Chen Fubao. He said:

> After the entry into Nanking, unlawful acts were committed by Japanese troops, and I remember having examined into these cases. I also remember Commander Matsui calling all officers together and telling them of the occurrence of such cases and giving strict orders for the maintenance of military discipline with the greatest severity.
>
> Four or five officers were involved in the above cases, and the rest were mostly trifling ones committed by privates. The kinds of crimes were chiefly plunder, rape, etc., while the cases of theft and injury were few, and the cases of death caused by those were few, to the best of my knowledge. I remember there were a few murder cases, but have no memory of having punished incendiaries or dealt with mass slaughter criminals. The above crimes were committed at different places, but a considerable number of cases, I believe, took place in the refugees' quarters in Nanking (IMTFE no. 2548).

Not only does he consider looting, rape, and murder to be "trifles," but he first claims that only "four or five officers were involved" and then claims "a considerable number of cases" took place in the Safety Zone. His evasive manner of speaking does not match at all with his claim that the cases were deeply investigated. On cross, Sutton immediately had to "refresh" Tsukamoto's memory. After some questioning, Tsukamoto admitted: "After the entry of troops into Nanking various incidents happened, including looting, rape, and so forth." Matsui consequently ordered that "the troops should be more careful so that those incidents would not happen again." Tsukamoto then denies having prosecuted any of the cases about which Sutton attempted to refresh his memory, holding steadfast to his claim that he had tried only 10 cases, and that he did not know who had given Matsui information about Japanese atrocities (Yang 2006, 534–539). Tsukamoto's claim that he had "no memory of having punished incendiaries or dealt with mass slaughter criminals" has become a great prop for Japanese right wing Rape of Nanking deniers.

Hidaka Shinrokuro was a counselor in the Japanese embassy in China during the Rape of Nanking, who was later promoted to consul-general in Shanghai in March 1938. He visited Nanjing four times between December 1937 and March 1938. In his affidavit he repeated the fairy tale about Matsui's great benevolence and unwillingness to harm the Chinese people. He makes the following claims in his sworn statement: after the fall of Nanjing, military and civil organs all absconded from the city, and nobody was left in charge. All foreign diplomats left the city after the fall, leaving nobody authorized to have talks with the Japanese army; all the foreign correspondents were desirous of getting out of Nanking to send telegrams to their main offices. Within a few days after the fall of Nanking, they all went to Shanghai, taking advantage of facilities offered by the Japanese Army in Nanking; only 200,000 people were in the city after the fall, and all of these entered the Safety Zone. Although the zone was not officially recognized, there was neither battle nor casualty in the area when Nanking was captured. Hidaka recounted the stealing of civilian clothes by Chinese soldiers as something he had observed personally. This demonstrates that he must have, while in Shanghai, heard of the reports made by Associated Press reporter McDaniel and *New York Times* reporter Abend (IMTFE no. 2537). Hidaka's statements were "completely at variance" with statements of all witnesses already cross-examined, including all witnesses who testified on Matsui's behalf; so prosecution attorney Tavenner declared it would be a "waste of time" to cross-examine Hidaka, also asking the tribunal to note the massive amount of pertinent evidence contrasting his accounts, particularly the interrogation records of Matsui and Muto. Tribunal President Webb did ask a few questions, however: "On January 1, 1938, the witness was deeply impressed to find that Matsui had not been aware of such facts, that is, misbehavior of the troops in Nanking, until that time. At what time did the witness hear about it and what did he hear?" Hidaka answered: "On January 1 I went to General Matsui's place to express felicitations on the new year, and on that occasion, in accordance with Japanese custom, proposed a toast to each other. At that time we were carrying on an informal conversation. There were no questions put by me to him, but in the course of the conversation General Matsui said there were some among his subordinates who did something very wrong and that it was extremely regrettable and unfortunate" (Xiaming 2006, 579–580). Hidaka's response was directly at odds with his long-winded affidavit, and more damning was that the two foreign reporters he mentioned had written reports on the Rape of Nanking. McDaniel wrote this in a wire of December 17, 1938 from Shanghai: "December 14 – Watched Japanese throughout city looting. Saw one Japanese soldier who had collected $3000 after demanding civilians in safety zone give up at bayonet point. Reached north gate through streets littered with dead humans and horses. Saw first Japanese car enter gate, skidding over smashed bodies... December 15 – Chinese thankfulness siege over became despairing disillusionment. Went with embassy servant to look for her mother. Found her body in ditch. Embassy office boy's brother also found dead. This afternoon saw some of the soldiers I helped disarm dragged from houses, shot and kicked into ditches. Tonight saw group of 500 civilian disarmed soldiers, hands tied, marched from safety zone by Japanese carrying Chinese 'big swords.' None return." (Sheng 2005, 117). Hallett Abend writes in a report from Shanghai of January 24, 1938 published in *The New York Times* the following day: "If we peel away the excuses put up by the Japanese such as military necessity, the naked truth that remains is the chaos and barbaric atrocities in Nanjing" (Sheng 2005, 152). Hidaka's testimony was obviously mendacious, but his rubbish is a treasure of today's Japanese right wing.

11.3 Testimony and Cross-Examination of Matsui Iwane

Matsui's affidavit and his answers on cross-examination were the primary components of his defense. The truth covered up by his lies and prevarications merit our careful examination.

There are 12 major points to Matsui's testimony, of which three focus on the macro perspective, while the rest constitute the basic supports to his defense. The following is a summary of his testimony: "The object and mission of the Expeditionary Force was to reinforce our naval force and protect the lives and property of our residents in and about Shanghai... I was always firm in the belief that the strife between Japan and China was a quarrel between brothers in the so-called "household of Asia" and that it was an unavoidable expedience for Japan to rescue by force the Japanese residents in China and to protect our endangered rights and interests. It was no different from an elder brother thrashing his young and recalcitrant brother after putting up with him for so long... I felt keenly that the above-mentioned Chinese attitude and the long and bitter fighting had estranged the Chinese Army and people in Central China from the Japanese Army, causing a hostile feeling between the two. Meanwhile, I instructed my officers and men to give protection and be decent to the Chinese people and to have a regard for the foreign rights and interests in China." The Shanghai Expeditionary Army and 10th Army were merged to form the Central China Area Army (note: Matsui commanded both the Central China Area Army and the Shanghai Expeditionary Army until December 7, when Prince Asaka took up command of the latter): "...its mission was to unify the command of these two units. However, since it had only seven staff officers, its duty was limited to giving operational instructions to the two headquarters, and had no authority to dispose the entire intendance and medical matters of the army in general... my relation with the officers and men in the field in regard to the command and supervision was entirely indirect... "Notwithstanding my scrupulous care in capturing Nanking, in the busy and unsettled condition at that time, it may have been some excited young officers and men committed unpleasant outrages, and it was to my great regret and sorry that I, afterward, heard rumors of such misconduct. At the time of capturing Nanking I was sick in bed at Soochow, some 140 miles away, and I was unaware of any such outrages committed contrary to my orders and received no reports thereof. After entering Nanking on 17 December, I heard about it for the first time, from the Commander of the Kempei[113] unit, and I, at once, ordered every unit to investigate thoroughly and pun-

---

113 Japanese for military police (translator's note).

ish the guilty men. However, it is a well-known fact that, in war time, the Chinese troops and some outlaws almost always commit acts of violence and looting by taking advantage of the confusion. Not a few of those crimes were committed by the Chinese troops and peoples when Nanking fell, so to hold the Japanese officers and men responsible for all the crimes is to distort the facts... In short, during my stay in Shanghai after the fall of Nanking until February, 1938, the only thing I heard was a rumor towards the end of December 1937 to the effect that there were some cases of illegal acts in Nanking but I had received no official report about such fact." Consequently, that constituted the first time he had heard of the alleged massacre in Nanjing. "It is possible that a great number of Chinese soldiers and civilians were killed or wounded by bombs, artillery shells and rifle bullets during the Nanking campaign, but I do not believe that there is a bit of truth in the prosecution's charge that there were cases of planned massacre in the fight of Nanking... In view of the situation at that time, it is needless to say that I did everything in my power to as commander of the Central China Area Army to take measures to prevent the occurrence of such unfortunate incidents to give severe punishment to the guilty and to compensate for the damages. However, it is to my great regret that the result was not perfect due to the hectic condition of wartime... Incidentally, when I heard the rumor of outrages in Nanking after returning to Shanghai, I issued a warning again to the officers and men then staying in Nanking by despatching especially one of my subordinate staff officers at the end of 1937 and ordered a thorough investigation of the rumor and quick punishment for anybody found to be guilty. However, up to the time of my leaving the post, I received no authentic reports concerning the above matters... After returning home I built a temple near my temporary abode at Mt. Izu, Atami and enshrined the souls of those victims of the two countries and prayed for the repose of their souls. Moreover, I built the statue of Kwannon, the Goddess of Mercy, in the precincts of the temple with the soil brought from the blood-covered fields of battle in the southern area of the Yangtze River. And with the help of her great virtues, I have been day and night offering, like other people who have faith in this Kwannon, prayers for the repose of all the souls of friends and foes, for the light of East Asia, and finally for the coming of the peace of this world" (IMTFE no. 3498).

There are great contradictions within Matsui's statements. For example, he commends himself for being very cautious in commanding the Central China Area Army and rigorously punishing disciplinary violations, yet he also claims that he was only in charge of headquarters and was not directly involved with troops or officers in the field to deflect guilt. He even claimed "no authority to dispose" of their actions. Upon arriving in Nanjing, he heard from the Kempei (military police) about crimes committed by "excited" soldiers, yet he extended blame for this onto the Chinese as well. He claimed to have punished the guilty, yet "the result was not perfect."

These contradictions all demonstrate that Matsui was aware of the Rape of Nanking, yet he used any available opportunity to avoid cognitive dissonance and push the blame elsewhere. For the prosecution, a veritable mountain of evidence from not only Chinese victims, but also from third party witnesses and the Japanese themselves, had already substantiated the truth of the event. Their cross-examination of Matsui proceeded on two lines: first, that Matsui had received reports on atrocities committed by his forces in Nanjing through multiple channels, and second, that Matsui had the ability and responsibility to take resolute actions to put a stop to them, but he did not. In the process, they deflated Matsui's lies about his love for peace.

Nolan begins his cross-examination nonchalantly, asking Matsui about the constant stream of reinforcements to the Shanghai Expeditionary Army and Central China Area Army. Then he suddenly pounced on Matsui's claim about wanting to prevent escalation of armed conflict, saying: "...before you left Tokyo in 1937 you made known your desire to push on to Nanking after the capture of Shanghai." It was well known that at the time of the "August 13 Incident," Japanese government and military authorities had limited the range of combat to Shanghai and its environs, and had no plans for the capture of Nanjing. It was rather the bellicose Matsui who had been the primary force pushing for escalation of hostilities and ultimately for officials in Tokyo to approve of the taking of Nanjing. Matsui gave the only response he could: "I did have such thoughts at the time." His claims of loving peace melted into oblivion.

Nolan then asked about Matsui's claim that "some officers and men may have committed unpleasant outrages in Nanking." Matsui, flustered, answered "Yes, I said so. I did not see it with my own eyes, but I knew of it from reports." When asked the nature of the outrages, Matsui answered: "Rape, looting, forceful seizure of materials." Nolan, realizing that Matsui had proffered new information, asked him where the reports had come from. Matsui answered: "From the gendarmery." Nolan kept up the press, asking if Matsui heard reports from anywhere else upon arriving in Nanjing. Matsui admitted to hearing "reports – stories of a similar nature from the consul." When asked why this was not included in his affidavit, Matsui prevaricated: "This is because I did not hear it as an official report. I merely heard stories from him about this in the course of our conversation." As we noted above, Matsui was in Nanjing at the time Westerners in the city were lodging protests with the Japanese embassy. In court, however, he claimed only to have heard "stories" about these reports. Nolan clearly recognized that he was going back on his own statements and brought up the testimony of Nakayama, who claimed that Matsui had received reports from "commanders and divisional commanders under your command, as well as from diplomatic organs." It is easy to envision Matsui's feelings in this predicament. He prevaricated again: "...the reports that I received from the commanders of the armies were in regard to the general war situation. I did not receive any reports from them on outrages." Nolan later brought up Tsukada's testimony, asking if Matsui had received reports on "outrages committed by troops under your command?" Matsui admitted: "He did report to me, saying that this was a report he had received from the gendarmery, from the Kempei."

After some back and forth, the prosecution exposed Matsui's lies about knowing nothing of atrocities committed in Nanjing. After the first cracks appeared, Matsui's entire defense crumbled like a house of cards.

Nolan asked Matsui: "Did the General Staff in Tokyo communicate with you regarding the conduct of your troops at Nanking?" A few answers later, without having "the conduct of your troops" even linked with atrocities, Matsui admitted: "I do remember, however, that towards the end of January, 1938, when Major-General Homma was sent to my headquarters from the General Staff, he said that the authorities in Tokyo were very worried about reports of outrages committed by Japanese soldiers in China." Here Matsui not only tells us that high authorities in the Japanese military leadership knew about the atrocities, but admitted to knowing of such through yet another channel. He had reports from "the gendarmery," from diplomatic organs, from journalists, from high-ranking officials, and now even from the General Staff. Matsui's lies about not knowing about the atrocities had no more legs to stand on.

Nolan, still not satisfied, continued: "But that was late in January. I am talking now about December and early in January. Did you receive any complaints from any government official, authority, or military authority in Tokyo regarding the conduct of your troops in Nanking?" When Matsui said no, Nolan took a step back, asking Matsui if he had not called his officers together "after the ceremony on the 17th of December." Matsui answered: "That was because on the previous 17th I had received, through my Chief of Staff, the report of the command of the gendarmery in regard to outrages committed by the Japanese soldiers, and I gathered these officers together for the purpose of giving them instructions directly." Again Matsui exposed his own lines by explaining the reason for the meeting on the 18th. Nolan then moved in for the kill: "How long did the atrocities go on in Nanking, General Matsui? Do you know?" Matsui instinctively told the truth: "I don't know. I think most of the outrages were committed immediately after our entry into Nanking." Nolan then resolved to prove to the court that Matsui knew that atrocities were committed over a long time. He asked Matsui if he heard the testimony of Magee and Bates about the atrocities lasting for six weeks after the city's fall. Matsui answered: "I heard their testimony given before this Tribunal, but I don't believe it." Nolan then fought fire with fire, demonstrating through his cross-examination that Consul-General Hidaka Shinrokuro in Shanghai had investigated "reports of foreigners" at Matsui's bidding! Matsui prevaricated that Hidaka had not reported to him, but he had no choice but to admit that the prosecution was already in possession of such reports!

As the prosecution had already accomplished its two main goals, Nolan finished by shoring up a few details. Colonel Morrow had interrogated Matsui at Sugamo Prison on March 8, 1946, at which time Morrow asked: "You stated that you went in to Nanking on the 17th. Did you see any bodies of dead civilians, women or children? Anything of that sort?" Matsui's answer was: "they had all been removed by this time. I saw a few dead Chinese soldiers near the west gate." Nolan asked: "Do I understand from that answer that the bodies of the dead civilians, women and children had been removed by the time you got there?" Matsui tried to lie, but unintentionally revealed his unconscious conclusion: "I don't know whether I said that or not, but if there had been, it was my idea then they should naturally have been removed from the scene." In his interrogation with Morrow, Matsui mentions having proactively sought meetings with *New York Times* reporter Hallett Abend. Matsui told Morrow: "I requested Mr. Abend to see me as I had heard rumors and I wished to quell these by putting the facts before Mr. Abend." Nolan asked him what rumors in particular, and Matsui responded: "...the many outrages alleged to have been committed by the Japanese troops in Nanking..." Nolan asked: "Who was alleging that these atrocities had been committed?" Matsui admitted that it was "one of my subordinates"! Then, over a painfully long stretch of cross-examination, Matsui again violated common sense by repeatedly declaring that maintaining "discipline and morals" among his ranks was not his responsibility, but was rather the responsibility of division commanders (Yang 2006, 409–422).

We see through Nolan's cross-examination that Matsui's role and responsibility in the Rape of Nanking is extremely clear, yet Matsui's lies about his ignorance of the event and the supreme discipline of his troops have caused much ink to be spilled by the modern Japanese right wing. So now we will examine both Matsui's own diary and those of other Japanese officers on the ground at the time to fully expose those lies.

Hata Shunroku, who replaced Matsui as commander of the Central China Expeditionary Army, writes in his diary entry of January 29, 1938: "As one chapter of the war in China came to a close, the expeditionary forces' military discipline gradually broke down. There seem to have been many instances of looting and rape, the kinds of things most taboo in the military." Consequently, "we will send the reserve forces summoned back to Japan and bring in active-duty troops to replace them. Also, General Matsui in Shanghai should be replaced by an active-duty officer..." (Weixing 2005, 1). Hata, in Japan at the time, heard a great deal about atrocities committed by Japanese troops in Nanjing; are we to believe that Matsui, who visited Nanjing personally several times, heard nothing? Hata, Matsui's successor, pointed out the relationship between relieving Matsui of his post and the Rape of Nanking. Truly, considering his many dashing victories, about which he brags not a little, why would he have been replaced for only a few isolated atrocities? Okamura Yasuji, commander of the 11th Division under the Central China Expeditionary Army, writes in his diary on July 13, 1938: "After arriving in the central China battlefield, it was only after hearing reports from Advance Staff Officer Miyazaki, Central China Expeditionary Army Staff Officer and Special Service Organ Section Chief Major General Harada, Hangzhou Bureau Chief Major Lieutenant Colonel Ogiwara, and others that I learned that mass executions of prisoners, committed by front line troops of the Expeditionary Army on pretense of supply difficulties, had become a bad habit. During the Battle of Nanjing, as many as 40,000 to 50,000 died in the great massacre. It was mostly these same people who engaged in looting and raping the people of Nanjing" (Weixing 2005, 6). His diary entry of September 26 tells us why there are so many photos of atrocities taken by Japanese soldiers themselves available for our viewing today: "What's worse is that they often took pictures of their cruel deeds to send home. This is truly the height of insanity..." (Wang 2005, 10)

Okamura's diary entries demonstrate that the Rape of Nanking was common knowledge among Japanese officers of the time, and that Chinese soldiers were the first target of massacres, followed by civilians. During an interrogation in Sugamo Prison on April 22, 1946, Muto Akira confessed: "In the Nanking Incident, the original plan was for two or three battalions to enter the city. Nevertheless, all units ended up entering the city, and that is what resulted in the great Nanjing catastrophe." He went on: "After atrocities in Nanking and Manila, I felt, as a member of the General Staff at the time, that Japanese military instruction was missing something." He then tried to explain: "The units that committed atrocities in Nanking and Manila were recruited in haste. They never received proper military instruction" (Yang 2006, 278). On the witness stand, he further confirmed that Matsui knew what really happened in the Rape of Nanking: "After the formal entry at Nanking was held on 17 December, General Matsui heard for the first time from Chief of Staff Tsukada that most of the units had entered the city against the commander's order; that, following the entry of the units, plunder and rape cases occurred" (IMTFE no. 255).

Despite conscious attempts to conceal the truth, glimmers of truth about the massacre shine out from Matsui's battlefield diary. In his diary entry of December 20, 1937, he writes that looting and rape were "difficult to avoid." This demonstrates that his admonitions to officers on December 18 about shoring up discipline were mere lip service. He writes in his entry of December 23: "I pray fervently that there will be no more unexpected problems in discipline." On December 29 he writes: "There have been more incidents of soldiers looting cars and other goods from foreign embassies in Nanjing. I am quite enraged by the stupid and crude actions of these soldiers. The prestige of the Imperial Army will be destroyed by such incidents. This is extremely regrettable." Here the use of the word "more" tells us that atrocities were happening on a recurring basis. The great heartache he expresses here demonstrates that this was not an isolated event. On January 13, 1938, Matsui writes: "Per a report from Expeditionary Army Staff Officer Onishi, he discovered through an on-the-ground investigation that all units in the area occupied by the Area Army have occupied and taken measures to protect local materials, and that this has become an obstacle to restoring local self-government." Here Matsui tactfully describes the emergence of "local requisitioning." Matsui gives a detailed account of his impression of 16th Division Commander Nakajima Kesago in his entry of January 24: "The 16th Division has come to Shanghai because it has been assigned to relieve a garrison in North China. Based on my observations of his speech and behavior, I find him to be a crude man. In particular, he amazingly exhibits a blasé attitude when discussing looting among his units. This is truly regrettable." Nakajima's 16th Division was one of the primary perpetrators of the Rape of Nanking. Does not Matsui give us a living picture of the man? Matsui's entry of February 6 demonstrates that he knew that the Rape of Nanking was still ongoing: "On the one hand, the slack discipline of the units has not been fully restored. On the other hand, some unit commanders have adopted over-lenient attitudes about disciplinary violations to avoid creating bad feelings. The propaganda and pacification work being actively performed by our troops are causing harm without bringing benefit, and running counter to our desired outcomes." Matsui was not alone in having these feelings. He continues in the same diary entry: "His Highness Prince Asaka has discussed problems with military discipline among the ranks, primarily with the 16th Division and its subordinate units." The military discipline problems he discusses in his diary are clearly very egregious. Matsui presided over a memorial ceremony held for dead Japanese officers and soldiers in Nanjing on February 7, but he writes that he "felt no pride of a victor whatsoever." Why? He continues in his diary: "Maybe I feel so sorrowful because of the various misdeeds of the units or the fraught progress in the work of building a local autonomous regime since our occupation of Nanjing" (Weixing 2005b, 153, 154, 156, 163, 168, 175–176).

The "Summary of Matsui Iwane's Diary Entries on the China Incident" that was later put together constitutes something of a confession for the Rape of

Nanking. He lists out "Incidents of Atrocities and Looting by My Army" as an independent portion, with much more detailed and candid records on the Rape of Nanking. He writes that he demanded stricter military discipline before he entered the city, but "what I had not expected was that my troops committed a great number of atrocities and looting incidents when they entered the city. These incidents greatly damaged the prestige and benevolent image of the Imperial Army." Matsui goes on to analyze the reasons that these atrocities occurred: "1. My forces were constantly engaged in ruthless, bitter fighting from the moment they landed at Shanghai. This fighting created intense feelings of enmity toward enemy forces on the part of my troops. 2. During the intense and rapid pursuit of the enemy, my forces did not receive prompt resupply of provisions and other materiel." Think about that for a second: why would Matsui expose himself to criticism by analyzing the reasons for these atrocities unless he was sure they had occurred? After analyzing the reasons, he admits: "I am at fault, because I did not maintain thorough control over unit commanders from the outset." Matsui's frankness here is extremely important. First, it demonstrates that it was precisely Matsui's leniency that allowed for competitive atrocities to be committed by the units under his command. Second, it demonstrates that Matsui's courtroom claims about not having the authority to control his subordinate units were lies. Third, it demonstrates that Matsui could have controlled these units but took no forceful measures to do so. In what reads like an appendix to the IMFTE verdict, Matsui writes: "These bad deeds (committed by the Japanese army) all occurred during chaotic fighting; consequently, it was impossible to try all the instigators for their misdeeds… What's more, I specially launched a rigorous investigation into the looting behavior of the troops after their entry into Nanjing, and took all compensatory measures possible. Particularly when it came to the looting of officials and civilians of various other countries, our diplomats became involved and handled these issues as amicably as possible. Nevertheless, as for the lives and property lost by foreign parties as a result of fighting, all we can say is that we had no alternative" (Weixing 2005b, 193–195).

In summary, there was a well-established clear relationship between the Rape of Nanking and Matsui. The IMTFE's verdict reads:

> Wholesale massacres, individual murders, rape, looting and arson were committed by Japanese soldiers. Although the extent of the atrocities was denied by Japanese witnesses the contrary evidence of neutral witnesses of different nationalities and undoubted responsibility is overwhelming. The orgy of crime started with the capture of the City on the 13th December 1937 and did not cease until early in February 1938. In this period of six or seven weeks thousands of women were raped, upwards of 100,000 people were killed, and untold property was stolen and burned. At the height of these dreadful happenings, on 17 December, Matsui made a triumphal entry into the City and remained there from five to seven

days. From his own observations and from the reports of his staff he must have been aware of what was happening. He admits he was told of some degree of misbehavior of his Army by the Kempeitai and by Consular Officials. Daily reports of these atrocities were made to Japanese diplomatic representatives in Nanking who, in turn, reported them to Tokyo. The Tribunal is satisfied that Matsui knew what was happening. He did nothing, or nothing effective to abate these horrors. He did issue orders before the capture of the city enjoining propriety of conduct upon his troops and later he issued further orders to the same purport. These orders were of no effect as is now known, and as he must have known. It was pleaded in his behalf that at this time he was ill. His illness was not sufficient to prevent his conducting the military operations of his command nor to prevent his visiting the City for days while these atrocities were occurring. He was in command of the Army responsible for these happenings. He knew of them. He had the power, as he had the duty, to control his troops and to protect the unfortunate citizens of Nanking. He must be held criminally responsible for his failure to discharge this duty (IMTFE verdict).

The tribunal also held that Muto Akira knew about the Rape of Nanking, but wrote of his culpability: "In our opinion Muto, in his subordinate position, could take no steps to stop them [atrocities]. Muto is not responsible for this dreadful affair" (IMTFE verdict).

The cross-examination of defense witnesses by the prosecution, statements of the accused, and in particular Matsui's own statements all influenced the tribunal's final decision.

That the court found Matsui not guilty on eight counts (1, 27, 29, 31, 32, 35, 36, and 54) and that Muto was found not guilty in the case of the Rape of Nanking demonstrates that the tribunal did pay attention to the defense's arguments.

11.4 The Inheritance of the IMTFE Defense's Legacy by the Japanese Right Wing

The trees long for peace, yet the wind never stops.[114] The Japanese right wing has been stirring the pot, not only refuting the IMTFE's verdict of Matsui, but denying that the Rape of Nanking even took place, since the 1980s. As they have constantly expanded the theaters of combat in their war against the truth, their body of evidence has steadily developed into a vast system of cancerous thought. We do not have the space here to analyze and refute their assertions one by one. We will, however, describe how the Japanese right wing has inherited the defense put up by the accused in the IMTFE, how their major arguments were "plagiarized" from defense arguments at the time.

---

114 From a poem by Han Ying, who lived around 150 BCE (translator's note).

In our opinion, the Japanese right wing has adopted the following primary "legacies" of the defense arguments from the IMTFE, directly or indirectly:

1. Matsui Iwane was a lover of peace, striving anxiously toward resurgence in all countries of East Asia. He issued several orders demanding strict observance of military discipline before and after the occupation of Nanjing, which officers at all levels rigorously obeyed.

Masaaki Tanaka was part of the Japanese forces that invaded China and worked under Matsui at the Greater Asia Association. Like Okada Takashi, he held up Matsui's erection of the "Pan-Asian Goddess of Mercy" to be proof of the general's love of peace. Tanaka writes: "The general set aside the pursuit of fame and wealth, saw through our mortal world, and made sacrifices to the souls of soldiers killed in action with all his heart." Tanaka quotes Matsui: "This earth (note: the earth used to build his Goddess of Mercy statue) is soaked with the blood of Chinese soldiers. The dead make no distinction between friend and foe. They were all martyrs in the fight to revitalize Asia. Looking to the long term, every single person who died on the battlefield from both Japan and China sacrificed themselves for the prosperity and development of the peoples of East Asia. Asia will rise again one day and cast off Western colonial rule. The time of co-prosperity across East Asia will inevitably come." Tanaka goes on to claim that in Sugamo Prison, Matsui persuaded Okata Shumei and Tojo Hideki to convert to Buddhism (Tanaka 1985, 50–62). As for the attack on Nanjing, Tanaka quotes from Hidaka's testimony to demonstrate that Matsui gave orders to treat prisoners and civilians kindly, and that money was given for items requisitioned, and that Matsui forbade the firing of artillery in the city to protect cultural relics.

He quotes Armored Platoon Commander Uemoto Masaki, part of the Japanese forces that occupied Nanjing: "There may have been some radical behavior on the part of some men, but on the whole the situation was good; these were highly disciplined crack units" (Tanaka 1985, 139–140, 199). As for conditions after the occupation, Tanaka was "forced" to quote from Matsui's battlefield diary and "Summary of Diary Entries on the China Incident," specifically Matsui's orders that discipline be rigorously maintained, claiming that despite there only being "a few" disciplinary violations, the general did express regret for these. Tanaka gives several reasons for Matsui's own admissions of atrocities, concluding: "The general faithfully did all that was in his power. ... He was falsely accused for the 'Rape of Nanking' and other crimes. It was such a pity that he befell these misfortunes!" (Tanaka 1985, 168–182). Shudo Higashinakano similarly takes great pains to repeat Matsui's claims about orders given before entry into the city to maintain strict discipline and protect foreign interests, quoting from Nakayama Yasuto's testimony to demonstrate that the reason all Japanese units swarmed into the city despite the original plan for only a few to do so was the need to sweep up enemy forces continuing to resist, and that they furthermore had no choice but to enter the city as Chinese soldiers and civilians had destroyed the areas outside the city to such an extent as to make them inhabitable, lacking even drinking water (Higashinakano 2000, 15–20).

2. There had been no mention of the Rape of Nanking before the Tokyo trials. The great casualty numbers were the result of fierce combat. There were no planned massacres carried out on orders. No prisoners were massacred. They were treated well, sometimes even released.

Matsui's claim that he heard of the massacre only after the war was torn to shreds by IMTFE prosecutors, but that has not stopped the Japanese right wing from repeatedly dredging up this shipwreck of a defense. According to Yoshimoto Sakae: "The first mention of this 'Nanjing Massacre Incident' was made in Japan on December 8 in the 20th year of Showa (1945). On that day, a special notice provided by U.S. Supreme Command was published in the *Asahi Shimbun* under the name 'History of the Pacific War – Collapse of the False Military Power Japan,' postscripted 'provided by the Allied Supreme Command.' ... This was as shocking as lightning on a clear day for the Japanese people of the time" (Sakae 1998, 7–8). Itakura Yoshiaki writes: "The 'Rape of Nanking' first became an issue during the International Military Tribunal for the Far East. In truth, the term 'Rape of Nanking' did not exist at that time" (Yoshiaki 2000, 408–409). Akira Suzuki writes: "It was because of the 'Tokyo trials' that the 'Rape of Nanking' became known to the world" (Suzuki 1999, 408–409).

In his book *What Really Happened in Nanjing: Refutation of a Common Myth*, Tanaka hammers this point over and over, and in 1994 he repeated the claim in a speech: after retreating out the Yijiang Gate, Chinese forces "were hit by machine gun fire from the Sasaki Unit. Consequently many Chinese soldiers died here ahead of their time. Those who managed to survive grabbed anything they could get their hands on and attempted to cross the Yangtze to Pukou. ... The 3rd Fleet, advancing up the river, opened fire on them. That is why there were so many corpses there. This is precisely what gave rise to the rumor of the great massacre in Nanjing. That is war." Tanaka writes that the remains housed in the Memorial Hall of the Victims in the Nanjing Massacre by Japanese Invaders "are nothing more than the remains of those who died in the fighting at Xinhe Town." Tanaka writes that he could find only 49 cases of murder in all reports made by the International Committee (in addition to 44 cases of injury, 361 cases of rape, 390 cases of abduction, and 170 cases of looting). "There were only 49 cases of murder. How can that possibly be construed as a great massacre?" He writes that the verdict in the cases related to the Rape of Nanking were made by six judges, from the U.S., China, the UK, the Soviet Union, New Zealand, and Canada; he even excludes the Australian Webb. Tanaka thinks that the opinion of the Indian judge Radhabinod Pal should have been adopted: that all should have been proclaimed not guilty (Tanaka 1995, 358–365).[115]

Tanaka specifically brings up the issue of prisoners, citing the example of the Yamada Battalion of the 13th Division mentioned above, claiming that the battalion released more than 14,000 prisoners to the north of the river. A prisoner insurrection occurred that night, resulting in chaotic firing by both Chinese and Japanese, with casualties on both sides. Most Chinese prisoners escaped, and in no way was this one-sided massacre. At Sanchahe, some prisoners were released, and the rest were handed over to the garrison. The prisoners at Xianhe Gate and Yaohua Gate were treated the same: "In summary, more than 10,000 prisoners were held in three prisons and two detention centers in Nanjing." Tanaka then quotes documents claiming that Chinese prisoners and their Japanese custodians got along well. We must make particular note of the fact that here Tanaka "frankly" notes the following in an attempt to demonstrate that there were no massacres of Chinese prisoners: "He (note: Yamada) had just received orders from Staff Officer Cho Isamu (note: a staff officer in the Central China Area Army) to 'kill prisoners'" (Tanaka 1985, 151–154).

Nakamura holds that civilians were killed, but he writes: "There were unlawful killings of ordinary Chinese, but this occurred only in sudden, scattered outbursts on the part of some troops. In no way was this planned behavior" (Nakamura 2001, 67).

Higashinakano Shudo quotes Osui Hiroshi's IMTFE testimony about the Japanese soldier tied to a tree and shot to death near the south gate of Nanjing and concludes: "That is what war is like." On this logical foundation, he claims that Chinese soldiers hiding in the Safety Zone did not come forward to surrender, and so these soldiers lost their "qualification as combatants" under international law, as well as their rights as prisoners. This gave the Japanese the right to attack and execute them. He similarly explained the release of Chinese prisoners by the Yamada Battalion, quoting from the handwritten notes of Morozumi Gyosaku detailing that Japanese forces had begun to convey Chinese prisoners to the north of the river, but were then hit by artillery fire from the Chinese on the other side. Panic broke out among the assembled Chinese when they heard the shots, as they assumed that the Japanese had begun to massacre them, and so they scrambled in every direction, giving the Japanese no choice but to fire on

---

115 Here Tanaka subtly perverts the truth. The truth is that only Hirota Koki was found guilty of charges related to the Rape of Nanking by a six to five vote.

them: "On the whole, Battalion Commander Yamada and Regiment Commander Morozumi took great pains to disband surrendered prisoners from the battlefield, but they nevertheless caused results that would have ensued had the division commander's orders been obeyed" (Higashinakano 2000, 50, 128–130, 91–96). Most interesting here is that he confirmed that the division commander had given a massacre order in his defense of the Yamada Battalion.

Matsumura Toshio denies the existence of survivors Li Xiuying and Xia Shuqin, whose existence is proven by a mountain of documentary and film evidence, by picking at microscopic discrepancies between statements made at different times. He admits that the Japanese army massacred 1,200 prisoners outside the city wall on December 12, 1937, but he specifies that this should be viewed as a "special case" and that Japanese forces released 5,500 prisoners at Xiaguan. He writes: "The Safety Zone was unbearably crowded within only two weeks of the fall of the city. This fact alone completely negates claims that massacre, looting, and rape persisted for over three weeks." He goes on: "From total numbers of population and Chinese troop strength in the city at the time, it is impossible that 300,000 were massacred in and about Nanjing" (Toshio 2001, 260–275, 38, 165, 218).

Takemoto Tadao and Ohara Yasuo write: "Over the course of sweeps, Japanese troops arrested many Chinese soldiers, who were all detained in the Nanjing prison within the city. There were about 10,000 prisoners held there. Half of these were dispatched to Shanghai as laborers at the end of December, and the rest were conscripted into the army of the Nanjing Government established in 1940 by Wang Zhaoming. There was no reason whatsoever to execute them" (Tadao and Yasuo 2000, 73).

3. There was a peaceful order and normal living conditions in occupied Nanjing. There were very few bodies. Japanese soldiers got along well amicably with Chinese and foreigners. Japanese soldiers did not loot or set fires; looting and arson were committed by Chinese soldiers and civilians. There was no widescale raping. Some Chinese women even actively seduced Japanese soldiers.

Matsumura Toshio cites the "scorched earth tactic" of Chinese military units fleeing the Battle of Nanjing as the primary reason for the great losses incurred in the city and grossly exaggerates the Chinese firing on their own routing forces at Yijiang Gate prior to the city's fall (Toshio 2001, 8–16). He cites Rabe's description of his house as being peaceful and in good order to demonstrate that the Japanese military did maintain strict discipline, yet he accuses Rabe of being extremely biased: "It was the Japanese army that suffered most from fires in the city. Rabe, not able to clearly judge even this, cannot be considered a third party witness of good faith. If it was the refugees that engaged in constant looting and plundering, then it must have been these same refugees who set fires to cover their tracks and create chaos" (Toshio 2001, 185, 170). On the basis of the few reports written by Westerners of Chinese civilians taking to thievery amid the chaos, Toshio conjures this image: "The refugees entering the Safety Zone first entered the houses of foreigners and rich Chinese, stealing many things. ... All foreign embassies were looted because they had nobody watching over them" (Toshio 2001, 94).

When former General Yamawaki Masataki took the stand in defense of Itagaki Seishiro at the IMTFE, prosecutors produced a document titled "Army Records of the China Incident" in rebuttal. The document was marked "Top Secret Document 4460 No. 0 – strictly forbidden to copy – in no circumstances is this document to be leaked." In part it reads: "At XX we captured a family of four. We played with the daughter just as we would with a harlot. But as the parents insisted that the daughter be returned to them we killed them. We played with the daughter as before until the unit's departure and then killed her. Our company commander unofficially gave instructions for raping as follows: 'In order that we won't have problems, either pay them money or kill them in some obscure place after you have finished.' If the army men who participated in the war were investigated individually they will probably be all guilty of murder, robbery, or rape. In the battlefield we think nothing of rape. There are even some men who resisted with firearms when discovered by the military police in the act. In the half a year of battle about the only things I learned are rape and burglary" (Hora 1973, 336–337).[116] Fujiwara Akira cites this in his book to demonstrate that there was a "suppression order" in the Japanese army regarding the Rape of Nanking. Matsumara Toshio, however, sees this as "chatter of soldiers returning home" and thinks this document was meant to "ban 'rumors' on the part of antiwar activists and thinkers" (Toshio 2001, 278–279). We infer from the document that Japanese soldiers, having slaked their bestial passions on the battlefield, were delighted to brag about their "war gains" upon returning home, to the point that Japanese authorities felt they needed to step in to suppress the talk. That said, how could such a disgraceful document help suppress "rumors"?

Higashinakano Shudo stresses that Chinese forces in the east of the city and at Xiaguan enacted tactics of strengthening defenses and clearing fields, connecting this tactic with the great fires in Nanjing. He willfully limits the scope of the Rape of Nanking to the International Safety Zone, and casts doubts like this: "If 100,000 to 300,000 had really been massacred in such a small space, there would have been bodies piled as high as mountains." He quotes an article

---

[116] Mei Ru'ao recalls that the IMTFE attached great importance to this document and "gave it a very high evidence appraisal" (Yang 2006, 631).

of January 10, 1938 from the *Yomiuri Shimbun:* "The first stage of resident surveys, begun at the end of year, ended after seven days, with 1,600 remnant forces arranged to take shelter in refugee camps. Now it is possible to stride about proudly with head held high in Nanjing" (Higashinakano 2000, 25–26, 155, 158). Tanaka Masaaka first stresses that Chinese forces were in the habit of looting, quoting the words of Japanese Battalion Commander Kusaba Tatsumi, who fought in North China, before making his own inference: "It is thus not difficult to imagine the wanton plundering of Nanjing by Chinese soldiers on the 12 and 13 – stealing clothes and food to facilitate their escape – certainly this must have resembled hell on earth even more than in Major General Kusaba's report." For more proof he quotes the *Asahi Shimbun* of the time to describe the benign nature of the Japanese army occupying Nanjing: "Before when residents saw a Japanese, they turned their heads and hid. Now that has completely changed. They are befriending Japanese soldiers and approaching them with wide grins. Although prices have increased 10-fold since before the war, vendors selling matches, candles, salt, and tea from stalls are doing brisk business. … In the plaza behind the Japanese embassy, one observes Japanese soldiers distributing snacks and cigarettes to residents and milk powder to old women holding infants. It is quite a lively scene" (Tanaka 1985, 124, 204). Tanaka then quotes from the testimony of Wakisaka Jiro, commander of the 36th Regiment, part of the forces attacking Nanjing, who claimed that a Japanese first lieutenant was reprimanded for picking up the embroidered shoe of a Chinese woman (IMTFE no. 3395), to demonstrate the high degree of discipline enforcement among these Japanese forces. He also quotes from the affidavit of 10th Division Judicial Officer Ogawa Sekjiro: "…it was not rare on the part of the Chinese women to take a suggestive attitude towards Japanese soldiers…" (Tanaka 1985, 199–202)

4. Testimony of Chinese and Western witnesses at the IMTFE was unreliable or perjured; the tribunal was not fair.

Just like defense attorneys during the IMTFE, the Japanese right wing of today almost completely denies the validity of testimony given by Chinese witnesses. Tanaka cites the cross-examination of Xu Chuanyin by Kanzaki Masayoshi and then writes: "This scene came to a close when even witness Xu Chuanyin was reduced to silence." He then quotes the private opinion of Judge Pal, claiming that Chen Fubao had perjured himself. Tanaka describes the findings of the Nanjing Enemy Crimes Commission to have been an exercise in literature, and the claims of witness Lu Su (who provided a written statement but did not testify in court) about the massacre of more than 57,000 people to be fantastical and absurd (Tanaka 1985, 250, 251, 254, 257).

Higashinakano Shudo raises nine doubts based in minor discrepancies in written records to deny the truth of witness Xia Shuqin's testimony. He further maligns as perjury Xu Chuanyin's testimony regarding the murder of Xia's entire family (Higashinakano 2000, 165–170).[117] Matsumura takes aim at Chen Fubao, claiming that his testimony is "contradictory" (Matsumura 2001, 49).

Western witnesses were neutral third party observers to the Rape of Nanking, and as such their claims should be beyond suspicion. Their "overwhelming" evidence[118] was an important prop of the verdict ultimately reached in the IMTFE. The Japanese right wing, knowing very well the role of this evidence, has spared no effort to attack and defame these witnesses. Take Bates as an example. Shohei Sammoji Shohei was unable to make a dent in his testimony on cross-examination. Tanaka Masaaka, however, cites an article in the *Tokyo Nichi Nichi Shimbun* of December 16, 1937 that purports to quote Bates, who had allegedly encountered a Japanese reporter: "Once the well-ordered Japanese army entered the city, Nanjing returned to peace quickly. This was better than anything else" (Tanaka 1985, 246). He then uses this article as proof that Bates lied to the IMTFE. Is it possible that Bates actually said those outrageous words to a Japanese reporter? Let's take a look at the letter titled "Some Pictures from Nanking" written by Bates on the very day that he was alleged to have spoken with the Japanese reporter: "…in two days the whole outlook has been ruined by frequent murder, wholesale and semi-regular looting, and uncontrolled disturbance of private homes including offenses against the security of women. … From a house close to one of our foreign friends, four girls were yesterday abducted by soldiers. Foreigners saw in the quarters of a newly arrived officer, in a part of the city practically deserted by ordinary people, eight young women" (Zhang 2005, 2–3). Does this not completely expose the *Tokyo Nichi Nichi Shimbun* article as a forgery? Higashinakano Shudo, however, repeats Tanaka's claim that the article exposes Bates's testimony to the IMTFE as perjury (Higashinakano 2000, 258).

---

117 In November 2007, a Tokyo court ruled in favor of Xia in a libel claim against Higashinakano.
118 There was a great quantity of third-party evidence tendered during the Tokyo trials, including not only American diplomatic documents, German diplomatic documents, Documents of the Nanking Safety Zone, letters from International Committee Chairman John Rabe, letters of German Ambassador Trautmann, official records of the International Committee by McCallum and others, but also documents written by Professor Bates, Rabe's diary, Minnie Vautrin's diary, Grace Bauer's diary, records from the German Foreign Office, Siemens China records, American diplomatic files, documents from the German Günther and his Danish colleague Sindberg, reports in major American and British journals such as *The New York Times*, *Washington Post*, *The Times* of London, *The Chicago Daily News*, *Time* magazine, and others. We think that in light of the volume of evidence, the verdicts stand the test of time.

11.4 The Inheritance of the IMTFE Defense's Legacy by the Japanese Right Wing — 599

That was not the only such article fabricated from whole cloth. An article in the *Tokyo Asahi Shimbun* of December 19, 1937, concocts a pleasant and tranquil image of Nanjing: "In the residential district, boys and girls climbed on broken horse carts, singing and dancing. ... Tranquil eulogies issued forth from the church. This is Pastor John Magee leading his now calmed Chinese congregation in the climax of prayers after the smoke of gunpowder had cleared. Today is Sunday. ... Today in the square within the Japanese embassy compound, Japanese soldiers are issuing refreshments and rice cakes to refugees, as well as cow's milk and cans for the mothers of infants. It is the living image of good will" (Zhang 2005, 242). Magee, the leading figure in the article's idyllic representation of Nanjing, was put the question by defense attorney Brooks in his IMTFE cross-examination about how many atrocities Magee "personally witnessed." Tanaka's standard is likewise that Magee must have been at the scene during the commission of an act, to have "personally witnessed" it: "American Pastor John Magee testified over the course of two days about over a hundred acts of massacre, rape, looting, and other atrocities committed by Japanese forces, yet other than three acts, one of murder, one of rape, one of looting, all the rest were hearsay and rumors, or possibly fabrications or imaginings, or maybe even entirely concocted by himself" (Tanaka 1985, 249). The truth is that it is the Japanese right wing that possesses the most fertile imaginations. For example, Magee testified that Japanese soldiers repeatedly broke into Chinese dwellings, but once Westerners appeared, they scampered off. Tanaka deduces that when Magee arrived, "those who 'scampered off immediately' were probably Chinese soldiers dressed as Japanese soldiers" (Tanaka 1985, 188).

Not only have all the Westerners who testified at the IMTFE been slandered, but all foreigners with any link to the Tokyo trials at all have been sullied by the Japanese right wing. Since their testimony is ironclad, the right wing has resorted to defaming their characters. The book *What War Means: The Japanese Terror in China* by *Manchester Guardian* reporter H.J. Timperley was an important piece of evidence for the prosecution. Kitamura Minoru alleges that per the memoirs of Zeng Xubai, head of the KMT Central Information Department, Zeng and Timperley had a secret meeting in Hankou where they agreed that per the plans of the International Information Section it would be inappropriate for the Chinese to relay information on Japanese atrocities abroad, and that it would be better for an international friend to tell the truth about the War of Resistance and Chinese policies on their behalf. As such, it was agreed that Timperley and Smythe, with funding from the KMT, would author two volumes on witness accounts of the Rape of Nanking, and this is just what Timperley did (Kitamura 2001, 43). Even as their governments sat on the sideline idly observing the Japanese invasion of China, all foreigners with consciences who sided with China's just fight declared the truth about Japanese atrocities to the world. This was an act of extreme righteousness, one that had no impact at all on the force of evidence tendered in the trials, yet Kitamura uses this as his basis for casting aspersions on Timperley's work. Kitamura also alleges that George Fitch, while transporting the 16 rolls of film shot by Magee recording Japanese atrocities in Nanjing, stopped on his way to the U.S. in Hong Kong, where he met with Chinese lobbying the American government to intervene in the War of Resistance. On that basis Kitamura claims that Fitch's funding was obviously provided by the Central Information Office, which also planned his activities. He then deduces that Fitch and Magee were not neutral, and thus their testimony is unreliable (Kitamura 2001, 53–57).

International Committee Chairman John Rabe neither appeared in court nor provided any written statements, but a letter from him to Ambassador Trautmann was included in the German diplomatic files available to prosecutors. The letter discusses arson, massacre, looting, and other atrocities committed by Japanese soldiers, and was tendered as evidence to the IMTFE by the prosecution (Yang 2006, 186–187). Consequently, there has been an unending attack on Rabe from the Japanese right wing. After the publication of his diary in 1996, the Japanese right wing launched a frenzy of slander. Tanaka Masaaka had no idea that Rabe had kept a detailed diary when he was writing *What Really Happened in Nanjing: Refutation of a Common Myth*, yet he arbitrarily posits that Rabe's claim of 20,000 cases of rape was "utterly unjustifiable" (Tanaka 1985, 252). Higashinakano could not completely write off Rabe's diary, but he does assert that Rabe "construed rumors and slanders as truths" and describes the diary as "excessively polished" and "barefaced distortion." He even goes so far as to describe the rape cases described by Rabe as "self-written and self-acted rape theater" performed by Chinese soldiers hiding in Rabe's house (Higashinakano 2000, 268–283). Masaki Unemoto, part of the Japanese occupation forces in Nanjing, wrote an entire book dedicated to distorting and slandering Rabe's diary, calling it "exaggeration, hearsay, and conjecture", "influenced by the author's religion, standpoint, view on history, and view on war." Unemoto claims that the book is rife with "obvious fabrications, contradictions, awkwardness, and irrationality" (Unemoto 1999, 1, 120).

In addition to slandering Chinese and Western witnesses as perjurious, the Japanese right wing also accuses the IMTFE of being "biased." All witnesses called by the defense, even those like Ishii Itaro who "revealed divine secrets," were trying to protect Matsui Iwane and the other defendants. But for reasons discussed above, their testimony was insufficient to extricate Matsui and the others ultimately convicted. The Japanese right wing has taken this grievance to heart, castigating the tribunal for not entering into evidence statements from

Greater Asia Association Secretary-General Nakatani Takeyo and others, "coldly overruling testimony and evidence provided by defense witnesses, while accepting absolutely all testimony and evidence tendered by the prosecution – even obvious lies and fabrications." In Tanaka's opinion, Nakatani "proved that General Matsui upheld the legacy of Sun Yat-sen to the last, indefatigably propagating the spirit of Sun Yat-sen, engraving Sun's words as the cardinal principles for Japan-China peace onto his heart." Yet they exult Wakasaki Jiro's testimony: "By order of Commander Matsui, military discipline was maintained in such a manner, and even a bit of unlawful act was never overlooked." (IMTFE no. 3395). Clearly, the Japanese right wing has adopted a double standard, holding Japanese witnesses as bastions of truth and all other witnesses as malicious liars. Even Japanese witnesses like Tanaka Ryukichi, whose testimony was beneficial to the prosecution, are also swept aside by the right wing (Fuji 1988, 389).

5. Other methods

During the Tokyo trials, defense counsel used every harsh and shameless shyster tactic available to negate prosecution witnesses to in an attempt to lighten sentences or outright exonerate their clients. These techniques have been adopted as a model of today's Japanese right wing for their "originality."

(1) Shamelessly posing as medical experts

Ever since Okamoto Masaichi clashed with Robert Wilson over the onset of symptoms in the second stage of syphilis, Japanese right-wingers have shamelessly discussed physiological issues of female victims in Nanjing. Higashinakano writes: "European statisticians estimate that as many as 20,000 women were raped in the Bosnian War. This gave rise to a spike in births among victims, as well as the tragedy of abandoning infants. The situation was similar in Rwanda. Nevertheless, there are no such records among the 'Records of the Nanking Safety Zone.' Does this not demonstrate that it is not possible that 20,000 women were raped?" (Higashinakano 2000, 184) To represent Higashinakano's brazenness as mere ignorance does not go far enough. In a letter to his wife of February 13, 1938, Bates writes: "Now the long-foreseen problem appears. A woman has brought her daughter to the University today, asking for abortion to relieve the engaged girl from continuing a pregnancy resulting from Japanese rape" (Zhang 2005, 30). Albert Steward, a doctor in Kulou Hospital, writes in a diary entry of December 1938: "Accompanying the mass murders there was wholesale rape of many thousands of women in the city. ... During recent months many of these unfortunate women have come to the University Hospital for help, and Dr.—has relieved a number of them of their unwelcome burdens, though there has been some division of opinion among the doctors as to whether or not it was right to do so. I understand that abortion is usually regarded as legal in cases of rape. Dr.—calls himself the No. 1 Jap destroyer of Nanking" (Zhang 2005, 299–300).

(2) Basing arguments in ignorance

Matsui Iwane claimed to have no knowledge whatsoever of the Rape of Nanking at the time. Japanese right-wingers have deduced in reverse that if there was truly a Rape of Nanking, then there should be documentary evidence of it with both the KMT and the CPC. Right through 1995, in an article titled "The Fictitious 'Rape of Nanking,'" Tanaka was still claiming: "Magazines, newspapers, and reports of that time from both the KMT and the CPC all included detailed reports on war conditions and damages. However, I can find no mention of the Rape of Nanking no matter how hard I look." (Historical Research Association 1997, 362). Higashinakano devotes a long section of his book to listing out magazines, newspapers, and leaders' speeches from the KMT and CPC to prove that nobody at the time mentioned the Rape of Nanking, and thus it must be fictitious (Higashinakano 2000, 223–253). For brevity's sake we will not list out the abundant KMT materials from the time describing the event, but on the CPC side, a Xinhua ribao article of May 30, 1938, describes the event in detail, noting: "Not fewer than 100,000 of our compatriots were slaughtered in Nanjing." As Higashinakano is well aware, Guo Moruo wrote the preface to the Chinese edition of Timperley's What War Means: The Japanese Terror in China. In 1939 the Yan'an Current Affairs Research Society published the book Riben diguo zhuyi zai Zhongguo lunxian qu [Japanese imperialism in fallen areas of China]. The first section of the book's third chapter recounts atrocities committed by the Japanese army in Nanjing per the letters of protest submitted by the International Committee to Japanese authorities. Mao Zedong wrote a special preface to the book titled "Yanjiu lunxian qu" [Studying fallen areas], in which he calls for everyone to earnestly study political, economic, and military conditions in areas fallen to the Japanese and inscribes the book's abbreviation of "Riben zai lunxian qu" [Japan in fallen areas].

The Rape of Nanking is a particularly barbarous chapter in the history of the Japanese invasion of China. All historical precedents were blown out of the water by its scale, and it caused irreversible damage to the image of Japan and grave suspicions of its purported objectives. As one observer noted, the atrocities committed in Nanjing reminded the world that Japan "not only threatens the Orient, but will one day also threaten the Occident. The world should know the truth about what is happening there" (Zhang 2006b, 262).

Nobody likes to have the ugly truth exposed about oneself, least of all Imperial Japan flying its banners of "liberation," "co-prosperity," "peace," and "just war." It is precisely for that reason that the Japanese began whitewashing, and covering up the truth from the moment the Rape of Nanking began, and propagating a concocted image of peace in the city (discussed above). Western witnesses saw straight through this guise. For example, when multiple Japanese media outlets reported that the people of Nanjing "spontaneously celebrated" the founding of the puppet Autonomous Committee, this was George Fitch's response, as recorded in his diary: "When I called at the Japanese Embassy this afternoon they were busy giving instructions to about 60 Chinese, most of them our camp managers, on how the New Year's was to be celebrated. ... At one o'clock New Year's day the dive-barred flag is to be raised above the Drum Tower, there will be 'suitable' speeches and 'music' (according to the program) – and of course moving pictures will be taken of the happy people waving flags, and welcoming the new regime" (Zhang 2005, 81). The Japanese army declared to the media of all foreign countries that they had offered relief to the refugees of Nanjing even while their own supplies were short. To this point, Secretary Georg Rosen of the German embassy writes in a report to the German Foreign Office on March 4, 1938: "The Japanese have brought along pretty full-color picture posters featuring an affable Japanese carrying a box of rice with a Chinese child on his shoulders and the child's poor, sincere peasant parents gazing with gratitude and happiness upon this kind-hearted uncle. The pity of it is that this color picture poster has nothing to do with reality, and should be thought of only as an advertisement to boost the tourism business!" (Zhang 2005, 430) International Committee Secretary Lewis Smythe paints an even more "vivid" picture in a letter to his family of March 8, 1938: "We now better understand Japanese news propaganda. During their flagrant and lascivious abuses of power in January, a Japanese news team enacted a farce in which children were given candy and a Japanese doctor gave 20 children a physical. Why are these scenes not reenacted when the cameras are not present!? In propaganda meant for the U.S., Japan describes itself as protecting foreign interests and stopping the spread of communism in China" (Zhang 2005, 283). In this sense, the Japanese right wing of today is repeating old lies from the defense in the Tokyo trials and creating some new lies to boot, all in an attempt to "create truth" by citing the history of the trials.

The IMTFE did not, however, strip defendants of their right to a defense. On the contrary, their defense was played out in the spotlight of the Japanese and international media. Hundreds of reporters and observers from around the world witnessed every facet of the trials, from the anxiety of Xu Chuanyin on the witness stand to Shohei Sammoji's awkwardness on cross-examination, prosecution attorney Sutton's brilliance, and the embarrassment of Matsui and other defendants after their lies had been exposed. The prerequisite to a fair decision by the tribunal was a fair process, and it is only on that basis that the Tokyo trials can be considered to have been conducted in good faith.

The long but necessary trials exposed the covered-up history of Japan's actions in the war to the entire world, putting on display the harm caused by militarism for all to see. The IMTFE's aim was to push Japan onto a road of peaceful development, "swords to plowshares" as they say, on a foundation of seeing history clearly and learning from its lessons. The political advances made in postwar Japan were to a large extent based on the distinction between right and wrong ascertained during the Tokyo trials.[119]

---

[119] A portion of this chapter was published under the title "Dongjing shenpan Nanjing datusha an de bianhu – yi kong, bian shuangfang zhizheng wei zhongxin de kaocha" [Defenses in the Rape of Nanking cases of the Tokyo trials – observations based in cross-examinations by the prosecution and defense], *Kangri zhanzheng yanjiu* 4 (2008), with Qu Yi'an listed as co-author. Before inclusion in the book major revisions and additions were made by Zhang Sheng.

References

References cited in book:

Old Newspaper articles:

Dagongbao [Ta Kung Pao] in Wuhan:

December 25, 1937. Mei bao jielu dijun baoxing Niuyue Taiwushi Bao zhu Hu fangyuan xiangdian yinqi Meiguo renshi shenke yinxiang [American report reveals enemy atrocities – New York Times reporter in Shanghai sends detailed telegram – creates deep impression on Americans].

January 28, 1938. Jing Mei shiguan mishu bei ribing ouda – nanmin qu shiliang kongkuang – dijun jing bu xu goumai [Secretary of American Embassy in Nanjing beaten by Japanese soldiers – food panic in refugee zone – enemy army amazingly won't allow purchases].

February 13, 1938. Dijun xinyi saodi – roulin Nanjing nanmin qu – jianyin lülüe bing tusha wugu – Ma shizhang han guoji weiyuanhui – qing xiang di yanzhong jiaoshe zhizhi [Enemy army sweeps in good faith – ravage Nanjing refugee zone – rape, kidnap, and massacre innocents – Mayor Ma asks International Committee to solemnly negotiate a halt with enemy].

February 16, 1938. Guoji juankuan – di yi tu zhiran [Enemy intends to take cut of international donations].

March 28, 1938. Bao di shouxing shijie zhang wen Ying bao jielu dibing zhengning mianmu [World hears of bestial atrocities by enemy – English report reveals savage face of enemy soldiers].

Minguo ribao:

December 21, 1945, first edition. Jiang Zhuxi guannian Jing shimin, shoushou chensu wangqu hanjian [Chairman Chiang cares for the people of Nanjing, receiving letters on wrongs suffered].

Shenbao:

November 28, 1937. Nanjing sheli anquanqu waiqiao renwei yu poqie yidan bei gongji pingmin sunshi qizhong Nanjing ge shangpu xian yi taiban tingye Ying qiao zhuzhai zhantie Zhong Ying wenzi tiao [Safety Zone established in Nanjing – Foreigners think very urgent – once attacked civilian losses will be particularly severe – most shops in Nanjing already closed – English residents post notices in Chinese and English on their houses].

January 6, 1946. Shoudu renmin chenshu hanjian jiajin fenlei zhengli zhong [Capital residents urgently classifying and organizing statements].

February 8, 1947. Nanjing da tusha an zhenli ge zhengren fenkai chenci [The truth in the cases of the Rape of Nanking – all witnesses indignantly testify].

February 12, 1947. Nanjing da tusha an zhujue Gu Shoufu shoushen ji [The trial of Tani Hisao, main character in the Rape of Nanking].

July 1, 1947. Chufa zhanfan bu zai baofu [Punishing war criminals is not about revenge].

January 27, 1949. Zhanfan anjian quanbu shen bi [All war criminals cases have been tried].

Xinhua ribao:

May 30, 1938. Nanjing tongbao canzao di roulin shoushang guanbing jin zao tusha lao you funü ji bei quan jian [Nanjing compatriots endure enemy ravaging – wounded soldiers all massacred – nearly all women, old and young, raped].

Zhongyang ribao:

September 2, 1937. Jing shimin shi wuyu, Xiaguan liangjia pizhi, cunhuo shanji laiyuan shen duo, ge di fengshou xiaoshu bu chang [No food worries for capital residents, Xiaguan grain prices sluggish, reserves enormous and sources many, bumper harvests everywhere and nowhere to sell].

November 17, 1937. Jing shi cunliang chongyu, daohuo changwang, mi jia pingding [Abundant grain reserves in Nanjing market, more continuing to arrive, rice prices stable].

July 29, 1946. Songjing Shigen ying lai Jing fuzui [Matsui Iwane should come to Nanjing to atone for crimes].

January 25, 1947. Bai yu zhengren zai Zhonghua Men linshi ting jianju Gu fan zuixing [Over a hundred witnesses report crimes committed by Tani in temporary court at Zhonghua Gate].

January 28, 1947, second edition. Fucha caichan sunshi, renyuan jijiang jueding [Re-investigating property losses, people about to decide].

Archives:

Academia Historia Office. Taibei:

No. 301–830(2), Taibei. Executive Yuan Reparations Committee Files, 301–830.

No. 129–212. Ministry of the Interior files. October 1945. Neizhengbu kangzhan sunshi diaocha weiyuanhui huiyi (er) [Ministry of the Interior Wartime Losses Commission meeting (two)].

No. 3–780.6/6. November 13, 1945. Zushe peichang weiyuan hui an [Files on forming the Reparations Commission].

Executive Yuan Archives.

No. 2–5390. August 11, 1944. Xingzheng Yuan Kangzhan sunshi diaocha weiyuanhui xiuzheng kangzhan sunshi chabao xuzhi [Points of attention on rectifying reporting of the Ministry of the Interior Wartime Losses Investigation Commission].

No. 2(2)-2652. August 5, 1946. Kangzhan sunshi diaocha weiyuanhui quanguo renmin shangwang kangzhan sunshi xiangmu shuoming [Explanation of the project of reporting nationwide casualties and losses from the war to the Wartime Losses Investigation Commission].

No. 21(2)-601. February 1, 1946. Kangzhan sunshi diaocha weiyuanhui cun diren duiyu Nanjing zhi huihuai ji baoxing yi ban [Wartime Losses Investigation Commission notes on enemy destruction and atrocities in Nanjing].

No. 301–822(1). Reparations Commissions File. Nanjing shimin caichan sunshi baogaodan [Reporting form for property losses of Nanjing residents].

No. 301–826(1). Nanjing shimin caichan sunshi baogaodan [Reporting form for property losses of Nanjing residents].

The Second Historical Archives of China files:

No. 2–5390. August 11, 1944. Executive Yuan files. Xingzhengyuan kangzhan sunshi diaocha weiyuanhui xiuzheng kangzhan sunshi chabao xuzhi [Points of attention on rectifying reporting of the Ministry of the Interior Wartime Losses Investigation Commission].

No. 12(2)-1234. September 21, 1945. Neizhengbu kangzhan sunshi diaocha weiyuanhui xiuzheng kangzhan chabao xuzhi [Points of attention on rectifying reporting of the Ministry of the Interior Wartime Losses Investigation Commission].

No. 12(2)/1393. April 21, 1945. Xingzheng Yuan guanyu kangzhan sunshi diaocha weiyuanhui gaili Neizhengbu deng qing xunling [Executive Yuan order on making Wartime Losses Investigation Commission under purview of the Ministry of the Interior and other matters].

No. 171/156. Kangzhan zhong renkou yu caichan suo shou sunshi tongji (jiezhi 1940 nian 12 yue di) [Statistics on losses to property and population during the War of Resistance (as of the end of December 1940)].

No. 398(2)-1439. October 19, 1938. Nanjing Jiaotong Yinhang Huang Yu fu Jing diaocha baogao [Investigative report of Huang Yu of Communications Bank on visit to Nanjing].

No. 416(2)/37. October 15, 1938. Huang Yanpei deng jianyi zhongyang zhengfu sheli kangzhan gong si sunshi diaocha weiyuanhui zhi Guomin Canzhenghui ti'an [National Assembly proposal of Huang Yanpei et al on the central government's founding a commission for investigating wartime public and private losses].

No. 718(4)/4711. Guomindang Zhongyang Xuanchuanbu Guoji Xuanchuanchu wei tuijian Ying jizhe Tian Bolie suozhu <wairen mudu zhong zhi Rijun baoxing> yishu he ge bumen de wanglai hanjian [KMT Central Information Department International Information Office letters to all departments on promoting the book *What War Means: The Japanese Terror in China* by English journalist H.J. Timperley].

No. 718(5)/14. Guanyu Rikou dui Zhongguo zhengzhi jingji de pinglun, zai Dongbei de junshi zhunbei, qin Hua baoxing ji Riben zhanshi jingji weiji deng xiang Jiang fei de yi chengjian [Commentary on political economy of China under Japanese invaders, military preparations in the Northeast, and translated letters on atrocities in China and Japanese wartime economic crisis submitted to the Bandit Chiang].

No. 718(5)/15. Guanyu Rikou dui Zhongguo zhengzhi jingji de pinglun, zai Dongbei de junshi zhunbei, qin Hua baoxing ji Riben zhanshi jingji weiji deng xiang Jiang fei de yi chengjian [Commentary on political economy of China under Japanese invaders, military preparations in the Northeast, and translated letters on atrocities in China and Japanese wartime economic crisis submitted to the Bandit Chiang].

No. 782–76. April 10, 1941. Guomin zhengfu Junshi Weiyuanhui kangzhan suo shou sunshi shangwei tianbao congsu bubao xunling [Nationalist Government order on quickly reporting any losses not yet reported to the Military Affairs Commission].

German Foreign Ministry Archives (Politisches Archiv des Auswatigen Amts):

1938 nian 3 yue 10 ri de baogao fujian [Appendix to the report of March 10, 1938]. No. 240/948/38.

A'ertengbuge gei Deguo Waijiaobu de baogao (1938 nian 3 yue 10 ri) [Report from Altenberg to German Foreign Office (March 10, 1938)]. No. 240/948/38.

Bidder. Ji wang Deguo zhu Hua dashiguan (Hankou) de baogao (1937 nian 12 yue 30 ri) [Report to German embassy in Hankou]. No. 2722/4279/37.

Bidder. Ji wang Deguo zhu Hua dashiguan (Hankou) de baogao (1937 nian 12 yue 30 ri) [Report to German embassy in Hankou]. No. 2722/4379/37.

Deguo zhu Hankou dashiguan 1938 nian 2 yue 12 ri bianhao 102 de baogao fujian [Appendix 2 to report No. 9 of the German embassy in Hankou of January 5, 1938]. No. 2722/1057/38.

Deguo zhu Hankou dashiguan 1938 nian 2 yue 12 ri bianhao 102 de baogao fujian [Appendix to report No. 102 of the German embassy in Hankou of February 12, 1938]. No. 2718/1789/38.

Deguo zhu Shanghai zong lingshiguan gei Deguo zhu Hua dashiguan de baogao (1938 nian 7 yue 2 ri) [Report of German consulate-general in Shanghai to German embassy to China (July 2, 1938)]. No. 5720/4637/38.

Feishe'er zhi Luosen de xinhan (1938 nian 1 yue 21 ri) [Letter from Fischer to Rosen (January 21, 1938). No. N/A.

Kelisidi'an – Keluoge'er zhi Deguo zhu Nanjing dashi de xin (1938 nian 1 yue 11 ri) [Letter from Christian Kröger to German embassy in Nanjing (January 11, 1938)].

Luosen gei Deguo Waijiaobu de baogao (1937 nian 12 yue 14 ri) [Report from Rosen to German Foreign Office (December 14, 1937)]. No. 2722/8432/37.

Luosen gei Deguo Waijiaobu de baogao (1938 nian 1 yue 20 ri) [Report from Rosen to German Foreign Office (January 20, 1938)]. No. 2722/1011/38.

Luosen gei Deguo Waijiaobu de baogao (1938 nian 2 yue 7 ri) [Report from Rosen to German Foreign Office (February 7, 1938)]. No. 2722/1096/38.

Luosen gei Deguo Waijiaobu de baogao (1938 nian 2 yue 10 ri) [Report from Rosen to German Foreign Office (February 10, 1938)]. No. 2722/1113/38.

Luosen gei Deguo Waijiaobu de baogao (1938 nian 3 yue 4 ri) [Report from Rosen to German Foreign Office (March 4, 1938)]. No. 2722/1896/38.

Luosen gei Deguo Waijiaobu de baogao (1938 nian 3 yue 24 ri) [Report from Rosen to German Foreign Office (March 24, 1938)]. No. 2718/2404/38.

Luosen gei riben zong lingshi Fujing de kangyi xin (1938 nian 1 yue 17 ri) [Letter of protest from Rosen to Japanese Consul-General Fukui (January 17, 1938)]. No. 5719/1004/38.

Taodeman gei Deguo Waijiaobu de baogao (1938 nian 1 yue 6 ri) [Report from Trautmann to German Foreign Office (January 6, 1938)]. No. 2722/1105/38.

Taodeman gei Deguo Waijiaobu de baogao (1938 nian 1 yue 28 ri) [Report from Trautmann to German Foreign Office (January 28, 1938)]. No. 2722/1508/38.

Taodeman gei Deguo Waijiaobu de baogao (1938 nian 2 yue 23 ri) [Report from Trautmann to German Foreign Office (Feburary 23, 1938)]. No. 2718/2081/38.

Taodeman gei Deguo Waijiaobu de baogao (1938 nian 2 yue 28 ri) [Report from Trautmann to German Foreign Office (February 28, 1938)]. No. 2718/2174/38.

Taodeman gei Deguo Waijiaobu de baogao (1938 nian 3 yue 12 ri) [Report from Trautmann to German Foreign Office (March 12, 1938)]. No. 2722/2452/38.

Taodeman gei Deguo Waijiaobu de baogao (1938 nian 3 yue 22 ri) [Report from Trautmann to German Foreign Office (March 22, 1938)]. No. 2718/2608/38.

Taodeman gei Deguo Waijiaobu de dianbao (1938 nian 1 yue 15 ri) [Cable from Trautmann to German Foreign Office (January 15, 1938)], no. 25, non-confidential.

Taodeman gei Deguo Waijiaobu de dianbao (1938 nian 1 yue 20 ri) [Cable from Trautmann to German Foreign Office (January 15, 1938)], nos. 35 and 36, non-confidential.

Weizizeke gei Deguo zhu Dongjing dashiguan de dianbao (1938 nian 1 yue 22 ri) [Cable from von Weizsäcker to German embassy in Tokyo (January 22, 1938)], no. 30, non-confidential.

Zhu Shanghai zong lingshiguan zhi zhu Hankou Deguo dashiguan de baogao (1938 nian 1 yue 11 ri) [Consulate-general in Shanghai report to German embassy in Hankou (January 11, 1938)]. No. PO: 4, L, 8.

International Military Tribunal for the Far East (IMTFE) files. National Archives II of the U.S., College Park, Maryland:

Field Diary kept by member of Japanese medical corps, Rg 153, Entry 180, Box 5, Location: 270/2/23/7.
IMTFE EXHIBIT No. 204, Rg 238, Entry 14, Box 128, Location: 190/10/21/03.
IMTFE EXHIBIT No. 205, Rg 238, Entry 14, Box 128, Location: 190/10/21/03.
IMTFE EXHIBIT No. 206, *IMTFE EXHIBIT No.207*, Rg 238, Entry 14, Box 128, Location: 190/10/21/03.
IMTFE EXHIBIT No. 255, Rg 238, Entry 14 (PI-180), Box 303, Location: 190/10/1/03.
IMTFE EXHIBIT No. 306, Rg 238, Entry 14, Box 137, Location: 190/10/21/03.
IMTFE EXHIBIT No. 307, Rg 238, Entry 14, Box 137, Location: 190/10/21/03.
IMTFE EXHIBIT No. 309, Rg 238, Entry 14, Box 137, Location: 190/10/21/03.
IMTFE EXHIBIT No. 328, Rg 238, Entry 14, Box 137, Location: 190/10/21/03.
IMTFE EXHIBIT No. 2548, Rg 238, Entry14, Box 246, Location: 190/10/23–24/1–4.
IMTFE EXHIBIT No. 2537, Rg 238, Entry 14, Box 245, Location: 190/10/23–24/1–4.
IMTFE EXHIBIT No. 2577, Rg 238, Entry 14, Box 246, Location: 190/10/23–24/1–4.
IMTFE EXHIBIT No. 3287, Rg 238, Entry 14 (PI-180), Box 290, Location: 190/10/24–25/5–1.
IMTFE EXHIBIT No. 3393, Rg 238, Entry 14 (PI-180), Box 301, Location: 190/10/25/1–9.
IMTFE EXHIBIT No. 3395, Rg 238, Entry 14 (PI-180), Box 301, Location: 190/10/25/1–9.
IMTFE EXHIBIT No. 3398, Rg 238, Entry 14 (PI-180), Box 301, Location: 190/10/25/1–9.
IMTFE EXHIBIT No. 3399, Rg 238, Entry 14 (PI-180), Box 301, Location: 190/10/25/1–9.
IMTFE EXHIBIT No. 3402, Rg 238, Entry 14 (PI-180), Box 301, Location: 190/10/25/1–9.
IMTFE EXHIBIT No. 3409, Rg 238, Entry 14 (PI-180), Box 301, Location: 190/10/25/1–9.
IMTFE EXHIBIT No. 3498, Rg 238, Entry 14 (PI-180), Box 306, Location: 190/10/25/1–9.
IMTFE Verdict, Rg 153, Entry 169, Box 8, Location: 270/2/21/03.
Ministry of Defense Defense National Institute of Defense Studies [Japan] Library. China Incident Files:
North China no. 128. 《第六師団戦時旬報第十三、十四号》(昭和十二年十二月一日一十二月二十日).
North China no. 223. 《第百十四師団戦時旬報第五号》(昭和十二年十二月十一日一十二月二十日).
North China no. 333. 《步兵第三十三聯隊南京附近戦闘詳報》.
Archives of the Nanjing Wartime Losses Investigation Commission
Nanjing Municipal Archives
1002–19–7.
1002–19–8.
1002–2–1044. August 27, 1938. Wang Xie shi cheng [Report of Wang-Xie]. Puppet Nanjing Municipal Government Secretariat Archives.
1002–2–1045. August 3, 1938. Nanjing shi di si qu gongsuo wei Shao Li shi cheng zhi shehui chu gonghan deng [Letter to the department of social affairs from the 4th district office of Nanjing in the matter of the report of Shao-Li and other matters]. Puppet Nanjing Municipal Government Secretariat Archives.
1002–2–1045. October 9, 1938. He Gao shi cheng [Report of He-Gao]. Puppet Nanjing Municipal No. Government Secretariat Archives.
1002–2–1499. September 29, 1938. [Nanjing shi baosong zaiqu nanmin diaocha chengwen gao [Questionnaire form for refugees in disaster area from Nanjing City]. Puppet Nanjing Municipal No. Government Secretariat Archives.

1002–2–1796. June 19, 1938. Luo Wenxi wei Shuixi Men wai Cheng Tai Ji deng muhang zao Rijun fenhui diaocha sunshi baogao [Report of Luo Wenxi on the investigation of losses from the Japanese army's burning of the lumber businesses Chengtaiji and others outside Shuixi Gate]. Puppet Nanjing Municipal Government Secretariat Archives.

1002–19–9. March 13, 1938. Shi zizhi weiyuanhui wei xingban shizheng xuyao ge xiang shiye jihua shu zhi Futian han [Autnomous Committee letter to Fukuda on plans for the establishment of all enterprises needed by the municipal government]. Puppet Nanjing Municipal Government Secretariat Archives.

1024–1–34512. 1945. Shijie Hong Shizihui Nanjing fenhui Minguo 26 nian zhi 34 nian cishan gongzuo baogao shu jielu [Excerpts on the report on charitable work performed from the 26th to the 34th year of the ROC by the Nanjing branch of the International Red Cross Society]. Puppet Nanjing Municipal No. Government Secretariat Archives.

1003–13–44. April 1946. Nanjing shi kangzhan sunshi diaocha weiyuanhui gongzuo baogao [Working report of the Nanjing Municipal Wartime Losses Investigation Commission]. Nanjing Temporary Municipal Assembly Archives.

1003–13–44. September 1, 1947. Nanjing shi zhengfu tongji chu busong kangzhan sunshi diaocha biao yibai fen qing yu tianbao gonghan [Nanjing municipal government statistical bureau letter requesting 100 more forms for the Wartime Losses Investigation Commission]. Archives of Nanjing Municipal Government Statistics Department.

1003–17–1. April 22, 1947. Nanjing shi zhengfu xianqi cui bao kangzhan sunshi bugao [Nanjing municipal government notice on urging reporting of wartime losses within a time limit]. Archives of the Nanjing Wartime Losses Investigation Commission.

1003–17–1. August 30, 1946. <Dagongbao> guanyu Nanjing shimin zaoshou sunshizhe xun xiang shifu dengji shenbao xinwengao [News articles in the Dagongbao about the urgent reporting to the city government of losses suffered in the war]. Archives of the Nanjing Wartime Losses Investigation Commission.

1003–17–1. September 1946 Nanjing shi kangzhan sunshi diaocha weiyuanhui gongzuo jielu [Excerpts from the work of the Nanjing Municipal Wartime Losses Investigation Commission]. Archives of the Nanjing Wartime Losses Investigation Commission.

1003–17–1. December 23, 1945. Nanjing shi kangzhan sunshi diaocha weiyuanhui shenling renkou shangwang diaochabiao ji caichan sunshi baogaodan gonggao [Nanjing Municipal Wartime Losses Investigation Commission notice on picking up forms to report population and property losses]. Archives of the Nanjing Wartime Losses Investigation Commission.

1003–17–9. January to February 1947. Nanjing shi zhengfu deng shoudu shimin kangzhan sunshi diaocha yuyi yanqi wanglai hancheng gao [Letters between the Nanjing municipal government and others on extension of reporting of wartime losses of capital residents]. Archives of the Nanjing Wartime Losses Investigation Commission.

1003–17–9. January to February, 1947. Xingzheng Yuan peichang weiyuanhui guanyu Nanjign shimin shangwang he caichan sunshi tongji xian yu shencha zaixing fabiao wanglai handian [Executive Yuan Reparations Commission telegrams on re-investigation of statistics of Nanjing casualties and property losses]. Archives of the Nanjing Wartime Losses Investigation Commission.

1003–17–9. July 1946. Li Boqian chengwen [Report of Li Boqian]. Archives of the Nanjing Wartime Losses Investigation Commission.

1003–17–9. September 1946. Nanjing shi shimin caichan zaoshou kangzhan sunshi tongjibiao [Nanjing municipal city residents statistical form for reporting losses suffered in the war]. Archives of the Nanjing Wartime Losses Investigation Commission.

1003–17–9. December 10, 1945. Nanjing shi kangzhan sunshi diaocha weiyuanhui di yi ci huiyi jilu [Records from the first meeting of the Nanjing Wartime Losses Investigation Commission]. Archives of the Nanjing Wartime Losses Investigation Commission.

Supreme War Council no. 782–76. May 21, 1941. Guomin zhengfu junshi weiyuanhui chaofa hua yi kangzhan sunshi caichan deng banfa xunling [Nationalist Government Military Affairs Commission orders on measures for unifying accounting of property losses from the War of Resistance].

Yale University Divinity School Special Collection, the Archives of the United Board for Christian Higher Education in Asia:

Bates, *National Affairs (October, 1936)*, Rg 10, Box 87, Folder 690.

Bates, *Public Affairs (November, 1938)*, Rg 10, Box 87, Folder 690.

Bates to Lilliath (November 14, 1937), Rg 10, Box 1, Folder 7.

Bates to Timperley (March 14, 1938), Rg 10, Box 4, Folder 65.

Bates to Timperley (March 21, 1938), Rg 10, Box 4, Folder 65.

Biographical Information: Dr. Miner Searle Bates Professor of Mission, Rg 10, Box 126, Folder 1132.

Forster to American Embassy (March 10, 1938), Rg 8, Box 263, Fold 8.

Forster to His Family (February 10, 1938), Rg 8, Box 263, Fold 8.

Forster's letters to His Wife (December 3, 1937), Rg 8, Box 263, Fold 9.

Forster's letters to His Wife (December 5, 1937), Rg 8, Box 263, Fold 9.

Forster's letters to His Wife (January 24, 1938), Rg 8, Box 263, Fold 9.

Letter from Robert O. Wilson to multiple people (August 22, 1937), Rg 11, Box 229, Folder 3875.

Letter from Robert O. Wilson to multiple people (August 24, 1937), Rg 11, Box 229, Folder 3875.

Letter from Dr. Wilson to his family (December 18, 1937), Rg 11, Box 229, Folder 3875.

Letter from Dr. Wilson to his family (December 19, 1937), Rg 11, Box 229, Folder 3875.

Letter from Dr. Wilson to his family (January 3, 1938), Rg 11, Box 229, Folder 3875.

Letter from Dr. Wilson to his family (January 9, 1938), Rg 11, Box 229, Folder 3875.

Nanking Nan Ming Chu, *Order Recovered, All Shops Opened for Business*, Rg 10, Box 102, Folder 864.

Preliminary Report on Christian Work in Nanking-Winter 1937 (February 18, 1938), M.S. Bates and W. P. Mills, Rg 8, Box 263, Folder 8.

War Relief in Nanking (April 30, 1938), Rg 10, Box 102, Folder 868.

General References:

Akahoshi Yoshio. 《揚子江を埋めた屍》 [Bodies Buried in the Yangtze]. In Soka Gakkai Youth Club Antiwar Publishing Committee. 《揚子江が哭いている――熊本第六師団大陸出兵の記録》 [The Yangtze River is crying—Kumamoto 6th Division Continental Convoy]. Daisan Bunmeisha. 1979.

Asaba Town History Commission. 《淺羽町史》(資料編三·近現代) [History of Asaba (Compilation Three: Modern Era)]. 2017.

Bates, Miner Searle. *Relief situation in Nanking*. Rg 10, Box 102, Folder 866, the Miner Searle Bates Papers, Yale University Divinity School Library Special Collections. 1938.

Bates, Miner Searle, and W.P. Mills. *Preliminary Report on Christian Work in Nanking Winter 1937* Rg 8, Box 263, Folder 8. The Archives of the United Board for Christian Higher Education in Asia, Yale University Divinity School Library Special Collections. 1938.

Central Archives (of China), The Second Historical Archives of China, and the Jilin Province Social Sciences Institute, eds. *Riben diguo zhuyi – qinhua dang'an ziliao xuanbian* [Japanese imperialism – selected files and materials on the invasion of China]. 1990.

Central Archives (of China), The Second Historical Archives of China, and the Jilin Province Social Sciences Institute, eds. *Nanjing da tusha* [The Rape of Nanking]. Beijing: Zhonghua shuju, 1995.

Chang, Iris. *Nanjing haojie– bei yiwang de da tusha* [The Rape of Nanking – the forgotten holocaust of World War II]. Translated from English to Chinese by Yang Xiaming. Beijing: Dongfang chubanshe, 2007.

Chen, Qibo. "Liang Hongzhi yu wei weixin zhengfu [Liang Hongzhi and the new reformed government]." In *Jiangsu wen shi ziliao jicui* [Collection of the best literary and historical documents of Jiangsu] (comprehensive edition), edited by Jiangsu Literary and Historical Documentary Editing Bureau. Nanjing: Jiangsu guji chubanshe, 1995.

Chen, Qianping, Lianhong Zhang, and Yuanzhi Dai, eds. *Deguo shilingguan wenshu* [Documents of German embassies and consulates]. Volume 30, *Nanjing da tusha shiliao ji* [Compilation of Rape of Nanking Historical Materials], edited by Zhang Xianwen. Nanjing: Fenghuang chubanshe and Jiangsu renmin chubanshe, 2007.

Chen, Renxia. *Zhong De Ri sanjiao guanxi yanjiu (1936–1938)* [Study of trilateral relations between China, Germany, and Japan (1936–1938)]. Beijing: Sanlian shudian, 2003.

Cheng, Zhaoqi. *Nanjing da tusha yanjiu – riben xugou pai pipan* [Rape of Nanking research – criticisms from Japanese fictioneers]. Shanghai: Shanghai cishu chubanshe, 2002a.

Articles:

Cheng Zhaoqi. "Zai lun "bairen zhan" [New discussion of the "contest to behead a hundred people"]. *Jiangsu shehui kexue* 6 (2002b).

Chi, Jingde. *Zhongguo dui Ri kangzhan sunshi diaocha shishu* [History of investigations of losses in China's War of Resistance Against Japan]. Taibei: Academia Historia Office, 1987.

China.com. Nanjing datusha xingcunzhe Zhang Xiuhong shouci gongkai zuozheng (zutu) [Rape of Nanking survivor Zhang Xiuhong publicly testifies for first time (with photos)]. 2007. http://www.china.com.cn/law/txt/2007–11/23/content_9312760.htm.

The Second Historical Archives of China, ed. *Zhonghua minguo shi dang'an ziliao huibian* [Compilation of files and materials from the history of the Republic of China]. Nanjing: Jiangsu guji chubanshe, 1997.

The Second Historical Archives of China, ed. *Zhonghua minguo shi dang'an ziliao huibian* [Compilation of files and materials from the history of the Republic of China], 5th Edition Volume 3 *Waijiao* [Diplomacy]. Nanjing: Jiangsu guji chubanshe, 2000a.

The Second Historical Archives of China, ed. *Zhonghua minguo shi dang'an ziliao huibian* [Compilation of files and materials from the history of the Republic of China], 5th Edition Volume 3 *Caizheng jingji* [Finance and Economy]. Nanjing: Jiangsu guji chubanshe, 2000b.

The Second Historical Archives of China, ed. *Kangri zhanzheng zhengmian zhanchang* [Direct battlefields in the War of Resistance Against Japan], volume 1. Nanjing: Fenghuang chubanshe, 2005.

Articles:

Di'er zhanqu songhu huizhan jingguo gaiyao [Summary of course of events in second battle zone, Battle of Shanghai].

The Second Historical Archives of China and Nanjing Historical Archives, ed. *Qin Hua Rijun Nanjing da tusha dang'an* [Files on the Rape of Nanking perpetrated by the Japanese army invading China]. Nanjing: Jiangsu guji chubanshe, 1981.

The Second Historical Archives of China and Nanjing Municipal Archives, ed. *Qinhua Rijun Nanjing da tusha dang'an* [Files on the Rape of Nanking perpetrated by the Japanese army invading China]. Nanjing: Jiangsu guji chubanshe, 1997.

China News. Ta ruci conghui weihe zisha? Mei xuezhe jie Zhang Chunru zisha zhimi [Why did she kill herself if she was so smart? An American academic unravels the mystery of Iris Chang]. November 23, 2007. http://www.chinanews.com/cul/news/2007/11-23/1085900.shtml.

Committee for Compiling the History of the 45th Infantry Regiment. 《步兵第四十五聯隊史》 [History of the 45th Infantry Regiment]. 1981.

Compilation of documents on Japanese issues [*Riben wenti wenjian huibian*]. Volume 1. Beijing: Shijie zhishi chubanshe, 1995.

Connerton, Paul. *Shehui ruhe jiyi* [How societies remember]. Shanghai: Shanghai renmin chubanshe, 2000.

Dai, Yuanzhi. *1937–1938: Rendao yu baoxing de jianzheng – jingli nanjing xingfengxueyu de Danmairen* [1937–1938: Witness to humanitarianism and atrocities – the Dane who lived through the Nanjing carnage]. Nanjing: Jiangsu renmin chubanshe, 2010.

Directorate General of Accounting, Budget, and Statistics (DGABS). Kangzhan zhong renkou yu caichan suo shou sunshi tongji (jiezhi 1944 nian 6 yue di) [Statistics on losses of population and property during the War of Resistance (through end June 1944)]. Executive Yuan Reparations Commission Archives no. 301/057–2.

Foreign Relations of the United States (FRUS) Diplomatic Papers, 1932, The Far East, Volume III, edited by Gustave A. Nuermberger, Victor J. Farrar, John G. Reid, and William R. Willoughby. Washington: United States Government Printing Office, 1948.

Foreign Relations of the United States (FRUS) Diplomatic Papers, 1941, The Far East, Volume IV, edited by John G. Reid, Louis E. Gates, and Ralph R. Goodwin. Washington: United States Government Printing Office, 1956.

Fuji, Nobuo. *Wo suo jiandao de Dongjing shenpan* [The Tokyo Trials As I View them]. Tokyo: Kodansha, 1988.

Gellner, Ernest. *Minzu yu minzu zhuyi* [Nations and nationalism], translated from English by Han Hong. Beijing: Zhongyang bianyi chubanshe, 2002.

Guo, Biqiang, and Liangqin Jiang. *Rijun zuixing diaocha weiyuanhui diaocha tongji* [Statistics from the Commission for Investigating Crimes of the Japanese Army], Volume 1. Volume 19 in the series, edited by Xianwen Zhang, *Nanjing da tusha shiliao ji* [Compilation of Rape of Nanking Historical Materials]. Nanjing: Jiangsu renmin chubanshe and Fenghuang chubanshe, 2006a.

Guo, Biqiang, and Liangqin Jiang. *Rijun zuixing diaocha weiyuanhui diaocha tongji* [Statistics from the Commission for Investigating Crimes of the Japanese Army], Volume 3. Volume 21 in the series, edited by Xianwen Zhang, *Nanjing da tusha shiliao ji* [Compilation of Rape of Nanking Historical Materials]. Nanjing: Jiangsu renmin chubanshe and Fenghuang chubanshe, 2006b.

Guo, Biqiang, et al., eds. *Ri wei shiqi shimin chengwen* [City resident reports during the era of the Japanese puppet government]. Volume 66 in the series, *Nanjing da tusha shiliao ji* [Compilation of Rape of Nanking Historical Materials], edited by Xianwen Zhang. Nanjing: Fenghuang chubanshe and Jiangsu renmin chubanshe, 2010.

Halbwachs, Maurice. *Lun jiti jiyi* [On collective memory]. Translated from French to Chinese. Shanghai: Shanghai renmin chubanshe, 2002.

Han, Lih-wu. "Chouzu Nanjing lunxian hou nanmin qu de jingguo [My experience organizing the Safety Zone after the fall of Nanjing]." *Chuanji wenxue* 41, no. 3 (n.d.).

Han, Qitong, ed. *Zhongguo dui Ri zhanshi sunshi zhi guji: 1937–1943* [China's estimated losses in the war against Japan: 1937–1943]. Shanghai: Zhonghua shuju, 1946.

Higashinakano, Shudo. *Nanjing da tusha de chedi jianzheng* [The Nanking Massacre: Fact versus Fiction]. Translated from Japanese to Chinese by Yan Xinqun. Beijing: Xinhua chubanshe, 2000.

Historical Research Association [Japan], ed. *Da dongya zhanzheng de zongjie* [Summary of the Greater East Asia War]. Translated from Japanese to Chinese by Dong Ying. Beijing: Xinhua chubanshe, 1997.

Hojo, Yasuo (pseudonym). 《南京大虐殺》 [Nanjing Massacre]. In Soka Gakkai Youth Club Antiwar Publishing Committee. 《鮮血に染まる中国大陸――加害者体験の記録》 [Mainland China stained with fresh blood – a report on the perpetrator's experience]. 1983.

Hora, Tomio, ed. 日中戦争資料 南京事件 [Materials on the Japan-China War – the Nanjing Incident]. Tokyo: Kawade Shobo Shinsha Publishers, 1973.

Hora, Tomio. *Nanjing da tusha* [The Rape of Nanking]. Translated from Japanese to Chinese by Mao Lianghong et al. Shanghai: Shanghai yiwen chubanshe, 1987.

Horiba, Kazuo. *Riben dui hua zhanzheng zhidao shi* [History of the guidance of the Japanese war of Invasion in China] (internally issued). Beijing: Junshi kexue chubanshe, 1988.

Hosaka, Akira. Rg. 153, Entry 180, Box 5, U.S. National Archives II, Maryland. n.d.

Hu, Jurong. *Zhong wai junshi fating shenpan Riben zhanfan* [Chinese and foreign military trials of Japanese war criminals]. Tianjin: Nankai daxue chubanshe, 1988.

Hu, Jurong, ed. *Nanjing shenpan* [The Nanjing Trials]. Volume 24 in the series, *Nanjing da tusha shiliao ji* [Compilation of Rape of Nanking Historical Materials], edited by Xianwen Zhang. Nanjing: Fenghuang chubanshe and Jiangsu renmin chubanshe, 2006.

Huang, Dexin. "Jinghuhang guofang gongshi de shexiang, gouzhu he zuoyong [Plans, construction, and use of Nanjing-Shanghai-Hangzhou defense works]." In *Bayisan songhu kangzhan – yuan guomindang jiangling kangri zhanzheng qinli ji* [August 13

Battle of Shanghai – personal battle records of former KMT military leaders], edited by CPPCC Documentary Research Committee. Beijing: Zhongguo wenshi chubanshe, 1985.

Huang, Donglan. "Yuefei miao: chuangzao gonggong jiyi de "chang" [Yuefei Temple: the "place" where public memory was created]." In *Shijian – kongjian – xushu* [Incident – space – recounting], edited by Sun Jiang. Hangzhou: Zhejiang renmin chubanshe, 2004.

Huang, Huiying. *Nanjing da tusha jianzhengren labei zhuan* [Biography of Rabe, witness to the Rape of Nanking]. Shanghai: Baijia chubanshe, 2002.

Iguchi, Kazuki, Junichiro Kisaka, and Masaki Shimozato, eds. 《南京事件·京都師団関係資料集》 [Collection of materials related to the Nanjing Incident and the Kyoto Division]. Aoki Shoten. 1989.

Imai, Takeo. *Jinjing wufu huiyilu* [Memoirs of Imai Takeo], translated from Japanese to Chinese by this book's translation team. Shanghai: Shanghai yiwen chubanshe, 1978.

Imai Seigo. 《南京城内の大量殺人》 [Mass murder in Nanjing]. 《特集 文藝春秋——私はそこにいた》 [Bungei Shunju feature: I was there]. 1956.

Inaba, Masao, ed. *Gangcun ningci huiyilu* [Memoirs of Okamura Yasuji]. Translated from Japanese to Chinese by the Tianjin Municipal CPPCC Translating and Editing Committee. Beijing: Zhonghua shuju, 1981.

International Treaties (1917–1923) [*Guoji tiaoyue ji (1917–1923)*]. Beijing: Shijie zhishi chubanshe, 1961.

International Treaties (1934–1944) [*Guoji tiaoyue ji (1934–1944)*]. Beijing: Shijie zhishi chubanshe, 1961.

International Treaties (1945–1947) [*Guoji tiaoyue ji (1945–1947)*]. Beijing: Shijie zhishi chubanshe, 1961.

Isa, Kazuo. 《步兵第七聯隊史·上海——南京戦》 [History of the 7th Regiment in Fighting from Shanghai-Nanjing]. 7th Infantry Regiment Comrade Club. 1967.

Itakura, Yoshiaki. "Zhenxiang shi zheyang de Nanjing da tusha [This is what the Rape of Nanking was truly like]." In *Nanjing da tusha yanjiu – Riben xugou pai pipan* [Study of the Rape of Nanking – criticism of Japanese deniers], by Zhaoqi Cheng. Shanghai: Shanghai cishu chubanshe, 2002.

Iwasaki, Shoji. 《或る戦いの軌跡——岩崎昌治陣中書簡より》 [Trajectory of a certain battle- from the letter of Shoji Iwasaki]. Kindai Bungeisha. 1995.

Japanese Ministry of Defense War History Bureau. *Riben junguozhuyi qin hua ziliao chang bian* [Uncut Materials on Japan's Militaristic Invasion of China] volume 1, translated from Japanese to Chinese by the Tianjin Municipal CPPCC Editing and Translating Committee. Chengdu: Sichuan renmin chubanshe, 1987.

Japanese Ministry of Foreign Affairs Diplomatic Archives. *Waiwusheng jingcha shi: zhina zhi bu (zhongzhi): zai nanjing zong lingshi guan* [Ministry of Foreign Affairs police history: China division (China detachment): consulate-general in Nanjing], Volume 48, no. 5–23. Tokyo: Fujishuppan, 2001.

Jiang, Liangqin, et al., eds. *Qianqi renkou shangwang yu caichan sunshi diaocha* [Surveys of early casualties and property damages]. Volume 15 of *Nanjing da tusha shiliao ji* [Compilation of Rape of Nanking Historical Materials], edited by Xianwen Zhang. Nanjing: Fenghuang chubanshe and Jiangsu renmin chubanshe, 2006.

Jiangsu Province Local History Compilation Committee. *Jiangsu sheng zhi – liangshi zhi* [History of Jiangsu Province – food history]. Nanjing: Jiangsu renmin chubanshe, 1994.

Jing, Shenghong, et al., eds. "Nanjing shi zhengfu ershi nian siyue zhi ershiwu nian shi'er yue gongzuo gaikuang – dui wu jie sanzhong quanhui de baogao [Summary of work by Nanjing municipal government from April of year 20 to December of year 25 – report on five plenary sessions]." In *Nanjing da tusha shiliao ji* [Compilation of Rape of Nanking Historical Materials] in Volume 1 of *Nanjing da tusha shiliao ji* [Compilation of Rape of Nanking Historical Materials], edited by Xianwen Zhang. Nanjing: Fenghuang chubanshe and Jiangsu renmin chubanshe, 2005a.

Jing, Shenghong, et al., eds. *Zhan qian de Nanjing yu Ri ji de kongxi* [Pre-war Nanjing and Japanese air raids]. Volume 1 of *Nanjing da tusha shiliao ji* [Compilation of Rape of Nanking Historical Materials], edited by Xianwen Zhang. Nanjing: Fenghuang chubanshe and Jiangsu renmin chubanshe, 2005b.

Articles:

Abe, Nobuo. Zhina shibian zhan ji · haijun hangkong zhan [Records of the China Incident War · the navy's air battle].

Kane, Penny. *Zhongguo de da jihuang (1959–1961)* [Famine in China (1959–1961)]. Translated from English to Chinese by Wenxin Zheng, Jiankang Bi, Longji Dai, et al. Beijing: Zhongguo shehui kexue chubanshe, 1993.

Kasahara, Tokushi. *Nanmin qu bai ri* [One hundred days in the Safety Zone]. Translated from Japanese to Chinese by Guanglian Li and Zhijun Wang. Nanjing: Nanjing shifan daxue chubanshe, 2005.

Kawabe, Torashiro. 《市ケ谷台から市ケ谷台へ― 最後の参謀次長の回想録》 [From Ichigayadai to Ichigayadai—Reminiscence of the Last Deputy Chief of Staff]. Jiji Press Ltd., 1962.

Ken magazine. The sack of Nanking. June 2, 1938.

Kirby, William C. *Jiang Jieshi zhengfu yu Nazui Deguo* [Germany and Republican China]. Translated from English to Chinese by Qianping Chen, Hongmin Chen, et al. Beijing: Zhongguo qingnian chubanshe, 1994.

Kitamura, Minoru. *Nankin Jiken no Tankyū: Sono Jitsuzō wo Motomete* [The Politics of Nanking: An Impartial Investigation]. Tokyo: Bungeishunju, 2001.

Koo, Wellington (Gu Weijun). *Gu Weijun huiyilu* [The Wellington Koo memoir]. Translated from English to Chinese by the Chinese Academy of Social Sciences Recent History Institute. Beijing: Zhonghua shuju, 1985.

Li, Youtang. "Erzhan hou Riben zhanfan shi ruhe shenpan de [How Japanese war criminals were tried after the Second World War]." *Zhongguo dang'an bao*, August 27, 2010. 4th edition.

Li, Zongren. *Li Zongren huiyilu* [Li Zongren's Memoirs]. Nanning: Guangxi renmin chubanshe, 1988.

Liang, Jingdui. *Kailuo huiyi* [The Cairo Conference]. Taibei: Shangwu yinshuguan, 1975.

Liaoning Provincial Archives. "Mantie dang'an zhong youguan Nanjing da tusha de yi zu shiliao [A group of historical records from the Manchurian Railway related to the Rape of Nanking]." *Minguo dang'an* 2 & 3 (two parts, 1994)

"List of Important Japanese War Criminals [Riben zhongyao zhanfan mingdan]." *Beijing dang'an shiliao* 1 (1991).

Liu, James T.C. "Kangzhan chuqi deguo juzhong tiaoting zhi jingguo [Germans as mediators in the early period of the war]." Translated from English to Chinese by Peilong Duan. *Chuanji wenxue* 34, no. 4 (n.d.).

Liu, Yanjun. "Nanjing da tusha de lishi jiyi (1937–1985) [Historical memory of the Rape of Nanking (1937–1985)]." *Kang Ri zhanzheng yanjiu* 4 (2009).

Ma, Zhendu, ed. In *Nanjing baoweizhan* [Battle for the Defense of Nanjing], volume 2 of *Nanjing da tusha shiliao ji* [Compilation of Rape of Nanking Historical Materials], edited by Xianwen Zhang. Nanjing: Fenghuang chubanshe and Jiangsu renmin chubanshe, 2005.

Matsumura, Toshio. *Nanjing da tusha da yiwen* [Great questions surrounding the Rape of Nanking]. Translated from Japanese to Chinese by Xiaming Yang. Beijing: Xinhua chubanshe, 2001.

Matsuoka, Tamaki, ed. *Nankin-sen· tozasareta kioku o tazunete – moto heishi 102-ri no shōgen* [The Battle of Nanjing – seeking sealed off memories]. Shakai hyōron-sha. 2002.

Matsuoka, Tamaki, ed. *Nanjing zhan – Xunzhao bei fengbi de jiyi* [The Battle of Nanjing – seeking sealed off memories]. Translated from Japanese to Chinese. Shanghai: Shanghai cishu chubanshe, 2002.

Matsuoka, Tamaki. *Nanjing zhan – bei gelie de shouhaizhe zhi hun – Nanjing da tusha shouhaizhe 120 ren de zhengyan* [The Battle of Nanjing – the souls rent from survivors – testimony of 120 Rape of Nanking survivors], translated from Japanese to Chinese by Weifan Shen. Shanghai: Shanghai cishu chubanshe, 2005.

Mei, Ru'ao. *Yuandong guoji junshi fating* [The International Military Tribunal for the Far East]. Falü chubanshe. 2005.

Mie Prefecture History Compilation Bureau. 《軍人後援会関スル書類綴――神奈村軍人後援会》 [Military Supporters Association Seki Sur Documents Spelling—Kannamura Military Supporters Association]. n.d.

Military History of the Kumamoto Corps Editing and Compilation Committee. 《熊本兵団戦史―支那事変》 [Military History of the Kumamoto Corps – China Incident]. Kumamoto Nichinichi Shimbun. 1966.

Mills, W. Plumer. *W. P. Mills to Nina (February 9)*, Rg 8, Box 141, Folder 12, The Archives of the United Board for Christian Higher Education in Asia, Yale University Divinity School Library Special Collections.

Ministry of Health and Welfare Repatriation Support Bureau [Japan]. 《岡村寧次大將陣中感想錄》 [Wartime impressions of General Okamura Yasuji]. n.d.

Nakamura, Akira. "Yinggai fanxing guoqu lishi de shi Zhongguo [China is the one that should reflect on history]." *The Seiron* 6 (2001). In *Nanjing da tusha yanjiu – Riben xugou pai pipan* [Study of the Rape of Nanking – criticism of Japanese deniers], by Zhaoqi Cheng. Shanghai: Shanghai cishu chubanshe, 2002.

Nakamura, Gentoku. Not for sale. Stored in the National Diet Library. We express gratitude to Professor Cao Dachen of the Nanjing University history department for finding this document and to Professor Lei Guoshan of the Nanjing University department of Japanese language for translating it. [日]中村元督编：《日支関係の現状及び将来》（須磨南京総領事の演説筆録），1937年4月20日东京印刷株式会社印刷, 同月24日社团法人日本工业俱乐部发行, 非卖品。Tokyo: Toppan Painting, 1937.

Nanjing Incident Investigation and Research Association [Japan], ed. *Nanjing shijian ziliao ji (di yi ce) Meiguo guanxi ziliao bian* [Compilation of materials on the Nanjing Incident (volume one) American relations edition]. Tokyo: Aoki Shoten, 1992.

Nanjing Local History Compilation Committee and Nanjing Food History Compilation Committee. *Nanjing liangshi zhi* [Nanjing food history]. Beijing: Zhongguo chengshi chubanshe, 1993.

Nanjing Local Records Compilation Committee. *Nanjing gongyong shiye zhi* [Records of Nanjing public enterprises]. n.d.

Nanjing Municipal Committee for Population Statistics. Minguo ershiwu niandu Nanjing shi hukou tongji baogao [Statistical report on the population of Nanjing in the 25th year of the ROC]. Nanjing: Nanjing tebie shi difang zizhi tuijin weiyuanhui, 1937.

Nanjing Municipal Government Secretariat. "Nanjing shizheng gaikuang" [General conditions of Nanjing municipal government]. In *Jindai Zhongguo shiliao congkan san bian* [Third edition of the modern Chinese history collection] no. 75 (748). Taibei: Wenhai chubanshe, 1938.

Nanjing Roads Management Office Historical Records Committee. *Nanjing jindai gonglu shi* [Modern History of Roads in Nanjing]. Nanjing: Jiangsu keji chubanshe, 1990.

Nanjing Special Service Organ. Nanjing shi zhuyao nongzuowu chan'e diaocha (Minguo ershisi nian) [Survey of yields of primary crops in Nanjing (24th year of ROC)]. In Nanjing shi zheng gaikuang (Zhaohe shiqinian san yue) [Summary of municipal administration in Nanjing (March, 17th year of Showa)]. 1943.

Nanjing University ROC History Research Center. Li Jingde koushu, Qu Shengfei, Dai Dai, Lü Min, Yang Rongqing 2006 nian 7 yue 4 ri caifang [Oral statement of Li Jingde and interviews of Shengfei Qu, Dai Dai, Min Lü, and Rongqing Yang (July 4, 2006)].

Nanjing University ROC History Research Center. Sun Dongcheng Koushu, Shen Dan, Li Linlin, Zhou Tian, Dong Zhujie 2006 nian 6 yue 26 ri caifang jilu [Oral statement of Sun Dongcheng and interviews of Shen Dan, Li Linlin, Zhou Tian, and Dong Zhujie (June 26, 2006)].

Nanjing War History Editing and Compilation Committee [Japan]. *Nankin senshi shiryōshū* [Nanjing War History Collection]. Tokyo: Kaikosha, 1993.

Nineteenth Mountain Artillery Regiment's 'Regiment History' Commemorative Publication Committee. 《山砲兵十九聯隊史》 [History of the 19th Mountain Artillery Regiment]. 1975.

Noguchi, Toshio. *Nara rentai senki* [Battle records of the Nara Regiment]. Yamato taimususha. 1963.

Nie, Lili. "Zhanzheng shouhai jiyi yu "lishi shishi" zhijian [Between wounded war memories and "historical facts"]." *Dushu* 9 (2006).

Nishihara, Issaku. *Sakusen nisshi* [Combat diary]. Yasukuni kaikō bunko. n.d.

Niu, Xianming. *Fomen binan ji* [Record of taking asylum in a Buddhist temple], edited by Zhang Sheng. Nanjing: Nanjing shifan daxue chubanshe, 2005.

Okumiya, Masatake. 《私の見た南京事件――日本人としていかに考えるべきか》 [The Nanjing case I saw-how to think as a Japanese]. PHP Institute, 1997.

Ono, Kenji, Akira Fujiwara, and Katsuichi Honda, eds. 《南京大虐殺を記録した皇軍兵士たち――第十三師団山田支隊兵士の陣中日記》. [Rape of Nanking – Battlefield diaries of Japanese soldiers]. Otsuki Shoten. 1996.

Ono, Kenji, et al., eds. *Nanjing da tusha – rijun shibing zhanchang riji* [Rape of Nanking – Battlefield diaries of Japanese soldiers]. Translated from Japanese to Chinese by Yijie Li et al. Beijing: Shehui kexue wenxian chubanshe, 2007.

Articles:

Endo, Takaaki. *Junzhong riji* [Army diary].
Miyamoto, Shogo. *Zhenzhong riji* [Combat diary].
Nakano, Masao. *Zhenzhong riji* [Combat diary].
People's Bank of China Office of the Head Adviser. *Zhonghua Minguo huobi shi ziliao* [Historical materials on currency in the Republic of China] 2nd edition. Shanghai: Shanghai renminchubanshe, 1991.
Powell, John B. *Baowei'er dui Hua huiyilu* [My twenty five years in China]. Translated from English to Chinese by Jianrong Xing, Mingyang Xue, and Yue Xu. Shanghai: Zhishichubanshe, 1994.
Qin, Xiaoyi, ed. *Zhonghua Minguo zhongyao shiliao chubian – dui Ri Kangzhan shiqi* [Initial compilation of important historical records from the Republic of China – period of the War of Resistance Against Japan], volume 2 *Zuozhan jingguo (si)* [War experiences (four)]. Taibei: Zhongguo guomindang "Central Commission", 1981.
Rabe, John. *The Good Man of Nanking: the Diaries of John Rabe*. Translated from German to English by John E. Woods, edited by Erwin Wickert. New York: Alfred A. Knopf. Kindle edition, 1998.
Rabe, John. *Labei riji* [Rabe's Diary]. Translated into Chinese from the German by Haining Liu, Jianming Yang, et al. (Zhang Sheng (ed.)). Volume 13 in *Nanjing da tusha shiliao ji* [Compilation of Rape of Nanking Historical Materials], edited by Xianwen Zhang. Nanjing: Fenghuang chubanshe and Jiangsu renmin chubanshe, 2007.[120]
Raginsky, et al. *Riben shouyao zhanfan de guoji shenpan* [International trials of primary Japanese war criminals]. Translated from Russian to Chinese. Beijing: Shijie zhishi chubanshe, 1955.
Republic of China Diplomatic Issues Research Association. *Zhong Ri waijiao shiliao congbian (qi) Riben touxiang yu woguo dui Ri taidu ji dui E jiaoshe* [Compilation of materials on China-Japan diplomatic history (seven): Japan's surrender, our country's attitude toward Japan, and talks with Russia]. Taibei: Zhongguo guomindang dangshi hui, n.d.
Rigby, Andrew. *Baoli zhihou de zhengyi yu hejie* [Justice and Reconciliation: After the Violence]. Translated from English to Chinese. Nanjing: Yilin chubanshe, 2003.

---

120 John Rabe's diary, originally written in German, is extremely long, over 1,400 pages in the original. The Chinese version, *Labei riji*, is a translation of the diary in its entirety, while *The Good Man of Nanking* is heavily abridged. In this book, I have quoted directly from *The Good Man of Nanking* wherever possible to stay as close to Rabe's original words as possible, using the citation (Rabe EN). Wherever a quote could not be found in the English version, I have translated from the Chinese version, itself a translation from the original German, using the citation (Rabe CN) (translator's note).

Ross, E.A. *Bianhua zhong de Zhongguoren* [The Changing Chinese]. Translated from English to Chinese by Maohong Gong and Hao Zhang. Beijing: Shishi chubanshe, 1998.

Rüsen, Jörn. "Weiji, chuangshang yu rentong [Crisis, trauma, and identification]." *Zhongguo xueshu* 1 (2002).

Saito, Chujiro. 《彷徨二千五百粁――兵狀の機微》 [Wandering 20005 km――The Sensitivity of the Soldier]. 1988.

Senmatsu, Takashi. 《鄉土部隊奮戰史》(一) [Fighting History of the Kyodo Unit (One)]. Oitagobun Shimbun. 1982.

"Shanghai Foreign Exchange Data (1926–1937)" [Shanghai guowai huishi biao (1926–1937)]. *Zhongyang yinhang yuebao* 8, no. 6 (1937).

Shekhovtsov, ed. *Di'erci shijie dazhan* [The Second World War] (10). Translated from Russian to Chinese. Shanghai: Shanghai yiwen chubanshe, 1987.

Shi, Quansheng. *Xiaguan kaibu yu nanjing jingji de fazhan* [The founding of Xiaguan and economic development in Nanjing]. Beijing: Fangzhi chubanshe, 1999.

Shigemitsu, Mamoru. *Riben qinhua neimu* [Inside Story to the Japanese Invasion of China]. Translated from Japanese by Qi Fulin et al. Beijing: Jiefangjun chubanshe, 1987.

Shimada, Katsui. 《步兵第三十三聯隊史――荣光五十年の步み》 [The history of the 33rd Regiment – 50 years of glory]. History of the 33rd Regiment Publishing Society. 1972.

Shoji Tokuji. Riben juliumin zhi [Japanese resident chronicle]. National Diet Library of Japan. Thanks to Professor Cao Dachen of the Nanjing University history department for finding this record and to Professor Lei Guoshan of the Nanjing University Japanese language department for translating it. 1940.

Shuhsu, Hsu, ed. *The War Conduct of Japanese War*. Shanghai-Hong Kong-Singapore: Kelly & Walsh Limited, 1938.

Smythe, Lewis S.C. *War Damage in the Nanking Area, December, 1937 to March 1938*. Nanjing: The Nanking International Relief Committee, 1938.

Society for the Preservation of the History of the Tsuruga Regiment. *Tsurugarentai-shi* [History of the Tsuruga Regiment]. 1964.

Sone, Kazuo. *Si ji Nanjing da tusha* [Private recollection of the Rape of Nanking]. In *Riben diguo zhuyi qin hua dang'an ziliao xuanji* [Selected files and materials on the Japanese militarist invasion of China], edited by Central Archives of China. Tokyo: Sairyusha, 1984.

Sun, Zhaiwei, ed. *Nanjing da tusha* [The Rape of Nanking]. Beijing: Beijing chubanshe, 1997.

Sun, Zhaiwei. *Chengqing lishi – Nanjing da tusha yanjiu yu sikao* [Clarifying history – research and considerations of the Rape of Nanking]. Nanjing: Jiangsu renmin chubanshe, 2005.

Sun, Zhaiwei, ed. *Yunanzhe de shiti yanmai* [Burying corpses of victims]. Volume 5 in *Nanjing da tusha shiliao ji* [Compilation of Rape of Nanking Historical Materials], edited by Xianwen Zhang. Nanjing: Fenghuang chubanshe and Jiangsu renmin chubanshe, 2007.

Suzuki, Akira. "Xin "Nanjing da tusha" zhi mi [New mysteries in the 'Rape of Nanking']." In *Nanjing da tusha yanjiu – Riben xugou pai pipan* [Study of the Rape of Nanking – criticism of Japanese deniers], by Zhaoqi Cheng. Shanghai: Shanghai cishu chubanshe, 2002.

Takasaki City Special History Commission. *Takasaki-shi-shi kenkyū* [Study of the history of Takasaki]. 2000.

Takemoto, Tadao, and Yasuo Ohara. "Zai shen 'Nanjing da tusha' – xiang shijie qingsu riben de yuanzui [The Alleged 'Nanking Massacre' – Japan's rebuttal to China's forged claims]. Tokyo: Meiseisha." In *Nanjing da tusha yanjiu – Riben xugou pai pipan* [Study of the Rape of Nanking – criticism of Japanese deniers], edited by Zhaoqi Cheng. Shanghai: Shanghai cishu chubanshe, 2002.

Tan, Yugan. "Nanjing shenchu Riben zhanfan qinli ji [My experiences trying Japanese war criminals in Nanjing]." *Wenshi tiandi* 6 (1995).

Tanaka, Masaaka. *"Nanjing da tusha" zhi xugou* [What Really Happened in Nanjing: Refutation of a Common Myth]. Translated from Japanese to Chinese by the PLA Academy of Military Science Foreign Military Research Section. Beijing: Shijie zhishi chubanshe, 1985.

Timperley, Harold John. *Timperley to Bates (March 28, 1938)*, Rg 10, Box 4, Folder 65, Yale University Divinity School Library Special Collections. n.d.

Tuchman, Barbara. *Shidiwei yu meiguo zai hua jingyan (1911–1945)* [Stillwell and the American Experience in China: 1911 to 1945]. Translated from English to Chinese by Zengping Lu and Zutong Wang. Beijing: Shangwu yinshuguan, 1985.

Unemoto, Masaki. *Zhenxiang: Nanjing shijian – jianzheng Labei riji* [Truth: Nanjing Incident – Refuting Rabe's Diary]. In *Nanjing da tusha yanjiu – Riben xugou pai pipan* [Study of the Rape of Nanking – criticism of Japanese deniers], by Zhaoqi Cheng. Shanghai: Shanghai cishu chubanshe, 2002.

United States Defense Savings Bonds and Stamps. "The Editors." In *Jap Beasts and His Plot to Rape the World*. The Library of Congress, Washington DC., 1942.

University Of Nanking Bulletin, University Hospital report. July 1, 1934 to June 30, 1936. Comparative studies of ratios between staff and patients. In Nanjing Municipal Archives, No. 1010–319. Cited from: Bi Gu, Nanjing da tusha qianhou de Gulou yiyuan yanjiu [Study of the Gulou Hospital before and after the Rape of Nanking]. Nanjing Normal University Social Development Institute masters dissertation, 2009.

Vautrin, Minnie. *Minnie Vautrin's Diary*. Box 134 of YDL Record Group No. 11, Archives of the United Board for Christian Higher Education in Asia, Yale University Divinity School Library Special Collections. All Chinese translations of Vautrin's diary used in this book from *Weitelin riji* [Vautrin's diary]. Volume 14 in *Nanjing da tusha shiliao ji* [Compilation of Rape of Nanking Historical Materials], edited by Xianwen Zhang. Nanjing: Fenghuang chubanshe and Jiangsu renmin chubanshe, 2006.

Wang, Jianming. *Kangzhan chuqi de yuandong guoji guanxi* [Far East international relations at the outset of the War of Resistance]. Taibei: Dongda tushu gongsi, 1996.

Wang, Shengzu, ed. *Guoji guanxi shi ziliao xuanbian (xia)* [Selected historical materials on international relations (two)]. Wuhan: Wuhan daxue chubanshe, 1983.

Wang, Shengzu, ed. *Guoji guanxi shi – di wu juan* [History of international relations volume five]. Beijing: Shijie zhishi chubanshe, 1995.

Wang, Weixing. "Lun Nanjing guoji anquan qu de chengli [On the founding of the Nanking International Safety Zone]." *Minguo dang'an* 4 (2005a).

Wang, Weixing, ed. *Rijun guanbing riji* [Diaries of Japanese officers and soldiers]. Volume 8 in *Nanjing da tusha shiliao ji* [Compilation of Rape of Nanking Historical Materials], edited by Zhang Xianwen. Nanjing: Fenghuang chubanshe and Jiangsu renmin chubanshe, 2005b.

Wang, Weixing, ed. *Rijun guanbing riji yu shuxin* [Diaries and correspondence of Japanese officers and soldiers]. Volume 9 in *Nanjing da tusha shiliao ji* [Compilation of Rape of Nanking Historical Materials], edited by Xianwen Zhang. Nanjing: Fenghuang chubanshe and Jiangsu renmin chubanshe, 2006a.

Wang, Weixing, ed. *Rijun guanbing yu suijun jizhe huiyi* [Memoirs of Japanese officers and soldiers and accompanying reporters]. Volume 10 in *Nanjing da tusha shiliao ji* [Compilation of Rape of Nanking Historical Materials], edited by Xianwen Zhang. Nanjing: Fenghuang chubanshe and Jiangsu renmin chubanshe, 2006b.

Wang, Weixing. "Rijun bushu ji zhanlüe yitu yu Nanjing da tusha de yuanyin [Strategic intentions of Japanese deployments and reasons for the Rape of Nanking]." *Jianghai xuekan* 6 (2007a).

Wang, Weixing, ed. *Riben guanfang wenjian yu guanbing riji* [Japanese official documents and diaries of officers and soldiers]. Translated by Lin Ye et al. Volume 32 in *Nanjing da tusha shiliao ji* [Compilation of Rape of Nanking Historical Materials], edited by Xianwen Zhang. Nanjing: Jiangsu renmin chubanshe and Fenghuang chubanshe, 2007b.

Wang, Weixing, ed. *Rijun guanbing huiyi* [Memoirs of Japanese officers and soldiers]. Translated by Ye Lin et al. Volume 33 in *Nanjing da tusha shiliao ji* [Compilation of Rape of Nanking Historical Materials], edited by Xianwen Zhang. Nanjing: Jiangsu renmin chubanshe, 2007c.

Wang, Weixing, ed. *Rijun wenxian* [Documents of the Japanese army]. Translated by Jun Liu et al. Volume 57 in *Nanjing da tusha shiliao ji* [Compilation of Rape of Nanking Historical Materials], edited by Xianwen Zhang. Nanjing: Fenghuang chubanshe and Jiangsu renmin chubanshe, 2010a.

Wang, Weixing, ed. *Dongjing zhaori xinwen yu Dumai xinwen baodao* [Reports in the *Tokyo Asahi Shimbun* and *Yomiuri Shimbun*]. Translated by Weixing Wang, Bin Li et al. Volume 59 in *Nanjing da tusha shiliao ji* [Compilation of Rape of Nanking Historical Materials], edited by Xianwen Zhang. Nanjing: Jiangsu renmin chubanshe, 2010c.

Wang, Weixing, ed. *Rijun guanbing riji yu huiyi* [Diaries and memoirs of Japanese officers and soldiers]. Translated by Lin Ye and Bin Li. Volume 60 in *Nanjing da tusha shiliao ji* [Compilation of Rape of Nanking Historical Materials], edited by Xianwen Zhang. Nanjing: Jiangsu renmin chubanshe, 2010d.

Wang, Weixing, ed. *Rijun guanbing riji yu huiyi* [Diaries and memoirs of Japanese officers and soldiers], volume 2. Volume 61 in *Nanjing da tusha shiliao ji* [Compilation of Rape of Nanking Historical Materials], edited by Xianwen Zhang. Nanjing: Fenghuang chubanshe and Jiangsu renmin chubanshe, 2010e.

Wang, Weixing, and Guoshan Lei, eds. *Riben junfang wenjian* [Japanese military documents]. Volume 11 in *Nanjing da tusha shiliao ji* [Compilation of Rape of Nanking Historical Materials], edited by Xianwen Zhang. Nanjing: Fenghuang chubanshe and Jiangsu renmin chubanshe, 2006.

Wang, Xiang. *Wang wei nanjing shizheng yanjiu* [Study of the Wang puppet government in Nanjing]. Nanjing University doctoral dissertation, 2009.

Wang, Yunjun. *Minguo nanjing chengshi shehui guanli* [Social Management of Nanjing City under the Republic of China]. Nanjing: Jiangsu guji chubanshe, 2001.

Wang, Zhengyuan. "Nanjing baoweizhan zhong de junhua zhuanxiantai" [Military hotlines in the Battle for the Defense of Nanjing]. In *Nanjing baoweizhan: yuan Guomindang jiangling Kangri zhanzheng qinli ji* [Battle for the Defense of Nanjing: personal experiences of former Guomindang military officers in the War of Resistance], edited by National Committee of the Chinese People's Political Consultative Conference Historical Materials Research Committee "Battle for the Defense of Nanjing" Editing Group. Beijing: Zhongguo wenshi chubanshe, 1987.

Wang, Zhuo. Zhonghua zhanying, shusi baoguo [Battle hawks of China, dying bravely for the country]. In CPPCC Documentary Research Committee, ed., *Bayisan songhu kangzhan – yuan guomindang jiangling kangri zhanzheng qinli ji* [August 13 Battle of Shanghai – personal battle records of former KMT military leaders]. Beijing: Zhongguo wenshi chubanshe, n.d.

Wen, Junxiong, ed. "Di 37 hao baogao (1938 nian 4 yue 2 ri) [Report no. 37 (April 2, 1938)]." *Minguo dang'an* 4 (2002).

Wood, John. W. to Irving. 1937, December 13–27. John W. Wood to Irving. Rg 10, Box 102, Folder 862. The Archives of the United Board for Christian Higher Education in Asia, Yale University Divinity School Library Special Collections.

Wu, Jingping. Kangzhan shiqi de Shanghai jingji [Shanghai's economy during the War of Resistance]. Shanghai: Shanghai renmin chubanshe, 2001.

Xia, Bei, Biqiang Guo, and Liangqin Jiang, eds. *Kangzhan sunshi diaocha weiyuanhui diacha tongji* [Statistics from surveys of War of Resistance Losses Survey Committee]. Volume 16 in *Nanjing da tusha shiliao ji* [Compilation of Rape of Nanking Historical Materials], edited by Xianwen Zhang. Nanjing: Fenghuang chubanshe and Jiangsu renmin chubanshe, 2006.

Xu, Xin. "Lun Youtairen mingji da tusha de fangshi [On the ways by which Jews remember the great massacre]." *Nanjing shehui kexue* 10 (2006).

Yamada, Masayuki. Xueshu shalong: Nanjing da tusha zhong xing baoli wenti de xinli yanjiu [Academic salon: psychological study of the issue of sexual violence in the Rape of Nanking]. n.d. http://www.sjhistory.net/site/newxh/xxdt-mb_a2007032915761.htm.

Yan'an Current Events Research Association. *Riben diguozhuyi zai Zhongguo lunxian qu* [Japanese imperialism in the fallen zones of China]. Yan'an: Jiefangshe, 1939. Reprinted in 1958 in Shanghai: Shanghai renmin chubanshe.

Yang, Daqing. "1938 nian 1 yue 17 ri "Guangtian dianbao" kaozheng [Textual criticism of the "Hirota telegram" of January 17, 1938]." *Minguo dang'an* 3 (1998).

Yang, Xiaming. "Lun Nanjing "anquan qu" gongneng de cuowei ji qi yuanyin [On the dislocations in functions of the Nanjing "Safety Zone" and their reasons]." *Kangri zhanzheng yanjiu* 4 (2000).

Yang, Xiaming, ed. *Dongjing shenpan* [The Tokyo trials]. Volume 7 in *Nanjing da tusha shiliao ji* [Compilation of Rape of Nanking Historical Materials], edited by Xianwen Zhang. Nanjing: Fenghuang chubanshe and Jiangsu renmin chubanshe, 2006.

Yang, Xiaming, ed. *Meiguo waijiao wenjian* [American diplomatic documents]. Volume 63 in *Nanjing da tusha shiliao ji* [Compilation of Rape of Nanking Historical Materials], edited by Xianwen Zhang. Nanjing: Jiangsu renmin chubanshe and Fenghuang chuban chuanmei jituan, 2010.

Yang, Xiaming, and Sheng Zhang, eds. *Guoji jianchaju wenshu · meiguo baokan baodao* [International prosecutors' documents – reports in American periodicals]. Volume 29 in *Nanjing da tusha shiliao ji* [Compilation of Rape of Nanking Historical Materials], edited by Xianwen Zhang. Nanjing: Fenghuang chubanshe and Jiangsu renmin chubanshe, 2007.

Yoshimoto, Sakae. "Fensui Nanjing da tusha de xugou [Smashing the fiction of the Rape of Nanking]." In *Nanjing da tusha yanjiu – Riben xugou pai pipan* [Study of the Rape of Nanking – criticism of Japanese deniers], by Zhaoqi Cheng. Shanghai: Shanghai cishu chubanshe, 2002.

Yu, Zidao et al., eds. *Wang wei zhengquan quan shi* [Complete history of the Wang puppet regime]. Shanghai: Shanghai renmin chubanshe, 2006.

Zhang, Jianning, Biqiang Guo, and Liangqin Jiang, eds. *Nanjing da tusha shimin chengwen* [Reports from city residents on the Rape of Nanking]. Volume 23 in *Nanjing da tusha shiliao ji* [Compilation of Rape of Nanking Historical Materials], edited by Xianwen Zhang. Nanjing: Fenghuang chubanshe and Jiangsu renmin chubanshe, 2006.

Zhang, Kaiyuan. *Nanjing da tusha de lishi jianzheng* [Historical evidence for the Rape of Nanking]. Wuhan: Hubei renmin chubanshe, 1995.

Zhang, Kaiyuan, ed. *Tianli nanrong – Meiguo chuanjiaoshi yanzhong de Nanjing da tusha (1937–1938)* [Intolerable injustice – the Rape of Nanking in the eyes of American missionaries (1937–1938)]. Nanjing: Nanjing daxue chubanshe, 1999.

Zhang, Kaiyuan, ed. *Meiguo chuanjiaoshi riji yu shuxin* [Eyewitnesses to Massacre: American Missionaries Bear Witness to Japanese Atrocities in Nanjing]. Nanjing: Jiangsu renmin chubanshe, 2005.

Zhang, Lianhong. "Nanjing da tusha shiqi de rijun dangju yu Nanjing anquan qu [Japanese military authorities and the Safety Zone during the Rape of Nanking]." *Jindai shi yanjiu* 3 (2001).

Zhang, Lianhong. "Nanjing da tusha zhiqian Nanjing shimin de shehui xinli [The social psychology of Nanjing residents before the Rape of Nanking]." *Kangri zhanzheng yanjiu* 4 (2002).

Zhang, Lianhong. "Nanjing da tusha yu Nanjing shimin de chuangshang jiyi [The Rape of Nanking and the wounded memories of Nanjing residents]." *Jianghai xuekan* 1 (2003).

Zhang, Lianhong, ed. *Xingcunzhe de riji yu huiyi* [Diaries and memoirs of survivors]. Volume 3 in the series, *Nanjing da tusha shiliao ji* [Compilation of Rape of Nanking Historical Materials], edited by Xianwen Zhang. Nanjing: Fenghuang chubanshe and Jiangsu renmin chubanshe, 2005.

Zhang, Lianhong, et al., eds. *Weitelin riji* [Vautrin's diary]. Volume 14 in the series, *Nanjing da tusha shiliao ji* [Compilation of Rape of Nanking Historical Materials], Xianwen Zhang. Nanjing: Fenghuang chubanshe and Jiangsu renmin chubanshe, 2006.

Zhang, Lianhong, and Chen Qianping, eds. *Yingguo shilingguan wenshu* [Correspondence of UK embassy and consulates]. Volume 31 in the series, *Nanjing da tusha shiliao ji* [Compilation of Rape of Nanking Historical Materials], edited by Xianwen Zhang. Nanjing: Jiangsu renmin chubanshe, 2007.

Zhang, Lianhong, and Yuanzhi Dai, eds. *Xingcunzhe diaocha koushu* [Oral statements in survey of survivors]. Volume 26 in the series, *Nanjing da tusha shiliao ji* [Compilation of Rape of Nanking Historical Materials], edited by Xianwen Zhang. Nanjing: Fenghuang chubanshe and Jiangsu renmin chubanshe, 2006.

Zhang, Renshou. "Gaizao Riben zhanfan shisi nian jishi [Records of actual events over 14 years of reforming Japanese war criminals]." *Zongheng* 6 (1997).

Zhang, Sheng. "Guomin zhengfu shiqi de Jinda [The University of Nanking in the nationalist era]." In the series, *Jinling daxue shi* [History of the University of Nanking], edited by Xianwen Zhang. Nanjing: Nanjing daxue chubanshe, 2002.

Zhang, Sheng, ed. *Waiguo meiti baodao he Deguo shiguan baogao* [Foreign media reports and German embassy reports]. Volume 6 in the series, *Nanjing da tusha shiliao ji* [Compilation of Rape of Nanking Historical Materials], edited by Xianwen Zhang. Nanjing: Fenghuang chubanshe and Jiangsu renmin chubanshe, 2005.

Zhang, Sheng. "Cong Nanjing da tusha kan Zhongguo kangzhan qiantu – Nanjing xifang renshi de guancha he yupan [China's prospects in the War of Resistance viewed from the Rape of Nanking – observations and predictions of Westerners in Nanjing]." *Minguo dang'an* 4 (2006a).

Zhang, Sheng, ed. *Ying mei wenshu – anquan qu wenshu – zizhi weiyuanhui wenshu* [British and American documents – documents from the Safety Zone – documents from the Autonomous Committee]. Volume 12 in the series, *Nanjing da tusha shiliao ji* [Compilation of Rape of Nanking Historical Materials], edited by Xianwen Zhang. Nanjing: Fenghuang chubanshe and Jiangsu renmin chubanshe, 2006b.

Zhang, Sheng. "Nanjing da tusha shouhaizhe PTSD chubu yanjiu [Initial study into PTSD among victims of the Rape of Nanking]." *Kangri zhanzheng yanjiu* 4 (2009).

Zhang, Sheng, ed. *Yelu wenxian* [Yale documents]. Volume 2 in the series, *Nanjing da tusha shiliao ji* [Compilation of Rape of Nanking Historical Materials], edited by Xianwen Zhang. Nanjing: Jiangsu renmin chubanshe, 2010.

Zhang, Sheng, ed. *Riben de junguo jiaoyu – bairen zhehe zhu ning shiguan shiliao* [Japanese militaristic education – Contest to kill a hundred people with a sword and documents from embassies in Nanjing]. Volume 26 in the series, *Nanjing da tusha shiliao ji* [Compilation of Rape of Nanking Historical Materials], edited by Xianwen Zhang. Nanjing: Fenghuang chubanshe and Jiangsu renmin chubanshe, 2007.

Zhang, Sheng, and Xiaming Yang, eds. *Dongjing shenpan shuzheng ji su, yi, de wenshu* [Documentary evidence from the Tokyo trials and Soviet, Italian, and German documents]. Volume 71 in the series, *Nanjing da tusha shiliao ji* [Compilation of Rape of Nanking Historical Materials], edited by Xianwen Zhang. Nanjing: Fenghuang chubanshe and Jiangsu renmin chubanshe, 2010.

Zhang, Sheng, et al., eds. *Xingcunzhe diaocha kousshu xubian* [Investigations and oral statements of survivors continued]. Volume 39 in the series, *Nanjing da tusha shiliao ji* [Compilation of Rape of Nanking Historical Materials], edited by Xianwen Zhang. Nanjing: Fenghuang chubanshe and Jiangsu renmin chubanshe. 2007.

Zhang, Xianwen, ed. *Zhongguo kang ri zhanzheng shi* [History of China's war of resistance against Japan]. Nanjing: Nanjing daxue chubanshe, 2001.

Zhang, Yan. Riben touxiang na yi tian [The day Japan surrendered]. *Renmin ribao*, August 14, 1995.

Zhu, Chengshan, ed. *Haiwai Nanjing da tusha shiliao ji* [Compilation of overseas historical materials on the Rape of Nanking]. Nanjing: Nanjing chubanshe, 2007.

References on Psychology from PTSD Chapter:

Cheng, Lingzhi, et al. "Jixing yingji ganyu de yuanze he fangfa [Principles and methods in preventing PTSD]." *Zhongguo linchuang fukang* 3 (2003).
Huang, Jing, et al. "Dizhen zaiqu qingshaonian shangyuan chuangshang hou yingji zhang'ai ji xinli, yaowu ganyu [PTSD and psychiatric and medical interventions among young victims in earthquake zones]." *Zhongguo yiyao zhinan* 10 (2008).
Ma, Lei, et al. "Chuangshang hou yingji zhang'ai de yichuan yiganxing yanjiu [Study of inheritability of PTSD]." *Shenjing jibing yu jingshen weisheng* 1 (2004).
Myers, David. *Xinlixue* [Psychology]. Translated from English to Chinese by Huang Xiting et al. Beijing: Renmin youdian chubanshe, 2006.
Wang, Huanlin, et al. "Zhongguo junren gexing tezheng de diaocha fenxi [Analysis of individual characteristics of Chinese soldiers]." *Zhongguo jingshen ke zazhi* 3 (1997).
Wang, Yao, et al. "Qiangjian shouhaizhe zhong de nvxing xinli yu xingwei wenti zongshu [Summary of psychological and behavioral issues among female rape victims]." *Shehui xinli kexue* Z3 (2007).
Xu, Wei, et al. "Te da baozha shigu xingcunzhe chuangshang hou yingji zhang'ai de chubu yanjiu [Initial study of PTSD among survivors of large explosions]." *Zhongguo xinli weisheng zazhi* 9 (2003).
Yang, Xiaoyun, et al. "Daxuesheng chuangshang hou yingji zhang'ai de fasheng tedian ji jiaoyu de qishi [The characteristics of PTSD occurrence among university students and lessons from education]." *Jiaoyu kexue* 2 (2007).
Yang, Xianju, and Yang Zhang. "PTSD ji qi xinxueguan fanying [PTSD and its effects on blood vessels]." *Xinxueguan bingxue jinzhan* 5 (2002).
Zhang, Ben, et al. "Tangshan da dizhen xinli chuangshang hou yingji zhang'ai de chouyang diaocha yanjiu [Sample study of PTSD after the Tangshan earthquake]." *Zhonghua jingshen ke zazhi* 2 (1999).
Zhang, Kerang, et al. "Chuanranxing fei dianxing feiyan huanzhe ji yixian yiwu renyuan he yiqu gongzhong chuangshang hou yingji zhang'ai de duizhao yanjiu [Comparative study of PTSD in SARS patients, front-line medical workers, and the masses in epidemic areas]." *Zhongguo linchuang fukang* 12 (2005).

References uncited in book:

1. Compilations and Archives

Archives of the Japan Foreign Affairs Archives. n.d.
Archives of the Social Bureau of Nanjing Special City. Nanjing Municipal Archives. n.d.
Central Archives (of China), The Second Historical Archives of China, and the Jilin Province Social Sciences Institute, eds. *Riben diguo zhuyi qin Hua dang'an ziliao xuanbian: Wang wei zhengquan* [Selected materials on the Japanese imperialist invasion of China: the Wang Jingwei puppet regime]. Beijing: Zhonghua shuju, 2004.
Library and Archives in the Library of the Japan Defense Ministry Research Institute. n.d.
Library of Japan archives. n.d.

Lu, Shuping, ed. *Nanjing da tusha: Ying Mei renshi de muji baodao* [The Rape of Nanking: eyewitness reports from British and Americans]. Hongqi chubanshe. 1999.

Nanjing Municipal Government Secretariat. *Shi nian lai zhi Nanjing* [Nanjing these ten years]. Nanjing Library Special Collection, 1937.

Nanjing Municipal Government Secretariat. *Yi nian lai Nanjing shizheng* [Nanjing municipal government this last year]. 1935.

Nanjing Municipal Government Secretariat. *Nanjing shizheng gaikuang* [Summary of Nanjing municipal government]. Taibei: Wenhai chubanshe, 1938.

Nanjing shi zizhi gongzuo gailun [Summary of autonomous work in Nanjing]. Nanjing Library Special Collection, 1937.

Nanjing Special Municipal Government Secretariat. *Shoudu shizheng yaolan* [Capital municipal government overview]. 1929.

Nanjing University summer investigations, 2004, by: Yuanyuan Wang, Dahai Chen, Ziyang Wu, Qin Cao, Lihua Shen, Min Mao, Runkai Wu, Xuan Liu, Wei Wu, Qing Liu, Yizhong Zhang, Qingrong Cao, Xun Sun, Wenting Gong, Suimeng Su, Qian Meng, and Xiuyi Ma. Chaired by Sheng Zhang, vice chairs Liangqin Jiang and Lingling Ren, coordinator Jun Yang. Files stored in the Nanjing University ROC History Research Center.

Nanjing University summer investigations, 2005, by: Ming Ye, Aihui Wu, Xiaoyan Wang, Zhaolu Yin, Yang Sun, Yin Zhou, Xiuyi Ma, Shengfei Qu, and Bingbing Wei. Chaired by Sheng Zhang, vice chairs Liangqin Jiang and Lingling Ren, coordinator Jun Yang.

Nanjing University summer investigations, 2006, by: Shuchi Wang, Dan Shen, Linlin Li, Min Lu, Dai Dai, Huamin Guan, Renren Tao, Dongjin Wang, Shengfei Qu, Zhenlong Yi, Wei Qiu, Ling Hu, Rongqing Yang, Weimin Dong, Dongdong Liu, Chaojun Ma, Xiaoping He, Xiangmei Sun, Zhujie Dong, Lihui Duan, Shoutao Zhang, Dasheng Shan, Yu Jiang, and Tian Zhou. Chaired by Sheng Zhang, vice chairs Liangqin Jiang and Lingling Ren, coordinator Jun Yang. Files stored in the Research Center for the History of Republican China, Nanjing University.

Nanjing weisheng xingzheng [Nanjing health administration]. Nanjing Library Special Collection. 1933.

National Capital Construction Technology Expert Office, ed. Shoudu jihua [Capital plan]. 1929.

Nationalist Government Civil Officials Office. *Guomin zhengfu gongbao* [Nationalist Government gazette]. n.d.

Qin, Xiaoyi, ed. *Geming wenxian di 91 ji* [Revolutionary documents volume 91]. Guomindang dangshihui. 1982.

Research Center for the History of Republican China, Nanjing University. Zhang Ruijiang koushu, Qiu Wei, Hu Ling, Sun Xiangmei 2006 nian 6 yue 26 ri caifang jilu [Oral statement of Zhang Ruijiang and interviews of Qiu Qei, Hu Ling, and Sun Xiangmei (June 26, 2006)].

Research Committee on Cultural and Historical Materials of the Chinese People's Political Consultative Conference, ed. *Nanjing baowei zhan* [The battle for the defense of Nanjing]. Zhongguo wenshi chubanshe. 1987.

Research Committee on Cultural and Historical Materials of the Chinese People's Political Consultative Conference, ed. *Ba yi san shibian – yuan Guomindang jiangling kang Ri zhanzheng qinli ji* [August 13 Incident – records of former KMT officers and soldiers who lived through the War of Resistance Against Japan]. Zhongguo wenshi chubanshe. 1985.

Research Committee of Literature and History of Jiangsu Provincial Political Consultative Conference, ed. *Jiangsu wenshi ziliao xuanbian di 16 ji* [Selected Jiangsu cultural and historical materials volume 16]. Jiangsu guji chubanshe. 1985.

Secretariat of Nanjing Municipal Government, ed. *Shoudu shizheng gongbao* [Capital government gazette]. n.d.

Siemens Branch Company Archives. Germany. n.d.

Tang, Meiru, ed. *Nanjing: yi jiu san qi nian shi yi yue zhi yi jiu san ba nian wu yue* [Nanjing: November 1937 to May 1938]. Translated by Kaiyuan Zhang. Sanlian shudian (Hong Kong). 1995.

The Library of Congress. Washington, U.S. n.d.

The National Archives. London, UK. n.d.

The National Archives II, College Park, Maryland, U.S. n.d.

The Second Historical Archives of China, ed. *Kang Ri zhanzheng zhengmian zhanchang* [Direct battlefields in the War of Resistance Against Japan]. Fenghuang chubanshe. 2005.

The Second Historical Archives of China, ed. *Zhonghua Minguo shi dang'an ziliao huibian (Di wu ji di er fulu xia)* [Collected files and materials on the history of the Republic of China (fifth volume second appendix). Jiangsu guji chubanshe. 1997.

University of Nanking. *Sili Jinling Daxue liushi zhounian xiaoqing jiniance* [Memorial brochure on the 60th anniversary of the founding of the private University of Nanking]. Nanjing University Library Special Collection. 1948.

University of Nanking Secretariat, ed. *Sili Jinling Daxue yi lan* [Overview of the private University of Nanking]. 1933.

Xianwen, Zhang, ed. *Nanjing da tusha shiliao ji* [Compilation of Rape of Nanking Historical Materials]. Volumes 1–8. 2005. Nanjing: Jiangsu renmin chubanshe and Fenghuang chubanshe.

Volumes 9 to 28. Nanjing: Jiangsu renmin chubanshe and Fenghuang chubanshe, n.d.

Volumes 29–55. Nanjing: Jiangsu renmin chubanshe and Fenghuang chuanmei jituan, n.d.

Volumes 56–72. Nanjing: Nanjing: Jiangsu renmin chubanshe and Fenghuang chuanmei jituan, 2010.

Yasukuni Bunko Library in Japan. n.d.

Zhang, Kaiyuan. *Nanjing da tusha de lishi jianzheng* [Historical testimony on the Rape of Nanking]. Hubei renmin chubanshe. 1995.

2. Books

Abend, Hallett. *Minguo caifang zhan: <Niuyue shibao> zhu Hua shouxi jizhe Aban huiyilu* [Republican China war of interviews: New York Times lead reporter in China Abend's memoirs]. Translated from English to Chinese by Yang Zhifeng. Guangxi shifan daxue chubanshe. 2008.

Anderson, Eugene N. *Zhongguo shiwu* [The food of China]. Translated from English to Chinese by Ma Ying and Liu Dong. Jiangsu renmin chubanshe. 2003.

Azuma, Shiro. *Dong Shilang riji* [Azuma Shiro's diary]. Translated from Japanese to Chinese by this book's translation team. Jiangsu jiaoyu chubanshe. 1999, first edition.

Bauman, Zygmunt. *Xiandaixing yu da tusha* [Modernity and the Holocaust]. Translated from English to Chinese by Yang Yudong et al. Yilin chubanshe. 2002.
Brown Miller, Susan. *Weibei women de yiyuan* [Against our will]. Translated from English to Chinese by Zhu Jifang. Jiangsu renmin chubanshe. 2006.
Chen, Anji, ed. *Qin Hua Rijun Nanjing da tusha guoji xueshu yantaohui lunwen ji* [Compilation of papers submitted at the international Rape of Nanking academic symposium]. Anhui daxue chubanshe. 1998.
Chen, Cunren. *Kangzhan shidai shenghuo shi* [History of life in the time of the War of Resistance]. Shanghai renmin chubanshe. 2001.
Chen, Jialiu. *Riben huanjing wuran de zhili he duice* [Environmental clean-up and responses to pollution in Japan]. Zhongguo huanjing kexue chubanshe. 1990.
Cheng, Zhaoqi. *Nanjing da tusha yanjiu – Riben xugou pai pipan* [Study of the Rape of Nanking – criticism of Japanese deniers]. Shanghai cishu chubanshe. 2002.
Cheng, Zhaoqi. *Riben xiancun Nanjing da tusha shiliao yanjiu* [Study of extant historical materials related to the Rape of Nanking in Japan]. Shanghai renmin chubanshe. 2008.
Dai, Junliang. *Zhongguo chengshi jianshe shi* [History of Chinese urban construction]. Heilongjiang renmin chubanshe. 1992.
Dong, Jianhong, ed. *Zhongguo chengshi jianshe shi (disan ban)* [History of Chinese urban construction (third edition)]. Zhongguo jiangong chubanshe. 2004.
Fujiki, Hideo. *Gonghai fanzui* [Pollution crime]. Translated from Japanese to Chinese by Cong Xuangong et al. Zhongguo zhengfa daxue chubanshe. 1992.
Furuya, Keiji. *Jiang Jieshi milu* [Secret records of Chiang Kai-shek]. Hunan renmin chubanshe. 1988.
Gao, Xingzu. *Rijun qin Hua baoxing – Nanjing da tusha* [Atrocities committed by the Japanese army invading China – the Rape of Nanking]. Shanghai renmin chubanshe. 1985.
George, Susan, and Nigel Paige. *Liangshi zhengzhi rumen* [Food for beginners]. Translated from English to Chinese by Huoqiong Li and Zhong Fu. Dongfang chubanshe. 1998.
Gulou Hospital History Compilation Office. *Nanjing Gulou Yiyuan yuan zhi (1892–1990)* [History of the Gulou Hospital in Nanjing (1892–1990)]. Jinlin tushuguan cang. 1993.
Guo, Qian. *Guomin shiqi tongzhizhe dui chengshi xiaceng shehui de shehui tiaokong* [Social controls on the lower levels of urban society by rulers in the Republican era]. Shandong University doctoral thesis, 2007.
Hata, Ikuhiku. *Nanjing da tusha zhenxiang – Riben jiaoshou de lunshu* [The truth about the Rape of Nanking – discussion of a Japanese professor]. Translated from Japanese to Chinese by Wenxin Yang. Shangwu yinshuguan (Hong Kong). 1995.
Higashinakano, Shudo. *Nanjing da tusha de chedi jianzheng* [A complete exposition of the Rape of Nanking]. Translated from Japanese to Chinese by Xinqun Yan. Xinhua chubanshe. 2000.
Hobsbawm, Eric. *Minzu yu minzuzhuyi* [Nations and nationalism]. Translated from English to Chinese by Jinmei Li. Shanghai renmin chubanshe. 2000.
Honda, Katsuichi. *Nanjing da tusha shimo caifang lu* [Interviews on the ins and outs of the Rape of Nanking]. Translated from Japanese to Chinese by Chunming Liu, Nenggou Baorong, Deli Wu, et al. Beiyue wenyi chubanshe. 2001.
Hora, Tomio. *Nanjing da tusha* [The Rape of Nanking]. Translated from Japanese to Chinese by Mao Lianghong et al. Shanghai yiwen chubanshe. 1987.

Hou, Yan. *Nanjing Guomin zhengfu chujian shiqi de shangye gaikuang (1927–1937)* [Summary of commercial conditions in Nanjing at the outset of the Republican era (1927–1937)]. Xiamen University masters thesis. 2003.

Hu, Hualing. *Nanjing da tusha zhong de Meigo huo Pusa – sheming baohu Zhonghua funü de Wei Telin* [American living Bodhisattva in the Rape of Nanking – Minnie Vautrin, who risked her life to save Chinese women]. Jiuge chubanshe. 2003.

Huang, Huiying. *Nanjing da tusha de jianzhengren – Labei zhuan* [Witness to the Rape of Nanking – biography of John Rabe]. Baijia chubanshe. 2002.

Hughes, J. Donald. *Shenme shi huanjing shi* [What is environmental history]. Translated from English to Chinese by Xueqin Mei. Beijing daxue chubanshe. 2008.

Imai, Takeo. *Jinjing Wufu huiyilu* [Memoir of Imai Takedo]. Translated from Japanese to Chinese by the Tianjin Municipal CPPCC Editing and Translating Committee. Zhongguo wenshi chubanshe. 1987.

Iris Chang Memorial Fund and the Global Alliance for Preserving the History of WWII in Asia. *Iris Chang and the forgotten holocaust: best essays from Iris Chang Memorial essay contest 2006*. Cozy House Publisher, 2007.

Iris Chang Memorial Fund. *The Denial and its cost*. Cozy House Publisher, 2018.

Jiang, Gonggu. *Xian Jing san yue ji* [Records of three months in a fallen capital]. Nanjing chubanshe. 2006.

Jiang, Lanxiang. *Huanjing fanzui jiben lilun yanjiu* [Study of the basic theories of environmental crime]. Zhishi chanquan chubanshe. 2008.

Jiang, Zanchu. *Nanjing shi hua* [Discussing the history of Nanjing]. Jiangsu renmin chubanshe. 1980.

Jing, Shenghong. *Nanjing lunxian banian shi (1937 nian 12 yue 13 ri zhi 1945 nian 8 yue 15 ri)* [History of eight years of fallen Nanjing (December 13, 1937 to August 15, 1945)]. Shehui kexue wenxian chubanshe. 2005.

Jing, Shenghong. *Wushidao xia de Nanjing: Ri wei tongzhi xia de Nanjing zhimin shehui yanjiu* [Nanjing under the samurai sword: study of the colonial society in Nanjing under the reign of the Japanese puppet regime]. Nanjing shifan daxue chubanshe. 2008.

Kasahara, Tokushi. *Nanmin qu bai ri – qinli Rijun da tusha de xifangren* [A hundred days in the Safety Zone – Westerners who lived through the great massacre by the Japanese army]. Translated from Japanese to Chinese by Guangqian Li and Zhijun Wang. Nanjing shifan daxue chubanshe. 2005.

Kirby, William C. *Deguo yu Zhonghua Minguo* [Germany and the Republic of China]. Translated from English to Chinese by Qianping Chen et al. Jiangsu renmin chubanshe. 2006.

Li, Enhan. *Riben jun zhanzheng baoxing zhi yanjiu* [Study of war atrocities committed by the Japanese army]. Taiwan shangwu yinshuguan. 1994.

Lin, Changsheng. *Nanjing da tusha zhi tiezheng* [Airtight evidence for the Rape of Nanking]. Zhongyang bianyi chubanshe. 2005.

Liu, Huishu. *Nanjing da tusha xin kao – jian bo Tianzhong Zhengming de "Nanjing da tusha zhi xugou" lun* [New considerations in the Rape of Nanking – refuting Tanaka Masaaka's theory of the fictitiousness of the Rape of Nanking]. Shenghuo – dushu – xinzhi sanlian shudian Shanghai fendian. 1998.

Luo, Ling. *Jindai Nanjing chengshi jianshe yanjiu* [Study of recent urban construction in Nanjing]. Nanjing daxue chubanshe. 1999.

Matsumoto, Shigeharu. *Shanghai shidai* [The Shanghai era]. Translated from Japanese to Chinese by Cao Zhenwei et al. Shanghai shudian chubanshe. 2005.

Matsuoka, Tamaki. *Cong Riben laobing zhanzhi shuxin yu riji kan – Nanjing da tusha* [Looking at the Rape of Nanking from wartime correspondence and diaries of Japanese veterans]. Translated from Japanese to Chinese by Xi Peng et al. Nanjing chubanshe. 2007.

Miquel, Pierre. *Faguo shi* [History of France]. Translated from French to Chinese by Hongbin Cai et al. Shangwu yinshuguan. 1985.

Moriyama, Kohei. *Nanjing da tusha yu Sanguang zhengce* [The Rape of Nanking and the three alls policy]. Translated from Japanese to Chinese by the Tianjin Municipal CPPCC Editing and Translation committee. Sichuan jiaoyu chubanshe. 1984.

Onuma, Yasuaki. *Dongjing shenpan – zhanzheng zeren – zhanhou zeren* [Tokyo trials – responsibility for the war – responsibility after the war]. Translated from Japanese to Chinese by Zhiyong Song. Shehui kexue wenxian chubanshe. 2009.

Nanjing Normal University Rape of Nanking Research Center, ed. *Wei Telin zhuan* [Biography of Minnie Vautrin]. Nanjing chubanshe. 2001.

Niu, Xianming. *Huan su ji* [Records of resuming secular life]. Zhongwai tushu chubanshe. 1971.

Pan, Guxi, ed. *Nanjing de jianzhu* [Nanjing's architecture]. Nanjing chubanshe. 1995.

Peng, Jian. *Nanjing da tusha qijian liu Ning Meiguo chuanjiaoshi xintai yanjiu* [Study of the state of mind of American missionaries in Nanjing during the Rape of Nanking]. Central China Normal University masters thesis, 2002.

Perkins, John H. *Diyuan zhengzhi yu lüse geming – xiaomai, jiyin yu lengzhan* [Geopolitics and the green revolution – wheat, genes, and the Cold War]. Translated from English to Chinese by Zhaofei Wang, Xiaobing Guo et al. Huaxia chubanshe. 2001.

Qin, Feng, ed. *Minguo Nanjing: 1927–1949* [Republican Nanjing: 1927–1949]. Wenhui chubanshe. 2005.

Ren, Chunxiao. *Huanjing zhexue xinlun* [New theory on environmental philosophy]. Jiangxi renmin chubanshe. 2003.

Ren, Yong. *Riben huanjing guanli ji chanye wuran fangzhi* [Environmental management and prevention of industrial pollution in Japan]. Zhongguo huanjing kexue chubanshe. 2000.

Shirer, William. *Disan diguo de xing wang* [The rise and fall of the Third Reich]. Translated from English to Chinese by Dong Leshan. Shijie zhishi chubanshe. 1996.

Sun, Zhaiwei, ed. *Nanjing da tusha* [The Rape of Nanking]. Beijing chubanshe. 1997.

Timperley, H.J. *1937: yi ming yingguo jizhe shilu de rijun baoxing* [1937: What War Means: Japanese Atrocities in China]. Translated from English to Chinese by Ming Yang. Hubei renmin chubanshe. 2005.

Tsuda, Michio. *Nanjing da tusha he Ribenren de jingshen gouzao* [The Rape of Nanking and the psychological make-up of the Japanese people]. Translated from Japanese to Chinese by Zhaoqi Cheng and Yan Liu. Xinxing chubanshe. 2005.

Van de Ven, Hans. *Zhongguo de minzuzhuyi he zhanzheng (1925–1945)* [War and nationalism in China (1925–1945)]. Translated from English to Chinese by Yunhuan Hu. Shenghuo – dushu – xinzhi sanlian shudian. 2007.

Von Clausewitz, Carl. *Zhanzheng lun* [On war]. Translated from German to Chinese by Xianzhong Niu. Guangxi shifan daxue chubanshe. 2003.

Wakeman, Frederic E. *Shanghai lieshi – zhanshi kongbu huodong yu chengshi fanzui, 1937–1941* [The Shanghai Badlands: Wartime Terrorism and Urban Crime, 1937–1941]. Translated from English to Chinese by Chuanming Rui. Shanghai guji chubanshe. 2003.

Wang, Hao. *Zhaoshi: Zhongguo wei'anfu* [Public declaration: comfort women in China]. Qinghai renmin chubanshe. 1998.

Wang, Junxiong. *Minguo zhengfu shiqi Nanjing shoudu jihua zhi yanjiu* [Study of the Nanjing capital plan during the Republic Era]. Taiwan National Cheng Kung University doctoral thesis, 2002.

Wang, Xiang. *Wang wei Nanjing shizheng yanjiu* [Study of the puppet Wang Jingwei regime in Nanjing]. Nanjing University doctoral thesis, 2009.

Wang, Yunjun. *Minguo Nanjing chengshi shehui guanli* [ROC urban social management of Nanjing]. Jiangsu guji chubanshe, 2001.

Wang, Zhixin. *Zhongguo Jidujiao shi gang* [Summary history of Christianity in China]. Shanghai guji chubanshe. 2004.

War History Office, Defense Research Institute, Japan Defense Agency. *Zhongguo shibian lujun zuozhan shi* [Army combat history in the China Incident]. Translated from Japanese to Chinese by Fulin Qi. Zhonghua shuju. 1981.

Weber, Paul. *Lusenbao dagong guo shi* [History of the Grand Duchy of Luxembourg]. Translated to Chinese by the Nanjing University department of foreign langauges. Jiangsu renmin chubanshe. 1973.

Wu, Guangyi. *Qinhua Rijun Nanjing da tusha rizhi* [Japanese soldiers' diaries on the Rape of Nanking]. Shehui kexue wenxian chubanshe. 2005.

Winn, Dan. *Riben zai zhongguo de chaoji da tusha* [The super Holocaust in China]. Translated from English to Chinese by Ping Hao et al. Beijing daxue chubanshe. 2005.

Xin, Ping. *1937: shenzhong de zainan yu lishi de zhuanzhe* [1937: grave tragedy and a historical turning point]. Shanghai renmin chubanshe. 1999.

Xiong, Jie. *Nanjign jindai chengshi guihua yanjiu* [Study of modern urban planning in Nanjing]. Wuhan Polytechnic University masters thesis, 2003..

Xu, Zhigeng. *Nanjing da tusha* [The Rape of Nanking]. Kunlun chubanshe. 1987.

Xue, Bing. *Nanjing chengshi shi* [Urban history of Nanjing]. Nanjing chubanshe. 2008.

Yang, Bingde, ed. *Zhongguo jindai chengshi yu jianzhu* [Modern Chinese cities and architecture]. Zhongguo jiangong chubanshe. 1993.

Ye, Dewei, et al., eds. *Xianggang lunxian shi* [History of the fall of Hong Kong]. Guangjiaojing chubanshe. 1982.

Ye, Zhaowen. *Lao Nanjing – jiu ying qinhuai* [Old Nanjing – old reflections of the Qinhuai]. Jiangsu meishu chubanshe. 1998.

Yin, Jijun. *1937, Nanjing da jiuyuan – xifang renshi he guoji anquan qu* [1937, the great rescuing of Nanjing – Westerners and the International Safety Zone]. Wenhui chubanshe. 1997.

Yu, Zidao, Zhenwei Cao, Yuanhua Shi, and Yun Zhang. 2006. *Wang wei zhengquan quanshi* [Complete history of the puppet regime of Wang Jingwei]. Shanghai renmin chubanshe.

Zhang, Bin. *1928–1937 nian Nanjing chengshi jumin shenghuo touxi* [Complete analysis of the lives of Nanjing residents from 1928 to 1937]. Jilin University masters dissertation. 2004.

Zhang, Lianhong, Shenghong Jing, Hong Chen, et al. *Chuangshang de lishi – Nanjing da tusha yu zhanshi Zhongguo shehui* [Wounded history – the Rape of Nanking and Chinese society during the war]. Nanjing shifan daxue chubanshe. 2005.

Zhang, Sheng, et al. *Ri wei guanxi yanjiu – yi Huadong diqu wei zhongxin* [Study of relations between Japan and puppets – centered on East China]. Nanjing chubanshe. 2003.

Zhang, Xianwen, and Sheng Zhang, eds. *Jinling daxue shi* [History of the University of Nanking]. Nanjing daxue chubanshe. 2002.

Zhang, Xianwen, ed. *Zhongguo kang Ri zhanzheng shi* [History of China's War of Resistance against Japan]. Nanjing daxue chubanshe. 2001.

Zhang, Xianwen, ed. *Zhonghua Minguo shi* [History of the Republic of China]. Nanjing daxue chubanshe. 2006.

Zhang, Xianwen, ed. *Zhonghua Minguo shi gang* [Outline history of the Republic of China]. Henan renmin chubanshe. 1985.

Zhang, Xianwen, Lianhong Zhang, and Weixing Wang, eds. *Nanjing da tusha quan shi* [Complete history of the Rape of Nanking]. Jiangsu renmin chubanshe. 2012.

Zhang, Zheng. *Guomin zhengfu yu minguo dianxin ye (1927–1949)* [The Nationalist Government and the telecommunications industry in Republican China (1927–1949)]. Guangxi Normal University masters dissertation, 2006.

Zhang, Zitai, ed. *Huanjing baohu fa* [Environmental protection law]. Zhongyang guangbo dianshi daxue chubanshe. 2000.

Zhang, Kaiyuan. *Cong Yelu dao Dongjing: wei Nanjing da tusha quzheng* [From Yale to Tokyo: collecting evidence on the Rape of Nanking]. Guangdong renmin chubanshe. 2003.

Zhu, Chengshan. *Qin Hua Rijun Nanjing da tusha shi yanjiu chengguo jiaoliuhui lunwen ji* [Collection of papers from the conference for sharing results in study of the history of the Rape of Nanking]. Anhui daxue chubanshe. 1999.

Zhu, Chengshan, ed. *Qin Hua Rijun Nanjing da tusha xingcunzhe zhengyan* [Testimony of survivors of the Rape of Nanking]. Shenhui kexue wenxian chubanshe. 2005.

3. Papers

Askew, David. "The International Committee for the Nanking Safety Zone: An Introduction." *Sino Japanese Studies* 14 (2002).

Bao, Maohong. "Huanjing shi: lishi, lilun he fangfa [Environmental history: history, theory, and methods]." *Shi xue lilun yanjiu* 4 (2000).

Bu, Ping. "Zhong Ri gongtong lishi yanjiu zhong de lilun yu fangfa wenti [Problems in theory and methodology in China-Japan joint historical study]." *Kang Ri zhanzheng yanjiu* 1 (2011).

Chen, Anji. ""Nanjing da tusha shi" yanjiu de lishi huigu he jinhou de renwu [A historical look back on the study of the Rape of Nanking and tasks going forward]." *Minguo dang'an* 4 (1997).

Chen, Hongmin, and Fu Min. "Nanjing da tusha yanjiu de huigu yu qianzhan [A look back and a look forward for the study of the Rape of Nanking]." *Kang Ri zhanzheng yanjiu* 4 (2008).

Cheng, Zhaoqi. "Labei riji shi "wugen de bianzao" me? – dui zhenxiang – Nanjing shijian – Jianzheng Labei riji de jianzheng [Is Rabe's diary a "baseless fabrication"? Putting the

book Truth – Nanking Incident – examining Rabe's diary to the test]." *Jindai shi yanjiu* 2 (2002a).
Cheng, Zhaoqi. "Cong Dongjing shenpan dao Dongjing shenpan [From the Tokyo trials to the Tokyo trials]. *Shi lin* 5 (2007).
Cheng, Zhaoqi. "Nanjing da tusha shi Dongjing shenpan de bianzao me? [Was the Rape of Nanking fabricated during the Tokyo trials?]." *Jindai shi yanjiu* 6 (2002b).
Cheng, Zhaoqi. "Nanjing da tusha yanjiu de jige wenti [A few questions in the study of the Rape of Nanking]." *Shi lin* 4 (2010a).
Cheng, Zhaoqi. "Nanjing da tusha zhaji zhi yi [Notes on the Rape of Nanking part one]." *Shi lin* 3 (2002c).
Cheng, Zhaoqi. "Nanjing da tusha zhaji zhi er [Notes on the Rape of Nanking part two]." *Shi lin* 1 (2003).
Cheng, Zhaoqi. "Nanjing da tusha zhong de Rijun tusha ling yanjiu [Study of the Japanese army's massacre order during the Rape of Nanking]." *Lishi yanjiu* 6 (2002d).
Cheng, Zhaoqi. "Riben xiancun Nanjing da tusha shiliao gailun [General discussion of Rape of Nanking historical materials extant in Japan]." *Shehui kexue* 9 (2006).
Cheng, Zhaoqi. "Songjing Shigen zhanzheng zeren de zai jiantao – Dongjing shenpan youguan Nanjing baoxing zui beigaofang zhengci jianzheng zhi yi [Re-examination of Matsui Iwane's war guilt – examination of defense testimony related to Nanjing atrocities part two]." *Jindai shi yanjiu* 6 (2010b).
Cheng, Zhaoqi. "Xiaochuan Guanzhilang zhengci de zai jiantao – Dongjing shenpan youguan Nanjing baoxing zui beigaofang zhengci jianzheng zhi er [Re-examination of Ogawa Sekijiro's testimony – examination of defense testimony related to Nanjing atrocities part two]." *Jianghai xuekan* 4 (2010c).
Cui, Wei. "Zhangzheng jincheng yu Nanjing da tusha [progress of the war and the Rape of Nanking]." *Jiangsu shehui kexue* 3 (2005).
Dai, Yuanzhi. "Shi lun Labei riji bufen chatu [An attempted discussion on pictures inserted into John Rabe's diary]." In the collection of theses *Di'er ci Nanjing da tusha shi xueshu yantaohui*, November 2007.
Felber, Roland. "Guomindang Zhongguo de Deguo junshi guwen – jinqi yanjiu shuping [German military advisers in KMT China – a commentary on recent research]." Translated from German to Chinese by Qianping Chen. *Minguo dang'an* 1 (1994).
Ding, Zhaodong, and Qianping Chen. "Lüe lun wei Nanjing shi zizhi weiyuanhui de tongzhi [A summary discussion of the rule of the Nanjing Municipal Autonomous Committee]." *Minguo dang'an* 2 (2004).
Fitch, George. "Nanjing de huimie [The destruction of Nanjing]." Translated from English by Li Yuming. *Minguo dang'an* 3 (1995).
Gao, Fanfu. "Riben Tianhuang Yuren yu Nanjing da tusha [Japanese Emperor Hirohito and the Rape of Nanking]." *Nanjing shehui kexue* 8 (2004).
Gao, Fanfu, et al. "Riben junren de xing xinli yu wei'anfu zhidu [The sexual psychology of Japanese soldiers and the comfort women institution]." *Nanjign shehui kexue* 8 (2006).
Gao, Pengcheng. "Nanjing da tusha shiqi Hong Wanzihui huodong de liangmianxing [The two-sided nature of activities of the Red Swastika Society during the Rape of Nanking]." *Nanjing shehui kexue* 6 (2010).

Gao, Xingzu. "Nanjing da tusha shijian yanjiu xianzhuang he jinhou de keti [Current status of study of the "Rape of Nanking" incident and topics for future consideration]." *Kang Ri zhanzheng yanjiu* 3 (1996).

Gao, Xingzu. "Rijun di shiliu shituan Zhongshan Men wai tusha zhenxiang [The truth of the Japanese 16th Division's massacre outside the Zhonghua Gate]." *Lishi yanjiu* 4 (1995).

Gregor, Neil. "Nazui tusha yu Nanjing baoxing de yanjiu: fanshi zhuanbian yu bijiao qishi [Study of the Nazi massacre and the Rape of Nanking: paradigm shifts and the lessons of comparisons]." Translated from English to Chinese by Yang Xiaming. *Nanjing daxue xuebao (zhexue – renwen kexue – shehui kexue)* 3 (2010).

Guo, Biqiang. "Guomin zhengfu mimi zuzhi fu Ri jielu Nanjing da tusha zhenxiang shuping [Commentary on the secret trip of the nationalist government to Japan to reveal the truth of the Rape of Nanking]." *Nanjing shehui kexue* 12 (2002).

Huang, Huiying. "Labei zai "Nanjing da tusha" qijian de xingwei ji sixiang bianhua jianxi [Brief analysis of changes in actions and thoughts of John Rabe during the "Rape of Nanking"]." *Minguo dang'an* 4 (1997).

Jiang, Liangqin. "Cong Song Hu dao Nanjing: Jiang Jieshi zheng zhanlüe xuanze zhi shiwu ji qi zhuanxiang [From Shanghai to Nanjing: mistakes in strategic decisions by the Chiang Kai-shek regime and subsequent change in direction]." *Nanjing daxue xuebao (zhexue – renwen kexue – shehui kexue)* 1 (2011).

Jiang, Liangqin. "Nanjing da tusha de zhijie dongyin [Direct motivators of the Rape of Nanking]." *Jiangxi shehui kexue* 2 (1999).

Jiang, Liangqin, et al. "Cong shimin chengwen kan Nanjing da tusha [Looking at the Rape of Nanjing from citizen reports]." *Kang Ri zhanzheng yanjiu* 1 (2007).

Jiang, Liangqin, et al. "Nanjing da tusha qijian shimin caichan sunshi de diaocha yu tongji – ji yu guonei xiancun dang'an ziliao de fenxi [Investigation and statistics on property losses of city residents during the Rape of Nanking – an analysis based in extant historical materials]." *Lishi yanjiu* 2 (2012).

Jing, Shenghong. "Buqu de Nanjing minzhong – lunxian shiqi Nanjing shimin de zifa kang Ri douzheng [Unbroken Nanjingers – the spontaneous struggle of Nanjing residents at the time of the fall]." *Nanjing shehui kexue* 8 (2005).

Jing, Shenghong. "Lun Nanjing da tusha qijian xifang qiaomin de xuanchuan gongxian [On the information dissemination contributions of Westerners during the Rape of Nanking]." *Jianghai xuekan* 1 (2009a).

Jing, Shenghong. "Nanjing lunxian qianhou de xifang qiaomin ji qi dui Ri kangzheng [Westerners and their stand against Japan before and after the fall of Nanjing]." *Nanjing shehui kexue* 4 (2006).

Jing, Shenghong. "Rijun da tusha qian de Nanjing jianshe chengjiu yu shehui fengmao [Construction achievements and social features of Nanjing before the Japanese great massacre]." *Nanjing shehui kexue* 6 (2009b).

Jing, Shenghong. "Zhanshi Riben chuanmei dui Nanjing da tusha de yangai yu fenshi [Covering up and whitewashing of the Rape of Nanking by Japanese media during the war]." *Shi xue yuekan* 8 (2010).

Jing, Shenghong. "Zhanshi Riben dangju zai guonei shi ruhe fengsuo Nanjing da tusha zhenxiang de? [How did domestic authorities in Japan keep the truth of the Rape of Nanking a secret from their own people?]" *Jiangsu shehui kexue* 3 (2008).

Kasahara, Tokushi. "Nanjing da tusha qijian xing baoli de gouzao [The structure of sexual violence during the Rape of Nanking]." *Jianghai xuekan* 6 (2001).

Kasahara, Tokushi. "Nanjing da tusha yu jiaokeshu wenti [The Rape of Nanking and the problem with textbooks]." *Jianghai xuekan* 1 (2003).

Kasahara, Tokushi. "Ri zhong lishi gongtong yanjiu yu Nanjing da tusha lunzheng zai Riben de zhongjie [Japan-China joint historical research and the end of debates over the Rape of Nanking in Japan]." Translated from Japanese to Chinese by Yingying Gao. *Kang Ri zhanzheng yanjiu* 4 (2010).

Li, Hanmei. "Zhongguo xueshujie dui "Nanjing da tusha shijian" de yanjiu [Study of the "Rape of Nanking Incident" in Chinese academia]." *Taipingyang xuebao* 8 (2005).

Li, Yuan. "Nanjing tebie shi diyi ren shizhang Liu Jiwen [The first mayor of the special city of Nanjing Liu Jiwen]." *Jiangsu difangzhi* 5 (2004).

Lin, Ting, and Liu Weirong. "Minguo shiqi de Nanjing jianzhu [Nanjing architecture in the Republican era]." *Dang'an yu jianzhu* 9 (n.d.).

Liu, Huishu. "Nanjing da tusha shiqi de Nanjing nanmin qu guoji weiyuanhui [The International Committee for the Nanking Safety Zone during the Rape of Nanking]." *Xueshu yuekan* 8 (1995).

Liu, Jiafeng, and Peng Jian. "Jianzheng Nanjing da tusha de chedi jianzheng [Confirming the ultimate confirmation of the Rape of Nanking]." *Kang Ri zhanzheng yanjiu* 1 (2001).

Liu, Yanjun. "Nanjing da tusha de lishi jiyi (1937–1985) [Historical memory of the Rape of Nanking (1937–1985)]." *Kang Ri zhanzheng yanjiu* 4 (2009).

Luo, Yijun. "Shanghai nan shi nanmin qu shu lüe [Brief history of the Shanghai Safety Zone]." *Shanghai shifan daxue xuebao* 2 (1990).

Ma, Zhendu. "Rijun da tusha qijian Nanjing junmin fankang wenti yanjiu [Study of the issues of resistance by soldiers and civilians in Nanjing during the Japanese army's great massacre]." *Kang Ri zhanzheng yanjiu* 4 (2007).

Mei, Xueqin. "Cong huanjing de lishi dao huanjing shi – guanyu huanjing shi yanjiu de yizhong renshi [From the history of environment to environmental history – a perspective on the study of environmental history]." *Shijie lishi* 6 (2006).

Pan, Tao. "Nanjing anquan qu de zongjiao fuhao fenxi [Analysis of the religious overtones of the Nanking Safety Zone]." *Nanjing shehui kexue* 10 (2008).

Peng, Jian. "Bei hushi de shouhaizhe – Nanjing da tusha zhong Meiguo chuanjiaoshi de ling yi mian [Overlooked victims – another side to the American missionaries during the Rape of Nanking]." *Nanjing shehui kexue* 8 (2003).

Peng, Jian. "Chou Ri hu, fan Ri hu – shi xi Nanjing da tusha qijian Meiguo chuanjiaoshi dui Rijun zhi taidu [Angry at Japan, opposing Japan – an attempted analysis of the attitudes of American missionaries toward the Japanese army during the Rape of Nanking]." *Nanjing shehui kexue* 6 (2004).

Qu, Shengfei, and Sheng Zhang. "Nanjing da tusha shiqi nanmin shenghuo zhuangtai yanjiu [Study of the living conditions of refugees during the Rape of Nanking]." *Yuejiang xuekan* 1 (2010).

Shoji, Junichiro. ""Ri Zhong lishi gongtong yanjiu" zhi huigu – yi Nanjing shijian wei zhuti [A look back on "joint historical research between Japan and China" – with the Nanjing Incident being the primary entity]." Translated from Japanese to Chinese by Wenhao Yu. *Kang Ri zhanzheng yanjiu* 4 (2010).

Sun, Zhaiwei. "Lun Nanjing da tusha de beijing he fanchou [On the background and scale of the Rape of Nanking]." *Minguo dang'an* 1 (1995).
Sun, Zhaiwei. "Lun Nanjing da tusha de zhunbei, shishi he yanshen [On the preparations, implementation, and extension of the Rape of Nanking]." *Jianghai xuekan* 5 (2000).
Sun, Zhaiwei. "Lun Nanjing da tusha yunan renshu rending de lishi yanbian [On the historical changes to the appraised number of dead in the Rape of Nanking]." *Jianghai xuekan* 6 (2001).
Sun, Zhaiwei. "Lun Nanjing da tusha zhenxiang de zaoqi chuanbo [On the early dissemination of the truth about the Rape of Nanking]." *Nanjing shehui kexue* 6 (2004).
Sun, Zhaiwei. "Lun Nanjing da tusha zhong de xing baoli wenti [On the question of sexual violence in the Rape of Nanking]." *Minguo dang'an* 4 (2000).
Sun, Zhaiwei. "Nanjing da tusha suo zaocheng de shehui jingji houguo yanjiu [Study of the socioeconomic consequences of the Rape of Nanking]." *Nanjing shehui kexue* 2 (1996).
Sun, Zhaiwei. "Ruhe jiedu Dongjing shenpan dui Nanjing da tusha yunan renshu de rending [How to read the determination of the number of people killed during the Rape of Nanking made during the Tokyo trials]." *Nanjing shida xuebao (shehui kexue ban)* 6 (2007).
Sun, Zhaiwei. "Shi lun "Nanjing da tusha" zhong de anquan qu [An attempted discourse on the Safety Zone during the Rape of Nanking]." *Nanjing shehui kexue* 5 (1992).
Wang, Tianping. "Zhao xiang gong jiu yan yu Nanjing da tusha [Prince Asaka Yasuhiko and the Rape of Nanking]." *Dang'an yu jianshe* 2 (2001).
Wang, Wexing. "Nanjing da tusha shi guanbing xintai tantao [An exploration of the psychological states of officers and soldiers during the Rape of Nanking]." *Minguo dang'an* 4 (1997).
Wang, Weixing. "Yi bu chenzhong de lishi – ping Nanjing da tusha [A heavy chapter in history – on the Rape of Nanking]." *Jiangsu shehui kexue* 2 (1998).
Wang, Weixing. "Youguan Nanjing da tusha de Rijun guanbing riji [Japanese soldiers' diaries related to the Rape of Nanking]." *Kang Ri Zhanzheng yanjiu* 4 (2005).
Wang, Weixing. "Youguan Nanjing da tusha de yingguo waijiao dang'an de shiliao jiazhi [The historical value of British diplomatic records related to the Rape of Nanking]." *Dang'an yu jianshe* 3 (2002).
Wang, Xiaoyan. "Nanjing da tusha qijian liu Jing xifang qiaomin jiuji nanmin huodong [Relief activities for refugees by Westerners in Nanjing during the Rape of Nanking]." *Jiangsu jiaoyu xueyuan xuebao (shehui kexue ban)* 4 (2006b).
Wang, Xiliang. "Jiexi "Dongjing shenpan shiguan" ji qi shizhi [Explaining the "historical perspective of the Tokyo trials" and their substance]." *Shijie lishi* 5 (2008).
Wang, Xiliang. "Riben xueshujie "Nanjing da tusha shijian" lunzheng ji ge pai lundian pingxi [Analysis of arguments over the "Nanjing massacre incident" in Japanese academia and key points of all factions]." *Kang Ri zhanzheng yanjiu* 4 (2006).
Wang, Yongzhong. "Nanjing da tusha shiqi de Jinling daxue nanmin shourongsuo [The refugee shelter at the University of Nanking during the Rape of Nanking]." *Kang Ri zhanzheng yanjiu* 4 (2008).
Wei, Chuxiong. "Lishi yu lishi xuejia: haiwai Nanjing da tusha yanjiu de zhengyi zongshu [History and historians: summary of disputes in the study of the Rape of Nanking abroad]." *Lishi yanjiu* 5 (2009).

Wei, C.X. George. "Politicization and De-politicization of History: The Evolution of International Studies of the Nanjing Massacre." *The Chinese Historical Review* 15 (2008).
Wen, Lifeng. ""Nacui tu you he Nanjing da tusha guoji yantaohui" zongshu [Summary of the International Symposium on the Holocaust and the Rape of Nanking]." *Xuehai* 6 (2005).
Xie, Donghui. "Nanjing guomin zhengfu huanjing fazhi lunlüe [Outline of rule-by-law in the environment of the Nanjing nationalist government]." *Nanjing shehui kexue* 4 (2008).
Xu, Ligang. "Nanjing da tusha qianhou liu Ning Ou Mei qiaomin de neixin shijie [The interior world of Westerners in Nanjing around the Rape of Nanking]." *Minguo dang'an* 1 (2001).
Yan, Haijian. "Dui zhanhou Nanjing da tusha an shenpan de zai renshi [Getting to know the post-war trials on the Rape of Nanking again]." *Nanjing shifan daxue xuebao (shehui kexue ban)* 3 (2008a).
Yan, Haijian. "Qin Hua Rijun junfengji de tixi nei renshi – yi Gangcun Ningci huiyilu wei kaocha duixiang [Understanding the insides of military discipline of the Japanese army invading China – focusing on the memoir of Okamura Yasuji]." *Guangxi shehui kexue* 2 (2008b).
Yang, Xiaming, and Wang Weixing. "Yingguo waijiao dang'an zhong youguan qin Hua Rijun Nanjing da tusha shiliao yi zu [A collection of historical materials related to the Rape of Nanking in British diplomatic papers]." *Minguo dang'an* 1 (2002).
Yang, Xiaming. "Meiguo Shidai Zhoukan 1937–1941 nian youguan Rijun hongzha Nanjing he da tusha de baodao [Reports in Time Magazine on the Japanese bombing of Nanjing and the great massacre from 1937 to 1941]." *Minguo dang'an* 4 (2006).
Yang, Xiaming. "Meiguo guojia dang'an guan ziliao jilu de Nanjing da tusha [The Rape of Nanking in files of the U.S. National Archives]." *Kang Ri Zhanzheng yanjiu* 4 (2005).
Yang, Xiaming. "Nanjing baoxing: Rijun xingwei beihou de zhidu anpai [Nanjing atrocities: institutional arrangements behind Japanese military behaviors]." *Jianghai xuekan* 6 (2007).
Yang, Xiaming. "Shi lun "Nanjing anquan qu" gongneng de cuowei ji qi yuanyin [An attempt at discourse on dislocation in the functions of the Nanking Safety Zone and reasons]." *Kang Ri zhanzheng yanjiu* 4 (2000).
Yao, Qunmin. "Jiuguo shibao jielu Nanjing da tusha zhenxiang shuping [Commentary on exposition of the truth of the Rape of Nanking in Jiuguo shibao]." *Minguo dang'an* 4 (2005).
Yi, Qing, and Jiang Liangqin. "Nanjing da tusha shiliao guoji xueshu taolunhui zongshu [Summary of the International Academic Forum for Historical Materials on the Rape of Nanking]." *Kang ri zhanzheng yanjiu* 1 (2006).
Yuan Yin. "Mishi de ziwo – dui Nanjing da tusha de shehui xinli dongji yu xinlixue pouxi [Lost egos – social psychology motivations and psychological analysis of the Rape of Nanking]." *Xiandai chuanbo* 10 (2010).
Zeng, Ming. "Nanjing da tusha shiliao guoji xueshui taolunhui zongshu [Overall picture of the International academic symposium on historical materials related to the Rape of Nanking]." *Minguo dang'an* 1 (2006).
Zhang, Kaiyuan. "Daodi shi shei zai zhizao weizheng? – Bo Tianzhong Zhengming Nanjing da tusha zhi xugou dui Bei Deshi de dihui [Who's making false evidence? – refuting Tanaka Masaaka's slandering of Bates in What Really Happened in Nanjing: Refutation of a Common Myth]." *Lishi yanjiu* 2 (1999).

Zhang, Lianhong. "Jin ji nian lai guonei Nanjing da tusha yanjiu zongshu [Overview of research of the Rape of Nanking in China in the past few years]." *Jianghai xuekan* 5 (2000a).
Zhang, Lianhong. "Nanjing da tusha de houyizheng: xingcunzhe de chuangshang [Aftermath of the Rape of Nanking: wounds of survivors]." *Jianghai xuekan* 3 (2006).
Zhang, Lianhong. "Nanjing da tusha dui Nanjing shimin shehui xinli de yingxiang [The impact of the Rape of Nanking on the social psychology of city residents]." *Jiangsu shehui kexue* 6 (200b).
Zhang, Lianhong. "Nanjing da tusha qianxi Nanjing renkou de bianhua [Changes in the population of Nanjing on the eve of the Rape of Nanking]." *Minguo dang'an* 3 (2004).
Zhang, Lianhong. "Nanjing da tusha shiqi de Nanjing shi zizhi weiyuanhui yu anquan qu guoji weiyuanhui [The Autonomous Committee and the International Committee for the Nanking Safety Zone during the Rape of Nanking]." *Minguo dang'an* 4 (2007a).
Zhang, Lianhong. "Nanjing da tusha shiqi de Rijun dangju yu Nanjing anquan qu [Japanese authorities and the Nanking Safety Zone during the Rape of Nanking]." *Jindai shi yanjiu* 3 (2001).
Zhang, Lianhong. "Nanjing da tusha yunan renkou de goucheng – yi Nanjing shi changzhu renkou wei zhongxin [The composition of the dead in the Rape of Nanking – centered on long-term residents of Nanjing]." *Nanjing shifan daxue xuebao (shehui kexue ban)* 6 (2007b).
Zhang, Lianhong. "Ruhe jiyi Nanjing da tusha – Zhong Ri gongtong lishi yanjiu zhong de xueshu duihua [How to remember the Rape of Nanking – an academic dialogue in the common study of history by China and Japan]." *Kang Ri zhanzheng yanjiu* 4 (2010).
Zhang, Lianhong. "Zhong Ri liang guo Nanjing da tusha yanjiu de huigu yu sikao [A look back and thoughts on study of the Rape of Nanking in China and Japan]." *Nanjing daxue xuebao (zhexue – renwen kexue – shehui kexue)* 1 (2007c).
Zhang, Sheng. "Deguo dang'an zhong de Nanjing da tusha [The Rape of Nanking in German sources]." *Kang Ri zhanzheng yanjiu* 4 (2005).
Zhang, Sheng. "Cong Nanjing da tusha kan Zhongguo kangzhan qiantu – Nanjing xifang renshi de guancha he yupan [A look at China's prospects in the War of Resistance from the outbreak of the Rape of Nanking – observations and predictions of Westerners in Nanjing]." *Minguo dang'an* (2006).
Zhang, Sheng. "Qin Hua Nanjing da tusha de "Deguo shijiao" – yi Deguo waijiao dang'an wei zhongxin [The "German Perspective" on the Japanese army's Rape of Nanking – centered in German diplomatic documents]." *Nanjing daxue xuebao* 1 (2007a).
Zhang, Sheng. "Cong Nanjing da tusha de fasheng kan Rijun de zhanlüe shiji xuanze – yi Rifang silü wei zhongxin de kaocha [Looking at Japanese strategic and timing decisions from the occurrence of the Rape of Nanking – observations centered in Japanese considerations]." *Nanjing shifan daxue xuebao* 6 (2007b).
Zhang, Sheng. "Dongjing shenpan zhong Rifang zhengren de jiti weizheng ji qi houguo [Collective perjury of the Japanese during the Tokyo trials and its consequences]." *Zhongguo shehui kexueyuan bao*, September 7, 2010, third edition.
Zhang, Sheng. "Guoji Hong Shizi Hui Nanjing fenhui zai Nanjing da tusha qijian de gongxian [Contributions of the Nanjing branch of the International Red Cross Society during the Rape of Nanking]." In *Hong Shizi Hui yu cishan wenhua* [The Red Cross Society and the

culture of charity], edited by Zihua Chi and Ruyi Hao. Guangxi shifan daxue chubanshe. 2010.

Zhang, Sheng. "Meiguo wenben jilu de Nanjing da tusha [The Rape of Nanking in American documents and records]." *Lishi yanjiu* 5 (2012).

Zhang, Sheng. "Cong lishi dao jiyi: shenhua Nanjing da tusha yanjiu de luoji lujing [From history to memory: the logic of deepening the study of the Rape of Nanking]." *Nanjing zhengzhi xueyuan xuebao* 6 (2014).

Zhang, Sheng. "Wujin de zhuiwen: shiliao de lianhuan jiedu – yi Nanjing da tusha qijian de Aidehua – Shipeilin wei li [Unending questioning: the interlocked reading of historical materials – citing Eduard Sperling of the Rape of Nanking period as an example]." *Shehui kexue zhanxian* 9 (2017a).

Zhang, Sheng. "Guoshang yong huai nan wang – xie zai qin Hua Rijun Nanjing da tusha 80 zhou nian zhi ji [National martyrs live in our hearts forever – marking the 80th anniversary of the Rape of Nanking]." *Qiu shi* 24 (2017b).

Zhang, Sheng. "Lishi shuxie zhong de "qi ge W" – yi Nanjing da tusha shi shuxie weili [The "seven Ws" in writing history – taking the history of the Rape of Nanking as an example]." *Riben qin Hua Nanjing da tusha yanjiu* 1 (2018).

Zhang, Sheng. "The Nanjing Massacre as Recorded in American sources. 2017 fall." *Chinese Studies in History* 50, no. 4 (2017c).

Zhang, Sheng, and Rufang Chen. "Nanjing da tusha qijian de Gulou Yiyuan [The Kulou Hospital during the Rape of Nanking]." *Beihua daxue xuebao* 5 (2008b).

Zhang, Sheng, and Yi'an Zhai. "Dongjing shenpan Nanjing da tusha de bianhu – yi kong, bian shuangfang zhizheng wei zhongxin de kaocha [Defense of the Rape of Nanking in the Tokyo trials – observations centered on cross-examinations by the prosecution and defense]." *Kang Ri zhanzheng yanjiu* 4 (2008a).

Zhang, Weibo. "Jin shi nian "qin Hua Rijun Nanjing da tusha" yanjiu shuping [Review of studies on the Rape of Nanking in the past 10 years]." *Zhonggong dangshi ziliao* 3 (2006).

Zhang, Xianwen. "Nanjing da tusha shiliao ji de xueshu jiazhi he zhengzhi yiyi [The academic value and political significance of Compilation of Rape of Nanking Historical Materials]." *Nanjing daxue xuebao* 1 (2007).

Zhang, Yan. "Qing mo ji Minguo shiqi Nanjing jianzhu yishu gaishu [Summary of architectural arts in Nanjing in the late Qing and Republican era]." *Minguo dang'an* 4 (1999).

Zhu, Chengshan. "Qinli Nanjing da tusha de waiji renshi shukao [On the number of foreigners who lived through the Rape of Nanking]." *Kang Ri zhanzheng yanjiu* 4 (2005).

Zong, Yumei. "1927–1937 nian Guomin zhengfu de jingji jianshe shuping [Commentary on economic construction by the Nationalist Government from 1927 to 1937]." *Minguo dang'an* 1 (1992).

4. Periodicals and Local Histories.

Dagongbao (Ta Kung Pao).

Jiangsu Provincial Local Records Compilation Committee. Jiangsu sheng zhi – liangshi zhi [History of Jiangsu Province – grain history]. November, first edition. Nanjing: Jiangsu renmin chubanshe, 1994.

Jindai Zhongguo (Taiwan).
Jiu guo shibao.
La Stampa (Italy).
Minguo dang'an.
Nanjing City Museum, ed. Nanjing fengyun zhi [History of Nanjing's precarious situation]. Nanjing: Jiangsu renmin chubanshe, 1983.
Nanjing Municipal Local History Compilation Committee and Nanjing Municipal Grain History Editing Committee. Nanjing liangshi zhi [Nanjing grain history]. Zhongguo chengshi chubanshe. 1993.
Nanjing Municipal Local History Compilation Committee. Nanjing gongyong shiye zhi [History of public enterprises in Nanjing]. Haitian chubanshe. 1994.
Nanjing Municipal Local History Compilation Committee. Nanjing shizheng jianshe shiye zhi [History of construction of municipal government in Nanjing]. Haitian chubanshe. 1994.
Nanjing Municipal Local History Compilation Committee. Nanjing jian shi [Brief history of Nanjing]. Jiangsu guji chubanshe. 1986.
Pravda.
Reader's Digest.
Relazioni Intenazionali (Italy).
Shenbao.
The Chicago Daily News.
The New York Times.
The North China Daily News.
The North China Herald.
The South China Morning Post.
The Washington Post.
Zhongyan ribao.

Postscript

First, I would like to thank the Nanjing University Humanities Fund and Mr. Samuel Yin for their generous funding support. Their help made it possible for me to work at full capacity on this project with no distractions.

In 2002, my teacher Professor Zhang Xianwen began planning to compile historical materials on the Rape of Nanking. In winter of the following year, through a recommendation of my brother Zhang Hao via Mr. Zhu Paoping, I circuitously got my book into the hands of the governor of Jiangsu Province Mr. Liang Baohua. With Mr. Liang's kind help, I was allocated funds of 700,000 yuan to collect, organize, translate, and edit historical materials from around the world. Our funding has grown since then. Guided by Professor Zhang, a team of more than 100 experts in the field both Chinese and foreign came together to finish the monumental 72-volume work *Compilation of Rape of Nanking Historical Materials* in 2011. Young and untalented at the time, I was hired by my teacher to serve as deputy editor. With his encouragement and that of the rest of the team, I slowly entered the circle of the study of the history of the Rape of Nanking.

The Rape of Nanking Historical Research Institute founded in Nanjing University has produced one to two PhDs and two to three masters degree holders per year since its founding. Because of my posting there, I have had the opportunity to study and explore with the authors of this book Dong Weimin, Guo Zhaozhao, Yan Haijian, Qu Shengfei, Wang Jinjing, and others. Gradually the papers of these PhD and masters degree holders came togoether, along with the results of my own research, to become this book. Everybody's perspective is different, and every paper has its insights. I did not butcher their works in editing, but rather only made them read more smoothly, adjusted the format of their notes, and integrated them into the flow of the overall themes of the book to create a better experience for the reader. Unfortunately I was unable to include essays by Su Suimeng, Chen Rufang, and Wang Xiaoyan in this book, and for that I feel particularly sorry.

I have been cultivated in the history department of Nanjing University for 24 years, and I owe a debt of gratitude to department leaders Professor Chen Qianping and Professor Sun Jianglin as well as to Professors Fan Jinmin, Shui Tao, and Ji Qiufeng for their support and for allowing me to pursue my academic research without having to look over my shoulder.

I have had the fortune of close contact and frequent instruction with Sun Zhaiwei, Jing Shenghong, Ma Zhendu, Cao Bihong, Zhang Lianhong, Wang Weixing, Yang Xiaming, Guo Biqiang, Xia Bei, Jiang Liangqin, Cao Dachen, Lü Jing,

Lei Guoshan, and Li Bin over these past 10 years as a result of having edited materials with them. I have also been assisted in the collection of materials and their study through contacts with Bu Ping, Tan Ruqian, Yang Daqing, Mr. and Mrs. Cai Deliang, Wang E, Hans van de Ven, Takahara Tokushi, and Ono Kenji. Yang Jun also assumed many of my teaching duties, giving me more time and energy to concentrate on this work. I thank them all from the bottom of my heart.

The support of my family goes without saying. My work was never assessed in monetary terms, even at the time of flourishing materialism, and this allowed me to keep up my interest in and respect for academics. This is truly a luxury for a scholar.

From the academic perspective, this book is a kind of reconstruction of the past. In a broader sense, that makes this book a part of the "collective memory" of the Rape of Nanking. The Rape of Nanking is an important page in the modern history of the Chinese people and in the construction of our state. Of course, the framework, calibration, format, and orientation of this collective memory are all deeply imbued with Chinese characteristics, and are still developing. So one can imagine the "Chinese face" and stamp of the times on this book.

Naturally, as China continues to open, the Chinese people are becoming more knowledgeable and rational toward great world trends, and the study of the history of the Rape of Nanking is gradually coming onto the tracks of international trends. The publication of this book can be viewed as an effort toward creating a "transnational historical understanding" and collective memory shared by all of humanity.

That said, the study of the Rape of Nanking is a new field in history. Despite my best efforts, errors are inevitable. As such, I appreciate any corrections or instruction readers may deign to offer!

Zhang Sheng

January 2012

Postscript to the Revised Edition

During a visit by the mayor of Nagoya Kawamura Takashi to Nagoya's "sister city" Nanjing, prior to the 2012 publication of this revised edition, Kawamura "willfully" denied the truth of the Rape of Nanking. At the time microblogs were in full bloom in China. On my account I declared that I was willing to publicly debate him anywhere, at any time, and with any audience listening, on the basic history of the Rape of Nanking. As the saying goes, one stone can raise a thousand ripples, and the ardent reaction to my statement was something that I, long confined to studying books in closed rooms, had never experienced before. Particularly after great promotions by my friend Qiu Qiming, Sina Weibo, and CCTV, I unexpectedly became a "celebrity" for a moment, and I was able to feel the significance of the Rape of Nanking to the people of our country.

Nevertheless, I received no response from Kawamura. My attention then turned to another matter: the Central Organization Department and Central League were sending professors to different parts of China for on-the-job training, and I threw in my lot. About half a year later, I was notified that I had been chosen for an assignment in Hainan. In early December, Professor Zhang Xianwen held a press briefing for *Compilation of Rape of Nanking Historical Materials* in Beijing, which I attended before beginning my training. Then deputy executive of the Central Organization Department Shen Yueyue, then Communist Youth League Secretary Lu Hao, and the party secretary of Baiyin City, Gansu Province educated us political "greenhorns" on how to behave.

On December 18, 2012, I arrived at my post in Wuzhishan City, Hainan. Wuzhishan is a county-level city in the mountains with a population of only 100,000. Its average elevation is 800 meters above sea level, and its average temperature is 22 degrees Celsius. The negative air ion count in its air is 50,000 per cubic meter, and most surface water there is grade one. Such a beautiful, tranquil, simple city is hard to come by. At the time of liberation, when a hunter here killed wild prey, not only did passers-by get a share, but so did their dogs. Now it has been classified as a national-level poor county, with annual fiscal transfer payments of as much as one billion yuan. The poverty and backwardness are even more evident under the swaying coconut palms of the country. I wrote in my diary: "I stooped over to hug my mother earth so beset with misery and give service to my hard toiling fellow locals." An entire year later, I left Wuzhishan in the dim dawn light of December 18, 2013.

During my year there, I made many smart, amicable friends like Secretary Song Shaohua and got closer to grassroots society. The concreteness, systematicness, and troublesomeness of accomplishing deeds there did not negate the value of academic research. I'd rather say that it represented the division of labor at all levels of this country of more than 1.3 billion people. The ideas of caring for the nation and the people and the community of shared destiny that have derived from academic research have been filled out with practical contents in interactions between rural people who don't know each other at all. Wuzhishan was not invaded by the Japanese. What locals there remember is the legendary uprising of Wang Guoxing and Feng Baiju's steadfastly holding up the red flag for more than 20 years. Most who have received basic education do, however, have knowledge of the War of Resistance and the Rape of Nanking. The recounting of the history of the nation-state has integrated the histories of local ethnicities who remained in the primitive stage of *"hemuzhi"* only half a century ago, in something akin to what philosophers call the "original state" of humanity.

My head was still full of grassroots party and government operations when I returned to Nanjing University. I did not attempt to dispel these thoughts, but rather temporarily shifted them into another channel. The anthropological and sociological values of rural society in Wuzhishan frequently emerge in my thoughts, but it's the Rape of Nanking that most often pulls my heartstrings. Any social or academic plucking of the strings creates waves in my emotion. The event has become part of my psyche, frequently arising even when my conscious thoughts are elsewhere. The completed manuscript of the revised edition is the final answer to the questions I have been asking all these years.

As I was working on the revised edition, the history department of Nanjing University, which I had served for more than 20 years, was remade into an academy of history. The new history building, reportedly the largest building dedicated to the study of history in all Asia, rose suddenly from the ground in the Xianlin campus. It was there that my team and I finished proofing the 12 volumes of *Compilation of Documents on the Diaoyu Islands Question*. While we were busy working on that, I felt this new wave of history slap me in the face: East Asia, a big historical tangle for thousands of years, has become even chimerical in the present. It was as though a vast and powerful sea breeze reeking of fish has blown in from deep in the Pacific, overturning, agitating, and sweeping up everything in its path, whipping up waves that touch the sky, making people stagger as they walk, and making clear vision impossible. When giant tidal waves of history appear on the horizon, there is nowhere for historians to hide.

The participation in this revised edition of Professor Jiang Liangqin and Professor Wang Weixing is particularly worthy of mention. Their focused studies in the areas of public and private property losses during the Rape of Nanking and the Japanese perspective on the event, respectively, have long been known in our field. This edition was possible only because of their contributions.

I thank the Nanjing University Humanities Fund and Nanjing University Academy of History for supporting the publication of this revised edition.

I also thank my family and friends.

Finally I thank those who have passed on but whose memory lives on, who were part of the best times of my life.

Zhang Sheng

Tomb Sweeping Day, 2015